Critical Acclaim for Pulitzer P
Rick Atkinson's *The Lo*

"Remarkable stories, recounted in detail a... ...ith feeling."

—*People*

"As masterfully executed as it was conceived. *The Long Gray Line* is a significant contribution both to our national history and to our effort to understand and come to terms with post-Vietnam America. Through Atkinson's meticulous research, we are there during each phase of the cadets' epic journey, there to savor their successes and wince at their failures. We live with them and, in some cases, we die with them."

—Nicholas Proffitt, *The Philadelphia Inquirer* (front page)

"Told through the emotions and experiences of West Point's class of 1966, *The Long Gray Line* makes the best book out of Vietnam to date."

—David Griffiths, *Business Week*

"In *The Long Gray Line*, Atkinson achieves a kind of unabashed power rare in topical nonfiction and takes his place as one of the most important chroniclers of the Vietnam generation."

—Richard Currey, *New York Newsday*

"More than any book I have ever read, *The Long Gray Line* reveals the true heart and soul of the military."

—Bob Woodward

"Impeccable and absorbing . . . Atkinson's book is exquisitely crafted. It reads as smoothly as a novel, involving the reader emotionally as well as intellectually. . . . It has all the power and then some of *A Bright Shining Lie*, and a bushel more style."

—Steve Paul, *Kansas City Star*

"Rick Atkinson . . . brings keen insight to this work. . . . Probably the best book about military life since Ward Just's *Military Men*. Not only is it thoroughly researched, but it is written with a novelist's flair for color, style and often gut-wrenching emotion."

—*Minneapolis Star Tribune*

"A poignant, thought-provoking account of the struggles of young men who pledged themselves to 'Honor, Duty, Country.'"

—*Publishers Weekly*

"I don't think any book has penetrated so deeply into the West Point mystique with such a marvelous blend of sympathy and objectivity. It is that rarest of things, good reading and good—important—history. In short, the book is a monumental achievement."

—Thomas Fleming, author of *The Officers' Wives*

"A book of enormous significance and importance. A direct hit!"

—Col. David Hackworth, author of *About Face*

"A panoramic and affectingly realized account . . . Consistently absorbing."

—*Kirkus Reviews*

"A tremendously impressive work . . . Masterfully told."

—James Fallows, author of *More Like Us*

"Through these brilliant and moving portraits, *The Long Gray Line* gives us a fresh perspective on twenty-five years of American life."

—Digby Diehl, *Playboy*

"A sensitive, stunningly eloquent book."

—*Booklist*

RICK ATKINSON

The LONG GRAY LINE

The American Journey of West Point's Class of 1966

Picador

Henry Holt and Company
New York

www.picadorusa.com
www.twitter.com/picadorusa • www.facebook.com/picadorusa
picadorbookroom.tumblr.com

Picador® is a U.S. registered trademark and is used by Henry Holt and Company under license from Pan Books Limited.

For book club information, please visit www.facebook.com/picadorbookclub or e-mail marketing@picadorusa.com.

www.liberationtrilogy.com

Designed by Robert Overholtzer

Unless otherwise noted, all photos courtesy U.S. Military Academy Archives.

The Library of Congress has cataloged the Henry Holt edition as follows:

Atkinson, Rick.
The long gray line : the American journey of West Point's class of 1966 / Rick Atkinson. — 1st Holt paperbacks ed.
p. cm.
Originally published: Houghton Mifflin, 1989.
Includes bibliographical references and index.
ISBN 978-0-8050-9122-9
1. United States Military Academy. Class of 1966 Biography. 2. United States. Army—Officers Biography. I. Title.
U410.N1 1966a
355'.0092'273—dc21
[B]

99-15023
CIP

Picador books may be purchased for educational, business, or promotional use. For information on bulk purchases, please contact Macmillan Corporate and Premium Sales Department at 1-800-221-7945, extension 5442, or write specialmarkets@macmillan.com.

Originally published in hardcover in 1989 by Houghton Mifflin Company

D 20 19 18 17 16 15 14

For Jane and Rush and Sarah

We few, we happy few, we band of brothers;
For he today that sheds his blood with me
Shall be my brother; be he ne'er so vile,
This day shall gentle his condition.

SHAKESPEARE, *Henry V*

Contents

Foreword

to the Twentieth Anniversary Edition

IN THE TWENTY YEARS since this saga of the West Point class of 1966 was first published, the men who initially appear as boys in these pages have become grandfathers. In those two decades, the country for which they battled and bled has fought more wars, small and large, in places like Panama, the Persian Gulf, Afghanistan, and Iraq. The culture that embraced, then shunned, then re-embraced them has at last moved beyond bitter bickering over Vietnam. Their war is history.

The military academy that brought the class of '66 together continues to evolve. If today's uniformed cadets marching across the Plain to the strains of "Garry Owen" resemble the gray ranks of yore, the corps upon closer inspection more nearly reflects America than '66 ever did: women, African-Americans, Asians, Hispanics, and multiethnics of every hue bring a diversity to West Point unknown two generations ago. Even the nation's commander-in-chief is half black, half white.

West Point, which had commissioned some 26,000 officers in its 164-year history before the class of 1966 graduated, has since turned out almost 40,000 more. Cadets entering the academy today are as far removed from '66 as '66 was from the classes that mustered at West Point during the First World War (and which produced some of the Second World War's finest commanders).

At first those who arrived as new cadets on R-Day in July 1962 numbered 807. By graduation, on June 8, 1966, that had been pared to 579. Now they tally barely 500. At last, more have left this life from causes unrelated to Vietnam than died in the war. When those still living recite in unison the names of the dead, a ritual repeated at every reunion, the homage takes ever longer.

Yet the values they cherish—service, family, fellowship—endure undimmed, just as the virtues revered by West Point—courage, integrity, loyalty, and all the rest—remain chiseled in granite at Trophy Point. Annealed by fire, bound in brotherhood, they still believe. Their place in the long gray line holds firm.

RICK ATKINSON
Washington, D.C., June 2009

PROLOGUE

THE NATIONAL CEMETERY at West Point is a place of uncommon tranquillity, screened from the martial hubbub of the Military Academy by privet hedges and stone walls. The tombstones run to the river bluff in parallel rows that hug the gentle contours of the churchyard. Far below, the Hudson rolls toward Manhattan, broken only by the winking oars of an eight-man shell scooting along the same shoreline traced nearly four hundred years earlier by Dutch sailors.

Visitors enter the cemetery past the old cadet chapel, built in 1836; a building of dark stone and incongruous white Ionic columns. The chapel's interior walls are covered with marble shields memorializing the rebel generals of the American Revolution. One plaque, nearly hidden from view in the choir loft, is inscribed only "Major General — Born 1740"; it recalls Benedict Arnold, the one-time apothecary's apprentice whose perfidy in selling West Point's fortification plans to the British is repaid with this anonymity.

Cadets assigned to funeral duty frequently march through the cemetery in dress gray and tarbucket hats, arms swinging the prescribed nine inches forward and six inches back of vertical as they escort yet another old soldier to his grave. They pass the sarcophagus of Winfield Scott, Old Fuss and Feathers, who died, stout and gouty, in his room at the West Point Hotel in 1866. His epitaph celebrates him as "Warrior, Pacificator, and General in Chief of the Armies of the United States." A few paces farther stands a blunt obelisk marking the remains of George A. Custer, who graduated last in the class of 1861. "Lieutenant Colonel of the 7th Cavalry," the stone proclaims. "Killed with His Entire Command in the Battle of the Little Big Horn, June 25, 1876." Nearby stands a monument to Thomas E. Selfridge, a 1903 classmate of Douglas MacArthur's who, as the stone recalls, "gave up his life in the service of his country at Fort Myer, Virginia, September 17, 1908, in falling with the first government aeroplane." The pilot, an Ohio bicycle maker named Orville Wright, survived the crash.

Seasons fall heavily, unambiguously, on the cemetery. In winter, snow often covers all but the most ostentatious stones. Thrushes fill the budding dogwoods in springtime, and in summer the air thickens with fireflies. But it is autumn, with its blazing maples and hint of decay, that gives the churchyard a certain purity. "It might," as Shelley wrote of the Protestant Cemetery in Rome, "make one in love with death, to think that one should be buried in so sweet a place."

Section XXXIV in the northern quadrant is indistinguishable from the rest of the yard except for a long row of stones, numbered evenly beginning with 124 and chiseled with a common epitaph: CLASS OF 1966. Most of the markers are government issue — bone white, unadorned, and twenty-four inches tall. Partly shaded by a graceful mimosa tree, the graves form two rows, back to back like a mutual rearguard.

On a Saturday morning in mid October 1986, Section XXXIV was crowded with the quick and the dead. The living, three hundred strong who had returned to West Point for their twentieth reunion, gathered in a half moon around the graves. Some wore drab green uniforms with the silver oak leaf insignia of lieutenant colonels or the silver eagles of full colonels. Others stood muffled in civilian pullovers and jackets, shoulders hunched against the chill. Despite the bright sunlight filtering through a few mare's-tail clouds high overhead, a stiff north wind made the morning uncomfortably cool.

After the classmates had recited the Lord's Prayer and listened to a reading of Psalm 23, the academy chaplain moved to a microphone in front of the semicircle. Standing with a slight stoop, his Bible opened to Isaiah, he read in a strong, sure voice: "Hast thou not known? hast thou not heard? . . . They that wait upon the Lord shall renew their strength; they shall mount up with wings as eagles; they shall run, and not be weary; and they shall walk, and not faint."

Several classmates propped a wreath of chrysanthemums beside the graves as a bugler lifted the drear blare of taps. An honor guard fired three volleys, scattering a flock of blackbirds. The Army flag, a large banner of white and gold, was nearly obscured by the colorful battle ribbons lashed to the same staff. A hundred and sixty-eight of the streamers, including seventeen from Vietnam, knotted and unknotted in the breeze: Cold Harbor tangling with Ticonderoga, Tippecanoe with Third Korean Winter, Chapultepec with Tet Counteroffensive.

"We stand here in the shadow of death," the chaplain continued at the microphone. "You hold in your hands a list of your classmates who have died. Look at them for a moment. Familiar names. There's one who was a roommate; that one was a teammate. That one was my friend. These were people who responded to a call. When the country asked them to take a task, they took it. They are people who followed through on their commitment.

"There comes a nagging question: Does our society somehow recognize their contribution? Does a self-indulgent society like ours somehow make their sacrifice worthwhile? Probably not. Yet it seems that the strong soldier, the superior soldier, is always the one willing to give his life. Any great leader in any society probably gives better than he gets. That's just a fact of life."

Some of the mourners traced the names on the stones with an index finger: McKibbin, Booth, Johnson, Fera, Brown, Wilson, Niskanen, Snell. The two rows of graves held most of the thirty men from '66 killed in Southeast Asia, the highest toll of any West Point class. Earlier, one survivor had scanned a twenty-year-old photograph that had been mounted for the reunion. "That's me," he said, pointing with the steel hook that served as his right hand. "The guy on my left is dead now; so is the guy on my right. The three of us didn't fare too well in Vietnam. I came out the best."

With a final amen, the cemetery service ended, the quick and the dead again partitioned. For the survivors, a homecoming football game and a reunion dinner were still to come. Off to one side an officer leaned against a maple sapling, hugging his wife and daughter as they all wept. "Even after all these years," said a classmate, turning to leave with a shake of the head, "it doesn't get any easier."

But this time it *was* easier. Easier than the fifth reunion, when the dead were still coming home from the war. Easier than the tenth, when they had gathered here beneath black umbrellas in a foul rain, everyone sobbing openly. Easier than the fifteenth, in 1981, when they had read the names of the dead, in unison.

No, this wasn't easy, but certainly it was easier. And that was one of the most terrible things about it.

After the memorial service, some of the classmates strolled back to the academy parade field, known as the Plain. They paused at Trophy Point to admire the panoramic view of the Hudson gorge. Nearly a quarter century earlier they had stood here to swear the oath required of all new cadets. Only the river had remained unchanged since that summer day; everything else — the nation, the Army, the academy — seemed to have been swept up in a succession of upheavals. The men of '66 had fought the war, bravely, and lost. More than a hundred of the 579 men in the class had been wounded. Several remained shattered beyond repair. The survivors had come home to heckles and, in a few instances, spittle. They had heard their profession vilified and seen the Army virtually collapse in chaos during the early 1970s. Scores of them had returned to West Point as instructors, only to witness the devastating cheating scandal of 1976. In addition to the war dead, a dozen others were gone, including two who had been murdered.

Twelve classmates now had children in the Corps of Cadets. Two thirds of the class had already left the Army, finding a separate peace as doctors, lawyers, bankers, businessmen. Those men still in the service had just become eligible for retirement; a full generation of the Army's officer corps was passing. Forty or fifty of the men in uniform were full colonels, of whom perhaps ten or fifteen would become generals and command the Army of the 1990s. Collectively, the class had returned to West Point with a twenty-five-year accumulation of triumphs, failures, secrets, enduring hostilities, and an indissoluble bond.

A dozen benches lined the footpath at Trophy Point. Hewn from pink granite and presented to the academy by the class of 1934, each bench had been inscribed with a different virtue: DIGNITY, DISCIPLINE, COURAGE, INTEGRITY, LOYALTY. The effect was almost quaint, an anachronism like the naming of British warships: H.M.S. *Invincible,* H.M.S. *Defiance,* H.M.S. *Indefatigable.* Yet the benches were truly emblematic of what West Point wanted to be, a fortress of virtue, a preserve of the nation's values. Just as the country's silver depository was kept in a vault at West Point — a kind of poor man's Fort Knox — so the academy aspired to safeguard America's most precious ideals. That protective instinct was a little sanctimonious at times, as though the academy had a monopoly on probity. At times it was simply ridiculous, as in the mid 1970s, when the place was a citadel of corruption. Yet the impulse was righteous, even noble.

Before the football game on Saturday, the academy staged a homecoming parade. The honored guests included MacArthur's widow and William C. Westmoreland, who had been superintendent when the class of 1966 arrived at the academy. His familiar crown of white hair was instantly recognizable in the dignitaries' box. Two wives, their eyes rheumy from the cold, sat in the bleachers discussing the war. One woman pointed to the men of '66 who had gathered on the edge of the Plain. "They got over to Vietnam," she said, "just in the nick of time to die."

With a thousand other graduates, the class of 1966 milled about in the shadows of Jefferson Road. Stamping their feet to keep warm, some of them launched into a football cheer — "Army! Army! Rah!" — which was answered in a higher octave by a group of women cadets playing tennis nearby.

Never inclined to undersize its heroes, the academy had placed a massive bronze statue of George Patton above the street. He gazed into the middle distance. Fifty yards away a comparable likeness of Eisenhower, arms akimbo, scanned the northern horizon.

Then, as the Hellcats' drum and bugle corps played "When Johnny Comes Marching Home" at a somber tempo, the graduates glided four abreast onto the sun-washed Plain. Led by a member of '22, the long gray line stretched for two hundred yards from oldest to youngest — '39, '56, '61, '66, '71, '76, '81. As they neared the waiting corps of cadets, the grads grew miraculously younger. Silver heads darkened, ebbing hairlines filled in, paunches flattened, stoops straightened, crow's feet pulled taut.

Ten thousand spectators cheered. The corps marched in homage past the graduates, eyes right, swords and bayonets flinging shards of light. And the glee club sang:

> Grip hands — though it be from the shadows —
> While we swear, as you did of yore,
> Living, or dying, to honor
> The corps, and the corps, and the corps.

PART I

1

BEAST

EVEN ON the Sabbath dawn Penn Station was a busy place. Redcaps hurried across the concourse on crepe soles, pushing carts piled high with luggage. Vendors began to unshutter their kiosks, and the garble of arrivals and departures droned from the public address system. Although it was a gray beginning to what would be a gray day, the huge waiting room was awash with a hazy luminance. Light seeped through the windows high overhead and filtered down through the intricate ironwork. Chandeliers, each with eight yellow globes, dangled from the girders. This was the year before the station — which had been modeled on the Baths of Caracalla — would be razed for a new Madison Square Garden and a monstrously ugly depot. Now, though, the building was magnificent, with its arches and trusses and vaulting space as vast as the nave of St. Peter's.

Beneath the large sign proclaiming INCOMING TRAINS, five young men climbed the stairs from the grimy warren of tracks below. Each carried a small bag containing a shaving kit, a change of clothes, and, as instructed, "one pair of black low-quarter, plain-toe shoes." They had boarded the train in Newport News and traveled north, through the pine forests of southern Virginia, through darkened Washington and Baltimore. Without much success, they had tried to nap as the train rocked through Maryland and the slumbering villages of southern New Jersey, silent except for the hysterical dinging of crossing gates. Now, a bit rumpled but excited by their arrival in Manhattan, the five chattered like schoolboys set loose on a great adventure.

They walked quickly across the waiting room toward Eighth Avenue. In front of a newsstand, the day's edition of *The New York Times* had just arrived in a thick bundle. Under the paper's name and the date — July 1, 1962 — the front page offered a remarkable snapshot of an

America that was about to vanish and the America that was about to replace it.

LEADERS OF U.S. AND MEXICO HAIL NEW ERA OF AMITY, the lead story proclaimed. A large photo showed the president ignoring his Secret Service agents to grasp the hand of a boy on his father's shoulders in Mexico City as a huge crowd — more than a million — roared, "Viva Kennedy!"

On the opposite side of the page, the *Times* reported that the federal deficit topped $7 billion as fiscal 1962 ended, with "the virtual certainty of another deficit" in the new fiscal year. Other articles reported that former President Eisenhower, speaking from his Gettysburg farm, had declared that Republicans represented the party of business and were "proud of the label"; Dodger southpaw Sandy Koufax had notched thirteen strikeouts in pitching a no-hitter against the Mets; and an article from Detroit — '63 AUTOS TO ACCENT STYLING OVER THRIFT — noted that car makers were about to offer more chrome, automobiles two to seven inches longer than the previous year's models, and ninety varieties of bucket seats. The *Times* also documented developments in Algerian politics, Saskatchewan health care, and a call by Nikita Khrushchev for the Soviet people to diversify their diets by eating more corn flakes. "Americans and Englishmen," Khrushchev observed, "are masters of preparing corn in the form of flakes." The missile gap had been succeeded by the cereal gap.

Tucked into the lower right-hand corner of page 1 were two nettlesome articles with an exotic dateline: Saigon. The first reported that the South Vietnamese government "charged today that new weapons from Communist China had been given to Communist guerrillas. It demanded action against these 'flagrant violations' of the Geneva agreement." The second article said that "a massive combined operation against 'hard-core' Communist guerrillas along the Cambodian border has resulted in the discovery of two training camps for insurgents and the capture of enemy documents." A related story on page 22 reported that "the most avidly read book in Saigon is *Bend With the Wind*, a breezy tract put out by the United States Embassy for the big American colony here." The book contained advice on riots, invasions, coups, typhoons, and earthquakes; it also explained a sequence of alerts known as Conditions White, Gray, and Yellow. In the event of Condition Red — the most serious gradation — Americans were to "remain calm and prepare for evacuation."

The five young men stepped onto Eighth Avenue. The overcast sky threatened drizzle; New York City looked hard and scruffy, as though it too had been shortchanged on sleep. They turned north and walked six blocks to the West Side bus terminal. A ticket agent directed them to the proper bus, whose sign above the windshield advised in block capitals WEST POINT. They climbed aboard.

All five were the sons of Army officers stationed at Fort Monroe, a picturesque antebellum fortress on the Chesapeake Bay where Jefferson Davis had been imprisoned after the Civil War. All five were also good students, model citizens, and active in extracurricular activities. One was an outstanding marksman, another a champion middleweight boxer.

The youngest of the group was still six months shy of his eighteenth birthday. Just under five feet ten inches tall, he had his mother's blue eyes, high forehead, and fair hair. He laughed often, with an abrupt, high-pitched giggle that was easy to pick out in a crowded room. Although never a gifted athlete, he kept himself in good shape. His name was John Parsons Wheeler III, and he was nervous.

As the bus worked its way north through Manhattan, Jack Wheeler couldn't help wondering whether he was making a mistake. He had agonized over where to go to college. The decision seemed so momentous that he had avoided making it for weeks after the arrival of the academy's acceptance letter — Admission Form 5.413, dated 24 April 1962, which had declared him "fully qualified and entitled to admission." At Hampton High School, he had been editor of the yearbook and president of the Spanish Club. His classmates considered him warm, erudite, and serious. The word among the girls at Hampton High was that if you planned to go out with Jack Wheeler, you had better be smart. He'd even lectured one of them on the constellations, pointing out the Dippers and the North Star. During his senior year, his classmates had voted him "most likely to succeed."

Much of Jack's ambivalence was caused by another letter he had received, this one dated April 16, 1962, and embossed with the Latin phrase *Lux et Veritas*: "Yale University takes pleasure in advising John Parsons Wheeler III that he has been approved for admission to the freshman class entering in September 1962." Unlike West Point's free education, four years at Yale were very expensive, but Jack had won a National Merit Scholarship to cover the cost. The idea of going to New Haven to study literature and live like a normal college student had enormous appeal. There was no doubt about where his mother, Janet, wanted him to go; she nudged him persistently toward Yale, convinced that her elder son needed a place that would give his mind free rein.

Just as persistently, his father nudged him toward West Point, his own alma mater. He very much wanted his son to be a military man: the Wheelers hailed from a long line of soldiers, traceable to at least the seventeenth century. But when young Jack took the physical examination for the academy, Army doctors disqualified him because of a punctured eardrum. Not to be denied, his father had taken him to an Air Force doctor who was accustomed to seeing shattered ears in his pilots. "Mighty fine ears your boy has, Colonel," the doctor said cheerfully before certifying the young man as physically sound for the academy. As Colonel Wheeler pressed his campaign, Jack had to admit that West Point felt comfortable, like the succession of Army posts he was used to — Fort Riley, Fort Knox, Fort Hood, Fort Monroe. The academy would almost be like home.

When he had finally made up his mind, Jack came down to dinner one evening, pulled up to the table, and announced, "I've decided where I'm going to go." He paused dramatically before adding, "West Point."

Janet finished her meal and excused herself. She got into the car and drove aimlessly around the post, trying to calm down. Without even bothering to check the marquee, she parked next to the theater, bought a ticket, and walked inside. "The most desirable woman in town and the easiest to find," the poster next to the box office proclaimed; "just call BUtterfield 8." By the time the heroine — played by Elizabeth Taylor — perished in an automobile wreck, Janet had recaptured her composure. She drove home and congratulated her son.

The bus rumbled across the George Washington Bridge and north onto Highway 9W, following the western Palisades. Past Upper Nyack, the land seemed to muscle up, inclining slightly as the engine whined through a shift of gears. Yes, West Point was a known quantity, more predictable than the alien civilian world of New Haven. The academy also offered an engineering education, which seemed more pragmatic to Jack than the humanities. In the aftermath of Sputnik, he thought, his generation had an obligation to keep America pre-eminent in the sciences and technology. That polished steel beachball, beeping its eerie A-flat taunt as it orbited the earth, had triggered a bout of American self-reproach several years earlier. The Soviets had humiliated the United States, and the implication was that the rising generation would have to set things right. Jack took that mission seriously, and West Point seemed a good place to accept the challenge.

Colonel Wheeler had not been around to see his firstborn off to West Point. Once again duty had taken him from home, this time to prepare for command of a tank battalion at Fort Riley, Kansas. Big Jack's frequent absences stretched the emotional distance that Jack felt; the more his father was away, the more Jack craved his admiration and respect. He understood, perhaps intuitively rather than intellectually, that attending West Point was the surest way to please Big Jack.

With a few hours to kill before the train left for New York, Jack had paced restlessly through the house at Fort Monroe.

"Come on," his mother said, sensing that he needed to get out, "let's go have dinner at the Officers Club." While they were eating, a general stopped by the table to chat for a moment. When he learned that Jack was leaving that night for the academy, the general put a hand on his shoulder and said gently, "He's too young. Boys shouldn't leave for soldiering so young."

Finally the moment came and Janet drove her son to the Newport News station. It was a beautiful evening, the sky jammed with stars. At home in Laredo, Texas, during World War II, she had fallen into the habit of staring at the heavens, wondering whether her husband was alive or dead on some European battlefield. Now, hugging her son on the platform, she looked up again and silently prayed to her ancestors, *Please, please attend him.* His eyes flooded with tears; dry-eyed herself, she fought an impulse to hop on the train with him. With a last hug she whispered, "Go find your star, Jack." And then he was gone.

Now, ninety minutes after leaving New York, the bus rolled into the village of Highland Falls, drowsy with summer and Sunday. Diners and pubs lined the main street, where five-and-dime stores peddled "Go Army!" pennants and ceramic figurines of cadets with little bow mouths and ruddy cheeks. Ahead lay the academy's main entrance, Thayer Gate.

The sheaf of official documents Jack had received included a form letter with a veiled warning from the adjutant general: "You are to be congratulated on this opportunity for admission to the military academy, for it comes only to a select few of America's youth . . . Now is the time for you to reconsider your decision to become a member of the Corps of Cadets. You should reassess your ambitions most conscientiously in the light of the mission of the academy, which is the training of young men for careers as officers in the regular Army of the United States. Without strong determination to achieve such a career, many of the demands of cadet life will be irksome and difficult."

With a squeal of brakes, the bus pulled up to the Hotel Thayer. The young men stood up, yawning and stretching as they shuffled toward the door. Jack grabbed his bag and stepped onto the pavement, his full sense of high purpose tinged with a touch of dread.

The Thayer was an imposing brick hostel perched on a knoll above the Hudson. Its roof, like that of a castle, was ringed with battlements, and the lobby was often filled with old soldiers in various stages of fading away. The grand dining room featured octagonal pillars with gilded bas-relief vines and tendrils that climbed toward the oak-beamed ceiling. Like all formal dining rooms on Army posts, this one smacked of the Old Army — big steaks and blue cheese and undertipping alcoholics. But little imagination was required in the soft lighting to see a MacArthur in the far corner, strands of hair combed vainly over his pate, or an Eisenhower with his eyebrow cocked, hanging fire with his cutlery as he listened to an old friend from '15, the famous "class that stars fell on."

Now, hundreds of young men, all as nervous as Jack, crowded the Thayer. Most had never seen the academy; a few had never been on a military post. Many — those with their hands still clamped over their wallets — had just come through New York for the first time. Nearly two-thirds were the sons of military fathers, and they came as close to constituting an American warrior caste as the nation would allow.

Two-thirds also were Protestants; only 1 percent were Jewish. Compared with other new college freshmen with whom they had been surveyed, the new cadets smoked less, prayed more, cribbed less, napped more. Few were from either very rich or very poor homes; half, in fact, came from families with annual incomes of $10,000 to $15,000. They inclined to achievement and overachievement: most had been varsity athletes, student government or class officers, and members of the National Honor Society. The Army brats, like Jack, had grown up as nomads, moving an average of eight or ten times in their young lives. The upbringing encouraged a strange concoction of traits that made them cosmopolitan and self-reliant, yet rootless and somewhat insulated from the larger civilian world.

All of them were also sons of the 1950s. Had they been asked, they collectively could have belted out the theme songs to the Mickey Mouse Club or the Davy Crockett show ("Born on a mountaintop in Tennessee . . ."). They had been nurtured on *Wagon Train* and *Wyatt Earp,* and knew that DDT meant "drop dead twice." Most wore butch haircuts or flattops, and a few rebels had experimented by rolling their T-shirts above their biceps with cigarette packs secured in the sleeve. They universally admired John Glenn, another military man, whose three orbits earlier that year had earned him fame and glory; they agreed with Pablo Picasso, who had said of the smiling Marine from New Concord, Ohio, "I am as proud of him as if he were my brother." Finally, they were largely ignorant of many things, including women, failure, and evil.

Jack spied a familiar face in the crowd, a friendly, reassuring one. Jeff Rogers, whose father and uncle were both West Pointers, had graduated from Hampton High in 1961 and enlisted in the Army. He had spent the past year at the military academy prep school in Virginia, brushing up his math skills and memorizing thirty new words a week. As little boys at Fort Riley, Jack and Jeff had played in the same sandbox; their fathers had both been brown-boot cavalrymen who made the necessary transition to tanks during World War II.

"C'mon," Jeff said, after pumping Jack's hand, "let's go look around."

They strolled down to the river and past the old train station, a pretty little gingerbread building with gables and a steep slate roof. Jack saw sailboats tied up nearby — that also was reassuring. At Fort Monroe, the Wheelers lived in a three-bedroom house near the sea wall, where they were lulled by the slap of Chesapeake waves on the stones. The commanding general occasionally let the family borrow his boat and Jack had learned to sail on the bay. The Hudson, he thought, with its tides, current, and barge traffic, would provide a stiff challenge to his seamanship.

The river was also beautiful. During the Ice Age, a mile-thick tongue of glacial ice had pushed through here, notching a gap in the steep highlands. To the south, Jack and Jeff could see where the gorge cut between Bear Mountain on the west bank and Anthony's Nose on the east. To the north, the river sliced through another pass bracketed by Storm King Mountain and Breakneck Ridge. Henry Hudson and his sullen crew had threaded this strait aboard the eighty-ton *Half Moon* on September 14, 1609, futilely searching for passage to the western ocean. Later that century, Captain Kidd and other pirates had infested the river. Even now, after more than three hundred years of encroaching civilization, the gorge still held a pristine, New World charm.

During the Revolution, George Washington had pronounced the military garrison at West Point "the most important post in America." To safeguard the fort against the British, Washington entrusted its command to a man whose name became a synonym for treason. Benedict Arnold was swarthy, doughy, and given to duels; in 1780, he was also the finest warrior in the American Army, gallant at Ticonderoga, fearless at Quebec, badly injured at Saratoga. For six thousand pounds sterling, Arnold agreed to sell West Point's fortification plans to the British, who waited downriver with an assault force. Full of ill temper over perceived slights, and influenced by his new wife, Peggy, the daughter of a Philadelphia Tory, Arnold slipped the plans to a British spy, Major John André. But when André was captured and the incriminating papers discovered in his boot, the plot collapsed. Arnold galloped to his barge — Jack could see the precise spot across the Hudson — and ordered eight of his men to row him downriver to the British sloop *Vulture*. The traitor fled to London, but West Point was saved.

Jack and Jeff climbed up the steep hill from the train station and through the stone portal that led to the Plain. This was the precise path that Douglas MacArthur, after arriving on the West Shore Railroad, had walked sixty-three years earlier, towing his indomitable mother. She had ensconced herself for four years at the West Point Hotel — now gone — where she could clearly see room 1123 in the barracks and tell by the lamplight whether young Doug was studying.

Now, the orderly splendor of the Plain lay before the two young men. From the river bluff, the plateau ran west for half a mile before suddenly lifting into the dark green hills. Barracks, houses, and academic buildings ringed the parade ground. Jack felt excitement rising through his anxiety. West Point was a grand place, he thought, wonderfully laden with tradition and honor.

Afternoon shadows began to lengthen. The time had come to return to the Thayer. An arduous first day lay ahead, and both of them wanted to get a good night's sleep. Leaving the Plain, they passed the Patton monument. It was said that, as a boy, George had hauled a chicken carcass around his house to mimic Achilles dragging Hector around the walls of Troy. The statue here depicted a barrel-chested warrior with broad hips and a nose like the prow of a ship. Clutching his binoculars in both hands, a pistol the size of an anvil on each hip, he had become the American Achilles.

One day when he was in the sixth grade, Jack had discovered his father's binocular case in a closet. Inside the container he found ghastly black-and-white photographs of a concentration camp near Nordhausen that Big Jack had helped to liberate in 1945. Jack, who rarely showed much interest in his father's wartime adventures, had been shocked — and fascinated — by the images of the skeletal dead and the skeletal living. He was proud that his dad had fought to crush that kind of horror. Even so, the photos were fearsome. But warriors, he suspected, had to get used to fearsome sights. That was part of their trade, part of the initiation into the brotherhood of combat.

Returning to the Thayer, Jack and Jeff had Patton's advice to contemplate. "Pursue the enemy with the utmost audacity," the great battle captain warned, in words inscribed at the foot of his monument. "Never take counsel of your fears."

"Sir, New Cadet Wheeler reports to the man in the red sash, as ordered!"

Jack stood with his shoulders squared, eyes fixed on the glowering upperclassman in white gloves, white hat, and red sash.

"Drop the bag!"

Jack was ready. He instantly let his valise fall to the pavement. Around him in Central Area he could hear upperclassmen verbally mauling other classmates who failed to demonstrate sufficient alacrity.

"I said drop the bag, NOW! When I tell you something, you are to do it immediately. Do you understand?"

"I understand."

"Wrong, you dumb crot. The correct answer is 'yes, sir.' You are permitted only three answers: Yes, sir. No, sir. No excuse, sir."

"Yes, sir."

The ordeal had begun and it was instantly dreadful. The first two months of cadet life were known as Beast Barracks. Jack and his classmates would not even be plebes until September; for now, they were simply "new cadets." For the next eight weeks they would be treated like vermin by the small cadre of upperclassmen who had been left behind for the summer to supervise Beast. The physical and psychological stress was intended to weed out the weak and unworthy, beginning with this lesson in instant obedience.

The overarching question at the Thayer that Monday morning, July 2, 1962, had been whether it was best to report early or late within the eight A.M. to ten A.M. period allowed them on R-Day — Reception Day. Some cadets who had not come up to West Point the night before were just now arriving — including one who stepped out of a limousine owned by his baroness aunt. For breakfast, Jack had walked into Highland Falls to a diner, where he swallowed some coffee and picked at his Danish. When he could no longer stand the tension, he hurried back to the Thayer, retrieved his bag, and climbed onto a shuttle displaying a large white sign: NEW CADET BUS.

Even before ten o'clock the casualty list began to grow. One lanky teenager reported with a tennis racquet and a set of golf clubs over his shoulder; after a five-minute torrent of abuse from an outraged upperclassman, he executed a smart about-face and walked back to the Thayer for a ride home. Others had arrived without realizing that they owed the Army four years of active duty service following their four years at West Point. Those who had been in the Army — the "prior service" cadets like Jeff Rogers — and the Army brats like Jack Wheeler were better prepared, thanks to careful coaching by their fathers and friends. Yet the intensity of disdain from the upper-class cadre, who barked and shrieked until spittle flecked the faces of the pathetic creatures cowering before them, was unnerving.

R-Day was also a masterpiece of logistics, planned with lavish attention to detail. The man in the red sash directed Jack to the gymnasium, where he was weighed, measured, inoculated, and judged in pull-ups, push-ups, and how far he could fling a basketball while kneeling. He surrendered all of his cash — $16 — and ran to the barbershop, where he was scalped so rigorously that the contours of his skull could be read like a topographical map. He then was photographed and issued an identification card.

On the fourth floor of the cadet store, a tailor measured him for tight-fitting dress trousers. (In an earlier age the tailor asked new cadets whether they "dressed right or dressed left" — that is, whether they preferred to tuck their genitals into the right pants leg or the left). In the basement of the store, Jack received one cadet raincoat, two sweat suits, and two gray shirts. In the boxing room of the gymnasium he picked up eight pairs of cotton gloves, bathing trunks, two pairs of gym shorts, one bathrobe, twelve cotton undershirts, four white waist belts, eight white shoulder belts, two pairs of black socks, three white twill shirts, two pairs of suspenders, and a stack of white boxer shorts, known as drollies. Not least among the culture shocks for those who had spent their lives clad in snug cotton briefs was this required conversion to the baggy drollies.

On and on it went, hundreds of sweating, confused cadets dashing about like so many sheep, the white-gloved upperclassmen nipping at their heels. In the south boxing room of the gym, Jack collected a pair of uniform shoes, a pair of rubber overshoes, leather slippers, low-cut Keds, canvas basketball shoes, shower slippers, and a pair of shoe trees. He also received a gray uniform cap, two garrison caps, two fatigue caps, and a blue rubber rain cover for his uniform hat.

The academy divided the 807 new cadets into six companies, each of which was further split into four platoons. Each platoon contained four squads, with eight cadets per squad. The cadet barracks — known as Central, North, Old South, and the just-completed New South — stood in "divisions," built like row houses. A division contained four floors, with four rooms on a floor. The academy did not issue keys — honorable men, after all, had no need for locks — and many cadets who had forgotten their room numbers wandered about the division corridors, too frightened to acknowledge their negligence. Although the divisions abutted, new cadets could pass between them only by going through basement corridors, where the bathrooms, or "sinks," were located, or by exiting the front door of one division and entering the door of another. Only upperclassmen were permitted to travel along the stoops, the broad porches lining the division fronts.

The morning passed with numbing celerity. Jack found that he was assigned to the fourth platoon of Third New Cadet Company. His room, number 1732, measured roughly twenty by twelve feet, with large windows, a linoleum floor, and a small, spare alcove containing three cots. His father's old room lay diagonally across Central Area.

I can't believe this is happening to me, Jack thought as he stood by the window. For a moment he felt as though he were living outside his body, watching himself. The sight was not a pretty one. Sweat poured from his shorn scalp and cascaded down his forehead. An odor of new wool and new cotton filled the barracks, as distinctive as the upholstery smell in a new car. Everything seemed hazy, unreal. Is this really happening? he asked himself again. He already had amassed enough gear to outfit the Wehrmacht, yet there was another heap of equipment on his bunk. He stared at the pile. I know what that is, he thought; that's a helmet. That's a helmet liner. That's a poncho. That's a web belt. This is serious. This is the Army.

He hustled down to the orderly room in the barracks to collect a can of Brasso, a glass tumbler, linseed oil for his rifle stock, and a bag with fifty other odds and ends. Back in the room, he stared again at the intimidating mound on his bunk. Where would he put all this stuff? Clearly, every item belonged in a particular niche. West Point, evincing a rage for order, resembled a fine watch; each tiny part had its proper function and position. Disarray was calamitous. When cadets laid out their field equipment during an inspection, for instance, the pistol belt was to go at the top of the display, the gas mask at the bottom, the poncho at left center. There was a right way, a wrong way, and the West Point way.

Compulsive order also governed the barracks. "All books," according to one regulation, "should be pushed to the back of the shelves and not be placed tangent to the edges." Even the medicine cabinet possessed an inviolable harmony. Hairbrush, soap dish, and razor on top; toothbrush and toothpaste in the middle; shaving cream, deodorant, and water glass at the bottom.

Jack scrutinized the uniform list he had been given. The document comprised three single-spaced pages of required articles, including "belt, cartridge or pistol; belt, guidon bearer; belt, saber; belt, uniform; belt, white shoulder; belt, white waist." A separate, five-page dress code manual catalogued the appropriate uniform for every conceivable activity. The manual told him what to wear to the bowling alley, to the barbershop, to the movies, to model airplane clubs, to the telegraph office, even to a fire ("any uniform authorized for wear outside of barracks"). The document told him what to wear to a court-martial if he was a witness; it told him what to wear if he was a defendant. It told him that the long overcoat "will be worn to chapel, to review, and to inspection" and that "the short overcoat will be worn when the long overcoat is not prescribed." Implicitly, it told him that he had checked his free will at Thayer Gate.

"Let's go, everybody out in Central Area. Let's go. Gonna learn how to march, New Cadets." The squad leader moved through the barracks, barking commands.

Jack hurried into the hall and down the stairs, keeping to the outer wall of the stairwell, as required of new cadets and plebes.

"Rack that neck in, mister. You call that bracing?"

Jack jerked his head back. Except when they were in their rooms or in the showers, new cadets were required to "brace" by retracting their necks into their collarbones in what appeared to be an awful orthopedic affliction.

"Rack your neck in, smack," the upperclassman ordered again. "I want to see six wrinkles in that neck. Six wrinkles, come on. One, two, three, four, five, six — good — seven. Oh my God, seven wrinkles. Come look at this, Jim. Seven wrinkles. That's a new record. Congratulations, smack."

Jack and his squad mates stood braced in front of the 17th Division. Sunday's overcast had blown over, revealing a fine summer day, temperature in the mid 80s. Dressed in long-sleeve wool shirts, the cadets sweated like dray horses. Throughout Central Area, hundreds of other new cadets stood before their divisions, braced and sweating.

"All right, we're going to practice saluting. Show me a salute."

Jack lifted his right hand to his right eyebrow and returned it to his side.

"That looks like a damned parachute coming off your forehead, mister. Make it snappy. Do not, repeat, do not move your head into the salute."

Standing in the sun, they practiced saluting and the rudiments of marching. "The fundamentals of drill are established daily," Frederick the Great had proclaimed, and West Point took him to heart. "If these maneuvers are all accurately observed and practiced every day, then the army will remain virtually undefeatable and always awe-inspiring."

The cadre taught the new cadets to stand at attention with heels together and toes pointed out at a 45-degree angle. At the command of "for-ward," the men shifted their weight inconspicuously onto the right foot; at the subsequent command of "march," they stepped with the left foot. Proper marching required a thirty-inch step, arms swinging without bending at the elbow.

Left-face, right-face, about-face, column left, column right. After an hour of drilling they remained ragged, still a far cry from Frederick's "awe-inspiring." But for now it would have to do. The hands on the large clock near the 1st Division crept toward five P.M. The time had come to take the oath.

The commandant stood waiting. As he watched from Trophy Point, Brigadier General Richard G. Stilwell saw the new cadets marching toward him across the Plain for the traditional swearing-in. They weren't exactly the Coldstream Guards. But considering that the academy had owned them for only seven hours, they looked more like soldiers than anyone would have thought possible that morning.

A small crowd of parents also waited. The ceremony always provided a good show: mothers weeping, fathers beaming, cadets glassy-eyed with fear. Trophy Point had long been a favorite spot at West Point. The sweeping vista of the river had even been popular among French wall-paper manufacturers, who reproduced the view on Parisian salon walls in the early nineteenth century. Now the promontory was dominated by Battle Monument, a huge shaft of granite dedicated to "the officers and men of the regular Army of the United States who fell in battle during the War of the Rebellion." Fifty captured Confederate cannons had been melted down to cast the plaque on the monument.

A statue of *Fame,* arms raised high in triumph, crowned the shaft. The bosomy, winged figure supposedly was modeled on Evelyn Nesbit, a one-time chorus girl whose jealous husband had murdered her lover, the corpulent rake Stanford White, after she confessed to frolicking naked on a red velvet swing in White's love nest. Trophy Point also bristled with cannons, most of them captured during the Mexican War. And there were sixteen links displayed from the Great Chain, the barrier that had stretched across the Hudson during the Revolution to prevent the British fleet from severing New England from the other colonies.

On a summer day in 1934, Richard Stilwell had walked across the Plain to swear his allegiance here. He had been a poor boy from Buffalo; his father, a milkman, died when Richard was an infant. His mother remarried a cable splicer for the phone company, a man who spent a good deal of his life in manholes, soldering breaks. After a year at Brown, where he earned his tuition by working the graveyard shift in a bakery, Stilwell was offered an appointment to the academy. He leaped at the chance of a free education and an opportunity to raise himself. He had loved West Point from the first day of Beast and even now cherished the memories of his cadet years. "To describe Pinkie with one expression," the 1938 yearbook said of Stilwell, "we would say he has self-confidence to the *n*th degree." Years later, after he had served as chief of staff for the Military Assistance Command in Vietnam, he would also be described by one historian as having "an unwavering trust in authority that led him to place loyalty to superiors above other considerations."

Stilwell's peers considered him one of the most brilliant officers in the Army, with a tough, penetrating gaze that made lesser men squirm. Blond and stocky, he was addicted to work and occasionally spent the night in his office, stretching out on the floor or leaning over his desk for rest. Dick Stilwell was the kind of man who learned a new word every day and then actually used it gracefully in conversation. He had been at West Point for three years now; as second in command, he helped bridge the transition from the previous superintendent, the great reformer Gar Davidson, and the current supe, an up-and-comer named

William Childs Westmoreland. Stilwell had not really known Westmoreland before 1960, though they had crossed paths briefly in Normandy during World War II and again in Tokyo during the Korean War. Although the new superintendent lacked Davidson's intellect, Stilwell believed that Westmoreland was smart enough to leave alone those things which were working well and to focus on external matters, such as plans to double the size of the corps.

Stilwell looked forward to returning to the muddy-boot Army — he had less than a year to go in his tour at the academy — but he had enjoyed his tour as commandant. Despite West Point's isolation, or perhaps because of it, the world seemed to beat a path to the academy portals. Just that spring, William Faulkner, in one of the last public appearances before his death, had visited for two days in April, reading from *The Reivers* in his tweeds and ruminating on man's destiny in "a ramshackle world." Three weeks after that, MacArthur had delivered his famous valedictory, which still had the academy buzzing.

Then, just last month, John Kennedy came to address the graduating class of 1962. After landing in his helicopter on the Plain, right where the new cadets now marched, he had been whisked straight to the fieldhouse. The date, June 6, marked the eighteenth anniversary of D-Day, and the president had been in top form: bantering, sophisticated, masculine in this fortress of masculinity, a war hero among future war heroes. After hinting at his own re-election plans and making a pitch for the Army's Special Forces — his beloved Green Berets — Kennedy made two specific references to the communist insurgency in Vietnam.

"I know," he said, "that many of you may feel, and many of our citizens may feel, that in these days of the nuclear age, when war may last in its final form a day or two or three days before much of the world is burned up, your service to your country will be only standing and waiting. Nothing, of course, could be further from the truth."

Instead, a new type of war threatened freedom lovers, the president continued, a conflict "new in its intensity, ancient in its origin — war by guerrillas, subversives, insurgents, assassins, war by ambush instead of by combat, by infiltration instead of by aggression, seeking victory by eroding and exhausting the enemy instead of engaging him . . . These are the kinds of challenges that will be before us in the next decade if freedom is to be saved, a whole new kind of strategy, a wholly different kind of force, and therefore a new and wholly different kind of military training."

He had finished by recalling "the lines found in an old sentry box in Gibraltar: 'God and the soldier all men adore, in time of trouble and no more. For when war is over and all things righted, God is neglected and the old soldier slighted.' But you have one satisfaction, however difficult those days may be: when you are asked by a president of the United States or by any other American what you are doing for your country, no man's answer will be clearer than your own."

It was good stuff, precisely in line with Stilwell's own philosophy, which he had developed during a somewhat unorthodox career that included a stint with the CIA in the 1940s. These new cadets are lucky, Stilwell thought. They have a mission again; JFK had made that clear. Only six years earlier, Eisenhower complained that the Army appeared "bewildered." That was true enough. Nuclear weapons had seemed to make a large land force obsolete, and no one was certain what an army was for. But JFK knew: nation building, fighting insurgencies, providing officers who were warriors and statesmen — that was the Army's new role. After years in the wilderness, the American Army was back.

The cadets had arrived at Trophy Point, ruddy and damp in their new wool uniforms. This class was much larger than Stilwell's had been, twice the size in fact. He sometimes thought that '38 had been among the last of the close-knit classes, more introspective, more isolated, and thus more tightly bonded. Of course, four years from now the class of 1966 would be considerably reduced. In a few days the commandant would gather them in South Auditorium and pull one of his favorite stunts. Scanning the group, he would gesture to about one third of the class. "You," he would command, "everyone over here, stand up." When they were on their feet, the general would say, "That's how many of you will be gone by June 1966."

Stilwell had a great deal to say now, but this was a time for brevity. The cadets were too shell-shocked to absorb much. If he did nothing else before he left West Point next spring, the commandant wanted to make them understand that in the twenty years ahead they were likely to face a confusing array of assignments, circumstances, and predicaments. Their education at West Point would be one of the most important factors in determining how well they coped with the future. He was also convinced — and had said so publicly — that all of them were likely to be involved in Southeast Asia. Kennedy's speech had reinforced that conviction. Such discussions, however, were better saved for a later occasion.

As Stilwell stood at the podium, the cadets formed neat ranks near Execution Hollow, where deserters and other miscreants had been hanged during the Revolution. The commandant began by welcoming them into "the noblest of professions — the military service of our country." They had "been examined and stamped as raw material of passable grade." They would be "tested, retested, [and] tested again" to determine whether they possessed the mettle to be worthy of the corps.

"As was true for all of the 24,400 who have preceded you, this has been a day none of you will ever forget. It has been a tough one, and designedly so. There will be many others. West Point is tough! It is tough in the same way that war is tough. It calls for leaders who can stand straight and unyielding under the sternest of physical and moral pressures. The security of this nation cannot be entrusted to men of lesser mold."

They were apprentices, he continued. For the next year they would be annealed in a system that presumed one basic leadership principle: "If you can't learn to obey orders, explicitly, you will never be able to give orders properly.

"My constant theme, sirs," he concluded, "is that the history of the United States of America and the history of the United States Army and the history of the United States Military Academy are so closely intertwined as to be inextricable, one from the other. As goes the Army, so goes the nation."

Stilwell let that sink in for a moment. The huge green shoulder of Storm King Mountain loomed behind him. "Men of '66, your great adventure is under way. Now raise your right hand."

Amid a forest of hands, Jack Wheeler lifted his. He had removed the white glove and was holding it, as the upperclassmen instructed, in his left hand. "I, John P. Wheeler, do solemnly swear that I will support the Constitution of the United States and bear true allegiance to the national government; that I will maintain and defend the sovereignty of the United States, paramount to any and all allegiance, sovereignty, or fealty I may owe to any state or country whatsoever."

The oath taking for new military recruits was a ritual dating to the Roman *sacramentum*. But the larger ritual, a nation offering its sons in defense of the commonweal, was at least as old as Homer. With their newly acquired ability to about-face, the cadets turned and marched back to the barracks. None knew, none could possibly know, that his advance to the crest of Trophy Point had been the high-water mark of pax Americana.

Night crept gradually into the valley. Even when taps blew at ten o'clock, fingers of light lingered in the west. Bats skimmed the Hudson, trolling for insects. Mist coiled on the water, and across the river a soft orange glow seeped from one of the mansions set into the hills above the village of Garrison. Passenger trains periodically clattered along the far bank, their caboose lights burning red in retreat toward Poughkeepsie.

In the darkened barracks, most of the cadets were too exhausted even for regret. In room 1732, Jack Wheeler, wearing his new Army-issue T-shirt and the unfamiliar drollies, ruefully concluded that he had never in his life hustled through a more stressful day. The place required a curious humiliation of its initiates. Eight more weeks of Beast, then nine months as a plebe. Not every day could be this fatiguing, could it? *Could it?* They had even been required to scribble letters home and show the sealed envelopes to their squad leaders. Jack wrote:

Dear Folks:
Am fine. Must polish equipment. Also must write letter. Letter is written.
Love,
Jack

Five hundred yards to the east, barges worked the river, their deep hooting reminding the cadets that people remained free in the outside world, going and coming as they pleased, free to laugh, relax, slouch — yes, by God, even slouch. Only a day before they had been part of that world. Now they seemed to have been plucked from it forever. Never, the Patton statue had warned, never take counsel of your fears.

"Two minutes. Two minutes." Thomas Merrit Carhart III listened to the stentorian voice of the King of Beast booming from the public address system. If that wasn't the voice of God, it was as close to the Lord as most new cadets got in Beast Barracks. Tom fumbled with his name tag, trying to poke the pin through the flimsy blue bathrobe without impaling his thumb.

"One minute. One minute." He raced out of the room and down the stairs of the 15th Division, remembering to wrench his head back into the braced position. Throughout Central Area he saw hundreds of his classmates, flip-flopping into formation in identical cotton robes and shower slippers. "Time's up," the King announced. A few stragglers scurried out of the barracks and into the ranks, pelted with abuse by the upperclassmen.

Tom's squad leader strolled past, examining his charges. Since the beginning of Beast several weeks earlier these "clothing formations" had become a routine part of the hazing, but this was the first time that the entire battalion of new cadets was put through its paces simultaneously. The upperclassman in charge of the cadre — the King of Beast — would name a uniform and give them three or four minutes to change, police their rooms, and fall into ranks. The task seemed impossible, of course, and that was the point: the test of grace under pressure was considered vital in gauging the pluck of future combat commanders. The uniform combinations were endless: fifty-fifty, gym alpha, gym bravo, drill bravo, uniform sierra, uniform India, dress gray, full dress gray under arms, full dress gray over white. Each outfit included a dozen accouterments to clip, pin, button, or hook. Starched white trouser legs had to be pried open with a bayonet to avoid wrinkling them. Just getting the white cross belts to hang properly on the full dress grays was like tumbling into a cargo net.

Some preposterous mishaps had occurred, hilarious to everyone except the victim. When the order was first issued to wear white trousers under arms, several new cadets emerged from the barracks with their pants hoisted to the armpits instead of bringing their rifles. Some forgot their helmet liners so the steel pots drooped over their eyes, making them look like Beetle Bailey. John Oi, the Canton-born son of a Boston restaurateur, appeared in formation with his name tag upside down — IO — and was known forever after as Mr. Ten. Other cadets, after futilely fumbling with the little chain that was supposed to run across the tarbucket bill, had raced out with the links dangling beside their ears like a yeshiva boy's curl. Years later, men who had been in horrific combat in Vietnam would wake up shrieking from nightmares — not that they were about to be overrun by the Viet Cong, but that they couldn't find the proper hat during clothing formation.

"All right," the King announced, his amplified voice echoing from the barracks walls. "You will now switch to uniform gym bravo. You have four minutes."

Tom and his squad mates hurried back into the division. Gym bravo meant athletic shorts and shirt, jock strap, white socks, tennis shoes, and sweat suit. That required going down to the lockers in the basement sinks. The sinks had become a dreaded place, like the scene of a particularly vicious crime. Clothing formations often were succeeded by shower formations in the sinks. The upperclassmen forced new cadets to brace in bathrobes and shower togs. Sometimes the cadre backed a victim against a wall with a nickel wedged against the nape of his neck until he had squeezed out enough perspiration to make the coin stick to the tile. Or each cadet might have to "sweat a shadow" against the wall until the squad leader blew his whistle and ordered them all into an icy shower for two minutes.

For more than an hour the King of Beast kept the cadets sprinting in and out of the barracks. Seven times they changed their uniforms, even appearing once in the ludicrous ensemble of athletic shorts, Keds, full dress coats, and helmets. Finally, as the last light began to fade, the King dismissed the formation. Tom returned to his room, wearily picked up the clothes that lay strewn across the floor, and tumbled into bed.

The next afternoon, during a few minutes of free time, he sat near the window polishing his equipment. The relentless hazing had begun to wear him down, but the thrill he felt at being part of the Corps of

Cadets had not yet dissipated. Arriving at West Point for R-Day had been the most exciting moment in Tom Carhart's life; though rarely at a loss for words, he had been dumb struck with admiration for the upperclassmen strutting around the Hotel Thayer, their sleeves streaked with the chevrons of rank.

As a boy, Tom had been mesmerized by a television show called *The West Point Story,* which painted "that rockbound highland home" and her graduates — played by Clint Eastwood and Leonard Nimoy, among others — in hagiographic hues. What other school, he wondered, offered such an illustrious roll of graduates? Dwight Eisenhower, U. S. Grant, and Robert E. Lee. Stonewall Jackson, Black Jack Pershing, Jeb Stuart. The list also included Abner Doubleday, who had invented baseball, and James Allen, who discovered the sources of the Mississippi River, and George Goethals, supervisor of the Panama Canal construction. Some of the academy's most praiseworthy sons were hardly known to the public, men like Leslie Groves, the bluff, stout engineer — described by one subordinate as "the biggest sonovabitch I've ever met in my life" — who had first supervised construction of the Pentagon and then commanded the Manhattan Project in World War II. Commandant Stilwell was right, Tom thought: the history of the Republic and the Army and West Point were inextricably bound, at least in those things most dashing and clever and glorious.

Tom wanted to be worthy of the great tradition, and while they were not especially glorious, he would start with his shoes. Squatting on the floor, he tried to see his face in the shine of his black low-quarters. Tom's was a splendid face, actually, as he would have seen had the shine been better. Neither strikingly handsome nor painfully homely, his countenance was long and expressive, like one of El Greco's Spanish noblemen, with thick lashes over blue eyes and a jaw that was firm but not pugnacious.

Tom also wanted to be spoony, which was defined in the glossary of cadet slang as "neat in personal appearance." A good spit-shine didn't come easily, and cadets relied on the prep school graduates in the class for helpful hints, such as how to use the proper side of an old T-shirt — the outside — and how to mix a little alcohol with the polish. But the alcohol tended to cloud in the sun, so it was important to rub cold water over the leather just before going outside. Tom now also knew how to tuck in a shirttail with the flat of his hand before positioning his trouser fly, belt buckle, and shirt seam in perfect vertical alignment. Brass looked best if he massaged in the Brasso with an index finger and then rinsed it off in scalding water. Being spoony, he now understood, was a demanding art.

Attending West Point was the fulfillment of a dream for Tom, and he longed to be the perfect cadet. That didn't come easily — he was a scamp by nature — but he was working hard to repress his seditious streak. "At West Point, I have but one desire," he had written on his academy application form. "To succeed, to do everything I do, no matter what it is, in the best way possible. I believe that anything someone wants he can have if he wants it bad enough. I want to be a success at West Point more than anything else. I believe I will be." His efforts in Beast had already been noticed; the cadre had twice singled out Tom for honors, first as the best new cadet in his company one week, then as the best in Beast Barracks. In an effort to be a completely straight arrow, he had even reported himself for an honor violation when his parents, searching for a picnic spot during a weekend visit, unknowingly drove Tom down Lee Road in an area off limits to new cadets; after giving him a brief reprimand, the upperclassmen told him to forget the incident.

To be sure, some things at the academy disappointed him. The enforced letter writing to parents on Sunday nights seemed silly. One stormy Tuesday evening, his squad leader had staggered into the barracks, drunk and abusive, which to an eighteen-year-old Catholic virgin had seemed particularly offensive and disrespectful of the new cadets. And the mandatory dancing lessons for new cadets were nearly as humiliating as the clothing formations. A leather-lunged physical education instructor bellowed "one two THREE, one two THREE" as the cadets shuffled around the ballroom in Cullem Hall; sometimes the nearby women's colleges supplied female partners — invariably short on pulchritude — but more typically the men blundered through the box step in one another's arms, would-be officers dancing with would-be gentlemen.

Tom lacked the kind of pedigree that many of his classmates had. Some were second-, third-, and even fourth-generation West Pointers, like Jack Wheeler and John C. F. Tillson IV, both of whom, like Tom, had attended Virginia high schools. Tillson's great-grandfather had graduated with the class of 1878 and served as provost marshal in Peking after the Boxer Rebellion. His grandfather, class of 1908, had served as a cavalryman at Fort Apache and elsewhere in the Southwest. Tillson's father, class of '38, was a major general.

Not having a bloodline like that sometimes nagged at Tom. Usually, though, he was proud and even boastful of being what he called "a low-born, common-stock American mongrel," the grandson of a farmer and a greengrocer. As such, he reflected the academy's gradual tilt toward a more egalitarian corps. Smaller percentages of cadets now hailed from well-born Episcopal families; they were replaced by ever larger numbers of Catholics and Baptists from the lower social ranks. Before World War I, the academy had drawn nearly a third of the corps from the families of doctors, lawyers, and other professionals. But by the mid 1950s, sons of professionals made up only 10 percent of the cadets, and links to the upper class had been almost severed. West Point increasingly attracted military brats and sons of the working class.

Tom was both. His father had risen through the enlisted ranks of the Army Air Corps to earn a commission and his pilot's wings; during World War II, he had flown P-38s in Italy. The Carhart family, including Tom and his four siblings, had traveled a typical Air Force circuit — Alabama; Washington, D.C.; France; Minnesota; and back to Washington. The father, Big Tom, who was well over six feet tall and weighed two hundred pounds, tended to leave daily decisions to his wife, a diminutive, pragmatic woman who would decide what kind of car to buy and where to send the children to school. Once, when he was a little boy, Tom had ridden a train with his mother and aunt to his grandmother's house in upstate New York. Suddenly he spied an immense fortress of gray stone across the Hudson. "Look, Tommy," his mother said, "that's West Point up there. That's a school for soldiers."

"Can I go there?" the boy asked.

His aunt laughed. "Oh, Tommy, you could never go there. That's for rich people."

His mother, glancing archly at her sister, demurred. "You can go wherever you want," she assured him. As the train sped north, the boy watched the gray walls recede to the south like an enchanting, hidden kingdom.

Tom assumed that he was Irish, but that was only three-quarters correct. The original Thomas Carhart immigrated to the New World from Cornwall, arriving in New York on August 25, 1683, as secretary to Colonel Thomas Dongan, the English royal governor. Awarded a 165-acre tract on the south coast of Staten Island for his service, Thomas married a woman half his age, sired three sons, and promptly died. His will showed him to be a man of modest means. In addition to the land, he bequeathed a rapier, a pair of pistols "broken and out of order," "six good pewter plates and twelve ould ones," "an ould wagon," and some household goods.

The family scattered, with some members thriving in New Jersey and both downstate and upstate New York. During the Revolution, the New Jersey Carharts fought valiantly for the rebels, the downstate Carharts remained loyal to the crown, and the upstate Carharts sat out the war as neutrals. Tom's line was from Troy, upstate, but the neutrality must have been bred out in the subsequent two centuries. Tom Carhart remained neutral on very few issues. Like Jack Wheeler and scores of his classmates, Tom wanted to emulate his father by being an officer, gentleman, and war hero. He wanted to be a general.

Now, in the 15th Division, he finally had a fair shine on his shoes. They looked spoony, if he did say so. After cleaning up the polish, he stood holding the small tin of dirty water. The container held only a couple of ounces, but there was no place in the room to dispose of them. Walking all the way down to the sinks was a nuisance, and he wasn't prepared to drink the water, as some classmates did. Tom edged over to the window and peered outside. The roof covering the stoop below looked like a suitable catch basin. No one would be the wiser. With a quick flick of his right wrist, he dumped the tin.

"You, man, in the 15th Division, who just threw water out the window! Right now, hang your nob out!"

Oh, God! Tom thought, seized with terror. Slowly he reappeared in the window. An upperclassman, arms on his hips, stood directly below, elegantly dressed to meet his Saturday night date. Now that was spoony — all except for the tiny black flecks on his white hat and the shoulder of his white uniform shirt. Somehow the water had carried beyond the stoop and squarely spattered the cadet.

"What's your name, mister?" the upperclassman demanded.

"Sir, my name is Mr. Carhart."

"Mr. Carter?"

"Sir, Mr. Carhart."

"You have thirty seconds to get down here in six sets of sweats. Do you understand me?"

"Sir, if — "

"Six pairs of sweats in thirty seconds. Move!"

"Yes, sir."

Tom dashed frantically about the division, pleading with classmates to lend him their sweats. With each successive layer he moved more awkwardly. He couldn't believe it: his resolve, his high-minded determination had come to nothing. This was going to be very unpleasant. A small group of upperclassmen gathered below, waiting to pounce. In the time-honored expression of the corps, Tom could "smell hell" as he waddled into the corridor toward the stairwell. Clearly, he was destined to suffer what cadets crudely described as the classic West Point experience: "a $50,000 education, shoved up the ass a nickel at a time."

One afternoon during Beast, the cadre ordered the cadets into formation before herding them into South Auditorium. "Gentlemen," an officer said as the lights dimmed, "General MacArthur spoke to us here several months ago and what he said was important."

After a pause, a recording of the general's voice, freighted with glory, thundered in the auditorium.

"Duty, honor, country. Those three hallowed words reverently dictate what you ought to be, what you can be, what you will be. They are your rallying points: to build courage when courage seems to fail; to regain faith when there seems to be little cause for faith; to create hope when hope becomes forlorn."

The valedictory, which MacArthur had delivered in the mess hall on May 12, was the last performance by one of the nation's greatest actors. He had prepared meticulously, memorizing the entire speech of more than two thousand words while pacing in a long robe through his ten-room apartment at the Waldorf-Astoria, puffing on his corncob as an Asian butler stood nearby with a tumbler of water.

He arrived at the academy gaunt from a recent bout with the flu. His hands, as veined as autumn leaves, trembled at lunch; perhaps to hide that palsy, MacArthur occasionally holstered them in his jacket pockets. He had combed his thinning hair from a part on the left directly across his crown, thus forming a perfect perpendicular with his hawkish nose. He was eighty-two years old.

"Your mission," the general continued, "remains fixed, determined, inviolable — it is to win our wars. Everything else in your professional career is but corollary to this vital dedication. All other public purposes, all other public projects, all other public needs, great or small, will find others for their accomplishment; but you are the ones who are trained to fight. Yours is the profession of arms — the will to win, the sure knowledge that in war there is no substitute for victory; that if you lose, the nation will be destroyed; that the very object of your public service must be duty, honor, country."

In language that admirers and detractors alike always described eponymously as MacArthuresque, he evoked West Point's great heritage: "From your ranks come the great captains who hold the nation's destiny in their hands the moment the war tocsin sounds. The long gray line has never failed us. Were you to do so, a million ghosts in olive drab, in brown khaki, in blue and gray, would rise from their white crosses thundering those magic words: duty, honor, country.

"The shadows are lengthening for me. The twilight is here," he concluded. "Today marks my final roll call with you, but I want you to know that when I cross the river my last conscious thoughts will be of the corps, and the corps, and the corps."

The new cadets, many with goose bumps, filed out silently, armed with a manifesto. *If you lose, the nation will be destroyed.* In the coming months they would hear the speech again and again. In their classes, in their barracks, in their sleep, they would hear the general's call to arms.

Later, some would be troubled by the implication of West Point elitism; others would find the true Douglas MacArthur — solipsistic and often mendacious — to be less than the sum of his words. But for now he articulated an idealism that each of them had long felt. Amid the ordeal of Beast Barracks, the speech provided a vital and timely affirmation of a higher calling. The greatest of great captains had charged them with the fate of the nation. "The soldier, among all other men," he had declared, "is required to practice the greatest act of religious training — sacrifice."

They called him Saint Doug — and not in derision. They believed.

Three times a day, to the rapping cadence of a drum, the cadets marched through the oak doors of Washington Hall for meals. The enormous room had the ambience of a medieval mead hall. Portraits of past superintendents hung above the wainscoting, including a beardless, dark-haired Robert E. Lee, wearing a Union colonel's uniform. A seventy-by-thirty-foot mural covered the south wall, rendering more than two millennia of military exploits in a mass of spears, arrows, muskets, gas masks, siege engines, and elephants: Cyrus at Babylon, William at Hastings, Meade at Gettysburg, Joffre at the Marne. Above the main door of the mess hall perched a small balcony, known as the poop deck, which was reserved for distinguished diners; occasionally the cadets caught a glimpse of Superintendent Westmoreland at his private table, as godlike and elevated as Mars himself.

Nothing at West Point inspired more rituals than eating. After removing their hats at the foot of the mess hall steps, the cadets double-timed to the tables, each of which seated ten. There they stood at attention until an upperclassmen gave the order to "take seats." New cadets sat braced on the forward three inches of their chairs, eyes locked on the helmet of Pallas Athena embossed upon each plate.

A cadet ate each meal "squarely": he cut off a piece of food no larger than a sugar cube and conveyed it to his mouth with a fork lifted from the plate and moved at right angles. Before chewing — as slowly and deliberately as a ruminant beast — the cadet returned his fork to the plate by the same route and placed his hands in his lap. Then he repeated the process.

One cadet at each table served as the "gunner." He was responsible for ensuring that waiters kept the table supplied with food, dishes, and silverware. Those gunners who carved badly were ordered to the library to study *Carving and Serving* by Mrs. D. A. Lincoln, a volume requested so frequently that the special collections desk kept the book close at hand. Another cadet, designated the "coffee corporal," was responsible for knowing the hot beverage preferences of upperclassmen and keeping their cups full. His cold beverage counterpart was the "water corporal." Like everything else at West Point, meals had become an ordeal for the new cadets.

Perched on the forward three inches of his chair one August evening was a slender, rawboned nineteen-year-old from central Arkansas. His nose, broad and flat, had been broken five times when he played high school football. In photographs, his deep-set blue eyes often seemed widened with surprise. When he spoke, which he did as rarely as possible to avoid drawing fire from the upperclassmen, his words carried a thick drawl.

Like most of his classmates, George Allen Crocker was still hungry, even though the meal was nearly over. Unlike most of them, George Crocker rather enjoyed Beast Barracks. That came as something of a surprise: after a visit to the academy three years earlier, he had announced to his mother, "I wouldn't go to that dumb school for anything." Beast was not pleasant, and he certainly didn't like the daily torment. But it was already clear that he had a knack for the military side of West Point — what little he'd seen of it — and the academy held for him the promise of a vocation.

"Crocker," the table commandant barked, "what are you famous for?"

Answering this standard jibe was always delicate. Plebes who boasted of their high school accomplishments invited scornful sarcasm. As usual, George played it safe. "Sir," he replied loudly, "nothing."

Anonymity was one key to surviving Beast Barracks. George had witnessed — and often endured — the usual hazing, bracing, shower drills, clothing formations, and sundry acts of petty tyranny. The heaviest hand seemed to fall on those who stood out, either through singular ineptitude or a brassy reluctance to remain inconspicuous. New Cadet Crocker had tried to remain faceless, concentrating on the few enjoyable parts of Beast that helped to counterbalance the drudgery.

Marksmanship was one example. After the academy issued M-1 drill rifles, the cadets used paper templates to learn the different parts of the rifle and how to field strip it properly. Gradually, they became proficient in the manual of arms — left shoulder, right shoulder, present arms. A cadet who referred to the weapon as a "gun" was rudely braced and told, in tones commonly reserved for misbehaving dogs, that a soldier never referred to his rifle as a "gun." Then, alternately gripping his weapon and his genitals, he was forced to repeat fifty times: "This is my rifle. This is my gun. This is for shooting. This is for fun."

Early in Beast, the class had jogged to a field near the river for bayonet instruction. "What's the spirit of the bayonet?" the instructor demanded after teaching the horizontal and vertical butt stroke series. "TO KILL, SIR!" the cadets shrieked in reply before plunging their blades into the straw dummies.

Then came a week of "trainfire," in which soldiers from the 101st Airborne taught them how to shoot M-14s. They learned to zero the sights, adjust for the wind, and keep the stock firmly against the shoulder to minimize recoil. The range offered a sequence of pop-up targets from 50 to 350 meters away. For long-range shooting, each rifleman had ten seconds to spot the target, tuck himself into position, and fire.

George had scored a 70, not the best marksmanship in his company but good enough to qualify him as an expert. A rifle felt comfortable in his hands. His father, William, was a superb hunter and had gradually worked his son up from a single-round .410 shotgun to a 12-gauge. They had often hunted ducks together in Arkansas out of a boat or a blind.

Bill Crocker came from Alabama, the oldest of ten children. In 1931, he was hired as a surveyor by Brehon B. Somervell, who later became the Army's supply chief during World War II. The job was a godsend for a young man of limited education in the Depression, but when the nation mobilized for war, Bill tried to enlist in the Seabees. Medically rejected because of dangerously high blood pressure, he sat out the war at home — to his everlasting regret, particularly since his five younger brothers all joined the service. Bill continued to shuttle throughout the South as a construction engineer on dam projects for the Corps of Engineers.

In 1940, while working in Dardanelle, a small cotton town northwest of Little Rock, he met and married Adele Ellis, who worked in the box office of the Joy Theater. The daughter of a former soldier, Adele's earliest memory was of standing near the Rio Grande and watching her father, George Jefferson Ellis, ride out of Mexico with his artillery battery after chasing Pancho Villa as part of Black Jack Pershing's expeditionary force.

Bill and Adele Crocker continued to travel from dam to dam, wherever the corps needed Bill's growing expertise: Alexandria and Monroe in Louisiana, Fort Smith and Dardanelle in Arkansas. In February 1943, Adele gave birth to a son, whom she named George, after her father. When Adele discovered that she could have no more children, Bill was relieved, so fearful was he of never being able to love another child as much as he loved George.

Dardanelle, with a population of about fifteen hundred, prided itself on being a town where everyone knew one another — and one another's business — and where no one ever locked a door. Life for young George revolved around sports, hunting, the several newspaper routes that earned him a dollar a day, and the Arkansas River. In the mid 1950s, the Crockers moved to the bright lights of Fort Smith for a year; when they returned, George sported an Elvis Presley haircut, leather jacket, and boots. In time, they moved across the river to the bigger town and better schools of Russellville. George occasionally worked with Bill at the Dardanelle dam, which was being built to control the killing winter floods that periodically swept the bottomlands. He absorbed his father's penchant for hard work and his unflagging honesty.

West Point was Bill's idea. He admired the competence and commitment of the Army officers who came to work with him on the dam, and he could think of nothing finer than to have George become an academy-trained engineer. George and a friend had entertained the notion of becoming dentists together; still, when Adele arranged an interview with a congressman she knew, George agreed to meet him. The congressman's appointment to the class of 1965 was already filled, but he offered young Crocker the slot for '66. Despite his earlier misgivings — "I wouldn't go to that dumb school for anything" — George accepted. A free education was not something to refuse lightly, and the prospect of spending his life drilling teeth in central Arkansas no longer excited his imagination. Moreover, in the early 1960s the people of rural Arkansas accorded West Pointers something close to demigod status.

So, after a year at the University of Arkansas — where he joined the ROTC, pledged Sigma Nu, and partied relentlessly — George left for the Hudson highlands. His father drove him across Tennessee and up through Gatlinburg, following the Blue Ridge. At the Hotel Thayer on July 2, 1962, before returning home, Bill offered his son parting counsel: "If you don't make it, I'll still be proud of you. And if you don't like it, call me and I'll come get you."

George arrived as the latest levy of a type that had done very well in the American Army — the small-town Southerner. As recently as 1950, two thirds of the officer corps was drawn from farms or towns with fewer than twenty-five hundred people. In the South particularly, the values associated with physical prowess, service to the country, and social protocol still endured. There the notion persisted that for men who heard the calling, the military provided a fitting place to hone those values. In World War II, Arkansas among the forty-eight states had reputedly mustered into uniform more men per capita than any other; *glory* was not a word that made its citizens blush.

George was proud of that heritage, although he had found little glory in Beast Barracks. The past six weeks hadn't been easy, but he knew now that he could survive the physical challenge of West Point. The academic challenge was another matter. In two weeks Beast would end and classes would begin. George had been a fair student at Russellville High, but the academy's higher educational standards worried him. He was, as he later put it, "hoping for a miracle."

Now, in the mess hall, the upperclassmen continued to distract the new cadets by demanding that they recite the arcana of "plebe knowledge."

"Crocker," the table commandant asked, "how many lights in Cullem Hall?"

"Three hundred and forty lights, sir."

"How many gallons in Lusk Reservoir?"

"Ninety point two million gallons, sir, when the water is flowing over the spillway."

"How's the cow?"

"Sir, she walks, she talks, she's full of chalk, the lacteal fluid extracted from the female of the bovine species is highly prolific to the *n*th degree."

The din of recitation resonated throughout Washington Hall. By this time, George and his classmates had been forced to memorize more than seven hundred lines of trivia.

"Sir," bellowed another cadet, launching into "the Days" at an adjacent table, "today is Wednesday, 15 August 1962. There are two and a butt days until the weekend. There are 19 and a butt days until Labor Day. There are 76 and a butt days until Army beats the hell out of Navy in Philadelphia. There are 132 and a butt days until Christmas. There are 294 and a butt days until the class of 1963 graduates on June 5. The movie today is *Two for the Seesaw* with Miss Shirley MacLaine and, and — um — Mr. Jack Lemmon."

"Wrong," the table commandant interrupted. "Robert Mitchum. Pass out your plate."

The cadet surrendered his plate and watched wistfully as the waiter scraped the remainder of his pork chop, green beans, and strawberry shortcake into the garbage. In recent weeks, the authorities had halfheartedly tried to curb what was officially known as "food deprivation," even staging surprise garbage weighings in an effort to detect which tables had unusual amounts of refuse. But the tactic rarely worked, because mess hall waiters usually tipped off the upperclassmen at the targeted tables. Since Beast began, George Crocker had lost twenty pounds; some of his classmates were beginning to resemble prisoners from Bataan.

Scrounging a few extra calories had become a passion. George's roommate, Don Kievit of Canyon, Texas, had taken to swilling from a Lavoris bottle for the nutrition he fancied the mouthwash contained. Soon the entire 1st Division was nipping away. Other cadets bloated themselves with water; if that didn't quite quell the hunger pangs, at least it kept their stomachs from growling so ferociously. Still others ate toothpaste, or even sliced up the tongues of old shoes for something to chew.

Smuggling food from the mess hall was a venerable tradition. Cadets William T. Sherman and William Rosecrans, both destined to be Union generals, used to hide boiled potatoes in their handkerchiefs and stuff butter in their gloves, which they fastened beneath the table with fork tines until it was safe to retrieve the cache. But smugglers lived dangerously. Recently, one new cadet in the class of '66 had been caught with a piece of chocolate cake under his raincoat. "You like cake, huh?" the upperclassmen asked. Procuring two whole cakes from the kitchen, they forced him to eat both while he double-timed through the barracks in poncho and helmet.

In letters from home, parents responded to their sons' pleas by enclosing packets of Kool-Aid, flattened Tootsie Rolls, or any other "boodle" inconspicuous enough to escape detection. A few fretful mothers simply sprinkled the pages with sugar or cornbread crumbs. The cadets hid their boodle in laundry bags, nibbling furtively in the dead of night like a battalion of mice.

After supper, George and his classmates marched back to the barracks for the usual evening of brass polishing and harassment. At ten P.M., an upperclassman called out, "Smacks in the racks." In the corridors of the 1st Division, the so-called Wheelhouse, where many of West Point's most illustrious sons — Douglas MacArthur, John Pershing, Charles Bonesteel, Jonathan Wainwright — had once lived, the squad leaders arrived for a newly imposed ritual. Having failed to thwart the starvation tactics through garbage weighings, the authorities had decreed that every night each new cadet would receive a half pint of milk and a piece of fruit. Grumbling about "coddled smacks," the upperclassmen distributed an armful of bananas and apples. But George and the others couldn't care less if they were coddled. For hundreds of them, this nightly feeding was the only thing staving off malnutrition. The bedtime fare also provided the class with its epigraph. The official class motto "Fame will mix with '66" — had been replaced:

> With fruit and milk we'll get our kicks,
> For we're the boys of '66.

A bugler blew taps. As the final notes faded away, the barracks fell silent except for the soft rustling of a hungry cadet rummaging through his laundry bag, watched, no doubt, with amused detachment by the vigilant ghosts of the great captains.

Jack Wheeler paused outside the room of his squad leader, Jim Daly. Okay, he thought, here goes. He knocked sharply on the door and walked in.

"Sir, all that I am and all that I hope to be I owe to my squad leader, Mr. Daly," Jack said loudly, braced at attention.

Daly looked up. His roommate was sipping a Coke with his nose buried in a book. The phonograph played "Scotch and Soda" by the Kingston Trio.

"Very good, Mr. Wheeler," Daly said with a slight smile. "What else can we do for you?"

"Sir, request permission to make a statement."

"What is it?"

"Sir, I'm thinking of resigning."

Daly's roommate made an exaggerated gagging sound.

"Have you really thought this through?" Daly asked. He was no longer smiling. "Is there anybody you'd like to talk to about this?"

"Yes, sir. I think I'd like to talk to the chaplain."

Jack had not come to this decision easily. In fact, he hadn't really come to a decision at all. But Beast was so arduous, so unpleasant, that he felt compelled to force the issue. After weeks of being treated like an American Mameluke — a slave soldier — he had reached the breaking point.

"I think I'm having just a bit more than average trouble keeping in step at drill," he had written to his parents a few days before. "It's very hard here. I'm doing o.k., I guess. I'm just so scared. I have so little time. I miss home very much. How can I say how I feel? I'm crying. I love you both very much. It's all over, isn't it? If only I could be home again, see you every night."

He knew that his father would be disappointed. Even though the elder Wheeler had not been around much, Jack understood that he was thrilled to have a son following in his footsteps at West Point. Big Jack had gone to all that trouble with the ear business and the Air Force doctor. But Jack couldn't help thinking about what he had forfeited. The Yale freshman class of 1966 was preparing to go to New Haven now; he knew that the students weren't worrying about starving to death or polishing brass until their arms ached. Life here was petty, oppressive. In the academy's fifteen-page booklet on how plebes should be treated under the "fourth class system," one paragraph read: "Forms of maltreatment, ranging from undesirable verbal expressions to physical brutality, result in personal humiliation and indignity. They have no place in the fourth class system." Jack had scribbled a single comment in the margin: "Ha!"

The connection between what he was enduring and the eventual gold bars of a second lieutenant seemed very obscure. He could understand a remark once made by Eisenhower: "If any time had been provided to sit down and think for a moment, most of the 285 of us would have taken the next train out." And every cadet knew the old witticism which held that "West Point enjoys two centuries of tradition untouched by progress."

With Daly's permission, Jack walked slowly up the serpentine stone steps to Quarters 60, the chaplain's house. This would be his second encounter with the chaplain's office. A few weeks earlier, the assistant chaplain, the Reverend James D. Ford, had given a talk to the new cadets in North Auditorium and discussed the Cadet Prayer.

"Make us to choose the harder right instead of the easier wrong, and never to be content with a half truth when the whole can be won," the prayer asked. Jack had noticed, however, that Ford's version ended, "All of which we ask in the name of the great friend and master of men, Jesus Christ our Lord." The version printed in Jack's handbook ended with "master of men."

"Chaplain, how come you changed the Cadet Prayer?" he asked after the lecture.

Ford had looked down from the stage. "Well, the chapel board met," he replied, "and it was thought that we're in a Christian setting, so adding Christ's name was appropriate."

"Chaplain," Jack persisted, "it's the cadets' prayer. Why didn't you ask the cadets?"

The protest was audacious — B.J., in cadet parlance, meaning "bold before June," when plebes were officially recognized by the upperclassmen. Ford climbed down from the stage and peered at Jack's name tag. "Wheeler," he pronounced, turning away. "I'm going to remember you."

Then Ford had paused, turning back to Jack with a nod. "And you're right."

This, no doubt, would be a different kind of encounter. Over the years the senior chaplain, Theodore Speers, had counseled hundreds if not thousands of cadets who were on the verge of leaving. Already 150 members of the class of '66 had quit. Resignation was practically endemic at the academy. Some quit because of what they said were orders from the Lord — they were sometimes referred to derisively as the God Squad. Others quit to get married, or to attend "real college." And a few — the Brasso cocktail crowd — tried to kill themselves.

Among Jack's classmates, in fact, there had been at least one suicide attempt, by a boy from Nebraska named Jenkins. He was bright, scrawny, and instant prey for the cadre, who made him sit by his window and cheep like a bird. "Louder, Jenkins, louder," they yelled from their rooms. Then one morning, New Cadet Jenkins flung himself down a stairwell. Within an hour every trace of Jenkins had been eradicated from his room: name tags stripped, equipment removed, mattress folded double on the springs. It was eerie, as though he had never existed; it was like Benedict Arnold's name being chiseled off the chapel plaque.

Jack was not that desperate. Some things at West Point, he had to admit, were downright fun. Jim Daly was a decent man, not nearly the thug that some of the other squad leaders were. Daly took his duties seriously, but he also had a puckish streak. Sometimes he pretended that the 17th Division was a submarine; he would post Jack and his classmates on the top floor as though it were a conning tower while they made torpedo runs on the barracks across Central Area.

"*Ah-oooga! Ah-oooga!* Fire one! Fire two!" Daly would shout, as his crew flushed the toilets with a whoosh, pretending they were aboard the *Spadefish* or the *Wahoo*. Jack also enjoyed the rifle range: he had shot better than anyone else in the company with his M-14, winning three pints of maple walnut ice cream, which he shared with the squad.

"Have I changed?" he wrote to his parents midway through Beast.

> Am seven to 10 pounds lighter, probably down to 144. Long, tough pull ahead. Eleven months more, then only thirty days off. Four years more, actually. Really, I guess it's a lifetime more to go. Childhood's over. So are those teenage years, school days and parties that books and t.v. promised but were never delivered. What's life all for anyway? Who cares? I've got to shine my shoes.

Jack reached the chapel and walked around back to Quarters 60, where Speers ushered him inside. The chaplain listened patiently while Jack described his misgivings. A large, Old Testament figure with a booming voice and white hair swept back from his domed forehead, Speers was accustomed to homesick plebes.

"It's really hard, Chaplain," Jack said, sitting erect on the edge of his chair. "I'm just not sure what I should do."

"It's rough," Speers agreed with a nod, "but you can do this. I know you can make it."

"Maybe I want to be a doctor," Jack suggested.

The chaplain rarely counseled cadets to resign. Occasionally a young man was clearly ill suited to academy life or had joined the corps for the wrong reasons. But in most cases, Speers believed, the decision had to be made by the individual in consultation with his conscience.

"Why don't you give it a few days?" he asked Jack gently. "Let's talk in a week if you want to."

Jack trudged back down to the barracks, brooding over his course of action. He was not a quitter; even at the age of seventeen, he prided himself on completing whatever task he had undertaken. Yet the thought of four more years in this penal camp left him numb with despair. *Childhood's over. What's life all for anyway?*

"West Point is tough!" Commandant Stilwell had warned on R-Day. "It is tough in the same way that war is tough. It calls for leaders who can stand straight and unyielding."

George Patton believed that a man's military life amounted to a three-minute accumulation of nays and yeas that determined his career and could shape the course of history. Jack would burn one of those yeas now. He would hang on and see this through. He would stand fast, straight and unyielding, finishing what he had begun.

2

Year of the Tiger

Three months later, at a quarter of six on a mid November morning, Jack tiptoed past a trio of snoring upperclassmen. Feeling his way through the darkened room, he dimly saw their recumbent forms beneath the "brown boy" quilts that every cadet cherished. An icy draft poured through the open window. The radiator was here somewhere; Jack could feel the heat beating from the pipes. Plebes told horror stories of scaldings and "radiator dong." Still clad in T-shirt and drollies, he cautiously leaned across the hot fins and pulled shut the window sash.

Outside, the distant boom of a single cannon shot reverberated through North Area, signaling ten minutes until reveille. "Wheeler. That you, Wheeler?" a groggy voice asked from beneath one of the brown boys.

"Yes, sir."

"Close the window."

"Yes, sir. It is closed, sir."

At least the upperclassmen no longer required plebes to warm the toilet seats in the morning, as an earlier generation had. Closing the windows wasn't too bad, Jack thought: by requiring him to leave the comfort of his warm bunk, the task gave him a few extra minutes to get ready for reveille formation. He slipped out of the upperclassmen's room and returned to his own to finish dressing. Quickly donning his uniform, he scanned the room to be certain everything was in order, then hurried down the corridor. The sixteen rooms in the 54th Division had burst to life: upperclassmen were shaving, dressing, swapping ribald jokes.

Cold, dead air slapped his cheeks as Jack pushed through the door to fall in with the other plebes — five minutes early, as required. A trio of Hellcats struck up a brisk medley of drum and bugle calls while another plebe launched into the spiel of the "minute caller."

"Sir, there are five minutes until reveille formation. The uniform today is as-for-class under raincoats. Breakfast today is scrambled eggs with sausage and grapefruit sections. Five minutes, sir!" the minute caller bellowed from the stoop.

He repeated the cry periodically, counting down to six A.M. Throughout the barracks, uniform flags further informed cadets of the day's attire. On this Saturday morning the poles flew a black flag for raincoats and a green flag for rubbers. The weather was bad and that was good, Jack thought as he stood shivering; perhaps the parade would be canceled.

Now that Beast Barracks had ended, he felt that he had his equilibrium back. West Point was still oppressive but bearable. "Academics is pure grind," he had written his parents that week. "Every night, fight the books and sweat your performance in class, as well as put up with the plebe system. Two hundred and five days until June week. I love you all, and I miss my family worse every day, though sometimes I'm too numb even to notice. I love you — Little Jack."

He had gotten a lucky break in being assigned to Company M-2. By reputation and tradition, Mama Deuce was perhaps the most indulgent company in the corps, an island of forbearance in a sea of tyranny. Jack was pleased to find that upperclassmen permitted plebes to use the Coke machine on the first floor. Even the instruction given all plebes in the academy's famous honor code was undertaken with restraint in Mama Deuce. A cadet does not lie, cheat, steal, or tolerate those who do, an upperclassman informed them succinctly. Any questions?

The rigid simplicity of the honor code usually forestalled questions. In a world fraught with ambiguity, West Point sought to purge equivocation. "Quibbling, cheating, evasive statements, or recourse to technicalities will not be tolerated," the cadets were told. Of course, the tradition of West Point honor and the single sanction for any violation — swift expulsion — at first terrified the plebes. The grapevine buzzed with stories, many of them true, about cadets being dismissed for impulsively saying they had brushed their teeth or polished their shoes when they had not. But at least in M-2 no one tried to bludgeon plebes with the code.

When the upperclassmen had returned from leave in early September, the twenty-four hundred cadets in the corps were divided into two regiments, a dozen companies in each. Every company had roughly equal numbers of freshman, sophomores, juniors, and seniors — known as plebes (fourth classmen), yearlings (third classmen), cows (second classmen), and firsties. Like so many things at West Point, this organization was a legacy of Sylvanus Thayer, the "father of the military academy," who had served as superintendent from 1817 to 1833.

Obsessed with uniformity on the parade field, Thayer had also segregated cadets by height. Tall cadets — flankers — were assigned to companies that would flank the serried ranks. Short cadets — runts — were grouped in companies forming the center of the ranks. By tradition, runts tended to be foul-tempered sticklers about regulations; flankers were tolerant and possessed of sang-froid.

Height assignments had persisted until 1957, when, under Project Equality, the academy began composing companies on the basis of scholastic, athletic, and leadership abilities. Even so, the psychology lingered in 1962. M-2 was an old flanker company and proud of it. Rarely were the upperclassmen sadistic, preferring to use plebes as manservants rather than slaves. Jack's duties, for example, included writing letters of endorsement to an upperclassman's girlfriend: "Dear Samantha: You don't know me but I am a fourth classman at West Point and Mr. Johnson asked me to write to you. I wanted you to know that he is a wonderful man and an exceptional leader."

M-2 was housed in the 54th Division in a section of barracks called the Lost Fifties. An architectural afterthought to North Area, the Lost Fifties stood wedged between the barracks complex and the steps leading to the chapel. Because Mama Deuce was somewhat out of the way, officers in charge rarely wandered over at night, much to the delight of the cadets who lived there.

Jack was overjoyed not to have drawn D-1, known as Dogshit One, or I-1, Inquisition One. Every year these two old runt companies washed out between a third and a half of the plebes who had survived Beast Barracks. In addition to the upperclassmen, some companies had legendary martinets serving as tactical officers. (A "tac," usually an Army captain, served as the company commander, maintaining discipline and supervising the cadets' military education). One tac often stood outside the barracks at night, checking to see that all window shades were evenly drawn. Another infamous tac ploy was to wear a sneaker on one foot. Cadets in the barracks would listen for the early warning of a tac's metal taps as he came up the stairs; the silent sneaker fooled them into thinking he was approaching at only half his actual speed.

In North Area, the final notes of reveille drifted away. Not the slightest hint of dawn had yet appeared. Jack and his classmates stood as immobile as statues in the damp cold, prohibited from even wiggling their toes. In fluid mechanics class, cadets studied a principle known as the Venturi effect, which posited that any fluid conveyed through a constricted passage increased in velocity. Nowhere was the Venturi effect more evident than at West Point, where the Hudson wind swept into the gorge of Storm King Mountain and whipped out across the Plain.

As the last upperclassmen strolled casually into the ranks, Jack wondered what the academy was going to be like in February. It wasn't Thanksgiving yet, but already everything looked gray and frigid. Gray walls, gray sky, gray cadets. Except for — Jack blinked in amazement. There, among the upperclassmen, stood a beautiful girl. She wore a cadet uniform with her brunette hair tucked beneath a cap. Jack's jaw sagged in disbelief. She was gorgeous, one of the most beautiful creatures he had ever seen. The girl must have spent the night with someone and was now being smuggled out of the barracks. Jack was as dumfounded as a peasant at the village well witnessing an appearance of the Virgin — except that this woman was very real and, he suspected, no virgin.

The company came to attention and prepared to march to the mess hall. The cadets nudged one another gleefully, although no one outside their formation had noticed. This is incredible, Jack thought, stealing a sidelong glance down the ranks. Sneaking a woman into the barracks was, well, it was pure flanker. It was Mama Deuce. It was *all right.* You could bet that they didn't have any beautiful brunettes over in Dogshit One, marching off with *them* to breakfast.

Somewhere, somehow, the girl vanished before they reached Washington Hall. Marching four abreast through the oak doors, the cadets were still electrified by the apparition.

The din of the mess hall pulled Jack from his reverie. As usual, with the entire corps sitting down simultaneously to a thirty-minute meal, the hall roared with activity. Waiters hustled, plebes recited, upperclassmen heckled. The yearlings, only a few months removed from the torments of their own plebe year, histrionically dropped their silverware at any plebe infraction, shaking their heads in exaggerated disdain. At one table, an upperclassman stood on his chair, cracking an imaginary whip while the other cadets rowed an imaginary galley. A plebe squatted at the foot of the table, peering into the mist.

"Zowie, zowie, zowie!" another plebe bellowed nearby, pounding the table with both fists. "Sir, I'm a stuffgut and a glutton. This is me left meathook. This is me right meathook. These are me meathooks extended and joined. I weigh 153 and a butt pounds, and oh what a butt."

Sitting on the forward three inches of his chair at the foot of the table, Jack was ready to recite if called on. Because plebes were not permitted to leave the academy for the holidays, upperclassmen frequently demanded that they sing "I'll Be Home for Christmas," and Jack had memorized the lyrics. Every week he also filled several index cards with facts that each plebe was required to learn by rote, from the daily menu to the names of the Cabinet secretaries.

As waiters brought platters of eggs and sausage to the table, Jack kept his eyes on the figure of Athena's helmet embossing his plate. He had looked up Athena in his father's old *Webster's Collegiate,* which defined her as "a preeminent goddess, wise in the industries of peace and the arts of war." He liked that. Industries of peace: she was not just a sanguinary harridan.

"Wheeler," the table commandant called out, "how about serenading us with a song? Something original."

Jack was ready for this demand, too. While playing with his slide rule, he had invented some lyrics to the tune of "Surrey With the Fringe on Top." He stood and belted them them out:

In math class for solving equations,
Or out of class for special occasions,
Use your log log duplex decitrig sliii-ding rule.
Oh, the slipstick's slick for arithmetic,
The case is genuine leather.
It's waxed and polished, it will never stick
In case there's a change in the weaaa-ther.

"Very good, Mr. Wheeler." The table commandant applauded. "Well done. Okay, plebes, big bites, big bites."

Jack sat down. Another meal survived. Only six hundred more to go before the end of plebe year. What a strange place, he thought for the thousandth time. Here they were, preparing to lead the nation's Army someday, but at times it seemed as though West Point were located on another planet.

Even issues of war and peace were remote, unreal. Just three weeks before, the president had appeared on national television to announce "that a series of offensive missile sites is now in preparation" in Cuba. "The purpose of these bases," he declared, "can be none other than to provide a nuclear strike capability against the Western hemisphere."

From the poop deck in the mess hall, the corps had been informed matter-of-factly that some cadets would receive tropical disease inoculations — just in case. Plebes entertained a wan hope that the firsties would be graduated immediately, as earlier war classes had been, allowing the men of '66 to become yearlings and escape the rigors of their fourth-class year.

But no one, it seemed to Jack, appeared to give the crisis in Cuba a second thought. The world might be on the brink of Armageddon, but West Point allowed the corps scant time to worry about such things. In a sixteen-hour day, plebes had two unscheduled periods: 2:05 to 2:15 P.M., and 3:15 to 3:35 P.M. Even in those thirty minutes of "free time," cadets always had plenty to do, since a plebe never knew when he would have to sing for his supper or recite the Cabinet secretaries or declare with certainty that today's dinner menu featured pork tenderloin, succotash, and pumpkin custard pie. Isolation had long been considered a virtue at West Point, preserving cadets from "the contaminating impurities of the outside world," as one academy authority once put it. But sometimes Jack felt sundered from everything that happened beyond this little colony. Had his father's plebe class been as disengaged, he wondered, when the outside world rushed headlong toward catastrophe in 1939?

After the adjutant dismissed the corps from breakfast, Jack marched out of the mess hall with the other plebes. Morning classes began in a few minutes; unless rain intervened, the corps would then assemble at noon for the usual Saturday parade.

The Plain looked cold and forbidding as Jack headed back to the barracks to collect his books. In 1947, West Point had organized a huge horse auction here to empty its remaining stables. The event provided an extraordinary symbol for the end of an epoch: the sale of the horses also meant the end of riding classes, polo matches, the annual equestrian show, and other trappings of cavalry glory. By the time the auction concluded, only the Army mules remained stabled at the academy — "imperfect links," as one historian wrote, "to the romance of the equestrian past." Patton had claimed that the saddest moment in his life came when he stood at attention, weeping, as his cavalry regiment marched past to stack their sabers for the last time.

Jack was the first Wheeler in at least a dozen generations not to grow up on horseback. Service in the cavalry was a Wheeler tradition, virtually a birthright. Thomas Wheeler, who had emigrated with his father from Bedfordshire to the Massachusetts Bay Colony in 1635, had commanded Concord's cavalry troop against the Indians in King Philip's War; ambushed near the settlement of Brookfield on July 2, 1675, he had been mortally wounded. Another ancestor, Fightin' Joe Wheeler, had graduated from West Point with the class of 1859, and eventually commanded the Confederate cavalry in the western theater of the Civil War. Fiery and diminutive, he later served as a congressman from Georgia for seventeen years; at the age of sixty-three, he was remounted as a major general in the Spanish-American War, and routed the enemy at Las Guásimas in Cuba with the spirited if baffling cry, "Give it to them, lads, we've got the damned Yankees on the run!"

Jack's grandfather was born in 1887 on Maryland's Eastern Shore at Marengo, a plantation named for Napoleon's victory over the Austrian army in northern Italy. As the family's youngest son, he followed the path taken by youngest sons for centuries: he became a military man. Unable to secure an appointment to West Point, he entered the Naval Academy, only to flunk out in his second year after failing to penetrate the mysteries of steam engineering. Undaunted, he joined the cavalry, was commissioned a lieutenant in 1913, and arrived at Fort Huachuca in time to chase Pancho Villa through northern Mexico. In 1918, while he was fighting in France, his wife bore a son, John Parsons Wheeler, Jr.

The boy grew up in a saddle, with a polo mallet practically molded to his arm. After his father returned from France, the family spent most of the next twenty years shuttling from one remote, dusty outpost to another along the Rio Grande — the unenviable destiny of cavalrymen between the world wars. When young John was nine, he rode with his father's 5th Cavalry squadron more than two hundred miles along the border from Camp Marfa to Fort Bliss.

On Saturday mornings, Major Wheeler would organize polo matches on the parade field, teaching his son the finer points of the nearside backhand and offside forehand. Although the boy was later called Big Jack to distinguish him from his own son, he was more Fightin' Joe's size — a wiry, slashing All-State running back in football. His sole aspiration was to attend West Point and become a cavalry officer. After a year at Kansas State University, he landed an appointment and arrived for Beast Barracks two months before Hitler invaded Poland. As the academy yearbook noted: "Jack hit here from college with a cocksure attitude, a haircut that would shame a concert violinist, and a sport coat that could be heard for miles. A rugged plebe year fixed all but the coat."

Like his father, he was a poor student, consistently hovering near the bottom of the class of 1943. But with war erupting on two fronts, the Army desperately needed pilots. The cavalry clearly was going the way of the archer, so Jack applied to be an aviator. Cadets who successfully completed flight school in the summer would be commissioned directly into the Army Air Corps rather than returning to West Point. Jack breezed through basic training and was halfway through the advanced course at Randolph Field in Florida when he was involved in a "wing bumper" during night formation flying; neither plane crashed, but the accident sufficed to send him back to the Corps of Cadets.

Jack hadn't planned to go home during Christmas leave in December 1941. Pearl Harbor had been destroyed just two weeks earlier, and the academy consequently shortened the holiday break. But when his father received orders to ship out from Fort Clark, Texas, for North Africa, Jack changed his mind; he wanted to see the old polo player before he went to war. From Penn Station Jack caught the train to St. Louis, where he transferred to the San Antonio express. The coaches were crowded with holiday travelers, febrile with war. In his dress grays, he was walking through the dining car when he spied Senator Tom Connally, chairman of the Senate Foreign Relations Committee, who was returning home to Texas from Washington.

"Sir, you won't remember me but my name's Wheeler and you were instrumental in trying to get me into West Point. I just wanted to thank you," Jack said, steadying himself in the aisle. His eyes fastened on a beautiful young girl sitting across from Connally. She was about twenty, with wide-set blue eyes and porcelain skin.

"Thank you," the senator replied. "May I introduce Miss Janet Conly?"

After a moment of small talk, Jack excused himself and repaired to the observation car. But the next morning he found Janet again, alone this time. They talked nonstop all the way to San Antonio. He discovered that she was from Laredo and had met the senator two years before while working as a page for the Daughters of the American Revolution in Washington. Now she worked in New York at Bonwit Teller, selling ladies' handkerchiefs. "And I want you to know," Janet added firmly, "that I'm going home to announce my engagement."

John Wheeler was waiting for his son on the platform in San Antonio. They made a fine picture, father in his officer's uniform and son in cadet gray. Jack watched Janet intently across the platform, where her fiancé smothered her in his arms before sweeping her toward his Oldsmobile for the long drive to Laredo.

"See that girl over there?" Jack confided, gripping his father's hand. "I'm going to marry her."

Janet Conly did not need this complication. Her life was already complicated enough. The Conlys were an old Texas clan, fallen on hard times. On Thanksgiving morning 1924, when Janet was three, her father had been kicked in the chest while harnessing a mule, and died in agony several hours later. After a ten-year struggle against a relentless tide of Great Depression debts, Beatrice Conly sold the family farm in Dimmit County, packed up her six children, and moved to Laredo.

At her mother's urging, Janet had traveled to New York to attend the Tobé-Coburn School for Fashion Careers, where young ladies studied merchandising, window dressing, and other skills that might land them millinery assignments from Condé Nast. Living in Queens with her godmother, Janet rode the subway every morning from Forest Hills to midtown Manhattan and walked three blocks to the school on Fifty-seventh Street. She loved sitting in St. Thomas's Church before class, or stopping for coffee at Schrafft's, where the waitresses served delicate tea sandwiches with the crusts trimmed away. The experience had opened her eyes to city life, but now she was ready to settle down with her Laredo beau.

So the last thing she needed was this pesky cadet. And Jack was persistent. When Janet returned to Forest Hills after New Year's 1942 — with an engagement ring on her left hand — he had already called to invite her to an academy hop. He phoned incessantly; she kept ducking him, spinning excuses. She didn't want to take the bus. She didn't want to take the train. West Point sounded cold. "I'm from Texas," she complained, "and I hate snow."

Finally, she agreed to have her godmother drive her to the academy. With two Irish terriers bouncing around in the back seat of Aunt Grace's Cadillac, they pulled up to Cullem Hall. Jack was waiting for her. A year later, four hours after he received his diploma, they were married in the cadet chapel.

Because of the war, the class of 1943 graduated on January 19, six months early. The Army immediately sent Jack to Fort Knox for a five-month introduction to armor and then to the Mojave Desert, where his unit was training. After storing the wedding gifts in a shack behind her mother's garden in Laredo, Janet drove to California, more or less living out of her Chevrolet during the journey.

At first she moved in with several other lieutenants' wives who had rented a cabin in Crestline. They whiled away their days sipping coffee and holding contests to see which wife could best iron her husband's fatigues. After one week of insufferable boredom, Janet fled to Los Angeles. When the 9th Armored Division finished desert training, the unit shipped out for exercises in the swamps of Louisiana. Just before midnight on Christmas Eve 1943, the Wheelers arrived at Camp Polk, where they rented a garage apartment. Three months later Jack left for England to stage for the Normandy invasion. Janet went home, pregnant.

The wait was lonely and frightening. In addition to Jack, her four brothers were all in uniform: one as a Marine chaplain, two as artillery officers, and one in the Army Air Corps. Every time the Western Union boy pedaled past the house, Janet held her breath, hoping that he wouldn't turn down Beatrice's walk. Once he did, with the news that her brother John had been killed in a raid on Tokyo.

The bad news about Jack came to her in the Laredo hospital where their son, John Parsons Wheeler III, was born on December 14, 1944. Five days after delivering, Janet was about to check out when the telegram arrived: REGRET TO INFORM YOU YOUR HUSBAND MISSING IN ACTION. He had vanished during the Battle of the Bulge. That bloody fight already had claimed two other sons of prominent Laredo families. Janet checked back into the hospital and stayed there for two weeks.

Jack was not dead — he was just very lost in the Ardennes — but it seemed to take forever to get word to Laredo. By the time he was pulled out of the line for a rest near Bastogne on January 13, he had only three tanks left of the sixteen Shermans his company had had a month earlier. At Bastogne, he also learned that he had a new son.

Two months later, in March 1945, Jack and his men arrived at Remagen, elated to see that the Nazis had botched the demolition of the Ludendorff railroad bridge across the Rhine. Positioned on the west bank of the river, his tankers fired their main guns at any target that moved in the east and their .50-calibers at the diving Stukas attempting to destroy the span. The Americans seized the bridge and stormed into Germany.

When the war in Europe ended in May, Jack volunteered to fly to the Philippines for the invasion of Japan. But Tokyo surrendered just as he was about to board the transport plane in France. He was not disappointed, to be sure, but he had to admit that the war had been an extraordinary adventure; he loved being a soldier, and war was a soldier's ultimate challenge. In February 1946, he finally returned home, where he saw his boy for the first time, toddling about Beatrice Conly's back yard in Laredo.

After sixty days' leave, Jack returned to Europe to join the Army of Occupation. Janet and young Jack followed him as part of the first consignment of American dependents permitted on the Continent. Mother and son boarded the U.S.S. *Holbrook* in Brooklyn and had a rough and wretched crossing of the North Atlantic; whenever they ventured from their cabin on B Deck, Janet kept her son on a short leash. After berthing in Bremerhaven, they boarded a train and traveled through Germany to Linz, on the Danube in northern Austria. There, on orders of General Mark Clark, the dependents were greeted with flower garlands and a band with bagpipes playing "I'm in the Mood for Love." Big Jack was waiting, too. He drove them in a sedan to their new home, a two-story house originally built for workers in a Nazi airplane factory.

Sometimes the victors endured shortages of essentials. Meat and fruit were rationed; on commissary day, Janet stood in line for a liter of milk shipped all the way from Denmark. And occasionally, the Russians across the Danube cut off the electricity to the American sector, apparently for spite.

But life was wonderful. They had won. The tankers tromped about Linz in their pinching tanker boots, smoking cigars and sporting yellow scarves. Janet hired a Hungarian cook and a nanny who slept like a big cat on the floor beneath little Jack's crib. After years of separation, the Wheelers were finally united. In their little Austrian kitchen, the sweet smell of rationed oranges mingled with the aroma of percolating coffee, hanging in the morning air like the precise odor of happiness.

Now, on this November Saturday seventeen years later, Jack climbed the steps of the 54th Division to grab his calculus text, a turgid looseleaf tome known as Green Death. Then, with the quick-stepping, Charlie Chaplin walk required of plebes, he hurried to Thayer Hall. Once the academy's riding pavilion, windowless Thayer had become West Point's main academic building. Six days a week, seventy-five minutes a day, Jack came here for calculus.

The class would have seemed entirely familiar to plebes from the previous century: a dozen cadets sat in descending order of their grade point averages; each man recited daily; grades were assigned daily and posted weekly. The instructor, like three quarters of the faculty at West Point, was an academy graduate. The plebe curriculum required each cadet in the class of 1966 to take calculus, as well as engineering, physical education, military tactics, geography, and English. A plebe's sole option lay in the selection of which language he wanted to study; Jack had picked Russian.

He sat in the second chair of the calculus class. Every few weeks the instructors shuffled the classes to reflect ascents and descents in the cadets' academic standing. This was the first, or most accomplished section of plebe calculus, and Jack currently had the second highest ranking. Unlike his father and grandfather, he was an excellent student and looked forward to winning the brocaded gold stars worn on the uniform collar by "star men" — the top 5 percent of each class.

In this calculus section, Jack had taken a particular liking to the cadet sitting in the seventh seat. They had suffered in the same Beast squad together, sharing shatterproof eyeglasses during rifle practice and the maple walnut ice cream that Jack had won for shooting well. Jack found something about him immensely appealing; perhaps it was his self-confidence, bolstered during a year at Duke University, or his unaffected intelligence. Even as a plebe he spent many hours after taps tutoring upperclassmen in mathematics. Short but well proportioned, he had an open face and arresting eyes shaped like inverted half moons.

His name was Thomas Jay Hayes IV, and he was another cadet with a remarkable West Point lineage. Tommy's grandfather, who graduated with the class of 1912, had written the standard ordnance text used at the academy for years. Before World War II, he managed the Springfield

Armory, where he supervised the assembly line surge that enabled the plant to produce three thousand Garand rifles a day. Promoted to major general, he took on the Herculean job of organizing the Army's munitions production during the war.

Tommy's father was no less accomplished. He had graduated in 1936, the same year as William Westmoreland. As an Army engineer during the war, he built air bases in Greenland and the Bahamas. Later, he held a variety of engineering commands: head of slum clearance in Washington, D.C.; district engineer in Little Rock and Omaha; supervisor of ICBM silo construction for the Titan, Minuteman, and Atlas missiles; construction supervisor at the manned spacecraft center in Houston. He, too, had become a major general.

Jack, Tommy, and the other ten cadets in the class immediately rose from their seats when the calculus instructor gave the now familiar command: "Take boards." At the blackboard, Jack chalked his name and his company in the upper-right-hand corner. Then he carefully divided the board into quadrants, and soon covered each of the sections with drawings and equations. After finishing, he set the chalk in its tray and turned around as the instructor called on Tommy to explain one of the problems. Scanning Tommy's board, Jack quickly saw that his friend had made an error in the equation.

Tommy apparently recognized the mistake himself, because he glanced across the room at Jack's board.

"Sir, I will use Mr. Wheeler's board," he said coolly, walking across the room with a pointer in his hand. There was an old tradition at West Point that Jack had heard about but had never actually witnessed: any cadet who erred could still "max" a problem by using a classmate's board work, if he could adequately explain the solution.

Tommy maxed. Jack was deeply impressed. Any egghead could solve an equation. But that effortless aplomb, Jack thought, now that was something special.

What was the best way to educate a future officer? Were great captains born or could they be made? What classroom skills translated into battlefield prowess?

West Point had wrestled with these questions for 160 years. In his graduation speech of June 1962, John F. Kennedy had virtually ordered the academy to cultivate an officer "with a new and wholly different kind of military training" for the new type of war he envisioned. In addition to being soldiers, modern officers were expected to be diplomats, nation builders, and independent thinkers.

Yet many at West Point saw little need for change. The academy, they believed, had done an exceptional job of molding officers with an old-fashioned education to fight in an old-fashioned way — annihilating an enemy until he surrendered. As always at the military academy, those who admired the status quo were locked in combat with those who wanted change.

Tradition versus change, conservatism versus innovation, old versus new: such battles had been joined at West Point for the better part of two centuries. In the years after its founding by Thomas Jefferson in March 1802, the United States Military Academy had remained, in the words of one dismayed contemporary, "a puny, rickety child." No standards obtained. Cadets might be as young as ten and as old as thirty-four. The first superintendent, Jonathan Williams, resigned in disgust in 1803; persuaded to return, he quit again in 1812. The second war with Britain, which began that year, nearly became a national military debacle; Andrew Jackson's postbellum victory at New Orleans notwithstanding, the performance of the American Army was marred by incompetent and bickering commanders, rampant indiscipline, and logistical fiascoes.

West Point found its soul with the arrival in July 1817 of a new superintendent, the slender, stern, brilliant Sylvanus Thayer. A native of Braintree, Massachusetts, Thayer had graduated with the West Point class of 1808 after a year at the academy preceded by four years at Dartmouth. Returning as superintendent, he found the place in an uproar. Most of the 213 cadets had taken an unlimited holiday. Five senior faculty members had been arrested for impertinence after complaining to President James Monroe about conditions at the academy. The outgoing superintendent, the vain and deceitful Alden Partridge, simply refused to leave. Assembling the corps, Partridge announced to lusty cheers that he was resuming command. Thayer caught the next boat to New York, where he waited patiently until Partridge was arrested for mutiny and imprisoned on Governor's Island, much to the glee of the New York newspapers.

In the next sixteen years, by force of personality and vision, Thayer transformed the academy into an institution admired and emulated throughout the world. Deeply influenced by his years of study in France, he believed in small classes, daily recitation, and weekly ratings in academics and conduct. Favoritism was exterminated, discipline made iron. Thayer required cadets to keep their rooms in "a state of perfect cleanliness and order." Gentlemen, he decreed, "must learn that it is only their province to listen and obey."

Unlike the Continental powers, whose officers were drawn largely from the nobility or monied classes, the United States intended West

Point to be relatively egalitarian. Even so, many outsiders viewed the academy as an affront to Jacksonian democracy. Congress sniped continuously; a Tennessee politician named Davy Crockett offered a resolution in the House in 1830 that decried West Point as "not only aristocratic but a downright invasion of the rights of the citizens."

Undeterred, Thayer assigned tactical officers to live with cadets in the barracks so that discipline could be enforced even more rigorously. He logged cadet offenses in a report dubbed the "skin list." Thayer also established an informal academy honor code, which decreed that cadets would not lie, cheat, or steal. His final act as superintendent demonstrated how passionately this supposedly passionless man considered the issue of honor.

After the class of 1833 had performed superbly during final examinations, the president of the board of visitors, Joel R. Poinsett, remarked casually at dinner one evening that he could barely conceive how the cadets could have done so well without knowing the questions in advance. Thayer, in high dudgeon at the implied insult, ordered the entire class back to their desks for a meticulous re-examination; the cadets, sharing Thayer's sense of violated honor, performed just as capably as they had on the original tests. With the rectitude of the academy upheld, Thayer boarded a steamer for New York, leaving behind a West Point that was far advanced from the one he had inherited sixteen years earlier. Even Andrew Jackson, hardly the academy's staunchest ally, praised it as "the best school in the world."

Thayer's educational system made West Point the nation's pre-eminent engineering school before the Civil War. Horace Mann declared in 1849 that he had "rarely if ever seen anything that equalled the excellence of the teaching or the proficiency of the taught."

But that excellence soon waned. Isolated and inbred, the academy ossified. The academic board, comprising department heads who ruled their fiefdoms like feudal barons, stoutly resisted reform. The system became sacred; the instructors were often pompous and humorless. When one cadet jokingly suggested in 1878 that a + became a − on passing through zero because the crosspiece had been knocked off, the instructor had him arrested.

A ludicrous formalism took hold. When professors in their swallowtail coats met one another on the street, they doffed their stovepipe hats and offered deep, sweeping bows beginning at twenty paces. By 1920, Charles W. Eliot, president emeritus of Harvard, savagely attacked West Point as "an example of just what an educational institution should not be." He condemned the academy's "ill-prepared" cadets, "completely prescribed curriculum," and "teaching done almost exclusively by recent graduates." Yet West Point remained impervious to such grapeshot. As recently as 1954, the head of the academic board smugly argued that each cadet "has exercised a complete freedom of choice in his decision to come to West Point at all — he chose the prescribed curriculum."

In modern times, the cultivation of character was considered the sine qua non of a cadet's education. The techniques of commanding an infantry company or an engineering battalion could be picked up through experience or in the Army's numerous postgraduate schools; character, however, was best cultured within the walls of the academy.

Yet character was not easily defined. Choosing the harder right instead of the easier wrong, as the Cadet Prayer prescribed, was part of character. So was adherence to the honor code, which was based on an epistemological assumption that every cadet possessed an inner gyroscope to guide him between right and wrong. Deep down, a cadet *knew* what was proper. Harnessing that knowledge to action — duty — was character. The best way to teach it was by example — the example of older cadets, officers at the academy, the lives of the great captains.

The class of 1966 had arrived at West Point just as some of the encrusted academic tradition began to give way, largely through the efforts of Westmoreland's predecessor, Gar Davidson. A decendant of Chief Justice John Marshall and a member of the class of 1927, Davidson had been promoted to brigadier general at the close of the Sicilian campaign, when Patton pinned a pair of his own stars on Davidson's shoulders. After V-E Day, he presided over the first German War Crimes Tribunal. In Korea, Davidson had performed brilliantly against the Chinese, preparing a perimeter defense that bore his name.

Davidson believed that officers in the latter half of the twentieth century required an education that went far beyond math and engineering. Foreign languages, nuclear physics, communication skills, history and the other social sciences — all demanded greater emphasis. Davidson urged faculty members to publish in professional journals and to keep current in their fields through occasional sabbaticals; he required those assigned permanently to the faculty to obtain doctorates. (Only 10 percent of the instructors in 1962 had Ph.D.'s.) His most difficult battle came during a tumultuous five-day meeting of the academic board in February 1960. The question was simple yet critical to the academy's future: Would cadets continue to study a curriculum that was wholly dictated, or would elective options be allowed?

Finally, after intense discussion — Davidson later wrote that "blood was drawn but the wounded lived" — the board ruled that cadets would have two electives in their final year. A proposal to allow them to declare academic majors was firmly rejected. The forces of academic progress had won a tiny victory.

But after sixteen decades of hidebound tradition, the reform represented an important step away from the notion that all cadets should be stamped in the same mold. Whether it would lead to a "new and wholly different kind of military training" to fight a new kind of war, as John Kennedy had decreed — that remained to be seen.

"Ohhh-din. Ohhh-din. Ohhh-din."

The call reverberated eerily throughout the barracks. Like monks before vespers, the plebes chanted homage to Odin in hopes that the Norse god would wash out the parade. This time, however, the old ritual was not going to work. Walking back from calculus class, Jack Wheeler saw that the overcast had lightened. Already traffic streamed through Thayer Gate as the GAP — the Great American Public — poured onto the reservation for the parade and the football game.

Inside the 54th Division, Jack peeled off his class uniform and slipped on the dress grays. He made sure that the white cross belts were properly aligned and that the cartridge box in back hung over his coccyx, three finger widths below his belt. Having shined and reshined his brass until it gleamed, he paid particular attention to the little details; if overlooked, they could make life miserable for a plebe during inspection. When Tommy Hayes had failed to fasten one of his tunic buttons, for example, an upperclassman made him return to his room, snip the button off, and sew it back on five times.

Jack scanned his image in the mirror. Despite all the care it demanded, the uniform looked terrific. A tradition nearly as old as the academy itself, cadet gray was first selected in 1815 to honor Winfield Scott's troops for their defeat of the British at Chippewa. The Americans had worn rough gray kersey into battle, because regular blue uniforms were in short supply. That historical woof was a nice touch, Jack thought, but it was the heavy wool warp that would feel good on such a chilly day.

He collected his rifle, straightened the tarbucket shako, and hurried down the stairs, taking a look at himself one last time in the full-length mirror by the door before falling in with the rest of Mama Deuce. The band crashed out a stirring Sousa tune as the corps emerged in perfect cadence through the sallyport to the Plain. Jack canted his head slightly to offset the wind tugging at his tarbucket. As they crossed the Plain, cadets at the end of each rank muttered in a stage whisper, "Butt in" or "Butt out" so that the marchers could adjust the rifles on their shoulders for an exact alignment.

Jack knew that from the vantage point of the GAP, which stood four and five deep around the lip of the Plain, the corps looked impeccable. That was not surprising, considering how long West Point had been trying to perfect parade drill. Some of the commands were identical with those used by Scott's officers at Chippewa. And the drill procedures, originally designed to expedite maneuver on the battlefield, were not much different from those codified by Baron Friedrich von Steuben, who had been hired by Washington and Benjamin Franklin to instruct the rebel troops at Valley Forge.

Jack glanced at the crowd. Parades and dress gray: this was what most Americans thought West Point was all about. The corps and the corps and the corps: impassive, interchangeable, precise unto perfect. Individuals subsumed by the group. What the GAP could not see beyond the flashing sabers and the precise thirty-inch steps was the banter and horseplay in the ranks. When cadet officers shouted the command "Pass in review," throughout the corps sounded a *sotto voce* echo, "Piss in your shoes!" A practiced eye could pick out the bobbing tarbuckets of snickering cadets.

"Hey, Wheeler," an upperclassman called softly from behind. "What's the most dangerous animal in the jungle?"

"Sir, I do not know."

"A duck with a flame thrower. Why do elephants have flat feet?"

"Sir, I do not —"

"From stamping out burning ducks."

"Good one, sir."

"Hey, Wheeler. See that girl in the front row in the yellow dress? How would you describe her?"

"Sir, she has blond hair, medium height, and —"

"Her breasts, Wheeler, what about her breasts?"

"Sir, I —"

"How would you rate her, Wheeler?"

"Sir, I would say seven point zero."

"Wheeler, that's my fiancée."

"Sir, may I make a correction?"

"What's your puny correction, smack?"

"Sir, she is definitely a nine point five."

"Wheeler, do you hear that big bass drum? I want you to count every time it goes boom and report to me after parade exactly how many booms you count."

"Yes, sir."

"I want an exact count."

"Yes, sir."

And so the long gray line marched on, eyes right, 120 steps per minute, past the adoring public and back through the sallyport. Boom. Boom. Boom.

*

As autumn gave way to winter and winter yielded, grudgingly, to early spring, the class of 1966 continued to shrink, exactly as Commandant Stilwell had predicted during Beast Barracks. Several dozen cadets left West Point because of academic deficiencies; those who dropped below a 2.0 grade point average — out of a maximum 3.0 — were "found" and either dismissed or "turned back," forced to repeat their plebe year, as George Patton had. Calculus was particularly lethal, especially for those whose high school mathematics classes had not prepared them for West Point's rigors. George Crocker, the pride of Russellville, Arkansas, had discovered that his anxiety about academics was well founded; George flunked plebe calculus but avoided dismissal by passing a last-chance "turnback exam."

Others ran afoul of the academy's rigid disciplinary system. Tom Carhart, after his humiliating experience of spattering the upperclassman with shoe polish water, abandoned all pretense of being a perfect cadet; with swashbuckling imprudence he had begun to defy upperclassmen and tactical officers alike, though not with sufficient incorrigibility to provoke dismissal — not yet.

Tom, George, and Jack Wheeler had the common advantage of being in the corps' second regiment. As the flanker companies traditionally were considered more indulgent than the runt companies, so the second regiment generally was considered more forgiving than the first; in September, one sergeant had warned those headed for the first regiment, "Spread your feet, bend over, grab your ankles, and kiss your sweet ass goodbye." For plebes assigned to a first regiment runt company, life often was as relentlessly harsh as Beast Barracks had been.

No beautiful brunettes appeared for reveille in Dogshit One nor in Inquisition One. Matthew Clarence Harrison, Jr., could confirm that. At the beginning of plebe year, Matt originally had been assigned to a flanker company, but after qualifying for an advanced section of English he was inexplicably switched to the sinister I-1. Inquisition One indeed merited its reputation, and the number of plebes in the company steadily dwindled. Thirty-one had joined I-1 on Labor Day; now a dozen of them were gone, and Matt figured that he might well be next.

Matt Harrison was another Army brat, born at West Point to a coastal artillery officer, class of '41, who taught at the academy during World War II. A fine athlete and the president of his high school student council in Virginia, Matt had pursued an appointment to the Military Academy with little contemplation of his motives or ambitions; like Jack Wheeler and many other classmates, he felt drawn both to public service and to the military life, which was the only life he knew.

Military life he knew; life at Hell on the Hudson, however, had been a rude shock. His troubles began early in Beast, when he violated the golden rule for plebes: never make the same mistake once. One Friday morning, Matt had been ordered to move his trunk to the barracks basement. Before leaving his room, he put on an old belt buckle; if he wore the newer, shiny buckle, he reasoned, it might get scratched and the upperclassmen would have him squatting over a bayonet point or sitting in an imaginary "little green chair" until his thighs shook uncontrollably from the strain. But no sooner had Matt stepped into the corridor than he was braced by his squad leader, a scowling martinet named Hughes.

"Harrison, that buckle looks terrible," Hughes said. "If I ever catch you with that on again, I'll kill you."

That night, during a clothing formation, Matt had been fumbling with his uniform sierra when he reached for the new buckle. It was gone; evidently one of his roommates had picked it up by mistake. As the King of Beast counted down over the public address system, Matt frantically reviewed his options. He could hide. He could fall in without a belt. Or he could wear the tarnished buckle that had nearly cost him his life that morning. Sweating profusely, he took the old buckle, slipped it on, and ran outside. Braced in formation, Matt watched Hughes work his way down the line. Please make us change again, he begged silently. Don't let him see it.

The squad leader stepped in front of Matt and looked him squarely in the eye. Then he scanned Harrison's uniform. When Hughes got to the belt buckle, he did a vaudeville double take. His eyes bulged, and a crimson flush rose through his neck and into his ears. "Take my squad," he said to another upperclassman. "You," he said, swiveling back toward Matt, "to the sinks. Post!"

Thirty minutes later Matt staggered into his room as though back from the dead. Hughes had been incoherent with rage, shrieking wildly, slamming Matt against the wall, and forcing him to brace in postures that seemed physiologically impossible.

Now, nine months later, Matt was close to dismissal for excessive demerits. The academy alloted plebes one demerit for each class day; those exceeding their monthly ration were deemed "unsatisfactory in conduct." A board of officers then determined whether to extend probation or expel the miscreant from the corps.

Cadets also referred to demerits as "quill," a legacy from the days when infractions were recorded with feather pens. Dropping a rifle was worth four quill. An irrelevant question was worth two; a query deemed improper was worth four. Exhaustion carried its own sliding scale: five quill for sleeping in church, three for dozing in class, one for yawning in the ranks.

Egregious offenders, like those caught drinking beer in the barracks, were "slugged." That meant demerits, confinement to quarters, and twenty-two or so "tours." Each tour required an hour of solitary marching back and forth through the Area, usually on Wednesday or Saturday afternoon. Perhaps the only consolation was the knowledge that walking tours were more humane than some of the punishments meted out to an earlier generation. At one time, for example, fractious cadets had been consigned to the Black Hole of Calcutta, a dank, eight-foot pit with a heavy wooden lid.

Matt could not even affect the insouciance of some of his classmates. A few amassed quill with damn-the-torpedoes antics that dazzled the less brazen. Among the emerging rascals in the class were an irrepressible Kansan named Buck Thompson and that crazy Tom Carhart. For Matt, however, cadetship entailed a string of nickel-and-dime demerits for nickel-and-dime offenses.

He took some comfort in having drawn a good roommate. Ronald Cox, from Hawaii, was the tall, bright, and unflappable son of a carpenter who worked at Pearl Harbor. Matt sometimes felt bad that Cox drew more than his share of hectoring simply because he lived with Matt, who seemed to attract abusive upperclassmen. He also thought it curious that someone from Hawaii should be as uncomfortable around the water as Cox was. Matt had to admit, though, that there was much to fear in the academy's mandatory swimming classes.

Among other things, plebes had to leap into the pool with fatigues, boots, and a backpack stuffed with bricks. Occasionally a cadet simply sank. The instructor, a leathery baritone named Robert E. Sorge, would peer dispassionately at the desperate figure flailing on the bottom.

"Do not help that man down there," Sorge would command. "He is still struggling."

Eventually the waterlogged plebe would be hauled to the surface, gagging convulsively, and assigned to the Rock Squad for remedial instruction. The terrestrial counterpart to swimming was mandatory boxing — the Bleed Squad. Cadets squared off in a ring with a sign above it that declared EVERY MAN A TIGER. They blindly, savagely pummeled each other while the instructor bellowed, "Hit! React! Hit! React!" with precisely the same cadence used to teach the box step in Cullem Hall.

Ron Cox was singular for another reason: he was black. In the 160-year history of the academy, only fifty black cadets had graduated; the class of 1966 would add three more to the tally. Cox had been the only black at his high school in Honolulu, and he didn't consider his color to be an issue at West Point. All plebes were treated badly; if he took any extra abuse because of racism, Cox didn't seem to be aware of it.

On several occasions, however, Matt overheard slurs — including *nigger* — from several of the Southern upperclassmen. One ugly incident occurred after the Army-Navy game in Philadelphia. Traditionally each company rented a room at the Ben Franklin Hotel for a postgame party. Matt was in the I-1 suite when a cadet walked in and announced, "I just saw Ron Cox and he's on his way up here and he's bringing a white girl as a date."

One of the Southern cadets declared angrily, "I just can't accept that." Fortunately, Cox and his date never showed up and the issue didn't come to a head.

Yet the vestiges of racism at West Point were slight compared with the vicious treatment accorded blacks earlier in the academy's history. After the Civil War, the academy became a proving ground for blacks in American society. Integrationists, searching for a qualified Negro to break West Point's color barrier, settled on James Webster Smith, son of a South Carolina slave who had been freed by Sherman's army. After reporting to West Point in the summer of 1870, Smith endured a hateful plebe year, during which he was made to clean up tobacco spittle from the streets with his hands. Hot-tempered and understandably hostile toward his classmates, Smith eventually flunked out.

The first black graduate was Henry Ossian Flipper, born in slavery to a shoemaker in Thomasville, Georgia. Flipper, who had been taught to read by another slave at night in a woodshop, was a remarkably forbearing cadet, taking the slurs and ostracism in stride. Once he lent his algebra book to a classmate; it was returned with his name crudely slashed from the calfskin cover so that other cadets would not know that it had been borrowed from Flipper. Flipper graduated in June 1877.

But from 1889 until 1936, no blacks graduated from West Point. The re-erected color barrier was broken by Benjamin O. Davis, Jr., the son of an officer who would become the Army's first black general. Davis, a tall, commanding figure, was subjected to "the silence." During his plebe year, he roomed alone, ate by himself at a separate table, and was addressed by other cadets only when official business required communication. Of his classmates in '36, who included two future Army chiefs of staff, Davis later said, "If there were friends, they were silent friends and I mean that literally." He eventually became the Air Force's first black general, rising to three-star rank.

Even after President Truman had desegregated the Army by executive order in 1948, the academy barred black cadets from social hops and dancing classes until 1951 and from intercollegiate sports teams until the early 1950s. They were also prohibited from entering Officers Clubs with their classmates during summer trips and were forbidden to teach Sunday school classes attended by teenage white girls.

"You had to be two people," recalled one black graduate, who deliberately modified his walk and accent as a plebe in an effort to appear more "white." "The real you was offensive to the white majority. You were accepted in accordance with how white you could become."

For those who survived to join the officer corps after World War II, the Army was not much more congenial. An Army study released in 1940 had described blacks as having "less developed mental capacities" — at the time there were only five black officers, including the two Davises and three chaplains. And strains of that mentality persisted well into the 1950s. Bitter disputes erupted over the combat prowess of black soldiers during World War II and the Korean War. Even in 1963, black Army officers remained something of a novelty, accounting for fewer than 2 percent of the total.

Ron Cox let it lie; what was past was past. Having come from a multiracial society in Hawaii, he concluded that he was not attuned to subtle slights. One experience that did linger with him for years took place in New York after the corps had marched in a spring parade. As he stood in line with other cadets on a Manhattan street, waiting to stow his equipment on a truck, he noticed a black man watching him from the sidewalk. After Cox turned in his rifle, the man stepped forward with a smile and shook his hand, pressing a five-dollar bill into his palm.

The gesture was both touching and awkward, yet it reminded Cox of the pride others felt in what he had achieved. West Point was a symbol that could be interpreted in many ways: the academy represented America's military might, of course, and the tradition of battlefield valor. But West Point also served as a standard by which one could measure the height of two national ideals — opportunity and equality. Thirty years had passed since Benny Davis had again broken the color line, in the class of 1936. But for some black Americans, Ron Cox realized, it seemed like only yesterday.

On a crisp spring afternoon in 1963, the first captain — the highest ranking cadet — from the class of '36 stood waiting at the entrance to the cemetery. Sometimes it seemed like only yesterday to William Westmoreland, too. Thirty years earlier, right over there at Trophy Point, he had been upbraided by the commandant for mispronouncing three words while reading the Declaration of Independence during a Fourth of July ceremony; the memory still pricked.

Even standing erect — the only way Westmoreland ever stood — he was just of average height. That often surprised those who met him for the first time later in his career, after he had become larger than life in a bogeyman sort of way. He was forty-nine, his hair frosted with gray, further dignifying the handsome face. On his left cheek, legacy of a childhood auto wreck, was an old gash, which had passed for a dueling scar in his younger, European days.

The superintendent was waiting for Douglas MacArthur. That morning, he had received a phone call from Courtney Whitney, MacArthur's aide in New York.

"It's a beautiful day and the general would like to drive up to West Point and visit the cemetery," Whitney said. "He doesn't want any hullabaloo and he doesn't want to go anywhere else."

"I'll meet him there," Westmoreland replied.

This would probably be the last time that he played host to the old battle captain. Westmoreland was completing his third spring as superintendent; in a couple months he would leave to take command of the XVIII Airborne Corps at Fort Bragg, North Carolina. He was sorry to see the tour here end; among other things, West Point and the huge superintendent's house had been a splendid place to raise three young children. But the previous summer he had talked the chief of staff out of sending him to command a corps in Europe. Requesting another extension would be pushing his luck. Besides, every officer — especially the Army's pre-eminent "water walker" — had to expect frequent moves. They came with the territory.

Westmoreland was proud of his accomplishments during his three years at West Point. He hadn't known quite what to expect on arriving in 1960, and President Eisenhower had not been much help. Summoned to Washington from Fort Campbell, Kentucky, where he commanded the 101st Airborne Division, Westmoreland walked into the Oval Office to warm greetings from the president, who congratulated him on his new assignment at the academy. After twenty minutes of small talk — during which Eisenhower reminisced about his cadet days before World War I — Westmoreland peeked at his watch and stood up.

"Mr. President, I've taken much too much of your time and I think I'd better be excused."

Eisenhower walked him to the door before suddenly plucking at the new superintendent's sleeve, drawing him back into the office.

"I do have one instruction for you, General," he said seriously.

"What's that, Mr. President?"

"Do something about that damned football team."

Westmoreland tried. He hired Paul Dietzel away from Louisiana State University to coach Army; what an uproar that had caused. The *Times-Picayune* in New Orleans and Russell Long on the Senate floor had accused the superintendent of unethical conduct. That was nonsense, of course — he had cleared it with the LSU president before talking to Dietzel — but the incident had given him a certain national infamy for the first time.

In other areas, he had trod lightly. Dick Stilwell, the commandant, had kept the corps well in hand. Stilwell's recent departure was a loss, but Westmoreland thought highly of his replacement, Michael S. Davison, who had arrived in March. Mike Davison's appearance was a clear contrast to Westmoreland's. The superintendent had the trim look of a Hollywood general; Davison was gangly, with a prominent Roman nose and large ears folded neatly against the sides of his head. His face was almost too small to contain all of the character carried in its features. As a plebe in the class of '39, Davison had been so obstreperous that he was ordered to sit at the foot of Westmoreland's mess table in hopes that the first captain could brace some obedience into him. Yet only five years after graduating — "clean sleeve," with no rank chevrons — Davison had commanded a battalion in France. Now he was on his way to four stars, a classic example of how performance as a cadet was a worthless predictor of success in the Army.

The appointment of Westmoreland, a combat leader and a "soldier's soldier," had been widely viewed as an effort by the Army hierarchy to steer West Point back to military fundamentals in the aftermath of the Gar Davidson reforms. In fact, Westmoreland left the academic side of the academy almost untouched, particularly in his first year. Instead, in an attempt to double the academy's size, he spent time and energy proselytizing President Kennedy on the need to have West Point co-equal with the Naval Academy.

Priding himself on being an effective manager as well as a warrior, he also launched a string of efficiency campaigns. One summer, he ordered a money-saving sprinkler system installed in the Plain. Some of the old professors, ever suspicious of disturbing the smallest hallowed pebble, spread the rumor that the new superintendent was moving the parade ground. Westmoreland thought that was hilarious. Years later he would burst into raucous laughter whenever he thought about the episode.

As always, the fundamental question at the academy was how best to prepare cadets to become leaders of the Army. The world had changed immensely since the 1930s, when Westmoreland joined the artillery. At Fort Sill in those days, the Model 1897 French 75 howitzers were mounted on wooden wheels and drawn by horses. Officers still wore dinner jackets and black ties to evening meals; social life centered on horse shows and Sunday fox hunts.

Westmoreland knew that the Old Army was gone, but he still believed that young officers should be gentlemen. Each year during his superintendency he had invited small groups of first classmen to formal dinners at Quarters 100. The evenings were quite amusing, he thought, as a dozen nervous cadets anxiously watched every gesture made by the host's young wife, Kitsy. When she unfolded her napkin, they unfolded their napkins. She lifted her soup spoon; they lifted their soup spoons. She took a sip of water; they took sips of water. Westmoreland could barely contain his mirth.

Then there was that brushfire war in Southeast Asia. Like Stilwell, Westmoreland suspected that both he and the cadets would end up there; South Vietnam seemed to be rapidly disintegrating under the relentless pressure of the communist guerrillas. Caught up by the Army's sudden infatuation with counterinsurgency, Westmoreland had established mandatory lectures on the subject for the corps and organized a conference, featuring a keynote speech by an MIT professor named Walt W. Rostow, who had become part of Kennedy's brain trust.

To defeat insurgents, Rostow had urged, the military must take the offensive. "If you wait passively," he warned, "you will be cut to ribbons." Westmoreland thought that made sense and he mentally filed away the advice for future use. Duplicating a program he had begun with the 101st, the superintendent also set up a five-day indoctrination session for cadets after their plebe year. The training introduced them to the basics of small unit patrolling and other counterinsurgency tactics. He called it Recondo, a hybrid of *reconnaissance* and *commando*.

Still, the most important things West Point could teach were timeless, whether the enemy was a Vietnamese guerrilla or a Soviet tanker or God knows who. Westmoreland had some thoughts he wanted to pass along to the cadets. There wouldn't be time before he left in June but perhaps next year, during a visit, he could articulate his thinking. His message was aggressively optimistic — fundamentally American in its sunny outlook, fundamentally West Point in its disparagement of contemplation and excessive cogitation. When the message took final shape in an address to the class of '64, the speech was tantamount to a Westmoreland manifesto:

> In my view, the positive approach is the key to success and it's the one that has a strong influence over people. Men welcome leadership. They like action and they relish accomplishment. Speculation, knowledge, is not the chief aim of man — it is action. All mankind feel themselves weak, beset with infirmities, and surrounded with danger. They want above all things a leader with the boldness, decision, and energy that, with shame, they do not find in themselves. He then who would command among his fellows must tell them more in energy of will than in power of intellect. He has to have both, but energy of will is more important.

Now, Westmoreland waited patiently near the portico of the old cadet chapel, a few paces from the monument to Major Francis Dade, who had been slaughtered with his entire command by Seminole Indians in 1835. A sedan pulled into the circular driveway and MacArthur climbed out. He didn't look eighty-three, but he had aged since his speech in Washington Hall the year before; his cheeks had hollowed, and the skull beneath the skin hinted more boldly at mortality. As always, he carried himself with the proud imperiousness of a bird of prey. The general spent most of his days in New York seated in a Waldorf armchair, scrawling out his memoirs on a yellow legal pad. But today he had decided to remember the past in a different fashion.

MacArthur led Westmoreland into the cemetery, where late afternoon shadows were stealing across the graves. The men ambled past the keeper's cottage and the fountain memorializing Major Robert Anderson, the Union commander at Fort Sumter. Westmoreland could remember MacArthur on a June day long ago, when, as chief of staff, he had given the commencement address to the class of 1933. Saluting West Point as "the soul of the Army," MacArthur had added, "The military code that you perpetuate has come down to us from even before the age of knighthood and chivalry. It will stand the test of any code of ethics or philosophy."

The two generals wandered among the graves, alone except for the cemetery keeper, who trailed at a respectful distance. After the long Hudson winter, the thick grass had begun to green and new buds stippled the tree boughs; as always, each grave was meticulously maintained, the headstones as perfectly aligned as the Corps of Cadets on parade. They paused beneath a gnarled oak at Winfield Scott's sarcophagus, where MacArthur talked of Fuss and Feathers' burden in prosecuting an unpopular war. Thirty feet away, under a magnificent willow, Sylvanus Thayer slept in a simple granite crypt. At George Goethals' grave on the eastern edge of the churchyard, MacArthur reminisced about the remarkable feat of carving the canal through Panama.

Each headstone seemed to trigger another burst of memories. This man worked with me in World War I, the general recalled. This one was a division commander in the South Pacific. This one was in Korea. This was one of the greatest football players of all time.

Westmoreland said little. He assumed that MacArthur was trying to decide whether to be buried here. As a soldier and the son of a soldier, the old general had no true home to which he could return. His mother's family had lived in Norfolk, but MacArthur had spent his nomadic life in dozens of places: frontier cavalry posts, France, Washington, Manila, Tokyo, New York, and of course West Point. The academy — clearly his spiritual home — seemed to have as firm a claim to his mortal remains as any place else. The funeral here, Westmoreland knew, would be an extraordinary event, surely as grand as Winfield Scott's had been a century earlier.

After an hour and a half, MacArthur turned back to the car. Westmoreland thought he seemed reluctant to leave, almost wistful. The sun had slipped behind the western hills; dusk sifted over the academy, bringing a chill to the twilight air. As the superintendent helped him into his seat, MacArthur paused. "General Westmoreland," he said, "I want to thank you for your courtesy and hospitality, and for allowing me to visit my old friends."

The door closed and the car sped south, crowded with shades.

3

YEAR OF THE RABBIT

HE WAS LATE. In fact, he was very late. She began to feel a little forlorn as she stood on Fifth Avenue, holding the rose that matched her flaming hair. The big clock outside the Sherry Netherland Hotel served as a constant reminder that the afternoon was slipping away. His tardiness seemed unmilitary. Wasn't punctuality supposed to be a martial virtue? But then again, he had been uncertain about exactly when he'd be able to spring free.

She had his first letter, written on West Point's Athena-embossed stationery and mailed to her parents' house on Garfield Place in Brooklyn. The handwriting was tidy, if occasionally influenced by gravity at the end of the lines. Already he had adopted the Army style of putting day before month:

7 May 1963

Miss Marcia McGuire,

I was looking through Mrs. Holland's files the other day and came across your name. Since I will be in New York City, Saturday, May 18, I thought this would be a good chance to meet someone there. I have been to New York before, but I haven't really seen the place because I just don't know where to go. I was hoping, if you are free that Saturday, you could go out with me. I will be free after the Armed Forces parade.

I'm a country boy from Omaha, Nebraska. I have been 20 years old for all of three weeks now. I am a lumbering 6′3″ tall with dark hair. I wear glasses. Think you would recognize me now?

Well, we can make arrangements later, if you are able to go. I hope you can make it.

Cdt. Art Bonifas, '66
Co. A-1, USCC
West Point, N.Y.

Okay, she had made it, but where was he? Even for a blind date this was unorthodox. She checked the clock again.

Applying to the Corps of Cadets for a date had been little more than a lark. Marcia and several of her sorority sisters at St. John's University had written to Beatrice Holland, the cadet hostess; Marcia even enclosed a grade school photo of herself. But when the hostess's office — known as the Holland Tunnel — wrote back to say that she would have to come up to the academy for an interview, Marcia abandoned the idea. She didn't own a car, and the prospect of taking the bus to West Point to be grilled for a blind date seemed ridiculous. Then, out of the blue, she got his note.

Surprised and intrigued, she wrote back, agreeing to meet him on the eighteenth. He immediately sent her a second letter, dated 13 May:

> Our part in the parade should be finished around 3 or 4. We can eat and then catch a show or do anything you would like to do. I like to dance, but I sprained my ankle a couple weeks ago and I may be limited to a modest twist or slow dancing. I really enjoy just the view of the city at night. The return bus formation will be at 1 A.M. That is all I know.

Her mother had been skeptical. The arrangement appeared just a little suspicious to Harriet McGuire. But, of course, what didn't? Brushing aside her mother's warnings, Marcia caught the subway from Brooklyn to midtown. Now, that maternal skepticism did not seem so silly. She watched the traffic creep down Fifth Avenue. Clusters of uniformed cadets occasionally rambled past, and she scanned them for a lumbering, dark-haired country boy with glasses. What did someone from Nebraska look like?

Suddenly, she spied an older version of herself strolling up the street.

"Mother!" Marcia cried. "What are you doing here?"

"You can rent those Army uniforms at any costume place," Harriet replied. "I don't trust this person."

"You cannot stand here with me," Marcia said, shock giving way to pique. "Mother, *please.*"

Harriet McGuire shrugged and retreated through the revolving doors into the Sherry Netherland. Marcia was mortified. This is beyond the pale, she thought. I'm nineteen years old. How would this look, dragging my mother along as a chaperone? Who —

"You must be Marcia?"

As advertised, he was tall, dark, and bespectacled. His dazzling smile revealed two rows of perfect teeth.

"You must be Art?"

He apologized for being late. He'd had to walk all the way over to First Avenue to stash his rifle and tarbucket in the truck. The crowds were, well, she knew, didn't she? Being from New York and everything.

Harriet McGuire abruptly twirled out of the revolving door and brushed past, eying the cadet as if looking for a tag on his uniform tunic that said "Broadway Costume Rental." Art and Marcia lingered near the big clock for a moment, exchanging shy pleasantries that were made even more awkward by Marcia's surreptitious efforts to track her mother's movements. From the corner of her eye, she watched Mrs. McGuire cross the street and position herself by the fountain near the Plaza. When they began to stroll down Fifth Avenue, Harriet followed on the other side as Art chattered away, apparently oblivious of this sideshow. Watching the beacon of red hair bob in and out among the other pedestrians, Marcia half expected her mother to bump into them deliberately to get a closer look at this so-called cadet.

Art opened the door to 666 Fifth Avenue. Crossing the lobby, they rode the elevator to the Top of the Sixes, where he held the chair for Marcia in the bar. Her mother had vanished. We lost her, Marcia thought with relief. Now she could concentrate on this earnest young man with impeccable manners. He seemed awfully nice, and so polite. Girls these days weren't accustomed to having doors held open and chairs pulled out.

They began to talk about themselves, sizing each other up with that clumsy self-consciousness of two strangers thrown together on a blind date. Each appeared intriguingly different to the other. She had been born and raised in Brooklyn. At St. John's, in Queens, where she was finishing her sophomore year, she studied elementary education. Her father, Peter, was an attorney, the son of immigrants from Counties Cork and Kerry. During the war, he had been a counterintelligence security officer for the Manhattan Project. Her mother — what could she say about her mother? Harriet Hannigan, intelligent, attractive, and intrepidly outspoken, had been a Rockette for a time, and had also danced at the Diamond Horseshoe in the 1930s until her father found out and made her go to work for the gas company. She and Peter McGuire had married in 1942.

Marcia and her younger brother had been raised among the middle-class Irish families thriving in Park Slope, just west of Brooklyn's Prospect Park. The brownstone at 689 Tenth Street was a wonderful place to grow up, barely a stickball swat from the park. Sycamore trees lined the sidewalks, which were always crowded with children roller skating or playing hopscotch, and neighborhood life revolved around St. Francis Xavier's parish. In parish elementary school, the nuns tried — and failed — to "correct" her left-handedness; in high school, they had greater success in clipping the Brooklyn accent from her speech. Her world was strict, insular, and always lively. When she was old enough to date, her father offered one simple dictum: "You bring an Italian into this house," Peter McGuire warned, "and he goes out the front window and you go after him."

Art Bonifas, the saints be praised, was not Italian. His paternal grandparents had emigrated from Luxembourg, which to Marcia was even more exotic than Nebraska. His father, Ray, had grown up on a Minnesota farm and gone to work for the Wilson Packing Company. In 1941, he met Thelma Milnor, a schoolteacher, in Aberdeen, South Dakota. Thelma and Ray courted for a year before marrying, sometimes playing golf with wooden-shaft clubs in an Aberdeen cow pasture that featured sand greens. Art, their only child, was born in Hillsdale, Michigan, while Ray was in the Army during the war.

After Ray's discharge, the family moved to Bellevue, Nebraska, outside Omaha. In the early 1950s, Ray went into the food brokerage business, and traveled throughout the Midwest. Perhaps to compensate for his absences during the week, he was a stern father, demanding strict obedience when he came home on weekends. Thelma provided the softer counterpoint, often driving her son to swim meets at the Omaha YMCA and encouraging his fascination with books.

When Art reached high school age, the Bonifases enrolled him at Creighton Prep, a Jesuit school. Ray assumed that his son would eventually join him in business, but Art wanted out — out of Omaha, out of the Midwest, out of his father's jurisdiction. After a year at Creighton University, he was offered an appointment to West Point. That was out, all right, and Art packed his bags. He arrived at the academy, somewhat unconventionally, by boat from New York.

Biographies exchanged, Art and Marcia strolled through Times Square. She always enjoyed seeing New York through a visitor's eyes. Usually she was too busy to tour Manhattan or appreciate the city's sights, and she watched with amusement as Art gawked at the neon signs and the brilliant theater marquees. Long lines of moviegoers waited to see *Lilies of the Field* and *It's a Mad, Mad, Mad, Mad World*. Women hurried toward the Broadway theaters in pointed shoes with slender heels, pillbox hats crowning their bouffants. You didn't have to be a fashion designer to know where *that* influence came from: all three of the Kennedy wives — Jacqueline, Joan, and Ethel — were pregnant that spring. They seemed to be in the news constantly.

For dinner, Art took her to Steuben's, a favorite cadet restaurant that served frosty steins of German beer. Over lobster, he told her about plebe life. The year had been tough, very tough, but his fourth-class ordeal was nearly over. Exams were coming up. In just three more weeks he and his classmates would be yearlings, released on leave for the first time since the beginning of Beast Barracks more than ten months earlier. Marcia thought cadetship sounded even worse than the nuns trying to make her into a right-hander in elementary school. But Art seemed unscathed; he was guileless and cheerful.

After dinner, they walked to Third Avenue to see *The Courtship of Eddie's Father,* a movie with Glenn Ford and Shirley Jones about a little boy playing Cupid for his widowed father. By the time the theater let out it was nearly one A.M. and time for Art to report to the fleet of buses waiting to carry the cadets back to West Point. After demurely thanking him for the pleasant evening, Marcia caught a taxi home to Brooklyn.

"So?" Harriet asked when her daughter came in.

For a moment Marcia forgot that she was supposed to be furious with her mother. She smiled.

"He was nice," she replied. "He opened doors."

Three days later, he wrote her a note.

21 May 1963

Dear Marcia,

What a day. Those exams really put me in a bad mood. It hurts when you find out everything you don't know. I've taken two exams, and I don't have any results back yet. I feel like I really did poorly. Oh well. Time will tell.

I hope your exams are going better than mine. Just think of all the studying you missed Saturday night. I hope it wasn't boring seeing things you've seen all your life. Thank you for showing me a great evening. Everything seemed to fall into place.

Sincerely,
Art

Marcia had never before received a thank-you note after a date. Now what? she wondered. Should she send him a note? After giving the matter some thought, she decided to invite him back for the Fourth of July.

Art spent his three-week plebe leave in Omaha, and then flew to New York. He checked into the Piccadilly Hotel, an off-Broadway hostel that offered discounts to cadets. He had a pair of free tickets to *How to Succeed in Business* — his father had got them from the Bon Ami cleanser company — and Marcia met him in Manhattan. After the play he took her home in a cab, and was flabbergasted when the meter reached $25. He caught the subway back to the Piccadilly.

The next day, July 3, Marcia and a friend picked him up and drove to the McGuire summer house at Breezy Point, across Rockaway Inlet from Sheepshead Bay and Coney Island. Her brother had needled her about dating a rube from Nebraska. "Does he have straw in his hair?"

he teased. But when Marcia introduced Art to her parents before showing him around the beach, Harriet and Peter McGuire were impressed. They hadn't heard that many "yes, sirs" and "no, ma'ams" in New York since before the war. He was like a rare bird, though one with simple plumage. In fact, his shiny brown pants and sneakers caused something of a flap when they tried to take him to dinner at the Surf Club that night. After scouring the club, they finally found someone with a spare pair of black dress shoes, size thirteen. Yet Art seemed unfazed by the episode; he just smiled his remarkable smile.

He and Marcia spent July 4 on the beach. He had seen the sea only once before in his life and it fascinated him. Standing in the surf to his knees, he took countless snapshots of the ocean with his Brownie. When he left for West Point, Marcia was sorry to see him go; he was fun to be with. Nineteen years of living in Brooklyn, in the protective shelter of the McGuire household, had sharpened her instinctive wariness of strangers. But Art made her feel marvelously at ease. This boy can't be real, she thought to herself after he had gone. A person can't be this honest.

On July 5, Art was reunited with his classmates at the academy for the beginning of their second year. As plebes, they had worn no insignia on their uniform epaulets, but as third classmen, they proudly pinned on the small gold emblems of yearlings. At last, the men of '66 felt they were part of the long gray line.

The class immediately left for Camp Buckner in the western hills above West Point; after a year of learning how to be cadets, it was time to become soldiers. For seven weeks, under the tutelage of paratroopers from the 101st Airborne Division, the cadets learned the rudiments of the Army's combat arms. They spent thirty-eight hours studying basic artillery tactics and another seventeen hours on armor fundamentals. Ten hours of instruction were devoted to the machine gun and grenade launcher, four hours to mortars, and another ten hours to learning how to read a map. They practiced hand-to-hand fighting with pugil sticks in the sawdust pits, where the instructor warned them to avoid crushing one another's testicles. "Remember your favorite author," he said soberly, "honor de balls-zac." They took turns sliding down a slender cable from the top of a seventy-foot tower, dropping halfway into Lake Popolopen far below. They studied survival techniques under a twenty-five-year-old noncommissioned officer named Franklin Delano Roosevelt Smith. Sergeant Smith, who came from a West Virginia family of twenty-one children and who had received his first pair of shoes when he joined the Army, had a flair for capturing the attention of the novices: first, he pulled out a live snake, salted the reptile vigorously, and bit off its head; then he killed a rabbit, drank the animal's blood from a cup, and devoured the uncooked heart and liver. More than one cadet vowed privately never to get lost in the woods.

For most of its history, West Point had pursued cadet summer training with a genteel languor. In the 1820s, the corps marched to Boston, listened to a brief oration by John Quincy Adams, and marched back to the academy. Even after World War I, cadets summered on Trophy Point, where sentries strolled among the tents at night in their Gilbert and Sullivan uniforms, calling, "All's well." But in World War II, West Point toughened the training by designing a "fit to fight" course; at Lake Popolopen, engineers built concrete pillboxes, a mock freight train, and a small town for "combat in cities" skirmishing. Cadets crawled through tunnels and under barbed wire, slashed up dummies with their bayonets, and lobbed grenades into enemy trenches. After the war, the arduous training continued, and the academy began to dismiss cadets who lacked the aptitude for soldiering.

From Camp Buckner, Art kept up a steady correspondence with Marcia. Having someone to whom he could describe the rigors of Army training seemed to fortify his resolve to survive the summer. On July 17, he wrote:

> Dear Marcia,
>
> We lost seven guys on a reveille run Monday morning. But I made it. I told you I wouldn't fall out. It was a rough one. Tuesday was easier. This morning we ran with rifles. It's getting tougher again. Next weekend we have a parade carrying full field packs, rifles, shovels, etc.
>
> Yesterday we played around with the machine gun again and the 3.5 rocket launcher. I couldn't hit the broad side of a barn with the launcher. I guess shooting is not my best side. Today we got gassed in a chemical warfare demonstration. It was really bad. Guys were on the ground gagging and choking. The chemical people also gave us a demonstration of a new nerve gas they've developed. They put a drop on a rabbit and in three minutes it went into convulsions and died. I guess it works on people, too. Nice thought, huh?
>
> I was on the 9 to 11 and 3 to 5 guard shift. What a night. We had the worst storm I've ever seen in my life. A squall blew up in the afternoon and water just came down in sheets. And then it settled down to a good hard rain all night long. I put on three different sets of khakis throughout the night and I had an inch of water in my boots. On my guard tour, I challenged three cooks going to the mess hall, three bull frogs, and two raccoons. It was a very fruitful evening.

One weekend, Marcia rode the bus from Manhattan to West Point for a hop in Doris Barth Hall at Buckner. Although he was happy to see her, Art worried that this cosmopolitan young woman might find him a dullard. "I enjoy being with you so much," he wrote in one of his July letters, "but I am beginning to feel guilty for taking you out of circulation. Those nights were pretty tame, I'm afraid, compared to what you are used to."

Her warm replies reassured him. Slowly, perhaps without fully realizing it, they were falling in love. On August 1, he wrote:

> I froze Monday night. Boy it was cold. I'm just too long for that blanket. My feet hang out or my shoulders hang out. I just can't win. Tuesday we rode out a problem in personnel carriers. They were really wild. They can go anywhere and usually do. Most of the time we were peeling each other off the walls. Tuesday night we slept on a hill. Of course we rolled down the hill at least once in the course of the night.

He added a rueful postscript that shyly hinted at his feelings for her. "Wednesday we carried out an operation with helicopters. That was interesting. I just wished that they had pointed them for New York City." As always, he signed the letter, "Sincerely, Art."

One night midway through Buckner, the cadets paired off for an exercise in "night navigation." At nine P.M., the two-man teams gathered in a large field. Each pair received a compass and a card containing an azimuth and a distance in meters. Theoretically, that would guide them to a two-foot stake in the woods. At the base of the stake lay an ammunition box containing another azimuth and distance for each team. By moving from stake to stake, carefully following the successive azimuths with their compasses and pacing off the distances, the cadets could find their way to a truck that would haul them back to camp. The supervising sergeant instructed each team to chart the stake numbers, azimuths, and distances on a card. "I want you to take this seriously," he added. "Pretend like it's war."

Jack Wheeler found himself paired with Bill Hughes, another Army brat whom Jack had known from childhood. As Boy Scouts, they had practiced Morse code on a telegraph wire strung between their houses. Bill was a fine woodsman and a born infantryman; Jack thought that was fortunate, because he knew that he was no Kit Carson.

They set off in high spirits, but by two A.M. the two cadets were hopelessly confused. Briar thickets choked the dark forest, snagging their fatigues and clawing painfully at their hands and faces. The deadfall and ravines made walking a straight line and keeping a pace count all but impossible. They tried shining their flashlights along the azimuth in ten-yard increments — knowing that such a stunt would probably get them killed in combat. Even then it was difficult to navigate. Exhausted and dispirited, they stopped to rest at one of the stakes.

"This is about as tactical as the three little pigs," Jack muttered. "We'll be lucky to find the truck by eleven o'clock tomorrow morning at this rate."

They heard other cadets crashing through the woods; the yellow shaft of a flashlight occasionally pierced through the darkness, stabbing the underbrush. As Jack and Bill sat by the ammo box, several other befuddled teams wandered up to the stake. Suddenly, Jack had an idea. He gathered up their cards and held them under his light, studying the recorded azimuths and distances. All of the teams were using the same stakes, though in a different sequence.

He noticed that he and Bill — Team Five — were always grouped with Teams Seven and Nine. Teams Eight, Twelve, and Fourteen seemed to have "back azimuths" from theirs; in other words, they were walking a mirror image of the course. By plotting where all the teams had been, Jack deduced which stakes remained for each team.

He double-checked his calculations, using a couple of simple math formulas. The course was circular, so the sum of all the angles around a point had to equal zero; also, the sum of all the distances, if calculated by vectors and back azimuths, would have to equal zero. It all added up. In fifteen minutes he had filled out his card and the cards of several other teams, rubbing some sweat on them for authenticity. Pretend like it's war, the sergeant had said. All was fair in love and war, right? Jack thought. Reinvigorated, he and Bill plunged into the brush and found the truck before dawn.

Few cadets in the class of 1966 remained unchanged by the rigorous first year they had endured at West Point. Perhaps more than most, however, Jack had changed profoundly. Michael Fuller, who had worked with Jack on the yearbook at Hampton High and had traveled with him on the train to Beast, thought the transformation was shocking. Fuller's parents had bumped into Jack at the Hotel Thayer during plebe Christmas, but he seemed barely to recognize them. He was distracted and withdrawn, very different from the warm, gregarious boy they had known. Plebe year had hit Jack hard, Fuller surmised. If you didn't play the plebe system as if it were a game, he thought, it could be a debilitating ordeal. Inclined to take everything seriously, Jack had probably taken the torment too seriously.

Colonel and Mrs. Wheeler also noticed changes in their son. Before Buckner, Jack had spent his plebe leave with them at Fort Riley, where Big Jack's tank battalion was stationed with the 1st Division in the Flint Hills of eastern Kansas. Janet, who hadn't seen Jack in twelve months, immediately noted a difference. She had sent the academy a seventeen-year-old who was more boy than man; West Point returned to her a son who was more man than boy. He seemed older, harder, more sophisticated. And she didn't like his haircut.

But plebe year was over. Jack knew that the next three years would be easier. Yes, perhaps he had taken the plebe system too seriously, although he had done very well academically, finishing his second semester near the top of the class. If the harassment by upperclassmen had been an obstacle on the road to his becoming a competent officer, at least Camp Buckner now moved him closer to the real Army.

He also discovered that Buckner was fun. Life in the wooden barracks was high-spirited, practically a scout camp compared with the gulag of plebe year. The cadets held limbo contests and raucous bull sessions. (Their three favorite topics were sex, sex, and sex.) They staged practical jokes, such as ambushing the Beast class of '67 one night with a string of two-inch firecrackers as the new cadets marched through the woods nearby. On Saturdays, after inspections in their summer whites, they splashed through the lake or grappled in wrestling tournaments on the beach. At night, they watched movies in a little tarpaper theater or danced in Barth Hall. For the first time, they began to think of themselves as an indivisible band of brothers; for the first time, they began to love one another.

Yet for Jack and the other cadets the summer was not entirely an idyll. Almost imperceptibly, the war in Asia had begun to intrude. Periodically in the past year the cadets heard reports of U.S. advisers killed in Vietnam; before General Stilwell left in the spring, he had presented Purple Hearts during the noon meal to several wounded officers joining the faculty after a tour in Southeast Asia. *Viet Cong* and *Charlie* gradually entered the cadets' lexicon.

"Gemmun," one old sergeant drawled at Buckner, "they's a thousand ways to die. One of 'em is Mr. Charles. The rest is because you are stupid. Your brains are off. You are slow and sloppy."

As part of their counterinsurgency training one day, the cadets practiced an airborne assault, using a standard hammer-and-anvil tactic. One company — the hammer — was inserted by helicopter to drive the imaginary enemy against another company — the anvil — which had set up a blocking position a mile away. Jack, who was part of the hammer, thought the exercise effectively revealed how confusing it was to tumble from the clamshell doors of the helicopter, get organized, and move out in the right direction. This isn't something you would use against a Soviet mechanized division, he told himself. It's to kill guerrillas.

Later, they learned how to disarm a booby trap. Squatting on their haunches or kneeling in the dirt, they carefully probed around the plate with a bayonet to find the fuse. A cold beer stood in the middle of the trap as a reward for those who successfully defused it. The device also was armed with a small charge, a noisemaker really, but one with enough pop to scare the wits out of anyone who tripped it.

Even with nothing at stake but twelve ounces of Budweiser, Jack found the exercise nerve-racking. For the first time, he realized that fear was something he had to accommodate. How do you defuse that? he wondered. Where do you put it? Was this gnawing dread something that everyone else felt, too? It didn't take a genius to connect the dots between this beer-can simulator and the bloody stumps of some poor son of a bitch screaming for a medic.

The exercise gave him something to think about. And Jack, whose acute intelligence could be both a gift and a curse, thought about it a great deal.

Tom Carhart sauntered about Camp Buckner with the fluid, loose-jointed amble of the natural athlete: elbows cocked back slightly, head erect, hips and shoulders rolling in their sockets. Even after an exhausting day of crawling through the woods, his once-crisp fatigues wilting with sweat, he remained in vigorous good humor. Buckner built soldiers, and in Tom's mind that was the end-game at West Point, wasn't it? No, he would never be an exemplary cadet; his experiences in Beast had disabused him of that notion. But he could, someday, be an exemplary officer.

An average plebe, he had finished 38th in the class in physical education and athletics, though only 368th of 704 in the "general order of merit," which was the academy's standard for comparing the cadets' overall performance. In "conduct," he had collected 181 demerits during the year, out of a maximum 334. Tom conceded that he probably was an underachiever — on the College Board examinations he had scored 674 in verbal and 729 in math out of possible 800s. But his lack of academic distinction didn't particularly bother him. The point was to grab those gold second lieutenant's bars which awaited him in June 1966. That was his grail. Everything else was unimportant.

On his West Point application, Tom had written, "Through my father, I have been constantly associated with military career men, and I have decided that there is no more enjoyable, satisfying, and fulfilling station in life than that of an officer." That was admissions committee malarkey, of course, but the nub of it happened to be true. He could scarcely wait to be commissioned. Cadet gray was just something that had to be endured until he could cast it off for Army green.

Buckner had opened Tom's eyes to the real Army. The infantry training, he thought, was exhilarating. The cadets requisitioned mortars and machine guns from a hutch that displayed a model of the Combat Infantryman's Badge on the outside wall and large white letters that commanded FOLLOW ME; firing the heavy weapons gave the yearlings an inkling of the lethal power that would soon be theirs to command. Tom also had a new appreciation of artillery: how decisive the big guns could be on the battlefield and how technical the artilleryman's art was. And armor! Heirs to the glorious tradition of the cavalry, tankers charged into battle in fifty-ton M-48s, which could destroy targets more than two miles away. Tom thought that perhaps he would choose armor when the time came to select a combat branch. Rommel, Guderian, Patton, Carhart. It had a nice ring, didn't it?

Buckner also opened Tom's eyes to the inherent danger of his chosen profession — and the gritty nonchalance with which some soldiers viewed death. One afternoon, the cadets assembled on the bleachers next to Lake Popolopen for an exhibition by a Special Forces team that had just returned from Vietnam. The SF leader described his team's capabilities as the soldiers began to arrive in pairs. Two floated in by parachute. Two emerged from the lake in scuba gear. Two slipped from the woods disguised as local hunters. Then a helicopter swooped in at treetop level, hovering over an open field with two more men perched on the skids.

But something went wrong. One of the Green Berets, a young lieutenant, had too much slack in his rope; instead of rapelling to earth, he fell like a stone to his death, bouncing so high that Tom saw a quick flash of blue lake between the ground and the man's body. As medics rolled the lieutenant onto a stretcher and rushed him to the hospital, the team leader continued his narration, apparently unfazed. "If you will direct your attention across the lake," he told the cadets in a monotone, "you will see two men in a hollowed-out log paddling in this direction."

Goddamm! Tom thought. One of your men just jumped to his death and you hardly skipped a beat. The officer's cool behavior left Tom awestruck. What a man! he told himself as the demonstration finally ended. I'd like to be just like that.

What kind of army forged such warriors? At Camp Buckner in the summer of 1963, the answer seemed obvious to every cadet: the greatest military force the world had ever seen, the United States Army. And they, the West Pointers of '66, were heirs apparent to that magnificent fighting machine, the rightful successors to Eisenhower, Patton, Bradley, and the other triumphant commanders who had smashed the Axis powers. As in all of the nation's battles for more than a century, West Pointers had dominated the top ranks during World War II. Though they made up only 1 percent of the 900,000-man officer corps during the war, academy graduates had accounted for more than half of the Army's division commanders.

For an Army that historically depended on citizen volunteers and draftees to fill the ranks, West Point's sacred duty was to prepare a professional cadre of warriors capable of training and leading the non-professionals in combat. In George Washington's wry sentence, "An army of asses led by a lion is vastly superior to an army of lions led by an ass." Part of the tradition of the long gray line was its ability to rise to the occasion. That responsibility was repeatedly thumped into the class of '66. Although West Pointers had no exclusive claim to courage or competence in the officer corps, the academy was presumed to embody those values which the Army cherished most dearly and which were vital to military victory. West Point was bedrock.

Neither Tom nor his classmates, however, fully realized that, despite its wartime exploits, the Army had been in constant turmoil since 1945. After mobilizing ninety-one divisions during the war, the service had virtually imploded following V-J Day. From eight million men then, it shrank to two million by June 1946. The Army remained a huge force — far larger than any previous peacetime muster — but it was a paper tiger, as the first months of the Korean War demonstrated.

The birth of the atomic age produced further confusion. Who needed a large land force in an age of nuclear weapons? Initially, the Army tried to ignore that impertinent question. But there were persistent suggestions — often from gremlins in the Air Force and Navy — that the Army had become superfluous, given the capability of bombers and, later, missiles and submarines to deliver nuclear strikes.

Partly for survival, the service tried to adapt itself to the atomic battlefield. In 1953, the first atomic cannon was test-fired; it weighed eighty-three tons and had the mobility of a brontosaurus. In October 1956, the Army unveiled a new fighting configuration known as the "pentomic" division, a term that Chief of Staff Maxwell D. Taylor acknowledged was a "Madison Avenue adjective." The radical reorganization carved a division into five battle groups, each with five rifle companies. The intent was to allow a division to spread out, making it less vulnerable to atomic strikes.

This brainstorm marked the beginning of a series of upheavals, lasting into the 1980s, in which Army doctrine — the nitty-gritty of how to fight — was constantly reassessed and altered. In 1961, the pentomic configuration was scrapped, much to the relief of most ground commanders, who felt, as an Army historian observed, that they lacked "the weapons and equipment that were essential for the proper application of the new doctrine." Pentomic was succeeded by ROAD, an acronym for Reorganization Objectives Army Division. ROAD returned the Army to a more conventional structure similar to that used in World War II and Korea. A typical division of fifteen thousand men would include three brigades, each comprising two to five battalions.

ROAD also coincided with a new obsession: counterinsurgency. Pushed by President Kennedy, "c.i." swept through the Army with the rapidity of the Hula Hoop fad. No one knew how or where c.i. would work, but it provided the Army with a new raison d'être.

Another phenomenon that appeared in the officer corps following Hiroshima would be recognized and understood only after the bloody decade that was to come. A smug hubris — the "disease of victory" — infected the Army, as it infected much of the American government. Victory in World War II had been so absolute, so brilliantly American, that the notion of losing a war was unthinkable. The formula for triumph in Europe and the Pacific — superior firepower, superior manpower, superior technology — seemed prescriptive for any conflict. "The dominant characteristics of the senior leadership of the American armed forces," Neil Sheehan subsequently wrote, "had become professional arrogance, lack of imagination, and moral and intellectual insensitivity." Those characteristics would lead the Army's commanding generals wilfully to underestimate their enemies and overestimate their own battlefield prowess. Tragically, the only antidote to the disease of victory was the humiliation of defeat.

Nineteen-year-old Tom Carhart, of course, knew very little about such pathologies. He was preoccupied with trying to become a lion rather than an ass, and he showed clear promise toward that end. During one exercise at Buckner, the cadets skirmished against soldiers from the 101st Airborne who pretended to be French-Canadian separatists. Tom heard them in the woods, shouting in bad French accents: "Thees ees Jean Pierre. Come and find us!" During the exercise, Tom was separated from the rest of his patrol. He worked his way around a hill and spotted four paratroopers crouched in ambush. He carefully crept up behind them with his rifle. Hey, he thought, this is just like cowboys and Indians. They don't know any more than we do. With a bold rush, Tom captured all four soldiers. A major saluted him and shook his hand, congratulating Tom for his temerity.

Overall, his platoon leaders gave him mixed, even contradictory reviews for his performance at Buckner. "Average sense of responsibility, basically quite reliable," one evaluator concluded. "Has the ability to work with others and seems willing to work in harmony with others. Above average capacity, average ability. Has shown very little initiative.

Has been quite aggressive. Not very forceful. Good sense of humor. Works well under pressure. Average strength and endurance."

One August afternoon, Tom walked into the wooden barracks, ready to flop down for a rest. On the top bunk, naked and nipping from an ill-concealed bottle of Cutty Sark, lay another reason for Tom's perpetual good humor at Buckner. His name was Richard William Thompson, and already he was known throughout the corps simply as Buck. Propped up with his own pillow and Tom's, a book resting on his chest, he guffawed loudly between slugs of Scotch.

"Hey, Buck," Tom asked, "what's so funny?"

With a snort of laughter, Buck held up the book. It was Chaucer's *Canterbury Tales*. The Wife of Bath, in her sensual fashion, recounted the pleasures of marriage:

> The firste nyght had many a myrie fit
> With ech of hem, so wel was hym on lyve.
> Yblessed be God that I have wedded fyve!

Buck was a twenty-two-year-old Kansan. He had arrived at Beast in Army khakis, already wearing paratrooper wings. A man of the world, he seemed to know a little about everything and a great deal about most things, including women. Compared with Buck, Tom felt like a young bumpkin who had just fallen from the turnip truck.

For nearly two months Tom had lain in the bunk below Buck, smelling the illicit Scotch and listening to tales of life as a Jayhawk ne'er-do-well. This man, thought Tom as he tumbled onto his pillowless mattress, is going to be a great soldier. He's going to be a general. He's going to be chief of staff. Buck would be a lion leading an army of lions. Tom figured that if he couldn't be a flawless cadet, perhaps he could be something like Buck Thompson. For Tom Carhart, that goal meant a lot less distance to travel, anyway.

Buck had grown up in Atchison, a scrappy river-and-railroad town on the west bank of the muddy Missouri between St. Joseph and Leavenworth. His father owned Thompson's Restaurant, the kind of place with a big banquet room for wedding receptions and a sign out front that said ROTARY MEETS TUESDAY NOON. There had been six children, but an older brother was killed after falling out of an automobile the year before Buck was born. His mother, Dorothy, always thought that Buck was two people — the son who had died and Richard William.

Buck surely had enough character for both. As a three-year-old, he would stomp about in his cowboy outfit singing "Pistol-Packin' Mama" for the old railroad men who came in to the restaurant to drink black coffee and swap lies. Among other favorite antics were peeking under the revival tent at the Holy Rollers and climbing Haystack Hill to spy on the necking teenagers. The Thompson brood lived in a makeshift dormitory on the top floor of the family house, where young Buck peppered his older sister, Lee Ann, with detailed questions about her sex life.

Fair-skinned, with thinning, ash-blond hair, he had a chest that seemed built from barrel staves, and he walked with an ungainly waddle, which became his trademark and the source of countless family jokes. At Atchison High, Buck was All-Kansas in football, second in the state in the discus and shot-put, and third in his class academically. He rejected thirty athletic and academic scholarships — as well as appointments to West Point and Annapolis — in order to play football at the University of Kansas.

When he was a freshman in Lawrence, he pledged Sigma Chi and became an instant legend. Once — as he later told his academy classmates — Buck picked up his date at a sorority house and took her to the state penitentiary at Lansing, where he had passes to a hanging. On another occasion, he led some cronies on a foray to a nearby farm to buy an old swayback nag for $20. They dragged the horse up six flights of stairs to the top of a new girls' dormitory — the elevator had not yet been installed — where they shot it and left the carcass as a joke. Working at a grain silo one Fourth of July, Buck was chewed out by the foreman for drinking beer on top of a boxcar; he climbed down, flipped a rail switch, and accidentally derailed the car, spilling several tons of wheat.

Having worn out his welcome at the university, he transferred to St. Benedict's College in Atchison, where he earned straight A's. He joined the Army Reserve, and won his paratrooper's badge and another appointment to West Point, just squeezing in under the academy's age ceiling.

Buck's insouciance as a plebe made him immediate prey for upperclassmen, who capered around him, like jackals tearing at a wounded stag. "Hey," Buck once asked a senior cadet who was treating him with disdain, "if you're Jesus Christ, where are your sandals?" By the end of his second semester, he had qualified as a Century Man by walking more than a hundred hours of punishment tours, a distinction rarely achieved in four full years. A classmate, Bob Cresci, was surprised one morning to see him sitting on his bunk puffing a cigarette, trousers bunched around his ankles.

"Buck," Cresci asked, "what are you doing? We've gotta be in formation in two minutes!"

Thompson sighed, exhaling a long plume of smoke. "Not for me, Bob. I'm tired and I need a smoke." Five minutes later he emerged from the barracks with his trademark waddle, the jackals nipping as usual.

And when asked to explain in calculus class one day why his blackboard remained blank, he fixed a mournful eye on the instructor and replied, "Sir, I regret to say that the spirit was willing but the flesh was weak."

Only a year after arriving at West Point Buck had become, as he liked to say, tongue-in-cheek, "a legend in my own time." The surest way for a cadet to convene an instant audience was to ask, "Did you hear what Buck just did?" His classmates adored him — his irreverence and casual gestures of independence. He represented the rebel bottled up in each of them. He was their dissident, their maverick, their brigand. He was their beloved outlaw.

The civil disturbance of October 9, 1963 — better known as the Great Mess Hall Riot — began, innocently enough, with roast beef and a football rally.

At six P.M., as usual, Tom Carhart and twenty-four hundred other cadets poured through the great oak doors of Washington Hall. Tom and his classmates no longer anchored the foot of the tables. Now yearlings, they had happily surrendered those seats to the pariahs of '67 and begun the long migration toward the chairs reserved for first classmen at the other end.

After returning from Buckner on August 27, Tom had marched with a new resolve, though one not wholly consistent with the official ideals of the academy. He would endure but not surrender, listening to his own drummer amid the institution's more conventional cadence. In thirty-two months he would be Lieutenant Carhart, and this cadet world would be nothing but a bad dream. A cadet riddle asked, Can you use the F-word and the S-word in a three-word sentence? The answer was Tom's credo: Fuck this shit.

He already had accumulated an impressive list of demerits and slugs. His regimental tactical officer, Colonel A. L. Hamblen, Jr., wrote:

> Apparently Cadet Carhart, recognizing plebe year is over, has relaxed. His performance reports from Camp Buckner are glowing, whereas his ratings from his company are far from complimentary. His present company commander calls his attitude "extremely negative." Cadet Carhart informed me that upon his return to barracks after Camp Buckner, he became greatly disillusioned with the West Point system of handling plebes and with the fact that those who seem to get ahead in aptitude ratings are those who "polish apples" and those who lead a "wishy-washy"

existence — agreeing with everybody and doing nothing to "rock the boat." As a result, he treats plebes as he thinks best. Moreover, he sees no value in the aptitude system. Cadet Carhart's indifference, his resentment of correction, his uncooperative attitude and his poor personal appearance overshadow his apparent high potential and his high standings in other areas.

Okay, he was not Sylvanus Thayer. But so what? Tom decided that as long as they didn't throw him out, he would continue to skate around the edges just like Buck Thompson. Although life as a yearling was regimented and demanding, at least the mess hall had become a kind of sanctuary now that they were no longer forced to brace or recite the Days or any of that other plebe nonsense. They could joke, swap gossip, socialize.

From the poop deck came a steady patter of announcements, including the public proclamation of major infractions. Cadets particularly heeded any disclosure regarding men who had been caught *in flagrante delicto:* "Attention to orders. Disregard of regulations, United States Corps of Cadets. Gross public display of affection. Found in a firm embrace with a female in the vicinity of the gardens behind the Hotel Thayer at approximately 2300 hours, 27 September 1963. Cadet Michael Johnson is awarded twenty-two punishment tours, forty-four demerits, and two months' confinement." The corps would moan in sympathy, and each Romeo made a mental note to scratch the Thayer gardens from his list of trysting snuggeries.

Not least among the privileges of being an upperclassman in Washington Hall was the right to observe several customs denied to plebes. For example, if upperclassmen at a table voted for dessert all around, the Boston cream pie or sheet cake was carved into equal shares for those who wanted a piece. But if the table voted to "go big dick" — plebes, forbidden to use profanity as well as contractions, had to refer to it as "going large Richard" — then one cadet, selected by lot, could eat up to half the pie by himself. A second cadet could take up to half the remainder, and so on. The only stipulation was that the winner had to finish his portion by the time the adjutant excused the cadets from the table: "Bat-talions, RISE! Dismissed!" Otherwise, he forfeited dessert privileges for a week.

On this Wednesday night the corps had finished its roast beef and was well into the ice cream when the rally began. Army was scheduled to play Penn State on Saturday, and the cadets hoped to bolster the Black Knights with a spirited show of support. Beating the Nittany Lions was almost as satisfying as beating Navy or Notre Dame. The previous year, Army had won a thriller, 13 to 10, which cost Penn State the national championship; this year, the fifth-ranked Lions were undoubtedly eager for revenge. For days the West Point cheerleading squad, known as the Rabble Rousers, plotted how best to fire up the cadets.

Tom had just finished his dessert when he heard the signal: a cannon blast followed by a long, shrill whistle. Several hundred plebes, as previously instructed, leaped onto their chairs, peeled off their uniform tunics, and began whirling them over their heads. "Rally! Rally! Rally!" they shrieked. Out of the kitchen glided a dozen Rabble Rousers on roller skates, also swinging their tunics and yelling. The corps took up the chant: "Rally! Rally! Rally!" Several cadets barged through the front door, leading the Army mule on a tether.

At this point, for reasons never fully understood, the well-disciplined United States Corps of Cadets turned into a frenzied mob. Cadets tilted their tables on end, sending ten place settings crashing to the floor. Large slabs of leftover roast beef flew through the air. Cadets stripped off their belts and used them as slingshots to fling pats of butter at the ceiling and the vast mural at the south end of the hall.

"Stack tables!" someone hollered. The cry was taken up: "Stack tables! Stack tables!"

Throughout the mess hall, cadets lifted the heavy oak tables one atop another — three, four, five, six tables precariously stacked as firsties swarmed over them like pharaoh's overseers, ordering the plebe slaves to shoulder up yet another.

When the towers were high enough, cadets leaped onto the chandeliers and began swinging in wide arcs, yodeling wildly. Others opened half-pint milk cartons and heaved them across the room in streaming white parabolas. They flung ketchup bottles and globs of honey at the large statue of a Crusader standing in an alcove.

For twenty minutes the Walpurgisnacht roared on. The sole officer in charge flapped about in his ice cream-spattered uniform, yelling into the din, "Halt! This has got to stop!" Butter pats pocked the ceiling and the mural figures of Miltiades and Joan of Arc; ketchup splattered the oil portraits of past superintendents and most of the cadets. Broken crockery and glass littered the floor.

Finally, with a few last whoops and crashes, the uprising sputtered and died. The cadets, alarmed by their own fury, scurried off to the barracks to await a counterattack by the authorities. There had been mess hall disturbances before: when the class of 1861 graduated after Fort Sumter and every graduate swore an oath of allegiance to the Union, the younger cadets at supper that night had smashed their stools to splinters in appreciation. But nothing in memory came close to this rebellion.

Although outraged, West Point's senior officers were surprisingly tolerant, perhaps because they could not identify any ringleaders to draw and quarter. The academy tallied the damages and docked every cadet $1.27 from his monthly paycheck until the riot was paid off. The new corps morale booster — full of false bravado — became, "If that was a $1.27 rally, let's have a $5.00 rally." For many months, Tom and his classmates talked about the devastation with hushed tones and a shake of the head, as though describing the carnage of Gettysburg or Verdun. And in the end, the Rabble Rousers had accomplished their mission: Army upset Penn State yet again, 10 to 7.

George Crocker's seventeen-month career as a cadet had been nearly as checkered as Tom Carhart's. In Arkansas, after once being teased about getting good grades in school, George had declared in exasperation, "Mother, I'm not going to be a brain." "Okay, George," Adele Crocker had warned him, "but you're going to be sorry." Now he was sorry. His Beast Barracks anxiety over West Point's academic rigor had been well founded; any subject that required dexterity with numbers caused him trouble, and at times West Point's engineering curriculum seemed to be all numbers.

Each cadet kept all of his math tests in a folder; George's were covered with the instructors' red notations: WP for wrong procedure, or RTP for read the problem. Sometimes he tried to demonstrate his good intentions by noting plaintively at the top of the page that he had labored until the instructor gave the "cease work" order. Even so, he floundered near the bottom of the class, perpetually in peril of being turned back or of washing out.

Determined to make his mark somewhere, George had thrown himself heart and soul into the academy's military training. At Camp Buckner, he found his calling: the infantry. He loved solving the squad and platoon attack problems, which seemed close to being the pure distillation of a warrior's craft. In his eyes, the NCO instructors from the 101st Airborne were both energetic and competent, men born to lead other men in the dark of night. Several sergeants on the Recondo committee also behaved in wonderfully theatrical fashion, slashing themselves with freshly honed knives to test the blades' sharpness, or cramming scrambled eggs into their mouths with both hands before swaggering like John Wayne from the mess hall, belching loudly.

When he was his company's skit leader during the Buckner Revue, George had demonstrated the "nuclear hand grenade" — track shoes included in every kit for a quick getaway — and the LAMF, an acronym for "light air mobile flyswatter" or, for the cognoscenti, "like a motherfucker." The class roared with laughter. Returning for yearling academics, he knew that he was hooked on the Queen of Battle, the infantry — if he could survive until graduation.

George roomed in Company B-2 with another Southern yearling, a tall, serene cadet named Arthur Crawford Mosley, Jr. Art was born in the delta town of Clarksdale, Mississippi, but grew up on the coast of the Florida panhandle in Panama City, where his father chaired the school board. Mosley was as brainy in the classroom as Crocker was hopeless. "George still has a lot of Razorback in him," Art once explained. "He has plenty of smarts, but something awful happens when he gets near a book." Nevertheless, they found common ground in their fondness for hijinks.

One fad sweeping the corps — much to the chagrin of those who revered West Point's decorum — was the art of mooning. A cadet mooner kept a tally sheet, scoring a point when he succeeded in tricking others into looking at his bare buttocks. No credit could be taken for a "kill" unless a victim had actually looked, so cadets often walked into one another's rooms with their eyes locked on the ceiling. The lunar permutations included double moons, waxing and waning moons, harvest moons, half moons, new moons, crescent moons, and the dark side of the moon. Occasionally, an especially inventive cadet mooned an entire roomful of cadets before happily padding off to record four or five more hatch marks on his score card.

Boldly ambitious, George and Art decided to attempt a nuclear moon. Crouching in ambush in Central Barracks, they waited until the corps marched out of Washington Hall after noon meal. As hundreds of cadets passed directly below, the pair let them have it: a double-daylight, two-megaton, thermonuclear ka-boom moon. The corps erupted in an uproar, of course — that was the point. While cadets hurled snowballs at the apparition, several tactical officers pounded up the barracks stairwell in full throat, futilely baying after the culprits.

On another occasion, Mosley later recalled, George decided to test an old cadet superstition. Across the Plain stood a statue of General John Sedgwick; it had been cast from cannons captured by the general's VI Corps during the Civil War. According to legend, a cadet could guarantee himself passing grades by appearing before the statue at midnight in full dress gray under arms and spinning the rowels on Sedgwick's spurs.

George knew that he needed all of the supernatural help available; on the other hand, no one was likely to wager any cash on such a stunt. So he proposed a variation. Late one night, after Art and a few others in B-2 had put up $10 each, George pulled on several sets of sweats, wrapped a towel around his neck, and retreated to the sinks, where he flipped on the hot water in the showers. After steaming himself into a sweat, he ran up to the division door. The night was frigid, the Plain dusted with snow. George peeled off the sweats, took a deep breath, and dashed naked out the door and across the parade ground to the statue. Reaching up, he gave the rowels a spin and sprinted back to the barracks, where Art and the others waited with their noses plastered against the windowpanes.

"Hell," George drawled as he came through the door and collected his winnings, "I never even got cold."

A more conventional outlet for his considerable energy was playing tackle on the 150-pound football team. West Point competed in a league composed mainly of Ivy League colleges; the rules required that a player weigh no more than 154 pounds at five P.M. on the day before a game. For George, a husky six-footer, making weight was a weekly ordeal; at one point his waist measurement was nineteen inches, a half inch smaller than his thigh. Early in the week, after drinking a glass of dissolved magnesium salt crystals to ream himself out, he lived on lettuce and ice. Then, after the weigh-in, he would ingest a can of cashews, a carton of vanilla fudge royal ice cream, and a jar of Tang to build his strength back up before kickoff. Although the weekly weigh-ins were dreadful, George enjoyed playing football because of the camaraderie, the competition, and — not least — because the gridiron was not the classroom.

West Point also believed that athletics built character and served to ground the staggering voltage generated by twenty-four hundred virile, womenless young men. The academy required every cadet to compete in either intercollegiate or intramural sports. All sports were taken seriously, particularly if Navy was on the schedule. The current head basketball coach was Taylor Locke, whose assistant, soon to succeed him, was Bobby Knight. Fanatical about winning, both coaches had maniacal tempers. At half time, if Army was playing poorly, Locke might rip the door off a bathroom stall or make retching sounds into a toilet bowl to dramatize how nauseated the team's performance made him. Knight, who later won infamy at Indiana University, occasionally kicked the ball rack into the third row of seats or scattered the players' folding chairs like wheat chaff.

But football was king. The national championship teams of the 1940s were particularly stunning; after Army routed Navy in 1949, MacArthur cabled, "From the Far East I send you one single thought, one sole idea, written in red on every beachhead from Australia to Tokyo: there is no substitute for victory." After Westmoreland hired Paul Dietzel as coach, the superintendent proclaimed fulsomely, "It is to the national interest . . . that we, by our performance, create the image of a winner."

In fact, only two events could trigger the complete mobilization of the nation's military academies: war and football. Thus, on a Friday afternoon in early November, less than three weeks after the Great Mess Hall Riot, four long trains carrying the entire corps, the Army band, and two mules pulled out of West Point. At the same time, a similar retinue — with a falcon instead of the mules — left the United States Air Force Academy in Colorado Springs. Both corps headed for Chicago, where the gridiron heroes would clash the following afternoon at Soldier Field.

George, who had played in a 150-pound game Friday afternoon, arrived at the station only moments before the seventy-car train pulled out. Happy to have made it, and delighted by any opportunity to get away from the academy, he settled into his seat for the eighteen-hour trip. A crowd of eighty thousand, including President Kennedy, was expected for the game.

Few cadets, however, were aware that the Windy City had been in an uproar over the impending invasion of five thousand young men. Earlier that fall, Mayor Richard Daley had turned over the arrangements for the game to his special events director, a politician named Jack Reilly. Reilly had called a press conference to announce that the city planned to sponsor a postgame dance for the cadets and thus needed several thousand blind dates.

"Got that, press?" Reilly barked. "We need girls, lots of girls, average age eighteen, and maybe five hundred or so in the upper bracket of nineteen. Get cracking!"

Thousands applied. So many young women were so eager to dance the night away with a cadet that Reilly had to disconnect his telephone. Then he announced that the girls would be screened so that the dance would be "on a high level."

Reilly established a committee of thirty matrons to evaluate the girls during three sessions at City Hall. Three thousand young women showed up, all of them coiffed, manicured, and deeply anxious. Applicants filled out forms listing their age, weight, height in heels, and reasons for their interest. Among the responses: "It would be a thrill any red-blooded girl would delight in." And: "This will be a new experience. I never applied for a date before."

Then rumors, apparently well founded, began to circulate that the screening committee had secretly decided to select only college coeds. Outraged working girls and their mothers bombarded City Hall with protests, including such letters as this:

"My girlfriend and I went to City Hall, room 610, to apply for being cadets' dates . . A woman secretary or something told us, 'Oh, I'm sorry, didn't you know? It's just for college girls.' Well, we think we speak and dress as well as any college girls. What's wrong with us? After all, it's like civil rights, isn't it?"

Reilly insisted the rumors were "poppycock. Of course working girls will go to the party." At this point, however, the academies announced that only eight hundred cadets needed partners. Some cadets already had dates, some didn't want them, some didn't dance. Many of the surplus twenty-two hundred girls had already spent sizable sums on party dresses and accouterments. Under an even more intense barrage of criticism, City Hall pared the list of women to eight hundred; the deciding criteria were height, personality, maturity, and comeliness.

Oblivious of this melodrama, George and the other cadets climbed off the trains at Englewood Station shortly before ten on Saturday morning. Buses transported them to McCormick Place for lunch. Then they marched to Soldier Field for the first football game played there between academy rivals since Army and Navy had battled to a tie in 1926. A huge crowd, including the president, roared with approval as the perfectly aligned ranks of cadets filed into the stadium. In a hard-fought defensive battle, Army won, 14 to 10, no doubt further advancing "the national interest," as Westmoreland had foretold.

Those who chose to attend Reilly's fête reported to the Conrad Hilton at 6:15 P.M., where the eight hundred blind dates were introduced alphabetically before being escorted into the ballroom. (Reilly financed the $10,000 party by selling $25 subscriptions to Chicago businessmen, who were so eager to support the cadets that they bought $200,000 worth of tickets.)

George and thousands of other cadets who opted not to attend the dance stormed into the Loop and the Near North Side, where the locals welcomed them as if they were doughboys liberating France. In West Point gray or Air Force blue, they wandered through the taverns of Rush Street, astonished to find themselves mobbed by adoring girls who insisted on buying round after round of beer and bourbon.

At 1:15 on Sunday morning, the West Pointers staggered back to Englewood Station for the trip home. As the train cars rocked gently through the night toward New York, they swapped stories of an amazing night in an open-armed town. They had been lionized, accorded a respect and an affection that bordered on adoration. This, they presumed, was how men who had pledged their lives to the service of the country were supposed to be treated; few imagined that it could or would ever be otherwise. They could hardly wait for the corps' next expedition, the Army-Navy classic in Philadelphia on November 30. President Kennedy was expected to attend that game, too.

George thought the weekend had been splendid. He and his classmates were American heroes, whether returning home in their dress grays to little towns in Arkansas or storming through a broad-shouldered metropolis like Chicago. Like most cadets, he had often daydreamed about how pleasant it would be to pursue his education someplace other than Hell on the Hudson, someplace where there were no calculus tests or carping tactical officers. But the thought of quitting never really entered his mind. That would mean admitting defeat, failing. And American heroes did not fail.

4

YEAR OF THE DRAGON

IT WAS ONLY one-thirty, but at West Point in late November dusk always seemed imminent. The winter sun hurried through the afternoon, wanly hugging the southern horizon. Bear Mountain and Anthony's Nose blotted the fading light, and darkness, gathering in the hollows like fog, crept up the leafless hills. Cadets had coined their own term for the drear polar season that lasted from Halloween through late March: they called it Gloom Period.

The assistant chaplain, the Reverend James David Ford, pulled into the chapel parking lot and switched off the car ignition. Gloom Period didn't bother Jim Ford; he had grown up in Minnesota, where, he liked to tell people, "we had nine months of winter and three months of poor sledding." In fact, winter was his favorite time of year. As a teenager, he had been ski champion of Minnesota and was still famous in the north woods as the only man known to have vaulted off a ski jump backwards. On an icy February day in 1949, when Jim was seventeen, five friends had wagered a nickel that he wouldn't attempt such a foolish stunt. When he took the bet, four of them — each holding one of his limbs — had pushed him off at the top; the fifth yelled "Jump!" at the right moment, because Ford was unable to see the edge of the ramp. He had sailed into space, a dark figure curled into a question mark. On the first attempt, he fell. But on the second and third jumps, he landed perfectly on both skis.

Now, at thirty-two, Ford still had a preternatural sense of balance. Equilibrium was his dominant feature, as red hair or a large nose marked other men. He had big hands, an owlish look, and a habit of leaning forward when speaking, his torso canted as though feeling for a place to land. He was as natural a raconteur as he was a skier, with a laugh —

a throaty heh-heh-heh — that deepened when he told stories of getting someone's goat. An admirer once remarked that it was fortunate Jim Ford had become a man of the cloth, since he had more than a little of the devil in him.

Ford had set aside this Friday to drive down to Manhattan with Bill Deveaux, the curator of the chapel organ. The pulpit and organ on the east side of the church were uncomfortably dark, and Deveaux had offered to rig a small spotlight from the ceiling. After finding what they needed in a shop that sold theatrical lights, the two men ate an early lunch before returning to West Point. The little expedition had been enjoyable, and they chatted gaily as they stepped from the car.

The chapel, magnificent and austere, loomed over them. Built in 1910 on a hill above Washington Hall, its square northern tower rose 145 feet and offered an unparalleled view of the Hudson Valley; visitors to the parapet could also find several generations of graffiti — notably IKE EISENHOWER, MAY 1914 — scratched into the copper cladding. A "stringtable" molding of carved figures ran horizontally around the chapel walls, depicting a procession of knights, archers, minstrels, jesters, and other characters from Arthurian legend. On the tower, other carvings showed soldiers in everyday poses: carrying books, playing a drum, lugging a bucket and brush.

Ford and Deveaux entered through a small door on the chapel's west side. In Gothic symbology, the entrance represented the spear wound in Christ's side. Imitating the great cathedrals of Europe, the chapel builders had included other medieval touches: a dank chamber was a reminder of the ecclesiastical dungeons of old, and a vertical notch in the wall near the altar represented a hagioscope, often called a lepers' squint, because lepers and others kept outside the church had used it to watch the service.

The chapel interior was brightened by some of the most magnificent stained glass in the western hemisphere. On both sides of the nave, above a forest of eighteen thousand organ pipes, dozens of windows depicted saints and scenes from the Bible, culminating in a spectacular wall of glass in the sanctuary. Above the pews, which could seat fifteen hundred, fourteen old regimental and American flags further colored the interior. Even so, the church was a dark and imposing vault, the kind of place in which to murder a Becket at his prayers.

When Ford's eyes adjusted to the dim light, he stepped through the arched bay near the side door and into the nave. Red velvet cords blocked the center aisle; an oak plaque above his head still bore the white numerals of last Sunday's hymns. Glancing over his shoulder, Ford was startled to see a group of cadets sitting in the darkened pews. On Friday afternoon? he wondered. Scanning the chapel, he saw more than a hundred young men scattered about, some kneeling, all bowed in prayer. Oh, my God, he thought, something awful has happened. An explosion in one of the classroom buildings? A training accident?

He stepped over to the nearest cadet.

"What's the matter?" he whispered. "What's happened?"

"Haven't you heard?"

"No. I haven't heard a thing. What is it?"

"The president's been shot."

Ford hurried to the chief chaplain's house, which was attached to the north end of the chapel through a hidden passageway. Ted Speers sat before the television, and Ford slumped down next to him in time to see the networks relay the United Press bulletin: FLASH. PRESIDENT KENNEDY DEAD.

Below the chapel, on the Plain, in the barracks, in the administration buildings, a silence settled over the academy. In one economics class, the instructor, a major with a huge red handlebar mustache, announced, "Gentlemen, the commander-in-chief has been shot. In respect, we will cancel class. Dismissed." The dazed cadets walked back to the barracks, where the fatal news was repeated matter-of-factly over the public address system.

Later that afternoon, Jim Ford returned to the chapel and stood at the main door, speaking softly with the cadets as they entered and departed. The assassination was a tragedy for the nation, but in Ford's mind it was particularly painful for West Point. The academy had special ties to the president. He had been their commander-in-chief; he had spoken here; his youth truly made him seem one of them.

Ford and Speers quickly arranged three memorial services, which were attended by hundreds of cadets and officers. Ford offered a brief prayer for the nation and the Kennedy family, before reading from Psalm 121: "I will lift up mine eyes unto the hills, from whence cometh my help." He thought the psalm especially appropriate for hilly West Point.

Before the final service, the two chaplains stood outside on the stone terrace, watching the cadets slowly climb the 138 steps from the barracks to the chapel. Ford also noticed lights burning on one of the athletic fields just beyond the Plain. Peering into the distance, he saw tiny jersey-clad figures running about. It was the football team, practicing for the upcoming Navy game. "Look at that," he told Speers heatedly. "What a contrast. Here the president is dead and everything stops at the academy except football."

On Saturday morning at ten o'clock, the entire corps assembled on the Plain in full dress gray under arms. A light rain fell as the band played "Sabers and Spurs" and "America Exultant." The ritual of formally notifying the corps of a president's death and the succession of a new commander-in-chief was highly stylized, almost liturgical. At a similar formation in April 1865, cadets had listened to an official War Department order apprising them of the death of Abraham Lincoln. A few days later, on April 25, 1865, as required by Special Orders No. 67, the corps crossed the Hudson and stood locked at attention in Garrison as the train bearing Lincoln's body passed through on its circuitous route to Springfield.

Now, ninety-eight years later, the corps listened to the reading of General Orders No. 117. The new superintendent, Major General James B. Lampert, a classmate of Westmoreland's from '36, also read a brief statement from Defense Secretary Robert McNamara, mourning the loss of "a gallant spirit whose championship of freedom and opportunity will be recognized by history." A delegation of cadets began preparing to leave for Washington to march in Monday's funeral. For the rest of the day, until darkness fell, a cannon thundered from Trophy Point every half hour. Blue smoke rolled toward the river, and each angry roar carried down the valley for miles until finally swallowed by the wind.

The Army-Navy game, originally scheduled for Saturday the thirtieth, was postponed a week. But the memory of those black-and-gold jerseys scampering beneath the gridiron lights on that awful Friday night troubled Ford for a long time.

As a man of the cross among men of the sword, Jim Ford was to find himself at loggerheads with the academy on more than one occasion. Though respectful of authority and wary of confrontation, he instinctively resisted being subsumed by the academy. As the chapel was physically removed from the Plain below, so Ford sought to maintain his distance from the military world surrounding him. Religion and soldiering, he firmly believed, were not incompatible; on the other hand, God was more than a mere armor bearer for warriors preparing to give battle.

Ford was the son and grandson of Lutheran pastors who had settled in the Midwest among other families of Swedish origin. The Fords were modestly well heeled, inclined to moderation, and pious without being sanctimonious. James David was born in 1931 in Sioux Falls, South Dakota, but spent most of his childhood in Minnesota. Like his father and grandfather, he attended Gustavus Adolphus College, where he met and married Marcia Sodergren, who came from four generations of Swedish Lutheran clergymen. Jim Ford enjoyed politics almost as much as he enjoyed skiing. Raised as a New Deal Democrat, he often quoted

Martin Luther: "Send your good men into the ministry, but send your best men into politics." Nevertheless, when the time came to choose a profession, Ford followed the family calling. Before being ordained, he took a year's sabbatical in Heidelberg, living the life of a Bohemian expatriate in a single room on the Neckar, with one shiny suit to his name and his skis always waxed and ready.

For Ford's first ministry, the Lutheran bishopric assigned him to Ivanhoe, Minnesota. Wedged into the southwest corner of the state, the farm town boasted a population of 719, of which 191 were his parishioners at Bethany-Elim Lutheran Church. The local theater, called the Gem, had only six seats across; Marcia joked that the marquee was so narrow they had to show *The Old Man* one night and *The Sea* the next. In 1960, after two and a half years in Ivanhoe, Ford heard that West Point was searching for an assistant chaplain. Intrigued by the academy's tradition and eager to minister to a larger flock, he applied; despite stiff competition from forty-four other candidates, Ford won the job. He and Marcia and their children arrived in February 1961. They moved into Quarters 5, a two-story frame house with a screened porch and a majestic view of the Hudson.

He adored West Point — the heritage, the chapel, and, most of all, the cadets. For a time he spit-shined his shoes as diligently as any plebe until reading somewhere that Maxwell Taylor said it was permissible to use a brush. Not yet thirty years old, Ford established an easy and immediate rapport with the corps. He was delighted whenever cadets exhibited independence and spirit, as when Jack Wheeler challenged the modification in the Cadet Prayer. During the second week of Beast Barracks, Ford usually gathered the new cadets in South Auditorium. After expelling the upperclassmen, he would tell them:

"Gentlemen, the first day has come and gone and it will never come again. What do you think of that?"

As they cheered wildly, he would continue: "The first week has come and gone, and it will never come again. What do you think of that?"

And so on. Much of the summer he spent counseling new cadets who wanted to resign, particularly those who claimed the Lord had ordered them to leave. "If God called you here to be a cadet in July," Ford admonished, "He doesn't call you to quit in August."

He also adored Ted Speers. Ford was Midwest and Gustavus Adolphus and Lutheran; Speers was Park Avenue and Princeton and Presbyterian. "You're one of those people," Ford once chided, "who think there's just New York and California."

"And a lot of cows in between," Speers retorted.

West Point, with its emphasis on athletics and physical prowess, demanded what Ford called a "grunt-and-groan" religion. Being a champion skier gave Ford a certain cachet; for Speers, a fine athlete who had won the 1921 British hammer-throw championship as a college student at Cambridge, a tennis court was the place to prove his mettle. He would toy with Westmoreland in their frequent matches before putting away the much younger superintendent with a lethal forehand topspin. One day, Ford was watching the two exchange volleys when Speers drilled a shot close to the line. Westmoreland locked his gaze on Ford and asked, "Jim, that was out, wasn't it?" When Ford nodded, Speers yelled, "Well, Ford, thinking about your five kids at home, I guess you decided to agree with the general."

In fact, Ford cared not a whit for the general's stars. Before arriving at West Point, he had given little thought to the relationship between military and clergy. His own martial experience was limited to a spontaneous — and futile — effort to volunteer for Air Force pilot training during the Korean War. Now that he was at West Point, he believed his clerical collar was a great leveler of status.

"I'm the rank of the person I'm with," he often explained. "If he's a three-star general, I'm a three-star general. If he's a plebe, I'm a plebe. The cadets can salute me, they can wave, they can say 'Hi,' they can say whatever they want."

West Point's chief chaplain was appointed by the president; by tradition, the post always went to a civilian, a practice that had long irritated other Army chaplains, all of whom were members of the officer corps. Ford was a shrewd enough student of power and politics to recognize that the uniformed clergy envied both the magnificent academy chapel and large congregation — one that was ensured, since church attendance was mandatory for cadets. He also was aware of bitter complaints about the nearly unbroken succession of Protestants — particularly Episcopalians — who had been appointed to West Point's chaplaincy.

But Episcopalianism, with its emphasis on authority, ceremony, and mission, had long been considered the denomination most appropriate for Army officers. Until World War II, nine of every ten generals were Protestant and about half were Episcopal. In the nineteenth century, Catholics at West Point had even been barred from worshiping on post. In recent years, the increased size and egalitarianism of the Army had eroded that elitism considerably, and Protestant sects were gradually melding into the ecumenical worship of what was sometimes called "the Army God." The appointment of Ted Speers, a Presbyterian, reflected the diminishing influence of the Episcopal Church. Even so, Protestant domination — like all traditions at West Point — died hard.

So did mandatory chapel. Obligatory worship for American soldiers, first required in 1775, had been abolished in 1916. But West Point stoutly resisted a similar reform. For years, officers who missed Sunday services at the academy were required to submit a written excuse to the superintendent; those who bucked the enforced attendance found themselves transferred to a frontier post where the state of a man's soul was not an issue. Until recently, all cadets, Protestant, Catholic, or infidel, had even been required to audition for the Protestant choir. The choirmaster would order each man to sing an octave — Glo-ry to God! Most were dismissed with an impatient wave before they had finished croaking out even the first note.

Since Sylvanus Thayer's day, religion had been deemed critical to a future officer's character. No atheists lived in foxholes, and West Point seemed determined that none would find refuge at the Military Academy either. Chaplains, who for years taught a curious concoction of geography, history, and ethics, also instructed cadets in the virtues of honor and veracity. Chaplain John William French, for example, had used his own textbook in 1860 to teach that "with us, truthfulness is to be honored, not only as a religious, a moral, and a military virtue, but as one that is ancestral . . . Stratagems to deceive an enemy are lawful and right. But apart from this, a true soldier knows not how to violate the truth."

Not all cadets accepted this religious forced feeding gracefully. In 1840, the commandant had pleaded with the corps to stop staining the chapel floor with tobacco juice; one nineteenth-century cadet wondered why he and his classmates should be forced to attend church, since "all excesses are without our reach and in fact we are everywhere so hemmed in that it is almost as difficult to sin here as it is to do well in the world at large." A later generation admired Chaplain John Forsyth, a rotund, Falstaffian figure who was part owner of a brewery. Occasionally delayed for Sunday service because of a lively billiards game at the Officers Club, Forsyth was most revered for the brevity of his sermons.

Jim Ford resisted the notion that chapel should be a place to instill virtue or provide cadets with a moral road map. Religion and morality, he believed, were two different beasts, not to be cross-bred. In Ford's theology, the pulpit was a place to suggest the proper ideals of Christian soldiers — love, reconciliation, peace — but it was the parishioners' task to determine how best to embrace those virtues. Ford's was a respected, even a venerable ecclesiastical approach. Yet it would take the terrible pain of war to truly put it to the test.

Obligatory chapel also troubled him. Forcing cadets to attend church seemed both constitutionally dubious and antithetical to the spirit of religious worship. Why shouldn't they decide for themselves? Ford wondered. But every effort to nudge the academy authorities toward a policy of voluntary chapel was sharply rebuffed.

So it was that every Sabbath the corps assembled outside the barracks and marched to church. Tactical officers sometimes hid in ambush near the chapel door to quill cadets guilty of "high water trou" — trousers that rode too high on the ankle. Occasionally the enforced attendance was a pathetic sight, especially on those Sundays when the corps had returned only hours earlier from the Army-Navy debauch in Philadelphia. On such mornings, they sat as sinners beneath the battle flags and stained glass saints, dress grays clashing with their green faces, the most afflicted of them in stocking feet, vomiting violently into their black, low-quarter, plain-toe shoes.

On April 5, 1964, nearly six months after John Kennedy's death, Jim Ford was again asked to pray publicly for a fallen leader. This time he found the words much easier to summon than when the president had been murdered. Standing on the mess hall poop deck as the corps sat down to supper, Ford was introduced by a cadet officer: "Gentlemen, General of the Army MacArthur died this afternoon. I direct your attention to the chaplain." Ford offered an appropriate benediction for MacArthur's soul. As he concluded with a final amen, he was surprised by the quiet that pervaded the usually raucous mess hall. Cadets by nature could be savagely irreverent, but the passing of Saint Doug commanded their respect.

Before dawn on Wednesday morning, George Crocker and the rest of the corps boarded buses for New York. At eight o'clock in a drenching rain, they formed ranks at the head of the four-block funeral cortège outside Manhattan's Seventh Regiment Armory at Park Avenue and Sixty-sixth Street. As a bugle sounded ruffles and flourishes, a senior cadet barked, "For-ward *march!*" The procession marched south on a route that carried them down Park, across Fifty-seventh Street, and on to Broadway. Near the end of the parade, the cadets peeled away to stand seven-deep on Seventh Avenue between Thirtieth and Thirty-fourth streets. Locked at attention, they watched as six horses clopped past pulling the same caisson that had borne JFK five months earlier. Behind the bier came MacArthur's five-star standard and the same riderless gelding that had pranced skittishly behind Kennedy's coffin. The stirrups held a pair of boots, empty and reversed, symbol of a fallen warrior since the days of Genghis Khan.

George stood motionless as the raindrops beat a counterpoint to the funeral drum. How many times had they listened to MacArthur's famous speech in those first few months of plebe year? Duty and honor and country, the general had said, "make you strong enough to know when you are weak, and brave enough to face yourself when you are afraid." Yet MacArthur's death, at the age of eighty-four, seemed anticlimactic to a nation that had so recently mourned John Kennedy. A few old-timers watching the funeral could remember him as a young superintendent, sitting with his stocking feet propped on his desk, punctuating every sentence with an all-purpose French *bon,* saluting with a touch of the riding crop to his battered go-to-hell cap. Yet to most cadets he was remote, a figure who, even before his death, had belonged to the ages. Like the rest of his classmates, George just wanted to get out of the rain.

The cortège wheeled into Penn Station. MacArthur's casket — government issue and gunmetal gray — was hoisted onto a train for Washington, where it would lie in state in the Capitol Rotunda before burial in Norfolk. Whatever the general had seen on that spring afternoon in the cemetery with Westmoreland, it had not drawn him home to West Point.

Four days later, on Sunday, April 12, George's father was admitted to the hospital in Russellville, Arkansas. During a spring rainstorm, Bill Crocker, fifty-seven, had been "walking the track" around the Dardanelle dam to make certain that trees and other debris had been properly cleared. He caught a cold, which turned into pneumonia and knocked him flat. On Wednesday night, the Crockers called George to tell him that his father hoped to be sent home on Saturday.

But when Adele next visited the hospital, Bill was in an oxygen tent. "Adele," the doctor told her, "Bill has had a bad night. I hate to tell you this but he's not going to live through the day. He's got cancer of the lung and he's had an infarction."

At West Point, after being informed by a tactical officer that his family needed him, George immediately left for the airport. At eight P.M., before boarding the flight to Memphis — there were no Friday evening planes into Little Rock — he called home. His maternal grandmother answered the phone. "Your father's real sick," she told him. "Everybody's at the hospital."

George stepped off the plane in Memphis, confident that his father would pull through. But when he reached the gate and saw the face of Uncle Jeff, his mother's brother, his optimism vanished.

"My daddy's dead, isn't he?" George asked.

"Yes."

"What time did he die?"

"Seven twenty-five."

George finally arrived home at four o'clock Saturday morning, exhausted and numb with grief. He was due back at West Point on Monday, so the funeral was arranged hastily. On Sunday, April 19, Bill Crocker was laid to rest in a plot by a silver creek and a huge oak tree. After the services, Adele insisted that her son return to the academy. "Honey," she told him, "you just go back and pass and graduate. That's all I ask."

For two months, George brooded over his father's death. He often thought about the last time they had really spent any time together, during that long drive to the academy for the beginning of Beast. *If you don't like it, call me and I'll come pick you up*, Bill had said. *Even if you don't make it, I'll still be proud of you*. George wanted to make it, wanted his father to be proud of him even from the grave. But it was hard. A few weeks after the funeral, one of the tactical officers wrote to Adele that George seemed unable to concentrate and was having more trouble than usual in the classroom.

One detail in particular bothered George. He had called home from the airport at eight P.M. on April 17. His father had died at 7:25, yet no one had told him about it. Why had they deceived him? The Crocker family prided itself on telling each other the truth, on being foursquare and straightforward. Why had they pretended that his father was still alive? Not until Adele gave a full accounting of Bill's death when George returned home again that summer was the issue cleared up. Bill had died at 7:25 Central Time; he was, in fact, alive when George called. "Mama," he exclaimed after Adele had finally solved the mystery, "I always thought you were lying to me."

It was a simple misunderstanding, but the resolution seemed to lighten the family's grief somewhat. Bill Crocker was gone. But something precious had been restored between his widow and his only son, whom he had cherished more than life.

Tom Carhart was in trouble. Despite his flashes of brilliance in the classroom, he was on the brink of expulsion because of his boisterous antics. Hammered with low ratings in military aptitude, Tom plummeted in class rank to 612 out of the 645 cadets remaining in the class of '66. By early 1964, he ranked twenty-fourth among the twenty-six yearlings in his company. Although he was popular with classmates, five upperclassmen "poop sheeted" him by recommending that he never be commissioned. Tom's tactical officer, Captain Richard P. Hoy, summarized the indictment:

> Cadet Carhart has dropped sharply in aptitude for the service. Cadets resent his impulsive, immature, clownish behavior, his uncooperative, negative attitude, and his unresponsiveness to their corrections. In addition, his poor personal habits and poor personal appearance have been ad-

> versely noted by nineteen cadets [in the company]. It is my best judgment that these many shortcomings and difficulties should be brought to a board of officers. In my opinion, he can and will correct his obnoxious, boisterous, immature, clownish, inconsistent, abusive, shoddy, and indifferent behavior with experience and with the impetus he would receive from a board of officers.

An investigation by a regimental panel of colonels who had the power to expel him from the corps was not something that Tom had bargained for. Buck Thompson had survived two regimental boards as a plebe, so the ordeal wasn't necessarily fatal. Still, the chance of being "found" — forced to leave — was sobering. Leaving the academy of his own volition was one thing; getting kicked out was something else. Expulsion, he believed, would stain him indelibly.

Tom did not like West Point; indeed, he liked it less each passing month. Forbidden things drew him magnetically; he got a thrill from doing what the authorities prohibited. The American Good Bad Boy — Huckleberry Finn was the classic example — had a West Point analogue, the Good Bad Cadet. And Tom Carhart fit squarely into the tradition.

The academy had always attracted some unlikely battle captains, among them James McNeill Whistler, Edgar Allan Poe, and Timothy Leary. Rascals were as much a part of the lore as were the sons of Mars, and they surely did more to soften the academy's image of insufferable priggery. Jefferson Davis, ever the rebel, found himself in trouble for spitting on the floor, cooking in his room, and even firing a musket from the barracks window. Poe, who arrived in 1830 after two years in the Army, often swapped candles for brandy and delighted his roommates in Old South by scribbling doggerel about the shortcomings of upperclassmen; eventually he was dismissed — though he ranked third in the class — for obstinately refusing to drill. Whistler flunked out in 1853 after defining silicon as a gas during a chemistry exam; years later, he would titillate London drawing rooms by proclaiming that "if silicon were a gas, I would be a major general."

But historical antecedent was a poor defense, as Tom well understood. Trying to explain that he was simply the latest in a long gray line of Good Bad Cadets was not likely to save him. When the regimental board met to ponder his fate, he was petrified.

As he walked to the hearing room, all of his flippancy drained away. They were going to kick him out, weren't they? This was it, the end of the dream. He marched into the office of the second regiment's commander on the top floor of New North, near the Lost Fifties, and saluted an unsmiling colonel and two unsmiling lieutenant colonels.

"What do you have to say for yourself?" the colonel finally asked.

"Sir," Tom answered meekly, "I'll be good."

It was the best he could manage. The officers agreed to "condition" him, which meant that he could remain in the corps on probation. Tom felt immense relief. The time had come to buckle down, he thought, time to say "Yes, sir, yes, sir, three bags full."

When Captain Hoy evaluated him again in April, near the end of his yearling year, the tac again criticized Tom for "poor judgment, loud and obnoxious behavior, poor personal appearance, and an uncooperative attitude." Yet he also found that Tom was highly motivated, with definite officer potential. "In my opinion," the captain added in a note for the record, "he has made a significant improvement since the rude awakening of his first board."

Tom emerged from the session with Hoy feeling greatly relieved. He had weathered the storm. He knew now that he had to be shrewder, more politic. Despite his unruly behavior, he ardently believed in the traditional attributes of an officer: gentlemanly conduct, personal fealty, brotherhood, the pursuit of glory. Those ideals rang true for Tom, though he pursued them in his own fashion. Beyond West Point, he believed, dwelt a fraternity of officers united by their commitment to principle and to the nation. Tom longed to be a member of that fraternity; if the academy demanded more decorum as the initiation fee, so be it. He was willing to pay the price.

For two months, he behaved admirably. He studied hard, shined his shoes, and tried to be less of a burden to the long-suffering Captain Hoy. On June 3, with the graduation of the class of 1964, the men of '66 became "cows," exchanging their gold epaulets for gray and moving a few seats closer to the head of the mess hall tables.

To celebrate the midway point in their cadet careers, Tom and three classmates agreed to undertake a grand tour of Europe in the fashion of nineteenth-century gentlemen of leisure. In July, after several weeks of training as "third lieutenants" with various Army units in Germany, the four cadets met in Frankfurt for the beginning of their two-week lark. They rented an Opel Kadett, filled a pink wastebasket with ice and bottles of Heineken beer, and headed for France. In addition to Tom, the touring party included Bob Albright, the son of a Boeing engineer from Vashon Island in Puget Sound; Danny Crawford, the son of a Texas oil man; and George Crocker.

Tom and George had first met as plebes on the 150-pound football team. Although Tom left the team after one season, the friendship persisted. George admired Tom's audacity and intelligence; Tom admired George's integrity and composure. Similar in height and build, they shared a fondness for fast cars, alcoholic beverages, and daredevil stunts. Like the components of certain explosives, when kept apart they could remain relatively inert; when combined, they became combustible.

Arriving in Paris on July 13, the eve of Bastille Day, the four cadets celebrated so hard that they were in a stupor when the parade took place the next morning. "C'mon, c'mon, try not to look like tourists," Tom complained, as they mugged for snapshots at Notre Dame and Sacré Coeur, looking more American in their crewcuts and Levi's than the Hardy boys. At the Arch of Triumph, a street vendor asked whether they wanted to see some dirty pictures. *Mais oui, monsieur, certainement!* they answered, before doubling over with laughter when he flashed some *fin-de-siècle* postcards of plump women in corsets.

From Paris they sped south to Fontainebleau, where the Carhart family had lived from 1954 to 1957. Tom's father, assigned as a liaison officer to the French military, had worked in one of Napoleon's old retreats, with ceilings twenty feet high, candelabra on the mantels, and double doors fit for an emperor's entrance. Enjoying the strong dollar of the mid 1950s, the Carharts had rented a huge house that came with Empire furniture, a maid, and a gardener. A ten-foot stone wall surrounded the mansion; it had been Tom's solemn duty as eldest son to hop out of the family car and open the big iron gates to the stable, which was used as a garage. A grove of chestnut trees stood just inside the wall, and in spring each bough bore clusters of white blossoms on its tips.

Tom's French was still excellent — he had almost no accent — and as he pointed the way to the old house he listened to the radio, laughing at the jokes while the others chuckled, too, feigning comprehension. The mansion had been boarded up, so they drank some wine in the yard and climbed one of the chestnut trees; from the upper branches, they could see the steep roofs of Fontainebleau.

This trip, with its high spirits and camaraderie, had been precisely the diversion George needed following his father's death. After the funeral, he had balked at the thought of touring Europe while his mother stayed home alone in Russellville, but she had wisely insisted, and sent him $200 to underwrite the adventure. Now, after a few days of barreling through France with Tom and Bob and Danny, he felt like his old self again for the first time in three months. The shock of losing his father so suddenly would never vanish, but he was no longer mired in gloom.

In Barcelona they attended a bullfight, where they sat in the cheap sol seats with little centimo hats made of newspaper and jumped nervously every time one of Franco's thugs saluted the matador with a burst of machine-pistol fire into the air. In Nice, they rented blue Vespas — Bob Albright immediately drove his into the rear of a Fiat — and later buzzed the Grand Casino at Monte Carlo, where the bouncers waved them away with a scowl.

Near the base of the Zugspitze, they checked into the sprawling Eibsee Hotel and, true to form, drank too much at a local beer hall. At two A.M., Bob challenged George to a sprint in the hotel corridor; George pulled up short to watch the naked Albright streak down the hallway, where he bowled over an American major's wife coming out of her room. The MPs were summoned, lectures were delivered, and the major grudgingly agreed not to press charges in deference to their careers and the greater good of the United States Army.

It all came to a boil in Provence near Arles, the town on the Rhone that had once been Van Gogh's home. Lunching in the Opel on Bacardi rum and sardines, the four cadets happened upon a boisterous village festival. The town square had been blocked off, but most of the action seemed to center on a makeshift bullring. On the circumference, large wooden barricades had been driven into the ground, spaced just far enough apart to allow a man to squeeze through sideways to safety. In the center stood a stout tree with a platform girdling the trunk three feet above the ground. Several ropes dangled from the lower branches. A large bull — well muscled, black as midnight, and snorting indignantly — pawed the earth near the tree. One horn had snapped off several inches from the tip; a wooden cap the size of a croquet ball sheathed the other. Several young Frenchmen taunted the beast, nimbly eluding each charge by slipping between the stakes or scrambling up the ropes into the tree boughs.

Tom and George immediately sprinted into the ring, yelling and waving their T-shirts at the bull. Bob and Danny, who either had more sense or less rum, watched from a safe distance. Be careful, someone yelled in French from the crowd, the bull is very dangerous.

"It's okay, folks," Tom hollered back, waving like a grand marshal, "we're American cowboys."

George dashed through the arena, fanning his shirt like a cape. Determined not to be outdone by a bullfighter from Arkansas, Tom danced closer and closer to the bull, taunting the animal in French and English.

"C'mon, you guys," Albright pleaded, "let's go. Get back in the car. There's no future in this."

Suddenly the bull charged. Tom bolted for the safety of the tree and scrambled onto the bench. With astonishing agility, the bull leaped up next to him, hooves clattering on the wood. The crowd shouted with alarm as Tom circled the tree with the bull on his heels. Leaping from the bench, he sprinted toward the barricades. But halfway across the ring, the bull caught him from behind. The balled horn smacked Tom below the shoulder blades with enough force to fling him through the air. As he landed in the dirt, the bull charged again, goring him once before trampling his limp form. The gasps from the crowd turned to shrieks. Oh, my God, Albright thought, he's dead.

As several Frenchmen diverted the bull to the far side of the ring, Tom lay motionless on the ground — for about three seconds. Then he leaped to his feet, arms raised in that grand marshal wave.

"*Pas de problème! Pas de problème!*" he yelled. "It's not bad, folks! *Ne vous inquietez pas, il n'y a pas de problème.*"

There were bravos, of course, as the American cowboys strutted back toward their little Opel. *Bon voyage,* the Frenchmen called, whispering among themselves and pointing at the crazy gored one, who now walked with a bit of a hobble. Lunatic, *oui,* they agreed, but *très brave*. The good people of Provence knew moxie when they saw it.

One Saturday afternoon in the autumn of 1964, Marcia McGuire stood waiting in Grant Hall while a plebe called the barracks to tell Art Bonifas that his girlfriend had arrived. Brass sconces brightened the walls, illuminating oil paintings of Henry (Hap) Arnold, Omar Bradley, and Dwight Eisenhower, who had posed with his right hand resting rakishly on his hip. Once the academy mess hall, the huge room had been converted into a lounge where cadets could rendezvous with their dates. Overstuffed armchairs and sofas upholstered in green and red velvet gave the hall an atmosphere of high Republicanism, like the Union League in Philadelphia. With its stiff formality and parade of visitors, the setting hardly inspired romance, much less passion; Grant Hall was about as carnal as a funeral parlor.

Marcia had something she wanted to tell Art and she knew it would not be easy. She had decided to return his little gold Army pin; he had given her the A-pin on Valentine's Day. After seven months of going steady, she had concluded that they should resume dating other people, now that his cow year had begun. In some respects, her reasons had little to do with Art; he had turned out to be exactly what he seemed at Breezy Point the previous summer — a sweet, guileless Cornhusker. But she had grown weary of exclusively dating a West Pointer. The grinding routine had become a burden. Being a cadet was hard; being a cadet's girlfriend could be even harder.

The life of a "drag," as a cadet called his date, was an odd lot. Roles were strangely reversed. The girls picked up the cadets and later dropped them off; the cadets had a curfew, while most of the girls did not; and the cadets, rather than the girls, were chaperoned by sharp-eyed tactical officers, who zealously guarded the virtue of their charges.

Beyond these superficial quirks, however, the academy remained unflinchingly traditional. Enormous changes in sexual mores and the role of women in American culture had just begun to stir through the nation. But West Point remained a preserve of chivalry and chauvinism. Every year the cadet yearbook made fulsome references to "the fair sex" and So-and-So's prowess "with the ladies." Each cadet received a copy of *Cadetiquette,* an eighty-two-page booklet that advised:

> His attitude toward ladies will always distinguish a gentleman from a boor. Ladies are worthy of particular consideration and courtesy. At all times they must be sheltered and protected, not only from the elements and physical harm, but also from embarrassment, crudity, or coarseness of any sort . . . Ladies are sometimes very independent and will occasionally get themselves into difficulties when they have no escort to assist them.

The hostess's office distributed a companion booklet, *Hints for Lady Visitors*. Among the admonitions:

> Be considerate. Be prepared to pay some of the expenses of your visit. Don't smoke cigarettes. Don't park your car after Retreat with a cadet in it. Don't indulge in loud or daring clothing on the reservation. Don't loll about in provocative attitudes in public. Don't wear any part of a cadet uniform (although in a sudden rainstorm a cadet may offer his raincoat).

The proper role of a woman, the Army and West Point seemed to presume, was to bear children and keep the home fires burning for her soldier. Women were bused in to the academy for quick visits before being banished again to the distaff world outside. For many cadets, coming of age in the domain of the academy made it impossible not to think of women as a different species — either princesses to protect or chattels to deflower. Every soldier had heard the bromide a thousand times: if the Army wanted you to have a wife, it would have issued you one. Cadets, of course, were not permitted to have wives — they had even signed documents swearing that they had never been married — and girlfriends were barely tolerated.

Intimacy at West Point was exceedingly rare. As a consequence, deep and mature relationships were difficult to cultivate. Dates were supposed to be liquorless and kissless, although cadets often honored those prohibitions more in the breach. At dances in Cullem Hall or the gymnasium, hop committee vigilantes patrolled the dance floor, chastising or expelling couples who demonstrated the slightest hint of an amorous grind. (Even so, by the end of the evening the big brass uniform buttons would leave marks on the ladies' skin above their strapless gowns, as though imprinted in hot wax.) A rigid structure governed most hops, as *Cad-*

etiquette explained: "Three pieces of music make up one dance. The normal hop consists of twelve dances. These are the twelve dances that appear as numbers on your hop card . . . Dances numbered 4, 8, and 12, which are marked with an asterisk on your hop card, are dances in which cutting in is not permitted."

Any PDA — public display of affection — was punished with a severe slug. Simply holding hands could earn twenty-two hours of marching on the Area and two months of confinement. Cadets constantly hunted for secure places to be alone with their girls, routinely jiggling every doorknob they passed in hopes of finding an unlocked, empty room. Flirtation Walk — a sylvan path near the river — was tacitly considered a sanctuary, and in warm weather brassieres dangled from the dogwood branches as couples darted into the woods with a brown boy quilt stuffed in a typewriter case. Elsewhere, however, young lovers remained fair game. Tales abounded of zealous tactical officers making amphibious landings at Delafield Pond, as though it were Inchon, or, in winter, tramping in snowshoes through the forest above the chapel, searching for hardy, huddling twosomes.

Once, Marcia and Art were sitting on the balcony floor in Grant Hall. He had his arm around her and had unzipped his tunic at the top and bottom, as cadets usually did when they sat down. A tac abruptly walked in and demanded, "Name and company, mister." No matter that the scene was entirely innocent; Art was slugged for PDA. And several weeks later, even before Art finished walking off the first slug, the episode was repeated — another twenty-two hours of walking the Area for an innocuous public display. Marcia was incredulous. One of Art's classmates, John (Buz) Buczacki, began calling her Miss Slugoid.

"If I was going to do anything to deserve that," she complained, "I'd do a lot more."

Not all drags accepted their lot gracefully. Some rebelled, particularly the working girls who valued their independence, or the coeds from large, liberal arts universities, where the calculus of love was beginning to change forever. They objected to the term *drag* and complained that couples tiptoeing into the woods with typewriter cases resembled fifteen-year-olds playing spin the bottle. And a date never knew when she would suddenly find herself abandoned because her boyfriend had been confined to his room or ordered to walk the Area for some petty infraction. Many young women endured the restrictions — after all, love was at stake — but not without grumbling.

Marcia had put up with it. For a young woman raised in a strict home, West Point did not seem that repressive. But the routine had gradually begun to grate on her.

Twice a month or so on Saturday morning, she caught the ten o'clock bus from the West Side terminal in Manhattan. The local rolled through every Sleepy Hollow village in the lower Hudson Valley, taking more than two hours to cover the fifty miles. When the bus reached Haverstraw, about ten miles south of the academy, Marcia and the other drags pulled out their vanity cases and carefully applied their makeup.

At the academy, she usually stayed at Mrs. Mahan's big white boarding house for $2.50 a night, or in one of the Thayer's dormitory rooms. At the hotel, ten girls crammed into two rooms and shared a single bath, invariably running out of hot water. Each young woman brought her curlers and hair dryers — large, domed appliances that blew out the fuses. Often at night, after the cadet curfew, at least one girl in each room would return from her date muttering about damned West Point and that damned cadet and who the hell does he think he is anyway? And there would be the clatter of gold on the bathroom tile as she threw down the knave's ring or A-pin in angry frustration before bursting into tears.

For entertainment, Art took Marcia to hops or football games or the movies. They passed many hours in the Weapons Room, a snack bar with a jukebox on the first floor of the gymnasium. If it was the beginning of the month and he had just been paid, Art would spring for steak sandwiches, which cost a dollar apiece; otherwise, they settled for hamburgers. Sometimes, when he was able to get away, they met in New York. He played on the academy water polo team — a natural goalie, with that vast wingspan — and Marcia would watch him compete at the New York Athletic Club. Once she went to Trader Vic's before a match and saved the gardenia that came in her drink; later, with a grand flourish, she tossed the blossom into the pool like a princess saluting her prince.

Despite their usually impeccable manners, the West Pointers on occasion could be embarrassingly boorish. One night Marcia and Art went to dinner in Greenwich Village with two other cadets and their dates. The cadets gave the waiter a miserable time — sending back the wine and carping about other things. Although not in uniform, they let it be known that they were West Pointers. When the bill arrived, the men paid the $26 and each cadet put a quarter on the table for a tip. As the three couples left the restaurant and walked down the street toward a nightclub, the waiter stormed after them, cursing furiously. While the others looked on, too astonished to react, he grabbed Art's classmate Fred Bertolino and pinned him against the wall.

"My taxes go to pay for you!" the waiter shouted. "With all it costs me to send you to school, the least you can do is leave a decent tip."

Marcia cringed in humiliation. As the waiter stalked back to the restaurant, she privately vowed always to keep spare change in her purse to supplement the gratuities if necessary.

Now, as she waited in Grant Hall, Art walked in from the barracks next door, smiling as usual. Marcia knew that her visits were the highlight of his week. He was doing well at the academy, ranking in the middle of the class academically. But the two years had not passed easily. Sometimes his imperturbable nature drove her to exasperation. When he casually mentioned a classmate or an upperclassman who seemed to be exploiting his affability, she shook her head. "Art, you are being so naïve," she scolded once. "Why do you let people do that to you?"

Art had simply shrugged. "They're not hurting me," he answered evenly. "They're not going to change me or change my attitude. It's nothing."

But Marcia knew that what she was about to tell him *would* hurt. After they had chatted for a while she broke the news as gently as she could. She would be graduating in the spring, Marcia explained, and although she cared for him deeply, perhaps they would be wise to date other people. She was not interested in anyone else in particular, she assured him; not at all. But the routine — the long bus ride to West Point, the few hours together before he marched off to Sunday supper, the monotonous ride back to New York — had become tiresome. They could still see each other, Marcia added, but not exclusively.

Then she handed Art's pin back to him. The tiny double sixes of his class year were linked to the gold Army A with a slender chain. He looked both crestfallen and confused, as though uncertain how to persuade Marcia to change her mind. Marcia felt sorry for him, sorry for both of them really. When she got up to leave, Art stood silently, a tall, slender figure of dejection. His gray tunic was fully zipped. The tacs would have approved.

For cadets who lacked steady girlfriends — and the long list included Jack Wheeler, Tom Carhart, and George Crocker — social life at West Point could be monastic. During Gloom Period, the preferred pastime was sleeping, better known as "rack." Occasionally, a cadet fastened an A-pin to his quilt, explaining solemnly, "My brown boy will never leave me." On Saturday nights, they played handball or watched movies in the gymnasium. Radio station KDET incessantly aired songs by April Stevens, whose sultry voice was interpreted by cadets as the sound of lust. (It had long been an article of faith in the corps that the authorities spiked the cadets' milk with saltpeter to lessen their concupiscence; if so, the tactic failed profoundly.) Drinking was prohibited within a ten-mile radius of the academy flagpole, so the nearest legitimate tavern was a tatty dive on 9W called Snuffy's. On weekends, the bar was a boozy mass of cadet gray. Sometimes, the boredom and frustration exploded, as when two roommates once marched down Flirtation Walk after an argument, squared off in the woods, and brutally pummeled each other until they could no longer lift their arms.

Fortunately, New York lay only fifty miles to the south. Those who remained free off academic and disciplinary restrictions occasionally broke the monotony of rack, handball, and April Stevens with a twenty-four-hour visit to the Big Apple. West Point and the city had more or less come of age simultaneously. After discovering that cadets were selling their pay vouchers in the city to finance drink and debauchery, Sylvanus Thayer had forbidden the corps to leave the academy without permission. The rule was widely ignored; cadets in the nineteenth century sometimes placed bets on whether they could get to the city and back between morning and evening roll calls. Cadet MacArthur had once slipped away to Rector's, a nightclub on Broadway, where he greeted Diamond Jim Brady like an old comrade, swilled martinis, and then repaired to a nearby burlesque show. As superintendent twenty years later, perhaps recalling that adventure, MacArthur had authorized cadets to visit the city without chaperons and even alloted them $5.00 a month in spending money.

Now that they were upperclassmen, the men of '66 fled to New York as often as possible. After Saturday parade, they would hurry back to their rooms to change while every turntable in the barracks blared the Rolling Stones' "Satisfaction." But transportation to the city was a problem, since cadets were not allowed to own cars until the spring of their first-class year. Some took the bus or hitchhiked. Others hid cars in Highland Falls. Matt Harrison and his classmate Bob Cresci owned an ancient Ford, dubbed the Blue Hog, which they kept in a local garage for $10 a month. Both side windows were shattered, old blankets upholstered the seats, and only one windshield wiper worked. The Blue Hog also burned an entire crankcase of oil during the run to New York, so Matt and Bob, unable to afford new motor oil, kept a five-gallon can of sludge in the trunk. Whenever the red oil light flashed, usually under the Westside Highway, they would stop the car, pull on a pair of rubber surgical gloves, and slop a few quarts into the crankcase.

Wearing a uniform in the city carried no stigma—that would come later. In fact, New Yorkers held cadets in the same high regard the citizens of Chicago had demonstrated the previous fall. Strangers sometimes bought the young warriors drinks or dinner at restaurants like Mama Leone's in midtown. Many places also offered cadet discounts, which was fortunate, because they were always strapped for cash. Forbidden to draw extra cash from home, each man had to make do with his monthly stipend of half a second lieutenant's pay — $151 a month — to cover uniforms, books, and all other expenses.

Trolling for girls was the preferred pastime; the uniforms helped in that pursuit. ("One hundred and ten percent of twisted steel and sex appeal," they crowed.) Whether hustling the buxom blondes in the German pavilion at the World's Fair or wooing the working girls on the dance floor at the Tuxedo Lounge, the cadets enjoyed conspicuous success, although barracks boasting always exceeded actual conquest.

Sometimes they rented a room for $30 at the Astor or Great Northern and wedged twenty cadets into it — each man paying a buck and a half for the privilege of sleeping on the floor or in the bathtub. Such "hotel parties" stretched the terms of the cadet honor code. Was the innkeeper being defrauded? And what about the corollary honor questions? Could you tell a girl you loved her and not mean it? What if you weren't sure? What if you changed your mind? The cadet honor committee periodically debated such issues, mulling the pros and cons with the chin-stroking solemnity of medieval clerics pondering how many angels could fit on the head of a pin. For now, a loose constructionism prevailed, and hotel parties remained legitimate — barely. As for love, conscience was usually considered the final arbiter.

In truth, the only standing rule in New York seemed to be obligatory intemperance. Elated by their brief furlough, the cadets drank as though the world would end at dawn. And when it did not and they regained consciousness in some malodorous fleabag, surrounded by a dozen or more inebriated, snoring classmates, they slowly picked themselves up and prepared for the painful return to West Point.

"One of these days," George Crocker once told Bob Albright after both awoke with crushing hangovers, "I'm going to do something in New York that I can remember."

As cow year drew to a close, the men of '66 prepared to begin their final twelve months at the academy with a three-week tour of Army posts in Kentucky, Oklahoma, Texas, Georgia, and Virginia. A few, however, were barred from the trip because they were D — deficient — academically. George Crocker, to his alarm and chagrin, was among them. He had flunked Electrical Engineering 304, or, as it was better known, "juice" class. "I'm dumb as dirt in juice," he complained to Art Mosley. "I still don't know what an electron is or why the lights come on when you flip the switch."

Those struggling in EE304 often met at night for poop sessions in Bill

Kakel's room. Kakel, who ranked fifth in the class and was headed for graduate school at MIT, would help them "spec," or memorize, some of the required formulas with mnemonics, like the calculation involving electrical current and resistance: "Twinkle, twinkle, little star, E is equal to IR."

Kakel's best efforts notwithstanding, George was found in EE304. As the rest of the class left on their summer trip, he and a half-dozen other Foundlings moved into the Boarders Ward, an isolated section of the barracks reserved for cadets who either had been accused of honor violations or were on the verge of dismissal for academic reasons. In a few days, the academy would allow George one last chance to redeem himself by taking a "re-entrance" exam in electrical engineering; should he fail that, he would be relegated to the Immortals, the long gray line of former cadets who had flunked out of West Point. Instead of being the first Crocker to graduate from college, he now faced the prospect of returning to Arkansas in disgrace, with three years of hard work down the drain. Even worse, his father's dream would forever be unfulfilled. "You just go back and pass and graduate," Adele had urged after Bill Crocker's death. "That's all I ask."

For George, the EE304 debacle was the latest episode in a checkered spring. His unwavering enthusiasm for the military aspects of the academy had earned the respect and admiration of his tactical officers, who clearly saw his leadership potential. Military history and infantry tactics fascinated him. Like many classmates, he was increasingly eager to fight in Vietnam. He taught himself to strip and reassemble an AK-47 and the ChiCom — Chinese communist — machine gun with its distinctive round magazine. Practicing such skills, he believed, was a sensible way to begin preparing for combat. Sometimes he browsed through the academy museum, which allowed cadets to check out weapons as though they were library books. The museum also had a splendid collection of trophies: the sash Robert E. Lee had worn at Appomattox; Hermann Goering's ivory *Reichsmarschall*'s baton; Mussolini's round black cap; Yamashita's seventeenth-century samurai sword. It seemed fitting that such relics should be at West Point, symbols of the vanquished displayed by the victors. Perhaps someday the museum would display an object of Ho Chi Minh's as a trophy.

But George was plagued with bad luck. He had recently been selected to be a cadet captain at Camp Buckner later in the summer. One Sunday morning, as the spring semester drew to a close, he skipped breakfast in order to study. An overzealous officer discovered him in the barracks and assumed that George was sneaking some unauthorized rack time. That was a Class One offense, requiring a hearing before a commandant's board of senior officers. George wrote out his version of the incident, confident that he would be exonerated once the board understood that he had been studying. But on the day of the hearing the presiding colonel showed little interest in explanations. "Okay, Mr. Crocker," the colonel snapped, "we've read your report. Anything you want to change?"

"No, sir," George answered, presuming that the document spoke for itself.

"Two months' reduction to cadet private," the colonel said. "Send in the next man."

George was stunned. In ten seconds he had been busted to private for an infraction he had not committed. Appeal was impossible. He blinked, swallowed hard, saluted, and marched out of the hearing room.

Now Private Crocker was in danger of being kicked out of the corps altogether. George had always believed, though he had no firm evidence, that the academy found a way to keep those cadets who possessed, as he put it, "the right kind of heart and the right kind of attitude," even if their classroom performance was less than brilliant. His belief was about to be put to the test. Once again, he plunged into the EE304 textbook in an effort to master the mysteries of the electron and learn why the lights came on when he flipped a switch.

Shortly before the re-entrance exam, he was summoned to a meeting with Colonel Elliot C. Cutler, Jr., chairman of the electrical engineering department. Cutler, who had graduated with the class of 1942, had been wounded in Europe as an infantryman in World War II, fought with the 24th Division in Korea, and subsequently earned a Ph.D. at Georgia Tech. Before appearing at the chairman's office, George slipped on his best uniform, polished his brass twice, and got a haircut. The session was brief and informal, but George had the distinct impression that Cutler was sizing him up. Was this, he wondered, the real test?

On the morning of the exam, the Foundlings reported to the EE304 lecture hall. An instructor took the roll, then marched the anxious cadets into a classroom. After several hours of struggling with impedance and voltage and ohms, George returned to the Boarders Ward, uncertain whether he should begin packing his bags.

That afternoon, the results were posted. He had passed. "Congratulations," the instructor told him a short while later. "You're back with your class. You have the option of joining them halfway through their trip or taking an extra two weeks of leave."

Relieved and jubilant, George took the two weeks. He never learned whether he had actually passed the test or whether Colonel Cutler had detected "the right kind of heart and the right kind of attitude." Whatever the reason, he was once again a member of '66, without prejudice. The specter of returning home as a civilian — as a failure — vanished. After moving out of the Boarders Ward, he quickly caught a plane to Arkansas before the authorities could change their minds.

The reward for passing EE304 turned out to be much grander than simply fourteen days of extra leave. One afternoon in Russellville, George drove out to the lake. A thunderstorm had just passed through; several swimmers lounged on the shore, bemoaning the bad weather that had ruined their plans to go waterskiing. One of them, a small and very pretty young woman with curly brown hair, immediately caught George's eye. He ambled over and managed to strike up a conversation.

Her name was Vonda Jones. A native of Little Rock, she had just graduated from the University of Arkansas, where she had majored in home economics and was captain of the cheerleading squad. In September, she told George, she was scheduled to begin teaching home ec at Mount St. Mary's Academy, a private girls' school in Little Rock. Vonda's grandfather had been a circuit-riding Church of God preacher, spewing fire and brimstone until his death at the age of ninety-five. Her mother was a teacher from the Ozarks village of Green Forest; her father, J. Fred Jones, had grown up in the hamlet of Mt. Ida, in a section of western Arkansas so untamed that a panther once crashed through the roof of the family house. Fred Jones had literally walked out of the woods to attend college, which he financed by delivering laundry and moonshine. When he was a law student at the university, he had lived for a time in a tent. Now he was preparing to run for a seat on the Arkansas Supreme Court and Vonda was going to stump the state on his behalf.

With his droll humor — among other things he was a splendid mimic — George told Vonda about his boyhood in Dardanelle and his three years at West Point. She listened intently, attracted to this tall, polite stranger with the easy manner and perfect posture. After a few minutes, she and George excused themselves and went to buy cigarettes at a restaurant several blocks away. By the time they returned two hours later, Vonda realized that she had found her soulmate. She knew nothing about West Point or the military, but she and George seemed perfectly suited. Here, Vonda thought, is someone I could talk to forever.

They saw each other twice more that week before George flew back to the academy. Soon after he left, Vonda visited a friend who had recently married a young lieutenant from the Air Force Academy. "Okay," she insisted, "tell me what you did. I don't want to mess this up."

The first thing, her friend advised, was to "get a big picture made of yourself — touched up, of course." Several weeks later George received an eight-by-ten-inch portrait of Vonda, its sepia tint concealing any conceivable flaw. He kept the photo in his barracks room in Company F-2, where it served as a beguiling reminder that E equals IR, and so much more.

The class of 1966 had less than a year left before graduation. That meant fewer than a thousand meals in Washington Hall, and only three hundred more reveille calls. They were first classmen, at last; come next summer, Cadets Jack Wheeler, Tom Carhart, George Crocker, and nearly six hundred of their classmates would be second lieutenants in the United States Army.

Two events marked the ascension of '66 to the top rung. The first was the selection of the brigade commander, the so-called first captain. Every summer the commandant and regimental tactical officers anointed one cadet in the rising senior class who most embodied the ideals of the long gray line. The roll of former first captains contained such luminaries as Lee, McPherson, Pershing, MacArthur, Wainwright, Westmoreland, Rogers, and Dawkins.

From the class of '66, the authorities selected Norman E. Fretwell by a margin of one vote over Sam Champi, Jr., a popular football star from New Jersey. The son of a laundry truck driver from Joplin, Missouri, Norm Fretwell had the square-jawed looks and fullback's carriage considered vital in a first captain. A good student, with exceptional ratings in military aptitude, he was popular with the cadets, who admired his fundamental decency. Though some were wary of Norm's polished manner, which struck them as more suited to a politician than a military leader, his classmates nonetheless elected him class president.

Norm, determined to rise above the near poverty of his parents, harbored a desire — bordering on compulsion — to be pre-eminent in everything he attempted. But before he could wear the sleeveful of chevrons that signified his new rank, he needed polishing. On a summer day in 1965, he met for the first time on the Plain with a retired major who had been assigned to correct the new first captain's deficiencies.

"Captain Fretwell, you waddle like a duck," the major told him bluntly. "When you were just a cadet, you could hide in the corps. But now you're out front where everyone can see you. And what they'll see is someone who waddles."

Norm nodded, trying not to wince. Unfortunately, the major's words were true, but with the officer's help he was going to be de-waddled if it took all summer. Hour after hour, they worked on his marching. Norm practiced leaning into the wind to keep his plumed tarbucket from blowing off without making it look as though he was leaning. He sharpened his command voice, using his diaphragm to avoid tightening his throat and neck muscles. And he learned how to wield the saber, drawing it from the scabbard at a 45-degree angle with his right arm before pulling the pommel to within three inches of his chin, the blade canted 20 degrees forward.

The major's tutoring lasted several weeks, but eventually the waddle vanished, the voice boomed, and the saber flashed with precision. At last, Norm Fretwell was worthy; he moved into the Wheelhouse room traditionally reserved for the first captain, the same room once occupied by Douglas MacArthur.

The second event to coincide with the ascension of '66 was the selection of a new chaplain. After a long, agonizing battle with leukemia, Ted Speers died at the age of sixty-five. Jim Ford, who grieved as though his own father had passed away, conducted the funeral service in the main chapel. The mourners sang *Nunc Dimittis* — Lord, now lettest thou thy servant depart in peace — before walking two miles to the cemetery for Speers's burial.

Ninety-two ministers applied to succeed him. After the field was narrowed to a half dozen, Commandant Mike Davison walked into Ford's office one day and tossed a sheet of paper on his desk. "Jim, here's the application for senior chaplain," Davison said. "We'd like you to apply."

"I'm too young," Ford replied. "The chaplain has to be thirty-five. I'm thirty-three."

"No," Davison said, smiling, "we had a meeting and lowered the age requirement."

In early August, the White House announced that President Johnson had approved Ford's appointment. Delighted and surprised — Ford had expected a prominent clergyman from Louisville to get the post — he moved his family into Quarters 60 behind the chapel. The big house with its six bedrooms and six fireplaces provided ample room for a young man with a growing family, and Ford looked forward to living there for many years.

For three years, the men of '66 had been shielded from the impact of social and political events outside Thayer Gate. The academy's seclusion and busy regimen had always isolated the corps; Subaltern Winston Churchill of the Fourth Hussars once noted during a visit that cadets were "cloistered almost to a monastic extent." But as the class began its final year, nagging reminders of the waiting world intruded with increasing frequency. It was becomeing clear that, like their fathers and grandfathers, these West Pointers would have their own war to fight.

From the mess hall poop deck, funeral announcements for graduates killed in action in Vietnam became more common; widows and fatherless children periodically arrived at the academy to receive posthumous medals in somber ceremonies. Recently, Superintendent James Lampert had presented a Purple Heart and the Legion of Merit to the family of Captain James P. Spruill, class of '54, who had been killed by a mine. Following Spruill's funeral, the Army published his letters home in a propaganda pamphlet, which circulated at West Point.

"Please don't let them back where you are sell me down the river with talk of despair and defeat," the captain had written shortly before his death. "There is no backing out of Vietnam, for it will follow us everywhere we go."

5

YEAR OF THE HORSE

SHORTLY AFTER TEN P.M. on the third Saturday in October of 1965, Jack Wheeler stood watching the ballerinas emerge from their dressing rooms backstage at the New York State Theater. Singly and in pairs, they crossed the immense lobby to mingle with the cadets clustered around the bar and buffet table. Even out of costume, the slender dancers looked as graceful and athletic as they had on stage in *Stars and Stripes* and *Ballet Imperial* a few minutes earlier. Jack hoped he wasn't staring too intently. These women are ravishing, he thought. Their bodies are perfect.

In one corner of the lobby, encircled by cadets, George Balanchine delivered an animated lecture on the similarity between the West Point uniforms and those he had worn as a young dancer in St. Petersburg. Although he was now sixty-one, the legendary choreographer radiated the vigor of a man half his age; that aura of youthful vitality, Jack suspected, was enhanced by his notorious penchant for grooming and marrying young ballerinas in an apparently endless succession.

"And be sure to sit up high when you come again," Balanchine advised the cadets in his thick Russian accent. "Because when I choreograph my ballets it's not only the individual dancers who are important but the pattern they make collectively."

Jack knew very little about dance and music — his mother said he had a tin ear — but this evening's performance had dazzled him. And to think how close he had come to spending the evening alone in the barracks! When Captain John Sloan, one of the social science instructors at West Point, had phoned that morning with an invitation to the ballet and reception, Jack at first turned him down, pleading an overload of classwork. But after a few more hours of plowing through his engineering texts, Jack called Sloan back to ask whether he could change his mind.

Now he was delighted that he had. The excursion to New York on this warm Indian summer day had provided a pleasant distraction from the mountain of work waiting for him back at the academy.

Jack knew that he was studying too hard. His first-class curriculum included nuclear engineering, military history, English, Russian, ordnance, and military leadership — which the cadets called "leadersleep." Jack had also signed up for an extra language — German — and was taking honors civil engineering. He still ranked among the top ten men in the class academically, of course; no one more than Jack personified the "hive," a man diligent in his studies.

Yet there was a price to pay. At times he was too busy, too immersed in his books, to enjoy himself. Had he forgotten, he sometimes wondered, how to have fun? Jack now lived in Company E-2. Easy Deuce housed more than its share of free spirits, led by the matador of Provence, Tom Carhart; the company captain was Art Mosley, who had dropped the nuclear moon on the corps with George Crocker. But Jack was too much the hive to be part of that boisterous crowd. While they romped through the barracks or raced down to New York for a weekend spree, he usually remained at his desk.

Although he was diligent and studious, Jack didn't think of himself as dull. Earlier that summer, he had lost his virginity on the front seat of his blind date's car at Fort Knox. The entire trip — the class's initial outing as firsties — had been rambunctious: six hundred cadets in a half-dozen airplanes shuttling between Forts Knox, Sill, Bliss, Benning, and Belvoir. The three-week junket was intended to give the cadets a closer look at the Army's combat arms — armor, artillery, Signal Corps, infantry, and engineering — before each man selected a service branch in February.

Arriving at the various posts, they had swaggered onto the tarmac, tan and lean in their khakis, combat boots, and sunglasses. Jack especially liked Fort Sill, home of the artillery. Sill had given him a new enthusiasm for the big tubes and an understanding of how the mathematics skills needed in the artillery played to his strengths. Artillerymen were called redlegs, from the days when they wore a scarlet stripe down their uniform trousers. Jack thought he would like to be a redleg.

He knew with certainty that he didn't want to be an infantryman. Ever since he had seen Steve McQueen in *Hell Is for Heroes,* Jack had known that he was not meant to be a groundpounder; soldiering was a dangerous profession, but the infantry seemed insanely hazardous. He also knew that he wasn't the woodsman that George Crocker or Bill Hughes was. The artillery, he concluded, seemed the right fit for him.

One evening at Sill, the cadets had changed into their white uniform

India — also known as the Snow Machine or the Good Humor suit — for a party at the Officers Club. As usual, each man contributed a dollar to the "pig pool," the consolation prize for the classmate deemed to have the homeliest blind date; Buck Thompson, who was a genius at trading dates to win the pot, claimed the pool yet again at Sill. The cadets drank muzzleblasters, a local concoction of vodka, fruit juice, and innumerable liqueurs. After a few muzzleblasters, more than one man politely said excuse me to his date and collapsed on the floor in a fetal curl; those who remained conscious sang "Oklahoma!" and threw the post commander into the swimming pool. Later that night, Tom Carhart took bets that he could wrap his hand in newspaper and shove it unharmed into a huge floor fan. Just as the blades began to chew the fringes of the paper, Tom's roommate, Frank Cosentino, came sprinting across the room, bellowing "Car-haaart!" and threw a cross-body block that knocked Tom under a table, where he passed out.

But Fort Sill, Jack reflected, had been a temperance hall compared with Fort Bliss in El Paso. Attired in uniform India, as inconspicuous as a battalion of ice cream vendors, the men were bused on two consecutive evenings from Bliss to the nearby border, where they either walked across the Rio Grande bridge or flagged taxis to the Juarez red-light district. Little Mexican boys tugged at their sleeves, pandering for the prostitutes who lounged cross-legged on the nearby stoops. After washing down penicillin tablets with cerveza and tequila, many cadets headed straight for a dive that every man had heard about from the class of '65. La Cueva — the Cave — was dark and compact, with a low ceiling, tile floor, and a few rickety tables. A young girl with red hair and an hourglass figure turned tricks in a back room for $8.00; a long but fast-moving line formed outside the door.

La Cueva also featured a floor show. As one of the Mexican barkeeps collected quarters to feed the jukebox, an older woman sashayed across the dance floor. First she stripped down to a G-string. Soon she discarded that, flopped onto the tile floor, and invited the cadets to strip, too. Any man who could manage an erection while flat on his back with his arms pinned by the bouncers won the dubious honor of keeping the dancer for the evening. A few tried valiantly, thrashing around on the tiles with the dancer grinding above them and a hundred drunken classmates roaring their encouragement.

Yet beneath the hijinks, the first-class trip had had a sober undertone, reminding the cadets that they were less than a year from becoming warriors. Neither machismo in Juarez bars nor exemplary performance in the classroom, Jack knew, was a guarantee of proficiency in combat. As one of his electives, he had picked a course in political philosophy taught by Dale Vesser, a Rhodes scholar from the class of 1954 who would become a three-star general. Vesser had led his students through a provocative discussion of Plato's *Republic* and the philosopher's categorizing men as cast from gold, silver, iron, or brass. Plato believed that among the virtues of the ideal state were wisdom in the rulers, courage in the warriors, and temperance in common citizens. War is an art, he had declared, requiring a long apprenticeship and many natural gifts.

Courage, natural gifts, long apprenticeship: Jack had begun his apprenticeship at West Point, but what of courage and natural gifts? He knew that he had gifts, but were they those suited to a warrior? That was a difficult question — an uncomfortable question. It probably could not yet be answered. On a Friday night in September, the men of '66 had gathered in the mess hall to receive their class rings. Jack's was engraved with the Wheeler family crest, which included a Roman helmet, an eagle, and the Latin *Facie Tenus* — Stand Fast. The ring had moved him profoundly, emblematic as it was of his most heartfelt beliefs: duty, honor, country; family, service, tradition. After slipping the gold circle on his finger, Jack sat at the dining table, weeping. Some of his classmates — particularly those who had been browbeaten into ordering class rings — were astonished by his emotion.

Tommy Hayes was also in Vesser's political philosophy class. There was no question about Tommy, Jack thought. He had it, the stuff of warriors. Jack's admiration for Tommy had grown steadily. The year before, they had double-dated to the Army-Navy game; Jack had walked into their room at the Ben Franklin Hotel one night to find his friend sprawled on the bed with his date, her bare breasts wondrously exposed. Tommy had just grinned. This year, Tom was head of the cadet choir and chairman of the honor committee. Recently, he had driven to New York with Superintendent Lampert to meet with a citizens' group interested in West Point.

"Well, Mr. Hayes," one man had asked, "what's the most difficult thing about being chairman of the honor committee?"

"Sir," Tommy replied without hesitation, "it's trying to explain the honor code to a group of men who can't possibly understand it."

Very intrepid stuff, Jack thought, like working the calculus problem from Jack's blackboard when they were plebes. Coming from someone else, the retort might have seemed impertinent. But coming from Tommy, it just demonstrated once again that he was something special. No question at all about Tommy, Jack thought: he was a man of gold. Someday T. J. Hayes IV was going to be a great general.

Now, in the theater lobby, Jack continued to look at the ballerinas.

Forty dancers, roughly half the company, had showed up for the reception, although they seemed less than overwhelmingly interested in the cadets.

Jack spotted another ballerina emerging from backstage, a striking young blonde with dark eyes and elegant, tapering legs. Spying another cadet walking over to her, Jack all but knocked him down to get there first.

"Hi," he said, "my name's Jack Wheeler and I really enjoyed your performance."

"Thank you very much," she replied. "I'm Ginny Stuart."

She seemed taken aback by this figure in gray who had stormed up like a French hussar. But she smiled anyway, with a lovely flash of large, even teeth. As Ginny answered his questions about the performance, Jack tried to place her accent; she spoke with the flat vowels of a New Englander, perhaps a Bostonian.

An hour later, Captain Sloan led the cadets out of Lincoln Center to his station wagon for the return trip to West Point. Ginny Stuart climbed in next to Jack and they drove up Broadway for eight blocks to drop the dancer at her apartment on West Seventy-second Street, a stone's throw from Central Park.

Standing on the sidewalk, Jack said good night, asked Ginny for her phone number, and watched as she nimbly disappeared into the building. In the darkened station wagon riding north along the Hudson Palisades, he was elated. A ballerina! Imagine that, he told himself. Ginny was a member of the corps de ballet; he was a member of the Corps of Cadets. As coincidences went, this one seemed deliciously auspicious.

Two nights later, trying not to sound as eager as he felt, he called her. Two months later, they were in love.

Jack found himself spending every spare minute in New York; he was particularly adroit at eluding Saturday morning parades in order to get a quicker start for the city. The stage manager sometimes let him watch Ginny's performances from the wings. The ballerinas would flutter about him as they came offstage, dipping their toe shoes in rosin or breathing deeply from green oxygen bottles. It was like living in a Degas painting, seeing these splay-footed, panting creatures suddenly transformed into gracile nymphs, oblivious of gravity as they vaulted back out toward the footlights.

Ginny's was such a feminine, crinoline world, so different from the granitic masculinity of West Point. Jack found the contrast stunning. He felt a powerful sense of awakening, as though swept up in his private renaissance. He was entranced by the grace of the swans gliding across the stage in Balanchine's version of *Swan Lake,* and by the way Ginny stalked her prey in *The Cage,* Jerome Robbins's strange fable of a female insect flirting and mating with a male before killing him. Even a tin ear could recognize the sights and sounds of genius.

"Oooooh," Balanchine would wince when something went awry, "that wasn't even pret-ty."

"Oooooh," Jack and Ginny would later mimic, "that wasn't even pret-ty."

Virginia Stuart was nineteen years old. Her accent was, in fact, that of a Bostonian, a native of Dorchester, to be precise. She was the youngest of five children, daughter of the regional manager for Whitman's candy. When Ginny was ten, her mother had taken her to see a performance of the Royal Ballet. She sat transfixed; soon her whole life was wrapped around ballet. Hour after hour, year after year, she trained her limbs to go in unnatural directions until she could control every ligament, from those dictating the motion of the big toe to the fifty muscles needed to rotate the leg in its stationary hip socket.

In 1963, the Joffrey Ballet invited Ginny to tour the Soviet Union. Before going to Moscow, she danced at the White House for President Kennedy and his guest, Emperor Haile Selassie of Ethiopia. In the summer of 1964, when she was sixteen, Balanchine summoned her to join his New York City Ballet. The regimen was brutal — twelve hours a day, six days a week — and Balanchine expected the dancers to memorize very complex choreography almost instantly. Ginny quickly became one of his workhorses. Strong and rarely injured — except for one awful tumble, when she tore all the ligaments in her foot — she often was asked to fill in for other ballerinas at the last moment. Ovations from an audience meant little to her; for Ginny Stuart, the gratifications were internal, as she pitted her considerable talent against the bonds of gravity and physiology.

She had an impulsive, almost reckless side, necessarily restrained by the demands of dance. She loved to wander into Central Park by herself at dawn to swing in the playground as the city roused itself. Sometimes a lone violinist practiced in an arbor nearby. They formed an odd duo, the musician playing Vivaldi amid the roses while the ballerina pumped ever higher on her swing.

Jack's internal discipline was one of the things Ginny found most attractive in him. The iron regimen at West Point supplemented his natural rigor; he was always very controlled, she thought, almost unnaturally mature. Sometimes it annoyed her that he was so controlled. He had an impish streak, but it never drifted into irresponsibility.

After performances, Jack often took her to the East Side for a late supper of coquilles St. Jacques in their favorite restaurant, a snug French club called La Chansonette. A singer would perform an Edith Piaf song while her husband played the piano and interjected mildly ribald asides ("You're always so tiredddd," he would croon). Occasionally the club featured a three-piece dance combo. After huddling for a bit of choreography, Jack and Ginny would spring into an animated Charleston, wagging their fingers and scissoring their hands and knees.

Sometimes on Monday, her day off, Ginny took the train or bus to West Point. Usually she stayed with Colonel Edgar Denton, who coached Jack on the sailing team. The Dentons had a small spare room in their attic with a view of Thayer Gate. If the day was warm enough, Jack took her sailing on the river or gave her a tennis lesson. Once, as several hundred cadets looked on, he escorted her into an evening lecture, where she caused a sensation in her white coat and beret, blond hair cascading to her waist.

Just as he had lectured a high school date on the constellations, Jack enjoyed playing instructor to Ginny. He wrote love letters full of French words, then provided a glossary at the end. When she was about to tour Europe, he taught her a few phrases in German, beginning with *Danke, ich will nicht tanzen* — I don't want to dance, thank you.

She had never finished high school, so she enjoyed his pedagogy and his gentle attentiveness. He always seemed to sense when she was getting bored and it was time to move on to something else. And she never had to worry that he would suddenly be pulled away to atone for some infraction; in his entire cadet career, Jack had walked only three hours on the Area.

As they grew closer, the turmoil within Jack became evident to Ginny. He seemed to have an idealized notion of what a soldier should be. As rigid as Patton's statue, that ideal was based largely on his father — whom she envisioned as a kind of Warner Brothers colonel, blazing away at the Germans from atop his Sherman tank — and reinforced by West Point. In Jack's mind, combat was the truest expression of a soldier's duty. A soldier went to war, either to die for his country or, preferably, to make the enemy die for *his* country. But Ginny recognized the irreconcilable clash between that warrior ideal and Jack's temperament. She could not imagine him as a ruthless battle captain. And, she realized, he could not imagine it, either.

"Do you think I'll make a good soldier?" he asked her once.

"As far as I can see, you're excelling in everything," she replied, surprised by the question. "But I can't see you going into battle and killing someone."

He nodded pensively but said nothing further.

One day he walked Ginny up the hill for a tour of the chapel. The place struck her as a powerful blend of piety and martial fervor. Carvings of a shield and cross dominated the north face of the chapel, where the inscription *Quis ut Deus* referred to Saint Michael: "Who is like God." A series of stained glass panels depicted Abraham's sacrifice of Isaac, pointedly symbolizing parents who offered their sons. At the other end of the building, the vast sanctuary window illustrated victory over sin and self with intricate military scenes, including David's slaying of Goliath and Joshua's capture of Jericho.

Jack showed Ginny the silver plaque on the front pew bearing the signatures of all the superintendents who had occupied this seat — MacArthur, Maxwell Taylor, Westmoreland, and seventeen others. Who, she wondered, will be the heroes among Jack's classmates? Who will be Patton? Who will be MacArthur? When other cadets talked about the war in Asia, their greatest fear seemed to be that the shooting might stop before they got to Vietnam. Given the chance, they intended to storm across the Pacific, win the war, and return to ticker tape parades, as their fathers had. But she found it hard to picture these lively, twenty-one-year-old boys as warlords. As she stood by the pew, the image of them killing — or sprawling dead in the mud somewhere — seemed horrifying and preposterous, and she pushed the thoughts from her mind.

Jack, however, could not push the prospect of war from his mind. You are the ones trained to fight, MacArthur had decreed. The barracks bull sessions now often revolved around Vietnam, where suddenly 200,000 American troops were at war. The new tactical officer of E-2, a genial captain from West Virginia named Les Bennett, had just spent a year as an adviser to a South Vietnamese battalion.

"You know, there's a great job to be done in fighting this war," Bennett told Jack and the other first classmen. "But what you don't want to do is get yourself slaughtered. That won't help anybody, not you, not the Army, not your country. You don't need to win your Silver Star the first day in combat. There's plenty of time for that in a year. There's nothing more devastating to a unit than to have the leader killed. It's important that you learn how to survive before you try to be a hero."

As features editor of the cadet magazine, Jack assembled an article entitled "To the Corps: From Vietnam." He solicited advice from other West Pointers already in the combat zone. Should we wait to get married? he asked them. What would you have done differently at West Point? How confident are you in battle?

"If you aren't *very* sure you're ready to get married, don't," advised Lieutenant Robert L. McGarity, writing from Go Cong Province. "However, if you do think you have found the right girl, you probably should go ahead, since all I can say is good luck on having her wait from graduation until your return from Vietnam."

Lieutenant Bruce Heim, class of 1963, wrote from the 101st Airborne, "There is nothing the Army or West Point has in its training program that will prepare you to see your first dead GI, your first wounded child, your first crying widow. Military Art and Tactics never told you of the butterflies and near nausea that are continually with you as bullets fly over your head."

As Gloom Period deepened in his final winter at West Point, Jack shuttled back and forth between his two worlds. In New York, he and Ginny occasionally carried a picnic basket up to the rooftop of her apartment building, where they danced to a tape recorder and scanned the street below for Boris Karloff, who was said to live in the Dakota apartment house next door. To the south, they could see the roofs of Lincoln Center and the soaring towers of midtown beyond.

Then Jack would return to Easy Deuce in Central Area, where he was quilled five demerits for "flowers displayed on windowsill." In military art class, the cadets spent many hours studying insurgencies—how the Huks had been suppressed in the Philippines, how the British had crushed the communist guerrillas in Malaysia, how the French had been trapped at Dienbienphu. From the poop deck, the stream of KIA funeral announcements accelerated.

In ordnance class, they heard lectures on the ballistics of wounds. Once they watched a sequence of slow-motion pictures showing what happened when a spinning bullet struck flesh. Entering cleanly, the round began to tumble, end over end; cutting through the victim like a ripsaw blade, it exited from a jagged, explosive hole.

A beautiful ballerina and tumbling bullets. They had one thing in common, Jack thought: they both made life seem very, very real.

One afternoon in November, Tom Carhart strolled into Art Mosley's room in E-2.

"Hey, Art," he said, trying to sound casual, "if I miss a few formations, can you cover for me?"

"What do you mean, can I cover for you?" Mosley asked. "What do you want me to do? Lie?"

"No, no, no," Tom said, shaking his head. "Not like that. But I just need to get away for a weekend. To, uh, steal the Navy goat."

Mosley's eyebrows shot up. As the company captain, he knew very well that the Naval Academy was off limits to West Point cadets. Furthermore, the commandants of both academies had publicly assured each other that there would be no thieving of mascots.

"Look, Tom, I'm not going to cover for you," Art said. The stern expression on his face gave way to a smile. "I'm going to help you steal it."

Unlike his company mate Jack Wheeler, Tom had walked more than a few hours on the area. In fact, he had walked more tours than almost any cadet at West Point — 108 — and had joined Buck Thompson as a bona fide member of the Century Club. Now that he was a first classman, he figured, the authorities were not going to expel him, especially when the Army was desperate for lieutenants to fight the war. Tom was eager to go. Just give me those gold bars, he kept saying, and point the way.

Tom's first-class year thus far had been a succession of pranks and schemes, although he had also ascended in the order of merit from 519 to 373. He spent some of his spare time overseeing a bookmaking operation in the regiment, using yearlings as runners to collect bets and pay off the winners. He and Mosley had also purchased a thousand pairs of ladies' panties and a little printing press, which they used to stamp BEAT NAVY on the bottoms; at $5.00 a pair, the panties concession had proved a lucrative enterprise.

Now Tom was ready for his greatest caper, the theft of the Naval Academy mascot. Behind the passing of quarterback Roger Staubach, Navy had made life miserable for the Army football team in recent years. The midshipmen had won five of the last six games between the two arch rivals. In Tom's view, anything that would boost Army's morale was a sacred duty.

As soon as Art Mosley joined the plot, Tom began planning in earnest. Like Alexander surrounded by the Companions, he conducted nightly strategy sessions with Mosley and a half-dozen conspirators in the sinks of E-2 or the more remote K-2, which lay amid the Lost Fifties. Among others, Tom enlisted Bob Kesmodel, a small, tough lacrosse player whose family lived in Severna Park, Maryland, just a few miles from the Naval Academy. Kesmodel's father, a private school headmaster with a weakness for this kind of skullduggery, learned that the goat had been moved for security reasons to the Navy's top secret research and development center across the Severn River.

"It's in a well-lit pen, surrounded by barbed wire and guarded by Marines. With weapons," Kesmodel reported to Tom one evening. "Forget it."

"C'mon," Carhart urged. "Let's give it a try. Let's at least go down and take a look."

On Saturday, November 21, the conspirators drove down Interstate 95 to the Kesmodel house in a borrowed station wagon and a new

Chevy. Gathering on the porch that night, they listened to the latest intelligence report from Kesmodel's father. The news was discouraging.

"Boys," he said, "I highly recommend against it."

"What the hell!" Tom urged, dismissing the warning with a wave. "Let's do it anyway."

Infected with Tom's enthusiasm, Mosley and the others agreed to try. Wearing black turtlenecks, their faces darkened with burned cork, they drove down a side street near the main gate of the base. Kesmodel's father had not exaggerated. A ten-foot chain-link fence crowned with barbed wire surrounded the facility. Two stocky Marines guarded the gate. Beyond the guards, in a twenty-foot pen topped with more barbed wire, stood the goat.

After scouting the fence, the cadets found an unlocked pedestrian gate several hundred yards from the pen. At eleven-thirty, they slipped through the narrow gate and tiptoed toward the pen. At twelve-twenty, exactly on schedule, four girls who had been enlisted as accomplices drove up to the main gate and began flirting with the two Marines. Only twenty yards away, while the guards were distracted, the cadets made a final dash to the goat.

Using a crowbar wrapped in a black towel, they broke the padlock. The gate swung open. Inside a small hutch stood their prize, Billy XV. His huge horns had been painted Navy blue and gold.

While Art and Tom each slipped a rope over the goat, a third Marine walked through the gate, where the girls were still chatting with the guards. Whistling, he strolled within three feet of the cadets, who lay sprawled motionless in a heap of goat droppings. After the Marine passed, they leaped to their feet and sprinted back toward the pedestrian gate, a cooperative Billy trotting alongside.

After coaxing the goat into the rear of the Chevy, where the seat had been replaced with straw, they gleefully fled back to the Kesmodel house. We did it! they shouted, pounding one another on the back. Tom could scarcely believe that they had succeeded without getting caught. They took pictures of the goat on the porch — where the ill-mannered Billy fouled the Kesmodels' green rug — and then, anonymously, called *The New York Times* and the city's radio stations to announce that the Navy goat no longer belonged to the Navy. At two A.M., with the goat bedded down in the Chevy, they left for the long drive north.

They hid Billy in Tom's grandmother's barn in Eagle Mills, New York. Back at the academy, Tom chose to inform the corps of the deed by secretly mimeographing several hundred fliers on Monday morning and leaving them in the mess hall. When Superintendent Lampert stood on the poop deck during the noon meal to make an announcement, the corps erupted in a rambunctious chant: "We want the goat! We want the goat!"

The color rose in Lampert's neck as in a thermometer. He turned and glared at the first captain, Norm Fretwell, who quickly moved to the microphone and barked at the corps to sit down and shut up, "right now!" In ten seconds, the hall was utterly quiet.

Under pressure from the secretary of the Army, Lampert and the commandant threatened to confine the entire corps for both the Army-Navy game and Thanksgiving unless the goat was returned. Two nights later, after taps, Tom and his co-conspirators slipped out of the barracks in their black turtlenecks and stocking caps. Tiptoeing through the sallyport, they suddenly heard the voice of the regimental tactical officer.

"Halt! What are you men doing?" he demanded.

Tom snapped to attention. "Sir! We're going to get the Navy goat and bring it back to West Point."

A long pause followed. The tac nodded. "As you were."

Happily singing "Catch Us If You Can," they drove to Eagle Mills, retrieved the goat, and slipped the animal into the stable with the Army mule before dawn. After intense discussions about what to do next — including a proposal that they stew Billy and serve him to the corps for supper — they decided to present the goat to the football team captain in the mess hall. But to their chagrin, several military policemen snooping around the stable discovered Billy first.

Tom ran to one of the classroom buildings, where he barged into a physics class and dragged Art Mosley out past the perplexed instructor.

"Mose, the FBI is here," Tom whispered in the hallway. "They're up on the hill. It looks like they've got the goat."

"What'll we do?" Mosley asked.

"We've got to steal it again," Tom insisted. "We stole it from the Navy, we can steal it from the FBI."

Together they ran up the hill past the chapel to the stable. But they were too late. Billy XV was on his way back to Annapolis, safely locked in the cargo bed of a van.

Tom and Art raced back down to the barracks. Matt Harrison happened to be the cadet officer in charge of the guardhouse.

"Matt, how about letting us use the public address system to make an announcement about the goat?"

"Are you kidding?" Matt replied. "C'mon, guys, they'll have me in a sling if I do that. Why don't you just lure me out or something?"

Instead, they ran over to South Area, where Tom climbed onto a trash dumpster. Someone handed him a portable loudspeaker, which he used to recount the saga to several hundred cheering cadets.

Hearing the commotion, a colonel in the nearby guardhouse bullied his way up to Tom. "I don't know who you think you are or what you think you're doing, but I want your name."

"Okay, sir," Tom answered, grinning broadly. "Carhart, E-2."

One by one, the conspirators appeared before a board of officers to confess their crime. Then they marched, again individually, before the commandant, Brigadier General Richard P. Scott. Tom was the last to enter Scott's office.

"We've got to give you some punishment, so I'm going to remove your first-class privileges for two months," the commandant said. "But I want you to know I'd be proud to have you serve under me in the Army. Well done."

Tom was exultant. What was a trifling slap on the wrist, he thought, compared to the glory of the deed? For three and a half years, the United States Military Academy had tried to force him to fit a template of proper behavior. It had not worked. It would never work. Now that he was close to graduation, Tom believed he would be able to demonstrate his ability in the real Army, in a real war, where no one would give a damn if he had his shoes shined. Audacity, courage, celerity, will — those were the manly traits that would count.

Three months later, on a frigid Monday night in February, the entire class of 1966 filed into South Auditorium. Anticipation electrified the air; on this night, each man would move a step closer to the Army by selecting his combat branch.

The first classmen had filled out "dream cards," listing their preferences for branch, unit, and assignment after graduation. The Army had set quotas for each category. Despite repeated studies that showed little correlation between academic achievement at West Point and military success, the cadets would choose in order of class rank.

The class, 809 cadets in 1962, had shrunk to fewer than 600 men. Two classmates had just left within the past month. One was Jeff Rogers, Jack Wheeler's boyhood friend, who had resigned to pursue his dream of becoming a commercial artist in New York City. The other was Phil Gray, a popular, gregarious native of Milford, Connecticut, who was considered the finest athlete in the class. In late January, Gray was accused of improperly passing some military history notes to another cadet; shocked and frightened, he appeared at midnight before the honor committee, which quickly found him guilty despite his vehement denials. After a brief stay in the purgatory of the Boarders Ward, Gray was expelled from West Point. The expulsion stunned his classmates, who talked about it in hushed tones, as though discussing a death in the family.

Except for those men who had physical impairments that precluded their joining the combat arms, the cadets now gathering in South Auditorium were required to pick one of five branches — infantry, armor, artillery, signal, or engineering. Those who had served as enlisted men in the Air Force, or whose fathers were in the Air Force, also had the option of joining that service.

In some respects, the men of '66 could see the milestones of an Army career stretch before them even now. About sixteen thousand lieutenants would be commissioned in the Army in 1965 and 1966, of whom 7 percent would be West Pointers. Under a law first passed in 1838, Military Academy graduates were obligated to remain in the service for at least four years; June 1970 would be their first chance to resign.

For those who hoped to spend thirty years or more in an Army uniform, lifelong military service was not guaranteed. In an effort to breed a younger, more vigorous officer corps, the Army after World War II had adopted a policy of "up or out." Those passed over for promotion at some point in their careers were forced from the service; no longer could an officer remain a major for fifteen or twenty years, as had once been the case.

Any cadet who studied the promotion pyramid could see that of a hundred new second lieutenants, ninety-two eventually would be elevated to first lieutenant, eighty-four would become captains, seventy-two would become majors, sixty-four would become lieutenant colonels, thirty-four would become colonels. Only two would ever be promoted to brigadier general, and then only after twenty-two years or more in the service.

The wild card, of course, was the war. The Army was expanding dramatically. Draft calls had increased tenfold over the previous year. When the class of 1965 had met in South Auditorium a year earlier for their branch selection, only a few thousand Americans were stationed in South Vietnam. The bombing campaign known as Rolling Thunder had not yet begun, nor had Marines waded ashore at Da Nang. Now — instantly, it seemed — more than a quarter of a million U.S. soldiers were in Vietnam, and their numbers increased monthly.

At West Point, many viewed this escalation as extraordinarily good fortune. One instructor hung a sign on his office wall: "Fighting is our business, business is good." Wars accelerated promotions, enhanced careers, and broke the monotony of garrison life, a condition best described by Lord Burghley in 1555: "Soldiers in peace are like chimneys in summer." Many tactical officers encouraged the cadets to think of "tracks in two": because of the increased tempo of promotions during wartime, lieutenants could earn their silver captain's bars — tracks — just two years after graduation. The class of 1966 had also listened to pep talks from General Stilwell and other veterans about how grand it was for a young officer to have the opportunity to fight for his country.

A few cadets — Jack Wheeler among them — had doubts about this war, but they prudently kept their questions to themselves. The professional officer corps, and hence the cadets, tended to be profoundly conservative. More to the point, the men of '66, like fourteenth-century knights, were looking for valorous deeds to undertake, and concerned themselves little with political consequences. To the extent that they articulated any rationale for the burgeoning war, the cadets tended either to parrot Lyndon Johnson's talk of Asian dominoes and communist hegemony, or John Kennedy's inaugural vow to "pay any price, bear any burden . . . to ensure the survival and success of liberty."

Despite West Point's isolation, the first classmen were aware of the small but vocal antiwar movement that had begun to divide the country. A few protestors had recently heckled the corps at a parade in New York; the newspapers now routinely reported draft card burnings and other protests, such as a recent Vietnam teach-in at the University of Michigan. Most West Pointers regarded such dissidents with contempt. Opposition to the war, though still feeble, was considered close to treason.

In fact, the dissent merely fueled the cadets' enthusiasm for the cause. The nation had summoned them to battle; in MacArthur's phrase, the war tocsin had sounded. They spoke with bravado, repeating to one another, for example, the witticism uttered by one sergeant after a bloody skirmish in Vietnam: "The enemy could have held reveille in a phone booth."

"It's better," they agreed, "to fight them in Vietnam than in the streets of San Francisco." The Army was much given to such apothegms; they provided a vehicle for transporting the wisdom of the ages and, less generously, a substitute for reflective thought. For the class of 1966, however, thought was somewhat beside the point — "above my pay grade," in the Army vernacular. They were men of action. Fighting was their business, and it was good indeed.

Now, an officer stood at the podium in South Auditorium and began calling out names by class rank.

"Clark, Wesley K."

Wes Clark stood up, the first to choose his branch. Brilliant and intense, he had ranked at the top of the class for three of the four years and would spend his first years after graduation at Oxford as a Rhodes scholar.

"Armor!" Clark declared.

His classmates responded with a cascade of cheers and catcalls, which continued through each selection.

"Hayes, Thomas J."

Tommy ranked ninth. As a star man — in the top 5 percent of the class — he was entitled to attend graduate school before his first military assignment. But Tom had waived that option, fearful that the war would be over by the time he finished his master's degree. There would always be time for more schooling later. "Engineers!" he declared.

"Mosley, Arthur C."

Fighting in Vietnam held little appeal for Art; when one officer urged the star men to forgo graduate school for the "opportunity to serve in combat," Mosley had muttered, "Opportunity, my ass." He planned to attend Harvard Business School in the fall. "Engineers!"

"Wheeler, John P."

Jack's was the sixteenth name called. He was spending so much time with Ginny Stuart that his studies had suffered, knocking him out of the top ten. Although he admired the men volunteering for combat — and felt a twinge of guilt for not being among them — Jack wasn't ready to fling himself into the war. He planned to defer graduate school for a year, first taking an assignment at a Nike Hercules missile base near New York. That would keep him close to Ginny. "Artillery."

"Fretwell, Norman E."

By tradition, first captains joined the infantry; Fretwell continued the tradition. "Infantry!"

"Thompson, Richard W."

Buck was eager to fight. "It's our job," he kept insisting. "Infantry!" he yelled, provoking another round of cheers and jeers.

"Bonifas, Arthur G."

Art's uncle had been an artillery officer during World War II, and spent three and half years in a Japanese prison camp. Art had been fascinated by his uncle's war stories and tales of life as an Army redleg. "Artillery!"

"Carhart, Thomas M."

Tom hoped to join the 173rd Airborne Brigade, an elite infantry unit that had already seen considerable action in Vietnam. Although he loved tanks, there was little room for armor in the jungle. He believed that in this war all branches were simply support services for the groundpounders; the idea of being a supporting player rather than a star repulsed him. Tom wanted to be in the thick of the fight.

"Infantry!"

"Harrison, Matthew C."

Matt's father had served first as a coastal artilleryman and then as an engineer. But the infantry — the Queen of Battle — seemed to Matt to be the essence of the Army, especially in a war against guerrillas. He also hoped to join the 173rd Airborne. "Infantry!"

"Crocker, George A."

George was among the last to choose. Academically, he had continued to struggle, but he too was ready for war. At a recent meeting of the Military Affairs Club, a general visiting from the Pentagon had disclosed a secret proposal to put a new division in the Mekong Delta to fight a riverine war. George thought the plan sounded intriguing, almost romantic. The Korean War classes, he knew, had been forever cleaved between those who served in combat and those who did not. It would be a mistake for '66 to let that happen. Selecting a branch was easy; he had known since Camp Buckner that he was born to be an infantryman. "Infantry!"

After the last cadet had chosen his branch, an officer tallied the selections: infantry, 179; artillery, 167; engineers, 69; armor, 66; signal, 52. Sixteen others, most of them physically restricted from the combat arms because of football injuries and the like, chose administrative, military intelligence, or chemical branches. Eighteen selected the Air Force.

Ninety-eight men volunteered for Vietnam, among them George Crocker, Tom Carhart, Buck Thompson, Tommy Hayes, and Matt Harrison. Each volunteer was required to spend at least four months in training with a stateside unit before entering the war zone. By thus seasoning the young lieutenants, the Army hoped to spare the class of '66 the kind of mauling suffered by the callow class of '50, which had rushed headlong into the Korean War after graduation.

The first classmen walked out of the auditorium and back to the barracks with a bit of a swagger. Someone had read that in the Chinese zodiac — widely observed throughout the Far East — 1966 was the Year of the Horse, a lucky symbol. That information was also passed about, just like the quip about reveille in a phone booth. How can we go wrong in Vietnam, they assured one another, when it's the Year of the Horse?

But the zodiac was more complicated than they knew — and its portents for the class more ominous. The cycle of years, in addition to being divided among a dozen animals, was divided among five elements — wood, fire, earth, metal, and water. Paired together, the animals and elements offered sixty possible combinations, such as Water and Dragon or Wood and Rabbit. Each was freighted with certain fateful propensities.

Among the many combinations, that of Fire and Horse was considered particularly dreadful. In Japan, for example, that pairing was known as *hinoe uma*; women born under such a sign were considered predisposed to murdering their husbands. The birthrate plunged drastically during *hinoe uma* as Japanese parents tried to avoid such a destiny for their children.

For those who followed the Chinese zodiac closely, few heavenly configurations were less propitious. And 1966 was the Year of Fire and the Horse.

Beneath a pewter sky on Saturday afternoon, April 23, a squadron of powerful sports cars raced along the Palisades Parkway south of West Point. As the trees on either side of the highway whipped past in a blur of spring green, two new Corvettes pulled abreast of each other. A cadet sitting in the passenger seat of the car on the left rolled down his window and held out a box of Ritz crackers. The grinning driver of the car on the right grabbed the box and glanced at his speedometer: the needle was nudging one hundred miles an hour.

Every spring, swarms of salesmen descended on the academy's first classmen, peddling everything from silverware and crystal to automobiles and insurance. In mid March, more than a hundred cadets had purchased new Corvettes from A. & C. Chevrolet, which offered fleet rates. Today, after morning classes and inspection, a half-dozen of the new car owners had met in the cadet parking lot above Michie Stadium. In close procession, they drove to the state park at Bear Mountain, where they drank a bottle of wine near the garbage dump until a ranger ordered them to leave. "That's all right," the cadets retorted, "we've been thrown out of nicer places than this." From Bear Mountain, they wandered into several bars before buying crackers and cheese at a delicatessen in Highland Falls. Then they headed for the parkway, eager to test their cars' performance.

One of the Corvettes, painted a rich "rally red," belonged to George Crocker. George had paid $3762 for the car and now, as he pushed the accelerator closer to the floor, it seemed worth every penny. Powered by a 350-horsepower engine, the Corvette leaped forward effortlessly. George's only misgiving was that the engine would knock unless it was fed one of three brands of expensive gasoline, each of which cost about forty-five cents a gallon. But if the price of fuel was sending him to the poorhouse, George figured that at least he would be able to drive there in style.

After his close brush with expulsion in Electrical Engineering 304 and his reduction to cadet private, George had bounced back smartly. He was promoted, first to cadet sergeant, then to lieutenant. His romance with Vonda Jones had blossomed in spite of the thousand miles that separated them; after months of courting long-distance through telephone calls and letters, they had announced their engagement at Easter. George's sole proviso was that they marry in Little Rock after graduation so that he wouldn't have to endure the chaos of June Week weddings at West Point.

Even George's perpetual battle with the academic departments had settled into a satisfactory stalemate. He was going to finish near the bottom of the class, but he would graduate. Some of his classmates admired him as the champion of the "slug stopper" among the '66ers. Failure to turn in an assigned project was automatically punished with a hefty slug; an eleventh-hour submission that barely met the minimum requirements was known as a slug stopper, of which Cadet Crocker was the acknowledged master.

In eight or nine months, George calculated, he would be in combat. He believed the war to be a just cause; it also afforded a young soldier the chance to prove himself. Like many of his classmates, he shrugged off the potential danger with cheerful bluster. One of the national magazines had recently published a photograph showing a wounded officer on a stretcher in Vietnam. An intravenous needle had been inserted into his left forearm and a drop of crimson blood could be seen dripping from the stone in his West Point ring. George and Art Mosley had joked about their "$200 left hands," on which each wore a $119 Rolex watch and a $90 class ring. If you've got to have a hand blown off in combat, they agreed, it's cheaper to lose the right one.

Following a few yards behind George was another new Corvette, painted "mossport green"; it belonged to Bob Albright. Sitting in the passenger seat was a cadet who could bluster with the best of them, Tom Carhart. This spring had already been a triumphant season for Tom. A few weeks earlier, he had written and directed *The 100th Night Show,* a traditional satire by first classmen in their final semester. Everyone agreed that the script was brilliant, particularly the scene in which the Italians in the class had sung Verdi in Renaissance costumes before being pelted with rotten tomatoes. Tom also astonished his friends by scoring highest in the class on the Graduate Record Exam — 730 in verbal and 780 in math, out of maximum 800s. His assignments to the infantry and the 173rd Airborne were fixed. And, with Buck Thompson, he was plotting one final prank: using an acetylene torch and a ten-foot box, they planned to sever the reveille cannon from its metal base and move it to the roof of a barracks, as Douglas MacArthur had done sixty years before.

Most important, Tom was in love. During Christmas leave of his cow year, he had met a tall, slim woman named Melissa Jackson, whose father was an admiral stationed in Washington. For more than a year, Tom and Melissa had written to each other daily. During a visit to Melissa's college in the Midwest, Tom drove her to St. Louis, where they cooed over the newborn animals at the zoo and dined on the *River Queen,* an old paddlewheeler berthed on the Mississippi. Love, Tom explained to his friends, "was like falling backward down the stairs."

Three weeks earlier, on the first weekend in April, they had met in Washington, where the cherry blossoms were in bloom. In a bar called the Tombs, Tom proposed marriage, and Melissa promptly accepted. They agreed that his year in Vietnam would be their betrothal period. The next morning, after Mass, Tom cornered Admiral Jackson in his den and asked for his daughter's hand.

"Well, Tom," the admiral replied, "we'd be delighted. You have our full permission. But you'll have to ask her, not us."

"Sir, I've already asked her and she's consented."

"Well, that's great. Let's drink to that."

On the mantel above the fireplace was a model of the U.S.S. *Constitution,* sails unfurled. The admiral pushed a button on the deck; a brandy flask and two shot glasses popped from the hull.

"To your future," the admiral toasted.

"Yes, sir. Beat Navy!"

"Beat Army!"

For Tom, life had fallen snugly into place. He would go to Vietnam, serve with distinction, and return to marry his beloved Melissa. Then, of course, they would live happily ever after.

The late afternoon overcast thickened into dusk and a light drizzle began to fall. Tom and Bob Albright followed George and the others into a parking lot south of Highland Falls. They were all modestly drunk. Classmate Tom Beasley, driving his new Skylark, waved goodbye and took off for New York. After steering his car through a series of tight circles around the parking lot, George turned back toward the barracks.

Tom and Bob decided to cross the Hudson to Peekskill for dinner at a steak house. Having often joked about the Corvette's "tenuous agreement with the laws of physics," they buckled the seat belts across their laps and headed for the river. Albright sped around the traffic circle before veering east across Bear Mountain Bridge. The car streaked beneath the twin gray spans as the rain fell harder. Ahead loomed Anthony's Nose, rising through the fog a thousand feet above the dark river.

At the east end of the bridge, the road swerved nearly 90 degrees to the right toward Peekskill. Bob leaned into the turn but suddenly realized he was going too fast. As he stamped on the brake pedal, the tires skidded across the slick asphalt and the car careened out of control. Bracing himself, Bob bent the plastic steering wheel almost in half. With a terrible roar of shattering glass and crumpled metal, the Corvette plowed head-on into the granite Nose.

Tom reflexively threw up his hands to shield himself, but the impact whipped his torso forward. His face slammed into the dashboard, knocking the clock out of the instrument panel. Still belted into his seat, Tom slumped over in a silent, bloody heap.

By chance, a volunteer fireman was driving across the bridge just behind them and saw the accident. Pulling alongside the wreckage, he leaped out and ran to the Corvette. Bob was dazed but apparently not seriously injured. Tom was unconscious, his face masked in blood. He had stopped breathing and the dashboard had left a pronounced dent in his forehead. The fireman pried open Tom's jaw, cleared out the jumble of broken teeth, and began mouth-to-mouth resuscitation.

A few moments later, Major Robert G. Yerks, who was driving from West Point to see his family in Ossining, pulled up next to the shattered car. Yerks had been the tactical officer of Company H-1 and was now executive officer of the first regiment. Yerks didn't know Tom personally, but everyone had heard of the matador of Provence and the cadet who had stolen the Navy goat. The major flagged another motorist and sent him to summon an ambulance from the toll booth at the west end of the bridge. For fifteen minutes, until the state police and paramedics arrived, Yerks tried to keep Tom warm and dry while the fireman kept him alive.

During the ten-minute drive to Peekskill Hospital, the paramedics cut a tracheotomy in Tom's throat and suctioned the blood from his windpipe. X rays at the hospital showed multiple fractures of his facial bones and lower and upper jaws. Plastic shards from the dash were embedded in his sinuses. Both lips were shredded. Brain damage could not yet be determined, but for the moment that was almost beside the point. Tom lay very close to death.

Yerks called Tom's tactical officer, Les Bennett, who arrived at the hospital an hour later. Directed to a corner of the emergency room, Bennett pushed aside the curtain to one cubicle. He saw an unconscious young man lying on a gurney, his face horribly battered. That's not Tom, Bennett thought, peering closer to be sure. But in the next cubicle, Bob Albright was being treated for cuts and bruises. That obviously wasn't Tom either. Bennett returned to the first cubicle, where for a long minute he studied the mangled, swollen face before finally concluding that this broken body was indeed Tom Carhart's.

For four days, Tom remained in a coma. His parents, who had immediately driven to West Point from Massachusetts, remained constantly at his side. His classmates also kept a vigil at the hospital, incredulous that this could happen to the invincible Tom Carhart. Not Tom, they protested; he's bulletproof. On April 27, he regained consciousness and recognized his parents. Two days later he was moved by ambulance to the West Point hospital.

He began an agonizing, faltering recovery. Surgeons worked to piece his face back together, but no one was sure how to reassemble his mind. In his medical file, the doctors wrote:

> Was quite lethargic after surgery. He would arouse to verbal commands, however, and on occasions would recognize his parents. Taking fluids orally by third day after surgery. His mental picture remained unchanged during the first week postoperatively, with patient being conscious but with a cloudy sensorium. Would walk and sit in chair, and respond to questions, but his answers were generally inappropriate.
>
> Trac tube removed May 9 and opening closed the following day. Over next several days, the patient became very combative at times and uncooperative, especially at night. Slept quite a bit and rarely opened eyes even when awake. Disoriented most of the time and had periods of extreme irrational behavior.

Sometimes he seemed to be little Tommy Carhart, chattering to his pals in elementary school. At other times he was a fighter pilot in World War II, muttering, "Where are the Japs? Let me at 'em. Where are they?" He often kicked and flailed, as though in a fight, and nurses tied up the sheet corners on his hospital bed to keep him from tumbling onto the floor. Les Bennett thought Tom's ramblings provided a glimpse into a remarkable imagination; sometimes his hallucinations were so strange, so hilarious, that Bennett had to take a stroll in the hospital corridor to keep from laughing.

For others, the addled babbling was disquieting, even macabre. Once, when Tom Beasley was visiting, Carhart rose from the bed and walked straight toward him, eyes as vacant as the windows in an abandoned house. Beasley put a hand on Tom's chest and briefly wondered whether he was going to have to knock him down. But Mrs. Carhart grabbed her son's elbow and gently steered him back to bed.

As Tom gradually regained some of his memory and other mental faculties, Les Bennett noticed something curious. Tom was not only determined to graduate; he also had become remarkably enthusiastic about West Point. Bennett was amazed by the transformation. Gone was the indifference to the academy's strictures. Gone was the impertinence that had antagonized a succession of tactical officers. Although he didn't always make a lot of sense, Tom clearly had become the grayest of gray hogs. Bennett knew from his experiences in combat that men close to death often had their values clarified in short order, but he had never seen anything quite this dramatic.

In late May, the academy began considering some difficult questions. Should Cadet Carhart graduate? Stay back a year? Be given a medical discharge? Tom's IQ before the accident was measured at 139; now it was at an effective level of 108. After reviewing his case, the authorities decided that Tom could graduate if he passed his final examination in ordnance class. A steady parade of classmates and instructors trooped through Ward 2 to tutor him in the mysteries of explosives and weaponry while he sipped his puréed asparagus. The course required mastery of both physics and engineering, and Tom found the work to be far beyond his abilities; he felt fog-bound, unable to concentrate.

"No way this guy's going to make it," one tutor told Bennett. "He can add one plus two and get three, and he can add three plus five and get eight. But he's incapable of seeing any relationship between the two. If you asked him to add the two sums, he couldn't do that to save his life."

Tom took the test in two parts at the hospital in early June. After struggling through the morning session, he sat for ninety minutes while the oral surgeons painfully removed the wires from his shattered jaw. To avoid further clouding his mind, he refused an anesthetic. When the doctors finished, he marched back into the examination room and took the second half of the test.

He did poorly, very poorly, but with a wink and a nod the ordnance department passed him. Come June 8, the academy decided, Tom could graduate with the rest of his class, although his commission as a second lieutenant would be held in abeyance indefinitely. He would survive, but everything else — commissioning, Vietnam, marriage, even the question of whether Tom Carhart would ever again be Tom Carhart — remained terrifyingly uncertain.

Jim Ford's sermon on baccalaureate Sunday was entitled "The Good Is the Enemy of the Best." Led by Tommy Hayes, the choir in dress gray marched four abreast down the aisle past the packed congregation. They sang Rachmaninoff's "Open Thou My Lips, O Lord," as the organ pipes thundered overhead. Many among the fifteen hundred standing in the chapel found themselves blinking away tears.

"Sometimes," Ford preached, "you can do good in ways that allow you to hide from doing the best. Being a graduate of West Point requires you to do good. People expect you to do good. But sometimes doing good isn't enough."

First Classman Bob Luecke read from St. Paul's Epistle to the Ephesians:

> Put on the whole armor of God, that ye may be able to stand against the wiles of the devil. For we wrestle not against flesh and blood, but against principalities, against powers, against the rulers of the darkness of this world.

After First Captain Norm Fretwell collected the offering plates from the ushers and handed them to Ford, the chaplain dedicated a new stained glass window to the class of 1966. The window depicted Saint Valeria, who had lived during the reign of Nero. After her husband, a Roman army officer, was tortured on the rack for his faith and buried alive in Ravenna, Valeria had fled toward Milan. She came to a village where peasants were celebrating a pagan feast; refusing their demands to join them, she was clubbed to death.

As the cadets shuffled from the chapel, they could see Valeria gazing down from the west clerestory. Crowned with a blue halo against a ruby background, her face bore a smile that was at once beatific and slightly sensual, like Bernini's great sculpture of Saint Theresa. She seemed an unlikely patron for this new tribe of American warriors — a woman beaten to death by her own people.

On Tuesday, June 7, Tom Carhart was furloughed from the hospital so that he could march in the graduation parade. Several classmates helped him into his dress grays, and at four o'clock, in a chill rain, the class of 1966 formed up to cross the Plain for the last time as cadets. His face cross-hatched with suture scars, Tom fell in with Art Mosley, Jack Wheeler, and the rest of Easy Deuce. Midway across the field, he appeared to falter. Frank Cosentino and other classmates closed ranks and kept him steady through the rest of the parade.

Melissa had come for graduation. For the past few weeks, Tom had tried to picture her in his mind but he found it difficult to form a clear image. When she arrived, he felt confused and his battered face made him self-conscious. She was sweet and solicitous, but the glory of the cherry blossoms in early April was gone. Being together made them both feel awkward, as though they were meeting for the first time in an arranged marriage.

In Tom's most recent evaluation, a psychiatrist described his mood as "somewhat depressed but appropriate. His social judgment appears to be intact and insight does not seem grossly impaired." Another doctor wrote that there was a "large discrepancy" between "his high intelligence and high aspiration to lead combat troops and the signs of impulsivity and mild poor judgment that were elicited by some psychological tasks. For example, he indicated that a person who noticed a fire while sitting in the movies ought to 'yell fire and try to get the audience to walk, not run.'"

Tom's parents were preparing to move to Japan, where Colonel Carhart was to take command of the Air Force base at Yokota. They agreed with the academy authorities that Tom should go with them for further recuperation. Technically, he would remain on cadet status until another evaluation was conducted in six months. The examining psychiatrist warned that commissioning Tom now would "have the patient operating with a handicap where brain recovery and potential have not been completed."

Dimly, Tom began to realize that his classmates were about to go off to the great adventure of war without him. Nothing — not the scars or the pain or the estrangement from Melissa — was more disconcerting than the thought of being left behind. For four years they had been brothers, bonded by hardship and triumph; now, the prospect of being excluded from the greatest bond of all — the intimacy of shared combat — was almost unbearable.

On the night of June 7, after the parade, a graduation banquet was held in Washington Hall. The Wheeler family arrived in force, Jack's parents having flown back to the United States from Southeast Asia. Jack did not know it at the time, but his father — who was listed as a military attaché at the U.S. embassy in Thailand — was helping to run the secret war in Laos. From Bangkok, Janet had watched the fighting steadily intensify in Vietnam; she was sick with apprehension for her elder son. Seeing him now, she thought there was something very fragile about him. Young Jack and his classmates looked so dashing, yet so innocent. What did they know of war? Of killing? She still wished he had gone to Yale.

After the banquet, Jack escorted Ginny to the graduation dance in the gymnasium. In her tidy, swirling hand, she later wrote him a note inside the cover of the photograph taken of them that night:

> I recall the fragrance of gardenias in my hair at the graduation dinner and hop. You were breathtakingly handsome in your whites, and it was exciting dancing in your arms. We were tired, and very much in love. Thank you, sweetheart.
>
> Love,
> Ginny

These final hours at West Point were bittersweet for Jack. He was proud, not only to have survived at the academy but to have succeeded with distinction. He was proud that his father and mother had flown twelve thousand miles to see him become a new lieutenant in the United States Army. And he was proud of the comely ballerina on his arm. Earlier in the year Jack had taken Ginny to the observation deck of the Empire State Building — it was her favorite spot in New York, a thousand feet above the gritty, churlish streets — and given her his Army pin with its tiny double sixes. They were, as she had written, very much in love.

But his ambivalence about West Point — and the profession of arms he was about to join — had never disappeared. Just a few months before graduation he had halfheartedly discussed resignation with Colonel Denton, his sailing coach. "Sir, I've got doubts about a military career, about accepting a commission," Jack told Denton, echoing his own words to Chaplain Speers during Beast Barracks four years earlier. "I think maybe I'd like to go to medical school." Denton had listened patiently, sympathetic but noncommittal. As Ted Speers had, he urged Jack to think it through; Denton also pointed out that resignation as a first classman would probably entail a two-year obligation as an enlisted man. Jack dropped the idea. But his sense of unease, particularly as the distant thunder of Vietnam drew ever closer, had persisted.

When he awoke on Wednesday morning, the cool drizzle of the past few days had vanished. Graduation Day was going to be sunny and hot. Hustling around the room, Jack pulled on his clothes and finished some last-minute packing. He decided to keep the dress gray tunic; everything else went to charity. Somewhere in Harlem or the Bowery, some poor wretch would be warm and spoony in cadet gray.

For the last time, *The New York Times* was dropped outside Jack's door. A brief article inside the front section bore the headline WEST POINT CLASS OF 1966 EAGER TO FIGHT. Noting the day's graduation exercises, the story reported that nearly a hundred men from the class had volunteered for war duty. Rhesa H. Barksdale, a classmate from Mississippi, was quoted as saying, "I look forward to going to Vietnam. Every American has a definite commitment to go to Vietnam to do his part. I wish there wasn't trouble there, but there is, and we have to do something about it."

Rushing about, with a thousand details to attend to, Jack barely glanced at the newspaper. The day's first order of business was the commissioning oath. Each company held its own ceremony. Art Bonifas and Company A-3 gathered in the superintendent's conference room in Building 600; Matt Harrison of C-1 took the oath in the presence of his father, who had returned to West Point for the twenty-fifth reunion of the class of 1941.

Jack and the other first classmen in Easy Deuce — but not Tom Carhart — met in the old ordnance laboratory just below the Plain near Trophy Point. Big Jack administered the vow to his son:

> I do solemnly swear that I will support and defend the Constitution of the United States against all enemies, foreign and domestic; that I will maintain true faith and allegiance to the same; that I take this obligation freely without any mental reservation or purpose of evasion; and that I will well and faithfully discharge the duties of the office upon which I am about to enter.

Now they were lieutenants. But no one had time to admire the new gold bars. Graduation began at ten A.M. The class sat in folding chairs between the goal posts of Michie Stadium while twenty thousand spectators fanned themselves in the bleachers and listened to Vice President Hubert H. Humphrey lecture about "our so-called doves" and "our so-called hawks."

> Vietnam, my fellow Americans, challenges our military courage, our political ingenuity, and our ability and willingness to persevere. We must not be deterred. We must not falter. To be firm without being belligerent, to be strong without being bellicose — these must be our standards. Let us then, not pursue policies — or judge ourselves — in consonance with the passing of the moment. But rather let us pursue those courses of which, in the judgment of history, it can be written: "These were the paths taken by wise men." My congratulations to this class.

Then the men walked up individually to collect their diplomas. When Tom Carhart's name was called, his classmates gave him an ovation. After the 579th man — the goat — had shaken Humphrey's hand, they removed their hats and flung them at the sun with a great roar. More than a few felt like U. S. Grant, who once wrote that leaving West Point was "the happiest day of my life."

Vonda Jones and Adele Crocker had also come for June Week. Adele, who had never flown in a jet before, was frightened when the plane's wheels retracted with a deep *thump* as they lifted off the runway in Little Rock. "My God!" she exclaimed loudly, clutching Vonda, "we just hit a car!" Safe on the ground in New York, she enjoyed herself enormously during the June Week ceremonies, though she and George shared the same thought many times: if only Bill were alive to see his son graduate. George was not the engineer that his father had envisioned, but Bill Crocker nonetheless would have been bursting with pride.

After throwing his hat in Michie Stadium, George handed his diploma to Adele and ran down to the barracks. He had agreed to be the best man for his roommate, Don Kievit, who had procrastinated in reserving a wedding slot at the chapel and had to settle for the first service, at one-thirty. That was so typical of Kievit, George thought as he changed into his new Army dress blues. Recently, Kievit had tumbled down a flight of stairs and smashed the stone in his class ring; he fashioned a replacement out of a porcelain toothbrush holder, which he proudly displayed to admiring plebes as an example of rare "toothholderite." That, too, was typical of Don Kievit.

After the wedding, George loaded his Corvette — discarding all of his cadet paraphernalia except for the tarbucket — and immediately fled for Arkansas. Since the car had scarcely enough room for a driver, Vonda and Adele flew home. Stopping for gas in Tennessee, George inquired about the new construction on Interstate 40. How about the stretch from Nashville to Memphis, he asked; have they finished that yet? Yes, the attendant told him, it's finished but it isn't open yet. They've still got the barrels up blocking the entrance.

What the hell, George thought, no guts, no glory. Veering around the blockade, he floored the accelerator, praying that the Caterpillar graders on the apron of the highway would stay clear of his lane.

The speedometer jumped to one hundred miles an hour and kept climbing. One-ten, one-twenty, one-thirty, one-forty. One hundred and forty-two miles per hour. Holy smokes, he thought. That tenuous agreement between the car and the laws of physics seemed to be holding, which was a fortunate thing for a young man in a big hurry.

As Don Kievit had been first on the wedding docket, Buck Thompson was last. Forty-two I-now-pronounce-you's later, Buck's turn at the altar finally came round.

His bride was Fran Urstadt, an attractive biochemist at Burroughs Wellcome who had attended nearby Ladycliff College. She had cornflower blue eyes and an animation that moved instantly from full stop to fully engaged. Originally from the Bronx — a touch of the borough remained in her voice — she had grown up in Carmel, New York, where her father was a construction engineer.

Fran's first encounter with Buck had been disastrous. Substituting for her roommate on a blind date, she found herself matched with a hulking Kansan who kept trying to drag her down to Flirtation Walk. After two hours of hand-to-hand combat, she stormed back to Ladycliff. Contrite and pledging reform, Buck called persistently for weeks.

Reluctantly, she agreed to a second date after making certain he understood that she was a proper young woman with high moral standards. Buck behaved with decorum this time, although his disposition, as she told her friends, was "very, very hot-blooded." Other cadets began calling her Three Girdles, for the armor with which she protected her chastity.

Buck grew on Fran, as he grew on everyone. She was surprised to find that he loved opera; on one of their first dates he took her to see *Parsifal* at the Metropolitan Opera. She thought the performance was impossibly long; the theater was so dim that she couldn't read the program, and the action on stage was confusing. But Buck was mesmerized. Anything German fascinated him, especially German military history. Her grandfather had emigrated from Germany, and Buck would chat with him for hours about Bismarck and Ludendorff and the Junkers.

Fran's family adored him — his humor, his generous heart, and most of all his large spirit. Somehow even Buck's drinking — prodigious even by cadet standards — was acceptable. Fran would smuggle Cutty Sark to him at the academy, and when he visited the Urstadt home her father always climbed to the attic to dig out the gift bottles of Chivas Regal he had received for Christmas. Buck had a seemingly limitless capacity for Scotch, although he occasionally passed out on a lounge chair in the back yard. Once, in a particularly thick stupor, he had walked through a glass storm door; another time, Mrs. Urstadt discovered him urinating in the back yard and insisted that her husband wake Buck every hour to march him to the bathroom.

At graduation, he wore academic stars on his collar; during his last semester he had simply decided to prove that he could finish in the top 5 percent of the class. The entire Thompson clan had come from Atchison for the ceremony, occupying the nearby village of Cornwall throughout June Week like an invading army. So many Thompsons were at West Point that it was difficult to keep track of everyone. At one point, an aunt and a grandmother were inadvertently left behind after a picture-taking session at Trophy Point; they were finally reclaimed, angry and tearful. Fran's family came also, of course — the German Urstadts and her mother's sisters, all of whom had married New York Italians. It was as though they had their own American melting pot, right there at West Point.

The wedding began at four o'clock on June 11. Jim Ford, bleary from the four-day procession of brides and grooms, performed the ceremony in the chapel. "Richard," Ford asked, "do you take this woman, Frances, to be your lawfully wedded wife?"

"Affirmative!" Buck barked. The wedding party erupted in laughter.

After the nuptials, the celebrants drove to the Officers Club for dinner and a reception. A momentary crisis disrupted the festivities when a candle ignited a breadbasket, which in turn set fire to an entire table. But the flames were soon extinguished and the party went on.

The newlyweds had agreed to vacate the club by nine o'clock, but Buck persuaded the manager to let them linger. One advantage to being last on the marriage manifest was that no one pushed the new lieutenant and his bride to vacate the room for another reception. Sometimes the wedding turnover grew so hectic at West Point that the little cellophane-wrapped bride-and-groom figures would be plucked from one partly devoured wedding cake as it was wheeled out and stuck on a new cake being wheeled in.

Buck, as usual, intended to enjoy the moment. Whether ambling into a Beast Barracks formation or celebrating his own marriage, he did things at his own cadence, in his own inimitable style, drinking life, as he drank everything, to the lees.

When the reception ended, the Thompsons and the Urstadts drove merrily out the academy gate. After the frenzy of June Week, a stillness now settled over West Point. The Hotel Thayer emptied out; no one dined at the mess hall tables or worshiped in the chapel pews; the stone barracks stood dark and deserted. And silence fell across the vacant Plain, where only the bronze statues of Patton, Sedgwick, and the other battle captains remained behind, heroic and impassive, as though patiently awaiting reports from the front.

PART II

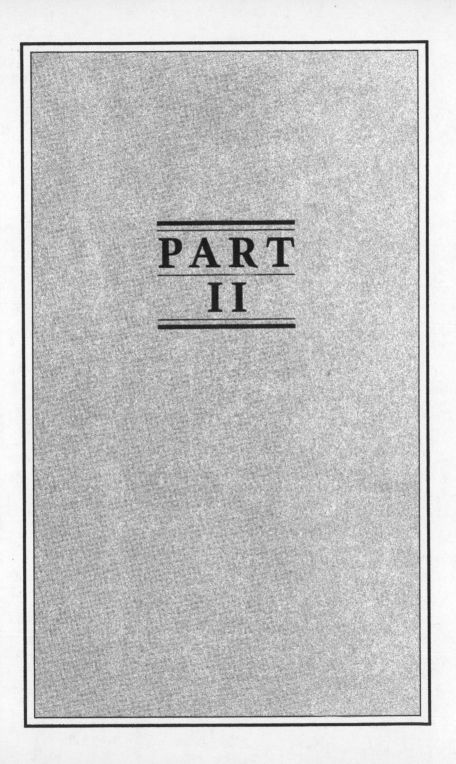

6

RANGER

IN ITS PEREMPTORY FASHION, the Army gave George Crocker only forty-eight hours' notice that he was to be at Fort Benning for the start of Ranger training on September 12, 1966. George and two classmates who also had been serving as platoon leaders in the 9th Division drove all night from Fort Riley, Kansas, to Georgia. When they reached Columbus, George insisted that they first stop at Ranger Joe's, a kind of haberdashery for cutthroats, where they bought jungle boots, fatigues, and the obligatory big knife.

They found Ranger headquarters in a section of Benning called Harmony Church, a hardscrabble patch of red clay with World War II barracks set among the pine trees. The popping of small-arms fire carried from a range in the nearby woods. A row of pay phone booths lined one parking lot. Black numbers had been stenciled on the corners of the buildings to distinguish one from another. When the three men rapped on the door of Building 4807, they were ordered to walk around to the side and knock on the wall for ten minutes. Okay, they told each other, so it's going to be like that.

The next morning at "O-dark thirty" all 212 Ranger candidates were rousted from the barracks bays for a brutally paced run, the point of which was to demonstrate that whatever kind of shape they thought they were in, it wasn't Ranger shape. In the sawdust pits, they practiced hand-to-hand combat, learning the overhead throw, rear takedown, and counters against a rear stranglehold. Outfitted with lacrosse helmets and pugil sticks, they paired off and thrashed each other until their urine ran red and sawdust stuck to their sweaty skin like feathers to tar.

Those who were timid had a fistful of sawdust crammed into their mouths before being matched against the NCO instructors, who made good on a promise to "clobber the living Jesus Christ out of you." Those who misplaced an M-14 were ordered to root around the pits on hands and knees, calling, "Here, weapon! C'mon, boy! Here, weapon!" And those caught with contraband chewing gum were forced to dig a six-foot grave in which to bury it.

The Ranger instructors showed no sympathy for the ill or injured. Any soldier who asked to go on sick call was ordered to crawl on his belly across several hundred meters of gravel, which gouged raw sores on his thighs and forearms. If you're sick enough to do that, the cadre sergeants explained, then you're sick enough for sick call. Most simply gritted out whatever ailed them, gobbling Darvon like jellybeans.

For the class of 1966, Ranger training was a required ordeal. As West Point was intended to build character, Ranger was intended to build soldiers — tough, indomitable soldiers, who were hard physically and harder psychologically. The course ran in nine-week cycles, with newly graduated West Pointers filling the late summer and autumn cycles known as Ranger 2, Ranger 3, and Ranger 4. Ranger 3 included George, Buck Thompson, Matt Harrison, and Norm Fretwell. Tommy Hayes also arrived, tanned and fit; he had labored so diligently to strengthen his upper body that he split a door frame with his chin-up bar. After three weeks at Benning, the men would undergo three weeks of mountain training at Dahlonega in north Georgia, followed by a final three weeks of jungle training in the Florida panhandle. Some classmates, like Art Bonifas, had already passed through Ranger 2; others, like Jack Wheeler, were scheduled for later cycles.

The first few miserable days at Benning — and the certainty that the training would get much worse — came as an unpleasant shock to the West Pointers after the relative comfort of their final year at the academy. As first classmen, they had been masters of the corps, with a thousand plebe lackeys to do their bidding. Ranger school abruptly jerked them out of their comfortable state, just as Beast Barracks had belted the coddled adolescence from them four years before.

They had all graduated with a blank slate. West Point achievements or shortcomings meant nothing after June 8; every man was a second lieutenant, sharing a date of rank and wearing the same rectangular ounce of brass on each shoulder. Ranger training was the first hurdle in the Army, and it would fell nearly a third of them in under six months. Failure to get the little crescent uniform patch, the Ranger tab, was not necessarily fatal to a career. But it was a smudge. Every year, the Army caught several officers wearing the gold tab fraudulently, having risked the shame of detection rather than acknowledge the humiliation of failure.

The 818 hours of instruction in course 7-D-F4, as Ranger training was officially designated, were intended "to develop a superb infantry soldier with exceptional endurance, skilled in the techniques of fieldcraft, survival, mountain, jungle, air-landed and amphibious operations." Beneath that bland and bureaucratic description lay another, implicit purpose in the fall of 1966: to keep men alive in Vietnam.

As the training intensified, they learned how to use a compass, read a map, call for artillery support, and place demolition charges. They learned how to set ambushes and establish a killing zone, how to calculate wind drift in resupply drops, how to cut landing zones for helicopter dustoffs.

They learned that if the dead could not be carried, they were to be buried at least three feet deep. One dog tag stayed with the corpse; the other remained with the living.

They learned in tracking an enemy that deep toe marks normally spaced meant the quarry was carrying a heavy load; deep toe marks widely spaced meant the quarry was running. They learned that water in a footprint would remain muddied for about an hour; that cigarette smoke could be detected four hundred meters away; that opened tin cans showed rust spots within twelve hours; that the height of blood on foliage sometimes provided a clue as to where an enemy was wounded. They learned that stealth in the woods at night — "noise and light discipline," in the Ranger vernacular — often kept the living from joining the dead.

For those who were not infantry officers — or who otherwise doubted the eventual utility of knowing how to snare a rabbit or employ the Malaysian fan technique on patrol — Ranger often seemed like 818 hours of pointless torture. At first, the West Pointers hung together. When a cadre sergeant ordered a miscreant to do push-ups — "Gimme twenty-five right now, mullet!" — sometimes as a show of unity the entire platoon would drop for twenty-five (plus one extra, the Ranger way).

At the academy, a phenomenon known as "cooperate and graduate" had long been part of the corps' heritage; that carried over into the so-called West Point Protective Association among Army officers. When classmates rated each other as part of the Ranger peer review, they often stacked the deck to make sure that everyone got at least a passing score.

But as the weeks wore on, fraternity wore thin. Tolerance for backsliders diminished. Yes, they were brothers, but it became evident that brotherhood in the real world had its limits. Those in trouble were still helped, sometimes to the point of literally being carried. But when the cadre had locked onto a potential victim — like lions culling a herd of wildebeest — there was not much the others could do but bolt for survival.

George was happy at last to be part of the real Army, although he felt guilty at abandoning his bride less than two months after their wedding. He and Vonda Jones had been married on June 25 at the First Methodist Church in Little Rock. Tom Beasley was his best man, showing up for the ceremony with a fetching young woman who he claimed was his cousin. Knowing that at some point he was supposed to kiss his bride, George had lifted Vonda's veil in the middle of their vows, only to be restrained by the minister. "Not yet," he cautioned George, provoking laughter from the congregation.

In early August, after a honeymoon in Key West, the Crockers loaded a U-Haul trailer — George said they needed it just for Vonda's shoes — and drove north to set up housekeeping as Lieutenant and Mrs. Lieutenant at Fort Riley. In the summer of '66, Riley was overflowing with 9th Division soldiers and officers preparing for combat. Even majors had trouble securing quarters on post, and a tornado in early June had wrecked a number of trailer parks and apartments near the post, further squeezing the housing possibilities. George finally found a flat about fifteen miles east of the fort in the town of Manhattan, where Vonda could take graduate classes at Kansas State University.

The Kansas summer was dreadful. Vonda spread out damp towels to cool the bed, watching in dismay as steam rose from the sheets toward the ceiling. George left every morning at four-thirty to join his platoon. Three times a week the men went into the field for training until ten P.M.; after returning to the barracks, George inspected the platoon, saw to it that the troops' rifles were securely locked in the rack, and waited in the orderly room until midnight before driving home to Manhattan for three or four hours of sleep. The 9th Division's destination was supposed to be classified; in a briefing for lieutenants at the division headquarters, a warrant officer confided, "We've been alerted for overseas deployment but we can't say where." Ever eager, George had almost raised his hand to spill the secret — "I know where, chief. It's Vietnam. We found that out back at West Point!" But he restrained the impulse.

The feverish mustering for war at Riley merely reinforced his hunger to join the fight. Like many of his classmates, he felt a limitless zeal and an unstinting faith in both the American cause and the Army's capacity to win this war or any war. Occasionally a disquieting report from Vietnam roiled his certainty; one magazine article that graphically described the fighting in the Ia Drang Valley in October and November of 1965 recounted several instances when units of the 1st Cavalry Division failed to maintain adequate security and properly read the signs of an enemy ambush. This suggestion of fallibility and the consequent deaths was chilling, but George brushed it aside, determined to profit from others' mistakes. Although he did not yet fully grasp his duties as a platoon leader in those first weeks at Riley — and was chagrined to find that his "veteran" platoon sergeant was a Signal Corps NCO who had never before been in an infantry unit — George was confident that a few months of training would turn the unit into one of the division's "mean, green fighting machines." Quintessentially American, he had the cocky ebullience of a twenty-three-year-old who presumed himself to be immortal.

Vonda also was a trouper. She learned to spit-shine George's boots to save him time. To save money, she ironed his fatigues rather than sending them to the laundry. Of his $325 monthly paycheck, $100 covered the rent, $85 went for the payment on her MGB roadster, and more than $100 was needed for his rally red Corvette. That left about a dollar a day for food and other expenses. It simply wasn't enough: reluctantly, they sold the Corvette and then the roadster, replacing the sports cars with a Volkswagen.

Vonda knew nothing of military life. Her older brother served in the Navy, but her first real exposure to the Army had come during the brief visit to West Point for June Week. Earlier in the summer, during the wedding preparations, she had worked in her father's successful campaign to win a seat on the Arkansas Supreme Court as an incorruptible Democratic alternative to the machine candidates. Part of her time was spent stumping through the rice lands of the southern delta counties, where voters wanted to know whether Judge Jones would match the opposition's bounty of a five-dollar bill or three beers for every vote.

Vonda knew that her husband would soon be going to war. She approved, though she was now pregnant and it was likely that the baby would be born just about the time George shipped out. She may not have known much about the military, but she understood duty. It was his duty to fight. It was her duty to support him. If that meant spit-shining boots or waiting like Penelope while he sailed off to conquer Troy, so be it. The way she saw things, they were a team — "till death do us part," as they had vowed. Some of the boys she knew from college were trying to dodge the draft by taking graduate courses, "underwater basketweaving and things like that," as Vonda contemptuously put it. She was a tolerant person, but dereliction irked her, irked her to no end.

As he had almost enjoyed Beast Barracks, George almost enjoyed Ranger school. The training amounted to a nine-week test of limits, but a test in which he didn't have to know what an electron was or why the lights came on. At West Point, much of the military curriculum had focused on the great sweep of armies — Napoleon's movement of corps and so forth. In Ranger, the lessons were tailored to small-unit survival — platoon tactics for platoon leaders headed for a platoon leader's war.

During the mountain phase of training, George learned to run a patrol. Typically, an exercise lasted three or four days. First, the men conducted area reconnaissance — deciding whether the terrain was suitable for a landing zone, drop zone, communications, ambushes, or track vehicles. They noted the width and location of bridges, roads, and streams, carefully marking each feature on a map. Were the locals hostile or friendly? If a bridge was to be destroyed, where should the charges be set? If an ambush was to be laid, was it better to use an L-shaped, a linear, or a box formation? Sometimes the most difficult task for a soldier was moving back through friendly lines without getting shot by his own nervous sentries, as Stonewall Jackson had been killed a century before.

Moving at night was always exacting, especially in the rain. A patrol leader had to count paces to keep track of how far he had traveled, either dropping a pebble in his pocket every hundred meters or tying a knot in a cord. Checking the map meant squatting beneath a poncho with a red flashlight beam while the instructor — the "lane grader" — quizzed the leader on his location, like some backwoods Socrates. "But why do you think you're here?" the lane grader would ask. "Why not over here? Have you crossed this stream yet? How many meters back was it?"

Getting lost meant flunking. If members of the patrol kept drifting apart, the lane graders sometimes lashed them together with dummy cords; if one Ranger stumbled — barking his shins on the deadfall and cursing with a harsh *goddamn* — everyone went down with him.

Losing a man on patrol also meant flunking. Each Ranger followed the two fluorescent cat's eyes on the back of the cap in front of him. Occasionally, a practical joker would put his cap on a stick and lead the man behind into a tree. The mountains were full of foxfire, a luminous fungus that could deceive an exhausted soldier into thinking the patrol had stopped when in fact he was waiting for an oak tree to move out.

The men averaged two hours of sleep and one meal of cold C-rations every twenty-four hours. "Rangers never use roads or trails," they chanted while trudging through the Chattahoochee National Forest. "Be a soldier," one cadre officer advised, "but don't be afraid to think like a bank robber."

Strange things happened in the mountains. One night, on the slopes of the Tennessee Mountain Divide, the men were so cold that they were allowed the unusual luxury of building a campfire. Buck Thompson collapsed in exhaustion next to the blaze and set his fatigue jacket on fire; he continued to snore peacefully while his classmates swatted out the flames.

On another occasion, they practiced pitching pup tents. As the Ranger captain strolled down the line, he nodded approvingly. Every tent was perfect — the canvas sides taut, the sapling poles perpendicular to the ground, the flaps folded back for inspection. Not bad, Rangers, the captain commented, not bad.

Then he came to Buck, who stood casually next to a shapeless heap of canvas. The captain glowered.

"What the — "

"Sir — " Buck interjected. He turned and commanded the heap of canvas, "Pup tent, 'TEN, HUT!"

As he jumped to attention, Buck removed his foot from a small sapling, which he had bent to the ground after threading it through the eyelet in the canvas.

The sapling snapped erect, pulling the tent into a perfectly taut little triangle.

His classmates roared with laughter, clapping one another on the back as Buck grinned impishly. Even in the wilds of north Georgia, the Buck Thompson legend continued to thrive.

For the most part, however, they were too hungry to laugh. Food became their abiding obsession. As one Ranger later put it, hunger advanced in three stages: in stage one, a man's appetite told him he was ready to eat his next meal; in stage two, hunger informed his every thought and motion; in stage three, a man was starving to death and his mind suppressed thoughts of food to the point of indifference.

Rangers remained perpetually in stage two, which resulted in a kind of hallucinatory hunger. "Look at this!" someone would cry. "A Hershey bar, right here on the ground!" The phantom candy was carefully unwrapped, divided into equal portions, and devoured with a loud smacking of lips. Extra cans of C-rations were auctioned for $10 or $12, or an IOU for a Kansas City strip at the Black Angus in Columbus. In the dead of night a shriek occasionally echoed through the woods — "Goddamn Coke machine ate my quarter!" — as another deranged Ranger bashed a tree trunk with his rifle butt.

One day, several men caught an eastern diamondback rattler. Just as they were preparing to cook and eat it, a cadre officer appeared. "If that snake doesn't make it back to camp alive," he warned, "you're out." For four days they took turns carrying the snake in a bundle, hobo-style.

Some were out anyway. By the end of the Georgia phase on October 23, 14 of the original 212 men in Ranger 3 had been dismissed for incapacitating sprains, fractures, and other medical ailments; an even larger number had either quit or been relieved because of poor performance. Another twenty stood on the verge of washing out. Under the complex grading system, each candidate had begun the nine weeks with 1050 points. The lane graders deducted points for any deficiency; to earn his tab, a Ranger had to finish with at least 683 points in his account. Moreover, the lane graders evaluated each man during four, five, or six patrols in the mountain and Florida phases; no soldier could collect a tab unless he had passed at least half of his patrols by the time the training ended on November 12.

Ranger revealed the inner man. Hunger, exhaustion, and stress quickly stripped away any façade. Classmates who thought they knew one another after four intimate, exacting years at West Point sometimes discovered a latent frailty — or fortitude. Those who appeared strong sometimes turned out to be surprisingly weak; the seemingly weak could be unexpectedly stalwart.

Sometimes, of course, those who seemed strong *were* strong. George found that his natural affinity for infantry life served him well in Ranger training. This was play war, to be sure, but in a few months it would be the real thing, with real ammunition and grenades. The imminence of combat imbued the training with a sharp and urgent relevance.

He had only one setback. His patrol was assigned to reconnoiter an outpost manned by soldiers from the 197th Brigade, who often played the enemy. George led the men through the woods, found the outpost, set up an ORP — objective rallying point — several hundred meters away, and began scouting the enemy activity. Suddenly, the enemy soldiers at the outpost dived for cover, pointing at the Ranger patrol and firing their weapons.

George was baffled; they were too well concealed to be detected. No way those guys saw us, he muttered to himself. Then, glancing over his shoulder, he saw the lane grader standing as tall and obvious as the Statue of Liberty.

You forgot to make sure that I was concealed, the lane grader told George. You have to be certain that every little detail is covered. I've got to flunk you.

George rolled his eyes. Like getting busted to cadet private for an offense he had not committed, this didn't seem fair. But he held his tongue. The mountain training was nearly over. The time had come to go fight guerrillas in Florida, where the Rangers were supposed to put together everything that they had learned in the past six weeks. This was one mistake he would not make again; every make-believe death in Ranger, he hoped, would mean one less dead man in Vietnam, where the bullets were real and a soldier paid for neglect with his life.

For their final three weeks of training, the Rangers moved to a remote airstrip in the swamps of the Florida panhandle. Auxiliary Field Seven lay near the Indigo River, hard by Bull Pond and Catfish Basin. Populated mainly by scorpions and the grand slam of American poisonous serpents — rattlers, water moccasins, copperheads, and coral snakes — the camp lay twenty miles from the nearest town. Other than a water tower and a cluster of spare, tin-roofed barracks, Aux Field Seven offered few amenities; the airstrip was, however, part of a proud heritage of American heroism.

In December 1941, the smoke had barely blown clear of Pearl Harbor when Franklin Roosevelt began planning to bomb the Japanese mainland. The sneak attack demanded repayment in kind, the president insisted, and as quickly as possible. Yet given Japan's dominion in the western Pacific, talk of a retaliatory raid seemed but hollow bluster. The logistical hurdles were daunting. Where would the American planes launch? Where would they land? Then, in early 1942, a naval staff officer had a brainstorm: why not fly long-range Army bombers from the deck of an aircraft carrier?

To plan the mission, General Hap Arnold summoned a remarkable aeronautical engineer who also happened to be one of the country's finest pilots. Jimmy Doolittle had been the first man to cross the United States in twelve hours, the first to execute successfully an outside loop, and the first to land an airplane blind. Now he would be the first to strike back at Japan.

By early March of 1942, Doolittle had assembled twenty-four bomber crews at Field Seven, where they practiced takeoffs from a five-hundred-foot runway — less than half the usual distance. The dismal location was well suited to top secret rehearsals. To strip his B-25s down to 31,000 pounds, Doolittle removed the bottom turrets and radio gear, and replaced the heavy conventional bombsight with a simple contraption that cost twenty cents. Extra gas bladders were installed, along with new propellers to add a few knots of speed. Dubbed Task Force 16, the Doolittle squadron left the Florida swamps in late March; by early April the squadron was steaming across the Pacific aboard the U.S.S. *Hornet*. The plan called for them to bomb Tokyo and other Japanese cities, then fly on to China or Vladivostok in the Soviet Union. On April 18, the B-25s launched from the *Hornet*'s deck at full throttle into a gale wind. Five hours and seven hundred miles later, Roosevelt's revenge whistled through their bomb bay doors.

On an afternoon in late October twenty-four years later, Lieutenants

Crocker, Thompson, Harrison, Hayes, Fretwell, and the other classmates remaining in Ranger 3 sat on bleachers in the same tarpaper shack that had once been used as the briefing room for the World War II bomber crews. They were waiting for the major.

After six weeks of brutal training at Benning and Dahlonega, the men of '66 were unrecognizable as the spoony cadets who had tossed their white hats in Michie Stadium four months earlier. All were thinner and some looked emaciated; their jungle fatigues hung loosely on bodies that were variously bruised, blistered, and bloodied.

The day before, after returning to Benning from the mountains, most of the half-starved Ranger candidates had invaded the Black Angus, where they gorged themselves on beer and rare steaks, each the size of a catcher's mitt. At Harmony Church, they received a mimeographed handout listing the gear they would need for jungle training in Florida; typically, an officer promptly countermanded the instructions. "Forget that crap," he advised. "Take only what you can carry on your backs."

Earlier this morning, the men had boarded buses for the 150-mile trip to Eglin Air Force Base in Florida. Near Field 7, after they had transferred to deuce-and-a-half trucks for the final few miles, the convoy drove through an ambush scene. A truck was ablaze, and soldiers lay on the ground in feigned death. "The enemy," one instructor warned ominously, "is all around us."

Oh, shit, the new lieutenants murmured, here we go. That was one thing everyone had heard about the major: he was nothing if not theatrical. Sitting in the dingy tarpaper shack, they wondered what would happen next.

Ka-BOOM! A deafening explosion rocked the shack. Two hundred drowsy Rangers leaped with fright, their ears ringing violently from the grenade simulator. Several even committed the mortal sin of dropping their M-14s, and rifles clattered on the bleachers like pickup sticks.

The door to the shack burst open and the major staggered in. He wore black pajamas, soaked and smeared with mud from a recent wallow in Holly Creek; his boots trailed a tangled clump of swamp weeds, and he carried an AK-47. Big and brawny, he had a parabolic slash for a mouth and jowls that looked like something from a meat locker. He spoke with the thick drawl of his native Schley County in south Georgia.

"I just came out from the swamp where I was fightin' the guerrillas. The guerrillas are mean and tough. They are not to be taken lightly." A mad glint lit his eyes as he paused, shaking himself like a Labrador retriever. "Here's what they did to me."

Ripping open the pajama top, he displayed a fearsome, knotted scar running vertically from navel to clavicle.

"If a man is bloody stupid," he continued, "his mother will receive a telegram and it will say, 'Your son is dead because he was stupid.' Let's hope your telegram just says, 'Your son is dead.' Or, with the training we're going to give you here, maybe your mother won't receive any telegram at all. So pay attention!"

Pay attention! Had he set himself ablaze like a Buddhist monk — a stunt that was not beyond his dramaturgy — they could have been no more rapt than they were now. Major Charlie A. Beckwith — also known as Chargin' Charlie — was already a legend. He was shrewd, profane, and animated with demonic energy. After three years in the 82nd Airborne, Beckwith had joined the Special Forces in 1958. Later, following a tour in Laos, he trained with British Special Air Service commandoes on Corsica and in Malaya, where he nearly died of leptospirosis. His admiration for British initiative, informality, and competence was unbounded, although his sermons on the subject had been largely ignored after his return to the United States. As a Green Beret commander in Vietnam, he recruited men for his unit with a flier that read: "WANTED: Volunteers for Project DELTA. Will guarantee you a medal, a body bag, or both."

Flying in a helicopter above the An Loa Valley in January 1966, Beckwith had nearly collected a body bag himself when a .51-caliber machine-gun bullet ripped through his abdomen. In triage, after surgeons had pushed him to one side as a hopeless case, Beckwith grabbed a nurse and snarled, "I ain't the average bear and I didn't come in here to pack it in." After five months in the hospital, he headed south from Detroit aboard his black Harley Sprint to take command of the Florida phase of Ranger training. The best way to teach survival, Beckwith believed, was to transform this patch of swamp into a little Vietnam.

"I hear you fuckers are a bunch of tigers in garrison and pussies in the field!" he bellowed. "Well, we'll find out. I'm glad you're here. The Florida Ranger camp has been overrun by the enemy and I really need you to help me drive them off. I'm gonna train you for a few days and then send you out to kill guerrillas."

With that, he picked up his rifle and galloped back into the swamp.

The Rangers left the shack buzzing about the apparition. The rumors were true, they agreed: Beckwith was a lunatic. Outside, a cardboard tombstone had been propped up for all to read:

Here lie the bones
Of Ranger Jones,
A graduate of this institution.
He died last night

In his first fire fight,
Using the school solution.
Therefore, be flexible!

Several days later, a cold snap hit the panhandle. Several dozen Rangers milled about on a riverbank, lashing their gear to poncho rafts for yet another amphibious crossing. That meant stripping off their fatigues, tying their boots to the little rafts, and plunging into the frigid water.

"Let's go, mullets," the lane grader yelled. "Quit dawdling. It's not gonna get any warmer."

Charlie Beckwith roared up in a jeep. As usual he wore only a red T-shirt and fatigue pants, with a stogie clamped between his teeth. Even before coming to a full stop, he was out of his seat. In four strides he hit the water; wading out to his chest, he flipped over and floated on his back as if it were an August Sunday at Ocean City.

"You pussies!" he yelled, the cigar still jutting from his mouth. "You've got to learn to be miserable. You've got to love this. This is infantry weather. You've got to love being wet and cold and miserable. Because the enemy is cold and wet and miserable, too. And that's when you step up and kill him."

He paddled to shore and stood up. Skim ice coated his thighs. "All right, now gimme ten. In the water."

One! Two! Three! Four! they counted aloud. Ten push-ups in knee-deep water and one extra for good measure, Ranger style.

None of the Ranger candidates had ever met anyone quite like Beckwith. (Fourteen years later, few men from the class of 1966 were surprised when the Pentagon disclosed that Beckwith had commanded the Delta Force attempt to free American hostages in Iran.) In the Florida Ranger camp, some wondered whether all field grade officers were as crazed as Beckwith. If so, they mused, twenty years in the Army would prove to be a long hitch. He was never offstage; even alone with his cadre he always seemed to be growling and muddy, like some swamp creature in a bad movie. For Charlie Beckwith, all the world was a prop.

In the middle of a moonless night, miles from Aux Field Seven, the Rangers would glance around and find Beckwith tagging along silently behind the patrol. At other times, he crashed through the swamp, screaming, "The VC are after me! The VC are after me!" He was so intense, so spooky, they almost believed him.

Having been tested physically for the preceding six weeks, they were now tested psychologically. To men who had not eaten in two days, Beckwith would promise food on the next helicopter and then make certain that the chopper arrived with nothing aboard except radio batteries. "Expect the unexpected," he commanded, "because in war things never happen like you think they're going to happen. Life is unfair." And in their dark, cold, foodless foxholes, strong men wept and fantasized about blowing his brains out.

The larger strategy of the war in Vietnam seemed to concern him not a whit. Beckwith's job was to help these lieutenants survive their year in the jungle, killing as many enemy troops as possible in the bargain. Ranger training, as he viewed it, was a kind of insurance policy. Some would die — that was war. But others who might have died would live, perhaps saved by what they learned during three wretched weeks in the Florida swamps.

When Beckwith had arrived in midsummer of 1966, he had found the training to be a series of unimaginative set pieces without the stress and confusion that were salient features of combat. Some very senior generals, he told the cadre, had authorized him to "make some changes." Florida was to be tough, rigorous, real; if there were casualties, they were part of the price of freedom. Periodically, a cadre officer would brief the doctors at the Eglin Air Force Base hospital. "You'll see spider bites, scorpion stings, snake bites, frostbite, twisted joints," the officer warned. "You'll also see malnutrition, exhaustion, and exposure. Treat them for their immediate affliction, but don't feed them. Not even a cracker. Treat and release."

Within a month of his arrival, Beckwith had completely overhauled the curriculum, shaping the three-week course into one continuous exercise. Occasionally, a bureaucrat drove down from Benning to complain that nothing in the files matched what was actually being done in Florida. Yeah, Beckwith nodded, that's right.

He built a cluster of hootches to simulate a Vietnamese village, peopling it with the wives and children of the cadre. The Ranger platoons took turns seizing the hamlet, determining whether it was friendly, and searching for weapons (while also rooting through the garbage for extra food). Tunnels and hootches were often booby-trapped, and if a Ranger was careless, Beckwith would shriek, "You're gonna die, son! You just killed half your platoon!" If a Ranger dropped his rifle in the woods, Beckwith painted his cap bright red and ordered him to carry a heavy log in place of his M-14 for several days; very few repeated the mistake.

For his cadre instructors, Beckwith recruited the best young combat veterans he could find. About fifteen officers and fifteen noncoms formed the cadre, and they were not just hot, they were "Ranger shit-hot." Beckwith asked every new instructor to write a three-page essay on how he had benefited in Vietnam from Ranger training, and what he had witnessed in combat that could be incorporated into the training, including new variations of booby traps. If an instructor was not up to Beckwith's standards, the major sent him packing to Benning in disgrace.

Eventually, the cadre built a pen for two large alligators, cheering like Romans at the Circus Maximus as they flung in chickens or hundred-pound snapping turtles with huge curved jaws. For cadre parties, the instructors received mission assignments, which they executed with the same shit-hot exuberance as if they had been told to storm Hanoi. One night, MPs ejected them from the Eglin beach club after a drunken smashing of furniture. On another occasion, they were thrown out of the base Officers Club after stampeding through the dining room in pursuit of a squealing piglet wearing a Ranger tab.

Although most of the '66ers simply tried to stay out of Beckwith's way, his ubiquity often made him difficult to avoid. One day in early November, Matt Harrison's squad was patrolling through the swamp when they came to a clearing. Matt knew what he was doing in the woods. He was a capable Ranger, but in Dahlonega he had flunked his first two patrols. During the second patrol, the squad had struggled up the Tennessee Mountain Divide in a torrential rain. The men were strung out for fifteen hundred meters down the slope when suddenly the lane grader appointed Matt as the new squad leader. He had no idea of their location or mission. The most important thing, Matt concluded, was to reach the crest of the divide and regroup. Climbing upward, the squad blundered into an ambush and was massacred.

About the same time, Matt's Ranger buddy and former West Point roommate, Bob Cresci, washed out. Hobbled with a festering blister, Cresci was summoned by the captain during a long run in the mountains. "What's the matter with you?" the captain asked, sneering. "You chicken?" "I really don't appreciate your mouth," Cresci replied boldly. "Okay," the captain said, "I think it's time for you to go low-crawl the airstrip." "That's ridiculous," Cresci answered. "I'm not doing that."

That was it. Cresci was gone and, although he didn't realize it at the time, so was his Army career. Now, staring at the quiet clearing, Matt knew that he could not afford another mistake. Standard procedure called for halting the column in the woods and scouting ahead for an ambush. With the squad concealed in the scrub oaks, Matt followed the trail into the clearing.

He saw bootprints in the sand. Following the tracks, he was surprised to find a soldier crouched in the bushes behind a machine gun. Other soldiers lay nearby, neatly camouflaged.

"Hey," Matt asked, "what are you doing here?"

"Uh, we were last night's aggressors," the soldier replied, "and we're just waiting for the trucks to pick us up."

Matt nodded. "Say, do you guys have any extra C-rations?"

He began working his way down the line, panhandling for food. Abruptly, he stopped. Of course, you knucklehead! he told himself. Ambush! Matt turned and fled back across the clearing, with the soldiers on his heels. When his squad saw Matt running toward them, they charged from the woods to counterattack. The encounter turned into a brawl; for several minutes, a couple of dozen men thrashed around in the sand.

Beckwith, purple with rage, raced into the clearing in his jeep. His little drama — which he had set up under the watchful eyes of a visiting general — had been wrecked by someone grubbing for food. "If I find out who did this," he roared, "you're out of the Ranger program!" Matt kept quiet.

Occasionally, Beckwith's realism took a sinister turn. One morning a patrol under the command of Ronald Bartek set out to observe what was described as a "guerrilla trail." Bartek was a gregarious, handsome Air Force brat; at the academy, as a cadet captain and regimental commander, he had been considered inordinately gung ho even by West Point standards. Following Bartek's lead, the Ranger patrol picked its way through the sloughs and scrub pines to the trail; after weaving camouflage covers for their foxholes, the men settled in to watch and wait.

Soon the guerrillas — played by soldiers from the 197th — walked past. Bartek duly noted their direction, numbers, and weaponry. He also noted that it was ten A.M. What he failed to notice was that the guerrillas were doubling back. Sneaking up on one of the foxholes, they yanked off the camouflage lid and captured the Ranger inside. They were tying him up as Bartek clambered out of his own hole. He had heard that being a POW, even in Ranger training, could be very unpleasant. This, he thought, was ridiculous.

"Time out, guys," he called. "War's over. You got him. It doesn't make any sense to take him off now."

The guerrilla leader shrugged. "Okay," he said, "we'll take you instead."

They bound Bartek's arms behind his back, wedged a stick through the crook of his elbows, blindfolded him, and lashed a noose around his neck. Then they plunged through the woods, shoving the prisoner face down into the dirt whenever a helicopter passed overhead.

Reaching their camp, the guerrillas stripped Bartek naked and made him kneel, painfully, on a bamboo pole. They looped the rope — its noose still cinched around his neck — over a tree limb and tied it to a bent sapling. "If you move," they warned, "you'll hang yourself."

After a couple of hours, his legs began to spasm. Bartek pitched forward, gouging his chest on a sharp stick.

"All you have to do is give us the names of your company commander, your battalion commander, and their location," the guerrilla leader said soothingly. "Then this can all be over."

When he refused, they smeared him with honey, even covering his genitals, and staked him to an anthill. The ants stung, but not as badly as his captors had hoped. They then dragged him into the sun, where he was staked spread-eagle. "Okay," the guerrilla said, "time's up. You're going to talk now."

They sloshed water down his throat from a five-gallon jerry can. When Bartek thrashed from side to side, they immobilized his skull by putting a two-by-four behind his neck and driving stakes into the ground on either side of his head. Flattening his nose so that he was unable to breathe, they began to pour again.

"This could be over," they told him repeatedly. "You're killing yourself."

Gagging convulsively, Bartek realized that he was in serious trouble. These guys are pissed, he thought. They're trying to teach me that everybody breaks. They could kill me. They're not fully in control of themselves.

"Enough," he gasped. "I'll talk."

When they propped him up, heaving and sputtering, he reluctantly began to recite names. Terry Stull. Bill McKinney. The names were phony. Terry and Bill had been his friends at West Point. Ron could hear the crinkling sound of paper unfolding. "No, no," a voice said. "That's not right."

Enraged by Bartek's effort to deceive them, the guerrillas brought out the jerry can again; another flood of water swept down his throat and into his lungs. He felt he was drowning. This was worse than being on the bottom of Mr. Sorge's swimming pool with the Rock Squad, deadweighted with bricks. It was so pointless, he thought, so unfair.

Finally he broke and told them everything. Names, locations, whatever they wanted. They jerked him to his feet and thrust him into a tiger cage, built so that he could neither sit nor stand. All he could do was crouch and tremble.

At five o'clock, seven hours after being captured, he was put on a truck and returned to his platoon. Bartek felt as though he had been gone for days. The ordeal left him badly shaken. Beckwith wanted stress. He wanted uncertainty. He wanted realism. He wanted his Rangers to understand in their bones that a soldier's life was perpetually imperiled. Ron Bartek understood.

*

Charlie Beckwith's mission in Ranger 3 was simple and straightforward: to teach his young charges the fundamentals of how to find and kill guerrillas. Yet few aspects of American military history were more perplexing than the country's approach to guerrilla warfare. No nation had more experience at irregular fighting. Beginning with Thomas Wheeler's foray against King Philip's renegades in the Massachusetts Bay Colony, the Americans for three hundred years had fought one guerrilla war after another. In the Revolution, Colonel Daniel Morgan and Francis Marion harassed the redcoats unmercifully, provoking Britain's Burgoyne to rue that "every private will be his own general and will turn every tree and bush into a kind of temporary fortress."

During the nineteenth century, the Army had exterminated a continent full of guerrilla fighters. A few campaigns, of course, had ended catastrophically. Barely a hundred miles from Auxiliary Field Seven, for example, lay the site where West Pointer Francis Dade had been massacred with his entire command of 107 men at the beginning of the bloody six-year struggle known as the Seminole War. Many American officers, however, showed exceptional skill at fighting unconventionally, including General George Crook, who crushed the Apaches by moving quickly, keeping his forces small and elusive, and using Indian scouts effectively. At the turn of the century, the Army fought another guerrilla war in the Philippine jungles against the Tagalogs; twenty-five years later, the Marines battled the guerrillas of Augusto César Sandino in Nicaragua.

But the lessons never seemed to stick. Each succeeding generation took up the art of guerrilla fighting as though discovering it for the first time. As the historian Russell Weigley wrote, "Occasionally the American Army has had to wage a guerrilla war, but guerrilla warfare is so incongruous to the natural methods and habits of a stable and well-to-do society that the American Army has tended to regard it as abnormal and to forget about it whenever possible."

Thus, when Omar Bradley was asked by a senator in 1951 whether the Army had learned anything new in fighting the North Koreans and Chinese, the chairman of the Joint Chiefs replied, "We certainly have been up against one type of warfare which we never had before, and that is the guerrilla type, in which you have infiltration of your lines by large groups."

That a commander as wise as Bradley could make such a comment was baffling to students of military history, evidence of a kind of mnemonic black hole. Dave Richard Palmer, who in the 1980s would become superintendent at West Point, explained such lapses as a failure of the Army to pay sufficient heed to military history. "The Army corporate memory," Palmer wrote in 1978, "was little more than one generation long, stretching back no farther than the experiences of the men in it."

John F. Kennedy had tried to fill the gap. One of the first questions he asked after his inauguration was "What are we doing about guerrilla warfare?" At his initial National Security Council meeting, Kennedy read aloud from Nikita Khrushchev's speech of January 6, 1961, in which the Soviet leader pledged Moscow's support for "wars of national liberation." At Kennedy's insistence, counterinsurgency — the political and military effort to defeat a rebellion — became the order of the day in the early 1960s. As he had during his 1962 graduation address at West Point, the president continuously talked of a "whole new kind of strategy." Those standing in the way — including Chief of Staff George H. Decker, who assured Kennedy that "any good soldier can handle guerrillas" — were purged. Promotions, the president hinted, would be awarded in part on the basis of enthusiasm for counterinsurgency.

At first, the Army complied with alacrity. Among other reasons, the service was still casting about for a sense of mission beyond the nuclear-oriented doctrine of massive retaliation, which had dominated the 1950s. By July 1962, the Joint Chiefs reported that "during the past eighteen months, nine special counterinsurgency courses for officers have been created" with more than two thousand officers participating. One skeptic, noting that the Pentagon had ordered every Army school to devote at least 20 percent of its time to counterinsurgency, reported that this requirement "reached the Finance School and the Cooks and Bakers School, so they were talking about how to make typewriters explode and how to make apple pies with hand grenades inside them."

The men of '66 had entered West Point in the midst of this tumult, and their Ranger training clearly reflected Kennedy's legacy. Many of the tactics Beckwith taught would have been recognizable to Crook or Dan Morgan or Robert Rogers, the New Hampshire woodsman who organized the first company of Rangers during the French and Indian War. But at "echelons above reason," as junior officers liked to call the senior brass, something quite different was happening.

Inexorably, the Army had begun reverting to old ways. The long-honored strategy of annihilating an enemy in pursuit of total victory was not easily abandoned, particulary for men baptized in the battles of World War II. Consequently, the military decisions made in Vietnam, in the Pentagon, and in the White House resembled those adhered to during the world wars and even that pursued by the Army of the Potomac: search out the enemy and destroy him; rely on superior firepower and superior technology; crush the foe with your gross national product. As adapted to war in Vietnam, the fundamental principles of that approach were: keep battalions intact; avoid letting rifle companies move beyond range of mutual support; minimize American casualties by relying on heavy mortar, artillery, and air bombardments before attacking; often cede the night to the enemy.

The strategy was doomed, in part because it was followed equivocally and in part because the American government underestimated the enemy's tenacity and grassroots support. The White House would not unleash the full fury of America's war power through mobilization or the eradication of Cambodian and Laotian sanctuaries. Whether a different formula would have succeeded is problematic. But one thing was clear even in the autumn of 1966: the traditional American war machine had begun to reassert its power. John Kennedy's call for "a whole new kind of strategy" had fallen on deaf ears.

At the end, on November 11, the men of Ranger 3 were ripe to be fooled. Rumors had circulated of a surprise conclusion to the training in Ranger 2, but that scuttlebutt was widely discounted. The unseasonable cold snap — during which they had been allowed to build campfires to ward off frostbite — lulled many into believing that humanity and common sense would prevail.

Beckwith's final exercise called for an assault on Santa Rosa Island in the Gulf of Mexico. The narrow spit stretched for forty miles from east to west but was rarely more than a few hundred meters wide. For several days, in teams of 15 or 20, the 178 surviving Rangers picked their way through the swamps to Santa Rosa Sound. After rendezvousing on the beach, at eight o'clock on the night of the eleventh, they climbed into twelve-man rubber rafts and began paddling into a chill, pungent sea breeze. Sixteen or seventeen rafts glided across the water, soundless but for the soft feathering of paddles and, once, the tiny *kersplash* of an M-14 accidentally dropped overboard. The dark silhouette of Santa Rosa lay a mile or so to the south.

After beaching their rafts, the Rangers fanned out into assault positions. Soldiers from the 197th guarded a mock missile installation a hundred yards ahead as the raiders crept through the sea oats, cradling their rifles. Occasionally they saw the bright orange pinprick of a glowing cigarette.

Almost as one, they opened fire. Dozens of rifles tore at the night, punctuated by the concussive boom of grenade simulators and the deep roar of machine-gun blanks. The howling Rangers charged the missile site; within minutes, all of the defenders were either captured or fleeing, dark figures scampering through the dunes.

"Well done, Rangers!" a cadre officer yelled. "That's it. We'll head back to Field Seven, get cleaned up, maybe get a little sleep. There's a big breakfast waiting for you. Graduation in the morning is at ten hundred hours. Everybody into the trucks over there."

With whoops and hollers — firing their remaining blanks at the black Gulf — they climbed into the dozen trucks that stood parked within a ring of sandbags near Route 98 on Santa Rosa. As the convoy rolled toward the bridge leading to the mainland, everyone tumbled into a dead sleep on the floor of the trucks. By now, it was midnight.

An hour later, the procession lurched to an abrupt halt. A lane grader banged on the truck beds with the flat of his hand. "Let's go. Wake up. Unass the trucks. Everybody out."

Groggy and disoriented, the Rangers stumbled onto the pavement, blinking in the glare of the truck headlights. Where the hell are we? they demanded with a swelling sense of dread. The convoy seemed to have stopped in a shopping center parking lot.

Not far from the trucks was a small building that appeared to be a bar. Suddenly the screen door flew open with a bang; out walked Beckwith. "Oh, God," someone moaned, "we've been had."

Beckwith leaped onto the hood of a jeep. "Men, Field Seven is under attack. We're going to have to leave the trucks here and march back to save it. We've got one more march to make, men, and I'm going to lead you. Let's go."

The camp lay seventeen miles away. Beckwith's rules were simple: they would march in two columns, one on either side of the road. They could sing, dance, or crawl. But those who didn't make it would not receive a Ranger tab.

The death march, as the trek inevitably became known, was the worst ordeal many of them would ever experience. The psychological shock, following the ebullience of the Santa Rosa assault, aggravated their exhaustion after nine weeks of little sleep and less food. Their feet, which had grown calluses in the mountains, were now soft from weeks in the swamp; the sand tore at them unmercifully. Before long, blood dribbled through the ventilation holes in their jungle boots. Some men sobbed openly with rage and frustration. Others vomited from the pain. A few bashed the ground with their rifles, cursing the cadre, their classmates, and God Almighty. Occasionally, a soldier with incipient dementia wandered off toward the woods, only to be tackled and dragged back to the column.

Beckwith led the way. Every few minutes he charged up and down the columns, shouting encouragement or whacking the Rangers on the back with a hail-fellow-well-met joviality. They responded with homicidal glares.

"Men, every night's a Saturday night, every day's a Sunday," he yelled. "Let's run. Rip open your shirt! Let some air in there! Over here! Over here! I gotta rut, men, I gotta rut! Easy walkin', men, easy walkin'!"

George Crocker marched at the front of the right column. Beckwith grabbed him by the collar.

"What branch are you, son?"

"Infantry, sir!"

"All right, all right. We've got an infantryman here!" Beckwith bellowed. "Last time, we had an air defense officer leading. An air defense officer! Can you believe that?"

A few paces behind, Matt Harrison found himself next to West Point classmate Gordon Kimbrell. After eight or ten miles, Matt stopped.

"Gordie, that's it," he said, shaking his head. "I've had it. I'm done."

Kimbrell nodded. "Matt, see that bend in the road up there? Let's just make it that far. Then we'll quit."

With a deep sigh, Matt picked up his rifle. They trudged the hundred meters to the bend. "Okay," Kimbrell said. "We made it. Let's quit."

"No," Matt said. "Up to that big tree up there. The one on the left. Then we'll quit."

"All right," Gordon agreed. And so they slogged on, mile after mile, one wretched benchmark at a time.

Not everyone who had assaulted Santa Rosa was forced to march back to camp. Fifteen men had been abruptly pulled from the group and ordered back into a truck. For them, Ranger school was over.

One of them was Bob Kesmodel, whose parents' house had served as Tom Carhart's command post during the heist of the Navy goat exactly a year before. At West Point, despite his small stature, Kesmodel was one of the best athletes in the class. Strong and agile, he had turned down an athletic scholarship to the University of Virginia to attend the academy because he cherished its ideals and what it represented. He was an excellent wrestler, a varsity lacrosse player, and second in the class on the obstacle course. A popular, convivial member of the Rabble Rousers, he also had been the main rider of the Army mule.

Kesmodel, who described himself as "physical, outdoorsy, and motivated," had assumed that Ranger would play to his strengths. He was assigned to the same Ranger platoon as Norm Fretwell and several other men who had been outstanding cadets. To his chagrin, Kesmodel found that he was intimidated; Fretwell and the others were princes, he was the jester. Physically, he was more than capable; he sometimes even carried the equipment of his bigger classmates. But the other men in his patrols would not respond to his leadership. Commanding men in the dark of night required a presence that he lacked. He was also surprised to discover that he was high-strung and easily rattled.

In the mountains, he had been the patrol leader for a mission in which they were to set up an L-shaped ambush. The lane grader fell asleep but later flunked Kesmodel anyway, claiming that the ambush had been set up incorrectly so that the men would have fired at each other. Kesmodel complained to the authorities that the lane grader had been dozing. "That's impossible," he was told. "Don't you ever say that again."

A week before the death march, he was again a patrol leader, this time during the bitter cold snap. Morale plummeted with the temperature as ice crusted the swamps. One Ranger — among the few who weren't West Pointers — was an older sergeant who had suffered frostbite in the Korean War. I can't go on, he told Kesmodel; I'm afraid of getting frostbite again.

Kesmodel's toes hurt, too. Everyone was in bad shape. Fighting off twinges of panic, he pulled the lane grader aside. "Look, we're out of radio contact. I can't believe they haven't called an administrative halt to this."

"What are you telling me?" the lane grader replied.

"I'm telling you I believe this thing should be halted. I'm sure that if we were in radio contact, they would tell us to stop."

"Well," said the lane grader, "you know what that means for you?"

"I don't care what it means for me. I'm concerned about this patrol. Who's in charge here?"

The lane grader gave him a curious look. "You are."

"Okay, I'm calling a halt. We're going to build fires and we're going to warm these men up before we go any farther."

At the end of the patrol, the lane grader flunked him. (Ironically, an administrative halt *had* been called to allow fires.) Now Kesmodel had flunked two patrols and passed two. On November 11 he was given a make-or-break chance. This time he was assigned to a different platoon. But the other men in the squad had finished their graded patrols, and they seemed wholly uninterested in his problems. "C'mon, quit grab-assing around," he ordered. They ignored him. Suddenly, he was no longer the popular, lacrosse-playing, mule-riding cadet he had been at West Point. He was a small man with glasses, struggling with his command in the deep woods.

Flunking the final patrol sealed his fate. After arriving back at Field Seven in the truck, he was ordered to the mess hall. Shortly after dawn on November 12, the death marchers limped into camp. They took a few minutes to clean up before reporting to the dining tables for all the steak and strawberry ice cream they could eat.

There, with the kitchen help, stood Bob Kesmodel. He had been pressed into duty as a waiter to serve his classmates their victory meal. It was a gratuitous, vicious humiliation of a decent man, an abasement that had been beyond his imagination and that left him shattered. Never again would he feel as he had about the Army or about himself.

Kesmodel's treatment was a brutal instance of the Army's ruthlessness. Only five months and four days had passed since the class of 1966 graduated from West Point, and already wheat and chaff had been separated, harshly. At ten A.M., the Ranger graduation ceremony began. Of the 212 men who had begun the training on September 12, 162 received the tab, including George Crocker, Matt Harrison, Buck Thompson, Norm Fretwell, and Tommy Hayes. Fifty did not. The Ranger attrition rate in the previous year had been 16 percent; this year it would be more than twice that, an increase widely attributed to Chargin' Charlie Beckwith's exacting reign in Florida.

Beckwith personally pinned on some of the tabs. In Ranger 2, according to one rumor, he had attached the little badges with a long straight pin through the skin of the biceps as one final test of mettle. This time, however, Beckwith simply saluted and wished the men well.

The few wives and sweethearts who showed up for the ceremony were shocked by the sight of their men. The contrast between this cracked tarmac on hell's half acre and the green grass of Michie Stadium five months earlier was stunning. The men looked as haggard and hollow-eyed as POWs. They reeked from weeks without a shower. Some had lost thirty pounds and would need special waivers before going on to airborne training, because they couldn't pass the minimum requirement of six pull-ups.

After graduation, the Rangers were supposed to jog past the reviewing stand. But that was too much to ask. A few gamely broke into a lame trot; most hobbled off to collect their gear, as feeble as arthritic octogenarians. The major was finished with them. The war beckoned.

7

BENNING

MARCIA BONIFAS — née McGuire — sat on the new gold rug in the living room. Thimbles, pairs of scissors, and scraps of cloth cluttered the floor. Her back throbbed from the hours she had spent hunched over the new curtains, trying to stitch a straight hem.

She held a finished set at arm's length, squinting critically. It was no use. The line of thread wandered across the cloth like a country road across a map. She had known at the outset that she was no Betsy Ross, but the material made the task even more difficult. At five yards for a dollar, the fabric was as flimsy as newsprint and the colors were uninspired: blue for the two bedrooms, white with gold fringe — to match the rug — for the living room. She had used the bamboo pole from the new rug as a curtain rod for the white set. But there was no avoiding the obvious: they looked awful.

Making curtains by hand had seemed the wifely thing to do. The house certainly needed something to brighten it up. Even the Army classified Quarters 18-E Lloyd Way as "substandard." As a second lieutenant, Art Bonifas collected $109 a month for a housing allowance; the rent on this place was only $75 and they were permitted to pocket the difference. That helped. The house was part of a single-story, brick six-plex, just off Benning Road. Known as Battle Park, the neighborhood was a dreary cluster of junior officers' quarters wedged between Columbus and the main part of post. Behind 18-E lay a thick patch of woods and a gully choked with kudzu.

A new lieutenant and his wife could not expect much in the way of amenities, but even so the living conditions on Lloyd Way were primitive. A visiting Saudi officer and his family, quartered a couple doors down, occasionally heaved their garbage out the back window. Marcia could handle that, but she had been furious when the children hacked down her beautiful elephant ear plants, which had been thriving beneath the air conditioner drippings.

The Bonifases didn't have enough money to buy furniture, so they had rented nearly everything in the house, including the sofa, kitchen table, and bed. Among their own few possessions was the bookcase separating the foyer from the living room. Art had built it to hold the Waterford crystal and some of their other wedding presents.

When Marcia's mother, the inimitable Harriet McGuire, arrived from Brooklyn for a recent visit, they gave her a quick tour of 18-E. After walking through each room, she told her daughter with a sympathetic sigh, "It's only for a year."

Later that evening, Art and Marcia took her to the Officers Club for dinner.

"Where are the lights in these military places?" Harriet complained, holding the menu up to her nose. "They don't use lights here? I can't see what I'm ordering."

"Mother, you're making a scene."

"What scene?" Harriet demanded, raising her voice even louder. "This is an Army camp. This isn't someplace where I need to worry about making a scene."

No, Marcia thought, probably not. Mothers-in-law probably had some form of undiplomatic immunity. Only wives needed to worry. Sometimes it seemed that a wife's principal duty was to fret over everything and anything that could possibly get her husband in trouble, from carrying the wrong calling card to wearing the wrong hat. In some ways, being Mrs. Lieutenant was even odder than being a cadet's girlfriend.

She brushed together the scraps of cloth, dumping the scissors and spools back into her sewing box. Regardless of how the curtains looked, at least they were hung. The front door swung open and Art walked in. His fatigues, which had been so crisp and starched that morning, had wilted during a long, hot day with his artillery battery.

"Hi, honey," he said cheerfully, giving her a hug.

His eyes locked on the white curtains hanging from the bamboo rod. She couldn't tell whether he was wincing or just tired. But without even sitting down, Art took her gently by the hand and led her out the door to the car parked in front.

"Where are we going?" Marcia asked.

He smiled. "To the Singer store. I'm going to buy you a sewing machine."

The estrangement following Marcia's return of Art's A-pin had lasted about four months. After he persuaded her to get back together with him, she had resumed the lot of the drag, once again shuttling to the academy for the limited pleasures of a hamburger at the Weapons Room and Saturday night in a Thayer dormitory room with four other girls and their roaring hair dryers.

In 1965, Marcia had graduated from St. John's and begun teaching second grade at P.S. 127 in the docks of Brooklyn's tough Red Hook section. By the second semester of Art's final year, they began to get serious. With his own graduation looming — and a tour in Vietnam ever more apparent — Art was eager to make their relationship permanent. He proposed and she quickly accepted.

The implications of her role as an Army spouse first became clear to Marcia during June Week at West Point, when she was invited to a midmorning coffee at Quarters 5749 for a "chat about Army life." The hostess, an officer's wife named Madge E. Fleeger, offered the ladies a four-page handout full of cheerful advice:

> You are about to become a Service Wife. It takes a bride quite a while to wade through her new cookbooks and I hope this will get you off to a good start at your first station.
>
> Perhaps you have learned to cook at home or have studied Home Ec at school. This is wonderful, but the first thing you will discover is that Mother's recipes are much too generous for two portions. There are some good books out on cooking for two and they will be well worth the price while you are waiting for your family to expand.
>
> Next, you should check on the altitude of your new post. Our first assignment was Fort Carson, Colorado, and it takes forever for potatoes to boil there.

Mrs. Fleeger went on to warn against cooking large roasts or hams "unless you know how to use the leftovers." The new bride, she added, should shop with a list, compare prices of meats, and always purchase staples and milk products at the post commissary, where prices were lower than in civilian stores.

Marcia was sure this was very useful information, but at the time she technically was not yet "about to become a Service Wife." Although she had agreed to Art's marriage proposal, she also insisted that he secure her father's permission. After graduation, on the evening of June 8, Art had followed the McGuires back to Brooklyn in his new Mustang, the only sporty car that would accommodate his gangly frame. Holding his commission in one hand and diploma tube in the other, he confronted Peter McGuire in the living room and asked for Marcia's hand. Art was made even more jittery by the knowledge that the McGuires were wary of him as a non-Catholic; his Jesuit education notwithstanding, Art was Lutheran.

Now the issue came to a head. "I didn't know you were really serious about getting married," Peter replied at last. "I can't say anything. You are not a Catholic and I don't think I can tell you yes or no. I think you'd better call Father Mike and see what his reaction is."

When the women were summoned and told of this impasse, Marcia nearly exploded with exasperation. What did it matter if he wasn't Catholic? Did that make him unworthy?

"This is a good man," she fumed. "Is the Catholic Church going to tell me I can't marry him?"

"I don't know," her father shrugged. "Ask Father Mike."

Marcia immediately called St. Xavier's and reached the priest, who seemed amused. "What's the matter with this guy, is he deformed or something?" he asked. "How long have you known him?"

"Three and a half years," Marcia said. "I think my father thought he'd graduate and just go away. He says he doesn't know what to do."

"He could say yes," the priest answered. "Is he out of his mind?"

With Father Mike's blessing secured, Peter McGuire relented. Art gave Marcia a West Point miniature ring for an engagement ring, puckishly hiding it in the bottom of a White Castle hamburger bag one night. They were married a few months later, but not before another brief religious schism. Art's mother, Thelma, grew irritated at the incessant Catholic demands for proof that her son had never been married.

"That's it, Arthur," she finally declared, after mailing off yet another batch of documents. "If they won't take our word for it, that's too bad."

The Church was finally satisfied. Joe Calek, Art's classmate and fellow Nebraskan, served as best man. Four cadets from the class of '67 drove down from the academy to hold their sabers like a stainless steel canopy over the newlyweds as they emerged from the church. After the reception on Governor's Island, Lieutenant and Mrs. Bonifas were ferried to Manhattan for a wedding night at the Plaza Hotel.

Art had been assigned to a unit in Germany, but after washing out of Ranger 2 — he, too, had flunked his last patrol — he was given new orders and was sent to the 2nd Battalion of the 10th Artillery at Fort Benning in late 1966. When he and his bride drove onto the post, Art stopped at the commissary. Marcia didn't have a military ID card yet, so he had to go in by himself.

"What do you want me to get?" he asked, climbing out of the Mustang.

"Gee, I don't know," she said. "How about TV Dinners?"

Well, it was a start. Like Fort Riley, Benning bustled with soldiers preparing for war. The 1st Cavalry had deployed to Vietnam in the middle of 1965, but thousands of "ninety-day wonders" were being transformed into second lieutenants at Officer Candidate School. The adjacent town of Columbus, Marcia soon discovered, offered few attractions other than a surfeit of liquor stores, tattoo parlors, and taverns catering to drunk GIs. Pawnshops and used car lots bracketed Victory Drive, the former decorated with neon and the latter with colorful spinning pinwheels.

As Columbus was an archetype of all Army towns, so the post had something universally military about it: the vast parade ground, the stucco senior officers' quarters, the red-roofed Officers Club. Next to the Infantry School stood several red-and-white paratrooper towers — each twenty-five stories tall — where a generation of jumpers had been slowly winched to the top with their chutes and their fears before sifting gently to earth.

Even with Madge Fleeger's chipper tutoring, Marcia felt unprepared for Army life. The protocol was so rigid and elaborate. Social position had nothing to do with financial assets or pedigree, as in the civilian world; instead, everything depended on rank. Even neighborhoods were carefully segregated by rank, as eggs were sorted by size.

Military etiquette was particularly daunting. The cocktail hour before a dinner party was supposed to last precisely forty minutes. Two car lengths were to be left vacant at the entrance to a party, one for the senior officer invited and the other for arriving and departing guests. Coffees were preferably held at ten, brunches at eleven-thirty, teas between three and five-thirty.

Children learned at an early age to stop play and stand at attention when a bugler blew retreat at five P.M. By tradition, officers neither carried umbrellas nor hung clothes on the line to dry. Marcia was to refer to her husband as Lieutenant Bonifas when speaking to social inferiors, but never as "the lieutenant." She could call him Art when speaking to other wives, but that was not an invitation for those of lower rank to do the same.

The Army, it was said, had a unique gift for turning pleasure into duty. Attendance at the battalion commander's New Year's Day reception was mandatory. In the Army, the concept of "fashionably late" did not exist: guests were early, on time, or tardy.

"This is a bunch of garbage," Art muttered as they converged on the colonel's door with a dozen other couples for one such party. "But let's do it and get it over with so I don't get in trouble."

Calling cards were attended by their own ritual. The cards, usually ordered from Tiffany in New York or Bailey, Banks and Biddle in Philadelphia, measured three and a quarter by one and a half inches, with shaded Roman lettering. An officer left one card for each adult member and each house guest of the family visited; his wife left one card for each adult woman older than eighteen, since she was *never* calling on a man. Neither caller, however, was to leave more than three. It was also improper for a wife to use her own name on a card; she was known by her husband's name, as in Mrs. Arthur Bonifas. Silver trays used to hold the cards also were either right or very wrong; for example, it was improper, as Marcia discovered the hard way, to use a tray engraved with initials.

Much of this etiquette was a legacy of the hat-and-glove Army that had existed before Pearl Harbor. Small and isolated from mainstream America, the prewar officer corps had resembled a gentlemen's club, in which order was preserved through routine, ritual, and hierarchy. Now, in a larger and more egalitarian Army, those rituals were gradually eroding — much to the dismay of many senior officers. But in 1967, military posts continued to resemble company towns, and many Old Army proprieties persisted, especially in a place as genteel as Fort Benning, which had once been a cotton plantation.

Perhaps paramount among the relics was the role of an officer's wife. "An officer's success," an Old Army adage declared, "depends on his ability, his conduct, and his wife." Along the same lines, a passage in the 1967 edition of *The Officer's Guide* noted that "a wife's attitude and conduct within the military or civilian community in which the officer performs his duty may have a profound bearing upon his effectiveness."

A boorish wife might not sink her husband's career, nor a charmer guarantee him general's stars. But in either case she could undoubtedly be a factor. Patton's wife had helped him translate French cavalry texts into English, enhancing his reputation as a fighter who could also think. George Marshall had a system worked out with his wife, Katherine, in which he would mutter "China" or "flowers" in a receiving line at Benning before the war, which allowed her to flatter the next guest by saying, "You served with Colonel Marshall in China, didn't you?" or, "Thank you for your lovely flowers."

Marcia was game. She drove to a hat outlet near La Grange to buy herself the required flowered bonnet. Once a month, she attended the Officers Wives Club luncheons, where spouses in each unit rotated responsibilities for making centerpieces or buying door prizes. She took her turn as a volunteer at the thrift shop, marking clothes in the morning, sitting by the cash register in the afternoon, and keeping an eye out for bargains all day.

Occasionally the ladies would be stymied by some conundrum of etiquette, as when the battalion commander's wife sponsored a luncheon at her house and no one knew whether hats were appropriate. (They were not, as it turned out.) As living quarters were sorted like eggs, so tacitly were wives. Reflecting their husbands, they were Regular or Reserve, off post or on post, retired or active, company grade (lieutenants and captains) or field grade (majors, lieutenant colonels, and colonels). A few believed that two additional categories existed: West Point and other.

There was no dearth of examples of how *not* to act. On one occasion, after the executive officer's young wife encouraged the junior officers to call her Sandra, several lieutenants impertinently called her husband, who was a major, by his Christian name. The major summoned his battery commanders for a tongue lashing: "You can call my wife by her first name, but don't you ever dare let any of your men call me by my first name again."

Discretion remained an abiding principle of the social code. Opinions, like emotions, were best muffled. The upper lip should remain stiff — and buttoned. Art and Marcia saw a clear demonstration of the importance of decorum at a party one weekend when the subject of the war came up. The discussion grew heated, with some of the lieutenants' wives openly disparaging a senior officer who had volunteered for a second tour in Vietnam.

"There's no way *my* husband is going to fight in that war," one wife declared. Once again there was a brief squall as the battalion commander upbraided his subordinates and ordered them to keep their wives discreet.

To gossip was human; to slander meant trouble. In such a crowded nest, vilifying another officer or his wife — especially a superior — inevitably caused a stink. Soldiers and their spouses were expected to observe yet another dictum: "All the brothers are valiant; all the sisters are virtuous."

Mrs. Arthur Bonifas tried to steer clear of those dangers. The Army's caste system bothered her, especially the social segregation between officers and enlisted. (She threw a party one Sunday afternoon for the NCOs from Art's battery and their wives. The gesture was considered unusual.) She also was annoyed by the imperiousness of some of the older officers' wives, like the Mrs. Major who often issued orders in the name of her husband.

But for the most part she tried to conform. All in all, Marcia liked Army life. The service did attract the valiant and virtuous in most cases. Despite the Army's talent for turning pleasure into duty, sometimes pleasure remained pleasant. The Bonifases' circle of friends steadily expanded.

For their first dinner party, Marcia cooked beef Stroganoff — the dish was not much more successful than the curtains had been — and nearly set the house ablaze while trying to flame bananas Foster for a recipe she had picked up during a visit to New Orleans. Despite the setbacks, everyone seemed to have a good time.

There was something bonding in sharing the lot of the other lieutenants, earning the same measly pay, living in the same cramped quarters, working the same long hours. The bonds between Art and his West Point classmates stationed at Benning seemed to strengthen, too. The private language of West Point was quickly supplanted by Army argot. Yet the common experience of the academy provided a fraternity within the larger brotherhood of the officer corps.

On Friday nights, the Bonifases often went to the Officers Club, which offered an inexpensive seafood buffet; on Sundays after church they indulged in brunch at the post golf course. And once a month, the battalion threw a hail-and-farewell party to greet newcomers and say goodbye to those who were leaving.

Also once a month, the club offered free drinks. Liquor companies provided Scotch, bourbon, vodka, or gin on a rotating basis. Drinking among the officers was as obligatory as hats for the wives. Units often held a "stand-to" on Friday night after work, when the men gathered at the club for twenty-five-cent drinks and shop talk. Although public inebriation was considered impolitic, the Army was an incubator for drunks. (A government study found that one in five officers was either an alcoholic — defined as a man imbibing at least five drinks a day, four days a week — or a binge drinker — a man periodically intoxicated for more than a day at a time.)

Military medicine also required getting used to, as Marcia discovered when she became pregnant in the spring of 1967. The monthly visits to Martin Army Hospital resembled cattle calls. Hundreds of women, many with bawling children, milled about in the waiting room for hours. Marcia never saw the same doctor twice. (When the baby, a daughter they named Beth, was finally born, Marcia's obstetrician was a stranger, the thirteenth doctor she had seen during her pregnancy.) Calls to the hospital exclusive of regular visits were discouraged unless the patient was moribund. The care was competent and free, but very abrupt. No one, however, dreamed of going to a civilian doctor. None could afford it for one thing; moreover, that would have meant rocking the boat.

Marcia was not a boat rocker. Yes, Fort Benning was a company town, she conceded, but it also was a family. And like most of the young wives, she was desperate not to do anything that would embarrass her husband. Every action had to be calculated with that in mind. She understood the adage about an officer's success depending in part on his wife. She understood the meaning of decorum.

Art knew that he was lucky. Having a wife like Marcia, who was a good sport with a terrific sense of humor, surely made life easier. It was important that she like the Army, because he was discovering that he loved it. He could think of nothing he would rather do for the next twenty or thirty years than be an artillery officer.

His career had started inauspiciously with the washout in Ranger 2. Those arduous nine weeks had reduced him from slender to skeletal. Because he was tall, Art often got saddled with the machine gun. Also, some of the lane graders seemed determined to take the West Pointers down a peg. "You have no rank!" the lane graders would yell. "Forget that you have rank. You are a Ranger."

But Art was not a Ranger, and that was something the artillery branch would not let him forget. Artillerymen who washed out received a truculent letter from their branch:

> Your failure to complete this important training reflects unfavorably on you as a Regular Army officer, and has the immediate effect of placing you behind your contemporaries in the competition for promotion, service schools, and subsequent assignments to positions of greater responsibility . . . Without self-improvement, your chances for a successful career in the Army are limited.

The letter had all the subtlety of a slap in the face. But Art had no intention of letting the threat just lie there. He requested another crack at Ranger after finishing his year at Benning; determined to prove himself, he would endure the whole miserable nine weeks all over again.

In the meantime, Art intended to become the best redleg he could. He had joined the 2nd Battalion of the 10th Artillery as a forward observer, became a battery executive officer, and finally was the commander of a battery with six howitzers. Some military historians believed that the American artillery, first founded by portly Henry Knox during the Revolution, had consistently been the most exemplary combat branch in the Army. In World War II and again in Korea, the artillery had been outstanding in its ability to respond quickly with massed firepower.

Art was proud of that heritage, but he knew little else about the artillery. The Army in its wisdom — and its appetite for lieutenants in the war zone — had excused the men of '66 from the basic branch courses in which young officers usually learned the rudiments of their craft. For infantrymen, bypassing the basic course was not much of a loss; Ranger helped to fill the breach. But it meant that the new lieutenants in more technical branches — especially artillerymen, tankers, and engineers — arrived at their first assignments fundamentally ignorant and consigned to what the Army called OJT: on-the-job training.

Art therefore relied on the more experienced officers and noncoms for instruction. He found a great deal to master, from such simple facts as the "kill radius" of a 105mm shell — thirty-five meters from the point of detonation — to the complexities of coordinating air and artillery strikes. Accuracy was determined by more than a dozen factors, including wind direction and speed at various altitudes (sometimes gauged with balloons); powder temperature (a round had less explosive force if it was cold); air temperature (the projectile would travel farther when it was warm and the air less dense); and even the rotation of the earth.

Calculations for elevation — the angle of the tubes — and deflection — the direction, or azimuth, of the tubes — were still performed manually with slide rules, logarithm tables, and firing charts. Over time, Art learned how to coordinate with the forward observer and how to establish blocking fires to prevent an enemy from escaping or being reinforced.

Like his classmates, he also was learning how to command other men — how to motivate them and how to deal with their fears and frustrations. Sometimes the best techniques were strictly instinctive. Art's classmate and fellow redleg Rance Farrell had recently used an unorthodox approach with his battery. When his men were weary and dejected from tedious preparations for going on maneuvers, Farrell gathered them together.

"I know you're tired and I know you're afraid we're going to get the sleeping bags wet and dirty," he said. "I guarantee you we'll get them clean. I don't know how, but we will. Okay, now I want you to repeat after me: Fuck!"

The men looked at each other quizzically.

"C'mon," Farrell repeated. "Fuck!"

"Fuck!" they answered.

"Louder!"

"FUCK!"

"Good. Now say: You."

"YOU!"

"Put it together!"

"FUCK YOU!"

"My shoulders are broad. I can take it."

Everyone laughed, breaking the tension.

Benning also required adjustments in moving from the idealized world of West Point into the real one of the Army. A cadet did not lie, cheat, steal, or tolerate such behavior in others. But the Army of 1967 engaged in a great deal of fibbing, especially about readiness. Each unit periodically reported its fitness for combat, and for those who were not C1 — ready to fight — there could be hell to pay, even if the reasons were beyond the commander's control. Depending on the unit and the tolerance of superior officers, an honest readiness report could sink an officer on his OER — Officer Efficiency Report.

As a result, mendacity pervaded many battalions, and officers often played mental shell games with themselves: "I know that truck's broken," they would rationalize, "but if I took the distributor off another truck and put it on this truck, it might be salvageable." For some West Pointers, the dilemma was painful, especially since no one — from buck sergeant to major general — seemed to question the practice. Like most moral quandaries, this one had to be resolved by each man according to his conscience.

Art figured it was all part of his apprenticeship. No one had ever promised that the craft of command would be simple. His hours were brutal, often stretching from dark to dark. Weekends never began earlier than 1400 hours — two P.M. — on Saturday. Sometimes holidays simply vanished beneath the welter of duty.

He and Marcia could expect to move at least once a year for the first three years, and once every two or three years after that. Of course, given their quarters on Lloyd Way, Art figured that was not all bad. Again, it helped to have a wife who took things in stride.

Sometimes on Sundays after church the two of them drove slowly around the post just to admire the more spacious quarters occupied by captains and majors and colonels.

"It's only going to get better," Marcia said once as they passed the attractive stucco houses of the field grade officers.

"Yeah," Art agreed, "it's only going to get better."

Not all of the new lieutenants' wives adjusted as gracefully as Marcia. Maxwell Taylor had once said that the Army, like the Church, was not for everyone. That undoubtedly had a distaff corollary: the Army wasn't for every wife.

Claudia Smith despised it. Ten days after the class of '66 graduated, Claudia had married Art's classmate Jeffrey H. Smith. The Smiths lived briefly at Benning before moving overseas to Schweinfurt — which was usually translated as Pig Crossing — in West Germany.

Claudia had grown up in Milwaukee, the daughter of a distinguished engineer who, like Peter McGuire, had worked on the Manhattan Project. Jeff was a tall, quiet Midwesterner from Clarinda, Iowa, the home town of Glenn Miller. Jeff's father had been one of Patton's battalion operations officers in World War II and won two Silver Stars as he fought his way from Normandy to Prague.

At West Point, Jeff threw the discus on the track team and roomed with a rangy, poetry-writing boxer named John Thomas Hoskins. Jeff would smuggle Taylor's New York State Burgundy into the barracks for them to sip while Hos read Stephen Crane's poetry aloud with wonderful feeling:

> Hoarse, booming drums of the regiment,
> Little souls who thirst for fight,
> These men were born to drill and die.

Jeff and Claudia met in the summer of 1961 in the lobby of Montreal's Queens Hotel. She was buying postcards at the cigar stand when he introduced himself. They discovered that they were both on their way to Scandinavia as exchange students. She was pinned to an older student at Northwestern University; Jeff thought of himself as a small-town rustic who didn't stand a chance with this vivacious, cosmopolitan young woman. The next summer, when he went to West Point and she went to Evanston, Claudia's sister told her, "It's really a shame. You look good together, but it will never work with him going so far away."

It almost didn't work. Arriving for her first visit during plebe Christmas, with a suitcase full of dresses and matching shoes, Claudia stepped off the bus at the Thayer and glanced around. The post was cold, gray, and dismal. This is awful, she thought to herself; this is like prison.

Her attitude never changed. She hated West Point, hated its rules, hated the way it made her feel like an interloper, hated sneaking about in the poison ivy for a little privacy, hated it most of all because it held Jeff. In Evanston, and later in Madison after transferring to the University of Wisconsin, she felt like the denizen of a very large world while his world was very, very small. In later years, whenever they returned to the academy for a visit, she felt smug, silently taunting the place as they drove through Thayer Gate: *Hah! I won! I've got him!*

Her hostility inevitably influenced Jeff. He had arrived at the academy full of JFK idealism, bent on becoming a Green Beret and rolling back the tide of communism in the Third World. Any young man worth his salt, he believed, wanted to be on freedom's team. When he visited Claudia at Northwestern for the first time, she was in the throes of the standard freshman identity crisis.

"Don't you just wonder who you are?" she asked him.

"No," he replied firmly. "I know who I am. I'm Jeff."

As time passed, however, some of his certainty ebbed. Sitting on the porch of her family's summer cottage in Wisconsin, he pondered resignation. But the thought of never again seeing Hoskins and his other classmates drew him back to the highlands. Even so, the ambivalence persisted: Jeff was among the few '66ers who seriously questioned the wisdom of the war, yet he also kept a framed copy of MacArthur's valedictory speech hanging on his wall.

After Jeff's graduation, Claudia transposed her dislike of the academy to the Army. Shortly before their wedding, someone gave her a copy of *The Officer's Wife;* she was horrified by what she read of calling cards and protocol and what was expected of her. The consequences of surrendering her career for the nomadism of an Army wife had not really dawned on her until late winter of her senior year, when she took a bus to Chicago with a group of other Wisconsin journalism students. Some of her friends were interviewing for jobs in the city. Together, they visited several older graduates who were already working. What an exciting life, she thought: living on the Near North Side, beginning a new career, blossoming as an adult. And then the realization struck her: I won't have this. I'm going to miss it.

Jeff gave Claudia a West Point miniature for an engagement ring, but she kept her wedding ring separate rather than having it soldered to the miniature, as some wives did. The idea of fusing the two, of bending the wedding band to fit the West Point gold, offended her. She had never thought of her engagement in terms of marrying the Army. She was marrying Jeff.

But being an Army wife, she soon discovered, was not that simple. At Benning one day, Claudia opened a letter from a dear college friend, Lynn, who wrote a diatribe against the war and those who fought it. "How can Jeff defend his line of work, i.e., killing?" Lynn demanded. Claudia was shocked. She knew Lynn opposed the war — that was hardly unusual at Madison, where antiwar sentiment had grown increasingly bitter. But this was absurd. Lynn was writing about Jeff, gentle Jeffrey, not someone with fangs. How could she ignore the human being beneath the uniform? How could she be so dogmatic? It had never occurred to Claudia that anyone could accuse her husband of being a killer.

She sent Lynn a bitter, caustic reply. "Come off it," she wrote, "these are *people* in the Army. You know Jeffrey. How can you say such things?" The exchange ended their friendship, but the pain lingered for many years.

In Schweinfurt, Claudia tried to play by the rules. She wore gloves and a hat and became secretary of the Officers Wives Club. The Army wife, according to *The Officer's Guide,* "is equally at home in a cabin or a mansion, a fine hotel, a transport. She is a good mother and rears her family, generally, under conditions which would seem impossible to her civilian sisters . . . Her sense of duty, honor, and country are those of the Army itself."

But Claudia, hard as she tried, could not accept the strictures. She began to think of Schweinfurt as she had West Point: a sad prison, a little cell without horizons. Once she was at a wives' club meeting when the battalion commander's wife walked in. Behind her back, another woman gestured to the women to stand. Claudia was appalled. Standing up for an elderly woman or someone particularly distinguished was one thing, but standing up for Mrs. Lieutenant Colonel was preposterous. Some of these women will go peacefully into this world, she thought, but I will go kicking and screaming.

As her alienation from the Army intensified, she clutched harder at Jeff. She thought of herself as locked in a struggle for him. The Army could send him wherever they wanted whenever they wanted. They could put him in harm's way at whim. They could rip you around, and you didn't have a damned thing to say about it. When he left for days or weeks at a time on exercises, Claudia was devastated. Always an extrovert, she hated being alone in the Schweinfurt apartment; the newspapers were full of news about Richard Speck, the madman who had murdered all those student nurses in Chicago.

Skewered by his absences, she felt a side of her emerging that she knew wasn't particularly appealing. Where was her self-sufficiency, her self-respect? Once, when he was leaving for a month, she followed him out the door like a shadow, pleading in a small, glum voice, "Don't go. Do we really have to do this?"

She envied the wives who seemed so plucky and contained, who gave their husbands a peck on the forehead and a pat on the cheek with a cheerful "Darlin', you just go and take good care of yourself." How do they do that? she wondered. What price did they pay, those wives who were left alone for weeks, months, years over the course of a marriage?

The Army does not begin to appreciate these women, Claudia thought. The military was a man's world, and women were just so much baggage. Those who thrived did so despite the Army, bolstered by their own strength and an unflagging love for their men. She wished that she could be more like them. She loved Jeff, no doubt about that. Why else would she be wearing white gloves and standing for some Mrs. Colonel in a place called Pig Crossing? But that inner peace . . . too bad *that* was not government issue, like helmets and rifles and the other things that protected you from harm.

In late October of 1966, nearly five months after his classmates had scattered from Michie Stadium with their diplomas and lieutenants' bars,

Tom Carhart returned to West Point for further medical evaluation. Tom's facial injuries had healed, leaving a cluster of scars, but the damage to his brain had proved more intractable. He too was searching for an elusive inner peace.

The academy seemed all too familiar. Plebes braced, terrorized by the yearlings and cows, while first classmen counted the days until June Week. Autumn tinted the surrounding hills, where the fading brilliance of the maple leaves signaled the impending arrival of yet another Gloom Period. From Trophy Point, Tom again admired the vista of the Hudson gorge between Storm King Mountain and Breakneck Ridge; as a cadet, he sometimes used to sit by himself on this spot, staring at the molten river and daydreaming of the glory yet to come. Now those moments of happy reverie seemed long ago, almost as distant in the past as glory was distant in the future.

A few weeks after graduation, Tom had been discharged from the hospital to fly to Yokota, Japan, to recuperate with his parents. He spent the rest of the summer slowly regaining his physical health and trying to brush away the fog that shrouded his mind. During the first two weeks of September, he underwent intensive psychiatric evaluations at the Air Force hospital at Tachikawa. Tom assured the doctors that he was no longer suffering from the confusion, headaches, and memory loss that had plagued him in the weeks immediately after the accident. He asked that the Army commission him. As one psychiatrist wrote in Tom's medical file, "He is extremely anxious to receive his commission and proceed with his military career. His motivation for military service is truly remarkable."

Another psychiatrist noted that Tom had handled the battery of psychological tests "amazingly well. The examiner was impressed by the lofty levels of patient's ambitions and by his extremely positive self-image. It appeared that there was some inflation of his self-image and ego-ideal, but it was obvious that this trend was present long before the patient's brain injury and has in no way been altered by this injury. There is no psychiatric contraindication to entry upon active duty."

In truth, Tom was shamming. Not the eagerness for duty — that was desperately sincere. But secretly he felt confused and adrift. His short-term memory remained riddled with holes. Emotionally, he was wobbly and volatile.

As his mind gradually cleared — in September his IQ was 120, compared with 108 in June after the accident — Tom grew ever more frustrated by the realization that he had been left behind by his classmates. They were headed for the great adventure of war, marching toward the sound of the guns, as all true warriors must. He was a captive in his golden cage in Japan. Yokota was pleasant and interesting enough — especially given his father's status as the base commander — but every day squandered in Japan meant sinking a little further from his classmates' orbit.

He knew that the old Tom had wanted to be an airborne Ranger — a commie-killing, snake-eating infantryman. The best plan now, he believed, was to stick to that scheme: go to war, serve the nation, be a hero, aim high for a general's stars. His only hope of catching up to Buck Thompson, George Crocker, and the others was to convince the doctors and the Army that he was healthy. At Yokota, he went to the library and studied medical texts on head injuries and behavioral psychology, looking for tips on how to act and feel normal.

The charade was difficult to sustain. One day in September, he strolled down the flight line at Yokota, trying to bluff his way onto a transport plane back to the States. He wanted to see Melissa — to recapture her affections — and then persuade the academy to commission him.

The airmen called Colonel Carhart. Tom's father showed up, also feigning nonchalance. He discreetly delegated several fighter pilots to lure Tom to the club for some camaraderie and a casual drink. But later, when Tom arrived home, the tensions exploded into an argument. It ended with his father in tears as Tom stormed from the house, slamming the door so violently that he broke a window. Stalking to the back yard, he cocked his fist and threw a haymaker at a tree trunk. The white streak of pain jolted the rage out of him.

That kind of behavior, obviously, would never do. He calmed himself and tried to be patient. This is going to take a little time, he told himself. Tom's outburst notwithstanding, Colonel Carhart minimized the tree-punching episode and assured the doctors that his son was making admirable progress. "The colonel has observed," one psychiatrist wrote, "that the patient is again extremely bright. . . . He reports that Thomas has been uncomfortable in his ambiguous convalescent state, but that Thomas has tolerated this frustration amazingly well, without resorting to any form of immature or antisocial acting-out of feelings."

His recovery seemed sufficiently steady for the physicians in Japan to approve Tom's return to West Point. Now, working part time in the Office of Military Instruction and running several miles every day to get in shape, he set out to prove to the academy that he was ready for duty. He also talked to an Army lawyer and a civilian attorney his father knew; Tom's insurance company was pressing him to seek restitution from Bob Albright for the injuries suffered in the wreck. Tom had misgivings about squeezing a close friend and classmate, even if the true target was an insurance firm. What, he wondered, was proper conduct in a case like this? He wasn't certain. But, reluctantly, Tom became a plaintiff in a negligence suit against Albright. The lawsuit, filed in White Plains, demanded $400,000.

Les Bennett, Tom's former tactical officer from E-2, watched him carefully. Bennett detected no trace of the scamp who had stolen the Navy goat. Impressed by Tom's courage and eagerness to recapture what had nearly been lost, Bennett recommended that he be commissioned. A cadet from the class of 1967 who had lived in E-2 with Tom also vouched for him in a letter to the authorities written on November 8: "It is quite apparent to all of us who knew him well that he is considerably more level-headed than he appeared before his accident. He appears just as lucid, if not more so, than before."

The doctors agreed. A neurologist at Walter Reed Army Hospital in Washington stated on November 9 that Tom was "completely free of neurological defects and fit for duty with no limitation." On December 13, he received his lieutenant's bars. The Army backdated the commission to June 8.

Tom's jubilation was tempered by a sense of unease. Although physically strong and strapping, he continued to feel adrift, unable to moor himself. Once he had floated through the world; now he trudged. He felt, as he later confided to a friend, as though he were "groping, grasping for reality."

From West Point, Tom reported to Benning for airborne training. Three weeks later, after successfully completing his five jumps and earning his paratrooper's wings, he walked into a Georgia pawnshop and paid $800 for an eighty-two-point diamond. He had the stone set in an engagement ring, flew out west, and offered it to Melissa. She accepted the ring, but after two awkward days, during which they tried to rekindle the flame that had once blazed between them, she handed it back. "I can't take this from you now," she said firmly. He pleaded his case but she was adamant. "Maybe later," she told him. "But not now."

Despondent and bitter, Tom returned to Benning for Ranger training in January 1967. Perhaps, he told himself, if he was persistent enough — if he could demonstrate that the old Tom she had once loved was back, body and soul — she would change her mind. Now, he tried to concentrate on becoming a good soldier. Most of his classmates had already finished Ranger — the first wave of men from '66 was just arriving in Vietnam — but Tom felt that at least he was back in the race.

At Harmony Church, Ranger began well enough. He handled the first phase at Benning without much trouble, showing particular ferocity at hand-to-hand combat in the sawdust pits. The mountain phase in north Georgia proved more difficult. The weather turned miserably cold, and he flunked his first two patrols. On several occasions he found himself crying, feeling sorry for himself in a way that would have disgusted the old Tom. Nevertheless, on arriving in Florida for Charlie Beckwith's jungle training, he stayed in the running for a tab. Just hang in there, he told himself; just buy a little time. Then, in late February, with less than a week to go, something happened that made him wonder whether he was star-crossed.

One night, while Tom was dozing in the swamp, an insect bit him on the face. He awoke feeling lightheaded. Within seconds, his eyelid swelled shut. When he tried to stand and hoist his rucksack, he collapsed and went into shock. The patrol leader radioed for help. By the time a jeep arrived and rushed him to Eglin Air Force Base, twenty miles away, Tom's pulse was very faint. Doctors in the emergency room revived the young lieutenant and admitted him to the hospital.

At first he felt relieved to be out of the swamp, away from the stress and the lane graders. But within two days, he understood the implications. Not only would he forfeit the coveted Ranger tab, but he might well be "profiled" — medically restricted from combat. The sting revealed an Achilles heel that he had kept hidden for years: he was severely allergic to certain kinds of insect venom.

Twice before he had suffered serious reactions. The first time, as a high school junior in Arlington, Virginia, Tom was painting gutters on the back of a neighbor's house when a hornet stung him on the right wrist. The welt hurt furiously and he went inside. As the neighbor rubbed the sting with raw onion, she suddenly exclaimed, "Tommy, you're getting hives!" She helped Tom into the back of her car. During the three-minute drive to the doctor's office, he began to hallucinate. He believed he was a three-year-old thrashing to the surface of a swimming pool.

Struggling up the stairs to the doctor's office, Tom had fainted and tumbled over backward. The doctor dragged the boy up by the wrists and laid him on the floor. Tom had the sensation of leaving his body; from across the room, he watched as the doctor grabbed a syringe and a vial, straddling the unconscious figure on the floor. The doctor paused to skim the instruction leaflet, which had a brown band across the top, like a letterhead. Isn't that funny? Tom thought, watching the drama. Dr. Bill has to read the directions.

The doctor filled the syringe and injected Tom. The next thing Tom knew, he was back in his body. He opened his eyes. The instruction leaflet — with its brown border — lay next to his head.

"I saw that from across the room," he told the neighbor thickly.

"Tommy, you almost died," she replied. "Your mind is playing tricks on you."

The allergy kept him out of the Air Force Academy, but West Point had granted a waiver. Then, at the end of Beast Barracks, he had been stung again during a hike. Again he was rushed to the hospital, although the reaction was less severe this time. For the next four years, he reported periodically to the cadet hospital for anti-allergy shots. During his final year he had pleaded with the Army doctor — a woman major — not to profile him.

"Look, Major, I really want to do the airborne Ranger Vietnam bit," he said. "You can screw me over or you can give me a break and keep it off my records. *Please.*"

Reluctantly, she had agreed. Now, lying in the hospital room in the Florida panhandle, he could not decide what to do next. What he really wanted was just to get away from all this, to find a safe place to hide. I want to go home, he told himself. But one drawback to being a military brat was that he had no home. He had already tried Yokota, and although he loved being with his family, he knew that he needed to push through this trouble on his own. He thought again of Crocker and Buck, his brothers, going to the sound of the guns without him. No, he thought, it's best to stick with the plan, as the old Tom would have done.

With a campaign of pleas and demands, he persuaded the Army to send him to Walter Reed for an evaluation. For a week Tom lived in the visiting officers' quarters near Georgia Avenue in Northwest Washington. Doctors stuck him with needles, studied his blood, and summoned him before two boards of examining physicians. When the week was up, they sent him back to Ranger to try again.

He struggled through the mountains, doing better this time, but when he arrived in Florida his luck turned bad once more. Beckwith was skeptical about Tom's having actually been stung, despite the undeniable fact that his head had swelled like a watermelon. Hell, Tom thought, I don't have to be out here again. It's not as if I enjoy this punishment.

One night he was walking point about a hundred meters in front of the rest of the patrol. As ordered, he followed a compass azimuth, but for some reason the patrol changed tactics and began contour patrolling, following the topography of a hill. When Tom doubled back, the other Rangers were gone. Damn, he thought, now what?

Standard procedure required Tom to find the nearest road, but he had no idea where that was. For more than an hour he crashed through the dark brush before stumbling onto a dirt track. He followed it until he came to a house, where he telephoned the Ranger headquarters.

In the meantime, a search had been launched. The patrol had been near a bombing range at Eglin, and when Tom was reported missing, the Air Force grounded its bombers and suspended air operations over the range. Search helicopters dropped flares in a hunt for the missing

Ranger. Beckwith was enraged. After Tom called, the cadre picked him up in a jeep. They drove for a few minutes before stopping.

"Out," the lane grader commanded. He unfolded a map and pointed to a road slicing through the swamp.

"You're here," he told Tom tersely. "There's this federal prison camp over here. It's seventeen miles away. Be there by dawn."

The jeep sped off, dust boiling in its wake. Tom knew that he was in for a long night, his own private death march. There would be no Ranger tab; that much was clear. But if nothing else, he was determined to salvage a small victory by reaching the camp before sunup. Angry, hungry, and humiliated, he shouldered his rifle and began tramping down the deserted road.

On the wall in one of the West Point hospital wards hung a brass plaque noting that Technical Sergeant Martin Maher had spent his last days in an adjacent bed before dying on January 17, 1961, at the age of eighty-four.

Marty Maher was one of the animating spirits of the Military Academy. Born in Ballyrine, Ireland, in 1876, he had immigrated to America at the age of twenty and landed a job as a civilian waiter at West Point. Two years and countless broken dishes later, he enlisted in the Army and in time became the academy's most revered physical education instructor. For more than half a century, Maher taught the manly arts to cadets, including men who became the great battle captains of the twentieth century.

Jack Wheeler studied the plaque for hours on end. He had little else to do, since he was immobilized in traction. At Fort Benning, during paratrooper training in the fall of 1966, Jack had ripped the cartilage in one knee. Rather than going on sick call and repeating the three-week course, he had hobbled through with the knee bound in an Ace bandage, nibbling bootlegged Darvon.

"Stand up!" the jumpmaster would yell. Suddenly Jack would be in the door of the C-123, ready to leap toward eternity. Looking down was considered sloppy; it could cause a paratrooper to tumble and tangle his risers. The proper procedure in jumping was to stare at the horizon, not at the true destination. After his final jump, Jack drove to West Point and checked into the hospital, where he soon lay with his leg hoisted high in an impious salute to the Maher plaque.

Jack cherished what Marty Maher symbolized: tradition, continuity, fraternity, a West Point beloved by all. Maher was the brogue-tongued embodiment of duty, honor, country. Among other things, Maher had taught swimming, though he reputedly never entered the water, since he couldn't swim himself. Instead, he used a block and tackle to demonstrate the strokes while suspended above the pool deck. His autobiography, *Bringing Up the Brass,* was made into a popular movie in 1955, renamed *The Long Gray Line* and starring Tyrone Power as Maher and Maureen O'Hara as his wife. The movie contained one scene in which Maher marked the yearbook photos of fallen West Pointers with black ribbons. The gesture, Jack thought, was both powerful and poignant.

Lying flat on his back, Jack also spent hours thinking about Ginny Stuart and savoring the memories of the summer they had spent together before jump school. Rather than going home during his long leave after graduation, Jack had landed a job as an assistant house manager for the opening season of the new Performing Arts Center in Saratoga, New York. Ginny and the rest of the New York City Ballet opened at the arts center in July. George Balanchine, who envisioned Saratoga as an American Salzburg, seemed less than thrilled by Jack's reappearance; although he held his tongue, the master would squint critically, as if to ask, "Doesn't this soldier have a war to fight somewhere?"

But Jack tried to make himself useful. There were no clocks backstage, so he bought clocks. The Saratoga stage was particularly hard on the dancers' feet, so he bought lamb's wool at a drug store to stuff into the toes of their shoes. "Five minutes," he would call, "five minutes till *Narkissos.*" When the corps performed *Nutcracker,* in July, a spillover crowd of seven thousand sat on the sloping emerald lawns outside; Jack tacked back and forth among them before the first act, collecting dollar bills in a grocery sack. Then he watched the performance from the wings as stagehands in the rafters shoveled out bushels of fake snow, which tumbled heavily through the oppressive humidity.

One day, Jack was surprised by a visit from a West Point classmate, Matt Harrison. Like Jack, Matt had taken summer leave at Saratoga in order to be close to his girlfriend, a college student who worked as a waitress in the Saratoga Spa; Matt was employed as a dishwasher, spending eight hours a day half immersed in steamed garbage. Having lived in separate regiments at West Point, Lieutenants Harrison and Wheeler barely knew each other. But on discovering that Jack had an undemanding job with the Performing Arts Center, Matt looked him up for a heart-to-heart chat regarding a classmate's duty to take care of his comrades. Jack delivered; he got jobs for both Matt and his girlfriend as "publicists," distributing fliers throughout the area.

The month was idyllic. Saratoga seemed to Jack every bit as grand as it must have been at the turn of the century, in the glory days of Caruso and John McCormack and Diamond Jim Brady, who used to arrive at the spa with twenty-seven Japanese houseboys and Lillian Russell in tow. The gambling casinos were gone, of course, but the sulfur baths remained popular and the thoroughbreds were preparing to run in August.

Saratoga also allowed Jack and Ginny for the first time to be together for longer than a weekend; as the month passed, their love — and friendship — ripened into something richer and more mature. After rehearsals, they occasionally shopped together at the supermarket, where Ginny would dance down the aisle to the Muzak in her jeans, sneakers, and braided hair, pirouetting between the canned beans and Rice-A-Roni. They swam in Ballston Lake, and on the Fourth of July Jack rowed her to the middle of Lake Saratoga, where they lay in the boat to watch the fireworks, cushioning their heads on life preservers. Later, they squeezed into a little booth to mug for instant photos; the grainy strip of black-and-white pictures showed a tanned and handsome couple, kissing, without a care in the world.

Lying in his hospital bed beneath the Marty Maher plaque, Jack thought how delightful — and how odd — the interlude at Saratoga had been. After four years of rigorous preparation to become a soldier, his first job had been working backstage at *Nutcracker,* worrying about clocks and lamb's wool. While his classmates were steeling themselves for combat, he had distributed ponchos to keep the ballerinas dry during a sudden squall. Curiously, the only disquieting thing at Saratoga for Jack had been Matt Harrison. Here was this graceful, wonderfully wry classmate, barreling around the countryside with a stack of ballet handbills, just killing time before going to Vietnam. Matt had been a reminder — really the only reminder — that there was a war going on.

After his knee healed and he was discharged from the West Point hospital, Jack traveled to Fort Bliss, Texas, for three weeks of training as a Nike Hercules fire control platoon leader. He had been scheduled to attend Ranger 5, known as Frostbite Five. (Survivors sometimes sewed the tab on their uniforms with blue thread to commemorate the cold.) But those orders changed abruptly; Jack's Nike unit was so shorthanded that after finishing at Bliss he was directed to skip Ranger and report directly to Franklin Lakes, New Jersey.

On arriving at Missile Master Site No. 75, he found a startling contrast between the subterranean world of attack dogs and humming computers at the Nike base and the benign surface world of north Jersey, with its glens and ponds and commuter traffic. As a platoon leader, Jack was responsible for guiding the antiaircraft missiles if enemy planes suddenly appeared over New York. He and his men spent many hours practicing "intruder" drills. Without warning, the command code for battle stations would sound: "Blazing Skies!" Jack would sit with his eyes glued to the radar screen, his face bathed in its soft green glow; outside, on the hill above the fire control trailers, the oblong radar antenna swept its endless circles, scanning the Hudson Valley and northern New Jersey for enemies. A dozen white Nike missiles, named for the Greek goddess of victory, slept in their silos in the adjacent hills. Each was a graceful cylinder nearly forty feet long, capped with either a high explosive or nuclear warhead.

What is it this time? Jack would ask himself. A hundred and fifty Bears at twenty thousand feet? Not likely. That was World War II stuff, the kind of raid launched to firebomb Dresden. No, it was more probable that the enemy planes would zoom down the river gorge below radar level, swooping past Poughkeepsie and then Newburgh, rattling the stained glass in the cadet chapel, before popping up past Anthony's Nose to fling their payloads at Manhattan.

He would have just a few seconds to adjust the target-tracking radar and identify the intruders as friend or foe. The trailer contained twin safes, one for the yellow team — the officers — and one for the red team — the enlisted men. The safes held codes used to authenticate the president's war orders. On a nearby hill, the rocket jockeys in the launching platoon hoisted the Nikes until they poked above the ground like outstretched fingers. Jack would pick his warheads — conventional or nuclear — then flip up the safety cap covering the launch toggle. "Ready to fire . . . FIRE. Missile away."

In a real battle, a series of white flashes would blossom high above the earth. He once had read an account of Japanese antiaircraft gunners in Hiroshima. Staring up at the *Enola Gay,* their eyeballs had melted when the Little Boy atomic bomb detonated. Jack had a persistent image of a small child in New York with his head tilted upward, instantly blinded by a Nike Hercules airburst.

If the Americans were lucky, the Nikes would destroy the entire enemy formation. If they were not lucky, the bombers would atomize New York, including Ginny's apartment on West Seventy-second Street, twenty miles to the southeast. At least one of the Bears, he knew, would also have Missile Master Site No. 75 in Franklin Lakes as its target.

The duty was nerve-racking. Less than ten years old, Nike Hercs were already obsolescent, with their fickle vacuum tubes, a 1950s technology soon to be outdated by improvements in modern electronics. The system was only one generation removed from ack-ack guns and the Nike Ajax, a short-range missile with a puny conventional warhead. Some experts — particularly those in the Air Force, which had lost a bitter fight with the Army in the 1950s over who would man American air defense sites — expressed skepticism that the Nikes could stop anything.

Crew performance had to be flawless if there was to be any hope of parrying an attack. Sometimes B-58 Hustlers simulated enemy raids down the Hudson; on other occasions, B-52s would soar in at high altitude, using the pinnacle of the Empire State Building as ground zero and turning Jack's screen a snowy white with their radar jammers. It was depressing, he thought, to see how so many bombers managed to get through in the drills.

Nevertheless, Jack liked the work. Technical know-how and quick wits were his long suits. This job pushed him to the absolute limit of his ability to concentrate, analyze, and act. At West Point, the cadets had never really dissected the issue of killing someone, much less killing the thousands who would die if nuclear warheads ever detonated. It was always assumed that West Pointers would kill when they had to, just as it was assumed that if Jack received a proper war order, he would fire his missiles. The business of killing was somewhat like the business of getting married: when the time came, a soldier stepped forward and did it.

The best aspect of Franklin Lakes was its proximity to Ginny. She lived less than an hour away. That, of course, had been his reason for selecting air defense and requesting the assignment to Site No. 75. One day, Ginny came out to Franklin Lakes for a tour. Jack explained the screens and the radars and how the system was tied into NORAD. She was impressed and asked good questions, although he laughed when she spotted his name plate — 2LT. WHEELER — and wanted to know what a "two-let" was. At the end of her visit, he pulled her aside and confided in a whisper, "I can't give you any details, but I can tell you that, yes, there are UFOs." She laughed at *that*.

Secretly, the notion of protecting his sweetheart with his battery of missiles appealed to Jack. He wryly envisioned himself as a modern knight, shielding his damsel from harm, ready to fling a dozen nukes at any dragon that dared disturb the peace.

During war drills at Site No. 75, the men used code words for various levels of defense readiness. Fade Out signaled the lowest condition, the equivalent of "all's quiet." The phases rose through stages of tension and hostility: Double Take, Fast Pace, Quick Draw, Big Noise.

Big Noise Applejack Delta meant total war. Just the phrase sent shudders through those privy to the code. But Jack could see himself hunched over the radar tube, the screen greening his blond hair, coolly firing Nikes in a volley of smoke and flame till kingdom come. *Missile away. Missile away. Missile away.* Even in Big Noise Applejack Delta, he would be a dutiful soldier. Of that, he was certain.

8

United Hearts and Minds

Heat whooshed through the rear doors of the C-141, rudely cuffing the hundred soldiers in the cabin. As the pilot cut the four engines, George Crocker peered out at Bien Hoa Air Base through the tiny porthole. We've landed in a furnace, he thought. The temperature had been a brittle 19 degrees when they left Fort Riley, Kansas, the day before and subzero in Alaska during refueling at Elmendorf Air Force Base. At Yokota, where the plane again stopped to refuel, snowplows had been scraping the runways.

There were no snowplows here. The jet exhaust and tropical heat made everything shimmer and blur, as though the world had lost its firm edges. But through the haze, George saw that Bien Hoa was bustling. Cargo planes, troop transports, and Chinooks crisscrossed the tarmac in an elaborate dance. Every few seconds another jet landed or took off with a deep roar. The stink of JP4 fuel and burning human waste — which was incinerated beyond the runway in fifty-five-gallon drums — drifted into the cabin, along with the *thacka-thacka-thacka* sound of helicopter blades that was the mantra of Vietnam.

George hoisted his duffel bag and followed the column across the tarmac into a briefing room. The torpor of the long flight fell away like a cloak from his shoulders. At last I'm finally here, he said to himself. He felt an electric sense of high adventure, of being called to arms. He had read about the excitement that soldiers often felt as they prepared for war — the volunteers mustering before Bull Run, for instance, or the American doughboys striding into France in 1917. Now, on this day in late January of 1967, his turn had come.

At West Point, the war had remained an abstraction. George had listened intently to the lectures delivered by officers returning from Southeast Asia; one of his tactical officers had been an adviser in Laos before the American build-up in Vietnam began in earnest. Yet he rarely felt emotionally engaged by those stories. They seemed remote, almost as distant as the military art lectures on the Napoleonic campaigns. Nearly every great captain, the cadets were told, had been tested in combat early in his career: Lee and Grant in Mexico, Pershing and Marshall in the Philippines, Patton and MacArthur in World War I. The clear implication, of course, was that the men of '66 should be grateful for the chance to be annealed in combat and prove themselves as young warriors. But those had been textbook wars and textbook heroes. A cadet could not smell JP4 and burning feces in the classroom. This was real. After years of preparing for this moment, George felt ready. More than ready, in fact: he felt invincible.

Ranger school and the months of training at Fort Riley had invested him with strong self-confidence. He knew the importance of stealth, of fire control, of using artillery and air support prudently, of avoiding ambushes by steering clear of well-traveled trails. He had a sketchy understanding of the past twenty years of fighting in Indochina: the catastrophic French defeat at Dienbienphu; the Gulf of Tonkin incident in 1964; the First Cavalry's big battle in the Ia Drang Valley in 1965. He felt certain that what he now knew about soldiering could keep him alive.

But there was also a great deal that he and his classmates did not know. They did not understand that for nearly two thousand years the Vietnamese had fought valiantly against foreign invaders and occupiers, Chinese, French, and now American. They were unaware that this protracted resistance had shaped a culture that was martially competent and infinitely patient, one that placed a premium on superhuman courage and sacrifice. They did not know that Ho Chi Minh was a nationalist first and a communist second, and that his relatively recent alliance with Moscow and Peking was a marriage of convenience rather than the manifestation of a cohesive international Marxist plan. They did not comprehend that the Americans had allied themselves with a clique of corrupt and discredited Vietnamese mandarins. Nor did they realize that to many, if not most, Vietnamese the Americans were as emblematic of colonialism and social injustice as the French, whose ill-fated effort to reassert France's glory in Indochina after World War II had been heartily supported by Washington.

In a young lieutenant such ignorance was forgivable, perhaps even necessary. Twenty-three-year-old junior officers who spent their time pondering geopolitical nuances would probably make poor platoon leaders. West Point had taught history that, understandably, was skewed to the prevailing American view of the world, imbued with the unique native blend of blind optimism, self-righteousness, and genuine beneficence. The lieutenants were hardly more benighted than the most senior echelons of the United States government and the American Army. What Lieutenant George Crocker did not know on arriving at Bien Hoa he could not have been expected to know; what the president, the secretary of defense, the Joint Chiefs, and the Army's top generals did not know would cost 58,000 American lives and lose the war.

In the airport briefing room, a young officer recited a welcoming monologue already heard by tens of thousands of American soldiers:

> Gentlemen, welcome to Vietnam. Gentlemen, here you will complete your in-country processing. Gentlemen, it is very hot today and I know that you will all want to complete your in-country processing as soon as possible, and therefore you will pay attention at all times.
>
> Gentlemen, you will refrain from talking. There is a snack bar and ice cream shop next to the finance building. Gentlemen, these facilities are off limits to you until you have completed your processing.
>
> Gentlemen, when you have finished processing, you may write a letter to your families and tell them you have arrived safely in Vietnam. You can tell them that you are twenty-two miles northeast of Saigon. And, of course, you can tell them that you are having a wonderful time.
>
> Now, gentlemen, you are in a combat zone. If a siren goes off, you can assume we are under attack — either incoming rockets or a mortar attack. In the event of such an attack, do not attempt to help. You will only hinder. Are there any questions?

Three hours later, George sat in the back of a truck heading northeast up Route 1 to Cu Chi. This was not exactly what he had expected. He was eager, but the abrupt departure for the combat zone surprised him. Back in the States, he had heard repeated assurances that new lieutenants would have at least a few days to get "acclimatized" by undergoing in-country training at the Army's replacement stations, known as repo depots. None of those guarantees now seemed to hold true.

At Fort Riley, it was conventional wisdom and a point of pride that the 9th Infantry Division had been assembled and packed off to combat faster than any American division since the Spanish-American War. Some soldiers had arrived at Riley before completing basic training; a few units lacked recoilless rifles or starlight scopes and had been forced to borrow M-60 machine guns from the Kansas National Guard. Some battalions had only five captains, though the authorized complement was fifteen.

Even so, the three brigades of the 9th were ready for war. By training and deploying together, the division initially avoided the peculiar chemistry of most in-country units, where green and eager newcomers were mixed together with cautious, war-weary short-timers. In the 9th, nearly everyone was eager and green; morale was very high. While still in Kansas, George's brigade, commanded by Colonel William B. Fulton, had been given two weeks of Christmas leave, and not a single man went AWOL. Everyone came back for the fight. The enlisted troops, who had been pulled from ten different reception stations around the country, included a fair number of Cat Is and Cat IIs — the Army's highest mental categories — as well as a few NCOs who were pulling their second combat tour.

To season his young officers and noncoms, Fulton had decided to fly them to Vietnam ahead of the troops, who would arrive by ship in two weeks for eventual operations in the Mekong Delta. The colonel had been authorized to bring an advance party of 18; instead, he had showed up at Bien Hoa this morning with 385.

George and several classmates were headed for the 25th Division, where they would shadow experienced platoon leaders for a fortnight's apprenticeship. More than two dozen of the 9th's lieutenants had graduated from West Point the previous June, including many of the division's platoon leaders. William Westmoreland, who had complained in 1966 that Vietnam was bogging down in "a protracted war of attrition," now reported that he had enough troops to "go over to the offensive on a broad and sustained basis in 1967."

This first wave of West Pointers from the class of '66 was part of that critical mass. Like George, most remained full of *pro patria* exuberance and tactical department enthusiasm for "tracks in two." But already they could see that the sword cut both ways: word was spreading of the class's first battle death. Billy W. Flynn had been killed on January 23, two days after his twenty-fourth birthday. There would be no tracks in two for Billy Flynn.

The convoy slowed to a crawl and finally stopped in Cu Chi. George grabbed his duffel bag again and hopped out of the truck. The countryside for their twenty-mile trip had displayed an exotic blend of twentieth-century war technology — jeeps and tanks and helicopters — and sixteenth-century Asian peasantry — bullocks and carts and rude huts. The base camp at Cu Chi had been built the year before on an old peanut farm, near the Fil Hol rubber plantation. The camp sprawled across fifteen hundred acres, with a six-mile perimeter. The Army had wasted no time turning the place into a little corner of America, with ice plants, walk-in refrigerators, sports fields, chapels, clubs, swimming pools, and even a miniature golf course.

George still wore his starched uniform from Riley. The first order of business, he figured, would be to find some jungle fatigues and draw his ammunition. Then perhaps he would have time to look around.

A young officer with a clipboard bustled over. "Lieutenant Crocker? See that chopper over there? The one that's landing? Go get on it."

George's eyes widened with surprise. "Me?"

"Now," the officer replied.

The sun was setting when the Huey dropped him off in a jungle clearing. As he ran out from beneath the whirring rotors, he could hear small-arms fire, distant at first and then suddenly much closer. He felt confused, lost. Where the hell was he? Somewhere near the Saigon River in War Zone C, but other than that he wasn't sure. He had been in-country for about six hours and already he was on the fringe of a firefight. As a cadet, he had been told repeatedly to go to the sound of the guns, but he never expected to be asked to do so quite this quickly.

Someone directed him to a tent ringed with sandbags near the landing zone. Inside, the company commander, a plain-spoken young captain named McCarthy, returned George's salute.

"It's a little late to send you down to your platoon on the perimeter," the captain said. "I don't want to get you shot or anything on your first night."

"Thank you, sir."

McCarthy pointed to an extra cot in the tent. "My first sergeant's away. You can have his bunk tonight and we'll link you up with the platoon in the morning."

That night, George lay on the cot, listening to the chatter of automatic weapons. Things were clearer now. He was with a company in the 27th Infantry, which called itself the Wolfhounds. A distinguished outfit with a long history, the 27th's motto was *Nec Aspera Terrant* — Frightened by No Difficulties. During the Korean War, the 27th had been perhaps the finest regiment in the Eighth Army. It was commanded for a time by John H. (Mike) Michaelis, a West Point classmate of Westmoreland's who had been the academy commandant in the early 1950s and later rose to four-star rank.

George had blundered into preparations for one of the largest operations of the war, a massive sweep codenamed Junction City, after the town in Kansas adjacent to Fort Riley. Currently, the Wolfhounds formed part of a blocking force. They were supposed to snare the Viet Cong as other American units drove the enemy from their sanctuaries. The principle was that of an ancient hunting technique, in which beaters pushed the game toward the hunters, but, as usual, the quarry here refused to cooperate.

Pap! Pap! Pap-pap-pap! As George lay on the cot, several rounds punched through the tent, ventilating the canvas with holes the size of a quarter. They sounded like fat raindrops. The sandbags outside had been piled two feet high, but the cots stood about two feet six inches off the ground. George stifled the urge to dive for cover, not wanting to move before the captain did. He watched McCarthy from the corner of his eye. Damn, he thought, why don't we all just get on the floor?

The captain rolled over casually, as though waking from a nap on the beach. He took the handset from his radio telephone operator, who lay prudently on the ground. "Tell B Company," McCarthy said slowly, "that we're taking some rounds up here."

Crack! At that instant, with a fearful splintering, a bullet shattered the crosspiece of George's cot, two inches from his skull. The canvas collapsed and his head flopped down as though guillotined.

He lurched onto the floor, flattening out next to the radio operator. While he lay there, a few more rounds whizzed through the tent. More stunned than frightened, George suddenly thought of his ordnance professor at West Point, an affable colonel named Morris J. Herbert. This sudden immersion in combat reminded him of a story that Colonel Herbert liked to tell his students. Herbert had graduated from the academy as an artilleryman on June 6, 1950. Two weeks later, the Korean War erupted. He joined the 2nd Division at Fort Lewis, Washington, just in time to board ship. "Don't worry about a thing," his battery commander had said in mid Pacific. "We're going to Japan to train for a couple months because we haven't done anything at Fort Lewis except paint rocks for the past year and a half."

The battery commander was right about the rocks and dead wrong about Japan. Herbert was shocked when the ship pulled into Pusan harbor in southeast Korea. The North Koreans had pushed American and South Korean forces all the way down the peninsula and were within fifty miles of forcing another Dunkirk at Pusan. Just hours after walking down the gangplank, Herbert found himself directing artillery fire as a forward observer. "It was an unreal feeling," he had told his ordnance class. "I couldn't believe these guys were shooting at me. I was a nice guy and they were trying to kill me."

Colonel Herbert's tale seemed less amusing now. Thirty-four members of the 670 men in the class of '50 had been killed in Korea, most of them as green as grass when they died. Dying in combat was something that George Crocker had considered statistically improbable, like getting hit by a bus. But how many of those thirty-four dead officers had assumed that they too were immortal?

I was a nice guy, Colonel Herbert had said, and they were trying to kill me. Beyond the obvious instinct for self-preservation, George now had additional reason to stay alive. Twelve days before he left Riley, Vonda had given birth to the Crockers' first child, a daughter whom they named Cheryl. Leaving his wife and baby had been hard, but the separation was made bearable by his unshakable conviction that he was going to see them again in one year. Vonda had begun writing daily letters, which she numbered consecutively. George planned to read number 365; he hugged the ground a little tighter.

On his left hand he wore his West Point ring. Shortly before graduation, an officer had given a brief speech to Company F-2: "A lot of you will go to Vietnam. One of the questions that will come up is 'Should I wear my ring?' I think you should. It will be a constant reminder to do your duty, a constant reminder of duty, honor, country. Don't ever not wear it because of concern that you might lose it or because it will get dirty or because the stone might get knocked out in combat. That's the time when you most need to wear it, because the ideals that it stands for must step forward in combat."

Like Colonel Herbert's reminiscence of life and death at Pusan, that fragment of advice suddenly seemed especially relevant. George had not yet fired a shot at the enemy, but already he better understood what the officer had been talking about. The ring represented a mystical link to the past. It was a talisman, offering strength and courage drawn from the thousands of brave officers who had gone into battle before him. Even men who thought themselves invincible could use that kind of magic.

In McCarthy's bullet-riddled tent, George listened to the fading gunfire. The firefight seemed to be ending, but he decided to forgo the comfort of the cot for the safety of the floor; for the remainder of the night, he lay on the ground, dozing fitfully.

The next few days were among the strangest — and very nearly the last — of George's life.

In the morning, the Wolfhounds worked their way along the Saigon River, searching for Viet Cong. When the sweep failed to flush any enemy, Captain McCarthy organized a skeet-shooting contest. While one of his sergeants stood by with a handful of paper plates, the captain strolled down to the water with a shotgun, looking every bit like a quail-hunting squire.

"Pull!" he yelled.

A white plate glided out over the river before disintegrating in a swarm of buckshot. "Pull!"

When he grew weary of skeet, McCarthy took an M-79 grenade

launcher and began popping at coconuts high in the trees across the river. The troops, meanwhile, amused themselves by firing at flotsam coming down the Saigon on the premise that it could be a Viet Cong frogman. George watched with a mixture of chagrin and amusement. Nobody, he reflected, ever mentioned *this* in military art.

Later in the afternoon of his first full day in-country, he climbed onto a tank that was bulling its way through the jungle toward a suspected enemy position. Every few minutes it stopped long enough to fire the main gun. When a second tank came clanking up on his right, George shifted over to the left side of the turret. As he did so, the other tank's main gun roared.

Almost simultaneously came a second blast. A mine had detonated between the two tanks, apparently triggered by the concussion of the gun. The explosion flung George from the hull, and the spray of shrapnel spattered against the turret, precisely where he had been a moment before. A soldier standing near him was badly wounded, his side shredded with hot metal.

That night, George went on patrol with the platoon leader he was shadowing. Soon mortar rounds began raining around them. The other lieutenant caught a piece of shrapnel in the arm, and a medic knocked him out with a shot of morphine.

"Well, Lieutenant Crocker," the platoon sergeant said cheerfully, "I guess you're taking over now." They sat motionless in the jungle for the rest of the night. No one slept.

The following day, his third in Vietnam, the company was preparing to board a flock of Hueys for an airborne assault when George had another close call. Three helicopters back, perhaps fifty yards away, there was a gold flash from a soldier accidentally triggering his M-79. A split second later, the grenade landed at George's feet, close enough to spear with a first baseman's mitt. Nothing happened. The grenade was a dud.

George still had enough stateside in him to want to mark the dud for ordnance disposal. But an officer standing at his side moved first: enraged, he scooped up the smoking round in a rag, sprinted to the soldier, and, shrieking like a madman, thrust the grenade into his stomach.

George had experienced the near-fatal consequences of bad luck; now he witnessed the price of poor judgment. Late one afternoon McCarthy called his platoon leaders together for a briefing. While the lieutenants spooned up their C-rations on the perimeter of one of the tank companies, the captain discussed an ambush patrol that would be deployed that evening. The young officer assigned to lead the patrol was an ungainly lieutenant who incessantly pushed his glasses up on the bridge of his nose. George had few regrets at being left behind on this operation; the other lieutenant struck him as the type who, rather than following his instincts, would always pursue the "school solution" that the Ranger cadre had so often warned against.

At dusk, the lieutenant led his men outside the company perimeter to reconnoiter the terrain and select the ambush site; several hours later, he followed the same route back into the jungle. The patrol had been gone for only a few minutes when a volley of gunfire tore through the night. The enemy, apparently having watched the platoon scouts pick their site at dusk, had patiently waited to ambush the ambushers. Four Wolfhounds came running back to the camp, carrying their dead lieutenant on a rubber poncho; his body, not yet stiff with death, flopped about grotesquely. George watched as the four puffing soldiers collapsed on the ground inside the barbed wire. One of them tapped out a cigarette and lit it with his Zippo. His hands trembled and, as he took a deep drag, the orange glow illuminated a face twisted with fear. Every time the soldier inhaled he glanced at the dead man, then abruptly averted his eyes, as though he had seen something immodest.

George felt a churning of emotions. The initial shock of seeing this pitiful platoon leader flopping ingloriously on the poncho quickly gave way to scorn and seething anger, not at the enemy, but at the dead officer. He had made a fundamental mistake and had paid for it with his life. Here was terrible proof that the kinds of errors Charlie Beckwith had cautioned against could indeed be fatal. Needing someplace to ground the sudden rage that surged through him, George discharged it at the dead officer. You idiot, he murmured to the lieutenant, you dumb idiot. You couldn't have given the enemy a clearer picture of your plans if you had handed them a map. *Don't ever do that,* he thought, simultaneously rebuking the dead man and cautioning himself.

But the following night, Lieutenant Crocker came within inches of the same fate. His platoon set up another ambush next to a trail. Before long, two groups of Viet Cong blundered into the kill sack. In a furious burst of machine-gun fire and claymore-mine detonations, the Wolfhounds killed several soldiers and sent the rest fleeing through the jungle.

"Let's drag the bodies back before they come collect their dead," George whispered to the other lieutenant.

"Yeah," the lieutenant agreed, "good idea."

Across the trail stood a patch of chest-high grass. He wasn't certain — it was very dark — but George thought he had seen some of the enemy flee in that direction. Listening for moans, he plunged into the grass. Back and forth he shuffled, feeling with his boots for bodies.

After a few minutes of futile searching, he returned to the trail and grabbed one of the dead Viet Cong by the hair. He expected blood, but not the mask of ants that already shrouded the dead man's head. George jerked his hand away as though he had touched a hot skillet. Everything happened quickly in Vietnam; even the scavengers moved with astonishing speed.

In the morning, the Americans returned to inspect the ambush site. Plainly visible in the swatch of tall grass stood the vertical bamboo triggers of a half-dozen antitank mines. Equally apparent were George's tracks from the previous night, meandering through the minefield as if they belonged to a picnicker out gathering daisies. In several spots the matted grass showed that he had come appallingly close to blowing himself to Cambodia. He had made a mistake almost as foolish as the one that had killed the lieutenant two nights before.

A few days later, in early February, his eventful apprenticeship with the Wolfhounds came to an end. George and the other officers in the advance party traveled by truck to Bearcat, a base south of Saigon, where they rendezvoused with the rest of the 9th Division. At Bearcat, Crocker and several other new lieutenants were awarded the Combat Infantryman's Badge. The rectangular patch with a Kentucky long rifle on it carried a certain cachet among the arriving troops, who had just dropped anchor at Vung Tau. The CIB symbolized a kind of blooding, marking the final passage from cadet to warrior.

For George Crocker, the badge also represented a profound transformation in his attitude toward the war. He felt as though his two weeks with the Wolfhounds had aged him ten years. Gone was the eagerness he had felt on the tarmac at Bien Hoa. The four or five brushes with death, the sight and sound of the wounded, the sight and smell of the dead, had swept away the naïve belief in his own invulnerability. He was still confident of surviving the war; after so many close calls he even wondered whether he might be charmed. But the blithe sense of adventure had vanished, just as it had vanished from the soldiers who survived Bull Run or the first wretched weeks in the trenches of France. The name on his fatigue blouse still read CROCKER; but as he mustered his platoon for the move into the delta, he knew with absolute certainty that a different man now wore the uniform.

The deployment of the 9th Division into the Mekong Delta in early 1967 marked the resumption of a kind of warfare — riverine combat — that the U.S. Army had last experienced more than a century earlier. American soldiers had once had considerable expertise in fighting a river war. During the Revolution, one of the principal strategic struggles was over control of the Hudson–Lake Champlain–St. Lawrence axis; West Point itself had first been fortified as part of the thrust-and-parry of that riverine conflict. In the War of 1812, the Americans mounted a river force, and in the grim Seminole War a mosquito fleet of 150 schooners, bateaux, and canoes had hunted Indians in the Florida sloughs, where a fourth of the U.S. Army's regulars subsequently died. With the exception of a foray up the Yangtze during the Boxer Rebellion, however, the Army had not fought extensively on rivers since Grant bisected the Confederacy by taking control of the Mississippi.

Now, more than a century later, riverine fighting was about to come back into fashion. The 9th Division was determined to control the Mekong, one of the world's greatest rivers. Flowing for twenty-five hundred miles from the Tibetan plateau, the Mekong split into four main fingers south of Saigon before emptying into the South China Sea. Command of the river and its myriad tributaries and canals was essential to wresting the delta away from the Viet Cong. But the French riverine experience was not heartening; in 1954 alone, at the end of their Indochina war, the French had lost more than a dozen boats to the Viet Minh. Some of those carcasses still sat in the Mekong mud as a reminder of things gone wrong.

In early 1964, the U.S. ambassador to Vietnam, Henry Cabot Lodge, had remarked, "I would not be surprised to see the Mekong Delta totally cleared of communist forces by the end of 1965." Instead, by the time the 9th Division arrived, the Viet Cong had more than eighty thousand troops in the region. The guerrillas were well supported by the local population — swimming like fish in the sea, in Mao's phrase — and they moved with elusive ease by sampan throughout the delta.

The American strategy aimed to clean out the Viet Cong infrastructure, freeing Route 4 — the main road to Saigon — and the rest of the rice bowl from communist domination. If the delta, which had a population density comparable with that of Massachusetts, could be stabilized to produce enough food to feed South Vietnam, other parts of the nation could begin to industrialize. As a base for his riverine force, William Westmoreland picked a site on the northernmost of the four Mekong fingers, west of the town of My Tho. The camp was originally called Base Whiskey, but Westmoreland gave it a loftier name to fit his aspirations: Dong Tam. It meant "united hearts and minds."

George Crocker's first view of Dong Tam was disheartening. He had not expected Windsor Palace, but the camp was little more than a barren mudflat on the north bank of the river. The site was even less appealing than Beckwith's Field Seven had been; at least that had showed some semblance of human habitation. The only sign of life at Dong Tam, besides one pathetic mechanized company camped in the muck, was a large dredge, named the *New Jersey*. It sat in the middle of the river spewing fresh layers of mud on top of the old mud in an effort to build up the riverbank before the monsoon season. Now, with typical American vigor, the Army set out to transform Dong Tam into a thriving fortress. Shortly after he and his platoon arrived, George ordered the men to pitch their tents and begin building hootches from prefabrication kits, which came complete with blueprints, lumber, nails, and even hammers.

The thirty-five men in his platoon, which was part of the 3rd Battalion of the 47th Infantry Regiment, quickly discovered that soldiering in the delta was beset with problems. The mud and brackish water quickly ruined weapons that were not routinely disassembled, cleaned, and oiled. Every morning, George had his men remove the rounds in their rifle chambers, since they would often get damp overnight and cause the weapons to jam. Every three days, each magazine was emptied, and the dirty ammunition replaced with clean bullets. Once the river operations began, the platoon periodically rotated onto one of several World War II ships that had been converted into floating barracks. Offering clean sheets, hot showers, and air conditioning, the ships gave the men a chance to dry out and escape the fungi that thrived inside wet boots. Better still, the Navy returned their laundry clean and fragrant, unlike the *mama sans* at Dong Tam, who rinsed the fatigues in river water and left them smelling, oddly, like oatmeal.

On the day before a search-and-destroy sweep, the men cleaned their weapons and fueled the boats. In the evening, boat captains got briefings on the mission, steaming formations, radio codes, tidal currents, and the latest G2, or intelligence. Before dawn, George and his troops would stand on a pontoon pier, rummaging around in different-colored barrels for claymores, grenades, and smoke canisters. Then, with other platoons from the company, they climbed into eight or ten shallow-draught troop carriers. The boats, each sixty feet long, were protected with armor and a trellis of iron bars to deflect rocket-propelled grenades. Canvas awnings shielded the soldiers from the sun.

In the early morning light, the delta presented a lush palette of blues and greens. Water buffalo, ridden by scrawny peasant boys in conical straw hats, pulled crude plows across the paddies to prepare them for the green rice shoots that would be planted as the monsoon season neared. Like armored geese, the American boats puttered past in a V formation, often led by a minesweeper. Helicopters scouted ahead for enemy ambushes. Sometimes the river tributaries were only fifty to a hundred feet wide, clogged with fish traps or Viet Cong barricades. Banana and coconut groves lined the banks.

As they approached the landing site, the Americans would open up with "reconnaissance by fire," bombarding suspected Viet Cong positions on both sides of the water with a Monitor — a seventy-five-ton floating fortress — or artillery, which was towed on barges and anchored in the mud with sharp cleats. Later in the war, large flame-throwing boats called Zippos sometimes scorched the banks with thick tongues of fire. The infantrymen then splashed ashore and fanned out, always eyeing the dikes and tree lines across the rice paddies for signs of the enemy. Frequently, another U.S. force would be inserted by helicopter to block the Viet Cong escape routes. Sometimes the enemy stood fast to fight, but more typically the sweeps encountered only sporadic sniper fire or came up empty altogether.

Even so, there were constant reminders of death's ubiquity. The winnowing of the West Point class of '66, which began on the first day of Beast Barracks, had abated temporarily at graduation, only to resume in Vietnam in an infinitely more sinister form. As the war intensified, as ever more lieutenants were shuttled into combat, the manifest of KIAs grew steadily longer.

One of George's classmates who also served in the delta was a native of the Panama Canal Zone named Frank Rybicki, Jr. A man of irrepressible good cheer, Rybicki seemed perpetually happy, whether strumming his guitar, practicing his jitterbug, or simply talking to his friends. At West Point, as president of the Glee Club, he would write to the Miss America candidates from each state where the club was touring, soliciting dates. He adored John Kennedy and had studied on a desk blotter inscribed with the "ask not what your country can do for you" quotation. Rybicki's sister married his academy roommate, Terry Stull, who also joined the 9th as a platoon leader.

One day in late spring, two Viet Cong companies badly decimated Stull's platoon in a six-hour firefight. Rybicki's platoon was among those ordered to reinforce. "We're coming down to help you out," he told Stull on the phone. "About time we worked together again."

The platoon waded into the Rung Sat Special Zone, near the main shipping channel to Saigon. Also known as the Forest of Assassins, the Rung Sat was an ancient pirate haven, a 350-square-mile nightmare of mangrove trees and nipa palms. Shortly after arriving, Rybicki bogged down in the mud. Without flipping the safety on, he thrust the stock of his rifle to one of his men to pull him out. The soldier accidentally grabbed the trigger, and Rybicki fell dead in a burst of his own gunfire.

By chance, George happened to get word of the accident before Terry Stull did, and it fell to him to inform Stull that his brother-in-law had been killed. *Newsweek* magazine devoted an entire page to Rybicki's funeral at West Point, calling him "an integer in the unending statistics in an unending war," and noting that "he was the second to die in West Point's class of '66, the 101st academy graduate, one of 10,000 Americans lost in what has now become the fifth costliest war in U.S. history." Twenty years later, some of Frank Rybicki's classmates would recall his death with particular anguish; to them it seemed the ultimate metaphor of self-destruction in Vietnam.

In addition to conducting search-and-destroy sweeps on the Mekong, units from the 9th occasionally walked patrol duty near Dong Tam in an effort to thwart the Viet Cong mortar crews who frequently harassed the compound. One night, around the time of Rybicki's death, George had been out with his platoon for several hours on just such a defensive patrol when he heard a harsh whisper. "Sssst! Sir!"

One of his soldiers, flattened against the side of a dike, pointed across the rice paddy. George crawled to the crest of the levee and peered into the darkness. The perimeter of Dong Tam lay only a kilometer behind him to the east. Ahead, a hundred yards to the west, the next dike rose like a dark wall above the field. He saw nothing out of the ordinary and heard only the usual buzzing of countless insects.

He inched along the dike toward the soldier who had whispered. Taking the GI's sniper rifle, George hoisted the starlight scope to his right eye. The night instantly gave way to an eerie twilight. The scope sucked in all available moon- and starlight and painted the landscape with a pale green illumination, as if the world were covered with penicillin mold.

George saw him instantly. A solitary Viet Cong wearing his *ao baba* — the customary black pajamas — stood on the adjacent dike. George couldn't quite make out what the enemy soldier was doing. Sometimes, he knew, the VC liked to reverse the American claymores so that the blast would be directed back at the unwitting U.S. soldiers.

George watched for a while through the scope, the hunter stalking his prey. This was a rare opportunity to watch the enemy at work. But he didn't want the soldier to slip away in the paddy. Easy does it, he told himself. He steadied his breathing, drew a bead on the soldier's heart, and gently squeezed the trigger.

BAM! A single red tracer streaked across the paddy and struck the VC in the chest, knocking him over with a small *splat* sound that carried to the Americans.

Got you! George thought. Got you, you little son of a bitch! Adrenaline surged through him, again quickening his pulse and his breathing. The platoon crouched expectantly behind the dike, but no one returned the fire. The western front of Dong Tam remained quiet.

Back at the base, George exulted, replaying in his mind the red streak of the tracer and the dull noise as the round found its mark. As many of his classmates were also discovering, nothing in the world compared to the exhilaration of combat. Some soldiers never overcame their fear or their revulsion at the killing, but he could understand how others became adrenaline freaks. The world outside the combat zone — the peaceful world at home — seemed oddly tame by contrast, almost boring. Men, Homer had observed, grow tired of sleep, love, singing, and dancing sooner than of war. The enemy here was faceless and nameless — except for gook, dink, slope, or Charlie — and while George did not exactly hate him, killing him was not difficult. It was not difficult at all.

After but a few weeks in Vietnam, he was beginning to realize that war boiled down to a few irreducible truths. No longer did he see it as an adventure; war was brutal, often harrowing. No longer did he imagine that he was invincible; he knew death could claim him at any moment. And it was also true that the killing of the enemy was no longer cloaked in ideology or patriotism. George had heard little discussion in the war zone of the domino theory or just causes or checking the spread of godless communism. Killing was much more elemental, an accession of animal instincts and soldierly axioms: survival against a foe who was trying to kill you; revenge for comrades who had died; loyalty unto death to those who shared the fight; and a fierce determination to be better than the enemy. West Point did not — could not — teach these things; what the academy could teach, implicitly, was how to keep the killing within the warrior's code so that combat did not degenerate into blood lust, nor decent men warp into butchers.

In 1943, George Patton had written in his diary: "War is very simple, direct, and ruthless. It takes a simple, direct, and ruthless man to wage war." Combat required a certain implacability of the best. George Meade had been too much the genteel Philadelphian to crush the Confederates; it took U. S. Grant, that indifferent cadet and one-time Galena shopkeeper, to annihilate the rebellion, simply, directly, ruthlessly.

That requirement held true on Sicily and true at Spotsylvania Court House; now it was true in Vietnam. And Patton's dictum held true even for a young lieutenant in a place named United Hearts and Minds.

In early May, the brigade left Dong Tam and moved inland on a search-and-destroy operation. For three days the Americans tramped through the countryside looking for a fight without finding one. The troops discovered elaborate bunkers and even some new equipment. But the enemy always seemed to stay one step ahead.

On the afternoon of May 3, George was summoned by his company and battalion commanders. "We're going to pull the brigade out but leave a stay-behind ambush," the battalion commander told him. "You're it. Why don't you go up in the chopper now with the S3 and take a look around?"

Sitting in the Huey next to the battalion operations officer fifteen hundred feet above the ground, George saw many Americans but no Victor Charlie. He had few doubts, however, that the enemy was down there in force. Not far away was the hamlet of Ap Bac, now deserted, where in January 1963 the Army of the Republic of Vietnam (ARVN) and the Viet Cong had fought their first major battle. Three hundred and fifty lightly armed VC had humiliated an ARVN force four times its size and had shot down five U.S.-piloted helicopters. The senior American adviser on the scene, a legendary lieutenant colonel named John Paul Vann, had offered a candid assessment of ARVN combat prowess — "a miserable damn performance" — which made front-page headlines across the United States.

Now, four years later, the VC still maintained control. Long since abandoned to the war, the rice fields, dikes, and small banana plantations near Ap Bac had begun reverting to jungle. George, scanning the countryside, saw that an enemy division could hide down there without being detected. This is going to be interesting, he told himself.

Shortly after he returned to the camp, the brigade began to pull out. It took a long time to ferry more than two thousand troops back to Dong Tam in helicopters, and shadows had begun to stretch across the desolate paddies as the last Huey lifted into the sky. George and his platoon crouched in the elephant grass, straining to catch the fading beat of the rotors until even their imaginations could no longer pretend to hear it. They were alone — three dozen scared infantrymen left behind as bait.

George gestured to the platoon. "Okay," he whispered, "let's move out."

Holding their rifles high, they waded waist-deep into a swamp. Their objective was a small canal, perhaps thirty feet wide, about a mile away; from the air it had looked like a twisting black snake. The commander had suggested that they cut through an open area to reach the canal quickly, but George preferred the back door through the swamp. It was an old Ranger tactic: use the least expected route. By moving this way, the platoon would also be able to hear anyone who tried to follow.

As always in the tropics, night fell with the abruptness of a dropped curtain. After reaching a copse of small trees and grass near the canal, the men fanned out in a circle thirty yards in diameter. They couldn't dig in — the water table was only six or eight inches below the surface —

so the soldiers scratched small battlements for cover. George helped site the two M-60 machine guns and camouflage the claymore mines along the canal bank. The claymores could be devastatingly effective at close range: weighing three pounds, each mine contained seven hundred steel peas packed into a paste of C-4 explosive. When triggered with a hand-held detonator, a "clacker," the C-4 spat the pellets for about fifty yards with the force of a shotgun blast.

As a final precaution, George raised the artillery firebase on the radio. A battery of 105mm howitzers, mounted on triangular platforms, had been flown into the middle of a rice paddy six miles away. Before the brigade flew back to Dong Tam, George had been assigned an artillery forward observer — a nervous young lieutenant — and one of his sergeants. Using the grids on his map, the FO now called in several rounds, which soon exploded nearby. By registering the proper deflection and elevation, the battery would be able to respond instantly with fire on potential approach routes to the platoon's perimeter.

There was always a chance, George knew, that the rounds would alert the enemy to the platoon's presence. But random explosions were common in Vietnam; something was always blowing up somewhere in the middle of the night. In Beast Barracks, new cadets had been required to memorize a saw that seemed particularly apt now: "A calculated risk is a known risk for the sake of a real gain. A risk for the sake of a risk is a fool's choice." Registering the artillery was a calculated risk.

Once in place, the platoon remained utterly quiet. That was good, George thought, very good. In four months these men had been transformed into a fine combat team. Lieutenant Crocker had been insistent — at times even harshly demanding — that they religiously follow the precepts of Ranger training. He was convinced that all of Beckwith's tricks picked up from the British in Malaya — minimizing noise and light, avoiding smelly insect repellent, stressing guile and subterfuge — saved lives. Several soldiers in the platoon had been wounded, but no one had been killed yet. That was something to be proud of.

George's own flirtation with death, however, had not abated. The near misses he began having during his first week with the Wolfhounds had continued with the 9th. On one occasion, a sniper had wounded two American soldiers in the head and George moved up to the perimeter. He assigned each remaining man five trees to watch. See if you can spot any movement, he ordered, and we'll call in some artillery. Suddenly, another shot rang out and the branch a few inches above his helmet fell to the ground as neatly as if snipped with hedge shears.

Not long after that the platoon was deployed on Thoi San Island near Dong Tam. George's platoon sergeant was a savvy career NCO named

Diaz, who had been an outstanding instructor at the Army's jungle school in Panama. As they were patrolling across the island, Diaz grabbed George's arm. "Nobody move!" he yelled. "Don't step!" He pointed at the ground. "Look, sir. The banana leaf, but no banana tree." Carefully lifting the leaf, Diaz revealed an undetonated Air Force cluster bomb that had been converted into a booby trap.

When, soon after, the platoon again drew night patrol duty outside Dong Tam, George set out in his usual spot, fourth in the column. But when the men began to slow down and bunch too closely, he moved up front to see why. As he climbed onto a dike next to the point man, a Chinese antipersonnel mine exploded. Shrapnel and barbed wire blew back between his legs, severely wounding the soldier who had taken his place in the file. The fireball flung George into the air and knocked the rifle from his hands. Dazed and temporarily deaf, he called for a helicopter to evacuate the wounded. Then he ordered the platoon back a thousand meters while he and Diaz crouched in the weeds for an hour, vainly hoping to ambush whoever had placed the mine.

Each close call took its toll. The stress, the rush of adrenaline, the inevitable reliving of the episode at night as he tried to sleep, all wore him down. He felt fatigued, as though he had been treading water for a long time. His exuberance ebbed a little with each incident. Always calm, at times he now found himself jumpy and distracted when the platoon prepared for yet another air assault or river sweep.

The drone of a plane interrupted his thoughts. An old C-47 Gooney Bird on a psyops — psychological operation — mission flew past. A steady stream of Vietnamese blared from loudspeakers on the plane's belly, urging the VC to surrender. *You must give up, soldiers. Death will be your only reward if you continue this futile struggle.*

Suddenly, on every side of the platoon, the jungle erupted in a roar of gunfire. Hundreds of enemy soldiers fired their rifles furiously at the plane. Then the .50-calibers opened up, hosing the night sky with tracer rounds.

Still lying quietly in their hiding place, the men in the platoon gaped in disbelief. Tracers stitched green threads through the air. The Gooney Bird, apparently untouched, continued to babble for another minute before lumbering off to proselytize elsewhere. After a few final bursts, the night fell silent again.

George gestured to the men to remain motionless. He found the .50-calibers particularly disturbing. Division intelligence had estimated that only battalion-size VC units or larger were outfitted with the heavy machine guns. At least two or three .50s had been firing; perhaps more. Two or three battalions? Is that possible? he wondered. It would not take long for two or three battalions to overrun three dozen Americans.

Someone shook his arm and pointed at the canal. The black silhouettes of two sampans silently glided by. A moment later, in a crimson burst, several claymores on the canal bank detonated, raking the sampans with steel. A piece of hot plastic from a claymore casing struck George in the back of the neck; he flicked it away with his hand. The boats burned for a few moments before sinking; once again the silence returned.

Not a single soldier in the platoon had fired his rifle yet. George had stressed over and over the importance of not signaling their position at night with rifle fire. Explosions were anonymous, but the popping of an M-16 told the enemy that an American soldier was squeezing the trigger. So far, the men had been admirably disciplined, and that's what would keep them alive: discipline held an infantry unit together, allowing every man to draw strength from every other man. Good infantrymen had once been likened to dangerous vermin that were hard to brush from the seams of the soil.

The VC began to probe. Soon George heard them rooting off to the left. As the enemy moved closer, Diaz lay sprawled on the ground nearby, clutching a pair of grenades. It sounded as though six or eight of them had closed to within a few yards of the platoon.

Out of the darkness, two enemy soldiers came running toward the perimeter, spraying the brush with their AK-47s. Diaz popped the handles from the grenades, let them "cook" in his hands for two seconds, and flipped them at the charging VC. Both grenades detonated in midair, brilliantly illuminating the scene as the soldiers jackknifed and fell dead. George ordered each man to pull the pin on a grenade. On his command, thirty grenades bounced in front of the perimeter and exploded in a spray of dirt and shrapnel.

Things began happening very quickly now. Two hundred yards away, a large enemy force, still uncertain of the platoon's precise location, rushed at what they mistakenly believed to be the American position. George crawled over to the artillery FO. "Let's get some fire on that bunch over there," he ordered.

There was no response. Petrified, the artillery lieutenant stared blankly. George grabbed him and jerked him upright.

"You get hold of yourself," he growled, his face inches from the FO's. "You get to it or get your sergeant over here to do it."

The FO nodded and raised the firebase on the radio. A minute later, 105mm rounds began raining on the enemy position with the familiar express train sound of incoming artillery. The Americans heard shrieks and moans as the VC retreated, leaving behind the dying.

Half an hour later, the enemy tried again. Once again they missed the platoon by several hundred yards; once again a curtain of artillery fell on the attack. By dawn, it appeared that the enemy had melted back into the jungle. George called the battalion on the radio. Howard Kirk, a classmate from '66, listened on the network back at camp. He thought George's voice sounded cool, controlled, yet frightened: "The sun's up. We killed a few last night. We're searching the dead now and we'll be ready for extraction shortly."

George crawled over to the canal to look at the sampans. A dead VC floated in the water. The force of the claymore had wrapped his leg bizarrely around his neck, like twine around a finger. Several other soldiers came over to tug on the edge of a sunken boat in a search for booty.

Diaz snapped his fingers twice and without uttering a word, jabbed his finger at the air. George turned his head. In a woodline 250 yards away, stretching as far as he could see in either direction, were the unmistakable signs of an impending attack. He caught glimpses of black and the glint of metal in the morning light. The Viet Cong made no effort to conceal themselves. George heard whoops and yells followed by the trill of whistles.

He turned back to Diaz. "I guess they found us."

The battalion commander was already in the air aboard his helicopter when George reached him on the radio.

"Sir, I've got a big ground attack about to start and I need some gunships. Right away."

Small-arms fire began slicing into the foliage above the platoon, sporadically at first and then in a heavy fusillade that shredded the leaves and branches. For the first time, the platoon returned fire with their M-16s and M-60s. The artillery lieutenant, having composed himself after George's tongue lashing the night before, called in coordinates to the artillery battery; within seconds the treeline erupted in fire and smoke.

That stalled the first charge. The Americans heard shouted commands as the VC tried to reorganize in the midst of the artillery barrage. For a few minutes, the enemy firing faltered, then resumed even more intensely. Hugging the ground as closely as he could, George spread a red panel to mark his position for the gunships. The gunships, he wondered; where are the gunships?

Thacka-thacka-thacka. As if on cue, a Huey swooped overhead.

"Hey, we're taking some fire," the pilot complained over the radio. "We see you, we see them."

George pressed the radio key. "You want me to throw some smoke?"

"No, don't do that. We've got you. I'm going to make a pass at them." The gunship veered toward the woodline, raking the trees with machine guns and rockets before circling back.

"We make four or five of them hiding in a ditch right down beside you," the pilot radioed. "You want to go kill them, or do you want us to get them?"

George pressed the key. "Hell, let's not fool around. You get them."

Another ship came on station, followed by two others. A cacophony of gunfire, explosions, and rotor noise washed over the platoon. Enemy bullets had stripped the thicket in which they were hiding as clean as if it had been mowed with a scythe; leaves and small branches covered the ground. Between M-16 bursts, the men pressed their cheeks into the dirt in an effort to lower the crowns of their heads an extra inch.

The battalion commander came back on the radio. "We're getting you out of there. Be ready to extract back about three hundred meters in that open area we talked about."

"Yes, sir. We're ready."

George shouted above the din to Diaz and the squad leaders. "Get ready to go. That clearing over there, about three hundred meters. Ready — GO!"

Like sprinters coming out of their blocks, three dozen men exploded from the brake while the four gunships sprayed the treeline. Running as fast as he could, George passed a beautifully preserved old American M-1 rifle lying on the ground. He suppressed the urge to snatch it and kept sprinting. Several Hueys glided in just as the platoon reached the clearing; the men leaped inside and collapsed panting on the floor.

Once again, George felt the exhilaration of survival. What an immense sense of power there was in pressing a little microphone key and seeing the woods erupt in fire. As the ground fell away beneath the helicopter, he saw several more dead Viet Cong spread-eagled below, each body marking the green earth with a dark X.

After landing at Dong Tam, he counted heads and found everyone present and accounted for; the platoon had escaped without a single casualty. The brigade commander, Colonel Fulton, ordered the men into formation. Filthy and exhausted, they stood at attention as the colonel strolled down the line, awarding each a Bronze Star.

"How many did you kill, soldier?"

"I think I got two, sir."

"Good, good. How about you, soldier?"

"At least one, sir, maybe more."

"Good. Very good."

After the ceremony, George walked back to his tent on the southeast corner of the base. Fulton had given him a Bronze Star and also recommended that he receive a Silver Star for "conspicuous gallantry and intrepidity in action."

This small, anonymous firefight, George thought, offered further insights into men at war. However insignificant the battle had been within the larger conflict, it demonstrated, in microcosm, certain verities. The American military historian S. L. A. Marshall had written that most men in combat "are unwilling to take extraordinary risks and do not aspire to a hero's role, but they are equally unwilling they should be considered the least worthy among those present." What soldiers most desire, Marshall wrote, is the esteem of their comrades.

That seemed on target, but another of Marshall's conclusions from his study of American infantrymen in World War II did not track. He had estimated that only one soldier in four fired his weapon when closely engaged with the enemy; the majority, Marshall concluded, were paralyzed with fright or preoccupied with survival. George could not see that. It seemed to him that when told to fire, these men — all of them — had done so with exceptional discipline.

Something about courage was also clearer now. At West Point, the cadets — Cadet Crocker among them — had been full of bravado. They had joked about which hand they would prefer to lose in combat, blustering about how many enemy soldiers they planned to kill. But bravado was grounded in ignorance; true courage was possible only after one gained the visceral comprehension that death was the potential price of valor. The men in the platoon — Lieutenant Crocker among them — had been truly brave.

"Sir?"

Two of his squad leaders and two PFCs stood at the entrance to the tent. It was unusual to see them here. George had made a conscious effort to remain distant from the other soldiers. Any platoon leader could be a great friend to his men, but George believed that getting too close eroded the unit's effectiveness. The biggest temptation to overcome in combat, he had discovered, was the impulse to abandon everything and tend the wounded rather than continuing to fight with the platoon. In February, he had even summoned the squad leaders to make the point explicit. "Maybe it's best that we not get too friendly," he told them. "It might affect how we do business if I know I have to put you guys in body bags."

Now, he waved the four men in.

"Sir," one of the sergeants said, "we're a delegation from the platoon and we don't really know how to say it, but we want to just say thanks for being hard on us and making sure we didn't talk or smoke or whatever. We really appreciated that last night. We know that all the things you were trying to do are worth it."

George shook their hands. When they left, he sat on his bunk and smiled. These guys have learned, he thought; they're true soldiers. And that thirty-second speech was worth more than all the Silver Stars in the United States Army.

George did not write to Vonda about the close calls. Nor did he mention the Silver Star. She tried to read between the lines to learn what was really going on in that place with the strange name. Dong Tam — it was melodious, really, almost like the sound of a bell. *Dong-tam, dong-tam.* But hard information about the war was difficult to come by. George was naturally modest and self-effacing, but sometimes she wished that he were a little more forthcoming about what he was going through.

Vonda and the baby stayed in Kansas until May so that she could finish her graduate classes. A night owl, she often watched the late news while exercising, hoping for a glimpse of her husband in the footage from Vietnam. Her affection for Army life had not diminished after the men all thundered off to war. In part, it was enhanced by the wife of George's battalion commander, Mrs. Lucien E. Bolduc. Unlike some senior officers' wives, she was a free spirit, who hauled her many children about in a van, read French for fun, and didn't seem to care a whit about Old Army protocol. If the Army has other Mrs. Bolducs, Vonda thought, I'm going to like it just fine.

At the end of the college semester, she moved back to Arkansas. Adele Crocker had taken a job as a house mother at Arkansas Tech, so Vonda and Cheryl moved into the empty Crocker house. But Vonda and Adele still saw each other frequently, and at times their visits were difficult, tense. There existed an almost chemical instability between a widow whose only child was in the war zone and a bride left alone with a newborn baby. Vonda's mother counseled forbearance. "Now you just remember all the wonderful things she's done for you," Mrs. Jones urged.

Okay, Vonda agreed, she would try to remember. She knew that it was probably beyond her ability to understand fully the stresses involved when your only son was in combat twelve thousand miles away. Someday, no doubt, she and her mother-in-law were going to be good friends. But until George was out of harm's way, they remained a constant reminder to each other of his absence. Occasionally Vonda would slip a little dig into her daily letter to Vietnam: "I invited Mother Crocker to dinner and prepared this wonderful meal, but I guess she forgot about it because she didn't come."

Unfortunately, George was not going to be out of harm's way any time soon. The struggle for the delta had become intense and bloody, although from a platoon leader's vantage point — usually about six inches off the ground — the Americans seemed to be winning. The 9th

Division had secured portions of the countryside where only a few months before ambushes were a near certainty.

Dong Tam had mushroomed almost overnight from a mudflat to a large village, complete with basketball hoops and a club with a patio where officers could buy frozen hamburger patties and charbroil them on the grill. The men in the battalion domesticated the local fauna, including a snake named Python 6, which was fed a live chicken once a week amid a crowd of hooting spectators. The soldiers also kept a pet monkey named Sam, which was taught to leap onto the executive officer's shoulder and masturbate while the enraged major whirled in circles, threatening to shoot the "goddamn thing" with his pistol.

The growing delta war inevitably led to greater numbers of American casualties, and the men of '66 were not spared. One of the more popular platoon leaders was an Army brat of Norwegian descent named Denny Loftheim. Loftheim had been King of Beast in the summer of '65. He liked to reminisce about how he and his brother Jon, also in the class of '66, were once forced to hold hands and skip across Central Area during their own Beast ordeal. Assigned to a reconnaissance platoon in the 47th Infantry, Denny Loftheim sometimes bunked near George Crocker on the barracks ship; some of the other officers — not West Pointers — teased him affectionately about his alma mater by calling him Duty Honor Country.

Loftheim was unusually superstitious, particularly about a photograph that had been taken on the way to Vietnam after the 9th Division left Kansas. Among the young lieutenants in the picture, Loftheim was the only one who had not been killed or badly wounded. He was also disillusioned about the war. Sometimes it seemed so endless, so mindless, that his frustrations spilled out in letters to Jon. "Take the advice of your younger brother," he had written that spring. "Don't come."

On patrol one day, his platoon was crossing a stream when a booby trap detonated, wounding the point man. When Loftheim moved forward to help, a sniper triggered a second blast. The powerful 155mm artillery round blew the young lieutenant to pieces. Several GIs later traced the detonation cord to a blind in the jungle, which was littered with the sniper's cigarette butts. Denny Loftheim was buried at West Point, a few feet from Frank Rybicki.

Six months into his tour, George's command stint expired and he moved to a staff position as the S3-air, the officer in charge of air operations for the 3rd Battalion. The job offered a different view of the war, either above small-arms range at fifteen hundred feet or "flying contour" at treetop level. Typically, the artillery spotter sat on his right in the Huey and the battalion commander on his left as they directed the troops below.

In mid June, the riverine force boarded a flotilla of nearly seventy boats for an operation codenamed Great Bend. In miserable monsoon heat, the armada steamed from Dong Tam down the Mekong and into the South China Sea to Nha Be, southeast of Saigon. For four days, the troops plunged through the Rung Sat, where Frank Rybicki had been killed, in an effort to secure the Long Tau shipping channel, which led to the South Vietnamese capital. Failing to find the enemy, the soldiers reboarded the boats on June 18 and moved eight miles to the juncture of two small rivers for another sweep.

Shortly before noon on June 19, George was flying in a Huey above Long An Province, not far from where he and his platoon had been left behind six weeks earlier. Because the battalion commander, Lieutenant Colonel Bolduc, was on R and R, the executive officer had taken his seat in the helicopter. George happened to tune in to one of the other battalion networks when a desperate cry came over the radio.

"Oh God, oh God! Everybody's dead! We're all shot!"

He clapped the earphones closer to his head. The shrieking intensified. "I need help immediately! Please, somebody help us! We're all dying!"

George reached to his left and tapped the executive officer. "Listen to this, sir," he shouted above the rotor noise. "You can't really make out what the situation is, but it's serious stuff."

The major listened for a moment, his features tightening.

"Who is it?"

"I don't know yet, sir. I was just listening to the other battalion net."

Fifteen hundred feet below, explosions blossomed in red and white puffs, and the delicate green stitchery of Viet Cong tracers spread across the rice paddies. "Let's take a closer look," the XO shouted. The Huey pilot looked skeptical but nodded. He and the co-pilot had each wedged a pistol into his crotch for protection against stray bullets from below. The Huey canted onto its side and dropped several hundred feet.

Ping! Ping! Small-arms rounds began punching through the aluminum cabin and ricocheting off the armored doors in front. The artillery observer grabbed his radio and sat on it to avoid taking a round in the buttocks. Scrambling into his seat, the crew chief in back cinched his straps with a sharp tug. George felt the familiar rush of adrenaline as a bullet severed one of the fuel lines. Within seconds, a fine, malodorous mist filled the Huey. He watched the pilot's hands frantically turning the radio knobs to the emergency channel.

"Mayday. Mayday. Mayday."

An ominous succession of warning lights began winking on the control panel. As the RPM limiter flashed red, the engine wheezed and died. The pilot immediately pushed the collective control stick down with his left hand to neutralize the pitch angle. To autorotate the helicopter into an emergency landing, he had to keep the rotors spinning, or glide would turn to plummet. Dropping at thirty feet per second, the pilot peered through the Plexiglas, looking for a place to crash. "Hang on!" he yelled.

George figured that if he held on any tighter, blood would squeeze from his fingers. Thank God it's the delta, he thought. At least the terrain offered plenty of open rice paddies. Farther north, in triple-canopy jungle, autorotating choppers sometimes impaled themselves on teak and mahogany trees.

Fifty feet from the ground, the pilot yanked back on the big cyclic stick with his right hand. The nose of the Huey flared up, further slowing its descent. But as the skids smacked into the earth with a jarring thump, the tail boom nicked the ground and cracked. George and the others flipped their safety harnesses off, grabbed the radios, and raced across the wet ground to a spot forty yards in front of the Huey's nose. They waited for the helicopter to explode, but it just sat there, a pathetic hulk, its fractured tail boom canted at an angle. Feeling as vulnerable as sheep among wolves, the half-dozen men fanned out in a tight perimeter and called for help on the radio. A few minutes later, another Huey swooped in, plucked them from the ground, and carried them to the firebase. They immediately boarded a replacement command helicopter and returned to the battlefield.

The predicament of the ground troops had not improved. Six U.S. infantry companies from the 3rd and 4th battalions of the 47th Infantry had swept across the canals and paddies below while a South Vietnamese battalion tried to block the enemy near Ap Bac. Alpha Company of the 4th Battalion had moved across an open paddy, only to be ambushed by enemy soldiers hidden in an L-shaped bunker complex on the company's front and right flank. Pinned down without cover, some of the Americans lay so close to the enemy that the use of artillery and helicopter gunships was all but impossible. Furthermore, the stout enemy bunkers remained impervious to everything except direct hits with 90mm recoilless rifles or gunship rockets.

As the other five rifle companies maneuvered below, George again tuned in to the 4th Battalion's radio frequency. He heard Alpha Company's commander describing the scene.

"I can't see very far, but I can see four people who aren't wounded and four who are wounded but can still move. Everybody else is either dead or wounded so bad they can't move."

The 4th Battalion commander cut in.

"Everybody?"

"Everybody."

Then George heard another voice from below. This one was familiar. "Yeah, I'm okay but I've got a lot of wounded. We need to get somebody in here, get this thing stabilized so we can get some dustoffs."

The voice belonged to Fred Bertolino, a classmate who was one of Alpha's platoon leaders. Even in this jam, and in spite of his apparent wounds, Bertolino was soft-spoken.

George flipped back and forth between the battalion networks; his old platoon was down there with the 3rd Battalion. Once again the executive officer ordered the Huey to descend, this time to drop some smoke canisters requested by one of the companies. At one hundred knots the helicopter swooped in almost low enough to pluck at the rice stalks. As the case of smoke was pushed out the door, George heard the familiar crack of bullets puncturing the fuselage, and soon the red warning lights began blinking furiously again. Once again the pilot made an emergency landing; once again they scrambled from the crippled chopper; and once again a rescue Huey hauled them back to the firebase for a replacement.

As the afternoon wore on, Alpha Company's predicament slid from desperate to doomed. Most of those still alive remained trapped in eight inches of paddy water within easy range of the enemy. Every effort to send help was violently repulsed. Both George and Howard Kirk, whose platoon had been moved from the ships to about a quarter of a mile from Alpha, listened to Fred Bertolino's frantic cries for help.

"We're all gonna bleed to death," he pleaded. "We're all finished, including me, if you don't get some help in here." His voice grew weaker and less coherent.

The shooting ebbed with the sunlight. Once more that afternoon, the helicopter in which George was riding was shot down. By the third time, it almost seemed routine. After eight o'clock, the battlefield fell silent. At midnight, when they finally stopped flying to wait for dawn, George saw that both the corps commander and General Westmoreland had arrived. On his right sleeve when he came to the delta, Westmoreland always wore the 9th Division combat patch he had earned during World War II in Europe. That was good politics, but this clearly was not the usual morale-building official visit from Saigon. Like praying monks, the generals knelt in the dirt, poking at a map and wondering what to do.

During the night, the Viet Cong slipped out of their bunkers. They moved west across a stream called the Rach Nui before turning south. After sunrise on the morning of the twentieth, the Americans caught one VC platoon in the open and destroyed it. The rest of the enemy escaped.

Howard Kirk's platoon crossed the Rach Nui to police the battlefield. The dead from Alpha Company lay scattered through the paddy in sodden clumps. Kirk found Bertolino face down in the brown water, where he evidently had lost consciousness and drowned. Kirk helped lift him into a body bag. If Fred Bertolino's family wanted a West Point burial, a spot was waiting for him in the academy cemetery. Dry ground there was never hard to come by.

The firefight was over. Forty-six Americans had been killed and 140 wounded. The 9th Division claimed 250 enemy dead. George Crocker had again narrowly escaped with his life. Once more the thought flashed through his mind that perhaps he was charmed. He wasn't sure how else to explain why so many of his classmates died and he was spared.

George rarely dwelt on the dead. Like getting too close to the troops, that was fraught with danger. By temperament, he was not given to philosophical ruminations on cruel fate. But the death of friends like Loftheim and Bertolino hit him hard, further sapping the boyish excitement he had once felt about the great adventure of combat. Occasionally, as when he heard that Loftheim had been killed, he sat on his bunk at Dong Tam, brooding. It seemed so unfair that such men should die. Why, he wondered, did war seem to single out the best? Why couldn't at least the very best of the best survive? When such fine soldiers died, he thought, their loss was a waste, a pointless, tragic waste.

Robert E. Lee had once mused that it was fortunate war was such a terrible thing because otherwise men would grow too fond of it. The deaths of men like Frank Rybicki and Denny Loftheim and Fred Bertolino served to guarantee that men like George Crocker would never grow too fond of war.

9

EIGHT SEVEN FIVE

ON JUNE 8, 1967, exactly one year after graduation and eleven days before Fred Bertolino died in a delta rice paddy, the class of 1966 was promoted en masse to first lieutenant. The men swapped their single gold bars for single silver bars. By now, the Army was so swollen with lieutenants that some post exchanges ran out of silver rank epaulets for dress uniforms; a few enterprising wives simply painted over the second lieutenant's insignia with pearl fingernail polish. Promotion also meant a pay raise, from $303 to $504 a month, plus the extra $65 combat stipend due each man once he set foot in Vietnam.

Also one year after graduation, *Newsweek* magazine published a long article on the class of 1966, "West Point Goes to War." The cover story devoted nine full pages to pictures of the men at graduation, in Ranger school, and preparing for battle. One photo showed Lieutenant Peter Lantz in his dress blues, having just exchanged wedding vows at the West Point chapel with his bride, Dagmar; the train of her white gown drifted behind them like a vapor trail. The article portrayed the West Pointers as heroic, cocky, and certain of their mission. "It is a just war," one class member said of Vietnam. "We have to take a stand somewhere. I think we ought to be out there. The duty of a soldier is combat; unless a man can do it, he's no good to the Army."

Yet as the second wave of classmates from '66 mustered for war, this final season at home was vaguely unsettling. The newspapers began referring to it as the Summer of Love. The press also documented the growing vigor of the counterculture, which was best typified by a new Beatles album called *Sgt. Pepper's Lonely Hearts Club Band*. Released on June 1, the album would sell two and a half million copies by Labor Day. The *Times* of London called the album "a decisive moment in the history of Western civilization." A writer in *The New Yorker* insisted "that the closest Western civilization has come to unity since the Congress of Vienna in 1815 was the week the *Sgt. Pepper* album was released. For a brief while, the irreparably fragmented consciousness of the West was unified, at least in the minds of the young."

But Sgt. Pepper was not an American soldier. Real soldiers en route to Vietnam, including the lieutenants from the class of '66, usually passed through San Francisco, western command post for the Summer of Love. A bus company offered a "Hippie Hop" excursion to Haight Street in San Francisco; it was billed as "the only foreign tour within the continental limits of the United States." Sometimes the bus took an hour to ease through the long-haired, barefoot, incense-burning throng that jammed Haight between Clayton and Ashbury streets. The newspapers carried frequent reports about red, green, and blue pills containing 250 micrograms of lysergic acid diethylamide, better known as LSD. Down the California coast, fifty thousand rock 'n' rollers showed up for the Monterey International Pop Festival, which opened on June 16 and featured twenty bands, including the Who and a former GI named Jimi Hendrix. Antiwar sentiment, seemingly confined to the lunatic fringe just a year before, now had a noisy popularity. Circles with an inverted pitchfork inside — the new symbol for peace — sprouted like dandelions.

For twenty-two-year-olds who had spent the past five years in the cloisters of West Point and various Army posts, this was bewildering. The apprehension of going to war was intensified by the awareness that something peculiar was happening within their generation — and it was not particularly unifying either, the Congress of Vienna be damned. What on earth was going on? they wondered. Where was the nation's war psyche, that famous American determination to annihilate the enemy? Many Americans now seemed to doubt that there even *was* an enemy. In 1962, the men of '66 had entered West Point as the leaders of a generation that wore its hair short, its feet shod, and its patriotism on the sleeve. *That* was unity. Now, the West Pointers' most cherished beliefs were under fire from their own countrymen.

In June, Matt Harrison flew from California to Bien Hoa, northeast of Saigon. Despite the oppressive heat and humidity, Matt was pleased to be in Vietnam. After Ranger training and his sojourn at Saratoga, he had spent six long months commanding a reconnaissance platoon at Fort Hood, Texas. The unit included many 11-Hotels — Army jargon for infantry scouts — who had seen action in the Ia Drang Valley and were marking time at Hood until their enlistments expired. Those suffering from malaria would stumble into formation, ask to go on sick call, then shiver their way to the hospital. Others were simply crazy;

Matt figured that if one of the requirements for being an 11-H was a degree of instability, then a few of these soldiers were overqualified.

Besides affording him an escape from Fort Hood, the assignment to Bien Hoa pleased Matt for two other reasons. First, it signaled his entry into a war for which he had eagerly prepared. Experiencing combat — "seeing the elephant," as Civil War soldiers once called it — was a necessary way to establish his bona fides as an Army officer. That was how a young lieutenant moved from apprentice to journeyman.

Second, Bien Hoa was the venue of a reunion with other classmates from '66 who also were joining the 173rd. The counterculture and antiwar sentiment at home meant little here. Within this brotherhood, every man knew where he stood; the values they had shared since Beast Barracks would still abide. Just in the 2nd Battalion of the 503rd Airborne Infantry alone, seven other '66ers showed up at the same time as Matt. Among them was the Chaucer-reading, Scotch-swilling Buck Thompson.

Buck arrived at Bien Hoa flashing photos of his new son, born a month earlier at Fort Bragg. Because of his passion for German history, Buck had wanted to call the baby Gunther, but Fran persuaded him to give that name to their St. Bernard puppy instead. Then he leaned toward Wolfgang, so Fran bought him a duck on which to inflict that moniker. In the end, he settled for Richard William Thompson II, nicknamed the Deuce. Buck loved the Deuce beyond description.

Predictably, Buck's departure for Vietnam had been memorable. He spent the final week at home with his family in Atchison. The night before he was scheduled to leave, he got drunk and fell asleep in the bathtub with the door latched and the water running. After scaling a ladder and trying unsuccessfully to jimmy the locked window, his siblings finally removed the door from its hinges and shut off the spigots. Buck snored on, as oblivious as he had been when his fatigue jacket caught fire in Ranger 3.

The next morning, his sister Lee Ann drove him down to the old Kansas City Municipal Airport, along the bluffs of the Missouri River. Buck would not let Fran or the baby come; the separation was too painful. In the terminal, Lee Ann wept bitterly, certain that she would never see her brother again.

The reunion at Bien Hoa was brief. For five days, Matt, Buck, and the others tarried at the 173rd's former base camp, where the brigade had first arrived from Okinawa in May 1965 to protect U.S. planes during Operation Rolling Thunder. The lieutenants fired their new M-16 rifles at pop-up targets and practiced patrolling through the nearby rubber plantations, confused because every Vietnamese looked like every other Vietnamese. Then they flew north, first to Pleiku, then to Dak To, where they were farmed out to different battalions. Army intelligence believed that North Vietnamese Army (NVA) troops had massed in the mountains of the Central Highlands for an attack on the Special Forces camp at Dak To. The 173rd was sent to parry the blow with a countermove codenamed Operation Greeley.

Matt was assigned as a platoon leader in Charlie Company of the 2nd Battalion. Then, a few hours after his arrival at Dak To, about 250 men from Charlie and her sister company Alpha were airlifted southwest to hunt for the enemy.

Nearly three hundred miles north of Saigon, the war for the Central Highlands was fought vertically, at a perpendicular to the horizontal delta war being waged farther south. The ridgelines of the Annamite Range in Kontum Province rose to four thousand feet in "primeval confusion," as one historian later described them. In the triple-canopy jungle, teak and mahogany tree trunks often grew to eight feet in circumference. Bamboo brakes were so dense that visibility rarely exceeded five yards, and paratroopers swore that their M-16 rounds would not penetrate the thickets. Sometimes men simply vanished. On June 20, a patrol discovered a clutch of skeletons in the jungle — two Green Beret soldiers, eight Montagnard tribesmen, and one NVA.

Monsoons blew out of Cambodia in a black wall of water. Even when the rains eased, the mountains remained bearded in a gray mist called *crachin,* the French word for drizzle. A man might awake in the morning to find himself studded with thumb-size leeches. Soldiers in the 173rd could expect a court-martial if they failed to carry at least three pairs of socks. Feet were inspected daily for infections and fungal growth; like a bizarre centipede, a platoon of paratroopers would recline with bare toes extended while their sergeants or lieutenants peered closely, just as Siegfried Sassoon had described doing in Kitchener's army a half century earlier.

For two days the 2nd Battalion slogged southward. Matt Harrison's prevailing image was of thrashing through a dark, wet, pestilential closet. Although they saw no NVA soldiers, the paratroopers followed a well-traveled enemy trail. Just a few miles to the west lay a principal terminus of what the NVA called the Truong Son Strategic Supply Route, better known to the Americans as the Ho Chi Minh Trail; the mountains provided a ramp for enemy supplies and troops spilling into South Vietnam from the NVA's Base Area 609 in Cambodia.

Late in the afternoon of June 21, Charlie Company and its contingent of Montagnard tribesmen stopped for the night. Matt deployed his platoon as part of the company's defensive perimeter. Straddling the NVA trail, the men dug in and carefully positioned their claymore mines and M-60 machine guns. A small "clearing" patrol slipped from the camp to make certain that no enemy soldiers had crept within striking distance. Three thousand yards to the south, Alpha Company also laagered for the night along the trail. Their mission nearly complete, Charlie and Alpha were scheduled to ford the Dak Po'Ko River the next afternoon to rejoin the rest of the brigade at Dak To.

As the last light ebbed, reducing the paratroopers of C Company to dim shadows, a sudden fusillade of automatic weapons fire ripped through the jungle. Minutes later, the clearing patrol straggled into camp, and Matt saw his first dead man. The corpse was that of a Montagnard tribesman who had been shot through the throat during the brief skirmish with NVA soldiers. Matt watched as the body was wrapped in a poncho and trussed with nylon cord so that the paratroopers could carry the tribesman back to Dak To the next day. No sooner had the camp quieted down again than Matt saw his second dead man. An American private wandering outside the company perimeter to urinate was shot and killed by one of his own sentries. The dead private was also wrapped and trussed.

As heat and pressure convert the leavings of the living into anthracite and diamonds, so the sight of those two packages in their olive-drab winding sheets hardened something inside Matt that night. The precise point of this transformation was difficult to fix, although it probably lay in that corner of the anatomy which men had once — without blushing — called the soul.

Instead of eons, the process took only hours. But it forever left in Matt a small, dense pellet of comprehension that the dead were truly dead, defined wholly by what they were not: alive. No Hollywood director's whistle would raise them from their sprawl for yet another take. This carbonizing of mortality, simple as it was, proved extraordinarily useful during the grim forty-eight hours that followed.

As Charlie Company began to stir on the jungle ridgeline just after dawn on June 22, Matt heard shooting again. The sound drifted through the trees from Alpha's position in the south. After a brief lull, the battle sounds resumed with such intensity that the shots merged into a continuous roar.

"Let's go. Saddle up. Be ready to move," ordered Ron Leonard, the Charlie Company commander.

Leonard was a blunt, no-nonsense captain from the outback of western Kansas. He and Matt had served together at Fort Hood, where they developed a mutual admiration, and Leonard was the sole reason that Matt was not down the trail with Alpha. Like the general manager of a baseball team, the captain had arranged a trade. Matt came to C Company in exchange for one of his classmates, Richard Hood, a native of Winter Haven, Florida, who had arrived in Vietnam the same day as Matt. Also with Hood in Alpha was another '66er, Donald Judd of Batavia, New York. Don and Matt had been friends at the academy and had bunked together briefly at Bien Hoa.

"Hey, Matt," Judd had joked a few days earlier, "how about signing a paper that says if you get killed, I get to take your body home so I can get out of here?"

That wisecrack had provoked a knee-slapping guffaw, but no one was laughing now. The distant shooting was so intense that it had an almost human timbre, like a hysterical keening. From fragmentary radio reports, Leonard and his officers in Charlie realized that Alpha had been ambushed as the men broke camp, but rain and fog were preventing aerial observation. The battalion commander at Dak To radioed Charlie Company to sit tight and wait.

The morning passed slowly, and an ominous silence again descended over the jungle. Just before noon, Leonard summoned his platoon leaders.

"Battalion has ordered us to try to link up with Alpha," he told Matt and the other three lieutenants. "We can expect contact on the way. I want to stay off the ridgeline and away from the damned trail. If the NVA are waiting for us, that's probably where they have their ambush."

Lugging the two men who had been killed the evening before, the company set off in a diamond formation. The point team went first, followed by the lead platoon. Two other platoons fanned out on the wings; the weapons platoon trailed in the rear with its two 60mm mortars. If the enemy attacked, the platoons were to collapse to the center of the formation while the mortar crews laid down a barrage of protective fire.

Within minutes, Matt was soaked with mist and sweat. Leonard kept them one to two hundred yards down from the ridgeline, periodically dispatching scouts to the west in order to keep the company parallel to the trail. Progress was agonizingly slow. Grasping at saplings to keep from sliding down the steep slope, the soldiers slashed their way through bamboo thickets and the sopping undergrowth.

They took most of the afternoon to travel less than two miles. Around five o'clock, the company came to a clearing thirty yards in diameter where Alpha had hacked out a landing zone the preceding night; before the shooting began that morning the paratroopers had salted the clearing with CS crystals, a noxious chemical intended to prevent the NVA from using the spot as a mortar base.

"Put your gas masks on," Leonard ordered.

When they donned the masks, Matt and the others found that the filters inside were waterlogged and useless. The Montagnards balked and refused to walk through the CS, so the Americans carried them on their backs. Even tiptoeing, the soldiers kicked up little crystalline clouds with their jungle boots. By the time the company had crossed the clearing, the soldiers were vomiting and weeping, their faces and hands flushed and puffy.

They found the remnants of Alpha Company clustered on a small knoll about 250 yards up the ridge from the spot where three rifle platoons had been attacked. The company commander was still alive — he had been supervising the CS operation when the shooting began — and his weapons platoon had also survived. But nearly a hundred others were missing.

A few minutes later, a helicopter swooped in to drop off the battalion commander, Lieutenant Colonel Edward Partain, who had been a tactical officer at West Point when Matt was a plebe. Partain gathered the officers around a map and tried to determine the best way to reach the trapped paratroopers.

"I want you to try to probe down the hill, but break off if you have any contact," Partain told Leonard. "Don't throw good money after bad."

But it was no use. Hundreds of enemy soldiers from a battalion of the 24th NVA Regiment lay entrenched on both sides of the trail. Armed with AK-47s and RPD light machine guns, the enemy could aim plunging fire from one direction and grazing fire from another. Charlie Company immediately ran into a wall of bullets and grenades. Unable to flank the NVA through the dense jungle, Matt and the others pulled back and dug in around the knoll near the top of the ridge.

That night, expecting an NVA attack at any moment, Matt heard screaming and occasional shots as the enemy executed the wounded along the trail. A few survivors crawled back into Charlie Company's perimeter in the dark, including one soldier who was in shock from a deep gash across his face. Helicopters dropped chain saws for cutting another landing zone, and a Chinook lifted the remnants of Alpha back to Dak To. Gunships circled overhead throughout the night, periodically dousing the jungle with rocket and machine-gun fire.

At dawn, Partain ordered another probe while a third company, Bravo, closed to reinforce. The shooting had stopped as Matt inched his platoon down the ridge. *Don't throw good money after bad.* For an hour, they crept closer to the ambush site; finally, the Americans realized that the enemy had vanished during the night. Matt and his men moved cautiously into the killing zone.

The scene was unspeakable. Seventy-eight American bodies lay sprawled for a hundred yards or so along the trail, framed by the encroaching jungle. Eighteen lay piled on top of one another in a small circle, site of a desperate last stand. The NVA had stripped some of the bodies. Others were mutilated, their eyes gouged out or their ring fingers chopped off.

A few survivors had feigned death. One soldier had remained motionless as the enemy shot him three times in the back; another did the same while his finger was severed with a trench knife. He sat among the dead, trying to attach his finger to its bloody stump with a strip of adhesive tape from a smoke canister.

Matt wandered numbly among the corpses and the detritus of combat — shell casings, rucksacks, C-ration coffee packets, and little cans of fruit cocktail, which had been opened for breakfast just before the ambush was sprung. The ground was splotched red. Some of the dead had hollow cavity wounds, brains literally blown from their heads.

Matt stopped abruptly. On the jungle floor lay the body of Don Judd. His face was contorted with pain, lips pulled back in a frozen grimace. From one of the survivors, Matt pieced together his friend's last moments. Crouching behind a tree, Judd had listened to the anguished screams of one of his men who was shot in the stomach. Ignoring frantic warnings from the company first sergeant to stay put, he had yelled for covering fire, dashed onto the trail toward the wounded paratrooper, and been cut down before his second step.

Matt stared at the body, the image of Don Judd's face fixing itself forever in his memory. Dear God, he thought. Don was getting out of here after all. Maybe if he had lived a little longer, long enough to develop that small, dense pellet, that conviction of mortality . . . And here was Rich Hood. Matt saw a small hole behind one ear, as though he had been executed point blank. His ammunition gone, Hood had fought to the end with trip flares.

Matt moved slowly among the dead as Charlie Company began zipping them into body bags. Never had he imagined having to witness such carnage. The battlefield bespoke something primordial, something as timeless as warfare: the stench, the droning flies, the grotesque attitudes of corpses already ripening in the jungle heat. The mutilated bodies, lying singly or in small groups, were reminiscent of Custer's last stand. But the tableau also suggested a heartbreaking naïveté, like the *Kindermord,* the Massacre of the Innocents in 1914, when untrained German schoolboys had been slaughtered at Ypres.

The paratroopers unearthed nine or ten NVA dead in shallow graves, some wrapped in plastic sheeting. The Army would claim four hundred enemy killed, but no one believed that. Nor did they believe Westmoreland when he later told the 2nd Battalion that Alpha's gallant stand had prevented Dak To from being overrun.

Judd and Hood would win posthumous Silver Stars. Looking for a scapegoat after the battle, the brass fixed on Ron Leonard and accused him of failing to move down the trail with "sufficient alacrity." A few weeks later, Leonard was transferred to another battalion.

Matt had seen the elephant. Returning to Dak To, he understood that there was a corollary to the inner hardening caused by battle deaths. As the dead were defined by their immutable segregation from the living, so the living were defined by their ability to move beyond the dead. The incessant discussions of duty at West Point had been abstract, much as war had been. Now duty was tangible. Matt's obligation was to carry on, to keep the living alive, to fight the good fight. To do otherwise was a betrayal of those who had died bravely, of those who entrusted their lives to his leadership, and of the long gray line.

Were you to fail, MacArthur had warned, *a million ghosts in olive drab, in brown khaki, in blue and gray, would rise from their white crosses, thundering those magic words: duty, honor, country.*

How terrible the price to be able to comprehend fully that sentence. Seventy-eight more ghosts had joined MacArthur's million. But now the general's warning seemed more than just the rhetoric of a histrionic old man. Robert E. Lee, who had once worried about growing too fond of war, also claimed that *duty* was the most sublime noun in our language. Yet sometimes a young officer could not help noticing that it was also a four-letter word.

Three months later, in mid September, a solitary Huey hovered for a moment before lifting in the usual maelstrom of noise and dust. Peering down through the open door of the helicopter, the Reverend James Ford watched the Dak To airstrip quickly shrink away until it was just a barren rectangle stretching east to west through the valley. Soldiers crossing Route 14 gingerly felt for the boardwalk lying beneath the mud; one misstep and a man would sink to his crotch in the quagmire. What a place, Ford thought, what an awful place.

The helicopter leveled off and headed northwest. Ford relaxed, settling back into his seat. Having taken nearly a hundred helicopter and plane rides during his six weeks in Vietnam, he could instinctively tell now when they had passed above small-arms range. At fifteen hundred feet, tensions in the Huey seemed to melt away — until it was time to descend again.

Jim Ford had never really been frightened before coming to Vietnam, not even when he ski jumped backward for the first time. Apprehensive, yes. Nervous, yes. But not scared. Since arriving in Saigon, however, he had experienced raw fear twice, both times in a helicopter. The first was when they had wandered into a firefight. In an instant — Ford still couldn't believe how quickly it happened — explosions and tracers filled the sky. Even the door gunner seemed momentarily paralyzed with confusion.

The second time, the Huey was hugging the jungle in a heavy rain when suddenly two huge trees loomed dead ahead. Traveling at one hundred knots, they were too close to fly over or around the trees. An image flashed through Ford's mind of rotor blades snapping against the unforgiving trunks and the cabin tumbling like a stone. At the last possible instant the pilot kicked the helicopter onto its side, skittering between the branches by an eyelash.

All in all, Ford thought, it probably wasn't a bad thing to know what terror felt like. The experience brought him closer to the soldiers and gave him a better sense of what they were enduring. And that, ultimately, was a good part of his reason for being here.

Several times since becoming chief chaplain at West Point, Ford had thought of going to Southeast Asia on an extended visit. When Westmoreland came to the academy during a recent stateside trip, Ford had invited him into Quarters 60 after Sunday chapel. Over a glass of sherry, the chaplain asked permission to "make some pastoral calls" in Vietnam. That's a great idea, Westmoreland replied, and quickly assented.

For the first few days, the chaplain stayed at Westmoreland's compound in Saigon. Sometimes after dinner the table was strewn with maps and charts as the senior officers plotted strategy. "It's all right," Westmoreland would assure his deputies, nodding toward Ford, "he can be trusted."

Out in the field, Ford had visited nearly three hundred West Pointers. For the most part he just listened as they talked about the war, their families, their fears, their frustration at walking over the same bloody ground again and again. The conversations opened his eyes. He had not given much consideration to American goals in Vietnam, but hearing these men talk started him thinking. Where was the war heading? What were the objectives? Why were men dying if the killing ground was immediately ceded again to the enemy?

It was not Ford's way to press these issues, at least not now. He was no William Sloane Coffin, although he admired the outspoken Yale chaplain and would go out of his way to hear him lecture. Coffin's antiwar pronouncements had grown increasingly passionate. But Ford believed that his duty was to succor the men in combat, not question the cause for which they risked their lives. He was certainly no pacifist.

At one firebase, a young redleg asked him whether he wanted to pull the lanyard on a 175mm Long Tom artillery tube; without even thinking, Ford stepped forward and jerked the cord, sending the projectile God knows where. Later, after a volleyball game with the troops, a colonel stopped by his tent and handed him a pistol. Jim, the colonel said, we've had reports of some incidents in the area so I'm leaving my .45 with you. Ford kept the gun next to his pillow all night, happy to have it.

Historically, he knew, chaplains had fallen in and out of fashion on the battlefield. Henry V heard Mass three times and took Communion before Agincourt. The medieval French and English armies carried legions of priests with them. But by the early nineteenth century, men of the cloth were a rare sight in combat; Wellington, for example, permitted a few Church of England clergymen to accompany him on the Continent, but primarily to counter the pernicious spread of Methodism.

Of course efforts to invoke God in a fight were at least as old as Melchizedek assuring Abraham of Jehovah's help in defeating the kings of the East. In America, chaplains during the Revolution and Civil War often cited this or that scriptural passage as evidence of God's enthusiasm for their sanguinary causes. Some had even joined in the bloodletting. One Confederate clergyman had been so inflamed during a skirmish in Kentucky in 1861 that he shot two Yankees, knifed a third, and ran after the retreating enemy, shrieking obscenities. In World War II, the bellicose behavior of some chaplains provoked a warning from military authorities that the Geneva Convention protected clerics only as long as they kept their place.

That was not Ford's style. References to Vietnam as a holy cause offended him; the notion of blessing cannons or rifles — as some chaplains had done even in the twentieth century — struck him as downright medieval. He was here, as he had told Westmoreland, on some "pastoral calls." Fundamentally, that meant seeing the soldiers as men, not vice versa.

The Huey circled the landing zone once and dropped quickly to evade sniper fire. On the ground, Ford climbed out, reflexively ducking his head as he hurried over to the group of soldiers waiting in the trees.

"This way, sir," one of them said. "We've got a little ways to walk if you don't mind."

Following them along a narrow trail through the jungle, Ford had the sense of having reached the end of the earth. These mountains appeared so remote, so relentlessly green. Mud spattered his fatigues; the canteen on his web belt sloshed gently with every step. He felt oddly serene. This was the kind of place where very little came between a man and his Maker.

After a few minutes, they entered a clearing on the side of a hill. It was 3:30 P.M., and one company from the 173rd had just laagered here for the night. Coca-Cola cans littered the hill; several paratroopers sat reading letters from home. Two things struck Ford: the incongruity of the familiar red soda cans in this alien terrain, and the contrast of white stationery against the Asian mud.

He soon saw another incongruity — Peter Lantz. At West Point, Lantz had been something of a devil-may-care cadet, gliding through the academy on what was facetiously known as "care factor." Upperclassmen often accused him of polishing his shabby shoes with a candy bar. Jim Ford probably had more ties to Pete Lantz to than any other cadet. He had confirmed him in the chapel, married him to Dagmar shortly after the class of '66 graduated, and baptized their first child.

Lantz greeted him warmly and then pointed through the mist at the green ridgeline a short distance to the west. That's Laos right there, he told the chaplain. You've come about as far as you can come.

From a small case, Ford removed the chalice, wine, and wafers needed for Communion. For six weeks, he had resolutely declined all offers to conduct services in Vietnam. He figured the last thing anybody needed here was a wise man from the East elbowing the in-country chaplains aside. But he had accepted the opportunity to come out here to administer Communion. On this verdant hillside he would be anonymous — not the Reverend James David Ford, not the chaplain from West Point — just a man in spattered fatigues sharing the sacrament of the Eucharist, the Lord's supper.

Several dozen men drifted over to join him. Ford placed a wafer in each man's mouth with his right hand and tipped the chalice with his left. *This is my body. Take and eat. This is my blood. Take and drink.*

After the service, he lingered for a bit, chatting and joking, before hiking back down the trail to the Huey. As they flew back to Dak To, he was surprised by the emotion the trip had stirred within him. How vulnerable these men seemed out here in the middle of nowhere, twelve thousand miles from home. West Pointers like Pete Lantz, Ford believed, were different from civilians in three ways: they had shorter hair, they wore a uniform, and they had better posture. That was it.

How many times had he counseled cadets who were troubled by the contradiction between the Christian injunction against killing and the profession of arms? Part of his job was to affirm their calling, to reconcile that contradiction.

"The commandment 'Thou shalt not kill,' " he would tell them, "is best translated 'Thou shalt not murder.' " Intent was crucial. Was the act of killing intended to forestall a greater evil, such as Nazism? Was there purity of intent, such as an effort to secure freedom rather than to subjugate?

At heart, he believed, these men were not killers, certainly not murderers. Violence was not something they sought. No matter how battle-hardened they grew as men, he would always see in them the frightened eighteen-year-olds swearing an oath on the summer Plain. At heart, they were peaceful men, gentle men. Jim Ford was positive of that. And he loved them for it.

In the fall of 1967, about the time that Ford returned to West Point, Matt Harrison took command of the decimated Alpha Company. Searching for someone who could help sponge away the stain of defeat after the slaughter of June 22, Lieutenant Colonel Partain appointed Matt, though he was a new first lieutenant and the job traditionally went to a captain.

The battalion left the Central Highlands for several weeks to interdict the rice harvest and fight against a force of local Viet Cong along the coast, near Tuy Hoa on the Song Ba River. The interlude seemed almost pleasant to Matt, after the hellish mountains. The local Viet Cong lacked the manpower, weaponry, and training of the NVA regulars, so the Americans could assert their military superiority without fearing the kind of slaughter that had cost Don Judd and Rich Hood their lives. Occasionally, Alpha Company practiced some of Beckwith's Ranger tactics, including stay-behind patrols and cloverleaf ambushes. War, Matt saw, had an element of gamesmanship, and when the game was going well, morale soared. Mortality seemed less fragile, less besieged. During the weeks at Tuy Hoa, the company killed more enemy and captured more weapons than the rest of the battalion combined, without enduring a single friendly casualty.

After a skirmish, when the field was littered with enemy dead and Alpha had not suffered so much as a flesh wound, a surge of jubilation washed through the company, imbuing the men with the feeling of brotherhood that comes with victory and survival. Matt was reminded of scenes that he had viewed on television of a victorious World Series locker room, where the players romped about, incoherent with joy. The joy of combat was neither objective nor rational; it may not have been especially sane. You could convince yourself that you deserved it. You won because you were better than they were. You were faster, smarter, tougher, luckier. You had put it all at risk. And, for today, you were fortune's favorite child.

In late October, the Central Highlands began to heat up again. A defecting NVA sergeant and captured documents led Army intelligence to conclude that Dak To was threatened by six NVA regiments with at least seven thousand troops plus one Viet Cong battalion. On November 1, the 173rd flew back to Dak To aboard Air Force C-130s. The U.S. counterpunch this time would be called — of all sweet ironies — Operation MacArthur.

The Americans did not realize it at the time, but the enemy was actually engaged in an elaborate diversion. Inspired by General Vo Nguyen Giap, the NVA in the highlands hoped to keep U.S. forces occupied while preparations were under way for a secret plan known by the acronym TCK-TKN, standing for the Vietnamese words meaning "general offensive–general uprising." That offensive was scheduled for late January 1968, at the beginning of the New Year's holiday known as Tet.

The Americans took the bait. Operations steadily intensified in early November. Psyops planes dropped more than twenty million leaflets urging surrender, and engineers worked feverishly to keep Route 14 open to Pleiku in the south. The small airstrip at Dak To was burdened beyond its capacity and occasionally aflame with crash-and-burns, including more than one collision between cargo planes and bulldozers expanding the field. The Air Force dumped tons of herbicide to defoliate potential ambush sites or destroy suspected enemy rice fields.

Contacts in the mountains became more frequent and bloodier. On the morning of November 11, Jerry Cecil, the son of a Kentucky postmaster and one of the '66ers who had been featured in the *Newsweek* article, led his platoon out of its night position into a saddle between two ridgelines. Rather than rotate to a staff job after his six-month command tour was up, Cecil had come to an understanding with his paratroopers: he would remain with the unit for a full year, as required of enlisted men, in exchange for their absolute obedience and loyalty.

As they entered the dense saddle near the old French fort at Ben Het, not far from the three-border junction of Cambodia, Laos, and Vietnam, Cecil sensed a trap. "Open fire!" he yelled, abruptly spraying the jungle with bullets. His sudden action saved the platoon from annihilation. The Americans, having blundered into the open end of a horseshoe ambush, were instantly pinned down. As helicopters dropped more ammunition and chain saws to clear a landing zone, the platoon inched backward. It took the men half a day to cover a hundred yards. Even with grenade fragments in his hip, Cecil three times scrambled up the ridgeline to carry wounded men to the landing zone. By the time the firefight ended, every man but one in the platoon was dead or wounded. The Americans counted 154 enemy bodies. Jerry Cecil received a Distinguished Service Cross, the nation's second highest award for valor.

Two days later, Matt was wounded. Still with Alpha, he no longer commanded the company. Partain, the battalion commander, had departed, and his replacement objected to having a lieutenant leading a company when experienced captains were available. Matt became the unit's executive officer; Alpha's new commander was Captain Michael J. Kiley, West Point '64 and the winner of four Silver Stars during an earlier tour with the First Cavalry.

At 9:30 A.M., a scout dog with the company's reconnaissance squad pricked up its ears while nosing up a ridge. Almost immediately, from a range of only twenty yards, NVA fire raked the squad. Matt took command of the company's lead elements, maneuvering them around the left flank. After linking up with the men under attack, he tried unsuccessfully to seize the high ground above the enemy, who were entrenched in bunkers across the ridgeline. Kiley brought two other platoons forward, but when he began moving them up the hill, the NVA responded with grenades and recoilless rifle fire, killing two paratroopers.

Soon the Americans detected movement on both flanks as the enemy tried to surround Alpha and sever the company from the rest of the battalion. Kiley quickly ordered his men back 150 yards, below the field of fire from the bunkers. At eleven o'clock, he summoned air strikes. The fight dragged on sporadically for another three hours, as Bravo and Charlie companies arrived to reinforce Alpha. At two-thirty, the enemy broke contact, leaving four dead on each side.

A fragment from either a mortar or a grenade had nicked Matt in the hand. Though not serious, within hours the wound showed signs of infection. Kiley, who had taken shrapnel in the leg, went to the rear for treatment, leaving Matt in charge. When he returned and saw Matt's festering hand, the captain insisted that his XO get help.

So it was that Matt remained at the aid station near the firebase for several days. As a consequence, he missed the beginning of the most intense fighting of the war since the battle for the Ia Drang Valley two years before. For Matt Harrison, the painful nick in his hand proved to be immense good fortune.

Twelve miles southwest of Dak To and only four miles from the Cambodian border, in Area of Operations Hawk, rose yet another hill in the endless procession of green ridges. Topographically, this one was relatively benign, neither unusually high nor perilously steep. Botanically, it offered the usual triple-canopy welter of hardwood and bamboo. From the north, the hill sloped gently, providing a ramp toward the summit that was roughly a hundred yards wide; the ridge dropped sharply to the west and more gradually to the east. On the Army's 1:25,000 scale maps, the hill was known only by its elevation in meters: 875.

In late spring, the NVA had secretly prepared an elaborate nexus of interlocking trenches and bunkers along the crest of Hill 875, now neatly camouflaged by the fecund jungle. With as much as eight feet of dirt and teak logs for overhead protection, the fortifications were impervious to all but direct hits from the heaviest Air Force bombs.

On November 18, an eighty-man Special Forces team on the south slope detected the enemy entrenched on the top of the hill. Following two brief firefights, the SF team withdrew with ten wounded. The next day, after a medley of artillery shells and seventy high-explosive and napalm bombs, three companies of the 2nd Battalion of the 503rd Infantry moved into position to storm the ridge.

The monsoons had passed and the morning dawned clear and bright, with temperatures heading toward the low 90s. With Charlie Company on the right and Delta on the left, the paratroopers began pushing up the north face of the hill in eight snaking columns at 9:43 on Sunday, November 19. Among those leading platoons in the assault were Buck Thompson and Pete Lantz. Each rifleman carried four hundred rounds of M-16 ammunition, and the grenadiers carried thirty rounds of high-explosive grenades and forty shotgun shells. Twelve hundred rounds were spread among the platoon for each M-60 machine gun, and every soldier had at least two fragmentation grenades, a smoke canister, and a trip flare. Some also carried claymore mines. As the paratroopers came to a clearing strewn with trees shattered by the earlier bombardment, one scout whispered to another, "I smell Charlies."

At ten-thirty, the NVA opened fire on the advancing columns. Specialist Four Kenneth Jacobson, the point man in Delta's second platoon, was shot three times and killed instantly. A medic who crawled up to help him was also hit and died a few minutes later. The Americans dropped their rucksacks and began to close up their platoons; the enemy intensified the fire with recoilless rifles and rocket-propelled grenades. Another medic was killed while tending one of the wounded C Company scouts.

Both companies marked their positions with smoke as artillery and bombing sorties smashed the hilltop once more. After thirty minutes, the paratroopers began to crawl forward again. Several soldiers from Delta surrounded one bunker and heaved five grenades through the firing port; a moment after the detonations, the Americans dived for cover when several NVA grenades came flying back out in response, an indication that the bunkers were tied together by tunnels. Two U.S. artillery rounds fell short, wounding four men in D Company. One of C Company's platoon leaders was mortally wounded by automatic weapons fire; Pete Lantz threw an arm around the lieutenant and dragged him down the hill as bullets and grenade fragments ripped the underbrush around them.

The attack stalled. After ordering a thirty-yard withdrawal, the C Company commander, Captain Harold Kaufman, drew his pistol and fired in the air several times to prevent the retreat from turning into a rout. Barely a grenade throw from the forward bunker, and under intense fire, both companies began to dig in, using their knives and helmets for shovels.

Farther down the hill, Captain Kiley had deployed Alpha Company in a U formation, with the open end toward the top of the ridge. When the shooting began, he ordered his weapons platoon to begin chopping a landing zone about a hundred yards from the fighting. A helicopter dropped a kit containing chain saws, axes, and crosscut saws.

Meanwhile, the NVA prepared to spring the trap. Undetected by the Americans, enemy soldiers crept down the western slope of 875 on trails, which had been built with neatly squared steps and handrails. Shortly after two P.M., they began inching back up the hill, approaching the paratroopers from below.

Forty yards from the landing zone, guarding Alpha's rear, four soldiers crouched next to the trail with an M-60 manned by Private First Class Carlos Lozada. Hearing the snap of twigs, Lozada peered around a tree and spotted a group of NVA soldiers with blackened faces and rifles camouflaged in burlap. "Here they come!" he yelled.

The first sweeping bursts of his machine gun caught fifteen enemy soldiers in the open and slaughtered them. In actions that would win him the Medal of Honor, Lozada provided covering fire from behind a log while the other paratroopers scrambled uphill toward the LZ. Then, stumbling backward up the trail, killing at least twenty NVA soldiers, he continued firing the M-60 from his hip until the weapon jammed. An enemy round slammed into his head, knocking him across the legs of another paratrooper, who screamed hysterically. One squad leader reached down and rolled Lozada face up in hopes that the enemy would see that he was dead and not mutilate his body.

The trap had been sprung, the noose cinched. As the enemy continued their heavy fire from the crest of 875, scores of NVA soldiers pushed against Alpha from two directions below, killing more paratroopers by the minute. Thousands of bullets tore the air, each with a sound once described as "the ripping of a silk dress." The Americans couldn't fire fast enough to cut down the swarming enemy soldiers, some of whom were shrieking and laughing bizarrely. One platoon leader named Tommy Remington, a friend of Matt Harrison's, was shot in both arms and both legs. Kiley, who had been wounded on the LZ during a mortar-

and-rocket barrage, dug in with a lieutenant, two sergeants, and two enlisted men near his command position. Charging from the west, the NVA quickly overran the little group, slaughtering Kiley and the five others.

Dragging some of their wounded — others had to be abandoned — the survivors from Alpha scrambled up the hill, yelling "Friendly! Friendly!" to avoid being shot by paratroopers in Charlie and Delta companies. Soldiers from the three companies quickly formed a defensive circle. If the north slope of 875 was a watch face, with the summit at twelve o'clock, C Company occupied the perimeter from twelve to five, D Company from seven to twelve, and Alpha from four to ten, overlapping the other two. At three P.M., an officer from C Company reported on the radio to the battalion firebase that they were surrounded by several hundred NVA. In the space of seventy-five minutes, the enemy shot down three helicopters attempting to drop ammunition and water. NVA soldiers shinnied into the trees for a better angle on the Hueys and the 250 encircled Americans, who lay crowded inside a wagon train circle perhaps seventy-five yards in diameter.

Just before five o'clock, a Huey from the 335th Assault Helicopter Company managed to drop a pallet of ammunition, but the supplies fell with a thud fifteen yards outside the perimeter, halfway between the Americans and the NVA. Peter Lantz and another lieutenant organized a recovery team. Dashing in and out of the perimeter, they had successfully collected most of the ammunition when suddenly Lantz jerked once and fell flat, slain by a sniper's bullet. The recovery effort was abandoned.

Also on the perimeter lay the brigade's Catholic chaplain, Father Charles J. Watters, who had hosted Jim Ford's visit to the 173rd two months earlier. A legendary figure who wore camouflage vestments and conducted Mass from an altar made of C-ration cases, Watters had won a Bronze Star in May for continuing to administer extreme unction to a dying soldier while under heavy enemy fire. Now, he behaved like a man possessed. Three times he shook off paratroopers trying to restrain him and scampered outside the lines to drag wounded men to safety.

At the firebase four miles away, alarm and confusion gripped the battalion command post. Between air strikes, the half-dozen howitzers at the base pounded the hilltop, but apparently to very little effect. Darkness was less than two hours away; a relief expedition would not be able to punch through until the next day, if at all. None of the fifty or sixty wounded could be extracted, and the survivors had run low on ammunition and water. The battalion commander knew that Kiley, as well as many other officers and senior NCOs, had been killed.

Matt Harrison understood at first hand how bad the predicament was on 875. His wound having healed sufficiently for him to rejoin the battalion, Matt had boarded a Huey earlier that afternoon, but as the helicopter neared the battle, it was driven away by a swarm of bullets ripping through the fuselage. Now, the battalion commander ordered Matt to prepare to assume command of A Company. But how?

Squatting next to a radio at the firebase, he tuned into the C Company frequency. A familiar voice came on the network.

"Buck?" Matt asked, pressing the microphone key. "Buck? Is that you?"

"Matt? Yeah, it's me."

Matt could hear small-arms chatter and occasional mortar explosions in the background.

"Buck, how you doin'?"

"Mmmm. I'm okay, Matt. I'm, uh, I'm hit, but I'm okay."

In truth, Buck had been hit three times. Wounded by small-arms fire during the morning assault, he was shot a second time while sprinting between the squads of his platoon, shouting encouragement to the paratroopers. Both times he waved away the medic who tried to help him. As C Company pulled back inside the perimeter, Buck was wounded a third time while carrying his platoon sergeant into the lines.

"Hey, Matt?"

"Yeah, Buck."

"Do me a favor, huh? If I get killed, make sure I get the Medal of Honor so my son can go to West Point."

What a character, Matt thought. Joking around at a time like this. You'd think he —

"Harrison, let's go." The battalion executive officer waved impatiently.

"Yes, sir. What's up?"

"You're going to rappel in on a Swiss seat."

In stunned disbelief, Matt listened to the harebrained plan. A Huey waited on the LZ near the howitzers. Someone — at "echelons above reason" — had decided to lower Matt and two others into the perimeter. The scheme sounded like a grotesque parody of *deus ex machina*. Helicopters at full throttle were not surviving the sleet of enemy fire; what chance was there for an exposed man dangling on the end of a rope? No chance, Matt knew, no chance at all. He was going to die. That was suddenly very clear.

In a trance, he walked quietly to the Huey and sat in the seat as though he were a condemned man in an electric chair. An irresistible fatalism swept over him. This was too preposterous even to protest. Duty had taken a strange and ugly turn, not simply asking but demanding the last full measure of devotion. He could picture himself swinging in a slow pendular arc above the trees as every North Vietnamese soldier within five miles took a shot at him. His hour had come round at last. The helicopter engine whined in preparation.

Then, at the last moment, a senior officer stepped forward. "Wait a minute," he ordered. "This is crazy. We're not doing this."

Even the reprieve seemed surreal to Matt. Untying the harness, he climbed from the Swiss seat as dutifully and impassively as he had climbed into it, and walked away from the Huey to await further orders.

Back on Hill 875, a deep gloom sifted over the Americans as the sun set. Temperatures plunged as quickly as they had risen during the day, sinking toward the low 50s. The paratroopers huddled between one another's legs for warmth. Another artillery round fell short, killing one and wounding four in D Company. Someone called the firebase and asked them to please, *please,* add a hundred meters to the next salvo.

Periodically, the NVA walked five or six mortar bursts across the three companies. During the lulls, the paratroopers heard enemy snipers yelling derisively in the twilight, "Chieu hoi! Chieu hoi, you GI!" Chieu Hoi — Open Arms — was the amnesty program offered to NVA and Viet Cong soldiers who surrendered.

The American survivors wrapped their wounded in clothing and blankets scavenged from the dead, and laid them in shallow trenches, where they watched a full moon, orange and monstrous, float up through the trees. Buck Thompson, still alive despite his three wounds, lay among them.

What was he thinking? Certainly of Fran and the Deuce, who at six months looked more and more like his father. Perhaps he thought of his boyhood in Atchison, of the three-year-old in his cowboy costume who once sang "Pistol-Packin' Mama" for the railroad men in Thompson's Restaurant. Perhaps he thought of the Jayhawk pranks, of the swayback nag executed in the girls' dormitory, or the sorority queen taken to witness the hanging at Lansing. Perhaps he remembered the top bunk at Camp Buckner, where he nipped at his Cutty Sark and read *The Canterbury Tales* as Tom Carhart gawked with undisguised admiration. Or perhaps he recalled June Week and his wedding in the chapel, where he had barked his vows — Affirmative! — and later helped stamp out the flaming tablecloth at the Officers Club reception.

Whatever his thoughts, they were the final inner murmurings of a short and happy life that ended at precisely 6:58 P.M. At that moment, an American bomber streaked over Hill 875 from northeast to southwest, oddly contrary to the usual southeast-to-northwest vector that the planes had flown all day. In the gathering darkness, the trapped battalion on the hill could hear the throaty scream of the jet as it roared directly overhead. At least one and possibly two large bombs whistled from the plane's belly, falling squarely in the middle of the C Company command post, where the surviving officers huddled near the wounded.

With a terrifying concussion, the explosions gouged a crater deep enough to bury a bus. Flame and steel ripped across the command post, severing heads, tearing arms and legs from their sockets, and flinging a geyser of dirt, blankets, and weapons high into the air. Hot shrapnel riddled scores of soldiers. Anguished shrieks of pain and panic swept like fire through the company.

The explosions killed forty-two men, including Father Watters. Forty-five others were wounded. Those who survived wept in outraged incredulity. Among the dead lay Richard William Thompson, apparently killed instantly by the blasts. Those who knew him would find it almost impossible to believe — and perhaps it surprised him, too — but even Buck was mortal.

At 7:30 A.M. on November 20, a relief expedition of ninety-six enlisted men and four officers from B Company of the 4th Battalion set out for Hill 875 from Firebase 16. The company, commanded by Captain Ron Leonard, shunned the trails and moved through the jungle on a series of compass azimuths in the same prudent diamond formation that had caused Leonard such trouble after the June 22 massacre.

Again, Leonard was told to expect an ambush. He also learned that most of the officers and NCOs of the 2nd Battalion were dead (including, erroneously, Matt Harrison). Fractured with the strain of the past twenty-four hours, at least one senior officer wept as Leonard's men pushed off, heavily laden with extra ammunition, grenades, and mortar rounds.

Leading the third platoon at the head of the diamond was another '66 graduate, Lieutenant Alfred Lindseth, a fair-haired farm boy from North Dakota. Al Lindseth had roomed with Tom Carhart when they were plebes, and, like Tom, he had volunteered for Vietnam. After a stint as a weapons platoon leader in the 173rd, he had grown bored tending the company's mortars and volunteered to lead an infantry platoon, in time replacing a lieutenant who was killed.

With Lindseth in the lead, Bravo Company took the entire day to reach the base of the besieged hill. The toppled trees and debris from the bombs and artillery shells reminded Lindseth of the rubble of a collapsed twenty-story building. At an abandoned NVA base camp, they passed dead enemy soldiers — blasted to pieces by artillery — in a heap of bloody Chinese dressings. Moving cautiously through the position once held by Kiley's Alpha Company, they saw the ground on both sides of the trail carpeted with dead Americans and North Vietnamese. Some of the paratroopers had small holes in their foreheads, the mark of an execution. The relief column passed Carlos Lozada, slumped on a cairn of spent M-60 casings, still clutching his jammed machine gun. Lindseth had never seen more than one dead American at a time; here, dozens covered the ground.

At five P.M., unmolested by the NVA, Leonard's company pushed into the 2nd Battalion's perimeter. The survivors cried with relief at the sight of the rescue party, and the paratroopers distributed food, water, and ammunition.

An hour later, a single Huey — the only helicopter to get in on the twentieth — swooped down in a fusillade of enemy fire. Five of the most seriously wounded were hoisted aboard as three officers jumped from the bay, including Matt Harrison, who had orders to take command of A Company and "exploit the tactical situation."

Crawling among the 2nd Battalion in the fading light, Matt scanned a scene even more ghastly than the ambush in June. Later, he would describe it simply as "the third circle of hell." Bodies and pieces of bodies lay strewn across the enclave. Curses and moans poured from the wounded. NVA snipers, having crawled within twenty-five meters of the Americans, periodically sprayed the American position with gunfire. Enemy mortar crews had moved so close that the Americans could hear the *pumpf!* of rounds leaving the tube, followed a few seconds later by a jarring explosion on the ground or in the tree branches overhead.

Among the wounded, Matt found Tommy Remington, the lieutenant who had been shot in both legs and both arms. "Matt," he asked, "do you have a canteen?"

Another lieutenant lay next to Remington, his intestines spilling out. Again and again he whispered, "I'm not going to die. I'm not going to die. I'm not going to die."

Spotting an Alpha trooper huddled behind a log, Matt crept over to him.

"Where's our line?" he asked.

The soldier stared blankly for a moment, as dumfounded as if asked to explain a principle of quantum physics. "Shit," he replied at last, "I don't know."

After passing out ammunition and food, Matt helped to slide some of the dead into body bags, including Kiley, Lozada, and the torn corpse of Buck Thompson. Before long, a wall of stacked bags stood four feet high.

Two other companies from the 4th Battalion arrived around eight, following the route blazed by Leonard and Lindseth. Now the better part of two battalions had squeezed into an area slightly larger than a football field. The paratroopers dug in behind the barricade of shattered trees, firing their rifles and heaving grenades at any shadow moving beyond the perimeter. The enemy, evidently realizing that the Americans had been reinforced and were well fortified, chose not to launch a full-scale attack, but the sniper and mortar fire continued almost without pause.

In the middle of the night, Lindseth, lying behind a log, heard the wounded man next to him begin choking in a raspy death rattle.

"Medic!" Lindseth yelled. "Medic!"

Hollow-eyed with fatigue, a medic stumbled over and tugged the poncho from the wounded soldier. In the moonlight, Lindseth was horrified to see that there was nothing below the soldier's waist; both legs had been severed at the hip. The sight seared itself into Lindseth's memory, as the medic injected another syringe of morphine. A few hours later, the soldier died.

The next morning, Tuesday, November 21, the artillery firebases began a six-hour bombardment of Hill 875; the Air Force dropped fifteen tons of high explosives and seven tons of napalm on the crest of the hill. While Matt continued to reorganize Alpha Company and evacuate the wounded, three companies of the 4th Battalion planned a counterattack. Shortly after three P.M., they stormed out from the perimeter but covered less than ten yards before being pinned down. The paratroopers found it impossible to crawl under the fallen trees covering the hillside, and any effort to scoot over the logs offered the NVA a clearly silhouetted target.

Flame throwers were ineffective; few Americans knew how to operate them and someone had forgotten to send the igniting strikers anyway. At one point, Lindseth collected ten LAWs — light antitank weapons that resembled small bazookas. Standing exposed between two trees, he fired them in quick succession at a nearby bunker. But the LAWs exploded harmlessly against the outer wall of thick teak logs; the six-inch firing ports in the bunkers were too narrow to be penetrated. After two hours and more than fifty casualties, the attack was aborted. Only the extraordinarily high percentage of duds among the NVA's Chinese-made grenades kept the toll from being even higher. The Americans dug in for a third night on 875, singing an old paratrooper song to the tune of "The Battle Hymn of the Republic": *Gory, gory, what a helluva way to die . . .*

On Wednesday, November 22, both battalions pulled back a hundred yards down the hill. Rather than attempt another assault, the Americans spent the entire day and succeeding morning smashing the hill with air strikes and artillery salvos. Every four or five minutes, F-100 and Phantom jets streaked past at five hundred feet, dumping silver napalm canisters, which turned the remaining teak trees into giant candles. Matt watched in awe as high-flying B-52s flattened the adjacent hilltops. Without warning, like Gomorrah revisited, an entire ridgeline would erupt in a roaring escarpment of flame and black smoke. At the base of 875, a steady convoy of Hueys evacuated the wounded from a small landing zone supervised by Lieutenant Peyton Ligon, yet another classmate from '66 who had arrived with the 4th Battalion. Along with fresh troops, the helicopters brought several squads of journalists who had insisted on being allowed to cover the battle at first hand.

Shortly after eleven the next morning, the Americans counterattacked again. Three companies from the 4th Battalion surged toward the top of the hill. "Now I want you to get up there," someone yelled, "and get them sons of bitches!"

But there were few sons of bitches to get. During the night, most of the NVA's 174th Regiment had melted away into Cambodia. The Americans kept a curtain of mortar fire falling twenty-five yards in front of their line as they crept up the hill. Al Lindseth, moving up the left side with Leonard's Bravo Company, leaped into a bunker and was surprised by how deep and sturdy it was. Spotting a dead NVA soldier in one corner, Lindseth kicked him in the head to be certain that he wasn't shamming, then pressed on.

A few moments later, Lindseth's platoon sergeant, who was carrying forty pounds of satchel charges, was hit by a B-40 rocket. The explosion atomized the sergeant, blew Lindseth through the air, and wounded Captain Leonard in the left calf. Spotting a muzzle flash from an adjacent ridgeline, Leonard called in an air strike. After the Phantom dropped its payload, a spectacular secondary detonation lasted for several minutes; apparently a fuel or ammunition dump had been hit.

Twenty minutes after the assault began, the first paratroopers reached the top of 875, yelling "Geronimo!" and "Airborne!" The crest was blackened and blown bald by five days of bombardment. The Americans found few enemy bodies, but a revolting stench hung over the hill, mingling with the acrid odor of shattered earth.

On the heels of the paratroopers came the journalists. "Hey, Lieutenant," one reporter called to Lindseth, waving a whiskey flask, "how'd you like a drink?"

"Damned right," he replied.

Crawling into a bunker, Lindseth took a swig from the flask and was suddenly horrified when the walls of the bunker collapsed around him. For a moment he was certain that he was about to be buried alive but the cave-in covered him only to the waist and he was able to claw his way back to the surface.

As Matt Harrison trudged up the hill, he passed a television reporter who stood before his cameraman, speaking into a microphone.

"Today is November 23, 1967," the reporter intoned, "Thanksgiving Day on Hill 875."

My God, it *is* Thanksgiving, Matt thought. A sharp, hot streak of anger flashed through him. This bastard, he thought, is using us as a backdrop for his report. There was something almost sacrilegious about it. They had fought the battle of their lives here, and the reporter's flat recitation diminished the agony and sacrifice of the past five days.

Matt shook his head. From the breast pocket of his fatigues he pulled a roster of paratroopers still missing from the 2nd Battalion, American men reduced to a scrawl of surnames and serial numbers. Among those on the list was *Lantz, Peter J., 1st lieutenant.* Where was Pete? Matt wondered.

A few yards down the hill, he noticed a small mound beneath a charred bush. With one of his sergeants, Matt hiked back down the slope. The mound was a man all right, though he was burned far beyond recognition. Matt nudged the figure with his boot. "I think it's a black guy," the sergeant said.

Then Matt saw the left hand, now clenched in a blackened claw. On one finger was a jade ring, which Matt instantly recognized as Pete Lantz's distinctive wedding band. Once again, Matt helped lift one of his classmates into a body bag. Of eight men from the class of '66 who had joined the 2nd Battalion five months earlier, four were dead and two had been badly wounded.

Big Chinook helicopters began to descend on the landing zone that had been cleared on the crown of 875. The crews, cheerfully wishing everyone a happy Thanksgiving, unloaded thermite containers full of hot turkey, mashed potatoes, and cranberry sauce. Filthy, exhausted, and ravenous, the paratroopers sat in the ashes and bolted down the meal. Then, less than an hour after the hill had been taken, the evacuation began in a dreary drizzle. The living sometimes sat on body bags in the crowded Chinook bays, joking bleakly about "the dumb dead fuckers" and "the KIA Travel Bureau."

After first stopping at a nearby firebase, the soldiers returned to Dak To. The 173rd held the traditional paratrooper memorial service with the boots of the dead arranged in a neat row, as though mocking the daily foot inspections.

Obsessed as ever with hard numbers, the Army began to tally the price of Operation MacArthur: 151,000 artillery rounds; 2100 tactical air strikes; 257 B-52 strikes; 40 U.S. helicopters lost. An estimated 298 NVA soldiers had died during the five-day fight on 875; U.S. losses were 107 killed, 282 wounded, 10 missing. Of the 101 men in Alpha Company on November 19, 28 were alive on Thanksgiving.

One paratrooper had a more succinct summary when asked by a reporter what had happened. "What the fuck do you think happened?" he replied. "We got shot to pieces." As the reporter began to scribble in his notebook, the soldier added, "Make that 'little pieces.' "

Even before Hill 875 was completely abandoned by the Americans on November 24 — title reverting once more to the jungle and the NVA — there were pointed questions in the press and in the ranks about the strategy, the tactics, the cost. Once again the initiative in this war of attrition lay with the enemy, who decided when to fight, where to fight, and when to slip away. As so often happened now in Vietnam, Americans had fought and died valiantly for a meaningless terrain feature that was seized only to be immediately relinquished. The battle was a Pyrrhic victory once defined by Churchill as "bought so dear as to be almost indistinguishable from defeat."

More men had died in five minutes at Verdun or Antietam than had died in five days on Hill 875, but this anonymous ridgeline in Asia was of a piece with those more celebrated fights, a horrific drama of bravery and cowardice, leadership and obedience, lucidity and confusion, death and sweet life.

Matt Harrison, Al Lindseth, and the others who survived were proud of what they had done. They had slugged it out, boot to boot, with a worthy opponent, finally driving him from the field in search of sanctuary. William Westmoreland, in Washington for another official visit, explained the battle as "the beginning of a great defeat for the enemy," marking a juncture in the war "when the end begins to come into view."

Perhaps so. But those riding away in the twin-rotored Chinooks that Thanksgiving afternoon had to wonder whether the flinty nihilism that caused them to slander "the dumb dead fuckers" on the floor was really the feeling of victory.

The first Western Union telegram arrived on Saturday morning, November 25, at the Urstadt house in Carmel, New York, where Fran Thompson and her young son had been living since Buck left for Vietnam.

DON'T DELV BTWN 10PM & 6AM DON'T PHONE

Mrs. Frances Thompson.

The secretary of the Army has asked me to express his deep regret that your husband, First Lieutenant Richard Thompson, has been missing in

> Vietnam since 19 November 1967. He was last seen on a combat operation when engaged against a hostile force in a firefight. You will be advised promptly when further information is received. In order to protect any information that might be used to your husband's detriment, your cooperation is requested in making public only information concerning his name, rank, service number, and date of birth.
>
> Kenneth G. Wickham, Major General. The Adjutant General.

For two agonizing days, the family waited. On Monday morning a young lieutenant arrived with the fatal news. Fran, seeing him stride up the walk, refused to answer the knock at the door. Buck was alive; she was certain of that. This officer in his dress blues could say nothing to shake her conviction. Why bother letting him in?

"You have to," her father said. "You have to go to the door."

Fran shook her head, tears pouring down her cheeks. Finally, the Urstadts brought the lieutenant to the back of the house so that he could deliver the death notice in person, as required by Army protocol. The telegram this time was conclusive:

> Your husband died in Vietnam on 19 November 1967 as a result of metal fragment wounds received from incident previously reported to you. He was previously reported as missing. His remains have been recovered and have been positively identified. Please accept my deepest sympathy.

No, no, no! It isn't true, Fran insisted. It was a mistake. Sometimes the Army got these things fouled up. That was understandable, wasn't it? There were so many dying, so many bodies to look after. Buck had simply been confused with someone else, some other poor wretch.

All Fran wanted was to sleep. For days, she could not bear to look at the baby. Perhaps she could start over, pretend that none of it had happened — the wedding, the child, this foul lie about Buck. "Enough," her mother said at last. "Enough. You've got to take care of the baby."

The night before a memorial service was held in Atchison, Fran had a dream. She saw men in boxes stacked three and four high. The boxes remained open at one end, and the dead men's feet protruded. She stared at the feet. One pair was splayed, the ankles canted outward. They were Buck's feet, his trademark, the great family joke.

"There he is," said a stranger standing next to her. "Those are his feet. You have to look."

When the lid of the box was opened, Fran refused to peer inside. She ran around a corner and then stopped, sensing that someone was behind her. She turned; there stood Buck.

"You're supposed to be dead," she said.

"I am," he answered gently. "Won't you let me rest in peace?"

When Fran awoke, she knew it was true. Buck was gone forever.

Major Paul Wilson, the husband of Buck's sister Lee Ann, flew home from Vietnam to meet the body at the military's huge mortuary in Dover, Delaware. Fran wanted to view the remains to be absolutely certain there was no mistake, but she was persuaded to let Paul do it instead. He saw a macabre sight. The body had a sickly green hue, like the color of a blank television picture tube. More than fifty wounds had been charted by the mortician. The family did not know — and would not know for twenty years — that Buck had been killed by an American bomb.

Buck was to be buried at West Point; meanwhile, five hundred mourners turned out for the ecumenical memorial service at St. Benedict's Abbey Church in Atchison, where he had briefly gone to school between the University of Kansas and West Point. The college announced the establishment of the Buck Thompson Scholarship Fund Memorializing Vietnam Veterans. Although Fran had finally accepted his death, Buck's mother could not. She had always believed that Buck was two children: Richard William and the older brother who had been killed in a car accident shortly before Buck's birth. If Buck was dead, then she had lost two sons, and that was too much to bear. The family worried over her sanity. When the American prisoners of war came home from North Vietnam six years later, Dorothy Thompson was convinced that Buck would step off the plane with them. Not until the last man had raced into the arms of his family did she acknowledge that her boy was gone.

The funeral at West Point was held on December 4, a day of bitter cold. Ice disfigured the statues of Patton, Sedgwick, and the other bronze immortals. Tree boughs sagged beneath the heavy glaze. It seemed to Fran that the day had been specially arranged to be as gloomy as possible, providing a savage counterpoint to the sunshine of June Week only eighteen months before.

Beneath the painting *Peace and War* in the old cadet chapel at the cemetery entrance, the Reverend James Ford stood waiting in his white vestments. The organist played the Call to Worship as the pews slowly filled between the black marble shields commemorating the generals of the Revolution. Ford had now buried several dozen dead from Vietnam — as many as three in one week — and there was no end in sight. They were all hard, but this one was especially wrenching. He had married the Thompsons, baptized their son, and had seen Buck during his visit to Dak To.

The funerals were enervating, sapping Ford of his youth. On the night before a service, he would usually visit the bereaved family at the Hotel Thayer. Often that was more difficult than the burial. For some reason he felt a special tie to the fathers of these dead soldiers. The widows and mothers were kept busy, the center of the mourning party, but the fathers appeared lost. Their role was to drive the car and remain stolid, even when ravaged by grief.

At the Thayer, the family would stare at Ford — with their son or father or husband lying in a casket at Hogan's Funeral Home in Highland Falls — and ask the simplest and most difficult of questions: Why? It was more proclamation of despair than query, and he did not have an answer.

The service was ready to begin. Fran and the Thompsons sat in the front pews. From beneath his robes, Ford pulled out a dog-eared volume called *The Occasional Services*. He had taped a copy of the Cadet Prayer and several psalms inside the red leather cover. The book offered services for marriage and baptism, confirmation and ordination, visitation of the sick and dedication of a church. But, as always these days, the book naturally fell open to one chapter: "Burial of the Dead."

"We're gathered today in loving memory of Richard William Thompson and to hear God's words of hope and strength.

"I am the resurrection and the light, saith the Lord," Ford read, his deep voice rolling through the chapel. "He that believeth in me, though he were dead, yet shall he live.

"O God, before whose face the generations rise and pass away, the strength of those who labor and repose of the blessed dead, we rejoice in the communion of the saints, we remember all who have faithfully lived and all who have valiantly died, especially those most dear to us."

Ford had penciled in the adverb "valiantly" after crossing out the original "peacefully."

"O God, who healest the broken in heart and bindest up their wounds, look with tender pity and compassion upon your servants whose joy has turned to mourning."

That was the nub of it, he thought: joy turned to mourning. No phrase better captured the reversal of fortunes, this black grief contrasted to the pride and delight that parents and sweethearts felt on seeing their new lieutenants in their June Week whites. Out of the depths have I cried to Thee, Ford thought, recalling Psalm 130. O Lord, hear my voice.

God would deal with the dead, Ford believed. There was no need to worry about them; His grace sufficed among the shades. These words, these incantations from the red-bound book spread before him, spoke to the living. The conviction that what he had to say brought some consolation was the one thing that kept Ford going. These ancient phrases of redemption and hope represented the only comfort that the families had, however meager it seemed. What else was there? A flag? A medal? A letter from the secretary of the Army?

In the midst of suffering, people wanted meaning. Why? Why? If he could not answer that awful question, he could answer a different one: Now what? At other times, he believed, his words from the pulpit were either unheard or irrelevant. But at a time like this, his voice felt strong and powerful, the echo of a God who had created life once and could do it again.

He read, as he always did at funerals, from Psalm 121: "I will lift up mine eyes unto the hills, from whence cometh my help. My help cometh from the Lord, which made heaven and earth . . . The Lord shall preserve thee from all evil: he shall preserve thy soul."

The organist played one stanza of "Alma Mater" as the casket, wrapped in a flag, was carried from the chapel. The cortège moved slowly through the icy yard to Section XXXIV, a hundred yards to the north. The yawning grave lay just a few feet from the most conspicuous monument in the cemetery, an outlandish, thirty-foot pyramid housing the remains of General Egbert Ludovicus Viele, class of 1847, and his wife, Juliette. Viele had been the chief engineer for both Central Park in Manhattan and Prospect Park in Brooklyn.

Fran was struck by the poetry of the site. Several years before, Buck had brought her here one afternoon to see Custer's grave. Wandering over to this granite pyramid, they had climbed past the pair of stone sphinxes and found the iron gate open to the burial chamber inside. Viele and his wife lay in matching sarcophagi. The general's image, the apotheosis of Victorian propriety, with its handlebar mustache and aquiline nose, was carved in bas-relief.

"Wouldn't it be ironic," Buck had said, "if I was buried near here? When I die, I want to be buried at West Point."

How long ago that was! Those days seemed impossibly distant, like the faintest recollections of a previous life. Fran thought of their honeymoon, sitting in the webbed seats of a plodding Air Force transport for twenty-four hours from Charleston to Rio de Janeiro. No Niagara Falls for Buck Thompson and his bride, no sir! After a month in Brazil and Surinam, before he went to Ranger 3, they had lived in a top-floor apartment on Palmer Avenue in Yonkers, where Fran worked as a biochemist. Buck spent much of his time cooking — he was a wonderful cook, having learned the art while growing up in a restaurant — and writing short stories. Sometimes he listened to his record of MacArthur's 1962 speech, which he kept on top of a cabinet. The album had inadvertently been left behind when they moved out; months later, Fran received a package from Yonkers with the record inside: *If you lose, the nation will be destroyed . . .*

She had tried to talk him out of going to Vietnam so quickly. Why don't you hold off, she pleaded; what's your rush? But he had been adamant — and bitterly disappointed that more of his classmates had not volunteered. "I can't understand it," he complained. "Only a hundred of us. That's our job. We ought to go."

They had planned to meet in Hawaii for R and R this month. Buck had resisted the idea, afraid that parting again would be too painful. But Fran insisted. She wanted to see him, wanted to get him away from the leeches and the filth that he mentioned in his letters. "I finally had a chance to get a shower after three months," he had written in one of his final letters. It tore at her heart that he had died before having a chance to get really clean.

Now she had nothing. Only his watch and wedding band had come back from Vietnam. His clothes, the countless pictures of the Deuce — everything had vanished. He had been recommended for a Silver Star. That was important, Fran thought, especially for his son someday. The medal was something to cling to, knowing that he had bravely tried to save his men. She wondered whether he didn't deserve a higher honor — the Distinguished Service Cross, perhaps. The Silver Star was great, but was it great enough? Did it measure up to the man?

The rifles cracked three times over the grave. Ashes to ashes, dust to dust. An officer presented the flag, folded into a trim triangle, to the widow. Now she had that, too.

After the ceremony, the family returned to the Thayer for a drink in the hotel bar. Lee Ann was sending her husband back to Vietnam. The Marine Corps was willing to let Major Wilson stay through the holidays, but Lee Ann insisted that he leave before Christmas. She could not be a wife and a grieving sister simultaneously. She knew that her behavior was odd, irrational. But she had a live husband and a dead brother, and that equation was hard to accept. She felt guilty about it, so guilty that it kept her from discussing Buck's death for years. In fact, nearly two decades would pass — until young Richard was a man himself — before Lee Ann and Fran could talk intimately about Buck without immediately dissolving into tears.

The next morning, December 5, the Thompsons and Urstadts packed their bags and checked out of the Thayer. Walking out the door, Fran was surprised to see the familiar face of another young woman coming in. It was Dagmar Lantz, arriving to bury her husband, Pete. There was a spot waiting for him, right next to Buck. Jim Ford was waiting, too.

10

Screaming Eagle

Like an avatar of the fallen classmate he adored, Tom Carhart arrived in Vietnam three days after Buck Thompson's funeral. It was December 7, 1967 — the anniversary of the Japanese attack on Pearl Harbor — and the irony was not lost on Tom that he was arriving in Saigon from Tokyo on a commercial airliner full of Japanese businessmen. As the plane prepared to land, he noted both the black fingers of smoke rising from a burning village and the lack of interest among his fellow travelers, who were too absorbed in their spread sheets to notice the war below.

Tom had reacted to word of Buck's death precisely as Fran Thompson first had: he refused to believe it. After hearing the news from a classmate, Tom placed a call to Fort Bragg, demanding confirmation from the Army. Even after verifying the death he found it hard to accept. Although he was unable to attend the funeral — he had agreed to visit his family in Japan before going to Vietnam — he mourned Buck as he would have mourned a lost brother. Yet his grief was a private affair, not to be confused or diminished by the issue of whether Buck had died for a proper cause. Tom's zeal for battle remained intact as the plane touched down at Tan Son Nhut Airport.

He was arriving in Vietnam with something to prove. For the twelve months since being commissioned, Tom had navigated almost entirely by the distant sound of the guns. His performance in the past year had been checkered at best, and he knew that the surest way to expunge the record was to show his eagerness and prowess in combat; the killing ground was where soldiering really counted.

After the painful ordeal of Ranger school, Tom had spent four months with the 82nd Airborne at Fort Bragg. He chafed at the tedium of garrison life, where much of his time seemed to be spent in the snack bar drinking cherry Cokes and gobbling french fries with fifty other bored lieutenants. His disdain for young officers hoping to avoid combat assignments quickly slid into contempt for all REMFs — rear-echelon motherfuckers. When other junior officers would boast about how they had arranged a safe billet for themselves in the rear at Cam Ranh or Long Binh, Tom hardly bothered to conceal his scorn. Not for me, he would reply; I'm going to the action. How much longer do I have to put up with this bullshit?

But despite the swagger, all was not well. The effects of Tom's head injury continued to haunt him. His short-term memory remained fickle and unreliable. While at Bragg, for example, he had taken jumpmaster training, an advanced course for paratroopers learning how to supervise an airborne operation. Though he studied assiduously, it was like throwing darts at a cinder block wall: the information simply would not stick. In a class of more than a hundred other officers and NCOs, Tom was the only one to fail.

Still, his classmates at Fort Bragg saw flashes of the old Carhart. The witty, self-assured, free spirit seemed to be slowly re-emerging, like the outlines in a brass rubbing. Arriving in Fayetteville, North Carolina, with a flat tire on his new Porsche, he drove the final ten miles to Bragg on the rim in a boil of sparks and shredded rubber. The story quickly made the rounds, always punctuated with, "Oh, that Carhart!"

But those who knew him best, including his former roommates like Mac Hayes and Frank Cosentino, saw that something was still out of synch. For one thing, Tom could no longer hold his liquor as he had during cadet days. And he seemed to be missing the natural grace that had once allowed him to float effortlessly through his travails; life had become a succession of small, tense struggles.

"For Christ's sake!" Cosentino stormed at him one evening. "Will you stop putting on this act? Give yourself a chance to heal. Physically, you've recovered. Now let yourself recover psychologically. You don't have to prove yourself to anybody."

Tom shook his head. His eyes flooded with tears. "There's only one person I have to prove myself to, and that's me. I'm not going to be any less than you."

In October, as his tour of duty at Bragg came to a close, Tom's superiors slapped him with a poor rating on his OER, the Officer Efficiency Report. Once, when the Army was small and clubby, evaluations had been informal and succinct. A commander's entire assessment of a subordinate might be boiled down to "a good man, but no officer," or "a knave, despised by all."

But the American Army was now one of the largest corporations in the world, and evaluations had become rigidly formal (though the grapevine still was an important source, particularly for inside information about the elite "water walkers" or "fast burners"). Under regulations first adopted in 1948, each officer's job efficiency was measured against that of other officers in the unit on the basis of nineteen factors. The Army also rated eighteen personal qualities, again comparing the officer with his peers. A few points one way or the other on an OER could make or break an officer's career.

"Lieutenant Carhart is an audacious officer in many ways, careless in many others," wrote Tom's company commander in the 82nd, Captain Juan A. Montes. "He is willing to assume responsibility dictated by position of higher rank, yet he lacks self-confidence, which he admits, and must be constantly supervised to obtain some results. He is bright with some ideas, but he is hesitant in his decisions." The captain closed his assessment by suggesting that "Lieutenant Carhart needs more time to adjust to the military life since he had the head injury in an automobile accident . . . He is undependable to a certain extent, does not inspire confidence, and may crack under pressure."

The battalion executive officer, Major Philip A. Pryor, was also blunt. "He is quick-witted and possesses an acute sense of humor. Lieutenant Carhart explains his performance as that of a field combat leader with a dislike for garrison duties. His manner of performance under field conditions, however, does not bear this out . . . I feel that due to Lieutenant Carhart's intelligence and background he has exceptional potential, although his demonstrated performance does not bear this out."

In assessing Tom's personal qualities, his superiors rated him "exemplary" in ambition, cooperation, enthusiasm, loyalty, moral courage, stamina, and understanding; yet he was considered only "average" or "below average" in self-discipline, judgment, and dependability. On a scale of 100, his overall rating was only in the middle 60s. Because OERs had become badly inflated throughout the Army, even mediocre officers often received near-perfect scores; Tom's rating was a crippling blow to the career ambitions of a young West Pointer.

While at Bragg one day, Tom confided to a major in his battalion that he still felt the effects of the car wreck. The major responded by formally requiring Lieutenant Carhart to be examined by a psychiatrist before being cleared for combat; Tom was furious, convinced that the major had betrayed his confidence. But the examination turned out to be perfunctory. Accustomed to seeing soldiers who were desperate to avoid Vietnam, the doctor detected nothing in this exuberant young lieutenant — someone who actually wanted to go to war — that should keep him stateside. Once again, Tom was waved through with a firm handshake and a pat on the back.

Just before leaving, he took another important step toward full recovery from his injuries. In October, Tom requested forty-five days' leave and went to West Orange, New Jersey, to stay with his sister Sally, a nurse. A plastic surgeon operated on him three times to repair the damage done to his face by the Corvette dashboard: first, the doctor broke Tom's nose with a hammer in order to reset and straighten it; then he removed the tracheotomy scar; finally, he patched the scars on Tom's chin and reshaped his shredded lower lip. Tom had to pay the bill himself, but the surgeon accepted documents from the pending lawsuit against Bob Albright as collateral against future payment.

The surgery raised his spirits enormously. After the last operation, he called Melissa from his hospital bed and asked whether he could visit her. She demurred, insisting that they wait until he returned from Vietnam before seeing each other again.

Even that rebuff couldn't tarnish his euphoria. His face looked more or less like the old Tom's, with its touch of the El Greco nobleman. The scarred mask was gone. Now, as he stepped off the airliner at Tan Son Nhut Airport, once again he felt like a whole man.

From Saigon, Tom flew to Phan Rang to join the first brigade of the 101st Airborne, the Screaming Eagle division. He was assigned as a platoon leader in A Company — nicknamed Abu — in the 1st Battalion of the 327th Infantry. The battalion, which boasted the motto "Above the Rest," operated out of Phan Thiet on the South China Sea, east and slightly north of Saigon. Tom took great pride at the division's eagle-head patch on his sleeve, particularly since the dominant colors were black and gold, just like West Point's.

His war started slowly. Despite Abu's constant patrolling, the enemy remained elusive. But he was glad for the chance to acclimate himself; Tom knew that the most dangerous period for a combat soldier was the first few weeks, when many men died before developing the necessary skills and instincts. He committed his share of rookie blunders on the initial patrols — sleeping on a noisy air mattress and removing his boots at night — until a friendly sergeant convinced him that such luxuries were foolish in the jungle. When the platoon first came under fire from a sniper, Tom brazenly stepped from behind a tree for a better view; the sergeant knocked him to the ground just before enemy rounds spattered against the trunk. Sightseeing is foolish too, the sergeant admonished.

Tom quickly learned that there were two ways to dress for combat. The first, of lesser importance, was physically. Like other soldiers in the field, Tom wore a helmet, jungle fatigues, and boots. (Few men in Abu wore socks and underwear; they took too long to dry.) Across his chest he strapped two ammunition bandoliers, each with ten magazines of eighteen rounds. He stuffed another six magazines into pouches on the suspender harness called the LBE, or load-bearing equipment. Initially, he carried a CAR-15, a relatively short rifle with a collapsible stock; George Crocker had recommended it in two letters to Tom and had even drawn a sketch of the weapon. But when the rifle jammed twice, Tom swapped it for a conventional M-16.

In his rucksack, he packed a poncho, C-rations, eighteen to twenty extra clips of ammo, and four or more spare canteens. Sometimes he flavored the water with Kool-Aid, a reminder of the packets that had once been surreptitiously enclosed in letters from home during Beast Barracks.

More important, however, was dressing mentally. The process was somewhat akin to the one followed by a professional athlete putting on his game face in the locker room before kickoff or the opening bell of a boxing match. Emotions, ranging from arrogance to raw fear, were stowed as carefully as the ammo clips in the rucksack, ready for deployment as needed. Tom had never known any experience that was as intensely absorbing as this psychological robing for war; everything not directly related to the prospective fight sloughed away in a little heap of superfluities.

He thought of death as something that he carried in the breast pocket of his fatigues. It was handy there, close to the heart. Tom soon recognized that life in the combat zone was not merely at risk; it was constantly under siege. What did the old sergeant used to say at Camp Buckner? *Gemmun, they's a thousand ways to die. Mr. Charles is just one of them. The rest is because you are stupid.*

It was odd, Tom thought, that West Point had made no effort to prepare its sons to deal with death on the battlefield. Almost by definition, West Pointers were expected to be rock-jawed and steely-eyed, like the gallery of superintendents' portraits in the mess hall. But no one had ever said, "Cadets, you're going to see a great deal of death and gore, and here are some possible ways to accommodate it." That omission struck Tom as a serious oversight, almost like sending a man into combat without proper training in marksmanship.

In the 101st Airborne, the code words for a wounded American soldier were "Dogwood eight." A dead American was a "Dogwood six." A dead enemy soldier, of course, was simply a "dead gook." Yet, Tom soon discovered, even enemy corpses could be haunting.

Shortly after he joined the 101st, the battalion moved from the coast to the Song Be Valley, near the Cambodian border north of Saigon. Again the enemy remained elusive, until one day the platoon stumbled across what turned out to be an NVA hospital hidden in the jungle. The surprised enemy guards began shooting, and soon the air thickened with smoke and automatic weapons fire. One NVA — carrying a pistol in one hand and forceps in the other — sprinted out of a thatch-roofed bunker. Tom and several of his men fired at the running figure, which abruptly fell in an awkward sprawl. When Tom examined the body after the shooting stopped, he saw that it was a woman. Her hair was knotted in a bun and she wore rubber surgical gloves.

The sight of this slain woman lying in the dirt at his feet — was she a doctor? a nurse? — sent a shiver through Tom. He felt a revulsion well up from deep within him, and his hands trembled uncontrollably. Who would have expected to find a woman out here? A dead gook, he realized, was sometimes more than just a dead gook. Death had countless manifestations. Like fingerprints or snowflakes, no two deaths were identical. Perhaps that was part of the fascination — the terrible miracle of singularity.

He took a deep breath to calm himself, trying to suppress the image of the dead woman. The hospital had to be searched and there were prisoners to interrogate. Once again, he carefully stowed away his emotions. But the breast pocket, he realized, was best left unbuttoned.

A few days later, shortly after ten A.M. on January 24, 1968, Tom's platoon was second in line as the company moved down a trail through a valley. Despite the lack of sustained contact with the enemy, the paratroopers had discovered a base camp with elaborate trench fortifications and other signs suggesting that the region was infested with the NVA. Dense vegetation reduced Tom's visibility to about ten yards. On his left, a stream ran parallel to the trail.

As the lead man in his platoon reached a small rise ahead, the enemy opened fire. Diving for the ground, Tom could hear the roar of several RPD machine guns from across the stream. By now, he had heard enough enemy gunfire to distinguish the sounds made by different weapons. An AK-47 sputtered in short, popping bursts; an RPD emitted a deep, vile whine, like an industrial lathe or some other immense machine. The noise from an RPD was terrifying, Tom thought, particularly since the only sure way to make it stop was to move toward the sound and kill the gunner.

Mortar rounds began bursting in the tree branches overhead, pocking the ground with shrapnel. One explosion knocked out the platoon radio; nearly paralyzed with fear, Tom kept fingering the useless microphone key as though trying to coax it back to life. Eight or ten of his men lay sprawled on the ground around him. Tom realized that they had to cross the stream toward that dreadful whine.

"Everybody," he yelled, "get down to the edge!"

The platoon crawled through the brush to the stream bank. In Ranger training, one tactic he had learned for crossing a creek under fire was to have the men dash across simultaneously. Tom hollered out his order: on the count of six, everybody across.

"One, two, three, four, five, SIX!"

Like a herd of spooked horses, the men splashed through the water as enemy bullets kicked up tiny geysers around them. One soldier was killed in the crossing and two others were wounded. Crouching on the opposite bank, Tom estimated that he was down to about twenty-five men. The enemy concentrated most of its fire on another platoon, but some of the NVA seemed to be flanking Tom and his paratroopers to the left. He set his M-16 on rock 'n' roll — fully automatic — and emptied a clip into the jungle.

"On line!" he yelled. "Let's take that hill!"

Standing up, Tom saw a narrow clearing, perhaps thirty yards wide, that had been defoliated by Agent Orange. Just as he spotted a dark movement in the jungle, a burst of AK-47 fire came from the trees across the clearing. Five green tracers swarmed toward him. On a rifle range, tracers had always seemed to move slowly enough for a man to dodge, but now they traveled with unbelievable velocity. Four of the green rounds whizzed past into the underbrush; the fifth one slammed into Tom's right thigh, two inches above the knee. The impact knocked him to the ground.

A spasm of pain streaked through him, more intense than anything he had thought possible. He couldn't scream, couldn't breathe. Everything seemed to be shutting down, as though his body had no room for anything except the raging fire in his right leg. At first, the sensation reminded him of being hit by a baseball. But as the pain intensified it seemed impossible that a single bullet could cause such agony. Maybe, he thought, I've been hit with a grenade.

Tom reached down to make sure his leg was still there. Both hands were instantly gloved in red. Is that really blood? he wondered. The viscosity was all wrong, more like wine or dyed water. The crimson liquid spurted too freely. Ripping through the back of his leg, the bullet had blown out a hole nearly the size of his fist.

Flat on his back, Tom watched as tracers shredded the leaves above him. He heard intense gunfire to his left. Rolling over and picking up his rifle, he emptied another clip into the jungle. He knew he had to move back or risk bleeding to death. Crawling to the stream, he stood and hobbled through the water, fully expecting to be shot in the back. A Phantom streaked overhead, and an instant later the jungle behind him erupted in flames. You bastards, he thought, take that.

In a clearing not far from where the platoon had first been ambushed,

Tom collapsed among twenty other Dogwood eights. Several Dogwood sixes lay to one side, their bodies limp and spongy. Tom glanced at the dead men, then looked away. More wounded soldiers from another platoon stumbled into the clearing. Jesus, he thought, so many casualties. The company was going to be lucky to have half its strength left.

He still clutched his M-16. The sweat on his palms helped wash away some of the sticky blood. As a medic bound his leg, Tom silently ticked off a checklist. Both legs — check. Both arms — check. Both eyes — check. Genitals — double check. Slowly, the pain and fear ebbed, replaced by a tide of relief. He was going to make it.

Harassed by sporadic enemy fire, the Americans hacked a landing zone from a bamboo grove, and Hueys began to evacuate the wounded. When Tom's turn came, two soldiers lifted him onto a stretcher and shoved him into the helicopter bay with three other wounded men. As he had never known pain comparable with those first few minutes after being shot, now he was gripped with a joy that seemed almost crystalline in its purity.

The Huey soared above the treeline. Below, the dead lay in a little huddle, as though caucusing over their grievances. The afternoon sun hung in the sky off to the right, a yellow globe above the green jungle. Tom thought the sight was indescribably beautiful. I'm alive, he told himself again and again. I'm alive. I'm alive.

The Year of the Monkey began on Tuesday, January 30, 1968, the first and holiest day of Tet. To Americans, the week-long Vietnamese celebration of the lunar new year seemed to combine Christmas, Easter, Halloween, the Fourth of July, and New Year's Eve into one huge holiday. To celebrate, both sides had agreed to a thirty-six-hour cease-fire.

Tom hoped to spend most of the holiday in Japan, recuperating at Yokota Air Force Base with his family. His father had received a garbled telegram that Tom was missing in action, followed by an even more garbled message that he was presumed dead. After two frantic, horrible hours, Colonel Carhart received an accurate notification that his eldest son was WIA — wounded in action.

Once he was evacuated from the Song Be ambush, Tom had been flown first to Tay Ninh and then to the 94th Evacuation Hospital at Long Binh, where surgeons labored over his right leg for nearly three hours. By the time he awoke, his lower thigh and knee had swollen hideously. A crimson incision circumscribing the limb was held shut by transparent gut stitches and metal staples.

From Long Binh, Tom was moved to the Air Force hospital at nearby

Bien Hoa. He was placed in a ward of wounded, moaning soldiers awaiting evacuation. Scanning the long row of beds, Tom saw how lucky he was. On either side of him lay amputees and burn victims, beautiful young men who had been shattered beyond repair and now were simply clinging to life.

The scene was sobering, but Tom was not inclined to ask himself any hard questions about the cost of the war. The doctors told him he would need two months to recuperate, yet already he was eager to get back with the Screaming Eagles. He was a West Pointer; a West Pointer's place was at the front, even in a conflict where there was no front.

Never having had any second thoughts about the war, Tom wasn't about to entertain them now. He was apolitical. Wasn't that the way professional soldiers were supposed to be? Wasn't that what West Point taught, a rigorous neutrality? Humphrey, Nixon, LBJ — Tom could not see a nickel's worth of difference between any of them. He wasn't even registered to vote. Issues of war and peace were properly decided by the democratically elected government; for a lieutenant to second-guess that government showed arrogant bad faith.

Tom held a few simple truths to be self-evident: communism was bad; America, freedom, and West Point were good. That was the extent of his political philosophy. More to the point was his conviction that those asked to place their lives on the line should do so without hesitation. That was part of the code, and the code was what separated a professional officer from a hired gunman. West Point, he believed, had taught a kind of samurai self-abnegation, a submerging of self to the larger cause. Death, while hardly something he sought, was irrelevant. If the country asked him to draw his sword and die, he was ready to do so.

Shortly after three A.M. on January 31, Tom awoke to a commotion in the ward. He heard hoarse whispers. Several shadows darted past. Flashlight beams careened wildly across the recumbent wounded.

"Hey," he yelled, still groggy with sleep, "what's going on?"

A voice answered from the dark, "The airfield is under attack."

For an instant, the lights flashed on until someone bellowed in protest, and darkness again swallowed the ward. Tom heard the distant booming of mortar-and-rocket fire. So much for the Tet cease-fire. The Viet Cong, he assumed, had probably lobbed a few rounds at Bien Hoa just to keep the Americans on their toes. But the explosions kept coming closer, like the footfalls of an approaching giant. Suddenly, two shells exploded right outside, shaking the ward.

"Get on the floor," a disembodied voice commanded from the end of the room.

Oh, Jesus, Tom thought, this can't be happening. Attacking a hospital?

He dragged himself onto the cold cement floor as medics scurried about, trying to comfort those in traction and those too gravely wounded to move. More explosions detonated nearby. "That ain't mortar fire," someone shrieked in a voice squeezed with panic. "Those are hand grenades or satchel charges. They're in here with us!"

A medic stopped in the aisle to wriggle into a flak jacket. He leaned an M-14 against Tom's bed.

"I'm Lieutenant Carhart. Gimme that weapon."

Tom took the rifle — it felt oddly heavy compared with the M-16 he was used to — as the medic dropped four magazines onto the floor next to him. Tom slapped a magazine into the rifle and flipped off the safety. A major on the floor across from Tom ordered the medic to lash the door shut. Someone sobbed; several men recited the Lord's Prayer.

The sounds of furious fighting were very close now. Smoke and dust drifted into the ward, and the chatter of AK-47s and M-14s rattled the windows. The beds seemed to levitate momentarily from the concussion of a nearby explosion. Flashes of yellow light stabbed the darkness. Someone yelled that a sapper had blown the door off an adjacent ward with a satchel charge, wounding several patients.

Moans and shouts from the other ward mingled with calls for help. *Medic! Medic!* Another patient, his right arm bandaged in a stump at the elbow, crawled past, cradling an M-14. He propped himself against a bed frame across the aisle from Tom. Their muzzles pointed at the door, the two men sat motionless for more than an hour, like twin sentries guarding a tomb.

The rifle fire gradually died out and the sound of explosions receded, as though the giant were lumbering away. At five A.M., two hours after the attack began, a medic took Tom's rifle and helped him back into bed. Fragmentary battle reports drifted in. The Viet Cong had destroyed an ammunition dump at Long Binh and even succeeded in overrunning the defensive bunkers at the east end of Bien Hoa. But the fighting was much more widespread than just an attack on those two American compounds, as the reports soon made clear. The enemy had also struck the U.S. embassy, Tan Son Nhut Airport, the presidential palace, and a thousand other targets. Many of South Vietnam's cities were in flames.

There would be no recuperation in Japan for Tom; he was bumped from the flight to Tokyo by the new wave of American casualties requiring immediate evacuation. Instead, he could mend in the 5th Convalescent Center at Cam Ranh Bay. It was a hell of a way to celebrate the new year, he thought. According to Chinese custom, Tom's luck for the next twelve months would be determined by the personality of the first person to come calling during Tet, and that first caller had been Victor Charlie. The Year of the Monkey promised to be lively.

Two months later, Tom was back in the field in I Corps, the northernmost sector of the war zone, inching his way up a ridgeline so steep that it seemed vertical. It was just after four A.M., and a chill rain muffled the sounds of the platoon clawing up the hill behind him. Tom had taken the point position, blindly whacking the relentless undergrowth with a machete until his arms felt like rubber. The men were too exhausted even to swear.

On the far side of the hill somewhere, Bravo Company had been ambushed the previous afternoon. Tom and his paratroopers had been trying to reach them since dusk, moving at the glacial pace of two hundred yards an hour. At times, the only way to keep the men from getting lost or sliding back down the hill was to have them hang on to each other like a soggy conga line.

Well, Tom thought, this is what I get paid for, isn't it? At least it beat lying in a hospital bed or malingering with the REMFs in some bunker, listening to the war over the radio nets. All in all, he felt pretty fortunate. After rejoining the 101st two weeks before, he had replaced the malaria-stricken commander of Tiger Force, the battalion's long-range reconnaissance platoon. The sixty-eight Tigers were a special breed of volunteers — flamboyant shock troops who enjoyed setting up ambushes and operating independently. The typical Tiger believed that he could rip open his shirt and let bullets bounce off his chest.

Tom fit in well. His leg had mended completely, leaving him only a nasty scar, a Purple Heart, and memories of that bizarre night on the ward at Bien Hoa during Tet. On several occasions, he had bumped into classmates serving in the rear, and no matter how brief Tom's visit, he invariably left the units in an uproar by insulting them as REMFs. He was immensely pleased with his special fatigues and the floppy hat that a Tiger wore. The Tigers also pleased him: during his first week, they had killed nine NVA soldiers while suffering only two lightly wounded.

God help me, but this is fun, Tom thought as he slashed at the vines. Not bulling through the wet jungle in the middle of the night, of course, but killing the enemy. He had never known such excitement; no drug, he was certain, could possibly match the high of destroying men who were trying to destroy you. He was scared, to be sure; at times he was petrified. But that was part of it. The killing helped to release you from the fear.

Bam-bam-bam! Bam-bam-bam-bam-bam! Two sudden bursts of AK-

47 fire interrupted his thoughts. Instantly the Tigers flattened out. Two more more bursts erupted from a hundred yards ahead. Tom saw muzzle flashes as the green tracers streaked to the left. Who were they shooting at? It seemed unlikely that the Tigers were the target. The enemy would probably have used grenades rather than give away their position.

He radioed the battalion command post. The commander whose call sign was Red Grizzly, was away on R and R, and the executive officer, known as Cottonmouth, was in charge. Tom proposed that they wait until first light before pressing ahead. Cottonmouth suggested they move back down the hill, veer around the enemy position, and strike out for the summit again. Tom resisted; that would take hours, he explained, and the men were too exhausted to trudge up this ridgeline again.

But Cottonmouth was insistent. As Tom would later recount the conversation in his memoirs, the XO told him, "I realize the extremity of your situation, but you are on a rescue mission. It is imperative that you get to Bravo Company as soon as possible."

Tom flushed with anger and frustration. Goddamn it, who had a better sense of the situation, the commander on the ground or somebody sitting on his ass in a tent miles away?

"This is Tiger. I don't think you know what you're saying. My men are collapsing all over each other. We're huddled together like a pack of wet rats. If we run into an ambush now, we'll all be killed! Every one of us! Over."

Cottonmouth urged his young lieutenant to calm down. An ambush is unlikely, he told Tom. The enemy isn't expecting you to come up that steep hill. "Now you take charge, Tiger," the major added. "I want you on top of that ridge by dawn."

After two more hours of brutal climbing, the platoon reached the crest shortly after a gray dawn began to seep through the clouds. They had no further contact. Following a game trail in the rain toward B Company, the Tigers stumbled on an NVA mortar crew; they captured the 82mm weapon and killed three enemy soldiers. A fourth soldier was pursued into the brush — the Tigers roaring "Kill him!" — and dispatched with a knife.

By the time they reached B Company, around noon, the enemy had dispersed. Although pleased by the capture of the enemy mortar, Tom was weary and frazzled from the miserable march. When Cottonmouth arrived in his helicopter a few minutes later, he and Tom argued again. The major insisted that the Tigers retrace their steps to the mortar position they had destroyed that morning.

"Sir, wait a minute," Tom protested. "You don't want us to do that in this country. That's just inviting an ambush."

"Lieutenant Carhart, shut up," Cottonmouth snapped. "I'm giving the orders."

Tom and the Tigers returned to the trail early that afternoon. But just as he had feared, a short time later his scout patrol was bushwacked with an antipersonnel mine and RPD fire. Tom heard his men screaming for a medic — *Witch doctor! Witch doctor!* — as he radioed the battalion.

"We're in some shit!" he yelled, barely restraining the torrent of curses that clogged his throat. Seconds later, the first artillery rounds fell on top of the Tigers. Without bothering to summon his forward observer, Tom frantically dialed the artillery net himself.

"Redleg, this is the Tiger! Cease fire! Cease fire!" he yelled.

"Tiger, this is Redleg. If you want to talk to me, you go through your Foxtrot Oscar or your battalion net."

"Listen, you motherfucker," Tom screamed, "this is life and death out here. Cease fire and give me a roger out."

"Roger out."

By flanking the enemy to the right and relentlessly spraying the jungle with automatic weapons fire, the Tigers eventually managed to drive the NVA away. But the platoon had suffered eight wounded and four dead, including a sergeant, whose head and arm had been shredded by the Chinese-made claymore. A Huey lowered a stretcher basket to evacuate the two most seriously wounded. Tom felt sick as he watched the helicopter crew slowly winch up the men.

The battalion operations officer, whose codename was Sidewinder, raised Tom on the radio. Alpha Company is close to you, Sidewinder said. Give the rest of your casualties to them and continue your sweep.

Tom was astonished. That stupid shit, he thought, how could he possibly ask us to do that when we've already been ambushed once on this damned trail?

"You're crazy," Tom answered. "You'll get us all killed."

Sidewinder ignored the insolence and repeated his order. Tom signed off, his mind churning. The situation presented a clear choice. Either he could continue to the mortar site or he could do what was best for the men. Even through his fatigue, Tom recognized that he was facing a classic conflict of a leader's dual obligations: Should he execute the mission or preserve the troops?

I'm not going any further, he thought. I'm not going to get another man killed. The mission was unjustified; it was an objective in the mind of a man in the rear who had never been in combat. Tom was willing to take the consequences of refusing a direct order.

He summoned the platoon and announced, without elaboration, that they were turning around.

Back at the firebase that evening, numb with exhaustion and despair, he collapsed against his rucksack in a bunker. Four good men were dead, including a damned fine NCO. For what? He had done what he thought was right, to the point of mutiny. Was that wrong?

In an age of relativity, Tom steadfastly believed in absolutes. The foremost absolute, he believed, had been the preservation of his troops. Under fire, with his men dying around him, he felt protective, like a father trying to shield his children. In garrison, he had found it easy to imagine that he was going to war, where men were men and absolutes must triumph. That had seemed as clear as duty, honor, and country. Yet now the issue was so muddled. He had done his duty as he saw it, trying to tie his actions to principle. Maybe I screwed up, he thought, but I would do precisely the same thing again. Hadn't he done what West Point had taught him to do? Hadn't he demonstrated principled behavior under pressure?

Slumped against his pack, Tom fell into a deep, troubled sleep.

A few days later, Cottonmouth relieved Tom of command. The deed was done gracefully, almost gently. Tom was neither court-martialed nor reprimanded. His record would reflect no disgrace, no black smudge; instead, officially, he was being reassigned to the brigade staff. After the battalion had moved by truck to the division base at Camp Eagle — west of the Tet-ravaged city of Hué — Cottonmouth summoned Tom to his tent late one afternoon and told him of the change.

"I think you'll find that the pressures here aren't nearly what they were on line, and maybe you'll be able to relax," the major said. "Just try to calm down a little and get some of the violence you've been living out of your system."

Angry, confused, and frustrated, Tom argued briefly with the major, but Cottonmouth was adamant. Tom saluted and walked out of the tent.

One senior officer who monitored the perplexing case of Lieutenant Carhart with interest was the commander of another battalion in the 101st, Lieutenant Colonel Robert Yerks. Yerks was the former tactical officer at West Point who had driven across Bear Mountain Bridge just moments after Bob Albright and Tom had slammed into Anthony's Nose. He had watched Tom's recovery carefully and had been involved in the decision to commission him in the officer corps.

The division brass, Yerks knew, was concerned about the number of casualties incurred under Lieutenant Carhart's command. Tom was aggressive and courageous, no doubt about that; he probably deserved more medals for valor than he had won. But reckless abandon had its limits. Yerks believed that courage on the battlefield should be defined broadly. Sometimes reining in your fears in order to command the unit effectively took as much courage as charging up a hill with a bayonet clenched in your teeth. Yerks felt that it probably wasn't a bad move to let Tom decompress a bit on the brigade staff.

Tom disagreed. He knew that any hope of resuscitating his career in the Army depended on his ability to command a company after being promoted to captain in two months. To be considered for that command, he needed more experience as a platoon leader. In mid April, after Red Grizzly had returned from R and R, Tom made an appointment to see the battalion commander at Firebase Birmingham, near the mouth of the A Shau Valley.

Wrapped in a flak jacket and slouched in the cab of a five-ton truck, Tom played out an imaginary dialogue during the twenty-five-mile trip to the firebase. He would carefully explain what had happened with Cottonmouth while the commander listened pensively.

"Okay," Red Grizzly would say, "you had a disagreement. Have to be careful with that. Drive on. Don't fuck up anymore. Don't get in fights in the rear. Fight the war. Get out there and kill commies."

It was a fine script, but Red Grizzly declined to read his lines. The lieutenant colonel led Tom to a rocky outcropping near the tactical operations bunker, where both men sat down and removed their helmets. At first smiling and genial, the battalion commander turned as ursine as his codename as soon as Tom requested another platoon command.

"I know that war is hell, but you just couldn't take it when the going got tough, and we don't want you back," the commander said bluntly.

Tom felt his face flush. He tried to explain about the ambush and the near catastrophe from the artillery barrage, but Red Grizzly cut him short.

"I've heard all about what happened. How about the night before? Didn't you cry out on the radio that you were all going to die? Didn't you beg to stop because you were all tired? Didn't you try to get out of moving all night to rescue B Company?"

The tongue lashing continued without mercy for ten minutes; then Red Grizzly stood up and clapped his helmet on. "Don't come back and bother us anymore."

Tom saluted. "Yes, sir."

The return ride to Camp Eagle seemed endless. Tom felt as though the commander had pummeled him with his fists. Who would have believed that mere words could raise such welts and contusions? Red Grizzly's castigation was the most humiliating thing that had ever happened to him, much more painful than being shot.

Now what? Had his performance really warranted such scorn? Was he deluding himself in thinking that he had acted on principle? He still believed that he had properly followed his conscience, heeding the dictates of duty. But duty and honor and country now appeared more complicated than he had realized. Was he out of step, with his faith in absolutes? Tom didn't know. And right now he was too stunned even to begin sifting the wreckage for answers.

By the spring of 1968, most men in the class of '66 were either in-country or were preparing to report for duty in the war zone within the next few months. Some of the early volunteers had completed their first tours, and they awaited, with virtual certainty, the orders to return for yet another year in Vietnam. As the class neared the second anniversary of its graduation, nineteen men had been killed in action.

The West Pointers had served with courage and distinction. Lieutenant Colonel Yerks, the former tactical officer who was now with the 101st, thought the class of '66 was a particularly intriguing group. In the two years since they entered the officer corps, they had been caught in the crossfire of social protests and upheavals that aimed squarely at their profession. They had as much tugging at their collective conscience, Yerks believed, as any West Point class since the Civil War. He was proud of the magnificent way they were performing in combat: the class was in the process of amassing nearly a hundred Silver Stars and an even greater number of Purple Hearts, a symbolic tally of valor and shed blood that was far higher than might have been expected of a class of its size.

Among those whose performance had been most exemplary was Tommy Hayes. Having rejected the sanctuary of graduate school after West Point, Tommy had also left the relative safety of his engineering unit by volunteering to command the long-range reconnaissance platoon in the 1st Division, nicknamed the Big Red One. He subsequently was picked to lead the division's aero rifle platoon, a unit described by the corps commander as "the eyes and ears of the Big Red One." At least one close friend thought Tommy was trying to prove that he was his own man, not just the grandson of Major General T. J. Hayes, Jr., West Point '12, and the son of Major General T. J. Hayes III, West Point '36. In eleven months of fierce combat, he had collected a Silver Star, three Bronze Stars, and a fistful of other medals.

Tommy's tour was scheduled to end in May, but he had recently asked to extend for another six months. In a letter home — marshaling his thoughts with dispassionate reason — he explained why:

> First, I don't feel a man can accomplish much in a year over here. It takes several months to get acclimated, to know the tricks of the trade, and to learn how to stay alive. Second, I don't particularly look forward to the prospect of returning to Vietnam every other year. If by staying over here I can make my unit more effective and perhaps bring this war closer to conclusion, then I will stay. Third, I feel that my country has invested a great deal in me as a soldier. I should like to repay that investment by accomplishing that for which I have been trained, in addition to testing the effectiveness of that training.

That was to be his last letter. At daylight on April 17, five battalions of the 1st Division swept into the jungle north of Saigon in a spoiling attack intended to disrupt a suspected enemy offensive against the capital. Tommy's unit was assigned to screen one flank of the sweep, and at three P.M. his platoon flew to a landing zone outside the village of Binh Co. Almost as soon as the helicopters touched down, heavy fire raked the platoon. In the opening fusillade, the point man was shot only twenty yards from where the enemy was entrenched along a treeline. Tommy ran across an open field to drag the wounded soldier behind a paddy dike. When another man was also shot in the open, he again dashed out and pulled him to safety. A moment later, as he began to reorganize the platoon, another volley of automatic weapons fire burst from the treeline, and Tommy Hayes fell dead. His bravery would earn him, posthumously, a second Silver Star.

Word of Tommy's death spread quickly; by the time he was buried at West Point a week later, more than a dozen of his classmates had flown or driven to the academy for the service. General Hayes even arranged for a DC-6 to fly from Army post to Army post to pick up those who could attend the funeral.

Tommy was laid to rest behind the old chapel in Section VI, next to his grandfather — the Army's ordnance wizard in World War II — who had died the year before. Jim Ford conducted the ceremony; he had seen Tommy briefly in Vietnam the previous fall, mud-caked and grinning as he sat in a tree, goggles propped on his head. Now, as Ford spoke, a hard rain fell, spattering the fresh graves of Buck Thompson and Pete Lantz across the churchyard in Section XXXIV.

Mourners ringed Tommy's grave in a dark, distracted semicircle, as though re-creating Courbet's great painting *Burial at Ornans*. His classmates stood with their heads bowed. They included Art Bonifas, up from Benning with his orders to Vietnam in hand, and George Crocker, who had just returned from the delta three months earlier. Jack Wheeler and Art Mosley had driven from Cambridge, Massachusetts, where both attended Harvard Business School. Jim Peake, one of Tommy's closest friends, had brought the body home. Bob Kesmodel had arrived from Panama. The stoicism of the Hayes family perplexed the young lieutenants, who futilely tried to blink away their own tears. The family stood silently, as though cut from stone, displaying no trace of grief. It was the Army way.

Beneath his reserve, however, General Hayes was shattered by the death of his only son in ways that Tommy's friends could not begin to comprehend. He had his own doubts about the war, particularly Robert McNamara's lunatic scheme to build an electronic fence across the demilitarized zone. The piecemeal escalation of the war also offended him. Yet, when he wrote letters to thank his classmates from '36 for their condolences, his words to William Westmoreland were gracious:

> Although nothing can compensate for his loss, at least his death came while fighting his country's battle in a cause he believed in and doing the work he chose. And he gave his life while saving others. Many are less fortunate . . . This letter calls for no answer, Westy.

After the funeral, several classmates lingered under the green tarpaulin. Jack Wheeler was struck by the contrast between the combat veterans and those, like himself, who had remained stateside. George Crocker, wearing his jump boots and decorations, appeared harder, older. He looked, Jack thought, like a warrior.

Jack had nearly finished his first year of graduate school at Harvard. Although it was the self-styled "West Point of capitalism," the business school seemed like a liberal arts college after the rigors of the military academy. The school was casual, diverse, cerebral — even coed. But Jack's thoughts often returned to the academy, and above his desk in Chase Hall hung a framed epigram that one of his West Point instructors had given him: "War is my business; business is good."

"So, George," Art Mosley asked Crocker as they stood beneath the tarpaulin, "how is it out in the Army? How are things?"

George brightened. "It's really good, Art. It's not chickenshit. You'll really like it."

Mosley scoffed. "Me? Like the Army? C'mon!"

George blinked with surprise. The cynicism — the venom — in his old roommate's voice startled him. Was this the same guy who had mooned the corps with him five years earlier? Sure, Art had always had a rebellious streak. So had George; that was one reason they got along so famously. But his commitment to the Army had seemed heartfelt, even gung ho. *Me? Like the Army?* Why that tone of repudiation?

"George, what about the war?" Jack asked. "What do you think?"

As George turned to reply, Jack saw the muscles in his jaw clench, tightening like slender steel cables. His face darkened, as though abruptly cast in a deep shadow.

"This is a bad war," he answered at last. "We can't kill enough of them."

Now it was Jack's and Art's turn to be surprised. Jack had never seen such an expression of frustration and disgust. Crocker's words conveyed a cold fury, made all the more menacing by the low tone in which they were uttered.

After the round of goodbyes and handshakes, Jack and Art hurried through the rain to Mosley's car. As the windshield wipers slapped away the miles back to Cambridge, Jack sat lost in thought. Saratoga, the Nike base, Harvard — all had been hiding places from the war. Although he knew his own tour in Vietnam was likely after he finished graduate school in another year, Jack had almost willfully blocked the thought from his mind. He didn't share Art Mosley's disaffection, but the incessant antiwar demonstrations at Harvard had inevitably chipped away at what little zeal Jack had left for the cause. Each time he heard of a classmate's death, he had felt regret and even had mourned. But until now he had not really been forced to grieve.

Tommy Hayes was dead. Jack found that difficult to comprehend. Among the host of princes at West Point, Tommy had been the most princely, a man destined for greatness. No one on earth had elicited greater admiration from Jack. Since Mosley had called him with the bad news, he had repeatedly conjured up two images of Tommy: the first was of him as a plebe, working the calculus problem from Jack's board; the second was of Tommy leading the choir down the aisle of the chapel when they were first classmen, his booming bass carrying above the others as they sang "When Morning Gilds the Skies."

In his pocket, Jack carried a sheet of paper he had pulled from a bulletin board in the cadet barracks just before driving to the cemetery. In the academy's daily flier, sandwiched between information about married officers' quarters and commissary closing hours, was the funeral notice:

> Services for the late 1Lt Thomas J. Hayes IV, OF107736, CE, Class of 1966, USMA, will be conducted in the Old Cadet Chapel at 1430 hr., Tue, 23 April, followed by interment in the Post Cemetery. The remains will lie in state from 1330 to 1430 hr., same date. Death occurred on 17 April in Vietnam.

He wondered what a funeral would have been like in that cemetery in 1943, with Big Jack and his classmates standing around the open grave of a young lieutenant killed by the Nazis or the Japanese. The trappings of grief would have been similar: the flag, the bugler, the honor guard, even the military stoicism. But would there have been the same suspicion — like an open secret too terrible to voice — that here was a young man who had died in vain? Slaughtered for nothing? Not likely. Jack had sensed that awful secret while standing in the rain beside his friend's casket, and it filled him with a bitter desolation.

For Jack, this had been an afternoon of twin revelations. The first had been the sight of Tommy's casket and the sure, sudden knowledge that the price was too high. The second, even more powerful, was George Crocker's face. Jack could not block the image from his mind — that handsome mug, usually open and good-humored, clenched as tight as an angry fist.

I'm out, Jack thought. *This war is completely screwed up.* He had known that in his head — the framed epigram about war being his business was just blather. Now he knew it in his heart. He was afraid. He did not want to die. *I'm out.*

Even before some of the '66ers arrived for their initial tour in Vietnam, others were back for the second time. Among the first to return was Matt Harrison, who had spent only four months stateside before shipping overseas again.

At home, Matt had served with the Old Guard in Washington. He and Bob Cresci, who survived a nasty leg wound in the Central Highlands, lived in an apartment building south of the Potomac on Four Mile Run. After months in the jungle, after all the death and violence, the World, as veterans referred to life beyond Vietnam, seemed unreal at times. America was so far, far removed from the war. One night Matt went to a concert to hear the Jefferson Airplane. The marijuana smoke billowed in huge gray clouds as the band played "White Rabbit" for what seemed like hours. His imagination couldn't have concocted a scene more remote from the bloody flank of Hill 875. People at home had no idea of what the war was like, and most simply didn't care to know.

The Old Guard was an elite unit, providing honor detachments for funerals at Arlington as well as for some of the capital's pomp and ceremony. Matt was offered a position as aide to the commander of the military district of Washington, with the understanding that he would subsequently command E Company, which guarded the Tomb of the Unknown Soldier. Instead, he asked to return to combat.

His brother was the reason. Robin Harrison, three years younger than Matt, had enlisted in the Marine Corps Reserve in California after graduating from high school. Bright, gentle, and impressionable, he fell under the spell of several antiwar activists, who urged him to resist being part of the American war machine. In answer to his insubordination, the Marines called Robin to active duty and gave him orders for Vietnam. Matt, who had flown to California to urge both his brother and the Marine commander to avoid a confrontation, volunteered to go in Robin's place.

Two brothers could not serve in the war zone simultaneously unless they volunteered, and obviously Robin had no yen for combat. All you have to do, Matt told him, is sit tight for a year at Camp Pendleton until your active-duty time expires. But, ignoring that advice, Robin forced the issue by refusing to obey orders. Faced with a court-martial, he fled to British Columbia.

By the time his brother deserted, however, Matt was already back in Vietnam with the 25th Division near Cu Chi. As a captain — accelerated promotions, tracks in two, turned out to be a reality — he became a company commander. Now he waged a different kind of war from the one he had fought with the 173rd. Instead of fighting large numbers of NVA every two or three weeks, he battled smaller numbers of Viet Cong every two or three days. The most serious scrap took place in the Ho Bo Woods, an infamous enemy stronghold west of the Iron Triangle above Saigon. Ambushed by an enemy force hiding in a V-shaped bunker complex, the company slowly and methodically destroyed the fortifications and routed the enemy. Lightly wounded by a grenade fragment during the fight, Matt received a Silver Star.

It was a different kind of war in other ways, too. As the Army became more and more desperate for troops, the quality of soldiers steadily declined. So did the caliber of officers. During his seven months in command, Matt was appalled by the incompetence of most of the fifteen lieutenants who served in his four platoons. The Army, it sometimes seemed, was willing to commission anyone who could walk or talk.

Matt began to view his role as that of a civilizing force, a restraint on sheer barbarism. The first time he walked through a Vietnamese village with the company, he was surprised and angered by the looting. After pillaging the hootches, some of the soldiers scuttled off with chickens and watermelons under their arms. "Hold it, guys," he ordered. "Stop right here. Put it back. We are not going to steal these people blind."

He was also infuriated when he saw his troops swing their helmets violently at Vietnamese children who came up to beg for food. Some soldiers lured the children with chocolate bars and then flung the candy at them, point blank, as hard as they could. "Listen," Matt yelled after witnessing this scene one day, "the next son of a bitch who does that is going to regret it."

Once, he found a group of soldiers who had herded several villagers off to a corner, lashed ponchos over the villagers' heads, and were beating them with fists and rifle butts.

"What the hell's going on here?" Matt demanded.

"Sir," one soldier replied, "these people must be VC."

"No. We are not going to do this. If they try to shoot us, then we're going to kill them. But we are not going to torture anybody."

As he turned away, Matt heard someone mutter, "Chickenshit."

He wheeled back on the troops. "Yeah, well, fortunately I don't have to run for re-election until this time next year. Now knock it off."

Matt found the veneer of civilization appallingly thin, especially in combat. Back home in Topeka or Cleveland or Spokane, he knew, these soldiers would no more think of clobbering a child with a helmet than they would consider robbing a bank. But in the war zone — in this war zone — standards of conduct had become as fragile as blossoms. It was an officer's job, he believed, to guarantee that atrocities didn't happen. That was another manifestation of duty.

Often, while preparing to take the company out for yet another sweep, Matt wondered whether he had an enemy counterpart, a kind of Asian doppelgänger. Somewhere out there, he would think, is a North Vietnamese captain who is getting his guys saddled up to do whatever their job is today, whether it's to find us or to avoid us. He's probably a lot like me. I wonder if our paths are going to cross today?

The image made him uncomfortable — it personalized the enemy too much — but he was unable to banish it from his mind. Larger issues of the war — winning or losing, right or wrong — bothered him very little. On a tactical level, the Americans were superior; that was as much as a company-grade officer needed to worry about.

Matt had a thick stubborn streak, and as the war became more unpopular at home, his own belief in the ethos of a professional soldier hardened. Whereas the prospect of becoming a civilian after his four-year commitment had once seemed appealing, it now held little attraction. Quitting would be like dropping out of a race midway. The Army needed him, needed his loyalty and his competence. Damn it, he thought, I made a commitment to this and I'm going to see it through.

Among the changes in Tom Carhart's life was his relationship with God. Ever since he was a boy, Tom had been a devout Catholic; at West Point he would have attended Mass even if church attendance hadn't been mandatory. His brush with death in the car accident left him more religious than ever during the first months of his recovery.

But in Vietnam, Tom's orthodoxy began to ebb. For reasons that he couldn't fully explain, he found the Church less and less satisfying. It was too rigid, too intolerant, and he felt a need to step away from the Roman Catholicism of his youth. He believed that he had come to a understanding with God, in which he acknowledged the existence of a supreme deity while rejecting the Church as flawed and all too human. Tom felt at peace with this spiritual compromise, and he stopped attending Mass. In the field, he was usually too busy with survival to pray.

But on a morning in early June 1968, he found the time. After his humiliation by Red Grizzly and a brief tour of duty on the brigade staff, Tom had wrangled the command of another platoon in a different battalion of the 101st (even while assuring his mother in a letter that he was safely ensconced in the rear). As the battalion began a sweep into the A Shau Valley fifty miles south of the DMZ, Tom's platoon moved up a ridgeline. Near the crest, one of his men discovered an NVA latrine. Just as Tom realized that they had blundered into an enemy camp, a quick sequence of explosions rocked the ridge. Tom heard the familiar whine of RPD machine-gun fire. At first, the paratroopers seemed capable of holding the hill against the assault. Tom cautiously flanked one NVA position and killed two or three soldiers with his M-16. But within minutes the enemy had gained the upper hand, raking the Americans with rocket-propelled grenades and automatic weapons fire. An explosion landed so close to Tom that the concussion blew his helmet off; he scavenged another helmet from a dead paratrooper, only to have that one blown off too. When he radioed for artillery fire, Tom was told that the firebase was too busy helping another besieged unit to lend immediate assistance.

As the NVA pressed their attack, Tom sensed with stark clarity that he was going to die on this nameless ridge. Between explosions, he took a few seconds to pray, not for deliverance but for courage. Please, God, he asked, let me die well. All he wanted was a death that his family and comrades would remember proudly. His principal regret, as he would later recall in his memoirs, was that he would never finish the canteen of lime Kool-Aid hanging from his web belt. The NVA began to mass for what appeared to be a final assault.

But just when the Americans' predicament seemed most desperate, deliverance arrived. A flight of F-4s suddenly appeared overhead. Tom marked his position with smoke canisters, and the bombers roared in with several payloads of high explosives and eight strikes of napalm. The wall of steel and jellied gasoline allowed the paratroopers to escape back down the hill to safety. Much to his surprise, Tom had survived. A bullet had creased his right arm and shrapnel had painfully lacerated his buttocks. Metal fragments also had slashed his chin, ruining the fine work done by the plastic surgeon eight months before and leaving a tiny constellation of gouges that looked like smallpox scars. After evacuating the dead and more seriously wounded, Tom returned to the battalion aid station for treatment, amazed — and even perplexed — by his good fortune.

Others in the class of '66 were not so lucky. Every few weeks now he got word of yet another classmate who had died. John Hoskins, the rangy boxer from Louisiana who used to read Stephen Crane's poetry aloud in the barracks at West Point, was killed in the delta on an airboat. Shortly before his death, Hoskins had written his own elegy:

> I am washed in the blood of my men;
> Their lifeless bodies I have lifted from the ground
> And carried in my arms . . .
> I am dead with them.
> I am washed with their lives.

Another classmate, Arthur M. Parker III, was struck by a helicopter rotor blade near Hué while pushing his men to safety. For four days Parker lay on the hospital ship U.S.S. *Sanctuary* before dying. He left behind a widow and seven-month-old son. Tom, who had liked and admired Art Parker at West Point, sobbed when he heard the news.

The final act in Tom Carhart's Vietnam drama was played out in a delta province south of Saigon. In mid June Tom pinned on his new captain's bars — not without considerable satisfaction, considering the troubles he had endured to earn a commission. Because captains rarely served as platoon leaders, he was assigned to Mobile Advisory Team 85 in the delta. Advisers to South Vietnamese regional forces — known derisively as Ruff Puffs — were supposed to be "like the steel reinforcing rods in concrete," in the words of General Earle Wheeler, chairman of the Joint Chiefs.

But Tom needed less than a day to see why the province had the reputation of being one of the three safest in South Vietnam: the place was an R and R haven for the Viet Cong. There was no concrete to reinforce. Instead, a tacit nonaggression pact existed between province officials and the enemy; the Ruff Puff battalion commander, Tom discovered, was an incompetent drunk who scrupulously avoided contact and preferred to go fishing with hand grenades. Sitting on the bank of a stream, he would pull the pin on a grenade, toss it into a stream, and watch like a Turkish pasha while his men scooped the stunned fish from the surface.

Tom and his small team of advisers whiled away their days in the American hootch, dubbed the Ponderosa, playing Monopoly, listening to rock 'n' roll on Armed Forces Network radio, and reading old *Sports Illustrated* magazines. Bored and frustrated, he was ripe for recruitment by Operation Phoenix. The program was actually several different operations run largely by the CIA in an effort to capture or assassinate enemy leaders. Over the next three years, it would be credited with 21,000 kills and achieve a grim notoriety, but now Operation Phoenix was brand new.

Over a beer in the American club one evening, Tom struck up a friendship with a gregarious, ruddy American called Red, who was the province coordinator for the Phoenix program. Red provided Tom with just enough details about the operation to pique his interest; when they met again a few days later, Red asked Tom whether he'd like to work with the Phoenix team. I need somebody with experience at leading patrols at night, Red explained. Tom agreed to help. What the hell, he thought, at least here's somebody who wants to fight.

Not long afterward, on a night in the fall of 1968, Tom and more than a dozen others parked their jeeps on a muddy road next to a rice paddy. A full moon had risen, but a thick overcast absorbed most of the light. In order to move quietly, Tom pulled off his boots and left them under the jeep seat. Guided by a Viet Cong defector, for two hours he crept barefoot along the dikes before spotting the dark rectangle of a house a hundred yards across an open field. He flipped off the safety on his M-16.

According to Red's intelligence, a senior VC officer had come to the area on a recruiting drive. As Tom inched across the field, he saw narrow bands of light seeping from two windows and heard the static hiss of a radio inside the house. When he was thirty yards away, he climbed onto a low dike. The door opened and two shadows emerged. Tom raised his rifle, drew a bead, and squeezed the trigger.

The two shadows jerked violently and collapsed to the ground, as the rest of the Phoenix team also opened fire. Tom then emptied his clip into the house at knee level, swinging his rifle from side to side. For a mad minute the walls shook under the fusillade of small-arms fire and grenade bursts.

When the shooting stopped, Tom pulled a flashlight from his thigh pocket. He switched on the red beam, stepped over the bodies outside the door, and peered into the hut. Two more bodies lay inside. One was an older man with gray hair. Pinned to his black pajama top was a brass star decorated with a small hammer and sickle. Three AK-47s lay nearby, along with a leather satchel stuffed with documents.

"I think this is our boy," Tom said, showing the others the brass star.

Hurrying back to the jeep with the satchel under his arm, Tom was ecstatic. Now *this* was how to fight the war, he thought. They had killed four communists and guaranteed that many others wouldn't sleep quite as soundly in the future. He laced the boots back on his muddy feet and drove back to the base.

The next day, Tom's commander, an American colonel who supervised all of the advisers in the province, ordered him to leave Operation Phoenix to the CIA cowboys. Your job, he told Tom, is to help your battalion become an effective fighting force. That does not include tramping around the countryside at night on unauthorized assassination larks. Understood?

Tom left the meeting in a red fury. Goddamn it, he grumbled, doesn't anybody down here want to win this war? What are we here for, to kill fish with hand grenades or to destroy the enemy? All the colonel wanted, Tom surmised, was to maintain the status quo. If Saigon thought the province was as pacified as the colonel claimed, his career would flourish. But if someone rocked the boat and insisted on fighting, then the colonel's little sham would be uncovered. Tom had even witnessed one ugly incident in which the colonel falsified a Silver Star citation for the South Vietnamese province chief. The whole thing was just a charade, just a damnable, stinking charade. And the more Tom thought about it, the angrier he got.

"What do you think, sir?" one of the sergeants asked him as they left the colonel's office. "Should we give it up?"

"Naw," Tom replied. "Shit, what's he gonna do, send us to Nam? Send us to the line? We're fighting the war. Just ignore him."

Twice more he sneaked out on Phoenix missions suggested by the mysterious Red. Again Tom framed the issue in terms of principle. He could sit back on his haunches and pretend that everything was going well. That was the prudent course, he knew, for his own safety and his career. You can get your ticket punched, he thought, collect a nice letter for your file, maybe collect a medal.

Or he could take the fight to the enemy, doing what he was trained to do, sworn to do, yearned to do. His views on war were akin to those of the British naval reformer Admiral Sir John Fisher, who in 1905 proclaimed, "The essence of war is violence. Moderation in war is imbecility. Hit first. Hit hard. And hit anywhere." As Tom saw it, he had little choice but to hit hard.

In October, the colonel summoned him again.

"Captain Carhart, what the hell's the matter with you?" he demanded. "I ordered you to knock off that Phoenix stuff and you have deliberately disobeyed. Here is your Two-o-one personnel file and Officer's Efficiency Report. There's a flight to My Tho in half an hour. You're to be on it with all your possessions. Tomorrow you will make your way to Can Tho, where you're being transferred."

Tom picked up the two-page OER. Of a maximum 140 points, the colonel had given him 78. That was the kind of score awarded to heroin addicts who tried to kill their superiors. Tom understood instantly that he was finished. With only a month or so left in his Vietnam tour, he would never recover from this kind of drubbing.

"Am I being relieved, sir?"

"Yes, I suppose you could say that," the colonel replied. "Any more questions?"

"No, sir."

Heartsick, he wandered back to the Ponderosa to collect his gear. What the hell *was* the matter with him? Why was it that every time he tried to do what he thought was right somebody kicked him across the room? Maybe it was time to think about getting out of the Army.

A letter lay on his bunk. He recognized Melissa's looping handwriting, and his hopes soared. Thank God, he thought, she has finally come around. He had written to her twice from Vietnam, both times after being wounded. "Well," he joked the second time, "I'm bleeding again." He had tried to keep the desperation from his words, reminding her of the cherry blossoms in Washington, their visit with her grandparents in Missouri, their lovers' dinner on the *River Queen* in St. Louis. But Melissa had never replied.

Clutching the letter, he went outside and stood on the steps. He imagined that he could smell her scent in the paper. Smiling, he tore open the flap.

> Dear Tom,
> The *River Queen* has sunk. Grandma and Grandpa died six months ago. I am married now.

He slumped to the steps. Another lieutenant walking past called to him in alarm, "Tom! Tom! You okay?"

He nodded feebly. "Yeah, yeah, I'm all right. Bad letter."

Later, he sat down and wrote a panicked reply. "My God," he pleaded, "you can't do this." But she could, and she had. She never wrote to him again.

Tom spent his last weeks in Vietnam as a staff officer in Cao Lanh, manning the tactical operations center from midnight to eight A.M. The graveyard shift gave him ample time to reflect on the past year. How was it possible that things had gone so badly? He had been relieved of duty twice. His refusal to lead his men down the enemy trail after the ambush, he still believed, had been a proper and principled decision.

But he was less certain now about his stubborn insistence on participating in the Phoenix operations. Had that been justifiable zeal or willful insubordination? He didn't know. For nearly twelve months in combat, he had followed his impulses — including the impulse to destroy the enemy — and what had it earned him? Two Purple Hearts and a blistering OER. Duty, honor, and country — indeed, life itself — seemed infinitely more complex now than they once had.

West Point had taught its sons to seek glory — not personal aggrandizement, but rather a greater good for the nation. In his own fashion, Tom had sought that glory, but glory had eluded him. And as he boarded the plane at Tan Son Nhut to fly home on December 6, he had not the slightest idea where it might be found.

11

LONG BINH

JACK WHEELER pressed closer to the fence, wrapping his fingers around the mesh. The day was gorgeous, one of those cobalt summer afternoons, faintly redolent of eucalyptus, that seemed unique to Northern California. Even in the warm sun, the metal fence felt cool to the touch. The chain link diced his view of the tarmac into a grid of three-inch diamonds. Charter planes, mostly 707s and DC-8s, stood in a line to Jack's right; to his left stretched a row of Air Force C-141s, including several splotched with brown and green camouflage paint.

Less than fifty yards away baggage handlers loaded a stack of shiny aluminum crates onto the nearest C-141. Jack could see hundreds of the boxes; one by one they glided up a black conveyor belt to disappear into the belly of the plane. Ammunition? he wondered. No, that didn't make any sense; they wouldn't ship ammo in aluminum containers. Perhaps they were missile boxes, Sparrows or Shrikes for the Phantoms at Tan Son Nhut. If so, they weren't very heavy; the baggage handlers hoisted the crates onto the belt with ease.

Suddenly it struck him: coffins. Empty coffins. No-frills, government-issue, aluminum creels for the dead, bound for another load of mothers' sons in the mortuary at Bien Hoa.

Good God, Jack thought. The sight was enough to make a man genuflect. What a melancholy image on this sun-filled afternoon. Glancing at his watch, he saw that he had nearly four hours to pass until his plane left. Maybe he could catch a movie. He turned from the fence, stealing one last glance at the flight line, and began to stroll toward the base theater.

Jack regretted that his father hadn't been able to stay long enough to see him off. Now stationed at the Aberdeen Proving Ground in Maryland, Big Jack had flown out here to Travis Air Force Base the day before to spend a final day with his son. They rented a car and drove south to San Francisco for dinner at Fisherman's Wharf. Jack had tried to feign good cheer, but he suspected that his father easily saw through his smile and strained banter. How hard it must be to see a son go to war, he thought, harder perhaps for a professional soldier than for most parents.

Janet Wheeler had remained at Aberdeen, "scared stupid," as she put it. Here she was settling into another year of waiting for the Western Union boy, just as she had in Laredo a quarter century earlier. The bravado of the men only made her feel worse. Two other officers at Aberdeen had lost sons in the war, and she found herself looking for auguries, patterns. Death came to that house, she would think, and they're eight doors down from us. And death came to that house; they're four doors down. Are we next?

Colonel and Captain Wheeler had passed the morning at Travis over breakfast and a long, idle chat. Father and son were striking in their dissimilarity. Jack, though not a big man, loomed several inches above his father, who was all angles and cusps, as though specifically engineered to squeeze into a tank. The left breast of his uniform jacket was covered with a twenty-six-year accumulation of "fruit salad" — decorations and service ribbons. As Big Jack was about to get on the plane at noon for the return trip to the East Coast, Jack had given him a bear hug and a kiss.

"I love you, Old Man."

"I love you, Jackson."

Now Jack wandered across the base alone, halfheartedly looking for the theater. He passed a few other GIs in new fatigues; they milled about aimlessly, obviously beset with both anxiety and boredom as they waited for their flights. Returning their salutes, Jack was struck by their youth. The median age of American soldiers in Vietnam was nineteen; in World War II it had been twenty-six, Big Jack's precise age when he fought at the Bulge.

Jack's orders had arrived in the mail at Harvard that spring as he was finishing his final year of business school:

HQDA
WHEELER, JOHN P. III, OF 108030
RPT NLT 29 JUN 69
90TH REPL BN LONG BINH RVN

Report no later than 29 June 1969. Although he had expected the orders, a vague sense of doom settled over him once the assignment was official. As he had grieved for Tommy Hayes, he began to grieve for himself. Although he never considered not going — news accounts of West Pointers declaring themselves to be conscientious objectors shocked him deeply — he did consider everything else with his usual relentless internal interrogatory. What was required of him? Did duty dictate that he volunteer to put himself in harm's way, as Tommy had? Was he less of a soldier, less of a man, if he did not? Was he betraying West Point if he remained in the rear?

He remembered a line of Thackeray's that he admired for its trenchant brevity: "Bravery never goes out of fashion." Tales of classmates valiantly sacrificing themselves stirred in him an overpowering love and admiration. Jack was afraid, but he did not believe that he was a coward. Surely there were things for which he would willingly die. Why, then, did he feel so anguished by his reluctance to face the fires of Vietnam?

Not knowing where he would be sent once he reached the 90th Replacement Battalion in Long Binh was part of the anxiety. This obligatory abdication of fate didn't come easily. It required, he thought, an almost un-American fatalism. In an odd paradox, it also meant surrendering certainty. But wasn't that the birthright of his generation, an unshakable presumption that there would be a tomorrow and that tomorrow would be better than today?

During his two years in business school the entire country seemed to have wheeled around against the war and, by extension, those who fought it. Even a solid majority of the Harvard MBA class of '69 — a conservative group overall — had declared in an opinion survey that sending U.S. troops to Vietnam was a mistake.

Like Marty Maher, Jack had begun to slip black ribbons into his yearbook to mark the photos of classmates killed in action. No one at Harvard seemed to care. Once, when he had showed *The Howitzer* to a coed he was dating, she practically yawned with boredom as he flipped from Bertolino to Flynn to Hayes to Rybicki to Thompson. One of the newest ribbons belonged to Frank Meszar III, Jack's roommate during their first-class year. Meszar, who had a weakness for cards, Corvettes, and cosmopolitan women, had been killed in March with the 1st Cavalry while leading his company in an attack. Meszar's father, a brigadier general, had won a Silver Star in Korea; now young Frank had one, too.

Not long after Tommy Hayes's funeral, Jack applied for a transfer from the artillery to the adjutant general's office, which provided the Army's administrators. Switching from a combat arm to a service support branch was viewed with disdain by many line officers. Their scorn was illustrated by a derisive ditty that poked fun at the small shield worn as a collar insignia by members of the AG Corps: Twinkle, twinkle little shield / Save me from the dirty field.

Even after the approval of his transfer, Jack told himself there was a fair chance that the Army would not honor it once he got to Long Binh. Once a redleg, always a redleg, and if the artillery needed a battery commander somewhere in the boondocks, he was sure they wouldn't hesitate to requisition Wheeler, John P. III, OF 108030.

Goodbye, Columbus was playing at the Travis base theater. He went inside and felt his way down the aisle until his eyes dilated in the darkness. They widened even further at the sight of Ali MacGraw swimming nude in a pool. Her body was tanned and sleek. The movie was about young lovers seeking common ground, and in the end, she and the hero parted. That just deepened Jack's melancholy; he couldn't help thinking of Ginny. In his first year of graduate school, she had sent a telegram to his room in Chase Hall: HI HANDSOME WANTED TO SAY YOU'RE SPECIAL AND I LOVE YOU YOUR PRIVATE SUNSHINE GIRL VIRGINIA. But in the past year and a half — living in different cities and in very different worlds — they had drifted apart, slowly and gently. Jack wasn't sure why, but the prospect of spending their lives together no longer seemed inevitable. Neither he nor Ginny felt prepared to marry, and by mutual consent they had dated others. Now that Jack was leaving the country for a year, their love affair was yet another uncertainty in his life. Perhaps, he told himself, they could rekindle the romance after his return, but he suspected the fire was burning itself out.

He left the theater and returned to the airfield. As he watched the crowd of soldiers at the gate, he thought back to that night in Newport News exactly seven years earlier, when he had taken the train to New York for West Point. How idealistic he and his classmates had been! Convinced of their ability to improve the world, they had a faith not one whit different from that which propelled others into the Peace Corps. His idealism, he believed, remained remarkably intact. But Jack was not at all certain that his going off to help wage this war would make the world a better place.

The gate opened and the line of troops surged forward. The time had come to leave his doubts stateside. He was a soldier, sworn to do his duty, honor-bound as well as Vietnam-bound. Jack grabbed his bag and walked briskly to the plane, as though once again he were a seventeen-year-old marching off to Beast Barracks.

Long Binh sprawled across a sloping plateau about twenty miles northeast of Saigon. By the summer of 1969, it covered twenty-five square miles and had a population comparable to that of a modest city — say Moline, Illinois — with movie theaters, swimming pools, and even a cavernous Chinese restaurant, the Loon Foon. Unlike Moline, Long Binh was enclosed within a perimeter of concertina wire, claymore mines, and innumerable sandbagged bunkers, each manned round the clock by four soldiers with an M-60 machine gun.

Large air-conditioned buildings for the headquarters of the United States Army Vietnam (USARV) and the First Logistics Command occupied the high ground. A huge ammunition dump, supply facilities, and maintenance bays with cement slabs and corrugated roofs dominated the lower slope. The American generals and colonels lived in comfortable trailers with lawns and flower beds tended by some of the twenty thousand Vietnamese who worked at Long Binh as houseboys, waitresses, and gardeners. The officers' mess often served steak and wine; on the frequent occasions when distinguished visitors from the States visited the generals' compound, the usual fare was surf 'n' turf, that peculiarly American combination of lobster and steak.

In the late afternoon, a squadron of two or three dozen Vietnamese pimps would drive up and down the main road on motor scooters, with fetching young girls in tight-fitting *ao dai* outfits riding sidesaddle behind them. For soldiers who ventured into Saigon, another fifty thousand bar girls worked in 160 cabarets and 47 dance halls with names like the Blue Angel, Eve, and the Bunny Club. The journalist Michael Herr referred to those stationed at Long Binh as "Dial soapers"; life in the rear, he wrote, "was like sitting inside the folded petals of a poisonous flower."

Much to his relief, Jack found on arriving at Bien Hoa Air Base that he was not being sent to a line unit. Instead, thanks largely to Art Mosley's skillful maneuvering, he was assigned to work for a lieutenant colonel in Management Information and Data Systems, the office at Long Binh that ran the Army's computers in Vietnam. Art had arrived at Long Binh several months earlier and had watched for jobs that would suit Jack's prodigious organizational skills while keeping him out of harm's way. When a vacancy became available in the data systems office, Art casually suggested to a personnel officer that a certain Captain Wheeler, though not a trained computer expert, would be an admirable choice for the job. After reviewing Jack's file, the personnel officer agreed and arranged the assignment.

For the first couple of days in-country, Jack was afflicted with the same numb disbelief that he had felt in Beast when he saw the mound of new equipment on his bunk in room 1732: *Is this really happening to me?*

He also had pangs of guilt about being a Dial soaper while so many others were dying in the mud beyond Long Binh's concertina wire. Here he was safe; he had not even bothered to requisition an M-16. Occasionally a line soldier would pass through, often with the strut and imperious glare of someone who had just been in the Shit, and the distinction was as clear as it had been between the warriors and their stateside classmates at Tommy Hayes's funeral. Oliver Wendell Holmes, who as a young Union captain was critically wounded at Antietam, had once observed that his having served in combat forever distanced him from men who had not. Jack felt that distance acutely, and it gnawed at him.

For the most part, however, he flung himself into his work, ten hours a day, six days a week. Vietnam was the first computerized war: the Army had Univacs, IBMs, and NCRs at 140 compounds all over the country to keep track of everything from body counts to bullets. In Saigon, a special computer was used solely to invoice helicopter parts. At Cu Chi, the 25th Division fed its Univac 1005 and NCR 500 with data from every firefight, large or small, in the hope of analytically predicting enemy movements. Lists of known or suspected Viet Cong sympathizers were also computerized, as was the Hamlet Evaluation System, which rated the loyalty of every village in South Vietnam.

Tropical heat and humidity, not to mention electrical surges and occasional mortar attacks, played hob with the systems, which were relatively crude by later standards. Like everything else in Vietnam, keeping the computers humming was an elaborate logistical undertaking. As junior officer on the staff, Jack often flew to Cam Ranh, Da Nang, and other bases to help them with their problems, whether finding spare parts or experienced technicians. One of his proudest accomplishments was a program he'd written that enabled one master computer to keep track of all other Univacs in South Vietnam. As he had at the Nike base in New Jersey, he believed the job at Long Binh matched his talents perfectly.

Two other classmates also served at Long Binh. The first was Mosley, who had arrived on New Year's Day 1969 after finishing at Harvard a year ahead of Jack. Brown-eyed, left-handed, inclined to menthol cigarettes and a shambling gait that made him appear even lankier than he was, Art Mosley was widely envied for having the rarest treasure in Vietnam — an attractive round-eyed woman who worked as a civilian at Army headquarters. Art's enthusiasm for military life had waned completely, but his affection for baseball had endured. That spring, he wrote to a friend back in the World:

> March 1, 1969, had to come sooner or later, but that doesn't make it any less sad. It was a gray, dismal day. No one died, no international crisis developed, no bizarre crime was committed, no one was physically hurt in any way. But all over America little boys cried and big boys wished they could. Mickey Mantle quit baseball. I feel as though a little of me has quit with him . . .

The other classmate was Theodore Hill, a tall, barrel-chested native of upstate New York. Like Jack and Art, Ted Hill was a math wizard who had graduated among the top twenty in the class of 1966. Like Buck Thompson and Tom Carhart, he had been a Good Bad Cadet who often spent time explaining himself before regimental disciplinary boards. Contrary to regulations, at West Point he at various times owned a bicycle, an automobile, a television set, and a hamster named Elemrap — an anagram of the name of a particularly despised tactical officer — which lived in a little cage hidden beneath Ted's bunk.

He had once hollowed out his cartridge box and inserted a transistor radio; in formation, he liked to click it on to full volume for a few seconds at a time so that the Kinks would shriek GIRRRL, YOU REALLY GOT ME NOW! as the tactical officers raged through the ranks looking for the offender. On another occasion, he and four others unhinged the first American cannon to fire a shot at Vicksburg, then dragged it across the Plain — gouging a trench worthy of Verdun — and left it on an upperclassman's desk as a surprise.

Ted Hill loved adventure. On graduation leave, he had prospected for gold in the Peruvian Andes until bandits ordered him out of the mountains at gunpoint. In graduate school at Stanford, he played first-team rugby, wore sandals and long hair, and dated the sister of one of the members of the Grateful Dead. As a company commander at Fort Devens, he was involved in a mysterious episode on the campus of Wellesley College, in which three different police agencies pursued him. All Ted would say about the incident is that "shots were fired."

Arriving in Vietnam with a distaste for the war that was even stronger than Mosley's, he notified his battalion commander that he would prefer to take part only in "defensive actions." To test his courage, the commander made him the machine gunner on a jeep. Later, Ted wrote a letter to military intelligence suggesting — to no avail — that he was a security risk who should be discharged from the service because he talked in his sleep.

Ted also offered to complete his military obligation in the federal penitentiary at Leavenworth. Having glimpsed the frontiers of mathematics at Stanford — the knowledge gave him goosebumps, like a beautiful poem — he figured that a year or two in prison just to think would be splendid, even if his keepers deprived him of paper and pencil. Marijuana possession could earn up to seven years, which seemed severe; when the authorities told him they were going to ignore any infraction that drew less than a five-year sentence, he dropped the idea.

Given the breadth of Long Binh, Captains Hill, Mosley, and Wheeler yearned for a set of wheels. Ted and Art both worked for engineering units, and getting from job to job was a time-consuming nuisance. Hill went to see the authorities about requisitioning a jeep.

"No way," he was told. "There are even colonels here who don't have jeeps."

"Okay, listen," he persisted. "I'll buy a vehicle in Saigon."

"No. There's a regulation against having a POV."

"POV?"

"Privately owned vehicle. POV."

"Of course. Okay, I'll rent one."

"No. Still privately owned."

"Motorcycle?"

"No."

"Okay, how about this: I will buy a vehicle and I will donate it to the United States Army with the stipulation that I get to drive it for the next few months."

That seemed to stymie them for a few minutes until they responded with logic out of *Catch-22*.

"Sorry, Captain, but there's no provision for that. If there's a regulation against it, then the practice is forbidden. If there's no regulation, then it's also forbidden because there isn't a regulation permitting it."

Undaunted, Ted and Art huddled to consider their options. Scrounging was an ancient if not precisely an honorable wartime enterprise. Like snatching the Navy goat, scrounging a jeep would require careful planning. After scouting the various motor pools in Long Binh, they targeted a mechanized unit with a large fleet of jeeps, many of which appeared to be unused. Late one night, carrying a six-foot-long pair of bolt cutters, they slipped into the darkened motor pool and selected a jeep to their liking. As with most vehicles in Vietnam, the ignition required no key, but a heavy chain had been padlocked around the clutch and steering wheel. The bolt cutters snipped the links easily. They then drove into the hills outside Long Binh, where a Vietnamese entrepreneur had set up a body shop and was making a good living from U.S. soldiers who stole jeeps from one another. For two cartons of Salems, he painted new identification numbers on the fender.

A few friends, including Jack, were allowed use of the jeep with the understanding that the vehicle was unauthorized and that anyone caught would take the rap. "If you see a roadblock," Ted advised, "hit the ignition as though you've stalled. Then get out, lift the hood, and pretend to be tinkering with the engine until the coast is clear."

A couple of weeks later, Ted was kicked out of his unit for insubordination. After finishing a feasibility study on an engineering project, he had taken the paper for polishing to a soldier who had a master's degree in English. Then he took the study to his commanding officer.

"Colonel, here's that report you wanted."

The colonel nodded. "Thanks very much. I'll look it over tonight and let you know tomorrow if there are any changes I want you to make."

"Uh, Colonel, I don't think you understand," Ted protested. "This is the best I can do. If you have something you want to change, you'll have to do it yourself."

The colonel flushed with anger and stormed from the office. For the next two days, Ted and his friends spent considerable time speculating on which hellish corner of Vietnam would be his place of exile. They were stunned when he was appointed commander of a personnel company at Long Binh, with fourteen vehicles at his disposal.

"Here you go, Mose," he told Art with a grin, symbolically transferring title to the hot jeep. "I don't need this anymore."

Soon after, Art flew to Honolulu on R and R, leaving Jack custody of the jeep. One afternoon, an enlisted man running an errand for Jack was stopped at an MP roadblock. Asked to explain why the serial number on the engine did not match the identification number on the fender, the soldier confessed. "And," he added, "Captain Wheeler uses it. And Captain Hill. And Captain Mosley."

When a pair of military policemen from the Criminal Investigation Division showed up to question Jack, he told them what he knew, which was quite a lot. After being fingerprinted and having his mug shot taken, Jack called Art in Hawaii and warned him to expect trouble when he returned.

Because three West Pointers were involved, the case was referred all the way to the Pentagon. The maximum penalty for misappropriation of government property was four years in prison, but CID agreed that no larceny was involved, since the three captains had used the jeep principally for Army business in a combat zone. Instead, each of them was reprimanded, fined $300, and given an Article 15 — an administrative punishment known within the ranks as a Fifteen Fucker — "for conduct totally unbecoming an officer."

They had hardly committed a major war crime. Given the drug abuse, fraggings — killing or wounding of officers and NCOs by their men, usually with grenades — desertions, mutinies, murder of civilians, and other disciplinary problems plaguing the American Army at the time, the jeep heist was hardly more than a fraternity prank. Hill and Mosley, each possessed of flanker sang-froid, shrugged off the punishment.

For Jack, however, the episode was shattering. *Conduct totally unbecoming an officer*. The words were harsh, humiliating, wholly contrary to duty, honor, country. He was not a dishonorable man; of that he was positive. He was a good soldier. He believed in West Point's creed with all his soul. Art Mosley had written the one-paragraph blurb under

Jack's picture in the '66 *Howitzer,* concluding with: "He will never be satisfied in merely doing what he likes to do, rather he will do what he can and ought to do."

That was a fine, flattering tribute from a loyal friend, and Jack liked to think the words were true: he would always do what he ought to do. But he found it hard to square the sentiment with the damning indictment from the Article 15. *Conduct totally unbecoming* . . . The censure lingered, hot and shameful, burning him as surely as if he had been branded.

"How do we learn?" one of his professors had once asked in a class at Harvard.

Jack had raised his hand. "We learn," he offered, "through pain."

Art Mosley tweezed a shrimp from his plate with the chopsticks as the waitress set another bowl of steaming rice on the white tablecloth. The table seemed to sag beneath the dishes heaped with eggrolls, moo goo chicken, and beef with oyster sauce.

"What is this? C'mon. Are we supposed to watch our country go into bankruptcy and our friends die without saying anything?" Art said, popping the shrimp into his mouth. "This is $30 billion a year, not to mention all these lives. This isn't what we were taught at West Point. In fact, it violates many of the things we *were* taught."

"'Don't ever get caught in a land war in Asia,'" Jack interjected, taking a swig of ginger beer.

"Exactly. How many times did we hear that? I can remember being taught the lessons of the French war in Indochina. Dienbienphu was one of the top ten decisive battles in all of military history."

Art gestured with his chopsticks. "There is just no place where you can grab on to anything that is right or true about this war. I'm going to sign it."

Several other officers at the large round table nodded. The Loon Foon provoked polemics. The restaurant resembled an aircraft hangar, with corrugated metal walls and a high peaked ceiling that trapped and amplified the din from dozens of tables below. Although reputed to be a black market center that laundered large sums of military scrip, the restaurant also served first-class Cantonese food. It was clean, it was well lighted, and diners never failed to be struck anew by the surrealism of having a vast Chinese eatery in the middle of Long Binh.

The order of business on the table at the Loon Foon this November evening in 1969 was a petition that read, "We, the undersigned, support the Vietnam moratorium." Six hundred thousand antiwar protestors had just marched on Washington in the largest demonstration ever staged on the Mall.

At Long Binh, the driving force behind the petition was an earnest, twenty-five-year-old Army dentist from the Bronx named Alan Goldstein. To Art in his dental chair one day, mouth agape, Goldstein had begun talking of the responsibility of officers to voice their dissent. Suspicious of authority and animated by a sense of high moral purpose — and ignoring the crude threat scrawled on his door one night, referring to him as a "commie faggot jew" — the dentist had spoken passionately about the immorality of the war.

In this case, he was preaching to the choir. Art's misgivings about the war had led him to reject the offer of a company command when he arrived in Vietnam. Among other things, he found giving orders to be distasteful; he preferred doing a task himself rather than commanding someone else to do it. Art applauded Ted Hill's suggestion that there be a rule prohibiting any nation from waging war until it had executed its top thirty leaders. That, he concluded, would cut down considerably on martial enthusiasm.

Now, beneath the bright lights of the Loon Foon, Art pointed at the petition. "I don't see this as being disloyal or disrespectful," he said. "On the contrary, I think when you feel strongly about something, it's your responsibility to act. What do you think, Dick?"

Richard E. Radez, West Point '67, had been a plebe in Mama Deuce when Jack was a yearling. He too had just graduated from Harvard Business School. Now he was a staff officer in the controller's office at Long Binh, responsible for looking after the dozen or so military banks run in-country by Chase Manhattan and American Express.

Shortly after arriving in Vietnam, Radez had heard Secretary of the Army Stanley Resor claim on the radio that B-52 strikes were carefully controlled to prevent them from hitting within a mile of Vietnamese villages. A week later, Radez woke up to find his bed heaving from nearby B-52 bombs. Shit, he thought, Stanley Resor doesn't know what he's talking about. That suspicion soon extended to everyone else in the chain of command.

Now he sided with Mosley. "We're all opposed to the war. I think the whole thing is crazy. The question is, what's the appropriate way of making that known? What is appropriate for us in our position as officers and also as citizens?" He paused for a moment. "Yeah, I'll sign. Give me the damned thing."

The petition was passed to Captain Bruns Grayson, another of Al Goldstein's patients. At twenty-two, Grayson was a company commander who had served in Vietnam for nearly eighteen months. A native of Alameda, California, he had been expelled from both parochial and public high schools for offenses ranging from fighting, theft, and drugs, to general truculence. After his father threw him out of the house, he had enlisted in the Army and eventually graduated from Officer Candidate School.

"Naw," Grayson said, "I'm not going to sign."

"How come?" Jack asked.

Grayson shook his head. "I think the war's a shitty idea, but if I sign, I'll still have this company, these hundred and fifty guys working for me. And if they find out I signed an antiwar petition, I'm going to have to spend God knows how much time dealing with all the administrative crap when they all want to become conscientious objectors. It'll be a pain in the ass."

"Jack?" Art asked.

Jack had listened without saying much. As a matter of principle, he believed the people of South Vietnam should have the freedom to choose the kind of government they wanted. But the more immediate issue was whether the war was winnable. Vietnam reminded him of a huge trampoline with half a million Americans bouncing around on it uncontrollably.

He pushed himself away from the table and stood up. "I'm going to go see my boss."

"Why?" Grayson asked.

"I want to talk to him and get his advice. I think he's a wise man."

Jack turned away but paused in midstride. "Hey, Bruns, can you give me a lift?"

Grayson sighed. Not least among the reasons for his popularity with this crowd, he knew, was that he had a jeep. "Yeah. Sure."

The drive to the colonel's room took five minutes. Jack rode silently in the passenger seat, lost in thought. Grayson felt guilty about all the time he spent away from his company with Jack Wheeler and the other West Pointers, but he found them irresistible. They talked about ideas and politics with an intellectual agility that to him was new and enlivening.

Grayson had met Jack after signing up for a University of Maryland extension course in business administration. Class was held in a Long Binh double-wide trailer with fluorescent lights and blackboards. A notice on the bulletin board reminded students that "in case of mortar or rocket attack you are to evacuate to ditches outside." The instructor was Jack Wheeler.

Jack loved teaching, and he thought of the class as his command. He wrote a stock program to demonstrate the intricacies of the market and set up a mock labor negotiation, with half of his students arguing the management position and half arguing the union position. When the bargaining grew intense and the labor leaders shouted, "Management pigs!" Jack was delighted.

He took Bruns Grayson on as a special reclamation project and encouraged him to consider Harvard when applying to colleges. When the application form failed to arrive from Cambridge, Jack said, "Why don't we just make one up? They're all the same." So Grayson drafted his own form and mailed it to Nathan Pusey, Harvard's president. Pusey replied with a gracious note, and soon afterward Grayson was accepted to the class of '74, which would be entering the following September.

Such episodes led Grayson to conclude that Jack was a phenomenon of nature. A voracious reader, Bruns had come across Isaiah Berlin's extraordinary essay on Winston Churchill. Written in 1940, the description reminded Grayson in a peculiar way of Jack:

> Mr. Churchill sees history—and life—as a great Renaissance pageant . . . The units out of which his world are constructed are simpler and larger than life, the patterns vivid and repetitive like those of an epic poet . . . The whole is a series of symmetrically formed and somewhat stylized compositions, either suffused with bright light or cast in darkest shadow.

When men were noble, they were very, very noble. When men were ignoble, they were craven. Jack's world, Bruns Grayson thought, worked much the same way, although it was the present rather than the past that inflamed his imagination. Despite his intellect, Jack was not a subtle thinker. No matter how many times Grayson told him otherwise, Jack persisted in believing that an Alameda judge had given young Bruns the option of going to jail or enlisting in the Army. For whatever reason, the image of Grayson confronting that Hobson's choice conformed with a myth that Jack found important.

He had, Grayson knew, a genuine impulse to help others, to serve. With inexorable enthusiasm, Jack flung himself into one enterprise after another, whether it was Army computers or getting one of his students into a good college. Given his heritage and background, that notion of service required that a man desire to lead, as well. Great men were, ipso facto, leaders. That was a West Point truism.

But that was also the rub. Grayson believed that the most singular leaders possessed certain traits that Jack lacked. They often were manipulative and reserved, assuming a command presence that set them apart. Yet Jack was an open book, utterly incapable of hiding his sentiments. Grayson knew that few things in life terrified people more than perpetual earnestness. Dick Radez used to say that Wheeler was the kind of character they drew cartoons about in *The New Yorker*.

Grayson parked the jeep outside the colonel's quarters and switched off the lights. Jack bounded up the steps and rapped on the door. Grayson followed on his heels with a sense of foreboding.

"Evening, Colonel," Jack said cheerfully when the door opened.

The colonel, rangy and soft-spoken, smiled and beckoned them in. "Well, Cap'n Jack. What's up?"

"Sir, sorry to bother you at night, but I wondered if we could talk to you for a minute."

Jack quickly recounted the discussion at the Loon Foon regarding the petition. "It calls for support of the moratorium against the war. Some of the guys feel that it's their obligation to express their concerns in a way that isn't disloyal to the Army or to the country. I'm not sure myself and I'd be interested in hearing your views on it."

The colonel listened politely, but when he spoke his voice was as jagged as shrapnel.

"I think it's outrageous and despicable and the act of a coward and a traitor to sign it."

There was silence; the colonel's reply had brought the conversation to a dead stop. Jesus, Bruns thought, who's the naïve one here? He had always thought of himself as a hick compared with Jack, a man who had excelled at West Point, dated a ballerina, and gone to Harvard. But even a juvenile delinquent from Alameda knew that you didn't solicit the colonel's views on something like this.

"I see, sir," Jack said at last. "I'll consider that. I — "

"Who's responsible for this thing?" the colonel interrupted. "Where did this so-called petition come from?"

Jack backed toward the door, awkwardly parrying the colonel's demand that he identify the petition's author. Thanking the officer for his thoughts, and bidding him good night, he returned to the jeep.

As they drove away, Jack sat silently with his arms folded. Grayson glanced at him several times before blurting out in exasperation, "Well, Jack, what the fuck did you think he was going to say?"

Jack said nothing. And he did not sign the petition.

As New Year's slipped past and a new decade began, there were ominous signs of an American Army coming apart at the seams. Yet few military men cared to recognize the portents of disaster, given both their native American optimism and the relative success of the 1969 campaigns. Viet Cong strength had been broken by staggering losses in Tet of 1968, and Saigon now completely controlled 70 percent of the country's villages and enjoyed reasonable security in another 20 percent. Highways were safer than they had been since 1956. U.S. intelligence analysts estimated that Viet Cong manpower in the delta had plummeted to about two thousand troops.

But those were tactical triumphs. Strategically, the war was slipping away. The nation's will to win the conflict was evaporating and the Army was crumbling from within. Considering that the Army fielded in 1966 and 1967 was, in the estimation of some historians, the finest ever assembled by the United States, the collapse happened with remarkable speed. Desertion and AWOL rates began to soar, as did heroin addiction. In the next two years, the Army would suffer hundreds of fraggings. In an effort to caulk morale, the military began distributing medals so promiscuously that they became known derisively as gongs. In 1970 alone, more than half a million decorations were handed out, twice the number of U.S. personnel remaining in-country.

As they had from the beginning, lieutenants and captains bore the brunt of the casualties within the officer corps. (In eleven years of combat, only eight colonels and three generals would be killed; the number of lieutenants killed was seventeen hundred.) In part, this was because platoons and companies served as the basic fighting units of a mobile war against an elusive enemy. The changing style of combat leadership was also a factor, as senior officers gradually migrated to the rear in modern conflicts. In the Civil War, by contrast, the chance of a general being killed was 50 percent higher than that of a private; among both Confederate and Union forces, the proportion of all officers killed was 15 percent higher than dead enlisted troops.

Among the West Pointers from the class of 1966, the death toll continued to rise with monotonous consistency. Soon it proportionately exceeded even the Korean War losses of the class of 1950, a group widely regarded as having been mauled in combat. The chance of being killed in Vietnam was about one in twenty among the '66ers; the chance of being wounded was about one in six.

John Fera, who had fought at Hill 875, was later killed on a search-and-destroy mission. Charles Johnson died in a burst of automatic weapons fire from an enemy-held hamlet. Both were buried at the academy. Gordon Kimbrell, who had been George Crocker's Ranger buddy, was killed in Cambodia. Michael Grisafe and Martin Niskanen both died in air accidents. Louis Sustersic, David Wilson, David Brown, Allen Culpepper, Howard Pontuk — the list of dead went on and on.

In 1931, George Patton had written, "Success in war lurks invisible in that vitalizing spark, intangible, yet as evident as the lightning — the warrior's soul." Whether a cause or consequence of the waning support for the war in Vietnam, that spark was winking out through much of the officer corps. For the blood brothers from the class of 1966, each

KIA from their ranks made the price of the conflict that much harder to justify. Not everyone in the class, of course, soured on the war. Some true believers wholeheartedly endorsed the cause and would continue to do so ten years after Saigon had fallen. But many experienced war zone epiphanies that shook their certitude as surely as the sight of Tommy Hayes's casket had shaken Jack Wheeler's. Some of the episodes were improbable, some were amusing, but all chipped away at their martial zeal.

Jim Brunnhoeffer's first assignment with his engineering battalion in the delta was to repair war-damaged tennis courts owned by the Phillips Petroleum Company. Not long afterward, like the gentry of Washington cantering into Virginia to witness the Battle of Bull Run, he and another officer drove out to watch a firefight near Thu Thua. As an artillery battery rushed its howitzers forward on a highway, Brunnhoeffer was chagrined to see the artillerymen flagged down and ticketed for speeding by a military policeman who had set up a trap with a stopwatch and mirrors. That night, while the enemy slipped away into Cambodia, Brunnhoeffer had his first doubts that the United States was going to win.

About the same time, Mike Hustead upbraided an enlisted man for being in an unauthorized area. The soldier went to his tent, grabbed an M-79 grenade launcher, and fired a round at the operations center where Hustead and his sergeants had gathered. The grenade missed, but Hustead was left wondering who the enemy was.

Leigh Wheeler, a good-natured former rugby player from Rockville, Maryland, could chart with particular precision the benchmarks of his disillusionment as an infantry officer. First, there were the prominent villagers who had their heads chopped off by the Viet Cong as a warning to others who befriended the Americans. Then there were the bodies of the two U.S. advisers he found, one a sergeant, the other an air defense major ordered into the bush despite his lack of infantry training. The enemy had killed the pair easily; Wheeler found the major three hundred yards from the ambush site, where he had crawled before bleeding to death. The Army offered its usual elegiac rhetoric to the survivors about valiant deaths in a noble cause, but Wheeler would have none of it. "They died because they were stupid!" he shouted after hearing the official version of the incident. "They died because there was some goddamn bureaucratic order that said they should go out there without proper training."

Finally, there was the charnel house. During a firefight, the enemy wounded several of Wheeler's Montagnard tribesmen. Evacuated from Landing Zone Buttons, the tribesmen were listed on the helicopter manifest as Gook 1 through Gook 6. Because the Montagnard families didn't know what had happened to their men, Wheeler traveled to Bien Hoa a few days later to look for them.

He was directed to the graves registration office, which sat inside a refrigerated Butler building. Glancing overhead as he entered the warehouse, Wheeler was sickened by the sight of the naked corpses of several American soldiers dangling upside down from a steel frame. In various states of decomposition, the bodies had been hoisted by meat hooks through their Achilles tendons while morticians hosed them down before embalming.

Vietnam, Leigh Wheeler realized, had turned into an American abattoir. In a letter to his wife, he wrote simply, "This is crazy." Two months later, after his tour had ended and he returned home to Maryland, he was asked to address the Rockville Optimist Club. "The management of the war is wrong. The effort is wrong," he told the Optimists. "The overall policy may be right. I don't know. It's not for me to say. But the execution is just abominable." Soon afterward, Leigh Wheeler applied to medical school.

In April 1970, ten months after arriving at Long Binh, Jack Wheeler flew to Hawaii for a week of R and R. As the plane tipped into its approach to Honolulu International, he could see the south side of Oahu spread out like an emerald in a sapphire sea. There was Pearl Harbor, with the white rectangle of the *Arizona* memorial. Above the harbor, in the Waianae Mountains, lay Kolekole Pass, where the Japanese had swept in at dawn nearly thirty years before.

Jack checked into the Bachelor Officers Quarters at Fort De Russy, an Army beach resort on the western edge of Waikiki. Army families from Fort Shafter and Schofield Barracks capered in the sand beneath the coconut palms, or paddled out to two square rafts anchored thirty yards from shore. Diamond Head loomed to his left and the Ilikai Hotel, one of the first Waikiki high-rises, to the right. Hawaii was beautiful, as lovely as any place on earth, but Jack felt lonely and confused.

One night he went to see a performance of a kabuki play. The Japanese drama, dating from the seventeenth century, fascinated Jack with its exaggerated pantomime. The actors had boiled their emotions down to a few elements: surprise, anger, fear, joy. He was trying to do that himself, wasn't he, though in a plodding, Occidental fashion? What was true? What things were worth dying for? What was he doing with his life? If the Army wasn't going to be his vocation — and that seemed increasingly evident — what would he do with the rest of his life?

His commanding officer had recently sent him a handwritten note:

"Try to go easier in life." Jack wanted to; God knew he wanted to. But he felt himself floundering, like someone in Mr. Sorge's Rock Squad trying to tread water with a pack of bricks on his back. With the single-mindedness that had so impressed Bruns Grayson, he had grasped at some peculiar straws.

Between business school and his departure for Vietnam, Jack had spent a month in Northern California at the Synanon commune on Tomales Bay. That seemed an unlikely place for a West Point captain, but at Harvard he had been swept up in the Synanon fad after reading the book *The Tunnel Back,* about a man named Chuck Dederich. When a fellow student claimed that life at Tomales Bay was like flying through the air after living under water, Jack thought he would see for himself. Everyone else in his generation seemed to be experimenting in one way or another — with drugs or unusual life styles or Eastern mysticism — so, he concluded, why shouldn't I?

Dederich, a large, craggy man with a large, craggy ego, had founded Synanon in 1958 as a sanctuary for drug addicts, whom he treated as compulsive, stupid children. Although later discredited — Dederich was convicted in 1980 of trying to kill someone by putting a rattlesnake in his mailbox — in the late 1960s Synanon was considered a respectable if unorthodox social movement that had expanded far beyond antidrug therapy. Jack saw Synanon as a bold effort to heighten the sense of community.

Commune rules prohibited drugs, violence, promiscuity, homosexuality, and foul language, except in encounter "games." These were played in small groups as part of "attack therapy." Players would turn on one another with ridicule and ranting, trying to break down the walls of social convention to release, cathartically, the true feelings trapped inside.

As his contribution to the commonweal at Tomales Bay, Jack drove a garbage truck. The men in the detail sang as they made their rounds:

We're your Synanon garbage men.
We don't work for money.
Oh, we don't work for cash.
We work for the pleasure
Of taking out your trash.

Communal living was an invigorating experience; it was part of his effort to educate himself in ways that had been impossible behind West Point's gray walls. His enthusiasm for Synanon, however, was dampened by an incident that occurred just before he departed for Vietnam. During one game, when a woman said that she would like to go to church, others in the group ridiculed her so violently that the abuse came close to a physical beating. These people have no faith, Jack thought as he left for Travis; they have no center of gravity.

That was the heart of the matter: a center of gravity. West Point had provided it with duty, honor, and country. That was gravity, all right — like Jupiter's, where a normal earthling would weigh six hundred pounds — but Jack was not sure how those precepts applied if you didn't remain in the Army. And what if you remained in the Army but avoided battle command? He had asked himself that question many times, and by now he thought he knew the answer: Jack was fully convinced — and had said as much in his tapes and letters home — that he had purchased his life at the cost of shirking the West Point standard, the one met by Tommy Hayes and his other fallen classmates. They had fought and died for their ideals; he had lived but somehow felt diminished as a consequence. That conviction was a heavy burden.

On April 22, 1970, Jack drove to the University of Hawaii campus for Earth Day. A succession of speakers waxed poetic about the planet and its intricate ecology. They also denounced the defoliating, murderous American war machine. A boisterous crowd of young people in beads and long hair applauded and flashed the V symbol for peace with their fingers. Jack felt like a leper.

Later, he drove to the national cemetery in Punchbowl crater. A sea of small, flat grave markers filled the extinct volcano from rim to rim, covering more than a hundred acres. Brilliant tropical flowers — red ginger, white plumeria, orange bird-of-paradise — covered many of the stones. An inscription from Abraham Lincoln had been carved into a memorial at the west end of the crater: "The solemn pride that must be yours to have laid so costly a sacrifice upon the altar of freedom."

Engraved on a series of white stone walls were the names of eighteen thousand Americans who had been killed in the Pacific during World War II and whose bodies had never been recovered. Between Conley, Donald H., and Connally, Lanham C., he found:

CONLY, JOHN C. MAJOR 99 BOMB SQUADRON
9TH BOMB GROUP TEXAS

The name was that of his uncle, Janet Wheeler's older brother. Jack had a copy of John Conly's Silver Star certificate. It explained how, on March 10, 1945, he had commanded a B-29 in a raid on Tokyo. Returning to Tinian after dropping its payload, the plane was buffeted by a snowstorm, which knocked out all radar and navigational equipment. With fuel nearly gone and ditching imminent, the crew began jettisoning equipment through the open bomb bay doors.

> During this operation [the citation explained], some of the equipment, including two flak suits, became caught on the extreme lower part of the rear of the bomb bay and the doors would not close. Major Conly removed his parachute, lowered himself by his hands down into the bomb bay, and dislodged the equipment with his feet.

The crew closed the doors, but as the plane prepared to ditch Conly refused to return to the cockpit. He remained in the radar compartment, where he managed to get the scope working well enough to direct the pilot to a small island.

> Upon ditching, the aircraft broke in two and Major Conly, who was in the unpressurized compartment, was not seen again. The nine men who survived the ditching succeeded in reaching the island, which was only a quarter of a mile away. Major Conly's gallant leadership, courage, and devotion to duty reflect great credit upon himself and are exemplary of the finest traditions of the Army Air Force.

Jack was close to tears as he took a snapshot of the chiseled name. The plain block letters deeply stirred him. He was four months old when John Conly sacrificed himself for his men and for his country. Something about the simple name etched in stone — the same Christian name as Jack's — reduced the man's life to its essence, much as kabuki reduced an emotion to the raw element itself.

He slung the camera over his shoulder and walked slowly from the Punchbowl. His mother would appreciate the photograph. Bravery never went out of fashion.

The recreation center at Fort De Russy quickly filled up with wives and girlfriends, most of whom had just arrived in Honolulu to meet their men on R and R from Vietnam. A coffee urn and pitchers of pineapple juice sat on a table in the back of the hall. Marcia Bonifas settled into a chair as mothers hushed their fussing babies. Again Marcia wondered whether she had done the right thing in leaving Beth with her in-laws. She and Art had debated the matter in their letters and finally decided to spend the week alone. "We need some time to ourselves," he wrote.

Marcia listened carefully to a chaplain, a tall black man with a gentle, solicitous voice, welcoming the women and counseling forbearance. "Your husbands and boyfriends may be a little different," he said. "They may not be as jovial as they were when you knew them before. They have a lot on their minds and they've seen a lot. You need to bear with them. Just be patient."

The chaplain sat down and a social worker moved to the podium. "Your men may wake up with nightmares. That's not unusual and it's nothing to be overly concerned about," the woman advised. "We strongly suggest that you wait here rather than go out to the airport. Buses will shuttle them here immediately after they clear customs.

"Also, once in a while a husband or boyfriend isn't on the plane. Don't worry. There are people who will track them down and find out where they are. We'll find them. If they missed the plane, we'll get them on the next one."

Oh, great, Marcia thought. That was all she needed. The anxiety was bad enough without having to worry about whether Art had made his flight. They were going to have only a few days together; every hour counted. Please, Art, she thought, please be on the plane.

Like Jack Wheeler, Art was "short." He had only three months left in his tour and he already had orders for his next assignment: the advanced artillery course at Fort Sill, Oklahoma. Soldiers in Vietnam invented innumerable short jokes: "He's so short he needs a ladder to get into his tent"; "He's so short he can walk under the yellow line in the road." But the shorter Art got, the greater was Marcia's anxiety.

As planned, when Art left for Vietnam she had moved back to Brooklyn with Beth, into the McGuires' new house in Flatbush. Sometimes Marcia and the other waiting wives she knew in New York would meet for lunch to commiserate. She enjoyed living at home — and her parents loved to spoil Beth — but she was surprised by how quickly she had outgrown the past. She was an Army wife now. Brooklyn seemed alien; when her childhood girlfriends came to visit, she found that they didn't seem to have much in common. Most had married local boys and settled somewhere in the borough, close enough to drive home for Sunday dinner with their parents. They still thought it odd that Marcia had done something as unorthodox as marry a soldier.

Even in Flatbush the antiwar feeling was hard to avoid. Twice someone dumped sugar into the gas tank of Marcia's car; it had a Fort Benning sticker on the bumper. Once, while taking Beth to the pediatrician at Fort Hamilton near the Verrazano-Narrows Bridge, she had driven through a boisterous demonstration of draft protestors. On another occasion, when her brother was home from Georgetown University, the dinner discussion turned to the war.

"How can you stand having your husband over there when it's so wrong?" he demanded.

She nearly exploded in anger. "You can say that before or after, but not while he's there doing his job. We'll discuss this after Art comes back. Alive."

Art did not miss his flight to Hawaii. At midnight, two green Army diesel buses pulled up beneath the palm trees next to the recreation center. Art walked down the steps, anxiously scanning the throng of women waiting on the lawn. When he spotted Marcia's red hair, his face lit up with the familiar grin. He wrapped his long arms around her, and she felt safe again. This was where she belonged.

Their six days together flew by with depressing speed. The Spartan austerity of their small hotel room in Waikiki reminded her of the Hotel Thayer, although Honolulu's flying cockroaches provided an exotic new touch. To finance the holiday, Marcia had been earning $78 a day as a substitute teacher once or twice a week. The money enabled them to afford some wonderfully camp activities on the island, like riding an outrigger canoe and sailing on a catamaran. They toured Pearl Harbor and watched the surfers on the North Shore and wandered through the International Market Place. For dinner they went to the Ilikai or the Cannon Club at Fort Ruger on the flanks of Diamond Head.

Marcia had brought along a spool of new home movies. They found a camera store that would develop the film and let them watch the reel on a monitor. Art was astonished by how much Beth had grown. She's practically a young woman, he said as he watched her toddle about, and I'm missing it.

Despite the chaplain's warning, Marcia found Art to be unchanged. He was gray and gaunt from lack of sleep — after six months of staff duty with the 4th Division in Vietnam, he now had his own artillery battery in the Central Highlands — but other than that he seemed the same old Art. His belief in the war remained strong, although he didn't want to talk much about his experiences. Occasionally things slipped out that disturbed her. Once, while attending the Don Ho musical revue, they shared a table with a young lieutenant. When Art discovered that the officer was an artillery FO, a forward observer, he muttered to Marcia, "Well, *his* life expectancy isn't very long."

On the sixth day she took him to the airport. He squeezed her tight. "I'll be home before you know it," he promised. "It won't be long now."

With six hours remaining before her own flight back to the mainland, she returned to the hotel room to pack and pace. When Art had left for the war the previous summer from his parents' home in Omaha, she and Beth had seen him off at the airport, and she had wept bitterly as the plane taxied down the runway. A stranger had touched her elbow.

"Can I help you?" he asked kindly.

"Yes," she wailed, blotting her eyes, "get my husband off that airplane!"

Now she felt the same way, perhaps even emptier and more frightened, even though Art would be out of Vietnam in another few months. *Get my husband off that airplane.* But there was no stranger to touch her elbow, no one to comfort her, nothing but the flying roaches and the distant hiss of the Pacific washing over the amber beach.

Even before he was shot in the head midway through his second tour in Vietnam, George Crocker knew that war was no longer the glorious adventure it had seemed four years earlier when he first stepped off the plane at Bien Hoa. In 1967, during his initial tour, he had learned a great deal about the cost of combat; during his long stay at home, those lessons had been grimly reinforced by the periodic reports of another classmate's death. Gordon Kimbrell was dead. Tommy Hayes was dead. Buck Thompson was dead. And, beyond that small circle of fallen friends, fifty thousand other Americans had died.

Before returning to Vietnam in September 1970, George tried rigorously to augment his visceral understanding of combat by learning more about the war's origins. During the advanced course for infantry officers at Fort Benning, he read everything he could lay hands on about the conflict: *War Comes to Long An*, *Street Without Joy*, *Hell in a Very Small Place*. The last, a fine account by Bernard Fall about the debacle at Dienbienphu, seemed to have uncanny parallels to that night on the stay-behind patrol near Ap Bac when his platoon was surrounded.

He was dismayed by his ignorance. As a new lieutenant, he had known that the French were routed in Indochina in the 1950s, but his knowledge barely extended beyond that. Now he had a broader appreciation of how protracted the struggle was for the Vietnamese: how the ancient enmity between China and Vietnam played out, how strategically important the Plain of Jars was in Laos, how the American troops arriving in 1965 were just the latest wave of warriors in a struggle that had lasted for decades.

George's attitude toward the war remained ambivalent; he was unaware of the powerful impact his steel-edged comments about "a bad war" had had on Jack Wheeler and Art Mosley at Tommy Hayes's funeral. In fact, Vietnam was an enigma to him. Who was winning? Militarily, the communists seemed to be losing. Large swatches of the delta that had been controlled by the Viet Cong during his first tour now were completely pacified. After years of ceding certain sanctuaries to the VC and NVA, the Americans had shown a new aggressiveness, which hurt the enemy and boosted U.S. morale; officers at the Infantry School had stood and cheered when the invasion of Cambodia was announced on April 30, 1970.

Yet the Cambodian and Laotian sanctuaries obviously had not been eradicated, and Washington gave no hint that the war would be carried to the enemy in the north except through bombing raids. Nor was there any hint that the communists were about to give up the struggle; the Americans had plainly underestimated the enemy's tenacity. The plans to turn the war over to the South Vietnamese seemed well conceived, but George had serious doubts about the ARVN's ability to fight successfully on its own. His boyish enthusiasm of four years before now seemed more naïve than ever. At twenty-seven, except for a slight weathering in his face, he looked unchanged from the eager lieutenant who had first galloped off to the sound of the guns. But in many ways he was older, shrewder, more reflective. He had not been pleased by the idea of returning to this war, although technically he had volunteered to come back. His hour had come round again, and of course he would do what needed to be done.

During his thirty-three months stateside, George's education had continued in other ways, too. He took airborne training and developed an enduring affection for jumping out of airplanes. He commanded a company at Fort Bragg with the 82nd Airborne Division. He served as a general's aide at the Army War College at Carlisle Barracks, Pennsylvania. He also was the honor graduate among fifty soldiers at Pathfinder training, learning to guide air drops, to organize helicopter landing zones, and to serve as a traffic controller for fixed-wing airplanes.

The year at Bragg was an eye-opener for both George and Vonda. On Highway 401, the road from Raleigh, a large billboard proclaimed FAYETTEVILLE IS KLAN COUNTRY. HELP FIGHT COMMUNISM. To the troops, however, the town was better known as FayetteNam. It was as violent and fractious as Tombstone or Dodge City had been.

Flocks of prostitutes often greeted soldiers arriving at the railroad station near the old slave market. The whores sometimes grabbed at the GIs' crotches, or mashed their breasts in a lascivious grind against the window glass of cars that paused for a stoplight on Hay Street. On the buses shuttling between the Bragg barracks and downtown, military policemen routinely frisked soldiers for knives, guns, and straightedge razors; even so, bloody fights erupted almost nightly. On payday the Crockers would see enlisted men wandering through the pawnshops and used car lots on Bragg Boulevard. The cash burning a hole in their pockets was practically incandescent. Others, having drunk their wages, crawled out of the topless bars on their hands and knees to vomit in the median strip. Signs began sprouting on lawns in Fayetteville's residential neighborhoods: DOGS AND SOLDIERS KEEP OFF THE GRASS.

George's classmate Bobby Seigle worked briefly at Bragg as a "survivor assistance" officer. He was perplexed to discover on his first case that the widow he was assigned to help — a spindly, twangy young woman, ugly as a hatchet — had been married at least three times to privates, each of whom was killed in action.

Aerial photo of West Point and the Plain as seen from above the Hudson River in the early 1960s. Buildings in the foreground include, from right to left, the Bachelor Officers Quarters, Cullum Hall, the Officers Club, and Thayer Hall. The chapel is in the background, above Washington Hall.

Learning how to salute on R-Day, July 2, 1962, in Central Area

John P. Wheeler III

Thomas M. Carhart III

George A. Crocker

Braced for shower formation in the sinks during Beast Barracks, 1962. As required, the soap dish is held open for inspection in the left hand, and a towel is draped over the left arm.

The Westmorelands and the MacArthurs meet shortly before the "duty, honor, country" speech of May 12, 1962. Left to right: Superintendent William C. Westmoreland, Douglas MacArthur, Jean MacArthur, Kitsy Westmoreland.

Thomas J. Hayes IV

Matthew C. Harrison

Arthur G. Bonifas

The Reverend James D. Ford, then the assistant chaplain, watches new cadets arrive on July 2, 1962. Note Ford's fingers, properly curled as required for a soldier standing at attention.

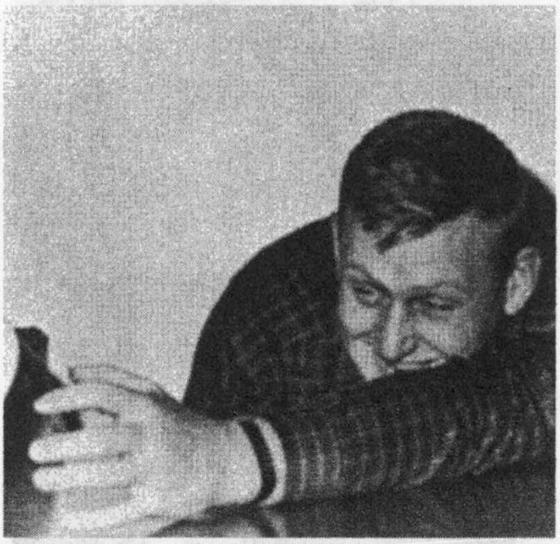

Richard W. (Buck) Thompson, reaching for a beer stein

Cadets in formation, wearing full dress gray uniforms, in Central Area. Note the barracks stoops on the left and the sallyport leading through the barracks in the background. (*Courtesy of John P. Wheeler III*)

Jack Wheeler and Ginny Stuart at the graduation hop, June 1966 (*Courtesy of John P. Wheeler III*)

The traditional tossing of hats at graduation, June 8, 1966

George and Vonda Crocker, married in Little Rock on June 25, 1966 (*Courtesy of George Crocker*)

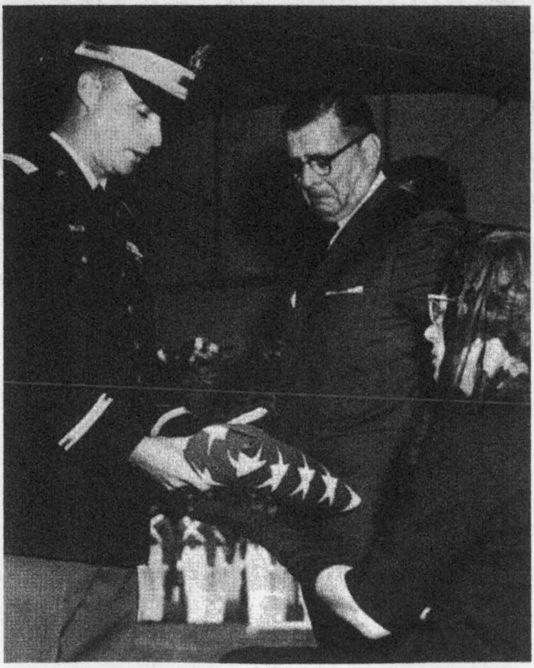

Funeral services at West Point for Frank A. Rybicki, killed with his own rifle in Vietnam on May 9, 1967. Terry G. Stull, Rybicki's classmate and brother-in-law, presents the casket flag to Frank's parents. (*AP/Wide World Photos*)

Colonel Charlie A. Beckwith, who commanded the Florida Ranger camp in 1966, seen here fifteen years later, after leading the unsuccessful effort to rescue American hostages in Iran (*AP/Wide World Photos*)

William G. Haneke

Bomb craters frequently offered the best protection during mortar attacks on Hill 875. (*U.S. Army photograph*)

During the final assault on Hill 875, on the morning of November 23, paratroopers from the 4th Battalion of the 173rd Airborne Brigade are temporarily pinned down by enemy mortar fire. (*U.S. Army photograph*)

A squad leader from D Company of the 2nd Battalion, 173rd Airborne Brigade, mans an M-60 machine gun along the perimeter of the American position on Hill 875. (*U.S. Army photograph*)

James Ford offers communion at a jungle clearing near Dak To, September 1967. (*Courtesy of James D. Ford*)

The Bonifas family in front of Battle Monument at Trophy Point before Art left West Point for Korea. Left to right: Beth, Marcia, Megan, Brian, Art. (*Courtesy of Marcia Bonifas*)

Art Bonifas resting after a run at Panmunjom, August 17, 1976 (*Courtesy of Marcia Bonifas*)

The fatal melee at Panmunjom on the morning of August 18, 1976. South Korean workers climb from the poplar tree as North Korean troops attack the white-helmeted United Nations Command personnel with axes and pikes. (*AP/Wide World Photos*)

The first West Point class to include women marches to Trophy Point to swear the oath of allegiance on July 7, 1976.

Lieutenant General Sidney Berry, fiftieth superintendent of the Military Academy, July 1976

Groundbreaking for the Vietnam Veterans Memorial, March 26, 1982. Left to right: Jack Wheeler, Senator Charles Mathias, Jan Scruggs, Charles Hagel of the Veterans Administration, Bob Doubek, Senator John Warner. (*Douglas Chevalier*/ The Washington Post)

The unveiling of the sculpture on November 9, 1984, by the artist Frederick Hart (left) and Senator John Warner (*Ray Lustig*/The Washington Post)

Elisa and Jack Wheeler dancing in Washington Hall at the twentieth reunion, October 1986 (*Lucian Perkins*/ The Washington Post)

Tom Carhart in the center courtyard of the Pentagon, September 1981 (*Rick Atkinson*/The Kansas City Times)

The author and Colonel George Crocker in the woods of Avon Park, Florida, during an exercise involving the 82nd Airborne Division, November 1987 (*U.S. Army photograph*)

(*AP/Wide World Photos*)

"Sir, wake up," Seigle's first sergeant admonished. "Some of these little farm girls, you think they're asleep, but they know the score. They make an industry out of marrying enlisted men heading for Nam. Death benefits, that's all they want. If one comes home alive, she just divorces him and looks for another one who's on his way over."

After living off post in a furnished apartment, the Crockers moved into captain's quarters on Knott Circle in Corregidor Courts. Vonda, not one to scare easily, was terrified. Army posts traditionally were safer than a Norman Rockwell village. Doors were never locked, thefts were rare, and violent crime was unthinkable. But by the late 1960s, the malignancy that had begun to afflict the Army in Vietnam began to spread at home.

There were rapes, many rapes. The men often went on maneuvers for days or weeks at a time, leaving their wives alone and vulnerable. A woman across the street from George and Vonda was assaulted one night; the Crockers awoke at four-thirty to find military policemen with M-16s swarming across their front yard. Not long after that, someone tried to break into a house down the street and was driven off only by the hysterical screams of a baby sitter. One wife set a trap after receiving a strange phone call; when two soldiers broke in and began to peel off their uniforms, the neighbors jumped out of closets and grabbed them. They were thunderstruck to discover that the would-be assailants were military policemen.

Vonda installed five locks on every door. "If there's a fire," she told George, "we'll all burn to a crisp before I can get the doors open." When he was away, she slept with two loaded pistols under her pillow. On weekends she drove out to one of the ranges in the Sand Hills and practiced her marksmanship, popping away at tin cans with increasing accuracy. When George's tour at Bragg ended, Vonda was delighted to leave FayetteNam behind — and dismayed to discover that Fort Benning was beset with similar problems.

When George returned to Vietnam, Vonda went home to Arkansas. On arriving in-country, Captain Crocker was assigned as an adviser to the ARVN 42nd Ranger Battalion. The most decorated outfit in the South Vietnamese army, the unit had earned three U.S. presidential citations. The battalion operated out of Can Tho, an elegant old French city that had once thrived on the Mekong River trade. He had tried unsuccessfully for an assignment to an American unit, but George took the adviser's job in stride, though he had no great affection for the South Vietnamese army. "If they're interested in fighting," he said, "I guess I will be, too."

One day in late 1970, his battalion moved through an area as green and flat as a pool table. The plain was bordered on one side with mountains, where the enemy had constructed caves so elaborate that ARVN soldiers could hear cows mooing and chickens clucking from deep within the earth, as though Old MacDonald had gone to hell.

As George watched the ARVN Rangers sweep toward a woodline, a sniper's shot rang out, and he fell like an oak tree. Blood gushed from the side of his head, just above the ear. He reached up with his hand, afraid to see how deep the wound was. But the bullet had struck only a glancing blow, cutting to the bone without penetrating his skull. The battalion medic stanched the bleeding and wrapped his head with gauze. The next day, George's commanding officer ordered him to seek further treatment at an aid station; when the helicopter arrived, he sprinted toward the Huey through a rice paddy as sniper bullets nipped the water all around him.

Once again, his luck had held. But several signs suggested that fortune was growing weary of the young captain. When the battalion moved to the Central Highlands for training, George contracted typhus. Evacuated to an Air Force hospital at Cam Ranh, he lay unconscious for two days with a dangerous fever. No sooner had he recovered than he was afflicted with worms so badly that his weight plummeted from 180 pounds to 150. He requisitioned a medical kit, gave himself a massive dose of tetracycline, and suffered through the long plane trip home to Arkansas to recuperate.

Back in Vietnam two weeks later, George happened to see the general whom he had briefly served as an aide at the Army War College. Lieutenant General William J. McCaffrey, West Point '39, had won a Silver Star as chief of staff of the 92nd Division in Italy in World War II. He won two more in Korea as a regimental commander and a planner of the Inchon landing. Capable and genial, he was now the deputy commander of the U.S. Army in Vietnam.

"George," McCaffrey asked, "why don't you come be my aide again?"

"Oh, no, sir," George replied. "Thanks, but I've got a Ranger battalion I kind of like." He declined to mention that he also was determined to avenge a young lieutenant who had been killed on his first day of duty.

But when George returned to the 42nd, the battalion was no longer his. Under Richard Nixon's Vietnamization policy, the ARVN Rangers did not require the services of an American adviser. He called McCaffrey. "Sir, if that job's still open, I'd like to take you up on it."

The time had come for a separate peace. He had done his duty on the line to the best of his ability. He missed his family desperately — he and Vonda now had a second daughter, Tara — and he was ready to go home. They were all ready. The bloody business had dragged out too long.

No one wants to be the last American killed in Vietnam. The press loved that sentence. George heard it again and again. He thought it silly. Of course no one wanted to be the last one killed. No one had wanted to be the first killed, or the hundredth, or the thousandth, or the ten thousandth.

Working for McCaffrey would give George a chance to see the entire country as the American war wound down. He had first seen the conflict from six inches above the mud; now he would see it from on high. During the week, they would fly from the Ca Mau peninsula in the far south to the DMZ in the far north, returning to Long Binh on weekends to labor over reports and paperwork. He would visit the Vietnamese military academy at Da Lat, where hunters had once stalked tigers in the cool mountains and Emperor Bao Dai had romped with his concubines. He would meet Vonda in Kauai on R and R and drink mai tais beneath the tiki torches.

He would become a Dial soaper at Long Binh. He would sleep in a tatty white trailer behind the plush cabanas that housed the general officers. He would meet the VIPs still swooping in from Washington with their briefcases and perplexed expressions. He would eat surf 'n' turf until he grew tired of it. He would ponder what had gone wrong and what had gone right. He would remember the dead. He would live.

PART III

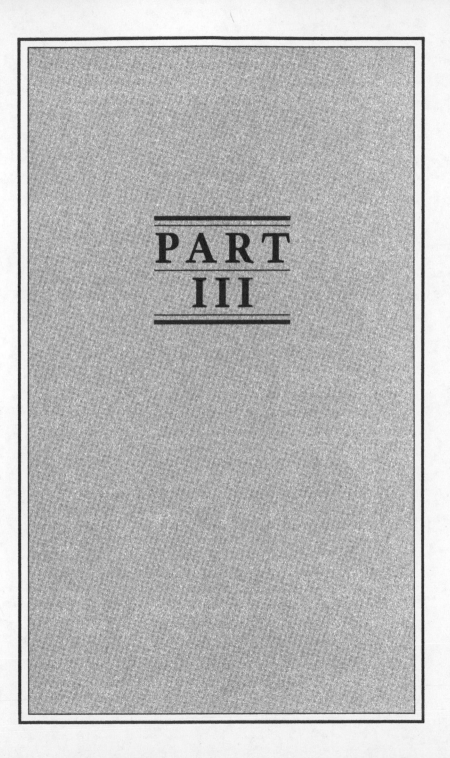

12

Wounds

Slowly and silently, the bookcase slid open on a steel track to reveal the hidden passageway between the rectory and the chapel. The ghost, a stocky, six-foot apparition, tiptoed into the transept bay. It paused, scanning the empty pews, before letting out a low wail. *Oooooohhhhh.*

Giggles echoed in the chapel. The ghost could see a child's head peeking in from the narthex at the far end and a pair of spindly legs crouching behind one of the clergy stalls next to the choir benches. Moaning and shrieking, it passed beneath four allegorical virtues — modesty, temperance, humility, and liberality — carved from stone in the east transept. Then, sweeping up and down the aisles, the wraith glided past the pews before vanishing back through the sacristy and into the rectory. The bookcase swung shut against a volley of childish laughter and taunts. *Nyaaah-nyaaah, can't catch us!*

The Reverend Jim Ford pulled the bed sheet over his head and folded it neatly, reminding himself to return it to his wife's linen closet. Exhaling loudly, he sagged into the chair behind his desk to resume work on Sunday's sermon. Not only was Quarters 60 a wonderful place to raise five children, he thought, but the chapel was surely the best clubhouse in the world. Sometimes the kids got gussied up with their friends and staged elaborate mock weddings; their favorite game, however, was luring Dad away from his work long enough to play spook.

Ford was pushing forty now. Gray had begun to fleck his dark hair, and the crimp of his clerical collar betrayed a few added pounds of encroaching middle age. He swiveled around in his chair, lost in thought while staring from his study window at the panoramic view of Washington Hall and the cadet barracks below. He always enjoyed the chance to romp with his children; fun had been a commodity in short supply at West Point these last few years. The academy's geographical isolation helped protect it from the rudest attacks on the war and the military establishment, but even so, the place at times resembled a fortress under siege.

As the war dragged on, Ford had often reflected on the contrast between Vietnam and World War II. He could remember walking down the street in Minnesota during his teens and seeing gold stars in the windows of those who had lost a son or father. There was a bittersweet pride in the sacrifice, and a sense that the entire community shared the loss. By 1944, American opposition to the war had dwindled to almost nothing; now, in 1971, the latest polls showed not only that half of all Americans opposed the war in Southeast Asia, but that they disapproved vehemently. And the worst part, Ford thought, was that those who had lost their men in Vietnam suffered alone.

After a decade at the academy, Jim Ford's burly figure was practically part of the landscape. But how life had changed in ten years. "There are two boats which are sinking today," he had recently quipped, "the military and the church. I've got a foot in both."

Wars, he knew, had always been hard on West Point. The academy lost many of her cherished sons; and when the nation wearied of combat — as the nation always did — Americans seemed to resent the Military Academy, as if it were the cause rather than an instrument of war. At the beginning of the Civil War, when a quarter of the cadets quit or were dismissed for their rebel sympathies, the defections provoked a hysterical round of attacks on the institution for supposedly nurturing such disloyalty. During the New York draft riots in 1863, anger toward the military spawned rumors of an impending raid on West Point, causing the superintendent to post sentries along the river and issue ball cartridges to cadets. Because the corps was at the bottom of the War Department's priority list, many cadets went shoeless and were reduced to wearing shirts cut from pillowcases.

During World War I, five classes had graduated early — from two months to nearly three years ahead of schedule — throwing the academy into turmoil. After the Armistice, gloom settled over the corps; daily life was marred by outrageous hazing, a cadet suicide, and frequent fights. Until MacArthur's arrival as superintendent, the academy had been run largely by retired officers summoned back to active duty and determined to recapture a past that was gone forever. Even after the Korean War, West Point had been able to fill only two thirds of its available vacancies; a booming economy and antimilitarism kept potential cadets in the civilian world.

Now, the schism over the war in Vietnam was reflected at West Point, though in a muted, discreet fashion that was difficult for outsiders to detect. New cadets often arrived with an iconoclasm and distrust of authority that would have been rare five or ten years earlier. Some upperclassmen hid wigs in the barracks, which they wore on leave in order to blend in with their long-haired college friends. Every qualified young man who wanted to join the class of 1972 had been accepted, and vacancies went begging. The tactical department remained as gung ho and hawkish as ever, but some of the academic departments — notably social sciences — held pockets of dissent. Instructors, many of whom had served one or two combat tours themselves, sometimes met over a beer at the Officers Club and wondered aloud at the war strategy, the cost in blood and money, and the growing national contempt for military officers. Some of the best and brightest young officers on the faculty were resigning from the Army.

But surprisingly few direct assaults had been launched at West Point. In the fall of 1969, a hundred Vassar students arrived from Poughkeepsie to preach peace and distribute daisies. They left a few hours later, frustrated by their inability to debate successfully against the cadets, who were well provisioned with statistics and syllogisms. One cadet graciously accepted a proffered flower, then ate it. Another excused himself from the picket line discussion by claiming that he was late for "poison gas class."

The rudest shock to the academy had come on March 17, 1970. At 12:30 P.M., the superintendent, Major General Samuel W. Koster, stood on the mess hall poop deck facing the corps and the flags of the fifty states. Koster, class of 1942 and a rising star in the service, had directed the Eighth Army's guerrilla warfare operations during the Korean War. Before arriving at West Point, however, he had commanded the division involved in the massacre at My Lai.

"I have been informed by my superiors," he somberly told the cadets, "that action has been initiated against me in connection with my performance of duty in the spring of 1968 while serving as commanding general, Americal Division, in Vietnam. I have therefore requested reassignment. I wish to say that throughout my military career the cherished principles of our motto — duty, honor, country — have served as a constant guide to me. I shall continue to follow these principles as long as I live." Then, in a final gesture of defiance, Koster added, "Don't let the bastards grind you down."

For ninety seconds the cadets stood on their chairs and cheered. Later they draped a banner from Washington Hall that read DON'T LET 'EM GET YOU DOWN. On March 18, the corps marched in homage, eyes right, past Quarters 100 while the general and his wife stood watching from the porch. (Some cadets kept their gazes straight ahead in a subtle protest.) The resignation — Koster was later demoted to brigadier for assorted "commissions and omissions" in failing to investigate the slaughter — brought the war home in ways that even the drone of KIA announcements from the poop deck had not.

Ford's doubts about the war gnawed at him constantly. They had begun with his six-week visit to the combat zone in 1967 and were stoked by the five or six dozen Vietnam funerals he had by now conducted. What was his obligation? Should he use the pulpit as a forum to question the limits of military power? Was the proper role of a chaplain to maintain a strict neutrality, or did conscience require that he speak out? He had always admired the prophets, from the biblical Amos to Yale's William Sloane Coffin, men who spoke with passion and conviction. Mankind, he believed, needed prophets to stir its sense of justice and righteousness, and to point the way for less intrepid souls.

At times Ford envisioned himself standing in the chapel and delivering a sermon that laid bare his thoughts. Wars, he would say, are fought by the military, but the decision to end them, like the decision to begin them, must be made politically. Every powerful military nation must ask itself: when do we go for the gun? The answer: Only as the last possible resort, certainly not as quickly as America had done in Vietnam. Wasn't it time to admit that the gun had been drawn too hastily?

But the words went unspoken. He was wary of dividing the congregation by forcing people to take sides. A pastor should unite, not cleave. And, as a deft politician, he knew that the academy's tolerance for dissidence and nonconformity was very limited. George Bean, a youthful and unorthodox Episcopalian who served as chief chaplain for five years during the 1950s, had raised eyebrows with a sermon on Paul's entreaty to the Romans: "Be not conformed to this world." That was not what the authorities liked to hear. Ford had even been rebuked by the academy's dean for using "sensitivity training" during a religious retreat he organized one weekend in 1967 for cadets and students from Yale and Vassar.

So he was circumspect. His sermons — with titles such as "The Amens of Life," "The Balcony and the Road," and "Saint Peter and the Spacecraft" — sidestepped topical controversy and focused on the four cornerstones of his theology: God's love, forgiveness, reconciliation, respect for family. Yet, Ford liked to think of himself as a liberalizing force; he even proposed at one point that cadets spend a year at a civilian college. Privilege irked him, including the old tradition of saving the choicest pews for senior faculty members; Ford insisted on abolishing reserved seating. "If there's one thing I'm certain of," he said, "it's that God doesn't care where you sit."

He encouraged tolerance and often tweaked those preoccupied with appearance and form. One day he was walking on the fourth floor of Washington Hall with Commandant Sam Walker, a brigadier general obsessed with short haircuts. On the corridor wall hung pictures of the academy's past commandants, including several from the nineteenth century who sported beards, mustaches, and long locks. Ford gestured at the portraits. "Hey, Sam," he said with a nudge, "we never lost a war during their time."

The academy motto, he told cadets, required explication. "Duty to whom? Honor by what standard? Country to what extent? The three words in and of themselves are insufficient. You have to think about them before they really mean anything, because the concepts have to be filtered through the experience of each succeeding generation." And he liked to quote one of his favorite generals, Donald V. Bennett, who had been superintendent when the class of 1966 graduated: "Cadets must learn whether it's appropriate to say 'Why, sir?' or 'When, sir?'" Although instant obedience was usually commendable, sometimes duty manifested itself most sublimely through a willingness to question orders.

Just as Ford was wary of using the pulpit to voice his questions about the war, he privately disdained those who displayed a smug certitude. Once, Lyndon Johnson's pastor, Dr. George Davis of the National City Christian Church in Washington, had spoken in the chapel as a guest preacher and virtually demanded moral support for the war as a kind of loyalty test. I wonder, Ford thought, whether he says that because he really believes it or because he's LBJ's minister.

He also was angered by those whose opposition to the war spilled over into scorn for soldiers or cadets. When the *New York Times* columnist Russell Baker wrote what Ford considered to be an attack on military men, the chaplain mentally scratched Baker from his list of required reading. On another occasion, he extended a speaking invitation to his own bishop, Dr. Franklin Clark Fry, head of the Lutheran Church in America; when Fry declined, pleading a busy schedule, Ford fired off an uncharacteristically impertinent note:

> Dear Bishop:
>
> These are busy times for us, too. We're in the middle of a war and these young men would love to have some free time. I'd suggest that it's important for you to come up here and give whatever comfort and counsel you can offer.

Fry apologized but Ford did not renew the invitation.

In hiring his assistant chaplains, he sought men who would resist being compromised by the institution. "Remember," he often cautioned them, "what we stand for started a long time before 1802. Don't forget it. We are not here at the academy's behest. We are a tenant using heat and light." Always intrigued by speed and balance, Ford spent much of his spare time in the woods on a trail bike or racing down the highway on a 750cc motorcycle. Soon he had converted all of his assistants to motorcycles; in the early 1970s, it wasn't unusual to see Ford and two or three others in clerical collars roaring about the Hudson Valley like members of a Brando brotherhood.

One of those cycle-riding assistants was a young Baptist from Dallas named Michael Easterling. Tall and graceful, with long fingers and an engaging smile, Easterling had been an Army officer for two years before attending seminary. An excellent athlete — another prerequisite for Ford, who took pride in never losing a racquetball game to a cadet — Easterling also was troubled by the war; the duties befalling the chaplain's office, he soon discovered, forced him to take stock of his conscience and convictions. Once, for example, he was asked to notify a woman living in nearby Stony Point that her husband had been killed in combat. Even before he reached the door, the widow spotted the somber cleric coming up her walkway and ran to the back of the house, where she had tacked a large map of Vietnam to the wall. With a dreadful keening, she ripped the map down and tore it into tiny scraps as Easterling watched helplessly.

Occasionally, when his turn came to speak in the pulpit, Easterling preached on the horrors of war. He reminded the congregation of Isaiah's injunction to beat swords into plowshares; he cited Eisenhower and other great captains on the terrible price of combat. But sometimes relatively innocuous homilies drew fire from the parishioners, as when Easterling discussed finding the will of God.

"We're put here for a purpose and each of us has to discover that purpose," he preached one Sunday. "It's a great mystery how we got here and why. We don't have much time, but we know that God wants us to develop as fully as we can."

Although the young minister considered the sermon harmlessly self-evident, his words immediately raised hackles in the offices of both the superintendent and the commandant. "These cadets already know what they're here for," a senior officer warned him. "They know what they're going to do. Don't confuse them."

One day, a yearling named Darryl Ellis came to see Easterling. "I think," the cadet confided, "that I may be a conscientious objector." After several counseling sessions, the assistant chaplain concluded that Ellis was sincere but fuzzy in his reasoning. "Keep thinking and keep reading," Easterling urged. By the fall of 1969, Easterling was convinced. "This guy's legitimate," he told Ford. "He's not kidding." Easterling provided Ellis with information on how to apply for release from the corps as a c.o. and advised him to retain a lawyer. While trying to mollify the brass, Ford stoutly supported his assistant.

"Conscientious objection has a long and honorable tradition and it's a responsibility of the chaplains to help protect that tradition," Ford explained, before adding wryly, "Easterling, you're going to get us all killed."

When Ellis showed up with a blunt, profane woman lawyer from a civil liberties organization in New York City, Easterling accompanied them to Washington Hall. "Hi, Major," the lawyer greeted the commandant's personnel officer. "Don't you think this situation has gotten all fucked up?" When the Army rejected Ellis's petition, he sued in federal court. An appeals court supported the cadet, and he was discharged from the corps. He asked Easterling as a final favor to officiate at his wedding. In a ceremony reflecting the times — the service featured guitar music and flower garlands — Ellis and his bride were married in Easterling's house, Quarters 7. After chapel the following Sunday, the superintendent paused at the door.

"Is it true that you married Darryl Ellis in your quarters?" he asked.

Easterling looked him in the eye and nodded. "Yes, sir, it is true."

The general sighed and walked out of the chapel without another word.

Although Jim Ford took pains to shield his assistants from the authorities, he rarely shared with them his own anguish about the war. (Easterling, for one, was struck by how strong Ford remained despite the heart-rending succession of funerals.) Whenever Ford was tempted to speak out, he recalled a sermon he had once delivered as a young minister in Ivanhoe, Minnesota.

"You farmers," he had told his parishioners, "you do not own the land. You are only stewards. God gave you the land and you must pass the land on to the generations that come after you. But how you do it is up to you. Go from this holy place armed with the good news of reconciliation with God — and figure it out for yourselves."

Figure it out for yourselves. That had been the proper approach then, Ford concluded, and it was the proper approach now. His job did not include providing men with a road map to their own consciences.

At other times, however, he recalled his year of study in Heidelberg. Ford's faith, Lutheranism, had been founded by a man with the courage to speak out, but in Germany in the 1930s the church had been silent. I am silent, he thought, out of a conviction that I can best serve my congregation by focusing on the eternal things of heaven rather than the daily concerns of earth. Is this the kind of pastor Hitler had approved of forty years ago?

Jim Ford would ask himself few questions in his life that were more painful — more terrible — than that one. It was unfair for many reasons, not the least of which was that he did not know the answer.

One hundred and thirty-eight steps down from the chapel portico and across the Plain, Tom Carhart sat with his feet propped up on a coffee table. In his left hand he held a volume of French verse, opened to a poem from Baudelaire's *Les fleurs du mal.* With his right hand, he scratched a few last notes on a sheet of paper.

From the west window of his corner suite in the Bachelor Officers Quarters, Tom could see Abner Doubleday Field, named for the graduate with the class of 1842. Snow powdered the diamond and outfield grass, and the sky was washed with Gloom Period gray. Yet winter at West Point was no longer as oppressive to Tom as it had been when he was a cadet. In fact, Gloom Period seemed downright cozy. The two-bedroom suite in the BOQ was comfortable and convenient — just a few steps from the Officers Club, where he took most of his meals — and his roommate was a likable Army lieutenant named Arthur Ashe, who seemed to be off playing tennis somewhere most of the time. The suite even contained a collection of Ashe's oversize trophies, the kind that had the heft of a bullion bar and was crowned with an elfin figurine frozen in an overhead smash.

Tom, as usual, had landed on his feet. After arriving home from Vietnam, he was assigned to command a basic-training company at Fort Polk, Louisiana. Polk was one of the Army's premier hellholes and Tom had seen enough of basic-training companies during his tour at Fort Bragg to know that he wanted nothing to do with them. The work seemed thankless and dreary — shepherding a couple of hundred sullen draftees, most of them headed for Vietnam.

But when he talked to the infantry personnel office in Washington about changing his orders to a teaching job at the academy, the major reviewing his file had scoffed. "We send only our very best to West Point, Captain," he replied, "and you have a very lackluster record." Undaunted, Tom appealed directly to Sumner Willard, his former instructor in West Point's French department. Now — presto — here he was, teaching three sections of French, with a promise that the Army would send him to graduate school in Paris next fall.

Tom's return to the States from the war zone had begun inauspiciously. He had planned to kiss the ground on landing, but as he stepped from the plane at Travis the gesture suddenly seemed mawkish; instead, he immediately caught a flight to Chicago, where he intended to spend a few days with friends. Still in uniform, he was strolling through the O'Hare terminal in search of a telephone when a group of hippie girls darted up and spat on him. The shock and pain could have been no more intense if they had slashed him with knives. Reeling with surprise and uncertain what to do, he did nothing. His assailants scampered off through the airport crush as Tom wiped the saliva from his face, now aflame with humiliation. That night he got into an argument about the war with his friends' daughter, who was home from college. This is great, he told himself sardonically. I'm back less than twenty-four hours, I get spat on, then I get hassled by my countrymen over a cause for which I just got myself shot twice. Welcome home, Johnny.

No one would spit on him at West Point. How was it possible, he wondered, that he had so despised this place just a few years before? The academy felt as comfortable now as a favorite slipper. Although no other classmates had been assigned to the academy yet — graduates usually didn't return to the staff and faculty until they had completed eight or ten years of Army service — Tom was not lonely. Teaching hours were easy — usually nine o'clock to four — with much of the time spent reading and preparing lesson plans. The skiing was grand, New York lay but an hour away, and he had met several attractive nurses to date. On a couple occasions, he had bought a case of beer and invited favorite cadets to his suite for a few hours of tipsy war stories. And one afternoon he drove north through Lee Gate to the little town of Cornwall, where two classmates' widows — Buck Thompson's Fran and Art Parker's Connie — were living on Patton Drive, which they had nicknamed Widows' Drive. On a living room couch he sat motionless for a very long time with one arm around Fran and the other around Connie, silently hugging them in a gentle, sorrowful embrace.

Yes, Tom thought, life was fine up here in this rockbound highland home. Perhaps, despite his setbacks in Vietnam, twenty or thirty years in the Army might still be an option. Things would have been nearly idyllic, in fact, if not for the nightmares.

He preferred to call them perturbations. Several times Tom had awakened abruptly, drenched in sweat and convinced that an intruder with a gun was in the room. Or he would dream that he was screaming a warning — *Look out! Look out!* — to someone who couldn't hear him. The dreams were disturbing but not altogether surprising, he figured, given his head injury and his recent exposure to combat. But when they persisted, he had walked to the West Point hospital and made an appointment to see a psychiatrist. Come back in six weeks, he was told; there's a waiting list.

Snapping shut the volume of poetry, Tom jumped to his feet to get ready for class. He straightened his tie and slipped on his uniform jacket. The only decoration he chose to wear on his left breast pocket was the

Purple Heart. The ribbon, a violet rectangle, bore a tiny bronze oak leaf to indicate his second award. On his right shoulder, he wore a hand-stitched 101st Airborne combat patch with the Screaming Eagle's head and an embroidered tab identifying him as a veteran of Tiger Force, 1st Battalion of the 327th Infantry Regiment. He smoothed the creases from his uniform trousers. Special "peg pants" — tailored to taper rather than blouse at the cuff — they were the same kind he had worn at Bragg with the 82nd Airborne. Scanning himself in the mirror, Tom thought he looked sharp, perhaps even spoony.

The class in Washington Hall went well. A lieutenant colonel from the dean's office sat in to observe while Tom helped a dozen cadets struggle through passages he had assigned from Molière's *Tartuffe* and from *Fleurs du mal*.

He loved teaching French. The language had a special place in West Point's heritage. Although Sylvanus Thayer's legacy of Francophilia suffered some neglect after the Franco-Prussian War, the tradition was as venerable as anything else at West Point — though not all of Tom's predecessors had displayed a mastery of the language. Tom, however, was fluent. He had even been able to brush up on both his speaking and reading skills in Vietnam, thanks to his liaison with an older Frenchwoman living in Saigon. Jacqueline Desmarais referred to herself as Tom's *marraine de guerre,* godmother of war; sometimes after they made love in her fourth-floor apartment, she helped him through the first two volumes of Proust's *À la recherche du temps perdu*. From her living room window he had also watched *The Green Berets,* a popular war movie that was being shown in the courtyard of the Majestic Hotel below. It was that kind of war: *Swann's Way,* John Wayne, and good sex, all in one evening.

After class, as the cadets filed out to collect their hats in the corridor, the lieutenant colonel who had observed Tom's teaching walked up to him.

"That was a fine class, Captain Carhart," the officer said heartily. "But we wear class A uniforms here. Green coat, green pants. Don't ever let me catch you wearing peg pants again in a class of mine or I'll throw you out."

Tom was stunned. Muttering a feeble "yes, sir," he collected his books and stumbled from the building. The cold nipped at his burning face as he crossed the Plain. Rear-echelon motherfucker, he thought, that son of a bitch! I don't need to take that shit. What's he gonna do, send me to Nam?

Instead of going to the Officers Club for lunch as usual, he returned to the BOQ and threw himself face down on his bed. I've got this great deal at West Point, he told himself, this cushy teaching job, and I'm about to screw it up. The colonel's words echoed in his head. Here was another humiliation, another jolt of pain in the succession of pains that now seemed so common in his life. He tried not to cry, but soon the pillow was wet with tears. Stop it, he commanded himself; stop it right now.

But he couldn't stop. He felt disembodied, almost like the teenager who had watched as the unconscious Tom was revived after being stung by a hornet. This isn't normal, he thought; a young captain fresh from the line doesn't break down because of a little chewing-out. This isn't Tom Carhart.

He sat up and dragged the back of his hand across his eyes. This isn't right, he told himself again. Something's wrong here.

The door to the ward shut behind him with a soft *click,* but in Tom's mind it slammed with an iron *clang!* He hoisted the suitcase onto his cot in the bay and pulled out a sports shirt and a pair of slacks. Peeling off his uniform — class A, to be sure — he draped it on a hanger and slipped into the civilian clothes. For the next — what? days, weeks, months, years? — the dress code would be casual mufti. He wouldn't have to worry about peg pants here.

Funny farm, loony bin, cuckoo's nest, booby hatch, nut house, cracker box, psycho ward. None of the derisive terms seemed particularly apt to Tom, given what he had seen thus far. The staff appeared to be friendly and kind, if somewhat overworked, and he thought the other patients in the officers' ward looked normal. No one ranted, no one raved, no one stood with arms tacked to an imaginary cross or with hand thrust into a tunic like Bonaparte. This place, he told himself, the Department of Psychiatry and Neurology at Walter Reed Army Medical Center, was where he would get better, not get lost.

When Tom had seen the psychiatrist at West Point, the doctor was cautious. After scanning the file and listening to Tom describe his nightmares and erratic behavior, the doctor said, "Well, here's what I think you ought to do. Let's face it, you're a special case. Because of your car accident and everything else, I think we ought to go talk to the hospital commander."

The commander remembered Tom well from the car wreck. "I'm not inclined to do anything here," the colonel said. "Given the severity of your head injury and how you fought to get commissioned, I suggest you go to Walter Reed for a full evaluation." Tom immediately agreed; having spent considerable time at Walter Reed after the car accident and his insect sting during Ranger training, he had faith in the Army doctors. He had tossed his possessions into the car and driven five hours from West Point to the hospital in Northwest Washington. On arriving, Tom parked the car, grabbed his suitcase, and signed in at the admissions desk: Carhart, Thomas M. III, Capt., USA.

He stayed for three months. It was frightening at first — terrifying, really. Look at me, he would think: the guy who stole the Navy goat and wrote *The 100th Night Show;* the guy who won the heart of the admiral's daughter and was going to win the war. Look where I've ended up. He felt as though fate, after toying with him for years, had tossed him onto a refuse heap.

At first, the doctors placed him on closed-ward status, a polite phrase for locking him in. The hospital, Tom learned, granted open-ward privileges partly on the basis of a peer evaluation. You mean, he asked himself, the crazies vote on who gets released? Some of the psychiatric wards were so crowded that extra beds had been placed on the porches outside; officers ate their meals with patients from one of the enlisted men's wards. Occasionally someone let out a leonine roar before heaving a tray of food across the room, almost like a sad parody of the Great Mess Hall Riot during Tom's yearling autumn.

When his name came up for open privileges after the first week, the other patients narrowly voted against him; his condescension had angered several of them. Okay, motherfuckers, he thought, I'll be good, I'll play the game. He behaved more graciously, and his courtesy was rewarded; after the second week, he received open privileges. That meant he could leave the ward after group therapy ended at nine A.M. Sometimes he wandered around downtown Washington, returning late in the evening, unless he had earlier appointments to see the psychiatrists or neurologists.

About twenty officers shared Tom's ward, including several West Pointers. One colonel, a former brigade commander who babbled incoherently, had undergone shock therapy. Another patient, a major with a graduate degree from Harvard, had suffered a nervous breakdown in the war zone. Yet another suffered from "hysterical conversion symptoms"; on getting orders to Vietnam, his fear manifested itself through lameness, and he had lost the use of his legs.

Although Tom briefly suspected a few of shamming, sympathy for most of the patients replaced disdain as he got to know them. These men were casualties, too, as surely as those in other wards who had been shot or burned. Combat fatigue — sometimes called "acute environmental reaction" — accounted for about 3 percent of all medical evacuations from Vietnam. This compared with 20 or 30 percent of World War II battle casualties. (The higher tally may have been attributable to the fact that soldiers in the World War often found themselves in combat "for the duration," rather than the fixed one-year tours common in Vietnam.) American psychiatrists believed that a soldier reached the peak of his efficiency after just ninety days in combat; a World War II study, *Combat Exhaustion*, concluded that "the number of men on duty after 200 to 240 days of combat was small and their value to their units was negligible."

Despite his sympathy, Tom felt distanced from the other patients. His problems, he knew, came from a wicked blow to the head, not battle stress. After weeks of poking and probing, the doctors offered hope. "The brain is the most protected part of the body," one explained. "But it's also the slowest organ to heal. It may take a full five years from the time of the accident before you've recovered as much as you're going to."

Five years. That would be April 23, 1971. He clutched at the date like an inmate cross-hatching a calendar until his parole. The doctors seemed to think he needed tranquillity, a haven where stresses were minimal, perhaps graduate school. Taking the advice to heart, Tom signed out for a two-week furlough and drove to New England to scout several colleges. One campus in Vermont particularly attracted him; there he could study French before going to Paris to study at the Sorbonne. I'm still on the mend, he told himself; I need to give myself time. The thought comforted him.

And he got married. He realized that it was an impetuous and rash thing to do. He also recognized that he was on the rebound from Melissa, who had jilted him so abruptly with her Dear Tom letter to him in Vietnam. But he didn't care. He wanted to be married. He wanted a partner, a bedmate, a companion. He wanted children. His bride, Susan Butler, was tall, blond, and buxom. Her father, like Tom's, was an Air Force officer. She had briefly dated Tom's brother, and Tom had seen her picture when he was in Japan on R and R midway through his Vietnam tour. When she and his brother broke up, Tom wrote her a friendly letter. The correspondence was followed by phone calls — Susan attended nursing school in the Midwest — and she came to visit him at Walter Reed. He picked her up at National Airport on a warm spring day two months after he had been been admitted to the hospital. Then suddenly they were engaged.

A few weeks later, after his discharge from Walter Reed, he and Susan flew to Japan. The wedding included three ceremonies, the first at the U.S. embassy in Tokyo, the second before the Japanese equivalent of a justice of the peace, and the third in the chapel at Yokota, his father's base. Tom wore his uniform, the only Army green amid the Air Force blue. Colonel Carhart borrowed a three-quarter-ton truck from the fire department and parked it, bedecked with flowers, outside the chapel. As the bride and groom sat grinning on two chairs in the back, the truck rolled slowly across the base to the reception, leading a procession of honking cars.

Following their honeymoon at a Japanese coastal resort, Captain and Mrs. Carhart flew home. After long consideration, Tom decided that the time was ripe for him to leave the Army. His career in the service, he concluded, had run its course; with his new wife he would make a new life. He applied for a disability discharge, and the Veterans Administration, after reviewing his medical file, set his impairment at 50 percent — sufficient for him to collect a government stipend for graduate school. But the Army calculated disability under a different schedule; it rated him only 10 percent disabled. That meant he would lose his ID card, access to the post exchange and commissary, and other military privileges. For severance, he was entitled to $3567 and an honorable discharge.

With the final papers spread before him, Tom briefly considered appealing. Now that the moment had come, he found it hard to cut the cord. His dream of serving the country for thirty years, of growing old in a green uniform with his classmates, of someday wearing a general's stars — he had given all that up at the ripe old age of twenty-five. And how quickly the dream had collapsed: his actual time in service, excluding stints in the hospital, totaled only two years, six months, and eight days.

In the end, Tom signed his name. By crossing the *t* in Carhart, he transformed himself into what had once been unthinkable: a civilian.

On the second floor of Walter Reed, not far from the main hospital entrance and a stone's throw from Tom's psychiatric ward, Mary Haneke's hands trembled slightly as she lit another cigarette. It was early winter now, and a chill draft swept through the wide corridor outside the Air Evacuation Office. She paced the linoleum, paused, flicked an ash, and paced some more. The waiting was the worst part. Not a very original thought, she figured, but truisms weren't novel. Since that first telegram about her husband nearly three weeks before, each hour had dragged past at an agonizing pace, as though life were gripped by a friction that slowed its normal rhythms. Even the C-141 hospital plane bringing Bill home was caught up in this malevolent dawdle; instead of arriving at nearby Andrews Air Force Base at two P.M., as scheduled, the jet had been delayed by a blizzard during refueling in Alaska. Now dusk was creeping over the capital. She stubbed out the cigarette and lit another.

The flurry of telegrams, first from Vietnam, then from Camp Drake in Japan, had raised as many questions as they answered. Making vague references to an explosion, the cables contained considerable medical gibberish about how badly wounded Bill was. When the surgeons in Japan began discussing further amputations, General Bruce Palmer, the Army vice chief of staff and a West Point friend of Bill's father from the class of 1936, had intervened to have the young captain flown home without further delay.

One phrase in the telegrams kept leaping out at Mary: "brain damage undetermined." Dear Lord, she thought, anything but that. Let him keep his mind. The idea of Bill as a vegetable was more than she could bear. In fact, she could hardly imagine him diminished in any way from the rangy, wise-cracking cadet she had first met in October 1964, when he was a cow and she a raven-haired teller at Scarsdale National Bank and Trust. They had dated for his final two years at the academy — how she had winced every time she heard the detested term *drag* — and then married six months after graduation. Please God, she repeated silently, let him keep his mind.

William Guernsey Haneke had joined the class of 1966 as an academic turnback — calculus was his downfall — from the class of '65. Bill's father, whose West Point classmates included William Westmoreland and Thomas J. Hayes III, had been stationed at Fort Monroe, Virginia, in the early 1960s, at the same time as Jack Wheeler's father; one of young Bill's favorite stunts was to catch big sand sharks from the sea wall at Monroe before dawn and slip them into the Officers Club swimming pool. He had attended prep school in Washington, where he earned an entire semester's tuition by digging out cars stuck in the snow along Pennsylvania Avenue on January 20, 1961. As he shoveled, Bill had listened on a portable radio to the new president's inaugural speech, those fine words about the new generation paying any price, bearing any burden, meeting any hardship.

The double doors at Walter Reed finally swung open, and the corridor began to fill with wounded men. Some could walk; others slumped in wheelchairs or lay on litters. Mary edged closer to her in-laws, who had driven to Washington with her that morning from Richmond. Major General Haneke had recently retired as chief of the Army's finance corps.

"I don't see him," Mary said. She stood against the wall with Bill's parents. Their heads swiveled in unison as they scanned the face of each passing soldier. "Maybe this is the wrong group."

General Haneke worked his way down the corridor, peering more closely at the name tags. He paused beside one litter that had been pushed off to the side. A shrunken, pathetic figure, hardly more than a pile of bones, lay huddled beneath a blanket, his head shaved and skin swabbed with petroleum jelly. The soldier looked to be in his forties, perhaps even fifty. Why, Mary wondered as she stared across the hallway, would such an old man be in the Army? The general edged back toward his wife and daughter-in-law. "That's the name," he said skeptically.

Mary walked over to see for herself. "No, it's not him. It's not," she called with a firm shake of the head. "You're wrong."

The tag said HANEKE, but this creature in no way resembled her husband. He weighed perhaps seventy-five pounds. His skin was a ghastly gray, almost the color of a cadet's dress coat. Two hundred and fifty metal sutures crisscrossed his head and neck like railroad tracks. His right leg was missing, as was part of his left foot. His right arm lay uselessly by his side; his left arm bore angry purple blotches and needle marks from the forty-eight pints of transfused blood that had kept him alive. A tracheotomy tube protruded from his throat; Mary saw black gaps where once there had been teeth. And he was blind: the left eye was intact but had been pierced with shrapnel. The right eye was gone completely, leaving only an empty socket.

For a long minute Mary studied the shape of his mouth. Slowly, very slowly, recognition stole over her. "Bill. It's him," she said at last. She was numb with disbelief.

Hearing her voice, the soldier began to cry. She saw him wince from the stinging salt of the tears cascading down his cheeks.

A man in a white coat walked up and began asking questions.

"What's your name?"

With his left hand, Bill covered the tracheotomy tube and spoke in a guttural whisper. "Haneke."

"Do you know where you are?"

"Washington, D.C."

"Do you know who I am?"

Good question, Mary said to herself. Who are you? She was astonished when Bill answered correctly.

"The psychiatrist."

"Yes. Do you know what day it is?"

Bill hesitated. "December third?"

"December second. You crossed the International Date Line."

Bill let out an odd little wheeze.

"December second," he repeated. "Our anniversary, Mary. Sorry. I didn't bring you a present."

*

Vietnam produced three kinds of casualties: the dead, the wounded, and the wounded who, by all medical odds, should have been dead. Bill Haneke was at the top of the third group, saved by the prodigies of modern battlefield medicine. He had no business being alive.

He had arrived in Vietnam somewhat later than many of his classmates, having first completed a tour of duty in Germany along the Czech border. In Vietnam, the Army assigned him as an adviser to remote Binh Thuan Province on the South China Sea. With twelve other Americans, Bill lived in an eight-acre compound about two miles from the beach. The camp contained an old French hospital that had long since been converted to a chicken coop; he spent hours shoveling out bird droppings and scrubbing the floor and walls with pHisoHex soap to make the place livable. Around the perimeter of the camp, dozens of unmarked French mines still lay buried. On hands and knees, probing with a bayonet, Bill and a sergeant had removed them one by one.

Several hundred Ruff Puffs — South Vietnamese local and regional troops — shared the compound, which was always full of farmers, fishermen, and other locals. When the Americans showed movies at night, Bill was certain that half of those sitting in the audience and cackling at Doris Day or Cary Grant were Viet Cong. The district was among the country's few desert areas — mountains to the west blocked the rains — and one of Bill's most valued possessions was a pair of polarized sunglasses that protected his eyes from the blinding dunes around the camp. The tallest tree for miles stood in the middle of the compound. One day he noticed a schoolgirl counting paces from the trunk to other buildings in the camp; suddenly he realized that the VC were using it for an aiming stake during their nightly mortar attacks. He ordered the tree chopped down.

Packages from home arrived periodically, bringing new socks, cans of Spam, and back issues of *Playboy*, which Mary decorously censored with a pair of scissors. A crack marksman who had been on the academy rifle team, Bill spent much of his time teaching the undisciplined Ruff Puffs to shoot accurately. Once he also made the mistake of showing them how to cook an unplucked chicken, Ranger-style. After wringing the bird's neck, he packed it in mud and baked it for several hours beside an open fire. When he peeled away the mud, the skin and feathers came with it. The delighted Ruff Puffs immediately plundered and baked every chicken for ten square miles. The Americans spent weeks paying reparations to angry farmers.

One night in mid September, the enemy overran the compound. Two Ruff Puff platoons defected, allowing the Viet Cong into the camp shortly after midnight. For nearly eight hours the VC ran amok, slaughtering scores of the remaining Ruff Puffs and blasting everything in sight with satchel charges and recoilless rifles. Bill and a dozen others hid in a bunker, protected by the debris from a shattered building, until air strikes drove the enemy away at dawn.

The Americans tried to stiffen the perimeter defenses. One of the most lethal devices used by Bill and the other advisers was a fifty-five-gallon drum of "fougasse," aviation fuel that had been thickened to the consistency of tapioca pudding. Bill would loop a detonator cord around the top of the barrel with a white phosphorous grenade attached; then he fastened two pounds of C-4 plastic explosive to the bottom. When triggered, the detonator sliced open the drum, the C-4 blew the fougasse out, and the grenade ignited the fuel so that a long tongue of napalm incinerated anyone in the vicinity.

On November 13, one of the fougasse drums had been left about 250 yards from the innermost perimeter of the camp. Bill's commander, an artillery major, wanted the barrel moved closer. Throughout the morning, Bill stalled; marriage to an Irish Catholic had infected him with Mary's Celtic superstitions, and he had an overpowering premonition — reinforced by the sight of an owl that had perched next to him on a radio antenna the night before — that something horrible was going to happen.

The major, growing angry at Bill's temporizing, persisted. "I've had enough of this stalling garbage," he said after lunch. "You and I are going to go out and get that drum."

"No," Bill replied. "I'll go out but you stay here. Something is going to happen to me. If you go, it's going to happen to you, too."

The major scoffed. "This is the biggest bunch of horseshit I've ever heard. Let's go. Right now."

Bill shrugged; he recognized a direct order when he heard one. Shortly before one P.M., he and the major passed through the barbed wire gate and scuffed through the sand to the barrel. Neither of them spotted the enemy soldier crouched with a detonator in a patch of weeds a hundred yards away. In the sand near the barrel, he had planted a five-inch artillery shell — probably an unexploded round originally fired from one of the American naval destroyers patrolling offshore. Beer and Coke cans, stuffed with broken glass and wire scraps, had been lashed to the shell, which by itself was powerful enough to sink a small boat. The sniper had smeared the contraption with human feces in a primitive but effective effort at germ warfare.

Canting the drum on edge, Bill and the major began to roll it up a four-foot knoll toward the camp. The major crouched behind him, pushing the barrel with one hand and Bill's back with the other. What are you doing? Bill wondered. Why don't you put two hands on the —

He never heard the explosion. The blast hurled him eighty feet through the air, draping his body sideways across a barbed wire fence and smashing his jaw against a steel stake, which had been set in concrete to prevent the Viet Cong from flattening the fence.

We're under attack, he thought dimly; I've got to get up. His ears rang so violently he felt as though a fire alarm were clanging next to his head. Though he could feel the hot sun, the world remained completely black. When he tried to move, the barbed wire held him fast. You're hurt, he thought; this is serious. You dummy, you've done it now — what's Mary going to say? She told you to come back in one piece. Fragments of teeth and bone clogged the back of his throat, making each gasping breath an ordeal. But whenever he attempted to wriggle a limb free of the wire, the pain flushed through him like fire, nearly causing him to black out. Oh, dear God, he prayed, please help me. I'm dying.

Something kept tapping his left shoulder, brushing against him with an annoying syncopation. Both the carotid artery and jugular vein had been slashed. The tapping was his own blood, spurting out every time his heart beat.

Then he heard the voice for the first time. It was soothing, supernatural. Turn your head to the left, the voice said. Try to be calm. I will see you through this.

He turned his head, partly pinching off the gush of blood. The tapping stopped.

Alerted by the explosion and column of black smoke, several Americans came running from the compound. The fougasse drum was intact, but the exploding shell had blasted a deep crater next to the barrel. The enemy sniper had vanished. The major also lay wounded, though not as severely as Bill, who had shielded him from much of the blast.

Several strong hands cut Bill free from the barbed wire and lifted him onto a jury-rigged stretcher of plywood and two-by-fours. Within fifteen minutes, a helicopter arrived with a medic, who started a plasma bottle and cut a tracheotomy in his throat. Flickering in and out of consciousness, Bill thought the gush of air into his lungs was the most wonderful sensation he had ever known. Again he heard the voice — and he never knew who or what it was. Be calm, it urged. Have faith. I am with you.

After intermediate stops at several aid stations, he arrived at the 24th Evacuation Hospital in Long Binh. Powder burns blackened his skin. He had lost his right leg and half of his left foot, one his lungs had been punctured with shrapnel, and a deep dent in his forehead indicated that part of the skull had caved in. The explosion had ripped large chunks of flesh from his buttocks, and shrapnel riddled every part of his body.

Because his dogtags and clothing had been blown off — except for the uniform shirt collar with his rank insignia — the hospital designated him Captain X. Not knowing that Captain X was an Episcopalian, a Catholic priest administered last rites. In triage, a harried surgeon glanced at him with a shake of the head and quickly assigned Bill to the lowest priority, the hopelessly moribund.

The voice spoke to him again: You must do what I tell you. Give them a sign that you are alive. Do it now.

Bill tried to cry out, but because of the trach tube, nothing emerged from his mouth but tiny wheezes. He thought that perhaps he had died and gone to hell. What, he wondered, have I ever done to deserve this pain? An intravenous tube protruded from his left leg. With all of his strength, he jerked his body so that the stand holding the plasma bottle crashed to the floor.

"Hey, this guy's alive," a corpsman yelled. "Hey, doc, this guy's still kicking."

"All right, get him ready. Table three just came open. Quickly, quickly."

Bill felt the stretcher being lifted. Someone cut away the shirt collar and remaining scraps of clothing. A dark wave of anesthesia flooded through him as surgeons and nurses began to cluster around the shattered body of Captain X, who had so stubbornly refused to check his mortality at the door.

The guest house at Walter Reed reminded Mary of the set from an old Humphrey Bogart movie. For $8.00 a night she got a sagging bed, a battered dresser, a naked light bulb — fly-specked, of course — and a bathroom, which she shared with a man in an adjacent room whose intentions seemed less than wholesome. "Got any aspirin, honey?" he would yell through the door. "Just leave 'em right here on the floor, unless you want me to come get 'em."

The place swarmed with white mice — offspring, apparently, of rodents that had escaped from the hospital laboratories. One Saturday night she ran down to the front desk to complain: "There's a mouse in my room."

The clerk gave her a sullen look. "Whaddya want me to do, sit shotgun?"

"No," Mary snapped, "I want you to catch him so he can pay his share of the damned room."

She bought a bag of traps at K mart and baited them with peanut butter. Every morning she hauled in the traps with the crook of an umbrella handle and scooted the dead mice into a paper bag. How, she asked herself, did a nice girl from Scarsdale end up in a dump like this?

Like Bill, she too had seen omens. With a mother born in County Mayo and a father born in County Leitrim, Mary had spent a childhood steeped in Irish superstition. The night before Bill was wounded, she was visiting her sister in Somers, New York. At three A.M. they pulled out the Ouija board. When is Bill coming home? *December*, the board answered. He was due home in August. Wounded? *Yes*. Not wounded badly? *Leg, foot . . .* Before it could spell anything else, Mary's sister picked up the board and dashed it across the room.

When Mary returned to her parents' home in Scarsdale the next day, she found that her wedding picture had fallen from the wall, splintering the frame. That night, after swallowing two sleeping pills, she was awakened at one A.M. by a crash against a window in the sun room downstairs. It sounded as if someone had put a fist through a pane, but as Mary lay listening she heard the rustle of wings. A bird, she thought; another evil portent. Padding down to make herself a cup of tea, Mary found her mother in the kitchen. When Mary told her about the Ouija board and the fallen picture and the bird, Mrs. Keegan cursed herself for filling her daughter's head with superstitious nonsense.

The next evening, just before midnight, an Army captain came to the door with the telegram. Occasionally, Mary knew, cruel practical jokers in New York dressed up as officers and delivered bogus KIA telegrams to waiting wives. She asked to see the man's ID card. Then she checked his shoes, figuring that a spit shine was one detail — a kind of military shibboleth — that would not be known by a fraud. The captain's shoes gleamed with frightful authenticity.

For three weeks, Mary could do little but read the Army's confusing telegrams about Bill's condition. But once he arrived at Walter Reed and moved into the officers' orthopedic ward, she devoted herself unflaggingly to his recovery. She was appalled by how many others at the hospital were in the same ought-to-be-dead category. One helicopter pilot had been struck by a .50-caliber slug that simply erased his face. Blind and lame, he was studying to be a lawyer. One of Bill's classmates and a fellow turnback from '65, William C. Rennagel, had lost his right hand when a grenade he was holding exploded prematurely. That such men were alive bespoke the medical miracles occurring every day in Vietnam, where the death rate among those who survived long enough to reach a medical facility was only 1 percent (compared with 5 percent in World War II and 14 percent among Union troops in the Civil War).

Every day, often from seven A.M. to one A.M., Mary hovered by Bill's bedside. She weighed only ninety-eight pounds, but her husband was so emaciated that she was able to lift him if he needed to be turned or moved to a litter for treatment. When he was able to drink liquids through a straw, she usually stopped at the guest house cafeteria — the Bug Hole, she called it — and ordered him a milkshake with two eggs blended in. Because his many wounds were suppurating, he needed a bath and clean pajamas several times a day. The bed sometimes was so full of shrapnel and other debris that worked its way out of his body that she called it the Gravel Pit. Yet ounce by ounce, Bill began putting on weight.

After doctors removed the sutures, she shaved Bill with a bowl and razor, stroking his face as carefully and gently as if she were powdering a newborn. For hour upon hour she read aloud from the sports pages — which she personally detested — often giving news about "smoo," until Bill finally realized that she was talking about Southern Methodist University, SMU.

Not all of the men were blessed with such devoted wives. Sometimes a wife came clicking through the ward in high heels, dragging an attorney in her wake. "Just sign here, honey," she would whisper to her wounded soldier. And as the poor wretch scratched his name to agree to the divorce or give her sole title to the house, the other patients turned their faces to the wall so that they wouldn't have to witness yet another atrocity. Occasionally, when Mary retreated to the day room for a cigarette, she heard the men talking: "Uh-oh. Look whose wife just showed up with a lawyer. Check out the attaché case." And later, when they noticed Mary smoking in a corner, their eyes would narrow, as if to ask, "Well, when are *you* going to sashay in with your high heels and your lawyer?"

Never. She was outraged just by the thought of such treachery. When an intern suggested that Bill might lose his other leg because of an unchecked infection, she crooked her finger: "Hey, you, Almost-A-Doctor, come here. Let's not have any more talk like that." Once quiet and demure, she became outspoken, referring to herself as Lippy Leroy. And when Bill contracted hepatitis — she was the first to notice his sallow complexion and the yellowing of his remaining eye — the doctor shook his head. "I'm sorry," he said, "but he's not going to make it."

"What's the sign of his making it?" Mary demanded.

"If he eats and his color gets better."

She stalked to his bedside and practically barked, "You're going to eat and your color's going to get better."

When the doctors said he would never stand again, that he had lost too many of the balance points in his left foot, she designed a special high-top shoe with laces in front and back. "Well, look," she suggested, "if you put some kind of weight on that side, wouldn't you have a balance point there? It'd be like a clock on a mantel — you know, the kind that won't work unless it's exactly balanced and you keep shoving matchbooks under one end." The shoe, constructed in the Walter Reed brace shop, worked perfectly.

Still listed in critical condition after three months at Walter Reed, Bill was moved to the Veterans Administration hospital in Richmond. Hugging Mary's special shoe to his chest, he was hoisted into an ambulance, which then rocketed down Interstate 95, its siren screaming for the entire ninety-mile trip. But soon, afflicted with a brain infection after his third neurosurgical operation, he was back at Walter Reed fighting for his life again. Crisis followed crisis. As quickly as one infection was arrested, another seemed to flare. When doctors removed skin from his thigh to graft onto his foot, the donor site became infected. Nurses covered the thigh with gauze soaked in saline solution; the dressing dried out and had to be changed every four hours. Fearing addiction, Bill refused to take codeine or other painkillers; unable to shriek because of the trach tube, he lay in the ward and wept silently.

Thirteen months after he was wounded, the Veterans Administration slashed Bill's benefits. For a year, while the glacial appeals process crept along, they lived on the wedding cash Mary had socked away. Pride prevented them from asking their parents for help. "This is wonderful," Mary told her husband sarcastically. "I've already got two strikes against me with your parents: I don't have a college education and I'm Catholic. I'm not going to let them think I'm pleading for money, too." When the VA appeals board convened in Roanoke, Virginia, Bill carefully placed his glass eye on the table and propped what remained of his left foot next to it. Even then the board restored the benefits only after pressure from a sympathetic congressman.

Slowly, Bill began to mend. He and Mary set weekly and monthly goals. The doctors had said he would never be able to sit, stand, or walk. Both Hanekes developed a fierce, almost belligerent pride in proving them wrong. Although he usually used a wheelchair, Bill could shuffle short distances with an artificial leg. Now the doctors said he would never have children and would never see again. He was determined to prove them wrong on those counts, too. Occasionally, when they were in public, someone would make a crack about Peg-Leg Pete or One-Eyed Sam. Bill let it pass; Mary never did. "What did you say?" she challenged loudly. "Peg-Leg Pete? Did your mother ever tell you that someday you were going to meet someone who was going to set you straight? Well, you just met her."

Bill never regretted having gone to West Point or serving his country in combat. "Bitterness," he said, "will only make it harder to get better. The enemy messed my body up pretty badly, but I'm not going to let him have my mind." He began to think about another career, perhaps in hospital administration, and he enrolled in courses at Virginia Commonwealth University. On a couple of occasions he was heckled by rabid antiwar protestors who blocked his wheelchair. "Murderer," they taunted. "Capitalist stooge."

Again, he let the insults pass, though he was not above ramming a few shins with the metal prow of his wheelchair. Capitalist stooge or not, Bill Haneke had places to go.

13

Farewell to Arms

Jack Wheeler nosed the Chevelle into the clot of cars on Wilson Boulevard. It was only two miles to the Pentagon from his apartment in Arlington, and although he occasionally wondered why he didn't just walk rather than fight the Washington commuter madness every morning, the short drive was pleasant enough. The Chevelle, purchased in the spring of his final year at West Point, was as reliable and undemanding as an old friend; when Bob Wheeler came up from New Haven for his brother's graduation in 1966, he had teased Jack mercilessly about parking such a drab, practical sedan next to his classmates' Corvettes and Mustangs in the firstie lot above Michie Stadium. "My God, Jack," Bob had exclaimed in mock horror, "it doesn't even have an FM radio!"

Yet now, five years later, many of those sports cars had long since gone to scrap, and the Chevelle kept puttering along. On the dashboard perched a pink cardboard heart from Ginny Stuart with a note she had scribbled several years before: "To my prince, Happy Valentine's Day, with lots of love to you from my heart." Jack smiled every time he noticed the memento; it appealed to his sentimental streak.

As the highway elbowed to the northeast, he saw the familiar tableau of the Iwo Jima Memorial. Dwarfed by those six bronze Marines, forever hoisting their flag on Mount Suribachi, a few early summer tourists ambled around the black marble base on which gilt lettering proclaimed UNCOMMON VALOR WAS A COMMON VIRTUE. Sometimes on Sunday afternoons Jack played touch football on the lush sward next to the statue. The setting was inspiring: a few hundred yards away, in the middle of the national cemetery, lay the Tomb of the Unknown Soldier and John Kennedy's grave, with its stabbing, yellow flame. Across the Potomac loomed the towering obelisk of the Washington Monument and the white shoebox of the Lincoln Memorial. Even as he zigged and zagged in a down-and-out pattern, Jack occasionally thought of how anachronistic the Iwo Jima statue seemed. Those six Marines were steely-eyed and rock-jawed, with their chin straps snapped and their ammo pouches buttoned. They came from a different war in a different age, when heroes were more easily oversized. Where was the Mount Suribachi in Vietnam? Hill 875? That seemed unlikely.

Leaving the Chevelle in North Parking, he walked briskly toward the inelegant gray mass of the Pentagon. Thousands of others converged on the building for the start of another workday. Jack felt anonymous, which, he conceded, was how a lowly Army captain was supposed to feel in the Pentagon, particularly since his current assignment required him to wear civilian clothes. He slipped through the doors of the river entrance, smartly hung a right in the E-Ring, and trotted down two flights of stairs to the sub-basement. After flashing his security badge to the guard, he worked his way through the labyrinth of the National Military Command Systems Support Center until he reached a steel door fitted with a combination lock the size of a coffee saucer. Jack twirled the dial to the proper sequence of numbers and pushed his way into the vault.

The thick-walled chamber — he often thought of it as a bunker — was divided into two rooms, both painted olive green. Six steel desks with their government-issue chairs stood pushed against the walls. Two technicians and two other officers — all wearing civilian clothes — huddled near the computer keyboard, examining the day's exercise for SAGA, the Studies Analysis and Gaming Agency. As a member of the Joint Chiefs' staff, Jack had the job of planning nuclear attacks against the United States.

Since December 1960, when the American nuclear arsenal contained only four thousand strategic warheads, the United States had had a secret plan for World War III known as SIOP — pronounced "sigh-op" — the Single Integrated Operational Plan. If a global war erupted, SIOP would determine the sequence of U.S. bomber, submarine, and intercontinental ballistic missile attacks on targets in the Soviet Union. As the arsenal grew during the 1960s, so did SIOP; the plan even carried its own security classification, known as ESI, or Extremely Sensitive Information. To keep the SIOP planners sharp, the Joint Chiefs had invented RISOP ("rye-sop"), Red Integrated Single Operational Plan. RISOP simulated the Soviet war strategy and analyzed the consequences of an attack on the American economy, population, and ability to retaliate.

Today's RISOP exercise was reasonably straightforward. Jack and his vault mates were instructed to assume that American forces remained in DEFCON 5, a "defense condition" that indicated normal readiness for war. They also were to assume that it was late winter in the United States, with the usual west-to-east wind patterns prevailing. Eighty percent of the Soviet strategic megatonnage stood ready for war. As always in these games, the Soviets would strike first, initially with submarine-launched missiles, then with ICBMs. The attack was to be a massive first strike that attempted both to "decapitate" — destroying the American command structure — and to cripple the U.S. nuclear retaliatory force. With help from the computer, the RISOP gamesmen had to determine when the United States would detect the attack and how quickly the nation would respond; their task also called for determining the extent of damage from the Soviet warheads: cities destroyed, military facilities knocked out, and percentage of the American gross national product obliterated.

Duly equipped with this grim program, the computer began its analysis, humming as blithely as if asked to calculate payroll deductions for every GS-12 in Washington. Even after a year of conjuring up such holocausts, Jack found the task intensely sobering. *Poof!* There would go Omaha, along with SAC headquarters at Offutt Air Force Base. *Poof! Poof!* San Diego. Norfolk. Washington, including ground zero here at the Pentagon would not be far behind. *Poof!* The duty was much more sinister, more real, somehow — than manning the Nike site in New Jersey in 1966. That seemed innocent by comparison, especially his fantasy of protecting Ginny Stuart with his missile battery.

Once, after a particularly tedious day of megadeath and destruction in the SAGA vault, Jack had told his brother, "You know what we ought to do, Bob? I'll call you when I know the bombs are about ready to go off and we'll get the family together and go down to Venezuela." But, in fact, Jack knew that he would stand his ground in this subterranean cave — just as he would have remained in his Nike trailer at Franklin Lakes — continuing to simulate Armageddon even as the real thing was bursting in a white, plasmatic hell overhead.

Since returning from Vietnam ten months earlier, Jack had edged ever closer to resignation. But leaving the military was not easy, as Tom Carhart and other classmates were discovering. He had a great deal invested in the Army — four years at West Point and almost five now in the service. More important, his identity was rooted in the military; having grown up as an Army brat, he had always owned a military ID card. The little plastic badge meant that he was part of the brotherhood, that he belonged. Where would he belong as a civilian?

More than ever before, Jack felt like an outsider within his own generation, a stranger in his own country. During his twelve months in

Vietnam, America had accelerated past him. Life was wilder. The music, the drugs, the long hair and frayed clothes, the hostility toward authority — all seemed foreign, as though much of the country spoke a dialect he could not quite understand. It reminded him of the lines from Yeats's "The Second Coming": "Things fall apart; the center cannot hold; mere anarchy is loosed upon the world."

Jack had arrived home at Travis Air Force Base at four-thirty on a July morning in 1970. He was met by Bruns Grayson, who had accompanied him when he solicited the colonel's views on the antiwar petition at Long Binh. Grayson, living at home in Alameda until fall classes began at Harvard, thought Jack seemed bewildered by his sudden return to the States. Of course it was entirely possible, Grayson knew, that Jack looked bewildered simply because he believed that was how a returning soldier ought to look; moreover, Grayson somehow had trouble distinguishing between Wheeler's temporary confusion and his inherent naïveté.

After sleeping until late the next afternoon, they arose to a turkey dinner cooked by Grayson's mother as an off-season Thanksgiving feast. Later they drove to Berkeley to see the movie *Woodstock*. Pickets stood outside the theater. When Grayson asked one what he was protesting, the picketer replied, "It's a ripoff of our culture, man. Exploitation. Don't go in."

Grayson shrugged. "C'mon, Jack. I'm just going to see a movie." As he and Jack walked toward the box office, the picketer yelled after them, "You're a scab on the people, man!"

The Wheeler family — Big Jack, Janet, brother Bob, and sister Janet Marie — met Jack at the airport when he flew back east. It was a glorious reunion, even for a family accustomed to being separated and reunited many times over the years. At the Aberdeen Proving Ground, Big Jack and Janet lived in a large house with a splendid view of Chesapeake Bay. The next day, Bob Wheeler drove his brother down to Georgetown, where they wandered through the shops along M Street and Wisconsin Avenue. Jack picked out some Levi's, a pair of leather sandals with toe loops, and a yellow-and-red fabric belt. Having costumed himself for the counterculture, he also bought two Edwardian suits at Britches.

Back at Aberdeen, Jack climbed into his Chevelle and drove north to Saratoga. He and Ginny had occasionally corresponded during his year at Long Binh; their letters were warm and confiding, if not as amorous as they once had been. Although he suspected that their romance had now lapsed into friendship, Jack wanted to see his ballerina at least once more. As he walked into the Performing Arts Center, he saw her rehearsing on stage; Ginny wiggled her fingers in greeting after spotting him in the audience. When the rehearsal ended, she bounded up and wrapped him in a big hug. He thought her even more beautiful and enchanting than she had been as a nineteen-year-old dancing in *Ballet Imperial* on that October evening at Lincoln Center five years before.

But the spark was gone. "I don't know what's happening," he confessed when they were alone together later, "but I'm thinking of you more as a sister than a lover." Her ego was bruised, yet she felt sorry for Jack; he seemed so sincere, so upset. Their common ground had always been a very narrow isthmus, and this moment had a certain inevitability. She still admired him enormously. His commitment to the commonweal struck her as noble, his values somehow more worthy than her own.

"I'll be okay," she said, knowing he needed to hear that. A sweet melancholy settled over them, and at last he got back into the car and drove away.

While attending Harvard, Jack had occasionally visited his brother at Yale. Bob's buddies, disinclined to take Jack as seriously as he sometimes took himself, had hung a nickname on him: John P. What-Are-You-Going-to-Do-With-the-Rest-of-Your-Life? Wheeler. He could laugh at the gibe, but the question persisted. What, indeed? Just as he had fretted endlessly over whether to attend West Point or Yale, so he agonized over resignation. "What's best for the Army?" he would ask Bob or Bruns Grayson or anyone who would listen. "What's best for the country? What should I do?"

More than anything else, he wanted to be part of America, a full participant in the nation's culture and in the unfolding destiny of his generation. Sometimes, after he began working in the Pentagon vault, he would slip on his Levi's and sandals and walk across Memorial Bridge to watch the antiwar demonstrations on the Mall. But he was always an observer, just as he had been observer in Honolulu on Earth Day, perhaps even as he had been a supporting player rather than a combatant in Vietnam. He also found that sailing and skiing no longer appealed to him, though they had once been his favorite hobbies. Every healthy man had a healthy boy inside him, he believed, and he wondered what had happened to the boy in Jack Wheeler.

He tried to review his options as analytically as the computer analyzed the RISOP nuking of America. The Army remained an option, of course. Some of his work in the past five years had been challenging and rewarding; at times Jack felt he'd even made a genuine contribution. During the summer of 1968, between his two years at business school, he had worked in the Pentagon on the staff of the assistant secretary of defense for systems analysis. Part of his job involved reviewing the military utility of biological weapons, such as anthrax bombs and other types of germ warfare. In a study of the issue, he asserted that there were no circumstances in which the president would conclude that biologicals provided a useful supplement to the American arsenal. The Pentagon sent the report to the National Security Council, and when Richard Nixon renounced the use and production of biological weapons in November 1969, Jack was told that his analysis had been a factor.

But that positive experience was outweighed by negatives. His countrymen's disdain for the military gnawed at Jack. In 1963, an opinion survey had ranked being an Army captain twenty-first in prestige among occupations, about on par with being a public school teacher; since then, public esteem for military officers had steadily plummeted, and they now ranked barely above bank robbers. Furthermore, America had been at war for twenty of the past thirty years. That was an odd turn of events for an avowedly peace-loving people and something that required contemplation by anyone considering military service for the next thirty years; he understood clearly now that he was not well suited to being a fighting man. Finally, although Jack had been told that the Article 15 for using a stolen jeep would not affect his military career, he realized that it remained a blemish nonetheless.

So, if not the Army, then what? He had very little appetite for being a captain of industry or devoting his life to amassing a personal fortune. It wasn't that he despised wealth; no one could spend two years in graduate school at the West Point of capitalism and come away sneering at businessmen. But he simply didn't care about becoming rich. For several weeks in business school, Jack had analyzed real estate transactions for Kidder, Peabody on Wall Street. As an intellectual exercise, the work had been interesting. But bottom lines ultimately bored him.

He toyed with the notion of going to seminary, perhaps even becoming an Episcopal priest. Jack had attended church services in Vietnam only once — Easter Sunday, 1970 — but his belief in God and in the Christian explanation of life had grown steadily in recent years. After visiting Ginny in Saratoga, he had driven to see his mother's brother, who was a priest at St. Andrew's Episcopal Church in Nashville. A life built on faith and service through the Church appealed to Jack, but it required an enormous commitment. Was he ready for that leap? He simply wasn't sure.

In the sub-basement vault at the Pentagon, the computer had completed its analysis. Jack scanned the results, which showed the progressive ripples of destruction after the initial detonations at H-Hour. Today's attack had been a holocaust. Men had needed nearly five centuries to build this part of the New World into the United States of

America, the greatest republic in the history of civilization. The RISOP team had required but a few hours to destroy the nation. Thirty percent of the American GNP was gone. Minimum casualties: twenty million, excluding radiation deaths. The printed list of cities reduced to rubble was as long as Jack's arm.

Although he appreciated the importance of the RISOP gaming — and had even been recommended for a meritorious achievement medal — Jack was weary of blowing up America. His future lay somewhere beyond this Pentagon vault, beyond the U.S. Army. In his heart, he knew what he needed to do now. He had to resign. John P. What-Are-You-Going-to-Do-With-the-Rest-of-Your-Life? Wheeler would answer the question when the rest of his life got here.

Sometimes, when he was upset or particularly gloomy, Jack toyed with the morbid thought that Tommy Hayes had the better lot. He had fought the good fight and died a hero. He would forever be twenty-four, forever preserved — in Jack's mind at least — as bronzed and oversize as those Marines gripping the flagstaff on the Iwo Jima Memorial. Tommy's slogging was over. No one would ask Tommy Hayes what he was going to do with the rest of his life.

On June 8, 1970, four years after graduation, the first men in the class of 1966 became eligible to leave the Army. (Others, like Jack, had incurred an extra year or two of obligation in exchange for their graduate schooling or specialized military training.) The stampede to get out began immediately. At the four-year mark, nearly a quarter of the class resigned; by December 1971, almost 200 of the 579 graduates had quit — fully a third of the class. The resignation rate was running 50 percent higher than it had in classes from the 1950s and early 1960s; in the war class of 1950, for example, only 11 percent had resigned after five years.

Alarmed by the departures, the Pentagon commissioned a study of the problem. "Why They Leave: Resignations from the USMA Class of 1966" ultimately trumpeted the obvious: most of them disliked the Army. The major factors cited by those resigning were family separations, another imminent Vietnam tour, promotions based on seniority, and uninspiring leaders.

Some of those leaving the service found the Army disillusioning, disturbingly different from the crisp, black-and-white values of West Point. They complained of senior officers obsessed with their careers and a craving to win general's stars at any cost; of a "ticket-punching" system that encouraged hopping from prestigious assignment to assignment; of a "zero defects" mentality in which a single blemish on a young officer's record would forever plague him.

Some found military life absurdly lockstep. "One former general's aide reports working in a headquarters in which every general maintained a wardrobe in his office," the study recounted. "As many as six uniform changes a day were required so that all generals in the headquarters would always be in the same uniform as the lieutenant general."

The Military Academy, which also worried about the resignation rate, followed up with further studies. Research psychologists scrutinized the character traits and backgrounds of the young officers for clues as to why some resigned and others did not. One study found that "careerists," those who intended to remain in the Army for at least twenty years, were twice as likely to have military fathers or fathers-in-law as the "non-careerists." The non-careerists attended church less, were more liberal politically, were less inclined to have completed airborne and Ranger training, and had spent less time in Vietnam than the careerists. Furthermore, the careerists tended to have wives who were content with frequent moves, Army social life and protocol, and an officer's social status.

Mass resignations by West Pointers had occurred in the past, usually triggered by a booming national economy and the lure of high-paying civilian jobs. But in the early 1970s, the phenomenon reflected morale problems that had spread throughout the Army. The resignation of thirty-three West Point faculty instructors in eighteen months — typically, only five to seven resigned each year — made front-page news in *The New York Times*. "It's really disastrous to see these people go because they are the brightest," an academy spokesman admitted to the newspaper. When firsties in the class of 1971 were asked whether they would attend West Point again if given the opportunity, more than half said no. In 1959, 90 percent of the first classmen had answered yes.

On a deeper level, of course, the resignations reflected an alienation between the Republic and its Army. With so many Americans insisting that the war in Vietnam was corrupt, there existed a corollary presumption that those who fought it were corrupted. For many soldiers, that contempt made uniformed life unbearable. Again, history offered many precedents for American antipathy toward the military; suspicion of the symbolic "man on horseback" had been indigenous since Colonial days. "Americans," Army Chief of Staff Fred C. Weyand observed, "have a long and proud tradition of irreverence toward and distrust of their military." Nor was antiwar sentiment unusual in the country's history. But as the astute Army historian Harry G. Summers, Jr., pointed out, "This dissent was usually directed primarily against the government rather than the military." Now the antipathy was more broadly aimed, and the men of '66 offered a convenient target: the first generation of West Pointers to join a losing Army.

Many in the class were surprised to find themselves resigning. Michael B. Fuller, who had traveled to West Point with Jack Wheeler in 1962 and had been captain of the academy rifle team, assumed before, during, and after his Vietnam tour that the Army would be his career. But a succession of incompetent commanding officers and the scorn of his countrymen wore him down. As a company commander with the Old Guard in Washington, he and his troops spent many weekends hidden in the hallways of the Treasury Building and Old Executive Office Building, waiting with M-16s and gas masks to repel any demonstrator daring to vault the White House fence. Ten years earlier, Fuller and his classmates had been the leaders of their generation; now they were pariahs. That struck him as both ironic and deeply unfair.

Al Lindseth, who had led the first relief platoon at Hill 875, did not want to wait ten or twelve years before his next opportunity to lead troops, as a battalion commander. Lindseth also concluded that the Army was a very unforgiving institution; he had no guarantee of getting that command should he make even a slight misstep during the next decade. He resigned to attend Harvard Law School, and eventually settled in Atlanta.

Sam Bartholomew, a West Point football star, felt himself demeaned by Vietnam. The lack of a clear objective, the on-again-off-again bombing, the policy of allowing the enemy to seek sanctuary in Laos and Cambodia — all troubled him deeply. "The hippie carrying a placard down Constitution Avenue in Washington is going to have more impact on America's future than I am if I stay in uniform for another thirty years," he complained. Bartholomew, too, resigned to attend law school.

For these men and scores of their classmates, resignation meant trying to re-enter the outside world that many had last seen as teenagers and that some — the military brats — had never seen. They bought three-piece suits instead of fatigues, went to hair stylists instead of the PX barber, and anchored themselves with hefty mortgages instead of pulling up stakes every couple of years. They shopped at supermarkets rather than commissaries, used the bathroom instead of the latrine, and awoke at seven o'clock instead of 0700. Packing away their salutes, they stopped punctuating every clause with "sir," and struggled, often in vain, to wean themselves from the military obsession with acronyms.

No resignation more stunned the class — and the Army brass — than that of Norman Fretwell, the first captain of '66. The poor boy from Joplin who had labored on the Plain to correct his waddle and to project his command voice was among the first to resign. At West Point, Norm, like every first captain, had been a symbol of his entire class; now he was a symbol of its discontent.

His first qualms came in Vietnam. Assigned to the 101st Airborne, he found the fixation with body counts so pervasive that platoon leaders had orders to open any grave they found, regardless of how old, in order to increase the tally of enemy dead. One morning during a patrol, his platoon's point dog froze. Norm ordered his men to fan out in a semicircle. Instinctively, he glanced over his shoulder just as a Viet Cong soldier stepped from the jungle thirty feet away. Their eyes locked for a brief moment of mutual terror and communication. Then, as the VC struggled to unsling his rifle, Norm blew the man's head off with his CAR-15. Why did I do this? he asked himself, staring at the faceless corpse. The platitudes about thwarting communist aggression had begun to sound hollow, and the image of that doomed enemy soldier lingered with Norm for many years.

Later, he was reunited with Charlie Beckwith, who had left the Florida Ranger camp to command one of the Screaming Eagle battalions. One day, a helicopter set Beckwith and Fretwell on a large bald hill to watch a firefight; no sooner had they landed than mortar rounds began bursting around them. For hours they huddled together in a circular Vietnamese grave. No, no, no, Norm thought between explosions. What am I doing here? Beckwith, who carried his revolver in a shoulder holster, had vowed to commit suicide rather than allow himself to be captured. Norm wondered who Chargin' Charlie would take with him.

He often asked himself why others died while he was spared. Sometimes the bullets flew as thick as Ozark mosquitoes, snipping holes in his fatigues. Survival seemed so arbitrary, more caprice than miracle. In his diary he wrote: "Am I willing to let life just happen to me?" Below the question he copied a doleful sentence he recalled from Jack London: "Life had become cheap and tawdry, a beastly and inarticulate thing, a soulless stirring of the ooze and slime."

Returning home on leave to Joplin after his year in Vietnam, Norm found the town changed. In 1962, when he left for West Point, he had been the small-town hero, the local boy about to make good. In 1966, he was still a hero — particularly after being selected first captain, like Missouri's own Black Jack Pershing — but his old friends kept a certain cool distance. "Hey, Norman," they would say, "it's great that you went off to West Point and earned all these honors, but what the hell are you going to Vietnam for?" Now, the coolness had become disdain, conveyed in a tone of voice, a cocked eyebrow, a smirk.

And after Vietnam came Berlin. As a plebe, Norm had roomed briefly with an Army brat named Robert Fergusson, whose father was a general from the class of 1936. Young Fergusson had left West Point honorably before graduation; after finishing college and commissioning in the Army, he had died heroically in Vietnam, where he won the Distinguished Service Cross. Remembering Cadet Fretwell's kindness to his son, General Fergusson, who had become the American military commander in Berlin, asked Norm to be his aide.

On the surface, at least, the tour offered splendid duty. Although Berlin's winters were as drab and bone-chilling as West Point's, the city was as much a victor's trophy as Goering's baton or Mussolini's black hat in the West Point museum. Norm lived in a top-floor apartment that had two bedrooms, two baths, and pricey Scandinavian furniture, all paid for by the West German government; he even had his own staff car, equipped with driver and telephone. Fergusson lived in a magnificent house that had once been a Nazi villa. As military commander, he also was entitled to a powerful speedboat and a summer cottage on the Wannsee, where leaders of the Third Reich had once met to draft plans for "the final solution," the extermination of the Jews.

"Norm," the general would say when the weather warmed, "let's go water skiing for lunch." Norm would make the calls, first to the cottage — "Hans, lay the suits out, *bitte*. We'll be there in thirty minutes" — and then to the boathouse — "Gas it up, *bitte*." After skiing, they would change and return to the office in the back seat of Fergusson's black Mercedes, where lunch was served on oiled wood trays. Norm once heard the visiting tire magnate Leonard Firestone say to the general, "Bob, *I* couldn't afford this."

Nearly every night Norm attended either a black tie gala or a cocktail party. When VIPs came to Berlin, whether it was the actress Elke Sommer or Mayor Sam Yorty of Los Angeles, Captain Fretwell usually escorted them. The publisher Hugh Hefner, who swooped into Berlin in his black Bunny jet, was the guest of honor one evening at a reception arranged by Fergusson. When the conversation turned to the war and Hefner loudly denounced American involvement in Southeast Asia, Fretwell pulled him into a side room. "Look," he said, "I don't care who you are. This party is being held for you. I want you to know that your host had only one child and that child was killed in Vietnam not long ago, and I'd really appreciate it if you'd just change the subject."

Life was good in Berlin, as broad and freewheeling as the Kurfürstendamm itself, yet he was unhappy. Sometimes the city under Allied rule seemed as corrupt and meretricious as the Berlin of the 1930s, a kind of *Cabaret* without the Nazis. Norm was contemptuous of what he privately referred to as "the backside of politicians," self-inflated men who would breeze in from Washington on official visits, invariably collecting their $50 government per diem even though their expenses had already been paid by the Army or the State Department. As the Army brass bowed and scraped — especially if the visitors sat on the House or Senate Armed Services Committee — the lions of freedom would pose for pictures next to the Berlin Wall before returning to their hotel rooms, where it was Norm's job to see that they were well stocked with liquor and other amenities.

Such episodes were trivial, to be sure, but they bothered Norm enormously. He felt soiled. Reconciling his life in Berlin to the ideals of West Point — which were not much different from those he had learned from the Boy Scouts in Joplin — was difficult at best. His wife, Barbara, who had been Norm's co-salutatorian at Joplin High before going to Smith College, despised the Berlin social whirl. "Those people," she would grumble after yet another embassy party, "they're so plastic."

He began to keep a diary in a blue, loose-leaf notebook with an UNCLASSIFIED stamp on the cover. On February 24, 1969, when his brother was visiting, Norm wrote, "I had an excellent discussion with Barbara and John in the evening about financial ventures and about the Army. I'm afraid that because of my bitterness I cast the Army in too dark a shadow." A week later, after watching a senior officer browbeating a subordinate, he worried about "the possibility of selling myself out if I remain in my present job much longer, or the Army for that matter." On March 4, he added, "People were created to accomplish more in their lives than to serve the fulfillment of their own selfish pleasures."

Some of the senior military officers were incredibly petty. Once he saw a brigadier publicly upbraided by a higher ranking general for having the button on his uniform cuff sewed on upside down. Holy shit, Norm thought, this is what I've got to look forward to?

Later he wrote, "Barb says I must be afraid of myself. And this may be true. But I want desperately to leap the chasm, to cross from being just good to being truly outstanding."

As the months passed, he gave more thought to resignation. But when he submitted the necessary paperwork, the Army balked. Europe was being "stabilized," the personnel office informed him, and Norm's services were required for at least another year. He appealed to Fergusson, who put the issue to his former classmate and the Army's chief of staff, William Westmoreland. Three days later the orders were cut. Norm went to Tempelhof Airport, boarded a transport jet, and flew back to the States without remorse.

"The Army at West Point was the epitome of what the Army was supposed to be like," he explained years later. "But I found that the Army in many respects did not correspond to that ideal. We were so naïve about what it really entailed. We'd learned a few drills at West

Point and we knew how to march pretty well. But we didn't know anything about killing. We didn't know anything about what life was really like. There was a toy-soldier element to West Point; it's as if we were being trained to be generals, not soldiers.

"My problem, and it wasn't a problem for me as much as it was a problem for the Army, is that I wanted to think too much."

In late July 1971, Jack Wheeler and Art Mosley decided to throw a party. They billed the affair as an FTA celebration; the letters stood for Farewell to Arms, or, for those in the know, Fuck the Army. Jack's resignation request was still mired in the bureaucracy somewhere, but Mosley already had begun working as a real estate developer in Washington. Thanks to Ted Hill, his classmate and partner in snatching the Long Binh jeep, Art had found a loophole. Scanning the fine print of Army regulations, Ted discovered that the military was required to notify officers in writing if they owed an additional period of service in exchange for their graduate schooling. Neither Ted's orders to Stanford nor Art's orders to Harvard had contained the necessary disclosure clause. The Army, which was shrinking anyway as the war wound down, made no effort to contest the appeal, and both men were honorably discharged more than a year early.

Art lived across the hall from Jack and his brother, who shared an apartment on North Rhodes Street in Arlington. The Wheelers' bachelor pad featured cinder block bookcases and a piano on which tin-eared Jack endlessly practiced "Mama's Little Baby Loves Shortnin' Bread." One afternoon, Big Jack and Janet had paid a surprise visit to deliver some pots and pans. As she rang the bell, Janet heard the frantic sounds of debris being shoveled into a closet and what sounded like someone slipping out a back entrance. "Sure is taking them a while to answer," mused Big Jack, who was slightly deaf from thirty years of working in tanks. When the door finally swung open, Jack stood there hyperventilating.

"Mom! Dad! What a surprise! Glad to see you," he said.

"Uh-huh. Sure you are," Janet replied dryly. She privately vowed never again to arrive unannounced.

For their FTA gala, Mosley and the Wheelers decided to leave the doors open to both apartments so that the party could wash back and forth between them. Art mixed a violent punch, a concoction hardly less potent than the Fort Sill muzzleblasters that had felled so many of his classmates during their first class trip in 1965. Next to the stereo Bob stacked the albums he wanted to play: Jimi Hendrix, Creedence Clearwater, the Jefferson Airplane, and others.

Among the guests was Bruns Grayson, who had finished his freshman year at Harvard. Earlier in the summer, Grayson, Mosley, Bob Wheeler, and John Tillson — another '66er — had spent a month floating down the Mississippi River from Hannibal, Missouri, to New Orleans on a twenty-five-foot raft made of planks and oil drums. Jack had remained in Washington, leaving the Huck Finn antics to the Good Bad Boys. "By the end of this trip," Mosley had predicted as they cast off, "we'll be so goddamn tough we'll be able to stick our dicks in the fire." No one tried to prove him wrong.

The party was a smashing success, even provoking a midnight visit from the Arlington police, who asked the revelers to keep the piano and stereo to a modest roar. As Bob adjusted the volume, one of Jack's co-workers from the Pentagon vault cornered him near the piano. "Jack, did you know you got a call today at the office from Army personnel?" he asked. "Your request for early resignation's been approved."

Jack started with surprise. "Really? Today?"

"Yeah. I didn't know whether you'd gotten the message."

Jack moved to the center of the crowded living room, a smile spreading across his face. "Hey, everybody!" he yelled loudly. "I'm out of the fuckin' Army!" And he let loose a long, high-pitched giggle.

Grayson rolled his eyes as he watched Jack accept congratulatory handshakes. Not everyone was amused. Several officers in the room, including a colonel, were clearly nonplused by the outburst. Grayson believed that Jack was wise to leave the service; a man of uncommon talent and sensitivity, he eventually would have been suffocated by the mediocrity now pervading much of the Army. Yet once again, Grayson thought, Captain Wheeler had displayed an uncanny capacity to snatch awkwardness from any situation.

A few days after the party, Jack put together his application to the Virginia Theological Seminary, an Episcopal school south of the Pentagon in Alexandria, Virginia. In the packet, he included a candid letter of recommendation from his uncle, the priest living in Nashville:

> Jack has a very ordered and logical mind regarding study — he is quick of mind and terse in expression, purposive in endeavor, competitive without meaning to be always, but primarily a searching mind . . . He is usually serious, doesn't care much for trifles in conversation.
>
> He lost his way with the church for several years, which bears on his current mode of mind. . . Jack has been one of the most self-centered of men by his own admission, and at least in intention and effort, he has changed this around completely . . . A few years ago, he admittedly cared for nothing but Jack. He is in suspense regarding his life work and this

> causes him some unrest. Despite all his strengths and capacities, he lacks confidence . . .
>
> He is the finest guy I know.

In his application essay, Jack wrote, "I need a chance and a place to get my roots down." Influenced by Dee Brown's *Bury My Heart at Wounded Knee*, which scathingly indicted the behavior of Army officers during the nineteenth-century Indian Wars, Jack fired a broadside at his alma mater:

> My conviction is that most West Pointers in the Army, especially general officers, are morally reprehensible because they blind themselves to much of the evil work that they do . . . My conclusion is that West Pointers in the service overindulge in fantasies of honorable service and significant contribution. They should balance their perception by accepting that their performance has often been despicable, not noble.

The words had gushed out, tapping a reservoir of bile and resentment that was deeper than even Jack had realized. Like many other officers, he had been shaken by the My Lai revelations; William Calley and the other junior officers involved were not West Pointers, but the massacre had left a dark stain on the Army. For the first time, Jack felt ashamed of his profession.

Even though he was accepted at the seminary, he remained uncertain whether to focus his new life as a civilian on the secular or the spiritual, so he pursued both. After leaving the Army on August 3, 1971, Jack moved into St. George's Hall at the seminary. His room, number 103, was comfortable if a trifle austere, and he softened its hard edges with a chair, desk, lamp, sofa bed, and colorful rug. Art Mosley drove down to visit once, but this new religious bent of Jack's made him uncomfortable. "I was afraid he'd reach out and sprinkle me with holy water or something," Art later joked. Bob Wheeler also was perplexed by his brother's retreat into a seminary, but he was no longer surprised by Jack's immersion in subjects that intrigued him. "Most people would take a few night courses at George Washington University to plug gaps in their education," Bob observed. "Not Jack. He goes right to the heart of the matter by learning Greek so he can read the Bible in the original."

To earn a living, Jack accepted an offer to be a senior planner for the new National Railroad Passenger Corporation. Better known as Amtrak, the company had been created by Congress to keep passenger train service alive in the United States. Jack's job, in the L'Enfant Plaza complex in Southwest Washington, involved compiling an inventory of the nation's rail stations to determine Amtrak's fair share of operating expenses. He would fly to Chicago or Los Angeles or New Orleans, where his first question was always "What does it cost to operate this station for a year?" More often than not, no one knew; the station might keep hundreds of different billing accounts, with the track account separate from the building account, which was separate from the account used to run common freight engines. Jack had to determine how much of the cost the railroads paid and how much they passed on to Amtrak. There was little likelihood, he knew, that the railroads had undercharged his company.

He found the work fascinating; it was like being an inspector general. The nation still boasted more than a hundred large depots, many of them called Union Station because they had been constructed by a union of railroads. Most were hemorrhaging money. In Cincinnati, for example, he found that the station, which had been built to handle scores of trains a day, now cost $500,000 a year for service that had dwindled to one morning and one afternoon train. The nation's railroads struck Jack as having a great deal in common with the Army: they remained largely a male domain — some even had male secretaries — with a strict chain of command and an imposing bureaucracy. They also appeared reluctant, at best, to show him their financial records. Once, after arriving in Ogden, Utah, after midnight, he called the president of the Southern Pacific at home to complain that the railroad was not cooperating. "The books were supposed to be laid out and waiting for me when I got here," Jack told the groggy executive. "They're not." After he made a few more persistent calls, the proper records were produced.

When he wasn't traveling, Jack left L'Enfant Plaza from eleven A.M. to one P.M. every day to drive down to the seminary for his class on the Old Testament. He was swept away by the stories of Isaac and Joseph and David, as though hearing the epic for the first time. From the "in the beginning" of Genesis to Malachi's "lest I come and smite the earth with a curse," the Bible seemed to him to be the musings of ancient authors who were trying, precisely as Jack was trying, to make sense of a life that was often not sensible. The recognition that there was one God, who manifested Himself through history and who loved His creation, struck Jack as the most profound and comforting truth imaginable.

Yet as the months rolled past, the old question persisted: What are you going to do with the rest of your life? Hovering between the worlds of the seminary and the National Railroad Passenger Corporation was not dissimilar to his firstie year at West Point, when he had flitted between the life of a cadet and the backstage life of Lincoln Center. The Amtrak work was challenging, much like putting together a complex jigsaw puzzle. But he found a certain hollowness in the job. Despite the intemperate attack on West Pointers in his seminary essay, Jack's impulse to render service for the common good remained strong; as Bruns Grayson put it, "Jack took off the uniform but he hasn't shed even one thin layer of duty, honor, country." Moreover, although he enjoyed the solitude and structure of the seminary, it became clear to him that he was not called to be an Episcopal priest.

Two things happened almost simultaneously that caused him to change course. First, he applied to and was accepted by Yale Law School. Three more years of schooling would give him time to ponder the future, and he figured the law would open up dozens of vocational possibilities. He would go to New Haven after all — ten years after his mother had first dreamed of sending him there.

Second, he fell in love with a woman named Elisa Lyles Desportes. Jack met her at a rainy picnic held at one of the high-rise apartment complexes in Bethesda, Maryland. She was fair-haired, with a cheerful, round face and a fetching Southern accent. Her family, originally French Huguenots, had settled in Columbia, South Carolina, where her father ran a large dental supply company. After receiving a master's degree in religion at the same seminary where Jack now lived, she had undertaken the study of Episcopal parishes: why some thrive while others founder. Though serious and committed, she had a vibrant sense of humor and an infectious, lilting laugh; Jack thought they were well matched, with innumerable interests in common. Perhaps, if things worked out, Elisa would follow him to New Haven; for now, he could commute to Washington for occasional weekends.

One trait that had remained constant in Jack was a flair for the dramatic. Whether solemnly informing his mother in 1962 that he had decided to attend West Point or announcing his departure from the Army in the middle of a crowded party in 1971, he had always shown a sense of theater. Thus, on the Saturday before leaving for law school, he rose at midnight, dressed quickly, and drove to the Lincoln Memorial.

Heat lightning split the sky to the west; thunder rumbled in the distance. Washington's summer humidity pressed against him like a damp cloak as Jack walked up the marble steps and through the double row of fluted columns, but inside the temple, the rectangular sanctuary was as cool and tranquil as a tomb. Lincoln, his craggy face beautifully floodlit, gazed into the middle distance at the shimmering image of the Washington Monument in the Reflecting Pool. His full lower lip seemed to verge on a marble smile.

Lincoln's Second Inaugural Address was carved on the north wall. Jack read the words slowly, murmuring the honeyed phrases as if reciting a prayer. *With malice toward none; with charity for all; with firmness in the right, as God gives us to see the right, let us strive on to finish the work we are in.*

Wheeling about, he walked to the south wall and read the Gettysburg Address with the same deliberation:

> It is rather for us to be here dedicated to the great task remaining before us; that from these honored dead we take increased devotion to that cause for which they gave the last full measure of devotion; that we here highly resolve that these dead shall not have died in vain; that this nation, under God, shall have a new birth of freedom; and that government of the people, by the people, for the people, shall not perish from the earth.

Jack trotted back down the steps, a lump the size of a goose egg in his throat. *Let us strive on to finish the work we are in.* Sometimes, he reflected, all a man needed for fortification was a few words of advice from an old country lawyer.

Tom Carhart, having touched bottom and begun what he hoped would be an ascent to the surface, also had decided to give law school a try. Looking for both a profession and a chance to stabilize his life, Tom, like Jack Wheeler, had concluded that the practice of law would be an honorable occupation.

The year following his resignation and release from Walter Reed had been difficult. He and Susan had moved to Amherst — "crash landed," as Tom put it — where he enrolled in the graduate business school at the University of Massachusetts. To earn money, he worked for several months at minimum wage as the dishwasher in a bar. Then he found a job supervising a five-man ditch-digging crew. For thirty-five hours a week, Tom labored in a warren of trenches being excavated for water, sewer, and power lines. The work usually left him too tired at night to study. At the end of the semester, he took incompletes in all his courses, which subsequently reverted to F's.

A company in Springfield then hired him to sell adding machines. Every morning Tom would make the rounds with sample machines on the back seat of his car. Within a few days, he recognized that he was a wretched salesman. "Where'd ya go?" the sales supervisor invariably asked at the end of yet another fruitless day.

Tom sighed. "Joe's Food Market."

"Who'd ya talk to?"

"Joe."

"Did he want a machine?"

"No."

"Why not?"

"Can't read."

After two months and only one sale, Tom was fired. He didn't care, happy just to leave the demeaning job behind. But now what? He had failed in the Army — there was no other way to put it, regardless of extenuating circumstances, and he was candid about his shortcomings as an officer — and now he was failing in the civilian world. A friendly guidance counselor suggested law school. Why not? Tom thought. He applied to Harvard, Yale, and the University of Michigan, and was accepted by the last.

For the first year at Michigan, his bad luck continued. Susan got pregnant, but the baby boy, premature, died at birth. At first, the shattering experience drew the couple closer; then they began to drift apart. Tom had seen in Susan a stirring creature whom he could refine and mold, but she had her own ideas about wedlock. When she suggested that they follow some of the precepts in a book she had recently read advocating marital independence, he assented, though such "liberal" notions ran completely contrary to his traditional notions of wedded bliss. Bit by bit, the emotional distance between them widened.

He nearly flunked out of Michigan after the first year. Achieving an undistinguished record of straight C's, he found that the gaps in his short-term memory were lethal in law school. Maybe I should quit, Tom told himself. Yet, lacking better options, he was reluctant to forfeit his Veterans Administration stipend. Moreover, since his stay at Walter Reed, Tom had placed great faith in the doctors' suggestion that the fifth anniversary after his accident would mark a significant benchmark in his recovery. When the date arrived — April 23, 1971 — Tom felt as though an enormous weight had been lifted from his shoulders. Instead of finding a summer job, he took two law courses, Evidence and Commercial Transactions, and earned a B+ in each. Hallelujah, he congratulated himself gleefully, I'm cured!

The fabled West Point Protective Association, he discovered, continued to operate even in the civilian world. Tom found two other academy classmates enrolled in law school at Ann Arbor, both of whom helped him wade through torts and contracts and other legal arcana. One was Norm Fretwell, who had recently returned from Berlin. The other, a year ahead of Tom in the law program, was Jeffrey Smith, the tall, quiet Iowan, whose wife, Claudia, had resented the constraints of being an Army wife at Fort Benning and Schweinfurt.

The Smiths had endured their own tribulations. Jeff, who was still in the Army while attending law school under an Army judge advocate program, was one of the very few '66ers who hadn't been to Vietnam, largely because of a quirk in the timing of his assignments. (Another was the West Point basketball star Mike Silliman, captain of the 1968 U.S. Olympic team in Mexico City.) Even as a cadet, Jeff had been skeptical about the war; now, in April 1971 as a second-year law student, he sent a letter to *The New York Times* applauding the court-martial conviction of William Calley for the My Lai war crimes but also suggesting that "until the nation is prepared to evaluate honestly the entire nature of the war, solitary trials will remain, regardless of their correctness, uncomfortable salients."

That measured, analytical approach was found wanting in Ann Arbor. One night at an informal dinner party with a half-dozen friends from the law school, Jeff and Claudia were sitting on the couch when a discussion of the war suddenly turned into an inquisition. How can you stay in the Army? the others demanded of Jeff. What's the matter with you? Why aren't you in Canada?

The hostility was disconcerting, even frightening. These people with their jabbing fingers and interrogatories were as hysterical as a mob of vigilantes. "You have to understand," Jeff replied, thinking of his old poetry-writing roommate John Hoskins, "some of my closest friends have fought and died there." When the others scoffed and continued to pound him with accusations, he regretted the rebuttal. By invoking Hoskins and his other dead classmates, he had, he felt, soiled their honor and cheapened their sacrifice.

On another occasion, Claudia was having lunch with a friend who said, "I think anybody who went to Vietnam was stupid." Here we go again, Claudia thought. She parried the insult. "My husband's class had one of the highest death rates in Vietnam of any of the classes from West Point," she offered. The other woman then cited a study which reported that among the twelve hundred students in the Harvard class of 1968, only two dozen went to Vietnam and none had been killed.

"Well," Claudia agreed, "the war has caused terrible divisions, I guess."

The other woman smirked. "Yeah, it tells you who's smarter."

Because of such incidents, the Smiths, though reluctant to take sides, found their neutrality difficult to maintain. The strident opponents of the war seemed to demand a quarantine of anyone who failed to embrace their dissent, and the Smiths began socializing only with those who had served or whose views were not girded with reproach. Even the movie *M*A*S*H* was upsetting; while the rest of the audience hooted with laughter, Jeff and Claudia sat in silence as they watched the painful allegory of war's absurdity.

The Smiths, perhaps because they ably bolstered each other, could withstand the isolation, but Tom Carhart was desperate not to be pushed away by his peers. He felt that he had done his bit, both in the jungle and in defending the war at home. One evening, when he still lived in Amherst, Tom had telephoned the student radio station during a call-in talk show about Vietnam. As he began listing the usual West Point debating points about the American commitment to the Southeast Asian Treaty Organization, the station cut him off. Fuck you! he shouted, slamming down the receiver.

Now, in Ann Arbor, near the birthplace of the radical Students for Democratic Action (SDS), he was determined not to be cut off again. Of all the injuries he had suffered in the past five years, none lingered more painfully than the memory of being spat upon at O'Hare Airport. Whatever it takes, Tom told himself, I don't ever want my countrymen to spit at me again.

What it took, of course, was acquiescence to the prevailing antimilitary sentiment. He began by smoking marijuana, frequently. That seemed a necessary initiation rite, and the habit was certainly pleasant enough. He let his hair grow and cultivated a mustache, a wild, brushy thing that became his trademark. Although he wore his Army fatigue jacket to class — adorned with Screaming Eagle patch, Combat Infantryman's Badge, jump wings, and the Purple Heart with its oak leaf cluster — he frequently joined in the denunciations of Richard Nixon and Henry Kissinger. When George McGovern opened a campaign office on South University Avenue, Tom volunteered to do some filing and other scut-work. He wrote letters to the student newspaper deploring the corrupt, tyrannical South Vietnamese government, and ran unsuccessfully for student council president on an anarchist's platform, vowing to "pave the Quad" and have janitors remove pubic hairs from the toilet bowls three times a day. He filled out an application form to join Vietnam Veterans Against the War, although when the organization asked for the $10 fee, Tom sent a copy of his Purple Heart citations with a note attached: "I already paid my dues."

To the delight of Jeff Smith and his other friends, Tom's old effervescence had returned. "Carhart's not a loose cannon," one classmate said; "he's a rocket without fins." Yet this relentless effort to fit in left him with a vague sense of disquiet. He had tied his fortunes to the anti-establishment strain of his generation at the expense of his truer self. And although he was happier than he had been in years, he still lacked inner tranquillity.

One piece of unfinished business from the past remained to be resolved while Tom was in law school. His $400,000 lawsuit against Bob Albright for damages from the Corvette wreck was about to come to trial, more than five years after the case had been filed. When the court was ready to hear the suit, Tom flew back to White Plains, New York; so did Albright, who was a captain stationed at Fort Lewis. The amount of money involved frightened Albright, but he still felt a warm friendship for Carhart. No one more than Tom, he thought, embodied those raucous, carefree cadet days, now gone forever.

Tom felt uneasy, even guilty. He was doing what his lawyers and insurance company said he should do, but suing a classmate and close friend was an unsavory business. Other men from '66 had inevitably picked sides in the case. The gist of Tom's allegation was that Albright had been irresponsibly negligent by driving after several hours of drinking; some believed that Tom was disingenuous in contending that he would have hesitated to get in the car had he known that the driver was drunk.

The accident had erased Tom's memory of much of the spring of 1966; the suit against Albright, he convinced himself, was one way to recapture that lost season. To assuage his conscience, he insisted that his lawyers secretly sign a document agreeing to accept no award higher than the $200,000 covered by Albright's insurance.

On the first day of the trial, the judge pressured both sides to resolve the matter out of court; the insurance companies agreed to a $35,000 settlement. Although Tom didn't know it at the time, the defense had a secret witness waiting in the wings. George Crocker, who had flown to New York from Erlangen, West Germany, was prepared to testify that Carhart also was drinking heavily with Albright on that Saturday afternoon. George's evidence of Tom's contributory negligence would have made for a very messy trial indeed, as attorney Carhart later realized.

Tom collected $9000 of the settlement after paying his legal fees and medical bills. He and Susan spent $5000 of it on a new Pontiac Bonneville. Yet Tom had never earned a less satisfying nickel in his life. In every respect, the price of collecting this small windfall was more than he could afford.

One other episode distracted Tom from his law studies at Ann Arbor and made him recognize that there were certain lines he would not cross, even in his new incarnation as a pot-smoking, left-leaning, Nixon-baiting aggrieved veteran. One day he received a surprise phone call from his classmate Ronald Bartek. The popular and articulate Bartek, who had been tortured by some of Charlie Beckwith's overzealous men during Ranger training, was now among the most vocal antiwar West Pointers in the country.

I'm calling some of the guys in the class, including you and Norm Fretwell, he told Tom, because a few of us in Washington don't feel we can remain silent anymore about some of the things we saw in the war, like phony body counts and the shelling of enemy hospitals. I'm going to testify before a congressional committee and want to know if you can help.

Tom hesitated. He admired Bartek as a dynamic leader, someone who could inspire others and who was passionately committed to public service. But Tom sensed that the water here was deep and dangerous.

I don't know, Ron, Tom answered. I'd like to help, but I don't know.

How about if we send someone out to talk to you about your experiences? Bartek suggested.

Sure, said Tom, I'll be glad to talk to him.

Not long afterward, Bartek and four other West Pointers testified before an informal House committee on "war crimes." Bartek, convinced of his duty to speak out, alleged that Major General Ellis Williamson, while commanding the 25th Infantry Division, sanctioned an artillery bombardment of an enemy hospital across the border in the Parrot's Beak region of Cambodia. He also told of hearing the corps commander, Lieutenant General Julian J. Ewell, lament that his units were "only killing two thousand of the little bastards a month," a complaint that allegedly resulted in monthly body count quotas.

The testimony received extensive coverage by the newspapers and television networks. That night, Bartek's father called him. "Well, Hot Shot, I saw you on television today." The senior Bartek paused. "I can't tell you how proud of you I am. I put in twenty-eight years in the military and I'm proud of it and proud of my country. I know you are, too. But I've watched this war and I know you have, too. I'm glad to have a son who sees what's right and tries to do something about it." Ron Bartek later repeated the story to Studs Terkel during a Chicago talk show, moving both of them to tears.

As agreed, Tom met in Ann Arbor with a lawyer who arrived from Washington to gather information that might support the dissident West Pointers. The whole business made Tom queasy. No stricture had been drummed into cadets at West Point more relentlessly than the notion that politics was none of a soldier's business; Dennis Mahan, one of the academy's most influential figures in the nineteenth century, had followed the precept to the point of refusing to vote while still in uniform. Even for ex-soldiers, the tradition was sometimes difficult to ignore.

More to the point, however, Tom had nothing to say. He had heard about inflated body counts, mistreated prisoners, and supposed violations of the Geneva Convention. But he had never witnessed such things, and he was not about to claim otherwise. "Were you just winking at the regulations?" asked the lawyer. He gave Carhart an exaggerated wink as if to demonstrate.

The gesture angered Tom. "No," he replied, in a tone of flat, cold finality. The lawyer left.

Bartek's charges soon blew over. Some of his classmates were pleased to hear him speak his mind, but the allegations infuriated others, including Matt Harrison, who had served part of his second tour as General Williamson's aide at Cu Chi. By chance, in a St. Louis bookstore one day, Matt came across a volume in which the transcript of the House hearing was reprinted.

Sitting crosslegged on the floor, he read the entire account with growing irritation. Most of the allegations, he felt, were drawn from innuendo and hearsay. We never had enough information to locate an enemy hospital, much less shell it, Matt thought, and there was no way that Williamson, at least, had ever pressed his commanders to falsify body counts. Yes, Matt agreed, some units inflated their body counts. But these assertions seemed appallingly flimsy.

He snapped the book shut and left the store, seething. Ron Bartek and the others didn't know what they were talking about, Matt concluded. He was convinced that their charges were not only wrong but dishonorable, since the furor undoubtedly had damaged Williamson's career.

For years, the matter rankled Matt. Sometimes when the subject came up, those near him noticed that the muscles tightened in his jaw, his brows knit into a frown, and his eyes seemed to darken, as though smudged with pain. It was yet another demonstration that even after the shooting stopped, the wounding continued.

14

A HARD PEACE

EVEN BEFORE the negotiators in Paris stopped bickering over the shape of the conference table and started to bicker over the shape of peace, the United States Army had begun to reap the whirlwind of America's ten-year war. Abraham Lincoln had believed in waging a hard war followed by a "soft peace" that would bind the wounds of the Civil War. Yet more than a century later, as another divisive conflict drew to a close, it was evident that the hard war in Southeast Asia would be succeeded by a hard peace. As the Army had borne the brunt of war, now the Army would bear the brunt of peace.

Ironically, the pain of peace was felt most acutely not in the United States but in Europe. In June 1971, a new general, four stars on his shoulders, arrived in West Germany to take command of the U.S. Seventh Army. Michael S. Davison, in a stellar career, had served as West Point's commandant from 1963 to 1965 and most recently commanded the American invasion of Cambodia. Returning to Europe was something of a homecoming for Davison, but the Seventh Army he had known as a twenty-eight-year-old battalion commander was a far different entity from the force he now led. Created before the invasion of Sicily, the Seventh Army by V-E Day, in 1945, had become one of the greatest fighting forces in the history of warfare: "Born at sea, baptized in blood, and crowned in glory," as Patton had remarked. Now it was crowned in chaos. Mike Davison arrived in Heidelberg largely unaware of how far the army had fallen in twenty-six years, but within three months the general offered a frank and public accounting: "The price of Vietnam has been a terrible one. In terms of the casualties, in terms of national treasure of both men and dollars that have been spent, it was a terrible price . . . The Seventh Army here in Europe is still suffering today as a result of Vietnam because we had to wreck the Seventh Army in order to keep Vietnam going."

A wrecked Army it was, a "bored and ignored" Army that had been bled white to keep the U.S. war machine in Southeast Asia supplied with officers, experienced NCOs, matériel, and money. In some respects the 300,000-man American force in Germany was less an army than an armed, savage mob of New World Visigoths. Standards had collapsed; morale was a farce; and discipline in many units resembled something very close to anarchy.

There were countless depradations, each assiduously chronicled by the German press. AMERICAN TERROR AS NEVER BEFORE, warned a headline in the *Neue Revue*. VIETNAM HAS POISONED THE U.S. ARMY IN EUROPE, echoed the *Berlin Tagesspiegel*. In the town of Neu Ulm, eight GIs kidnaped a sixteen-year-old German girl in July 1971 and gang-raped her. The following weekend, American soldiers committed eight additional assaults. Firemen in the town refused to respond to a blaze in the barracks for fear of being beaten. A month later, fifteen soldiers raped two girls camping beside the Danube. In Stuttgart, a hundred soldiers armed with knives and stones fought German police for five hours in what was described as the city's bloodiest fighting since World War II. In Wiesbaden, fifteen teenagers — all children of American soldiers — first beat up a German man tending his garden, then battered two local utility workers. When the police arrived, only by drawing their guns could they drive away two hundred counterattacking American high school students.

Every week, it seemed, soldiers committed another unspeakable crime. In the early morning of October 6, 1972, a deserter being returned to his unit aboard the Alps Express overpowered and shot his two guards near Göttingen, murdered a German rail hostess, and then heaved the three bodies from the train. Later that month, when a hashish deal turned bad in Augsburg, a trio of GIs shot two German boys, bashed their bodies with rocks, then kidnaped and raped a twenty-year-old German girl in a bizarre attempt to establish an alibi for the drug killings.

The list of crimes rolled on and on — murders, rapes, muggings, and robberies by the thousands. Gangs of soldiers roamed the streets of Munich and Nuremberg while citizens cowered behind locked doors like the terrorized townsfolk in a Wild West melodrama. Occasionally, the Germans retaliated. When an abusive soldier picked an argument with the manager of a Bamberg restaurant, twenty diners clubbed him to death and tossed his body into the alley out back. "One can safely assume," the local newspaper observed primly, "that in this case the pent-up emotions against American soldiers in Bamberg gushed forth like [water from] a broken dam."

Part of the Vietnam bequest was rampant drug addiction. As the war sputtered to a close, an estimated 10 to 15 percent of the American privates and corporals in Vietnam were heroin addicts. A fix that cost $40 in the United States was only $1.50 in Saigon. An eight-inch marijuana joint cost a nickel; for pocket change, a soldier could easily remain stoned for a week. In just the first three weeks of October 1970, thirty-five drug overdose deaths had been reported in Vietnam. Soon, similar problems cropped up at home. Fort Hood, Texas, became known as Fort Head; officers at Fort Dix, New Jersey, stopped posting armed sentries because their rifles were so frequently stolen by junkies, who sold the weapons on the black market.

As the epidemic spread to Europe, hashish became as common in many units as cigarettes or Life Savers. An enterprising soldier could earn $100,000 a year by driving to Munich once a month and buying wholesale a load of Peshawar black or Lebanese red, which Greek and Turkish hash merchants sold in planks three inches wide and a quarter inch thick. After returning to his unit and carving the planks into grams, suitable for retail sales, the entrepreneur could peddle each gram for $1.25 to $2.50. Some soldiers smoked more than a hundred grams a month, lighting up with the compulsive frequency of a three-pack-a-day Marlboro man.

Drug abuse among soldiers was hardly a new phenomenon. During the Civil War, and again in the 1870s, the American Army had endured rashes of opium addiction. Sometimes, intoxicants had even been officially sanctioned to bolster the troops' courage; Napoleon's soldiers received triple rations of brandy before the Battle of Austerlitz. Yet rarely if ever had a modern fighting force been as consistently high as the American Seventh Army. In one artillery unit at Neu Ulm, for example, authorities estimated that 50 to 80 percent of the sixteen hundred enlisted men were stoned on duty, and that half of them also used hard drugs.

The other cancer eating at the Army's vitals was racial hatred. Black rage, which had exploded in the States during the Watts riot in 1965 and the widespread disturbances after the assassination of Martin Luther King, Jr., in 1968, continued to fester in the military. Many black soldiers felt like second-class citizens; although 14 percent of the Army's enlisted troops were black in 1971, the officer corps remained 97 percent white. Blacks and whites often segregated themselves in the barracks, which became tinderboxes of tension. Graffiti were as ubiquitous on Army posts as on New York subway walls: KILL WHITEY; BLACK IS BEAUTIFUL; KKK, GET THE NIGGERS.

Court-martial boards sometimes acquitted AWOL soldiers, who argued successfully that the barracks had become so dangerous that sensible men had to flee for their lives. Lopsided brawls, in which a single white soldier or a single black was savagely pummeled by a gang of the opposite race, occurred so frequently that commanders openly longed for the days when GIs had settled their differences one on one in a bare-knuckled fistfight, surrounded by a ring of cheering spectators.

In Europe, blacks also resented the Germans, never known for racial understanding. Black soldiers endured outrageous discrimination in housing, restaurants, and even prostitution. (Hookers frequently doubled their fees for a black soldier.) Blacks committed a sharply disproportionate share of the crimes and atrocities against German civilians; during a twelve-month period in 1970 and 1971, black Americans in Germany were charged with three thousand violent crimes.

"They are supposed to protect us. But they rob, murder, and rape," a German magazine chided. "American soldiers in Germany arouse naked fear."

As the catastrophe befalling the Army in Europe and elsewhere unfolded, it assumed the proportions of classical tragedy. The victors of World War II had been filled with hubris, and by the early 1960s, the "disease of victory" had become malignant. What chance did a few barefoot peasants in Vietnam — those "raggedy-ass little bastards," as senior American generals in Saigon had called them — have against the world's mightiest military power? Who could believe that ideology and nationalism would triumph over napalm and carpet bombing? And, of course, those exhibiting arrogance and overweening pride always got their just deserts.

Certainly many of the Army's wounds appeared to be self-inflicted. As one government study concluded in late 1971, this was "an Army which bordered on self-destruction primarily because of internal factors." Even before the last body bag had been shipped home from Vietnam, everyone from lieutenant to lieutenant general recognized that the Army had made some regrettable mistakes: six-month command rotations; obsession with quantifiable indices such as body counts; oversupervision of junior officers and NCOs; micro-management from Washington.

The officer corps had become top-heavy, with officers now accounting for 15 percent of the Army; that was more than double the percentage during World War II. One Defense Department study called it "the most overmanned, overstaffed, overofficered" armed force in history. The Army, one colonel complained, had become "a dragon with a huge tail and tiny teeth."

Moreover, professional officers found it difficult to match the ideal; the warrior had become a manager. Two devastating studies by the Army War College in the early 1970s held up a clear looking glass in which the service could behold itself. Although the officer corps continued to pay homage to duty, honor, and country, the first report concluded, "there are widespread and often significant differences between the ideal standards of the Army and the prevailing standards."

What that meant, according to the second study, was the frequent appearance of the "ambitious, transitory commander — marginally skilled in the complexities of his duties — engulfed in producing transitory results, fearful of personal failure, too busy to talk with or listen to his subordinates, and determined to submit acceptable, optimistic reports which reflect faultless completion of a variety of tasks at the expense of the sweat and frustration of his subordinates."

The officer corps, to its enormous credit, never complained during or after Vietnam of being betrayed at home, never evinced the kind of bitterness toward the Republic that had poisoned some defeated armies. Yet a certain maundering self-pity was apparent. Even Westmorcland kept a small card in his breast pocket with a quotation from John W. Fortesque's history of the British army from 1899 to 1930: "The builders of this empire were not worthy of such an army. Two centuries of persecution could not wear out its patience; two centuries of thankless toil could not abate its ardor; two centuries of conquest could not awaken its insolence. Dutiful to its masters, merciful to its enemies, it clung steadfastly to its old, simple ideas — obedience, service, sacrifice."

The U.S. Army could likewise cling to those "old, simple ideas," but it could no longer entertain the illusion of invincibility. The war had been lost, the Army beaten. For many officers, that realization made the hard peace even harder. As the writer James Fallows later observed, "Whatever damage the war in Vietnam did to the self-confidence and certainty of the nation, it did that much, squared, to the professional soldier."

Like any army moving from war to peace, this Army was entering a period in which it would search high and low for its soul. Only the vanquished truly learn anything from the last war, according to an ancient maxim, and the issue now confronting America was whether the defeated nation and the nation's vanquished Army would learn anything from Vietnam.

All of these problems and more greeted Captain George Crocker on his arrival in Germany in the fall of 1971. Like General Davison, he had transferred to the Seventh Army directly from Vietnam, knowing little about the true state of American forces in Europe. In fact, George was badly misinformed. Europe had been "stabilized," according to the scuttlebutt at Long Binh; the problems of discipline and manpower shortages of the late 1960s supposedly were on the wane. About the only discouraging word came from West Point classmate Jim Dickens, whom George had seen shortly before leaving Vietnam.

"Erlangen!" Dickens exclaimed when he heard where Crocker was headed. "I just left there. It's terrible. You'll want to get out of the Army after you've been there. Go get your orders changed. Do it now, George."

George was taken aback for a moment, but he quickly brushed aside the warning. Having been a company commander at Fort Bragg between Vietnam tours, he knew that there was little excitement to be found now in the shrinking stateside Army. Living in Europe with Vonda and their two daughters would be an adventure; he had wanted to return ever since his brief stint as a "third lieutenant" before cow year at the academy. Besides, if he requested an ITT move from Vietnam — intertheater transfer — rather than a PCS from CONUS — a permanent change of station from the continental United States — his waiting time on the housing list for good quarters would be shortened by thirteen months. That was just one of the many acronym-laden tricks of the trade crucial to the pursuit of happiness in the Army.

After arriving by Pan Am charter in Frankfurt, the Crockers were driven in an Army staff car to Erlangen. The pretty university town, about ten miles northwest of Nuremberg, immediately enchanted them with its red-roofed buildings and narrow serpentine streets named after Bismarck and Hindenburg, Beethoven and Goethe. The *Altstadt* — old city — was founded in 1367, but Erlangen's enduring prosperity had begun in the seventeenth century with the arrival of French Protestant refugees, who established a leather and hosiery industry. Yes, the Crockers soon learned, there was a bit of anti-American sentiment — students occasionally demonstrated with the usual placards and boorish epithets — and you never knew when the *Polizei* would stop you at an Autobahn roadblock to search the trunk for fugitive terrorists from the Baader-Meinhof gang. But compared with what Vonda had endured at Forts Bragg and Benning, Germany at first blush seemed relatively subdued.

The Crockers lived off post in a top-floor apartment originally designed as maids' quarters. A long hall resembling a bowling lane ran from the front door to the rear of the flat; seven bedrooms and a large kitchen opened onto the corridor. Cheryl and Tara slept in bunk beds in one bedroom, and another was converted into a playroom with wall-to-wall mattresses. The sloped living room ceiling reflected the steep pitch of the roof, and a pair of doors led, respectively, to a room with a bathtub and another room containing several toilet stalls and a brace of sinks. But in its quirky, feather-duster fashion, the apartment was perfectly charming. They liked the neighborhood, too: a bakery down the street provided fresh bread and strudel, and on Sundays Bavarian families with wicker baskets full of roast sausage and berry wine sometimes picnicked beneath a big oak tree on the Schenckstrasse out front.

The families of American servicemen in Europe usually sorted into two categories. The first lived in American ghettoes, ate American food, and saved all their money to vacation at home in the States. The second was more adventuresome, enjoying life in the Old World as much as time and money would permit. The Crockers fit squarely into this latter group. Vonda kept the family on a tight cash budget — an Army captain only earned $875 a month — so that they could ski in the Alps near Garmisch-Partenkirchen, enjoy the Oktoberfest in Munich, and even travel to Spain. Closer to home, they might take tea with the Germans in the forest on Sunday afternoon or visit one of Bavaria's picturesque villages, where, after ratcheting down the price over a few beers, they commissioned a master cabinetmaker to build them a grandfather clock. In the summer of 1972, they drove to Munich one morning to see the field hockey and high-jump trials at the Summer Olympics, before watching in horror on television the next day as terrorists slaughtered eleven Israeli athletes and coaches.

As much as he enjoyed Europe, however, George soon realized that Jim Dickens had a point. The mechanized brigade of three tank battalions and an infantry battalion at Erlangen crowded a cassern barely a mile in diameter, with cobblestone streets and mustard-hued stucco buildings that had been used by the German army during the world wars. The brigade, George saw, was a true microcosm of the troubled Seventh Army. After a stint as the battalion S3 — the operations officer — he took command of C Company's 177 soldiers, of whom one-fourth were black. A significant number of both whites and blacks in the company were heroin addicts.

Racial brawls became commonplace. One night during a turf battle in a club off post, a half-dozen blacks were knifed and then heaved over the wall of stone and barbed wire ringing the cassern. Another time, a white and a black got into an argument over a girl at the enlisted men's club. The two soldiers stepped outside and a minute later the black staggered back into the club, clutching his bloody stomach and screaming, "Whitey cut me!" The ensuing rumble — fought with jagged beer bottles and chair legs — spilled from the club into the three tank battalions, one after another. The soldiers burned a barracks and a battalion logistics annex before MPs finally restored order. During yet another riot, George was summoned from the apartment to muster his company. As he drove toward the barracks, a mob of black soldiers appeared out of nowhere, engulfing his car. An image flashed through his mind of the vehicle being rocked, rolled, and set ablaze. But, like a flash flood roiling past a big rock, the men surged around him toward the motor pool. "Last time we had a goddamn riot they stole all our tools," one sergeant explained bitterly after George rolled down the car window. "So we're going over to guard our tanks. They ain't gonna get our stuff this time."

Other officers didn't fare as well. One day not long after he arrived, when most of the troops had left Erlangen on an exercise and the cassern was nearly deserted, George, sitting at his desk, heard a loud *pop*.

"Goddamn, sir!" exclaimed the battalion operations sergeant, John LeGow. "That was a shot!"

"Naw, Sergeant LeGow," George said with a shake of the head, "that couldn't have been a shot."

LeGow hurried to the window. "Goddamn, sir, take a look."

In the middle of an open area near the barracks lay one of the battalion commanders, writhing in pain. He had been shot through the fatty tissue of his potbelly. As a medic sprinted to the lieutenant colonel's side, George ran into the barracks. The shooter, a private who had just returned from the rifle range with a few smuggled rounds in his pocket, still stood by the window with his M-16. He was disarmed and arrested, and the colonel, after recovering from his wound, remained in command. The incident kept the cassern buzzing for weeks.

At Erlangen, George discovered that among the many changes sweeping through the Army was an erosion of the company commander's omnipotence. As recently as the late 1960s, a young captain had been invested with the power of a feudal thane. Within his company, he paid, fed, housed, clothed, and disciplined the troops; if a soldier bounced a single check, he could expect his company commander to confiscate his pay, draft a repayment schedule for the soldier's debtors, and dole out a weekly pittance of spending money like a stern father reining in a prodigal teenager. At Fort Bragg, George had even had the power of "blood stripes": an errant sergeant or corporal would be marched to the battalion sergeant major, who ripped off the soldier's rank chevrons and taped them to the sleeve of a more deserving man.

Now, much of that clout was gone. The company payroll, dining, housing, clothing, and even some of the discipline were under a central authority. No longer did the seventeenth-century officers' dictum apply: "Pay well, command well, hang well." Hanging, of course, was long gone. Pay was paltry at best — a private first class earned $282.65 a month — and signs of poverty among American troops in Germany became more evident as the value of the dollar plummeted.

About all that remained was to try to command well. At times, George wondered whether that was possible. This was the third company he had commanded, but none of his leadership experience had prepared him for men who were so alienated, so unmotivated, so high. The soldiers often expressed their indifference with the phrase "mox nix," a corruption of the German *machts nicht*, "it doesn't matter." General Davison's frank comments about the wrecked Seventh Army had simply disclosed to the world what had heretofore been an open secret in Europe: the American Army was the most fragile of paper tigers. George was stunned by how quickly it had collapsed.

He routinely ignored an edict prohibiting officers from entering the barracks alone at night. (One first sergeant had been stabbed in his bed by soldiers who kicked in the door and fell on him with flashing knives.) Strong, strapping, and not easily intimidated, George figured he could take care of himself. But the state of the barracks never failed to astonish him. Usually, all of the hall lights had been smashed, so the corridors were dark and unnerving. In the typical soldier's room, the door had been removed and laid across two Volkswagen tire rims to fashion a coffee table, invariably laden with several pounds of melted candle wax and incense ash. The windows were painted black. An ultraviolet bulb replaced the ceiling light, the better to highlight Day-Glo wall posters that depicted copulation positions — one for each sign of the zodiac — and President Nixon squatting on the commode. The bunk had been dismantled and replaced by a bare floor pad. In the corner stood an impressive pyramid of beer cartons, stacked to the ceiling.

The Army's temporary forbearance in permitting such hovels reflected an effort to make the service more attractive as the nation eliminated conscription and moved toward an all-volunteer military. Under Westmoreland, the Army abolished reveille and permitted beer-vending machines in the barracks. Basic training had been eased, and bayonet instructors replaced the traditional "Kill! Kill!" with a more sanitary "Yah! Yah!" Recruiting posters — which had once depicted a stern, finger-jabbing Uncle Sam — now were replaced by slick, Madison Avenue television commercials. "I Want YOU" was massaged into "Today's Army Wants to Join You." (Nothing more infuriated traditional officers and NCOs, who found the advertising campaign smarmy and unctuous.) "Commanders at all levels," the Pentagon decreed, "must challenge their noncommissioned officers to stay ahead of changes in the country and society."

Some of the VOLAR — volunteer Army — reforms struck George as appropriate and well intentioned. The impulse to treat men as adults rather than as recalcitrant children seemed sensible if the country wanted them to volunteer for Army service. But the timing was terrible. Coming as they did on the heels of the drug, race, and morale problems bred during the war, the reforms made a mockery of the discipline needed in any military unit. "Discipline is the soul of an army," George Washington had warned, and that was no different two hundred years later. So many officers and NCOs had been killed in Vietnam, or had subsequently left the service, that the Army's bedrock of experienced leadership was extremely thin. Moreover, the caliber of troops was poor; as often as not they were indeed recalcitrant children.

Once established in Heidelberg, General Davison began to take drastic steps. He relieved officers who seemed less than committed to eradicating racism, and he blacklisted and publicly identified German businesses that discriminated. Commanders began to ship home troublemaking blacks and whites, often with dishonorable discharges. In a hunt for drugs, commanders also conducted frequent searches of barracks and automobiles, force-marching suspected users to a physician for examination.

At Erlangen, the effort to turn things around began with the Great Raid. One day in mid 1972, George's new battalion commander summoned his officers. "Enough is enough," he decreed. "We're going to clean up the barracks, tonight, after duty hours. Go home for supper and come back at 1900 hours." That night, like revenue agents storming a speakeasy, George and the other officers swept through the rooms, kicking out the painted windows and tearing down the obscene posters. Debris cascaded into the yard outside, forming a small mountain of tire rims, beer cartons, and broken furniture. "Sir," one soldier confided to George, "to be honest, we're glad somebody finally told us to get rid of this junk."

In C Company, George began weeding out the incorrigibles through a new Army discharge procedure known as Chapter 13, which restored some of the commander's authority. He started with a group he sarcastically dubbed the Magnificent Seven, heroin addicts whose arms were peppered with needle tracks from wrist to biceps. Each had washed out of the brigade's drug rehabilitation program; each had four or five Article 15s on his record.

"You guys are getting chaptered out of the Army," George announced to them one morning as they stood before him, slack-mouthed and glassy-eyed. "I don't really know how to do it yet, but I know it's for the good of the unit and I know it's for your good. Cooperate as much as you can. Be where you're supposed to be when you're supposed to be there. We'll learn together how to do this together."

The tactic worked. In a few weeks, the Magnificent Seven were gone. Morale in C Company began to improve, as did discipline, permitting

George to devote more time to training his men. As always, the working hours for troop commanders were brutal, often dark to dark. One December the brigade spent so much time in the field that when George arrived back in Erlangen on Christmas Eve he had to admit to Vonda that he'd had no time to shop for presents. Sometimes the battalion traveled to Hohenfels for maneuver exercises, or to Grafenwöhr for live-fire training. In the grand scheme of NATO war plans against a Soviet invasion, the battalion was responsible for defending a four-mile sector along the Czech border. Occasionally trailed by spies driving Skoda automobiles, George and his platoon leaders spent hours studying the border terrain to plan their defense. They planted yellow poles to show where they would position tanks, blue poles for armored personnel carriers, and red poles for TOW antitank weapons. If the spies moved close enough to take pictures, George fudged the location of the poles slightly to avoid disclosing the actual defensive positions.

In March 1974, the Army assigned C Company to play the role of partisans in an exercise called Alpine Friendship. Under the rules of the game, George became a guerrilla chieftain in a Bavaria supposedly overrun by the Soviets. His orders were to link up with American Special Forces advisers from Bad Tolz and spend a month simulating demolition raids on bridges, dams, and military installations throughout southern Germany.

The first day nearly ended in disaster. As a helicopter dropped off C Company for the start of the exercise, German *Landpolizei,* who had been promised a fifty-mark bounty for every captured guerrilla, heard the rotor blades and gave chase. Running through the forest, the men heard the *ee-ooh, ee-ooh* of sirens, followed by the *wooof-wooof-wooof* of pursuing German shepherds. The barking grew steadily louder. Just as George began to envision spending a month in a German jail, nursing a nasty dog bite, he had an idea. "Get out your C-rations," he ordered. The men pulled the rations from their rucksacks, dumped the meat along the trail, and ran on. The barking soon stopped and the sirens faded away.

George led his band to a cavernous, three-story barn that had been leased as a kind of safe house. Five miles away lay the town of Landsberg and its famous prison, where, following the Beer Hall Putsch, Adolf Hitler had spent thirteen months in Cell Seven, munching on poppy seed strudel and dictating *Mein Kampf* to Rudolf Hess. In the Landsberg barn, the guerrillas grew beards and planned their campaign.

Armed Forces Radio transmitted their mission assignments in a code using a series of birthdays. "I'd like to wish a happy birthday to Sergeant First Class Joe Johnson in Schongau," the radio announcer might say.

"His special day is coming up on the twenty-third." Listening in the barn, like Resistance fighters monitoring the BBC, the guerrillas would immediately begin scheming how best to destroy the bridge at Schongau by March 23.

The missions went well. Usually the men moved on foot — George reconnoitering incognito in plumber's coveralls and gum boots — though occasionally they hid in the back of a dump truck or in Volkswagen buses. If the target was a dam, a squad would paddle through the water after midnight and, as guards overhead puffed unsuspectingly on their cigarettes, fasten a detonator cord and blocks of wood — simulating explosive charges — to the floodgates. Then they summoned one of the umpires refereeing the exercise to verify the "kill" and chalk up yet another success for Crocker's raiders.

On the last night of Alpine Friendship, the partisans staged a successful raid on the "enemy" brigade headquarters, located outside a small village. Back at Erlangen, George saluted as the battalion commander welcomed him home after a month in the field. "George," the lieutenant colonel observed with alarm, "all of your men are wearing beards." "Yes, sir," George replied, a grin on his bearded face. The next day, in a ceremony befitting the solemnity of the occasion, C Company shaved en masse. Crocker's raiders had once again become 177 ordinary, government-issue dogfaces.

Such pleasant diversions as Alpine Friendship helped break the tedium of garrison duty, but General Davison's "wrecked" Seventh Army was not easily repaired. Disciplinary headaches persisted, especially drug addiction. After ousting the Magnificent Seven from his unit, George cashiered another fifty-one soldiers from the Army, nearly all for drug abuse.

"Sir," a lieutenant once asked him after a particularly tiresome day of personnel problems, "why are you staying in the Army? I mean, look around. Is this what you want to do for the rest of your life, with these kinds of troops?"

That was a difficult question, one that George had privately put to himself on several occasions. What am I doing? he wondered. Had he been a brand-new lieutenant assigned to Germany in the midst of this demoralizing tumult, the odds were better than even, he now concluded, that he would have resigned.

As it was, he never seriously contemplated quitting, never even discussed the option with Vonda. He was hooked on the Army. In part, this reflected his affection for "doing men things in a manly manner with other men," as one of his subordinates once put it — whether staging mock assaults on German bridges, scouting defensive positions along the Czech border, or working on marksmanship at Grafenwöhr. He liked teaching young soldiers the importance of stealth, of avoiding noise and light when on patrol, of fire control — all of the skills that had kept his platoon alive in Vietnam. He found a certain comfort in repetition, in knowing that regard for these eternal verities of soldiering separated the living from the dead when the shooting started.

But an equally important reason for remaining in uniform was his fundamental confidence in the country, in the Army, in the future. "There will be dark days ahead, George," General McCaffrey had once predicted at Long Binh. "The Army has always had ups and downs, and we're heading for a down, especially the way Vietnam is turning out. But you have to have faith. Things will get better."

George often pondered McCaffrey's words. They made sense; you had to take the long view. He was a good enough student of history to understand that the general knew what he was talking about. The Army — and the Army's relationship to the Republic — might undergo shifts; but it always resumed a delicate balance. If one thing distinguished many of those in the class of 1966 who had stayed in the Army from those who resigned, it was faith in this equilibrium.

For men who took the long view, none of the present symptoms of an Army in chaos was unprecedented. True, the American Army had never lost a war; but even in the two centuries before this defeat, it had suffered some of the same ills plaguing the military in the early 1970s. Desertion was one example. The Army's desertion rate in 1971, nearly fivefold the rate for 1966, was only slightly higher than the desertion rate in 1944. In 1826, more than half of all new enlistees had deserted; in 1871, a third of the entire Army went "over the hill."

Indiscipline was virtually a historical trademark of American fighting men. George Washington, in a curiously precise choice of fractions, had lamented that "seven-elevenths" of his Army was rioting at the end of the Revolution. Foreign mercenaries like Von Steuben and Pulaski often expressed bewilderment at the contentious independence of American soldiers. The inspector general of the Army of Northern Virginia complained bitterly in 1864 about "the difficulty of having orders properly and promptly executed. There is not that spirit of respect for and obedience to general orders which should pervade a military organization."

Even the current national disdain for professional soldiers, while searingly painful for men who had risked their lives in the service of the country, was by no means unprecedented. Americans had always been fickle toward men in uniform. In the 1830s and 1840s, both the public and government showed open contempt of military men; Ulysses S.

Grant once told of proudly wearing his uniform for the first time, only to be ridiculed in the streets of Cincinnati by a ragged urchin. Congress thought so little of its Army in 1876 — the year of the Little Big Horn — that the lawmakers neglected to pass an appropriations bill, and soldiers served without pay until November 1877.

"We've been living in a kind of aberrated period since World War II," observed General William A. Knowlton, who had succeeded the disgraced Samuel Koster as West Point's superintendent. "We've been misled by the general high standing of the military in a society that's always been ambivalent about the military. Our traditionally strong antimilitary elements have been so sublimated that the people who have come of age in this period, and who have not gone back and looked at history, thought this atmosphere of esteem was the norm in American history."

Those inclined to stay the course in the officer corps would have to endure a hard peace, as they had endured the hard war. Some of the nation's best battle captains were officers who had gritted their way through times of national indifference or opprobrium — men like Black Jack Pershing, who languished as a lieutenant for nearly two decades. Indeed, West Point liked to think that the academy fashioned soldiers who would wait patiently to answer the summons of the trumpet when the country most needed them.

Consequently, when George Crocker was asked by his young lieutenant, "Sir, why are you staying in the Army?" he replied with words that echoed McCaffrey's: "This is the low ebb. You have to have faith. While the Army may be down now, it's just temporary. The Army is one of the great, enduring institutions. It's one of the things that have held us together as a nation. It will rebound. There are better days ahead."

He was in for the duration. He too would await the trumpet.

Three hundred miles northwest of Erlangen, Tom Carhart knew something about enduring a hard peace. The years since his return from Vietnam — Walter Reed, Ann Arbor, marriage, and then divorce — had been hardly less convulsive than combat. Tom had experienced moments when he felt utterly lost, wondering whether he would ever find a niche. But now, here in Brussels, where he had worked for nearly a year as an international attorney for the Archibald Law Offices, S.A., he had found at least a temporary haven. He felt like a runner who finally catches his breath after a long, uphill race. For the first time since the car wreck at West Point, Tom was at peace with himself.

On this brisk day in early spring, he had driven his Lotus into the southern suburbs to one of his favorite spots in Belgium, the battlefield at Waterloo. Like so many hallowed killing fields, this one possessed a dreamy tranquillity. As he walked the grassy slopes that had once been littered with the carcasses of forty thousand soldiers, Tom saw the battle unfold once again in his mind's eye. There, across that sunken road south of the forest of Soignes, the British army had mustered along a six-thousand-yard front. Napoleon had attacked at eleven A.M., first against the Château of Hougoumont, where the French broke into the walled garden, only to be trapped and slaughtered like seined fish. Over there Marshal Ney, having survived the loss of five horses killed beneath him, had ordered the desperate charge against Wellington's center. Tom could hear the piping of the Scottish regiments, the beating of the *pas de charge,* and the bullets smacking like hailstones against swords and scabbards. Here the surrounded British 40th Regiment, just arrived from fighting in America, was ordered to "make faces!" in a desperate effort to intimidate the enemy with fierce scowls. Some British soldiers had passed the few quiet moments between cavalry charges by reading letters pulled from the packs of dead Frenchmen or grilling chops in the scavenged breastplate of a fallen cuirassier.

Like most major battles, Waterloo had been a struggle decided by infantrymen besting infantrymen. Tom appreciated that, being an old groundpounder himself. Hadn't he always claimed that other branches were simply support services for the infantry? A British soldier who fought here was known for the rest of his days as a Waterloo Man; that single day of battle on June 18, 1815, was equivalent to a full two years' service in the calculations toward a pension. The British, at least, knew how to be grateful.

But it was the emperor who most fascinated Tom. In military art class at the academy, he had studied the campaigns from *A Military History and Atlas of the Napoleonic Wars,* a bulky tome with the heft of an ammunition box and a wonderful Napoleonic epigram: "I am a fragment of rock thrown into space." Tom had been particularly intrigued by the Battle of Auerstadt and Jena, where Bonaparte had turned catastrophe into triumph and chased the routed Prussians across half of Europe. Here at Waterloo, three months after the return from Elba, was where the adventure ended.

Tom let the Lotus carry him back into the city — one constant in his life was an affection for sports cars — and then parked on a side street in the Woluwe St. Pierre. He lived in a beautiful town house set two hundred feet back from the main avenue, giving the place a cloistered isolation even amid the urban crush. He had never really thought about the matter before moving to Brussels, but not until now had he ever lived alone. He'd always had roommates: fellow cadets or Arthur Ashe or his wife. Now it was just Tom, and the solitude enchanted him. He had many friends — including Michelle, an impeccably coiffed Walloon dowager who had become his mistress — and the $48,000 yearly salary from Archibald permitted him to lead the sporty life of a well-heeled expatriate. But he scrupulously reserved several evenings each week simply for being alone. That allowed him to cultivate a newfound streak of introspection and to nurture a promising friendship with none other than Tom Carhart. Somewhat to his surprise, he found that he enjoyed the man's company.

After a quick supper of cheese and bread, Tom poured himself two fingers of cognac, switched on the radio to a French music station, and settled into an easy chair next to the living room hearth. He had begun reading Proust again, but the visit to Waterloo drew him back to his favorite biography — the two-volume life of Napoleon by André Castelot. Each book was exquisitely bound in green leather with an endleaf reproduction of Jacques Louis David's painting *The Consecration of Napoleon*. Tom had paid $30 for volume one, and the law firm had generously presented him with volume two as a gift. Flipping past the epigraph — *"Quel roman que ma vie!"* — Tom found the chapter on the 18th Brumaire and plunged once again into Castelot's account.

What a novel is my life! Over the past few years Tom's life too sometimes had seemed the stuff of fiction, with an improbable plot that twisted, turned, and doubled back on itself. At the end of his final year in Ann Arbor he had applied for and been awarded the editorship of *European Taxation,* a journal based in Holland. He moved to Amsterdam, bought a Porsche, smoked prodigious amounts of hashish, and worked in an office set in the bell tower above one of the city's ancient gateways. From the tower balcony, Tom could watch the bustling cobbled street that ran between two canals below. Sometimes a flock of storks oared past for an evening meal at the nearby zoo. In autumn, the birds rose in a great, flapping cloud of white to begin their long migration to North Africa for the winter.

Susan had remained in the States; things were that bad between them. But in September 1973 she sent Tom a telegram: MY DARLING I LOVE YOU. MAY I COME TO AMSTERDAM? He cabled a reply: OF COURSE MY DARLING. Bullshit, Tom thought; she just wants a European vacation. He believed his skepticism was confirmed when, after three months in Holland, Susan flew home for Christmas, leaving Tom with an ultimatum: find a job in California or I'm leaving you.

Reluctant to see the marriage dissolve, he landed a position in Los Angeles as a policy analyst for the RAND Corporation, the think tank that had been founded under Air Force sponsorship in 1948. For

$45,000, the Carharts bought a town house on the south side of the San Fernando Valley. His work at RAND was eclectic and intriguing, drawing Tom into a variety of public interest issues. He wrote a ninety-page analysis of the War Powers Resolution, which Congress had passed in the wake of Vietnam to define the president's obligation during military crises. He also spent several months at Fort Hood, looking for efficient ways to maintain Army vehicles. And for the Justice Department he participated in a study on "hardened offenders," criminals who had been convicted of felonies at least three times. Tom puckishly recommended that such miscreants be executed; *that* got their attention in Washington.

Although he had acceded to Susan's ultimatum, the marriage continued to disintegrate. "You've got to quit dwelling on Vietnam," she would chide as he launched into yet another monologue on the war. "You're out of step, Tom. Put it behind you. No one cares." Her lack of interest left him sputtering with frustration. "You don't understand," he would say lamely. "You just don't understand." Soon after his arrival in California, Susan left him for good; Tom received the divorce papers in the mail.

Her departure was not unexpected, but still it hit him hard. Here was another failure. His views on women, he knew, were less than enlightened in this age of liberation. As a role model, his father had been very much the traditionalist, excusing himself from the dinner table every evening with a polite "thank you, dear, for a lovely meal" and wandering into the study while Tom's mother cleared the table, washed the dishes, and bedded the children. West Point had reinforced that Victorian concept; in the masculine world of military men, Tom had concluded, a wife was a possession, something a man owned as he owned a sword or a shako.

Yet even as he recognized his own shortcomings, Tom seethed with anger toward Susan. He felt used, exploited by a woman who took and took without giving in return. Partly in an attempt to begin his life with a clean slate, he interviewed for two jobs, one in Belgium and one in Indonesia. Offered both, he decided on Brussels because he spoke fluent French and knew his way around northern Europe.

Leaving Los Angeles, Tom drove across country and stopped on a whim to see his old West Point classmate Tom Beasley, who was practicing law in Nashville. For several days, they drank and caroused as though they were back in the academy barracks, the world once again their oyster. Beasley suspected that Tom was not entirely well, but he didn't press the point. One night during his visit, the Beasleys went to a party and left Tom engrossed in conversation with the baby sitter;

when they returned four hours later, Tom was still talking and the sitter's hair was standing on end. Beasley never knew exactly what was said during those four hours, but the sitter remained frightened for weeks.

Only in Brussels had Tom's life gradually come together. In this city, so cultured and self-assured, he enjoyed strolling across the Grand'Place or past the guild houses with their Flemish Baroque façades. He also settled into a comfortable routine at Archibald, researching tariff laws for British Leyland and the like. Typically, he arrived in the office at ten, lunched from one until three, then worked until eight or nine. For amusement, he had Paris, only three hours away by rail, and it wasn't much farther to the ski slopes at Tignes in the French Alps or the beaches of the Côte d'Azur. Tom envisioned himself settling in Europe, eventually earning a six-figure salary, and perhaps moving to Archibald's Paris office.

To the occasional classmate who ran across him, he was still "crazy Tom." Every spring, West Pointers around the world gathered to celebrate the anniversary of the academy's founding on March 16, 1802. Though the event was often stuffy, the Founders Day banquet in Germany always drew hundreds of graduates from across Europe. This year in Heidelberg more than a dozen classmates from 1966 had reserved a table near the podium; the guest speaker was General Alexander M. Haig, Jr., class of '47 and the supreme allied commander in Europe.

Tom showed up, thoroughly drunk, wearing his West Point blazer, royal Stuart plaid pants, and a crimson vest he had just purchased in London. He was the only civilian at the table. While Haig rumbled through his speech, Tom began to criticize the general's words in a stage whisper: "Aw, he's full of shit. That's bullshit." Although his classmates took Tom's performance in stride, older graduates at other tables tried unsuccessfully to silence the heckler with dagger glances and whispered reproaches.

"Goddamn it," he answered loudly, "this is Founders Day. This is the time when we stand up and celebrate." As Haig droned through an interminable catalogue of the threats to freedom, Tom stood and weaved his way from the banquet hall, much to the relief of his classmates. Suddenly, the noise of a ruckus carried to the podium from the rear of the hall. On the table reserved for the class of '74 stood Tom Carhart, a mustachioed pillar of red among the dress blues. As the younger graduates roared their approval, Tom bellowed, "Okay, we're gonna do the Rocket Yell!" Windmilling his arms, he let trill a piercing whistle and launched into one of the favorite cheers at West Point football games:

BOOM! — Ahhhh!
USMA Rah! Rah!
USMA Rah! Rah!
Hoo-Rah! Hoo-Rah!
AR-MAY! Rah!
Team! Team! Team!

His classmates clapped their hands over their eyes and shook their heads. That Tom, they muttered. Can you believe this? It was outrageous. It was impertinent. It was rude. It was wonderful. And they loved him for it.

Such antics notwithstanding, living alone in Europe encouraged a more reflective streak. Sometimes, in his armchair by the fire, Tom sorted out the advice he had received over the past twenty years: make a plan and stick to it; or forgo planning and live impetuously. At RAND, he had shared an office with a brilliant and profoundly fatalistic Indonesian, whose views Tom found attractive.

"Everything is fixed," the Indonesian had declared. "You cannot affect even the way you were meant to drive to work."

"Are there no decisions you can make for yourself?" Tom would ask.

"Well, yes, you can perhaps make a decision about what color socks to wear, but only between blue and black. You cannot chose red if you are destined to wear a darker color. The worst thing you can do is try to make something work if it's not destined to work. The only thing you'll accomplish is to make it worse."

Such a philosophy was utterly contrary to the underlying West Point assumption of man as master of his fate, and Tom could hardly accept completely the Indonesian's determinism. Yet he did not dismiss it out of hand, as he once would have; it was an oddly comforting view, one he drew on occasionally. Life would unfold as life was meant to unfold.

"You were dealt a very bad hand of cards," his old academy roommate Frank Cosentino had once told him bluntly in California, "and you played them badly." Yes, Tom could agree: he was flawed, a creature who at times was merely the sum of his deficiencies. But now he felt at ease with his imperfect self. Concerned that he was becoming too dependent on hashish, he abruptly quit; he also abandoned the strident rhetoric of the Ann Arbor student left. In Brussels, he gradually returned to a truer Tom, one who was fundamentally conservative in many ways.

He was no longer a warrior and would never be a general or a great captain. Sometimes he grieved for the lost dream. But he took great satisfaction from the knowledge that he had served, that he had fought and bled for his country. One of Tom's favorite quotes was George Washington's comment during the French and Indian War: "I have heard the bullets whistle and believe me, there is something charming in the sound." Tom also had been charmed by the whistling bullets, and he now drew strength from his combat experience, shedding his ambivalence. In terms of bravery and self-sacrifice — by the rigorous standards of the long gray line — he believed that he had passed the test. Having made his peace in this fashion, he could get on with his life.

One day when he was still in Ann Arbor, Tom was browsing through the sports pages of *The Detroit Free Press* and noticed the obituary of a former baseball pitcher. The highlight of the ball player's career, according to the article, was the day he threw a no-hitter against the New York Yankees in the 1930s.

Tom wondered what his own obituary would say. What had he ever done that could come close to pitching a no-hitter against the Yankees? He thought back to a day in the spring of 1968, when Alpha Company had been pinned down by three enemy machine guns in the highlands. Another platoon leader, frightened to the point of immobility, cowered behind a large tree. Tom was terrified too, but the sight of the craven lieutenant angered him into action.

"Fix bayonets!" he had shouted to his platoon. A metallic rattling followed as the men snapped their bayonets onto the muzzles of their M-16s.

"No quarter! Follow me!" Standing erect, Tom had stepped into the sunlight of the clearing, spraying bullets over the lip of the hill as he marched up the slope with the platoon at either side. He had been certain that he was going to die, but when he reached the crest he saw that the NVA had fled.

When Tom recounted this story at Walter Reed, the psychiatrist had written on his chart, "Has suicidal tendencies." That was a hoot, Tom thought; in other wars, they had a different name for it. Even in Brussels, he remembered that episode as clearly as if he had stepped into the sun-drenched jungle clearing only a week before. It was his no-hitter. Now he could imagine the words of his obituary: "Tom Carhart died today. In 1968, he lined his platoon up at the edge of the treeline at the bottom of a hill, stepped out into the sunlight, and yelled, 'Fix bayonets! Follow me!' "

Shortly after his visit to Waterloo, Tom received some terrible news from home. His sister Sally, who was a year and a half older than he, had been in a car accident in Los Angeles. Her head was badly injured, much as Tom's had been in 1966, and now she lay in a coma. Colonel and Mrs. Carhart flew from Massachusetts to be with her, and every day they called Tom in Brussels with a status report. One night at seven, Colonel Carhart called again. "It looks as if this is it," he said.

Tom caught a train to London and flew directly to California. Arriving in midafternoon, he hurried to the hospital, faint from fatigue and anxiety as he walked into the lobby. Sally lay in the intensive care unit, surrounded by life support equipment, her head wrapped in bandages. Tom leaned over and whispered in her ear for a moment. Her fragrance overwhelmed him; she had precisely the same clean girl-smell he remembered from their childhood. Tom kissed her and returned to the waiting room. A short time later, the doctor summoned the family. "Quickly," he urged, "she's going." As the Carharts stood by her bed, Sally died.

She was cremated and eventually interred at Arlington National Cemetery. Shattered by his daughter's death, Colonel Carhart lost thirty pounds over the next two months, and his salt-and-pepper hair turned white. Tom had returned to Brussels, but he feared for his father's life. He began considering a return to Massachusetts to look after his parents. Perhaps he could also set aside a few months to work on the Vietnam memoirs he had been writing fitfully. Taking advantage of Belgian work laws, he negotiated a severance agreement with the partners at Archibald and came away with nearly $15,000.

He packed up, sold the Lotus, and bade Michelle adieu. Brussels had been a wonderful interlude. He had arrived feeling lost, and the city had restored his confidence, permitting him to find a sense of balance and proportion. He would always be grateful, remembering Brussels as an anchorage that offered him refuge when he most needed it. But he now knew that the time had come for the expatriate to return home.

The innocence that the young men of '66 had carried to Beast Barracks more than a decade earlier had long since disappeared, like a boy's peach fuzz yielding to a man's beard. The common pains and disappointments attending every coming of age had removed most of their naïveté; the bloody business of war ripped away the rest. Yet if none was an innocent, few were cynics. Most retained their idealism, buttressed by West Point's categorical insistence that good men are governed by high principles. Presuming the world to be basically benign, they could still be surprised by evidence of evil. And thus, when the news circulated of another classmate's death in February 1975, they were distressed and confounded. For evil had plainly befallen John Oi on a snowy night in Boston.

Mild-mannered and cautious, John Oi was of average height, with thick brows and slightly bulging dark eyes behind black-framed glasses. After World War II his father, Henry Oi, had emigrated from Canton, where John was born, to Boston. There he made a name for himself as a successful restaurateur and secretary of the Chinese Merchants Association. John enlisted in the Army in 1959 and earned an appointment to the academy following a year at the West Point prep school. Many classmates best remembered him as Mr. Ten, the cadet who wore his name tag upside down in Beast Barracks one day. He had been good-humored and generous in helping those who struggled academically; on Graduation Day, John's roommate, Jerry Cecil, had waved his diploma and said, "This sheepskin belongs as much to you as it does to me, buddy."

After being commissioned as a signal officer, John endured the usual succession of far-flung assignments: Germany; Fort Hood; Vietnam, where he won two Bronze Stars; Fort Bragg; and Taiwan, where he served as a military adviser to the Nationalist Chinese army. While in Taipei, John married Cheryl Ann Lau, the daughter of a store manager from Hilo, Hawaii. A graduate of Smith College, Cheryl had a doctorate in ethnomusicology from the University of Oregon, where she had specialized in Asian and Polynesian music. In 1973, the Army offered to send John to graduate school for a master's degree in electrical engineering; he selected Northeastern University in Boston in order to be close to his family and because Cheryl longed for New England's cycle of seasons.

As John settled into the life of a graduate student, Cheryl landed a part-time job as moderator of a television show called *Asian Focus;* she also signed up for classes in school administration at Boston State and occasionally gave music lessons at the Wurlitzer Piano and Organ Company. The Ois rented an apartment in the southwest suburb of Norwood. Sometimes they helped Henry Oi at his restaurant; Cheryl worked the ten P.M. to two A.M. shift as hostess and John filled in as manager when his father was away. Like his late classmate Buck Thompson, John had profited from a childhood spent in a restaurant by becoming an excellent cook. Cheryl, who could barely boil water, often found him in the kitchen concocting yet another gourmet meal with his saucepans and wok.

Captain Oi also relished military service. His secret ambition was to be the first Chinese-American general in the U.S. Army. Sometimes he pulled his West Point sword from the closet to demonstrate the old cadet drills for Cheryl and their friends. But John, aware of the odds against promotion to general officer, hedged his bets. In Boston he continued to look for a prudent investment to fall back on should his military career end prematurely.

One of his closest friends was another Cantonese immigrant named Wing Gwong Chin, whom he had met when they were busboys in 1957.

Wing now had his own restaurant in Seabrook, New Hampshire. The Hawaiian Garden — the kind of place given to tiki torches and tiny paper parasols in the mai tais — was prospering, and Chin wanted to expand. He had his eye on Marietta, Georgia, a booming suburb of Atlanta that was home to a gigantic Lockheed aircraft plant. Marietta could use a good Chinese restaurant, Chin concluded. John invested $20,000 — more than half of it from Cheryl's savings — in the venture. Joining John and Wing Chin in the partnership were two other men, a mysterious relative of Chin's known as Uncle Harry, and the fellow who would actually manage the new restaurant, Armand R. Therrien.

Son of a New Hampshire logger who had emigrated from rural Quebec, Therrien had spent four years in the Air Force, five years as a ticket agent for Northeast Airlines, and nine years as a New Hampshire state trooper specializing in embezzlement cases. Tiring of police work after his promotion to detective corporal, Therrien had quit to become assistant manager of the Hawaiian Garden. "Schooling limited. Capabilities unlimited," he wrote on his résumé. "I have enjoyed and done well at all my occupations but to date have not found one that would consume my entire efforts."

He had a strong Gallic face, thick black curls, a compelling smile, and graceful aplomb; his manner would serve him well in the new Marietta restaurant. After securing a $166,000 loan from the First National Bank of Boston, the four partners each took out a $200,000 Aetna life insurance policy. Payable to the corporation, the policies helped guarantee the restaurant's solvency. "I don't think we can miss," Chin said.

On February 3, 1975, John and Cheryl treated Therrien and his girlfriend to dinner in Boston as a farewell celebration before Therrien took off for Georgia the next day. Wing Chin had flown to San Francisco, where he knew someone in Chinatown who would sell them attractive furnishings for the new restaurant at wholesale prices. Over dinner, Therrien gave the Ois a progress report on Hawaiian Garden South, which was under construction in an old Exxon station on Roswell Road in Marietta. The underground tanks had been torn out and workmen were converting the service bays to a large dining room. Therrien had leased a flat for himself only five minutes away. Everything was on track for a September opening. As they clinked their wine glasses in a toast, Therrien and John joked about who would buy the first Rolls-Royce.

A week later, on Tuesday, February 11, 1975, John and Cheryl drove to Fort Devens, northwest of Boston. Captain Oi was in line for promotion to major, and he wanted to be certain that all of the paperwork in his personnel file was in order. Light snow powdered the streets of Norwood as they returned just before four P.M. Cheryl, who had a graduate class from five to seven, quickly gathered her books and took the Mercedes, leaving the Grand Prix for John, whose own class at Northeastern began at eight.

At seven-thirty, Westwood police cruiser 92 turned onto a secluded stretch of Canton Street. Flanked by scrub pines and barren honeysuckle vines, the road sliced behind the Norfolk Golf Club before emptying on to Route 128. Behind the wheel of the cruiser was Patrolman William Sheehan, a fifty-seven-year-old widower who wore badge Number 1 as the senior veteran on suburban Westwood's twenty-nine-man force. His rookie partner, Robert P. O'Donnell, had been an ironworker out of Boston's Local Number 7 for eleven years before joining the force just four weeks earlier.

As they drove down Canton, the policemen spotted a red-and-black Grand Prix between light posts ninety-eight and ninety-nine. Easing past the car with their searchlight on, Sheehan and O'Donnell saw that the driver's head was slumped forward as though he were asleep. A man in the passenger seat waved the officers away. His curiosity aroused, Sheehan parked in front of the Pontiac and flipped on his blue roof flashers. Emerging from the cruiser with their flashlights, the patrolmen were greeted on the street by the man in the jump seat. He was smiling.

"My friend is sick," Armand Therrien said heartily, "but it's okay. I can handle it."

"What's a sick man doing driving a car?" Sheehan asked, pushing past Therrien.

Shining his light on the driver, the patrolman saw a man wearing olive drab Army fatigues beneath a beige coat. His eyes, open and vacant, bulged grotesquely and the whites were flooded with red. Blood poured from his left ear.

"Hey," O'Donnell demanded, "what's all the blood?" Hearing a soft click, the younger officer turned to see Therrien holding a .38-caliber Smith & Wesson in both hands. With a deafening roar, the muzzle flashed a foot from O'Donnell's face. The bullet grazed the rookie's forehead and powder burns blinded him for an instant as he pitched forward to the pavement. Therrien pivoted toward Sheehan and fired twice more, hitting him in the head and right arm. As O'Donnell grabbed the gunman's leg, Therrien emptied his pistol. One round shattered O'Donnell's belt buckle, driving metal fragments into his abdomen. Therrien then began clubbing the patrolman over the head with the Smith & Wesson while trying to jerk O'Donnell's service revolver from its holster. Unable to get the pistol free of the restraining snap, Therrien wrenched loose of the officer's grip and sprinted down Canton Street. O'Donnell drew his gun and fired six times, hitting the fleeing man in the shoulder and right thigh. As Therrien writhed in pain next to the police cruiser, O'Donnell hobbled up to him and leveled his revolver: "You make another move and I'll blow your head off."

"I'm sorry, sir." Therrien sobbed. "I'm sorry. I give up."

The phone was ringing when Cheryl Oi returned home at 9:20 after a late music lesson at Wurlitzer. Picking up the receiver, she noticed that her dog, Wong Tsu, was acting oddly, cowering and shivering as though frightened. The caller, a reporter from *The Boston Globe*, was pursuing a story about a man named Oi who had been shot two hours earlier. At first Cheryl assumed that the wounded man was one of John's relatives. But as the reporter supplied more details, Cheryl hung up and dialed Norwood Hospital, which confirmed that the victim was her husband.

When she arrived in the emergency room, John was in convulsive death throes. He had been shot once behind the left ear. Officer Sheehan had been pronounced dead on arrival, but O'Donnell's wounds were remarkably superficial. At 9:45, John Oi was pronounced dead.

Therrien underwent surgery at Massachusetts General Hospital. He would recover; in his coat pockets, police found a box of bullets, two pairs of handcuffs, and two billfolds with a total of $770 in cash. When he emerged from anesthesia, a policeman read him his rights and asked whether he had any questions. "I understand the charge," Therrien replied, "but I don't understand the reason." Two days later, he was carried on a stretcher into the white-tiled basement corridor of the Dedham district courthouse and formally charged with the murders of John Oi and William Sheehan.

Investigators spent months piecing together the crime. They found that Therrien had left Marietta on the afternoon of February 10 and driven all night to Boston, where he checked into a motel under a false name. At 6:20 on the night of the shootings, he had called Oi from a gas station and asked for a meeting to discuss an urgent matter regarding the restaurant. They had met in the parking lot of a restaurant on Route 1, where Therrien left his station wagon and got into John's Grand Prix. Police concluded that Therrien killed Oi for the $200,000 insurance policy. Although payable to the corporation, the sum would capitalize the restaurant sufficiently to repay the loan from First Boston and remove one of the restrictions that the bank had placed on the partners: a $15,000 ceiling on salaries, including Therrien's. The other partners, each of whom had a supplemental source of income, didn't care about salaries, the prosecutor alleged, "but Therrien cared. Because Therrien wanted to better himself."

The accused told a considerably different story. He had driven to

Boston, Therrien testified, to surprise his girlfriend. When he met John, the two men had argued over Oi's allegation that Wing Chin was going to cheat the other partners. Oi had struck Therrien twice, knocking him out. When he regained consciousness, Therrien said, the two policemen were standing near the car, arguing with Oi. One of them called John a "Chink." Then there were shots. O'Donnell had killed Oi, Therrien claimed, and then shot his partner.

The jury didn't believe him. After ten hours of deliberation, they found Armand Therrien guilty of murder, assault with intent to murder, and assault and battery with a deadly weapon. He was sentenced to two consecutive life terms and driven immediately to Walpole state prison.

Captain Oi was buried at West Point, not far from the tomb of Winfield Scott, the Great Pacificator. A small group of classmates attended the funeral, which featured the doleful bugle and cracking rifles of military interments. But the ceremony had an added distinction, a proper tribute to Mr. Ten, who had aspired to be the first Asian-American general in the U.S. Army. In keeping with Chinese custom, each mourner received a nickel to symbolize that John had died a prosperous man, and a small bag of candy, intended to remove the bitter taste of death.

15

DISHONOR

AT LAST the sea was calm. Knifing ever westward, the *Yankee Doodle* once again rode the swells with an easy grace. The Atlantic gleamed with phosphorescent plankton, as though mirroring the inverted bowl of stars overhead. Jim Ford eyed a shimmering patch of ocean in front of the sloop's bow and watched it drift past. He picked out another patch, then another. As each one passed astern, he whispered to himself, I'm thirty feet closer.

Even before setting sail from Plymouth, England, Ford had anticipated being homesick. But now, when he was midway between Madeira and Bermuda, the emotion had become a physical presence, squatting next to him on the deck like a brazen stowaway. The most difficult time always came during this graveyard watch from midnight to three A.M., when his two shipmates slept below. Watch yourself, he thought; don't let it get to you. You'll be home soon.

The hurricane had taken its toll, if not on the *Yankee Doodle* — which proved eminently seaworthy — then on Ford's nerves. For the third time in his life, he had known raw fear. The thirty-five-foot seas and seventy-five-knot winds had been every bit as frightening as his two close calls aboard the helicopters in Vietnam nine years before. Even before the hurricane hit, he had sensed trouble in the radio warnings of "cyclonic variables." But Ford didn't know what the term meant, and none of the reference books he had aboard mentioned it. Not until the wind began to scream, carving the sea into great green cliffs, did he understand that cyclonic variable was nautical jargon for bad storm. Several times, when the jade waves reared so menacingly that Ford had difficulty distinguishing horizontal from vertical, he took refuge in Psalm 31: "Be of good courage, and He shall strengthen your heart, all ye that hope in the Lord." He had even scribbled a footnote next to verse twenty-four in his King James Bible: "Read Mid-Atlantic on board Yankee Doodle, 25 May 1976. James Ford." Attempting to compose his own prayer, he settled on a four-word plea: "Lord, I've had enough."

Now, with the tempest stilled and less than three weeks left before landfall at West Point, the heaviest burdens were homesickness and ennui. To stay awake during his night watch, he had tried to kill time by re-creating an entire chapel service, from hymns to sermon. But after five minutes of belting out "A Mighty Fortress Is Our God" and recounting his parable "Saint Peter and the Spacecraft," he quit. Conducting the imaginary service was even more boring than watching the plankton.

Ford checked his watch. Nearly two A.M., time to get the radio check. For the past six weeks, he had been listening to stations in France and Africa. But in this stretch of the Atlantic, he expected to pick up the news, weather, and precise time from a powerful station in Fort Collins, Colorado, which skipped its signal off the underbelly of the atmosphere to cheer lonely seamen three thousand miles away. Standing and steadying himself, Ford moved to the console and began adjusting the frequency knob. The shortwave set was a Danish-made Sailor, one of the finest radios on the market, and the Reverend James Ford could spin quite a yarn regarding its purchase.

The story began five years earlier, in July 1971, when someone asked Ford on his fortieth birthday to list his goals for the rest of his life. Without hesitating, he ticked off four ambitions: "I'm going to learn to do crossword puzzles. I'm going to learn to play chess. I'm going to learn to ride a unicycle. I'm going to sail across the ocean."

In short order, he began doing two crossword puzzles every day, a habit that persisted for years. Soon he mastered chess, inaugurating a long tournament with his son in which one point was awarded for each hundred games won. Then he bought a unicycle and lugged it down to the concrete floor of the chapel basement. For the first forty-five minutes, the cycle was the toughest thing he had ever tried in his life; but within an hour he had it licked. Even at forty, Ford's sense of balance was dazzling.

The sailing expedition took a bit more preparation. For several years, he studied charts, read technical books on seamanship, interviewed experienced sailors, and practiced on the Hudson. Then a graduate from the class of 1965, Paul W. (Buddy) Bucha, suggested that he make the crossing as part of the American Bicentennial celebration. The notion of voyaging to the New World by sea — as his Swedish grandparents had — fired Ford's imagination.

In seeking a crew, he recruited two Rhodes scholars from the class of

1955. Harvey A. (Mike) Garn had resigned from the Army in 1963 and was now a research director at the Urban Institute in Washington. Colonel Lee Donne Olvey had been the '55 first captain and was now chairman of West Point's social sciences department. Neither Garn nor Olvey had ever set foot in a sailboat, but Ford's choice of the two landlubbers was intentional: "It's easier to pick good men who can be taught to be good sailors," he explained, "than it is to pick good sailors who have to be taught to be good men."

When the time came to buy a boat, Ford offered another tongue-in-cheek maxim: "Sailing the Atlantic isn't hard. You leave Plymouth harbor and hang a right. The wind is free; you just need $25,000 to catch it." Scraping together his savings and cashing in his life insurance policies, Ford ordered a customized twelve-thousand-pound, thirty-one-footer from a boat builder in southwest England. But that was only half the task. Virtually penniless, he couldn't afford to buy the radio, navigation equipment, life raft, and other crucial gear needed for the crossing.

Again, Buddy Bucha stepped in. Bucha knew a certain Annapolis graduate, class of '53, who had done well for himself in the business world. In fact, the man was a billionaire, and he had recently asked Bucha for a favor. The 1975 Army-Navy game was approaching; H. Ross Perot, the Texas industrial magnate, wanted to play a prank on his rivals at the Military Academy.

"Surely," Perot insisted, "there is someone at West Point who is corruptible."

"There is," Bucha agreed. "The chaplain."

Shortly after midnight on the eve of the big game — with embers from the pep rally bonfire still glowing on Abner Doubleday Field — Perot, Ford, and the academy bell ringer entered the chapel. Ford unlocked the main door and switched on the lights. On a table in the front vestibule, Perot carefully placed his trademark Stetson. The three men climbed the winding stone staircase that led from the narthex to a long vault concealed above the nave ceiling. Clambering along a wooden catwalk that ran the length of the chapel, they came to a brick chamber directly over the altar. In the middle of the belfry sat a contraption with a dozen wooden handles. Slender cables connected the handles to seven tons of chapel bells in the loft overhead. "Here you go," Ford said cheerfully, before backing into a hidden alcove beneath the eaves.

At 12:30 A.M., the tranquillity of the Hudson Valley was shattered by the deafening peal of a tune that turned any decent Army man's blood to froth:

Anchors, aweigh, my boys,
An-chors a-weighhhh!

This unholy din was followed by "The Marine Hymn" — *From the halls of Montezuuuu-ma, To the shores of Tripoli* — and the obnoxious trill of "Sailing, Sailing." Within minutes, hundreds of cadets raced up the hill from the barracks. Cursing and shrieking, they stormed into the chapel like avenging Crusaders, vowing to smite the interloper. Perot, who had locked the gate to the belfry, taunted them briefly before surrendering. The cadets manhandled him out of the chapel to the north portico, where they surrendered the intruder to the military police. Ford crept from his hiding place just in time to see the flashing red lights of the MP car recede down the hill, hauling H. Ross Perot to jail.

The next day, after quietly obtaining Perot's release, Ford held a special church service. The chapel, so heinously defiled by the infidel, was solemnly reconsecrated. (The chaplain's true role in the affair remained secret for years.) And in exchange for Ford's complicity, Perot happily paid the bill for a life raft, sextant, plane tickets to England, food, and the Sailor shortwave. "When I get to heaven," Perot later said, chuckling, "I'm not so sure I'm gonna find Jim Ford there."

Now, in the middle of the Atlantic, Ford put the radio to good use. At two A.M., he picked up the Fort Collins time check and set his watch. In an hour it would be time to wake Olvey, who would shoot the stars with his sextant and make any necessary adjustments to their course. Bermuda lay only a few days to the west; then they could begin the final leg to New York. Ford hoped there would be no further mishaps. A huge whale had charged the boat one day, veering away at the last instant. And Garn had accidentally crushed his finger under a deck plank; when he contracted blood poisoning, Ford discreetly read the chapter on amputation in his medical text and readied the two shots of morphine in his first-aid kit. Fortunately, the finger had healed on its own.

After the time check, Ford listened absentmindedly to the news. Jimmy Carter, having all but locked up the Democratic presidential nomination, was increasing the volume of his attacks on the incumbent, Gerald Ford. Bicentennial preparations continued throughout the nation. The Supreme Court, without comment, had upheld the court-martial conviction of Lieutenant William Calley.

But the next item caused Ford to sit bolt upright: "Officials at the United States Military Academy have confirmed reports that the entire junior class will remain at West Point following graduation exercises next week as part of the investigation into a massive cheating scandal."

Dozens of cadets, the report continued, had already been dismissed for unauthorized collaboration on an academic assignment.

Ford was dumfounded. He hadn't heard the slightest hint of this before leaving West Point in the spring. Dozens of cadets — was that possible? He knew the academy must be in an uproar, absolute chaos. And here he was, watching plankton on the high seas. Flipping off the shortwave set, he hurried belowdecks to wake his crew with the bad news.

Three months after the scandal had surfaced, Lieutenant General Sidney Bryan Berry was still in shock. These past months had been the most difficult time of Berry's entire fifty years. "I've never been in more of a combat situation than I am now," the superintendent had recently lamented, and coming from a man who had accumulated four Silver Stars in Korea and Vietnam, that was saying something. Even now, as summer settled over West Point, every week seemed to bring a new revelation, a new accusation, a new crisis. And there was no end in sight.

Sid Berry was a fast burner. Some admirers thought he was *the* fast burner among the Army's up-and-coming young generals. As a warrior, his credentials were impeccable. He even looked the part, with a spine that had all the curvature of an iron poker and piercing eyes that pinched into narrow slits whenever he let loose one of his rollicking belly laughs. In September 1970, *Life* magazine had profiled him in a fourteen-page article, "Case Study of an Army Star." "Nobody," the magazine declared, "looks more like a future chief of staff than Sid Berry."

He hailed from Hattiesburg, Mississippi, son of a country lawyer who rarely called young Sid anything but "boy." At West Point, a yearbook photograph of Inquisition One — Berry's company in the class of 1948 — described him as "our leader, the owner of the place." Desperate for a chance to fight, his only moment of despair at the academy had come when he heard the announcement of V-E Day while walking guard duty in 1945.

In Korea, he more than made up for the missed opportunity. Combat exhilarated him. "I sing all day as I ride in my jeep," he wrote to his wife during the hard winter of '51, "and get up in the morning whistling and singing." In the early 1960s, as Robert McNamara's military assistant, he had accompanied the defense secretary to Vietnam three times. Promoted to full colonel, Berry later served in the delta as adviser to a South Vietnamese division. One day an exploding grenade punched sixteen holes in him. "Picked up my second Purple Heart on Sunday," he advised his wife. "Doctor tells me my lung has made amazing progress. Just good, clean, vigorous living I tell him."

Before returning to Vietnam for a second combat tour, he spent a year at the Council on Foreign Relations in New York. One evening in Manhattan, Berry went to Broadway with his wife and father-in-law to see Tom Stoppard's masterly *Rosencrantz and Guildenstern Are Dead.* Waiting for the curtain to rise, he watched the theater fill with hundreds of powdered, furred, coiffed women and their sleek men, all reeking of wealth and the good life. Suddenly, he was swept with revulsion. None of these people had any idea of what was happening twelve thousand miles away in Southeast Asia; every day young boys were blown to pieces while these civilians glided through life in their designer clothes and fancy cars. Berry felt an overpowering urge to run from the theater, shrieking, "There are men dying in Vietnam!" Only through the most rigid exercise of self-discipline was he able to remain in his seat as the first act opened on a scene of appropriate absurdity: two characters flipping coins that landed on heads ninety times in a row.

In April 1974, he was summoned to Washington for a session with Chief of Staff Creighton W. Abrams, Jr., who officially informed Berry of his new appointment as superintendent. A burly tanker with a face like a rockslide, Abrams — who was to die prematurely of cancer five months later — had succeeded his classmate William Westmoreland as senior commander in Vietnam and then as the Army's chief. As Berry scribbled notes on a stack of three-by-five cards, the chief talked about the academy, the Army, the nation. West Point's ideals, Abrams said, leavened the Army, causing the service to rise. But the academy had to avoid elitism. "West Pointers often are prima donnas and spoiled brats," the chief continued. "They have to get down on their bellies in the mud with the soldiers and show them how to sight a machine gun." He urged Berry to "narrow the broad gap between the reality of West Point and the reality of the Army."

Three months later, Berry moved into Quarters 100 as the academy's fiftieth superintendent. The notion that he was taking command of an institution in trouble never crossed his mind, though there were, of course, perplexing issues to resolve. Morale needed bucking up, particularly after the winless 1973 football season, which had culminated in a 51-to-0 thrashing by Navy. The outgoing superintendent, William A. Knowlton, had spent much of his time defending the academy against litigation over everything from mandatory chapel to the honor system. But when Knowlton recited some of his concerns the night before he left West Point — characterizing himself as "the commander of a stockade surrounded by attacking Indians" — Berry privately thought that his predecessor's description was a bit overdrawn.

As he settled into the job, Berry discovered many tasks that demanded clear and decisive action. An eighteen-year-old cadet on the football team was charged with two rapes. Another crisis involved a plebe named Steven Verr, who had been convicted of lying in the fall of 1975 after concocting an elaborate fib to explain why he was crying as he left the mess hall one day; when Berry overturned the conviction on the grounds that there "was no intent to deceive" and that Verr had been treated shamefully during the honor board proceedings, some cadets responded with open dissent and even anonymous death threats against the plebe. And after Congress passed legislation requiring the admission of women to the corps, the superintendent found himself occupied with preparations for their arrival in July 1976.

Yet all of these things seemed manageable. Back home in Hattiesburg, the thing that most impressed Sid Berry's family and friends was that he lived in the house once occupied by Robert E. Lee. If anyone recalled that Lee had attributed the rapid graying of his hair to fretting over the Corps of Cadets in the early 1850s, that historical footnote went unmentioned.

Then, in the spring of 1976, the scandal broke. The cheating had first been detected in mid March. The required course Electrical Engineering 304, or "juice," was widely despised by the cadets as an exercise in "spec and dump" (memorize and forget). Even the West Point catalogue description made the class sound bootless: "Frequency selectivity in communication circuits. Characteristics and modeling of electronic devices. Diode circuits, amplifiers, oscillators and modulation methods. Radio and electronic systems. Laboratory exercises reinforce key points."

On March 3 and 4, 823 cows from the class of 1977 received a take-home examination worth 5 percent of their semester grade. The instructions at the top of the test, which involved designing a power supply to charge a battery or run a radio, explicitly warned, "There will be no collaboration on Part 1 of this problem . . . There will be *no discussion with anyone except* Department of Electrical Engineering instructors."

One of those instructors — in fact, the course director, who had written the design problem — was Major Billy Frazier of Cleburne, Texas. A member of the class of 1966, he had spent two years in the same cadet company as Art Bonifas. When cadets turned in their exams on March 17 and 18, one conscience-stricken cow had scrawled on the bottom: "I have received assistance on this paper." Billy Frazier impounded all 823 papers, locked them in a safe, and spent a three-day weekend carefully reading each one in his Bartlett Hall office. With growing apprehension, he found evidence of collusion on a huge scale. In some cases, the papers from cadets within the same companies had identical misspellings, similar arithmetic mistakes, or word-for-word wrong answers; one cadet had even painstakingly copied the margin doodle from another paper in the apparent belief that it was part of the answer. Not only had they cheated, Frazier concluded, but many of them had cheated stupidly.

On April 4, the department sent the names of 117 suspected cheats to academy authorities for disciplinary action. At the honor committee hearings, Frazier testified repeatedly as the faculty's expert witness. Within three weeks, fifty cadets had been found — expelled — and two others had resigned outright.

Clearly, the academy hoped to contain the damage. But some cadets and their attorneys were convinced of a rush to judgment by West Point and a willingness to convict scapegoats for the sake of expediency. On May 3, ten military defense lawyers wrote to Secretary of the Army Martin R. Hoffmann, advising him that the cheating was "widespread," that "upwards of three hundred members of the class of 1977" were involved, and that the honor committee "not only acted arbitrarily and improperly, but that certain of its members affirmatively conspired and acted to conceal and cover up violations."

The genie was out of the bottle. On May 23, Berry appointed an internal review panel of a dozen officers and five cadets to investigate. By alleging corruption in the honor boards, the accused had charged that one of West Point's most venerated institutions — the honor system — was tainted. Nothing was considered more sacred by most West Pointers than the thirteen-word vow of honor: "A cadet will not lie, cheat, or steal, nor tolerate those who do." Honor was the cornerstone of character, and without character West Point was just another trade school.

Curiously, cheating had not been considered particularly dishonorable in the nineteenth century; when Cadet George Armstrong Custer was caught pilfering the answers to an examination from an instructor's desk, he was permitted to remain in the corps. But in the modern age cheating had become a mortal sin. West Point had endured scandals before — notably the "football ring" in the early 1950s, when ninety cadets were expelled. More recently, from 1965 to mid 1973, 305 cadets had been found for assorted honor violations. The notion of hundreds of colluding cadets, though, was unthinkable.

Unthinkable, perhaps, but the evidence suggested it was true. As the dimensions of the scandal became clearer, Billy Frazier and others realized that cheating cells riddled West Point. All but three of the corps' thirty-six companies contained at least one guilty cadet, and expulsions stripped some companies of almost every cow. Usually the cells were made up of roommates or friends, who had swapped information in the barracks, in the hostess's office, or even in the bathrooms between classes.

But the worst part of the scandal for many officers was the certainty that what had happened in EE304 was an aberration only in that the culprits had been caught. Beating the system had become epidemic, with a disdain that became known as "cool on honor." The "hives" — those who studied seriously — were often ridiculed, and some star men stopped wearing the embroidered badges of academic distinction on their collars for fear of being mocked. If a majority of the corps was innocent and honorable, as the academy stoutly proclaimed, a sizable minority was guilty of at least tolerating the cheats.

Some of the alienation reflected a belief that the honor system had become a sham. Several companies routinely elected representatives to the honor committee who had a "liberal" attitude toward the code. An honor conviction required a unanimous vote by the twelve-man board, and there had been numerous 11-to-1 acquittals in recent years, particularly of accused upperclassmen with a loyal friend on the panel. Academy justice could also be absurdly arbitrary. One plebe — who turned himself in — had been expelled after stating that he had completed twenty sit-ups when in fact he had done only eighteen; yet an upperclassman, who had actually given the class of 1977 its initial indoctrination lecture on honor, was permitted to graduate even after being convicted of cheating. And the honor system, once a model of simplicity, now had a convoluted catalogue of do's and don'ts. For example, the stunt of "bedstuffing" — cramming pillows under a blanket to make it look as though a cadet were dutifully in his rack — was currently an honor violation, whereas an earlier generation had ruled that the practice, although contrary to regulations, was "certainly not dishonorable."

By mid June, Sidney Berry was heartsick. No less than in Korea or Vietnam, he felt as though he were fighting for the survival of his unit. The media covered the scandal fervidly; the cover of *Time* magazine on June 7 had depicted a cadet with his right hand raised to take an oath while holding his left hand behind his back with fingers crossed. Amid inquiries in the House and Senate and the endless recriminations, Berry wondered whether he had overlooked the warning signs of a disaster.

Early in his tenure he had appointed a study group to examine and assess the honor system. But when the panel asserted, in May 1975, that "the honor code is a clear and simple statement of an unattainable level of human behavior," the superintendent had largely ignored the findings. An old-fashioned believer in absolutes, Berry sharply disagreed with that conclusion. It smacked of relativism. If the honor code was anachronistic, then what was West Point's mission? Berry was convinced that one of the academy's greatest gifts to the nation was a set of enduring ideals, standards that remained inviolable during times of crisis and national soul searching. As West Point leavened the Army, so the academy helped to leaven America by preserving certain verities: duty, honor, country, truth.

Was that wrong? he wondered. Was he hopelessly out of date? Just what the devil did the country believe in? If these young men represented the best of America — and their statistical profile suggested they did — then what kind of country had this become? Perhaps the academy's greatest failure was its insensitivity to the colossal changes that had swept through the nation in the past ten years. Church, family, school — all of the temples of authority and moral instruction — had been weakened. A vice president and then a president had resigned in disgrace, as had a West Point superintendent. Skepticism, even cynicism, had become part of the national catechism. Berry believed that drugs, rock music, and flimsy standards of sexual morality were all symptomatic of these changes. And the war had done much to call everything into question. "Honor," Machiavelli once warned, "is impossible in a defeated country."

Unconsciously, West Point had presumed that the sons it received every July were precisely like those it had always received, imbued with a basic reverence for truth, honor, and authority. That presumption, regrettably, had been wrong. More than ever before, the academy would have to guarantee that its men — and, soon, women — were indoctrinated with a proper regard for the immutable principles.

Yes, Sid Berry was heartsick, but, as he told one interviewer, "By God, I've been heartsick in battle and done what I had to do." He would do what he had to do now, even if that meant decimating the class of '77. The academy would emerge stronger than ever. This too would pass. But until it did, West Point was in for a long, steamy summer.

The day was indeed warm and humid when George Crocker drove his brown Ford station wagon through Thayer Gate on July 1, 1976. The green mead of Buffalo Soldier Field, the Gothic parapets, the leafy tors looming above the Plain — all seemed as familiar as if he had graduated the previous month instead of ten years before. George hadn't really wanted to come back to West Point, if truth be told; given his druthers, he would have returned to the 82nd Airborne. But now he had to acknowledge a certain pleasure in coming home to alma mater. As one who had never been a paragon of good behavior when he was a cadet — and who had flunked EE304 during his own cow year — he appreciated the irony in his coming back as a tactical officer.

He would join sixty-four other classmates now assigned to the academy as tacs or instructors. Although all wore Army green, there were distinctions among the men of '66, of course. Some remained captains, but others, like George, had been promoted early to major. A few also sensed that a subtle schism would forever exist between those who had stayed in the combat arms and those who had repaired to the rear by transferring to support branches.

Yet such differences dissolved beneath the conviviality and delight of being part of a reunited band of brothers. Many returned with a reverence for West Point that would have embarrassed them a decade earlier. To Rance Farrell, who taught English, the academy resembled the great Gothic cathedrals of Europe. In constructing their spires and steeples, the cathedral builders had lavished devout care on the tiny filigree that only God could see; so too had West Point been built with a thousand loving secrets — some as invisible, as intangible, as tradition and love of country. Unseen by the three million annual visitors who wandered around the Plain, such secrets dwelt in the stones, perpetually sensed by those who lived here.

Right now, however, West Point hardly possessed the majestic tranquillity of Chartres or Notre Dame. With the scandal fully ablaze, General Knowlton's metaphor of a stockade surrounded by Indians seemed less and less outlandish. *Besieged* was a word that quickly came to mind as George looked around the academy. More than eighty military attorneys were ensconced in Thayer Hall. A tangle of telephone wires snaked across the floors of classrooms that had been converted into temporary law offices, and a large bulletin board displayed the names of accused cadets, with color-coded markers to show the stages of their respective legal proceedings. George had read and heard a great deal about the EE304 affair, but he was determined to suspend any final judgment. Just because the scandal had been on the cover of *Time,* he thought, didn't necessarily mean the academy was hopelessly compromised. He had resolved to wait and see for himself just how bad things were.

He was about to get a very close view. Normally, cadets accused of honor violations were segregated from the rest of the corps in the section of Eisenhower Barracks known as the Boarders Ward. There they remained until they were either expelled or exonerated and returned to their companies. But so many cows had been accused in the current scandal that the academy formed a separate unit called the Special Processing Detachment — SPD, or "Speed" — which had grown to about two hundred cadets.

Few of West Point's three dozen tactical officers wanted anything to do with Speed or its pariahs, many of whom had grown sullen, bitter, and preoccupied with their legal plight. (Affecting a gallows humor, they called themselves the Liars, Cheaters, and Thieves.) Because he had had experience in Germany with what was politely known as an "adverse unit," and was the newcomer in the tactical department, George was immediately assigned to serve as Speed's sole tac. When the academic year started in the fall, he would be shifted to Company A-1, one of a dozen companies containing the first female cadets. Vonda meanwhile remained in Arkansas with the children; until the Crockers' quarters were ready in the Stony Lonesome housing area above Michie Stadium, George would bivouac in a vacant cadet room next to Speed in New South barracks.

In the two years since leaving Erlangen, the Crockers had moved twice. In the summer of 1974, they were sent to Fort Leavenworth. George joined the first cluster of his classmates going through the nine-month course at the Command and General Staff College, where young officers were initiated into the mysteries of division and corps operations. Faced with the unpleasant prospect of joining a recruiting or a readiness unit after Leavenworth — either was anathema to an officer yearning to rejoin the troops — he asked instead to attend graduate school and then return to West Point. His request had been granted.

The subsequent year at Duke University in North Carolina had been exciting, both because Vonda gave birth to a baby boy and because it was George's first sustained exposure to the civilian world since his freshman year at the University of Arkansas thirteen years earlier. For a respite from the academic grind in Durham, he painstakingly restored a 1940 Ford two-door coupe, installing mohair upholstery and applying eleven coats of black acrylic lacquer to the body. But there was no respite from the postmortem soul searching about Vietnam and the American Army; even after the fall of Saigon and the triumph of North Vietnam, George found himself fighting an occasional rearguard action. At a dinner party one evening, the conversation inevitably circled around to the war and the role played by American dissidents like the actress Jane Fonda, who had vocally sympathized with the North Vietnamese cause and had even traveled to Hanoi.

"You don't understand," one history professor told George, "Jane Fonda may have saved your life."

"No," George replied sharply, "*you* don't understand. I would rather be dead than be saved under those circumstances."

Now, armed with a master's degree in psychology and counseling, he was ready for the unhappy cadets in Speed. Browsing through the *Tactical Officer's Manual* and other documents in his small office on an upper floor of Washington Hall, George could see that the academy had changed considerably in the past decade. The corps had doubled in size to forty-four hundred cadets. (Some critics felt that the rapid growth had contributed to the current scandal by making the institution more impersonal and unwieldy.) Bracing had been eliminated in 1969; shortly after, clothing formations and the Silence — the ostracism of cadets believed guilty of honor violations that could not be proven — also were banned. Other changes followed in quick succession: in 1972 the Supreme Court struck down mandatory chapel as unconstitutional; in 1973 the academy had pared down the bible of regulations, known as the Blue Book, from 183 pages to 64 (eliminating such gems as "No shoes shall be worn in the shower"); and in 1975 the number of drills and ceremonies had been reduced by a third, ostensibly to give cadets more time for study and other activities.

Some things, of course, remained eternal. West Point still worshiped the so-called God of Class Standing; even seating at football games was determined by class rank, and George — or, rather, #529-66 — found that his low standing put him only one seat away from the section in Michie Stadium reserved for the class of '67. And the academy's love of precision still ranged from the sublime to the ridiculous. In an attempt to define exactly how far sideburns would be permitted to migrate down a cadet's cheek, someone had discovered an obscure, cartilaginous part of the ear called the tragus. The discovery led to an edict: "No sideburns below the tragus."

Two reforms in particular were substantive. First, more than a hundred women would arrive with the class of 1980. Second, graduates no longer had to join the combat arms; newly commissioned second lieutenants could now select combat support branches (such as military intelligence) or combat service support (such as the transportation, ordnance, and quartermaster corps). Like many of his classmates — in fact, like Superintendent Berry and most of the Army's generals — George had deep reservations about both of these changes. He believed that West Point's foremost task was to fashion combat leaders. For nearly two hundred years, that was what made this school for soldiers distinctive. As for women, even though they were about to enter the service academies, federal law still barred them from combat units. That contradiction would almost certainly render them second-class citizens at West Point, and their very presence would destroy the atmosphere of this all-male sanctuary.

But for now, George's more immediate concern was Speed. Other than getting a little friendly advice and a clap on the back from his superiors, he was on his own. He began by summoning the group for a speech that was half pep talk, half threat.

"I don't know any of you," George said, "and I just got here. I don't know you personally, I don't have any opinion about any of this, and I don't know what your individual situations are. But you're supposed to act like cadets and do what I say. We're going to have physical-training runs every morning and we're going to try to behave like good soldiers."

So every morning Major Crocker led his two hundred grumbling charges on training runs through the academy streets. While permitting them ample opportunity to consult with their lawyers, he tried to keep them physically fit, mentally occupied, and away from the media — at least in the barracks. Much of his time was spent in informal counseling sessions. Some Speed cadets would come by to cry on his shoulder; others attempted to explain themselves; still others wanted to rail against the academy and the honor system. He listened patiently and, in a few cases, with considerable sympathy.

On the Fourth of July, those cadets still at the academy for the summer gathered with thousands of civilians from throughout the Hudson Valley to watch the academy's fireworks display. As one of the nation's historic showplaces, West Point had planned a grand celebration befitting the Bicentennial, investing a small fortune in Spiderwebs, Golden Dragons, Clustering Bees, and other pyrotechnic wonders. A flotilla of small boats assembled on the river, and a throng of expectant, festive celebrants lined the banks, etching the air with hissing sparklers. As the day's last light faded in the west, a technician ignited the first skyrocket. It rose a few feet, sputtered feebly, and tumbled to the ground. The same thing happened again. And again. And again.

Somehow, the entire display had become damp. The crowd could see an occasional distant burst of red, white, and blue from festivities in the small towns across the Hudson. But at West Point, the celebration amounted to little more than a depressing succession of fizzles. After the initial dismay, even some of the academy brass found the fiasco amusing. Given the way the Bicentennial year had gone thus far, they told one another, this debacle seemed only fitting.

It took but a few weeks for the grim presence of EE304 to cloud Jim Ford's euphoria following the *Yankee Doodle*'s triumphant return to a brass band and champagne at West Point's South Dock. When Ford and his crew had phoned home from Bermuda shortly after hearing the first radio report of the scandal, someone at the academy jokingly suggested that the sailors turn around and head back to England. Now, having been thoroughly briefed on the events of the past three months, the chaplain understood why. Nerves were frayed, tempers short, and a pall hung over the academy.

Every smoldering grievance about West Point seemed to blaze anew. Even the century-old hostility of the Army's military clergy toward the academy's civilian chaplains was inflamed. One morning not long after his return, Ford traveled to Washington for a meeting with Major General Orris E. Kelly, the chief of Army chaplains. As they lingered over breakfast on a pair of counter stools in the Sheraton Hotel restaurant, Kelly suddenly reproved Ford for his lack of military rank.

"How," Ford retorted, "do those two stars on your shoulder help you to minister to anybody?"

"These two stars help me because the people I minister know that I can relate to them," answered Kelly.

Ford scoffed. "If that's true," he replied, "how come you're not a private? We've got more of them."

That was an unusually impertinent riposte from Ford, but the tensions at West Point were infectious, making everyone peppery. He was doing the best he could at the academy to console and counsel; the job was difficult enough, Ford thought, without this brass-bedecked minister needling him.

As in the depths of the Vietnam War, Jim Ford was again perplexed by the proper role of the chaplain at a time of bitter controversy. Having spent hours talking to implicated cadets, and more hours talking to Sid Berry and Commandant Walter F. Ulmer, Jr., Ford felt great sympathy for both sides. One of his favorite words was *ombudsman*, a term of Scandinavian origin. An ombudsman investigated grievances by individuals against higher authorities. The West Point chaplain, he believed, should serve as an ombudsman; several times in the past he had leaped into honor disputes on behalf of cadets in whom he believed. He had testified for them at honor hearings, and once, in a case involving a cadet accused of cheating on a computer exam, Ford even retained an expert witness who won the young man's acquittal. But in the EE304 affair, he straddled the fence.

One day in mid summer, a young captain named Arthur F. Lincoln, Jr., showed up in the chaplain's office just north of the mess hall. Ford had known and liked Art Lincoln ever since he was a cadet in the class of 1966. Son of a Maine woodsman, Lincoln had attended law school at Boston College, joined the Army's judge advocate general corps, and served in Vietnam at the end of the war. In 1973, he arrived at West Point as a judge advocate officer and law instructor. Drawn into the EE304 case as an attorney appointed to represent several accused cadets, Lincoln was now the most controversial figure at the academy for his public insistence that West Point had turned a blind eye to the full scope of the scandal. He believed that at least six hundred cadets were involved to some degree, and it angered him that the academy refused to acknowledge any flaw in a system that had allowed so many young men to go astray.

Lincoln and the other defense lawyers had asked their clients to write detailed, confidential affidavits. A sympathetic Catholic priest, the Reverend Thomas Curley, had locked the documents in a safe deposit box at the Marine Bank in Highland Falls. The affidavits contained explosive allegations, accusing hundreds of additional cadets of cheating, lying, and other honor violations.

"I remember many instances in which 'poop sessions' were given by someone who had already taken an exam," one cadet wrote. "The size of the 'poop sessions' ranged from five to ten . . . and from there it spread to other companies, usually by word of mouth." The affidavits implicated twenty-two members of the honor committee, as well as the captains of several athletic teams and other prominent cadets.

Lincoln came right to the point with Ford. He wanted the chaplain's help. "These cadets have been wronged," he told Ford. "The institution isn't clean on this thing and I'd like your support on behalf of the cadets. What can you do for them?"

Ford hesitated. He felt bad for Art. A few of his classmates from '66 had rallied behind Lincoln, but most had ostracized him, convinced that he was disloyal and overzealous. Before long, Art and his wife stopped receiving invitations to parties and barbecues. "How can you do this to the academy?" one classmate pleaded.

Ford felt no such hostility toward Lincoln, but he was not prepared to become the lawyer's ally either. "Art, I just don't feel that I can put the weight of my office behind you," the chaplain finally replied. "I don't think that the facts are clear enough for me to make the kind of public statement that you want."

After a disappointed Lincoln left the office, Ford tried to sort out his own feelings. He had always been bothered by the honor system's mandatory expulsion of violators; it allowed no margin for extenuating circumstances, no way to temper justice with mercy. Although increasingly ecumenical — as chief chaplain Ford was administratively responsible for members of forty denominations plus Catholics and Jews at West Point — he remained resolutely Lutheran in his concept of grace, which he defined as "unmerited favor." Grace, he sometimes said, "is when you're loved by God and don't deserve it." All Christians shared the notion, but Lutherans lived it. The good things in life came as a gift. Jim Ford believed that with all his soul, but he recognized that the creed was absolutely antithetical to West Point. Nothing at the military academy was undeserved. Cadets who were slugged deserved to be slugged.

Cadets who wore stars deserved to wear stars. Cadets who cheated deserved to be kicked out.

Ford also thought another bit of Lutheran theology was apropos: *Simul justus et peccator,* simultaneously saint and sinner. That Latin phrase had been fundamental to Martin Luther and it was fundamental to Jim Ford. Every cadet, every pastor, every human being was incessantly tugged at by good and evil, he believed. In EE304, the *peccator* had gotten the upper hand. That did not make the young men immoral, he concluded; it simply showed them to be human. Ford measured morality by the inner desire of the heart to do the right thing. The cadets had obviously erred, but at heart, he held, they retained a basic goodness.

Having watched the academy closely for fifteen years, Ford knew that every significant trend sweeping American society inevitably showed up at West Point, albeit late and muted. Even the Supreme Court's abolition of mandatory chapel reflected the nation's ambivalence toward organized religion. Ford had welcomed that decision, though the ruling slashed Protestant cadet attendance by two-thirds and Catholic attendance by half; going to chapel, he believed, should be a voluntary act of worship, not a duty. To the extent that the cheating in EE304 was an act of defiance, he viewed it as an aftershock of the rebellions that had swept most college campuses years before. The scandal also was the result of a collision between an institution that continued to venerate a Southern rural military tradition — embodied by Sid Berry and even George Crocker — and a student body that was growing increasingly estranged from that tradition.

So what should the academy do? Ford wondered. What should *he* do? Ford had recently attended a lecture in the library by the former commander of the 82nd Airborne, James M. Gavin, one of the most celebrated Army generals of this century.

"Sir," a cadet had asked Gavin, "what's the most important thing about a West Point education?"

Gavin replied by citing a line from the Cadet Prayer: "Learning to choose the harder right instead of the easier wrong."

The cadets implicated in the EE304 scandal had chosen the easier wrong. They had to be punished, and though Ford regretted that the sole penalty was draconian, there seemed to be no recourse. He could not disagree with the authorities on this one. Nor would he sermonize on the issue; Ford had never been inclined to topicality in the pulpit. Like his farmers in Ivanhoe, like his congregation at West Point during the war, the cadets and officers at the academy would have to puzzle out this problem for themselves.

*

Just when it seemed that life at West Point could not get any more chaotic, 119 young women arrived and threw the academy into a new pandemonium. If traditionalists believed that the honor code contained the thirteen noblest words in the English language, then the ninety-four words in Public Law 94-106 — which abolished the all-male exclusivity of the nation's military academies — were considered the most ignoble. Had a company of Martians suddenly appeared on the Plain in dress gray and tarbuckets, there would have been no greater sense of invasion and outrage than was provoked by the arrival of ten dozen American females.

For several years, the male defense establishment had resisted the admission of women with a desperation worthy of Bataan or the Alamo. In April 1974, each of the service secretaries and uniformed chiefs issued statements adamantly opposing the idea. General Westmoreland, who dismissed the proposal as "silly," added, "Maybe you could find one woman in ten thousand who could lead in combat, but she would be a freak and we're not running the Military Academy for freaks." When Gerald Ford signed PL 94-106 into law on October 7, 1975, Sidney Berry had contemplated resigning in protest.

Instead, as Berry told one journalist, he decided "to put it behind me and do what the good soldier does." For the next nine months, the superintendent and Commandant Ulmer threw themselves into the preparations. They dispatched delegations to study other institutions that had recently gone coed, including Yale, the U.S. Merchant Marine Academy, and the Los Angeles Police Department. Berry and Ulmer flew to Fort McClellan, Alabama, to solict advice from the Women's Army Corps training center. "General," one female drill instructor told Berry, "don't ever be influenced by a woman crying. You can't trust a woman. If she thinks she can get away with something by crying, she'll do it."

The academy launched studies to establish an SOP — standard operating procedure — for everything from folding brassieres to dealing with menstrual cycles in the field. Berry personally reviewed any modification that would establish different standards for women. Should female cadets be permitted to wear makeup or perfume? Yes, it was decided, but in "tasteful" moderation. Should they participate in bayonet drills? Yes, why not? Should they be required to practice boxing and wrestling? No, because of possible breast damage, judo should be substituted. Should they live in the same barracks with the men? Yes, but for the first year only a third of the thirty-six companies would be integrated; at least eight to ten women per company were necessary to provide a sufficient "support group." Should they be permitted to date other cadets? Yes, but plebe women could date only other plebes, not upperclassmen. And sex in the barracks was strictly forbidden. (Later, when the inevitable violators of this dictum were caught *in flagrante,* they marched before a "fornication board," which harshly punished them for "engaging in acts of affection prejudicial to the discipline and good order of the U.S. Corps of Cadets.")

Berry announced that he expected male cadets to "clean up their language and manners." Engineers built new locker rooms in the gymnasium, as well as new sinks in the barracks (with chin-up bars to help the women develop their upper body strength). A group of fashion designers from Hart Schaffner & Marx sashayed into Ulmer's conference room one day — much to the disgust of the more macho tactical officers — with a portfolio of suggested uniforms that would better accommodate the female anatomy. One of the most contentious issues concerned the tails on the cadet full dress tunic, which ballooned unbecomingly around a woman's hips. After scrutinizing the derrières of several models who paraded past in a variety of jacket styles, Berry made what he described as "a major command decision": the women's coats would be shorn of their tails. The hem would stop at the waist like an Eisenhower jacket, or, less generously, like a waiter's jerkin.

Unfortunately, major command decisions had little influence on the ingrained male chauvinism of the United States Corps of Cadets. As Berry and Ulmer prepared West Point physically to receive the women, the academy's Office of Institutional Research surveyed the mental landscape. The OIR findings proved startling. One survey compared attitudes at West Point and the University of Texas. Not only were cadets more conservative in their views toward women than Texas students, the study concluded, but they were about as reactionary as the *fathers* of the Longhorn students. Fewer than half of the cadets agreed with the proposition that women should be considered equal to men in filling political offices or corporate executive suites.

Another survey revealed that cadets stereotyped women as either "the gentle kind" or "the talkative, emotional kind." A majority agreed that "the activities of married women are best confined to home and family." Among the cadet comments: "I think it is a disgrace for women to be here"; "West Point used to be the last bastion of male virility. Now our society has destroyed this"; "any woman that would even think of coming to West Point is not mentally straight."

In an attempt to lessen this misogyny, West Point's three generals — Berry, Ulmer, and the academic dean, Frederick A. Smith, Jr. — periodically met with large groups of cadets in question-and-answer sessions that became known as Stump the Stars. Although the queries were sometimes ludicrous and often cheeky, the generals tried to offer calm, reasoned explanations. But there were limits. Once, after Berry had explained that women would be permitted to wear their hair to the collar, a cadet from the class of '77 stood in the back of South Auditorium.

"Sir," he addressed Berry, "you say we're going to have the same standards for everybody?"

"Yes."

"Well, sir, why can't I wear my hair down to my collar?"

Before Berry could reply, Ulmer's patience snapped. Nearly leaping from his seat, he barked with sudden fury, "BECAUSE I SAY SO!"

The chastened cadet slumped back onto his chair as his classmates applauded the commandant's display of autocratic anger.

But despite their enthusiasm for Ulmer's outburst, few cadets were convinced that women had a rightful place at West Point. As one upperclassman declared on an opinion survey, "I feel it is my duty to the alumni and the entire Army to run out as many females as possible."

Such were the challenges facing George Crocker when he met with the nine plebe women in his company in early September 1976. His own misgivings notwithstanding, George was determined that the women would get every chance to succeed; the best guarantee of that, he believed, was to accord them equal treatment. Introducing himself as "a duck hunter from Arkansas," he gathered the women alone for the first and only time in Pershing Barracks shortly after swapping his Speed command for Company A-1.

"I'm not going to protect you," he said. "In my mind, the worst thing I could do is to somehow try to shelter you. That would make it twice as bad. You are trend setters, the first ones in a new territory. You're going to have it harder than every class after you, because there will only be one group that is the first class of women. But you're going to sink or swim on your own merit. You won't be harassed out of the academy, nor will you be coddled."

Despite Major Crocker's best intentions, they were harassed disgracefully. One of the nine women listening to George that day was Susan Puanani Kellett, a nineteen-year-old who had been valedictorian and student body president at Kamehameha High School in Honolulu. Arriving for Beast Barracks wearing a lei, jump suit, and high heels, she had encountered the usual shrieking abuse on reporting for the first time to "the man in the red sash," as tens of thousands had before her. ("Man, these guys are really in a bad mood," she thought naïvely.) But the standard hectoring that was a plebe's lot quickly assumed a sexist intensity, particularly when the entire corps returned after Beast in late summer.

"Good morning, sir," Susan greeted an upperclassman while walking across the Area one day.

"It's not going to be a good morning," he replied, "until you goddamn bitches get out of here."

Male cadets anonymously scrawled crude sexual slurs on the barracks walls, scattered condoms on the women's bunks, and sent vibrators to them through the mail. During a lecture in Mahan Hall one evening, when a psychologist made disparaging remarks about women in an effort to provoke a protective reaction from the cadets, the men stood and cheered. When Susan wore perfume to a showing of *The Longest Day* in Eisenhower Hall one night, the cadet next to her sniffed and said, "Miss, when you wear perfume, you should wear it conservatively. You stink." On another occasion, when she wore her uniform skirt, an upperclassman observed, "When I was home there were some *real* women there."

Some of the women cultivated a deliberate androgyny by artificially lowering their voices and refusing to wear skirts or makeup. Those considered too feminine by the men were "fluffs"; those too masculine were "dykes." "Whore" was a favorite all-purpose epithet. The men ridiculed the women for lacking a man's upper body strength and endurance and for having longer hair. (Some upperclassmen prowled the barracks with rulers, measuring locks that extended below the collar.) When some women began to gain weight from the daily four-thousand-calorie mess hall fare, they were badgered for contracting "Hudson hip disease." Many men resented the attention lavished on the women by the media and the GAP, the Great American Public; when a female cadet hurried along Thayer Road, tourists often shouted, "There's one!" and piled from their cars with cameras clicking. The women ruefully joked among themselves about being "bears at Yellowstone."

The women in A-1 viewed their Major Crocker as tough, fair, and clearly a bit discomfited at times by this squad of females who had so disrupted the masculine homogeneity of his company. One day he walked through the barracks with a roll of masking tape, marking a spot on the floor of each room to show how far the door had to be left open when a woman entertained a gentleman visitor. The women thought that was hilarious.

Another time, Susan and several others tied scarves around their heads, stuffed pillows under their cadet raincoats, and waddled about the corridor pretending to be "barefoot and pregnant." When George stumbled on the scene, he stared for a moment before wandering off with a shake of his head, as if to say "*This* is what happens when you let women in." The females thought that was hilarious, too.

Although an old flanker company, A-1 was now considered a no-nonsense outfit, and George continued that tradition. The men viewed him as reserved, formal, and a little intimidating, the apotheosis of the lean Airborne Ranger role model who wore a chestful of combat medals and brooked no debate when it came to carrying out orders. When the movie *Star Wars* came out, they presented him with a poster of the villainous Darth Vader, which he fastened to his office door.

Tactical officers competed fiercely for the informal accolade of commanding a "good company"; George and the other '66er tacs spent long hours debating leadership principles and how best to prepare cadets for life in the Army. Philosophies of discipline ranged from the relatively indulgent — like those of Mac Hayes of F-3 and Boyd Harris of H-4 — to the hard-nosed, like that of Inquisition One's Freddy McFarren. In a study conducted by the commandant's office, George was judged to be a "low quill-high slug" tac; he gave relatively few demerits, or quill, for minor infractions, but punished major transgressions with severe slugs, which had to be expiated by walking the Area. (Boyd Harris, who was "low quill-low slug," liked to quote Ambrose Bierce, who once defined a quill as "an instrument of torture yielded by a goose and wielded by an ass.")

Having viewed the corps both from the vantage point of Speed and from the tac's office in A-1, George saw subtle but significant differences from the cadets of his own day. The best cadets in the company, he concluded, "are better than we ever were." They were sophisticated, self-assured, and often much better prepared for Army life than the men of '66. On the other hand, he believed that the worst of the cadets he now saw would never have been accepted by the academy in the early 1960s. The doubling of the corps and the difficulty of attracting good candidates in the wake of Vietnam had led to the admission of some who were poorly motivated, physically marginal, and no credit to the long gray line.

Although he sympathized with some of those implicated in the EE304 affair — believing that they had simply been swept along by the "cool on honor" subculture — George was bothered by the extensive privileges now enjoyed by the upperclassmen. Nearly every weekend the firsties roared off to New York, abdicating responsibility for running the corps to a skeleton crew of lower ranking cadets. George saved his heaviest slugs for upperclassmen who failed to act like the young officers they were about to become.

While he never surrendered his conviction that West Point should have remained a polytechnic for the fighting Army's combat arms, George's experience in A-1 did moderate his views on women at the academy. For one thing, he thought the chauvinist hysteria was inane. The complaints that "women can't do pull-ups" or "women are brittle" seemed fatuous, and the wild rumors about A-1 and the other integrated companies being cadet brothels were contemptible. He was disgusted to discover that the upperclassmen in his company had even organized a secret contest in which the objective was to reduce every woman in A-1 to tears at least once.

George admired the response from one of the physical education instructors, who would answer complaints about women being "poor runners" with a brief lecture: "Okay, guys, physiologically the women have 40 percent more body fat, so just to make it even, let's give you a seventy-pound weight to carry. They have only 60 percent as much lung capacity, so let's degrade your breathing by making you wear this mask. They have a little mechanical disadvantage in their hip structure, so we'll put a brace between your legs to make you pigeon-toed. Now go run a mile, guys, and see if you can keep up with the women."

Women, without question, would play a crucial role in the volunteer Army. From less than 1 percent of the total force after World War II, they were now on their way to constituting 10 percent; jobs that had once been *omni vir* — all male — such as helicopter pilot and tank mechanic, were now capably filled by women. If West Point was going to be the leader of the Army, George reflected, then the academy damned well needed to be the leader in all respects, including the training of women officers.

Vonda tried to help in her own way. She had an unusual communication line to some members of the corps; at times it gave her a clearer sense than the tacs of what cadets were really thinking. Distressed by her vulnerabilty during their tour at crime-ridden Fort Bragg in the late 1960s, Vonda had taken up karate. Despite her diminutive size, she was a natural. One day, after a few months of study at Fort Leavenworth, she pointed to her loose-fitting robe. "Grab my *gi*, George," she urged. A split second after grasping her lapels, George lay on the floor, pleading for mercy. Vonda was delighted.

Now she was close to getting her black belt. Several times a month she met with a karate master and a group of male cadets in the old gymnasium. The workout began with a barefoot one-mile run, 180 sit-ups, and 50 fingertip push-ups. Then, after three hours of practice kicks and feints, they ran another four miles.

Once, when she was helping a novice cadet who was six foot six, Vonda failed to block his punch properly. He smacked her on the cheek with a two-knuckle jab that knocked her out. "Oh, God," the cadet wailed, holding Vonda's limp form, "I've killed the tac's wife!" The master laid her out on the floor and magically revived her with finger pressure on the soles and on a spot beneath her nose. Bouncing to her feet, Vonda waved away the cadet's profuse apologies. "Don't worry about it. I don't go home with any tales. I don't even remember your name."

Before long, the cadets treated her as one of the boys. Emboldened by her pledge of anonymity, they talked openly about their tacs, their professors, their girlfriends. They talked about the boodle hidden in their rooms, the best places to sneak a drink, and the mischief they hoped to perpetrate when on leave. They also ranted about the women cadets:

"They don't belong here. They're bringing down the standards."

"They're only here to get a husband. Why do they want to be here when they can't go into combat?"

"Some of them looked okay when they first got here, but now they're heifers. They've all got Hudson hip disease."

Although Vonda had agreed with George that admitting women to the academy was a mistake, she felt sympathetic toward them now that they were here. What had they done to earn this kind of disdain? Perhaps if they were more assertive and self-confident, even within the limits of the plebe system, life would be easier. Whenever the women from A-1 visited the Crocker house in Stony Lonesome for dinner, Vonda tried to lift their spirits. Once, when George was out of earshot, she offered a little advice.

"You know," she said in her soft drawl, "y'all could make the most of being women. There's nothing wrong with keeping your femininity. A little lip gloss could go a long way."

Ruefully, the cadets shook their heads. "You don't understand, Mrs. Crocker," one of them replied. "If we put on even a tiny bit of lip gloss or perfume or makeup, we get heckled. It's better not to put on anything than to deal with the grief we get."

Vonda nodded. They had a fair point, one that was difficult to refute. Even Darth Vader's wife — a black-belted model of perky self-confidence — could understand what it was like to be afraid. She pressed the issue no further.

On August 23, 1976, Secretary of the Army Martin Hoffmann announced that cadets who had left West Point after being implicated in the EE304 scandal — the number was climbing toward 150 — could be readmitted to the academy in the summer of 1977 after a one-year "period of reflection." Those who wanted to return would have the cheating episode expunged from their records; those who chose to remain civilians would not be required to put in two years of service as Army enlisted men, as was usual for upperclassmen who resigned. The year's absence, Hoffmann suggested, would give each cadet time "to mature, reflect upon his desire for a military career, and demonstrate his potential for commissioning."

The secretary's amnesty did not go down well with the West Point brass. Sidney Berry believed that Hoffmann — whom he described as having "a high regard for West Point, a high regard for the Army, and a lawyer's mind" — had not thought the issue through and was too quick to offer absolution. Walt Ulmer was also incensed. The commandant obdurately opposed readmitting the cheaters. Hoffmann, he believed, misunderstood West Point, misread public opinion, and had an unreasonable concern that Congress was about to intervene in the scandal. One Sunday afternoon in early September, when the secretary was visiting the academy, Ulmer finally gave voice to his frustration. "Every son of bitch with a briefcase and a three-day pass is trying to tell me how to do my business," the commandant said. "I really don't think I need all the help."

Hoffmann let the insolent remark pass — although he would not forget it — and proceeded to announce the appointment of a special commission to investigate the scandal. To chair the panel, the secretary selected two distinguished West Pointers: the Eastern Airlines president Frank Borman, a former astronaut from the class of 1950, and Harold K. Johnson, a member of the class of 1933 who had survived the Bataan Death March to become chief of staff in the mid 1960s.

The Borman Commission, as it came to be known, swiftly set up offices in the academy library and began sifting through a mountain of archives and confidential records. After several months of intense work, the commission released its report in Thayer Hall, the old riding arena where Cadet Sid Berry had once practiced his horsemanship. In addition to recounting in excruciating detail how the EE304 affair had come to light, the ninety-page study noted that the scandal was not unprecedented and followed a "recurring pattern [of cheating rings] during the preceding twenty-five years." Yet the current degree of disaffection in the corps and the palpable contempt for the honor code stood in "dramatic contrast" to the mid 1960s, when the academy honor system "was highly regarded, well understood, and strongly subscribed to."

Furthermore, the report cited irrefutable evidence that "board fixing" and corruption in the honor committee had persisted for several years. Thirty of thirty-five cadets found guilty of cheating by a special board of officers in the summer of 1976 had previously been exonerated by the cadet honor committee; one cadet had even been acquitted eight times of various honor code infringements, always protected by his friends on the committee. Although the academy leadership had been aware of gross inadequacies in the honor system, the report charged, "no decisive action was taken."

A subsequent study conducted by three Army generals painted an even starker portrait. West Point, it concluded, was plagued by

> poor morale, lack of supervision and planning, intellectual inbreeding of the faculty, resistance to change, negative attitudes toward learning among cadets, and a pervasive lack of humor . . . Problems are identified falteringly and solved hesitantly.
>
> There are doubts about the role of tactical officers, the place of women in the Army, and priorities in the education and training of cadets. Cleavages exist between faculty and non-faculty, academic and military, senior and junior, tenured and non-tenured, male and female, officer and cadet.
>
> A relatively humorless atmosphere seems to prevail . . . A certain grimness marks many of the cadets, an outlook which may blind them to many of life's humorous aspects and rob them of much of the enjoyment of their four-year experience.

When this was duly reported in *The New York Times,* a group of cadets slung a banner from a window in Grant Hall. Demonstrating that at least the corps' impish streak remained intact, the banner read, HOW CAN A NEWSPAPER WITH NO COMICS CALL US "HUMORLESS"? Even so, the scandal hurt. Several thousand cadets who had dutifully observed the honor code, and knew nothing of "cool on honor," felt unfairly impugned by the ridicule and bad press. Particularly grating was a different banner, this one unfurled in the bleachers by students from another university during a football game. It read, AT LEAST WE DON'T CHEAT!

As Hoffmann had foreseen, the public airing of dirty laundry by the Borman Commission led to a rapid dissipation of interest in EE304. The scandal was over — 93 of 149 dismissed cadets would return the following summer as members of the class of '78 — but not the bloodletting. There had been too much rancor to let bygones be bygones.

Attorney Art Lincoln, having been passed over for promotion to major, received orders to Fort Polk, Louisiana, for "career enhancement." Recognizing that he no longer had a career to enhance, Lincoln resigned from the Army halfway into what he had always assumed would be a twenty-year career. Sid Berry asked him, during a final conversation, "If you were superintendent for a day, what would you have done differently?" Lincoln smiled and replied tartly, "I would have listened to a guy like me a little more carefully."

Walt Ulmer, who considered the Borman report "unbelievably superficial," was scratched from the promotion list to major general and abruptly removed as commandant midway through his tour. Ulmer's admirers believed that he had been made a scapegoat, and many tactical officers angrily resented Berry for allowing his commandant to take the fall. Ulmer never felt that way about the superintendent, but before leaving the academy he gave a scathing interview to a reporter which appeared in a New York newspaper under the headline GENERAL OUSTED FROM WEST POINT CHARGES HE WAS TREATED UNFAIRLY. Although Ulmer's exile to Fort Hood appeared to mark the end of his career, he later was rehabilitated, and earned three stars and a corps command before retiring.

For Sidney Berry, the scandal left an indelible stain on an otherwise impeccable record. After finishing his three-year tour as superintendent, he took command of an Army corps in Germany. But there would be no fourth star. The man who had been lionized by *Life* as "an Army star" — whose face, the magazine said, lent "itself to carving in stone or minting on coins" — would retire to Mississippi without ever becoming chief of staff, as had been predicted for him.

One last, intriguing act, however, remained to be played out as EE304 passed from view. In the fall of 1976, Universal Studios asked Berry's permission to use the academy grounds to film a scene for the movie *MacArthur,* starring Gregory Peck. Although he had reservations about the disruptions caused by a Hollywood film crew — the academy already resembled Grand Central, given the investigators, journalists, and usual tourist hordes tramping about — Berry concluded that West Point and the Army could use some favorable publicity for a change. He quickly assented.

Led by the producer, Frank McCarthy, a retired brigadier who had served as George Marshall's military secretary during World War II, the seventy-five-member production team moved into the Hotel Thayer. By shaving Peck's hairline, nicking a bald spot on the top of his head, and combing a few gray strands across his skull, Universal's makeup artists transformed the sixty-year-old actor into an uncanny facsimile of the eighty-two-year-old Douglas MacArthur.

Late one afternoon, Berry invited the visitors to a cocktail party in the Quarters 100 library, known as the Five Star Room. When Peck and his wife arrived, they studied the portraits of the Army's five-star generals covering the library walls. Mrs. Peck glanced back and forth from her husband to the picture of MacArthur, ever jaunty in his open collar and go-to-hell cap. "You know, Gregory," she said at last, "he looks more like you every day."

As dusk fell, Berry escorted the actor across the edge of the Plain to the mess hall. Peck had assumed the shambling gait of an elderly man, and for a moment the superintendent had the eerie sense that it actually was the Old Soldier toddling at his elbow. "You must excuse me for walking so slowly, General Berry," Peck apologized, "but I've gotten myself so into the character of General MacArthur that I just can't throw it off easily."

In re-creating the scene of MacArthur's May 1962 valedictory speech, the producer and his crew took great pains to achieve historic accuracy. When the filming was about to begin, only two of the corps' four regiments were permitted in the mess hall; all women cadets, of course, were excluded. The director instructed the cadets not to look at the cameras and asked those wearing horn-rim glasses to remove them, since they had not been in fashion in 1962. Among those watching the preparations were George Crocker, who stood beneath the poop deck, and Jim Ford, who had been in Washington Hall on that Saturday afternoon fourteen years before.

When the sound, lighting, and camera equipment was ready, Peck faced the sea of gray uniforms. Hand pressed flat on the lectern, he launched into an abridged version of the original thirty-two-minute speech.

"Duty, honor, country," he intoned, a slight tremble in his voice. "Those three hallowed words reverently dictate what you ought to be, what you can be, what you will be. The long gray line has never failed us. You now face a new world — a world of change. The thrust into outer space of the satellite spheres and missiles mark the beginning of another epoch, and through all of this welter of change, your mission remains fixed, determined, inviolable — it is to win our wars. Only the dead have seen the end of war."

As Peck ended one take, Ford noticed that the director had omitted a historical detail. "When the general finished his speech," the chaplain pointed out, "he added a little flourish. He turned and saluted Mrs. MacArthur up on the poop deck."

The crew shot the scene again, this time incorporating Ford's suggestion. "The shadows are lengthening for me, the twilight is here," Peck repeated. "Today marks my final roll call with you, but I want you to know that when I cross the river my last conscious thoughts will be of the corps, and the corps, and the corps. I bid you farewell."

Wheeling about, he tossed a salute to the actress playing Jean MacArthur. As their predecessors had fourteen years earlier, the cadets paused for a heartbeat before exploding in a thunderous ovation that washed against the wainscoting and carried high into the rafters.

It was a moving re-creation, well directed and superbly acted. Given the events of the past few months, Sid Berry thought the performance provided a splendid lesson for the two thousand cadets who stood clapping and whooping with robust enthusiasm.

Yet the scene was not quite real. There was a slight hollowness to it, an air of contrivance. Too much had happened since May 1962. Those days, suffused with a golden innocence, were gone forever. The "world of change" that the general described had been more apocalyptic than he had foreseen. As MacArthur himself predicted, the Old Soldier had faded away. And not even Hollywood, not even Gregory Peck, could bring him back again.

16

THE POPLAR TREE

FRIGID in winter, searing in summer, tense and dangerous year round, the two-and-a-half-mile-wide demilitarized zone separating North and South Korea was sometimes called "the loneliest spot in the world." Bisected by 1292 yellow panels that precisely demarcated the border, the DMZ stretched for 151 miles across the waist of the peninsula, from the Sea of Japan in the east to the Yellow Sea in the west. Although a haven for pheasants, black bears, and Manchurian cranes, the strip was as much a no man's land in 1976 as it had been before the armistice that ended the Korean War twenty-three years earlier.

The American Army still classified the DMZ as a combat zone, and with ample cause. Since the signing of the truce in 1953, a thousand South Koreans, six hundred North Koreans, and forty-nine Americans had been killed in border clashes. North Korean infiltrators, often dressed in ROK (Republic of Korea) uniforms, were frequently detected sneaking into the south. Three times in the mid 1970s, ROK forces had discovered North Korean miners burrowing beneath the DMZ. The third shaft, discovered only two miles from the border village of Panmunjom, bored through solid granite 225 feet beneath the surface. The tunnel was wide enough for three soldiers wearing full packs to run abreast, and the floor canted at a slope of 3 degrees so that ground water would flow north, where it could be pumped out. As GIs in Korea liked to say, "There ain't no D in the DMZ."

Under the 1953 truce terms, North and South were each permitted to rebuild one war-gutted hamlet within the DMZ. South Korea chose a village near Panmunjom named Taesongdong, whose 225 inhabitants had subsequently become the country's most prosperous farmers. Each citizen of Taesongdong owned seventeen acres of rice land, compared with the average of one acre held by other southern farmers; as further compensation for living in the DMZ and abiding by an eleven P.M. curfew, the villagers paid no taxes and were exempt from military conscription.

The northern village of Paek Chon Ni, also within sight of Panmunjom, consisted of a weird cluster of pastel-tinted apartment buildings, where martial music and socialist slogans blared from loudspeakers all day long. Nicknamed Propaganda Village by the Americans, the hamlet was a Potemkin fake. Southern observers squinting through telescopes could see that the apartments were barren of furnishings. Every morning, the North Koreans bused farmers and their children into the DMZ, where they worked in the Paek Chon Ni fields until late afternoon. Then they were herded back onto the buses and driven away. At dusk all of the lights in the apartment buildings came on simultaneously, triggered by a master switch.

Of the 42,000 U.S. troops in South Korea in 1976, about a hundred served with several dozen ROK soldiers in a 166-man unit based along the DMZ at Camp Kitty Hawk, just south of Panmunjom. The unit's three platoons took turns manning observation posts and serving as guards during talks between North and South at a compound within the DMZ known as the Joint Security Area, or JSA.

Originally intended as a temporary, neutral site for the discussion of truce violations and other grievances, the JSA's Quonset huts and spare wooden buildings — crowded into a circle only eight hundred yards across — had become part of the landscape. Each side could have no more than five officers and thirty enlisted men at one time in the JSA, and automatic weapons were prohibited. The main road into the JSA from the south, Military Supply Route 1, had been built over an ancient trace that once stretched from Pusan in the peninsula's southeast corner all the way to Manchuria. Now the southern stretch of the road ended at the infamous Bridge of No Return, where both sides exchanged prisoners following the 1953 armistice and across which the crew of the American spy ship U.S.S. *Pueblo* had marched in December 1968 after nearly a year in North Korean captivity.

The JSA was the one spot in Korea where northerners and southerners stood cheek by jowl, invariably scowling. Open warfare had been succeeded by a blustery battle of intimidation, in which one-upmanship became an art form. Both sides, for example, built flagpoles on an Eiffel Tower scale. The four-hundred-foot North Korean tower stood a bit taller than South Korea's, but the southern flag was the size of a clipper ship's mainsail. The skirmishing over flags later carried into the armistice building, where each side began installing progressively taller flagstaffs until the poles would no longer fit in the negotiation room.

Physical confrontations had become commonplace in the JSA. North Korean guards frequently spat, shoved, or shouted threats and obscenities at the American and ROK soldiers; as recently as June 1975, Major William Henderson had suffered permanent damage to his larynx after being kicked in the throat outside the armistice building. After that, both sides selected soldiers in part on the basis of height and bulk. Few of the American or ROK troops were shorter than six feet or lighter than 175 pounds; some reportedly wore elevator lifts in their combat boots. Walter Winchell, commenting on American troops in Korea in 1950, had advised, "If you have a son overseas, write to him. If you have a son in the Second Infantry Division, pray for him." A quarter century later, prayers were still appropriate for soldiers posted in the angry perdition where the two Koreas collided.

For relaxation when they went off duty, the American officers at Panmunjom often repaired to a club known as the Monastery. Each member of the Merry Monks, as they called themselves, owned a brown, hooded monk's robe made of velveteen, which he wore during elaborate induction ceremonies whenever a new officer arrived. Each monk also owned a black baseball cap. Hung from hooks above the Monastery bar, the caps were arranged by seniority — not according to rank, but on the basis of time spent in the DMZ. The most veteran monk hung his hat on the last hook at the corner of the bar; when his year in Korea ended and the time came to go home, his robed comrades bade him farewell with a jolly ritual of toasts and then moved their own caps one peg closer to the end.

On Wednesday, August 18, 1976, the merriest monk of them all was Captain Arthur Bonifas. After 368 days in Korea, Art had three days left in his tour before returning to the States to pick up Marcia and the children, who had remained at West Point for the past year. His replacement — Captain Ed Shirron, who at six foot six and more than two hundred pounds was big even by Merry Monk standards — had already arrived. Art was spending his final days in Korea showing Shirron around, preparing for the change of command on the twenty-first, and planning one task that remained undone in the JSA — the trimming of a Normandy poplar tree that obscured the view of southern observers watching the Bridge of No Return.

Sometimes Art felt that he had been at the DMZ for fifty-two years instead of fifty-two weeks. The job was important — he had no doubt about that — but after a year away from his family, he yearned to go home. No one knew with certainty whether the American Army would remain in Korea much longer, since the Democratic presidential nominee, Jimmy Carter, had already hinted that if elected, he would consider removing the U.S. troops. Art thought such a move would be unfortunate; after spending 54,000 American lives and $40 billion to preserve South Korea's independence in the past quarter century, this was no time to retrench. Years before, the stalemate that ended the Korean War had felt like defeat to an America accustomed to total victory. When viewed through the experience of a genuine drubbing in Vietnam, however, preserving the status quo in Korea seemed increasingly satisfying, particularly given the economic boom sweeping South Korea.

Art was also eager to get back to his first professional love, the artillery. Six years had now passed since he had been a true redleg. After he returned from Vietnam, the Army had sent him to the artillery advanced course at Fort Sill for a year and then, in August 1970, to Syracuse University for a master's degree in mathematics. In graduate school he let his hair and sideburns sprout and even cultivated a mustache. The Army warned him to expect antimilitary feelings on the campus — remove the Fort Sill parking stickers from your car bumper, he and Marcia were told, so that protestors won't know who you are — but it wasn't so bad once they got there. While at Syracuse, Art had also converted to Catholicism, which pleased his in-laws.

In the summer of 1972, the Bonifas family moved downstate to West Point, where Art taught calculus. The three years at West Point had been idyllic in many ways. The family's third child, Megan, was born at the academy, joining Beth, who was born at Fort Benning, and Brian, who was born at Sill. Every afternoon, Art and the other instructors who lived in Stony Lonesome caught the "Daddy Bus" in front of Thayer Hall after work. Scores of children swarmed from the tidy brick duplexes when they heard the tortured grinding of the diesel engine as the bus crawled up Continental Road past the football stadium. Escorted into the house by his capering kids, Art would romp and wrestle with them for a few minutes before climbing the stairs to shed his uniform. He and Marcia fell into the habit of spending fifteen or twenty minutes alone in the bedroom — "private time," they called it — just hashing over the day's events or swapping gossip while Art slipped into mufti. For both of them, that brief interlude became the most special time of the day, drawing them closer than ever before.

In the summer of 1975, Art had considered a tempting offer to extend for a fourth year in the math department. He liked teaching, especially the lower sections of cadets who truly needed his help and who reminded Art of himself. (The old "Green Death" of his own cadet days had been replaced with a more conventional calculus text.) By now many classmates from '66 staffed the math department in particular and the academy in general, and they often gathered for a few rubbers of bridge or tailgate parties before home football games.

Yet Art wanted to return to the muddy-boot Army. That was important for his career, and, more important, he missed being with the troops. When offered the job of heading the security detachment in the Korean JSA, he accepted with enthusiasm; though the detachment was not part of an artillery unit, the assignment was prestigious and offered him an opportunity to command soldiers again. Marcia and the children moved into a dowdy, two-bedroom duplex on Clark Street at Stewart annex, a former airbase just north of West Point. The quarters were disappointing — among other things, the basement flooded routinely — but the Bonifases both knew that "waiting wives" rarely received better housing. Art had spent his last weekend at home cobbling together bunk beds for the kids.

A few days after arriving in Korea, Art wrote Marcia a letter, dated 18 August 1975:

> Hi, honey. Finally getting into my job. It will be great. I will practically run this camp. I am responsible for every person in it — all their equipment, plus I will deal directly with the North Koreans over the peace table concerning security between the North Korean guards and our forces in the Joint Security Area. I am also commander of the three platoons that go forward one at a time to guard the area. One of my platoons is in that area 24 hours every day of the year. It's really spooky. We live constantly within four miles of North Korea.
>
> The North Koreans are rotten people as you can imagine. They spit on our guards and do as much as they can to harass us into a fistfight as with Major Henderson. In the Henderson case, there was more to it than he stated. Our mission here is to take the verbal abuse, kicking, and shoving, but to not let it go any further. Major Henderson lost his cool and blew it. It's a natural reaction but he should have known better than to do that.
>
> I've driven up there three or four times now and their guards have been trying to figure out who I am and what I'm doing there. It is really interesting to see this and again to be thankful that we are U.S. citizens. I am so glad you and the kids are safe back home.
>
> We have some personnel problems, even though the majority of the people are great. Ten days ago, one boy was so upset about family problems that he committed suicide with a rifle.
>
> A lot of my old training is coming back and I think I can really do a great job here. Tell the kids I love them. Beth xxxxx Brian xxxxx Megan xxxxx. And, of course, I miss you the most, hon. Love, Art.

As the months passed, Art spent much of his time haggling over security issues with the North Koreans, who would shriek "U.S. imperialist aggressors" as many as three hundred times in a single session. Of the 35,000 truce violations alleged by South Korea since the war ended, the North had admitted to two; of the 150,000 violations alleged by the North, the South had admitted to fewer than a hundred. That was hardly the kind of conciliation likely to alleviate tension, much less reunify the nation; whenever he entered the JSA, Art wore a crash helmet and groin protector.

In February 1976, he returned home for several weeks to be with his father, who was dying of cancer in Omaha. When he visited Marcia and the children at West Point, Art brought a transcript of a recent negotiating session he had held with a captain from the Korean People's Army (KPA):

KPA: Your hooligan today drove his jeep like mad dog and the jeep run this way as showing the mark on his wheel and hit the structure and destroy it. In this way your hooligans continue to commit provocations against our personnel when on duty. Don't be seeking for a way to evade the responsibility for this criminal act. Admit and apologize for that.

BONIFAS: You will have to explain to me once more how this is a criminal act, a scratch on a cement foundation.

KPA: Don't make a silly attempt, but admit and apologize.

BONIFAS: Last night, someone attempted to break into one of our guard posts next to the Pan Mun Bridge. This is a very serious incident, I believe, more serious than standing here today talking about a scratch in some concrete. Will you investigate that matter?

KPA: Don't make nonsense.

And so on, for page after page.

As his tour drew to a close, Art began putting his affairs in order. He expected to be on the August promotion list, so he drove to Seoul to order new uniforms, a major's shoulder boards, and engraved invitations to the party he and Marcia planned to throw at West Point. Several times he called home to offer advice about their next move, which would be to an artillery unit at Hunter Army Air Field in Georgia in the fall. He also mailed a birthday card to his mother, on which he scribbled, "Things are fairly quiet here now with the KPA. Hopefully, they'll stay that way for some time to come."

Yet conditions on the DMZ were hardly as placid as Art's reassuring note suggested. Three North Korean infiltrators and three ROK soldiers had been killed in a firefight in late June, and machine-gun bursts had been exchanged on August 5. The North Korean leader, Kim Il Sung, had canceled a planned trip to Sri Lanka, complaining bitterly about the "deterioriating situation on the Korean border." Always tense, in the late summer of 1976 the DMZ was as taut as a bowstring.

The morning was already muggy at ten o'clock on the eighteenth as Art drove into the JSA to supervise the tree-trimming detail. His uniform fatigues blotted the perspiration from his back and shoulders, and a dog days' haze hung over the DMZ. Because of the border tensions, the tree operation had been planned carefully; a previous pruning attempt on August 6 had been aborted after KPA threats. During consultations on the seventeenth, Art's commanding officer, Lieutenant Colonel Victor Vierra, had told him, "Make sure you're firm."

Art's first stop was at Checkpoint 5, an observation post five hundred yards from the Bridge of No Return and the guardhouse — known as Checkpoint 3 — near the southern end of the bridge. Gazing down the pitch toward the bridge, Art clearly saw the offending Normandy poplar, which stood only thirty-five yards from CP3. Originally planted as part of a windbreak in 1941 when Korea was still under Japanese occupation, the poplar was now forty feet tall and full of noisy, nesting magpies. Once again, Art mentally noted which boughs blocked the view of the bridge and guardhouse. Before leaving CP5, he positioned a soldier with a camera and asked Ed Shirron to remain there also.

"You'll be able to see what's happening from here with binoculars," he explained, "and it will be clear to the North Koreans that there's just one guy in charge down there."

At 10:40, he drove to the tree in his jeep with two other officers: Art's ROK counterpart, Captain Kim Moon Kwan, and one of the platoon leaders, Mark T. Barrett, a twenty-five-year-old first lieutenant who had been in Korea for only a month. Following the jeep, a deuce-and-a-half truck carried five workers from the Korean Service Corps and seven guards armed with pickax handles. In keeping with JSA rules, the only firearms allowed were the officers' pistols. Art positioned the rest of Barrett's platoon at Checkpoint 4, about seven hundred yards from the tree; another platoon remained just south of the JSA entrance; the third platoon was off duty.

After leaning two ladders against the poplar trunk, three of the Korean workers climbed into the lower boughs. Each carried an ax. Hand saws, power saws, a hatchet, and a machete lay scattered on the ground. At 10:50, ten minutes after the pruning began, several jeeps bearing eleven North Koreans crossed the Bridge of No Return. Art recognized their leader, Senior Lieutenant Pak Chul. Nicknamed Bulldog by the American troops because of his saturnine scowl, Pak was a former KPA sergeant who had been commissioned in 1974 as a reward for kicking a U.S. officer in the testicles.

"What are you doing?" Pak demanded in Korean as he approached Art and his men.

Captain Kim replied that they were only trimming the tree, not cutting it down. Pak nodded. "Good," he replied.

But a minute later, the North Korean demanded that the work be stopped. "The branches that are cut will be of no use, just as you will be after you die," he threatened. Art ignored him, turning his back to watch the workers who hacked at the limbs while nervously aware of the confrontation below.

Pak whispered to one of his soldiers, who then hopped into a jeep and drove off. Moments later, a KPA truck roared across the bridge. As the truck halted near the tree, twenty more KPA soldiers spilled from the rear with metal pipes and ax handles. "Stop the work!" Pak shrieked. He carefully removed his watch, wrapped it in a handkerchief, and stuffed it into his pocket.

Art again ignored the bluster and gestured to the workers to continue, apparently unaware that Pak had maneuvered directly behind him. "*Chukyo!*" screamed the North Korean. "Kill him!" He leaped at the American captain's back, striking his neck with a karate blow that knocked Art to the ground.

Up at Checkpoint 5, Ed Shirron couldn't believe his eyes as he watched the brawl erupt a quarter mile away. The fight had begun so quickly. Through his binoculars Shirron saw the KPA soldiers viciously clubbing the Americans and ROKs, whose shouts and grunts carried up the ridge. Mark Barrett broke free of the melee and sprinted out of sight into a narrow gully, closely pursued by several club-wielding North Koreans. The South Korean workers dropped their axes and ran as the KPA pelted them with rocks. Several KPA guards picked up the abandoned tools and swung them with a wild, pendular frenzy. Shirron watched as five or six soldiers clustered around Art's prone figure. Again and again, they whacked at him, first with clubs, then with the blunt end of an ax.

"Jesus Christ!" an American soldier standing next to Shirron cried out. "Jesus Christ, they're killing him!"

Marcia hurried home from the Stewart Officers Club. She had never left the children alone before, and being away from them made her nervous. Beth was a very responsible eight-year-old, and several helpful neighbors lived nearby, but there was no telling what kind of mischief Brian and Megan would get into. She glanced at her watch: eleven A.M. She had been gone for seventy-five minutes.

A Lenox china platter rested on the car seat next to her, now empty of the baked goods that Marcia had taken to the Officers Wives Club hail-and-farewell. The final busy round of goodbyes had begun. In addition to bidding adieu to the half-dozen waiting wives who were preparing to leave West Point with their returning husbands, the Club had formally thanked Marcia and the other Red Cross volunteers who had worked at the Stewart clinic during the past year. Marcia appreciated the gracious gesture, but she was glad when the speeches ended and she could leave.

Was there ever such a thing as a normal move? she wondered. Even though the Army shunted its officers around every two or three years as routinely as chess pieces, anxiety always seemed to grab hold. She had long ago committed herself to Army life, but it took a couple of hardship tours — when your husband was halfway around the world for a year at a time — to earn your stripes. Marcia had now endured two such tours, Vietnam and Korea. If Art's absences had been hard on her, they had been harder on the children. She particularly worried that Beth, who had spent nearly two and a half of her eight years without Art around, was not as close to her father as she should have been. Marcia knew that Art was desperately eager to come home, and she was desperately ready for him. The strain of caring for three children alone had worn her down; unable to find Brian one day recently, she had panicked and summoned the MPs, only to discover him sleeping on the top bunk bed. So when Art had mentioned in his most recent phone call from Korea that he might stop in Omaha to see his dying father, Marcia begged him to return to West Point first. "Please, Art," she pleaded, "just come home and take care of Brian and me."

He had replied with as close to a rebuke as he was capable of delivering. "Marcia, I cannot guarantee that I am going to be home right away," he said sternly. "You have got to learn to take care of him yourself."

She did her best. Certainly she felt more self-reliant than she had during Art's year in Vietnam. The memory of her struggles with the checkbook that year always made her smile. "How is it possible," he had asked incredulously after coming home, "that anybody could make such a mess with so little money?"

This time, he would have nothing to complain about on that score. She also thought he would like the new house she had helped design in Savannah. It seemed so long ago that they had been Lieutenant and Mrs. Lieutenant at Fort Benning, driving around the post to gaze admiringly at the field grade officers' quarters. They had assured each other then that military life was only going to improve, and now that Art was a major — he was, in fact, on the promotion list that had come out this morning — they would finally have a fine house of their own. Marcia had selected a real estate agent from the back of *Army Times,* flown to Georgia, and — ever mindful of the $45,000 ceiling she and Art had agreed to — helped choose everything from the length of the windows and the wallpaper in the bathroom to the precise timbre of the door chimes. Before signing the house contract, she had even marched into the brigade commander's office to ask for his assurance that Art was going to remain at Hunter for at least two years. What brass! she thought, remembering how she had sat next to the colonel's desk sipping coffee while he called Washington and then guaranteed a minimum tour of twenty-four months. She couldn't believe that she had been so bold, but the recollection pleased her.

The decision to remain at West Point while Art was gone had been the right one. Moving in with Thelma and Ray Bonifas in Omaha had been out of the question. They simply were not up to handling three rambunctious children; after one five-day visit a few years before, Thelma had written, "Just a few more adjustments to the TV and a little more Ajax on the walls and the house will be as good as new." Marcia had given serious consideration to returning to her parents' place in Brooklyn, where she would have been more than welcome. But West Point was home. The academy, though beset by the EE304 scandal and the turmoil over the admission of women, was still a lovely place to live and raise a family. Most of her friends lived at West Point, and at this stage in her life she knew that she needed to be independent of her parents.

That reminded her: tomorrow was her birthday, number thirty-three. She made a mental note to bake a cake for the party the children would expect.

As Marcia pulled into the driveway, she noticed a gray staff car parked in front of the house. When she got out of her car, carefully hugging the Lenox platter, a young officer with a briefcase emerged from the other sedan and began walking toward her. Maybe I'm in trouble for leaving the kids alone, she thought.

"Are you Mrs. Marcia Bonifas?" the officer asked. He wore the silver bars of a first lieutenant, and she was struck by the deep flush in his face. Perspiration cascaded from his forehead.

"Yes." She nodded.

"On behalf of the president, the secretary of the Army, and the chief of staff," the lieutenant blurted out, "I regret to inform you that your husband has been mortally wounded."

"Wounded?" She felt her own face flush with confusion. Art had mentioned an officer in Korea named Dan Cronin who had been accidentally shot in the leg. "You mean, wounded like Dan Cronin?"

"Who?" asked the lieutenant, now as confused as she was. "I don't know — that name is not familiar. That's not the name of the other officer who was killed with Captain Bonifas."

"Was killed?" she echoed. Her confusion gave way to panic. *Don't drop the plate,* she told herself.

"Yes," the lieutenant said. "Killed."

Curiously, before she felt anything else, she felt pity for this hapless young officer who stood there sweating like a horse in the sun. He was so miserable, so obviously eager to be somewhere else, anywhere else. "Please," she said, "won't you come inside?"

They stepped into the cool hallway near the staircase, her eyes as wide and unblinking as if she had been slapped. Continuing into the kitchen, Marcia set the plate on the counter. The lieutenant asked if he could use the telephone to call his office at Fort Hamilton, in Brooklyn. When she nodded, he added, "If it's any consolation to you, there was another man shot with your husband."

No, that was not much consolation, thank you. She walked into the living room, gazing vacantly at the furniture. *Help me,* she thought, *help*. Things like this didn't happen in Korea. It was not Vietnam. The war was over. Korea was all bombast and spear shaking, not a place of mortal danger.

When the lieutenant finished his call, he mumbled his condolences and hurried out the door. She picked up the telephone and dialed the math department at the academy.

One of the secretaries answered. Marcia identified herself and asked to speak to the department chairman.

"I'm sorry," the secretary said, "he's not here. He's in Washington."

"Can I talk to somebody, please?" Marcia asked, trying to control the tremble in her voice.

"May I help you with something?"

"Art's been killed in Korea. I need to talk to someone."

The secretary screamed. Marcia heard an extension phone being picked up, and Rick Callahan, one of Art's classmates and fellow math instructors, came on the line.

"Hi, Marcia. Are you calling about the promotion list? I haven't seen it. Is Art on it?"

"No, Rick, I'm not asking about the list," she said, exasperated to tears by yet more confusion. "I am telling you that Art has been killed."

The next twelve hours passed in a blur. The house quickly filled with friends who came to comfort her but who ended up wandering through the rooms, as lost and helpless as she felt. A nurse injected Marcia with a sedative, which left her feeling logy and even more miserable. "That's it," she told the nurse. "No more of this stuff."

The Army owned the best communications system money could buy, and once the word was out that Art had been killed, the news blew through the world almost instantly. The number of people who knew kept growing exponentially. Telegrams began to arrive from across the States and overseas, including messages of condolence from people who had obviously found out she was a widow when she still happily presumed she was a wife.

"What do I tell my children?" Marcia asked her neighbor, Pat Kahara, whose husband had also spent the past year in Korea. "How do I explain this? I can't tell them the bit about Daddy now being an angel, flying around in heaven."

She gathered the three children together in the living room. Their hair was sun-bleached from spending so much time in recent weeks at the McGuire summer house on Breezy Point. "Something terrible has happened," Marcia began. After she had told them and hugged them and promised they would get through this together, Brian, who was six, went outside to sit on the stoop with little Jason Kahara. "My daddy's not here anymore," Marcia heard her son say. "Who's going to be my daddy now?"

At six P.M., she sat down to watch the evening news. The killings in Korea led the broadcast, complete with grainy, horrifying footage taken from the JSA observation post. For the first time, she understood exactly what had happened. By the time the U.S. quick-reaction platoon had arrived at the poplar tree, the four-minute melee was over and the North Koreans had retreated across the Bridge of No Return. The Americans broke out their ammunition and TOW antitank missiles, but there were no further incursions from the north.

Four U.S. soldiers and five South Koreans had been injured, in addition to the two officers who were killed. A rescue team found Mark Barrett's body in a clump of weeds, where he had been dragged down and executed. Captain Kim, who had fled after being beaten himself, had driven back to the tree, loaded Art into a jeep, and raced to Camp Kitty Hawk, where the American captain was flown by helicopter to Seoul. But he was beyond help. Art's skull had been crushed, his face mutilated.

As the account droned on, Marcia realized that Art had not been shot as she was told. He had been axed to death. She sobbed uncontrollably.

Outside the house, a flock of reporters and several television vans from New York set up a stakeout. West Point's public affairs spokesman, Major F. William Smullen, kept them at bay, but the killings had provoked outrage across the country, including demands for vengeance. President Gerald Ford, who was in Kansas City for the Republican National Convention, angrily condemned North Korea, as did Secretary of State Henry Kissinger. "Whatever the merits of the dispute about the tree," Kissinger intoned, "nothing could justify a premeditated act of murder."

As night fell, the McGuires arrived from Brooklyn. Marcia's father wandered outside with a beer to talk with the reporters. "We're Irish," he said, apologizing for the tears streaking his cheeks, "and we're very emotional people."

Harriet, as outspoken as ever, tried to buck up her daughter in her own fashion. "Listen," she told Marcia, "do something with your face and lose twenty pounds. You're on the market again."

After midnight, when the house had emptied out and her parents and children were in bed, Marcia paced around the living room, unable to sleep. She had begun to pack that week, and the house had the sterile, unsettled appearance of a place that was midway between vacancy and occupation. The oriental rug had already been rolled up and wrapped in brown paper. The curtains had been taken down and packed in boxes, awaiting the movers. Wanting desperately to keep busy, Marcia pulled out the new slipcovers that had just come back from the upholstery shop in Newburgh and tugged them onto the blue velvet wing chairs.

What was she going to do now with her life? Move to the new house in Savannah, even without Art? Move back to Brooklyn? Remain at West Point like some of the other widows she had seen around the academy, reluctant to cut loose from the only real home they had? All of a sudden she was thirty-three years old with three young children, no husband, no job, and forty or fifty years of loneliness staring her in the face.

She felt no anger toward the North Koreans. All day long there had been muttered imprecations about "those damned cowards" and "those bastards." From the news reports, she sensed that the entire country was working up a foul, vengeful temper. There was even talk of war. But Marcia didn't feel that way, perhaps because Art had written so often about how deep-rooted the KPA hostility was toward Americans. If Art had been killed in Vietnam, she would have been bitter, convinced that he had died in vain on behalf of an ally who did not deserve his sacrifice. But he had given his life for a job he believed in, trying to keep the peace in a country he admired. He wouldn't have liked this saber rattling any more than she did.

With a final tug at the slipcovers, she stood up and rummaged about for a pen and some stationery. In her tidy cursive, she scratched a brief note:

> I understand the anger you are feeling. But I feel, and Art would feel, that taking any further action will mean more widows and more children without fathers. If this had to happen to someone in the unit, Art would never have forgiven himself if he had sent someone else out unprotected. It is important that there be no more bloodshed.

Marcia signed the single sheet, folded it neatly, and addressed the envelope to "Officers and Men of JSA, C/O Lt. Col. Victor Vierra." At last, exhausted and frightened, having honored her husband in death as in life, she crawled into bed to await the empty deliverance of a widow's sleep.

For the first time since 1953, tensions in Korea caused U.S. military commanders to place the troops there on the heightened war alert known as DEFCON 3. A squadron of F-4 fighter-bombers flew from Okinawa to Korea, and another squadron of F-111 bombers arrived from Mountain Home Air Force Base in Idaho. B-52s began flying practice bombing runs from Guam, and the aircraft carrier U.S.S. *Midway* steamed toward the Korean coast with an escort that included a cruiser and four frigates. Art's classmate Edgar Wright III, who commanded an artillery battery in Korea, helped supervise the reactivation of some obsolete Sergeant missiles; Wright awaited orders to tip the Sergeants with nuclear warheads. North Korea responded to these preparations by placing its army in what was ominously described as a "wartime posture."

Even as Marcia's house filled with mourners, Kissinger, CIA Director George Bush, and top military leaders met in a rump session of the Washington Special Action Group, the government's senior crisis team. They discussed a range of responses to the killings, among them the mining of North Korean harbors.

As it happened, the commanding general of the Eighth Army in Korea was General Richard G. Stilwell, the former commandant who had administered the cadet oath to Art and his classmates on the first day of Beast Barracks in 1962. Stilwell, who had announced his impending retirement from the Army just two days earlier, was notified of the killings while having lunch at a hotel in Japan. He flew immediately to Seoul, where his staff presented him with three options: do nothing, start World War III, or do "something meaningful."

Not surprisingly, Stilwell decided on the third course. The poplar was "only a damned tree," he declared, but "it involves a major principle." He proposed cutting it down with a show of force in what was soon codenamed Operation Paul Bunyan. (The South Korean president, Park Chung Hee, with vindictive bellicosity suggested that if KPA soldiers intervened, they should be beaten to death with their own weapons.) Stilwell's plan was approved by the Joint Chiefs and President Ford, who, having turned back a challenge to his nomination in Kansas City by Ronald W. Reagan, was vacationing in Vail, Colorado.

To gather intelligence about the tree, an Asian-American engineering lieutenant from the Second Infantry Division dressed in a South Korean uniform and drove slowly past the poplar in a jeep. After debating whether to blow it up or push it over with a bulldozer, the Army agreed on a more conventional approach and scoured South Korea for thirteen chain saws. Medics began stockpiling morphine, soldiers fashioned clubs from mop handles and lead pipes, and two additional chaplains joined a U.S. infantry battalion north of the Imjin River. Under orders from Washington, Stilwell trained his forward artillery on a KPA barracks complex across the DMZ — just in case.

At 6:57 A.M. Korean time on Saturday, August 21 — it was Friday evening in Washington, where the military brass had gathered in the Pentagon with what was described as the expectant air of a ringside crowd awaiting a heavyweight prizefight — Lieutenant Colonel Vierra handed the North Koreans a message: "At 0700 hours, a United Nations Command workforce will enter the Joint Security Area and complete the task begun on Wednesday. Should there be no interference, the work will be completed and the workforce will be withdrawn."

Three minutes later, four waves of helicopters carrying 140 troops began setting down in a field near the poplar, protected by seven Cobra gunships, three B-52s, and a huge force assembled just outside the DMZ. As engineers stood on a dump truck to dismember the poplar with their chain saws, several dozen ROK soldiers battered the walls and windows of two KPA guard posts. Unable to resist the kind of meddling that had tormented combat commanders in Vietnam, senior officers at "echelons above reason" peppered the task force with questions during the operation, including "How old is the tree?"

Forty-five minutes later, the deed was done. About a hundred KPA soldiers stood watching from across the Bridge of No Return, but made no effort to intervene. The Americans vacated the JSA, leaving behind an ugly stump, waist-high and four feet in diameter.

Engineers hauled the poplar limbs to Camp Casey south of the DMZ, where they whittled the wood into swagger sticks. Stilwell's aides shipped a cross-section of the trunk back to the Pentagon; presumably the generals could count the rings themselves to determine the tree's age. Hung on a wall in the National Military Command Center, the trophy bore a plaque that read: "This wood was taken from a tree at Panmunjom. Beneath its branches two American officers were murdered by North Koreans. Around the world, the tree became a symbol of communist brutality and a challenge to national honor. On 21 August 1976, a group of free men rose up and cut it down."

With American rage thus channeled into the destruction of a tree rather than into another Korean war, border tensions began to ease. As Operation Paul Bunyan drew to a close, the mortal remains of Art Bonifas and Mark Barrett were flown home. After being embalmed in Japan, Art's body arrived at Travis Air Force Base on August 21, where it was met by his classmate Danny Crawford and an honor guard. At the Oakland Army Base mortuary, the body was clothed, prepared for burial by cosmetologists, and placed in a casket. Shortly after six A.M. on August 22, Art arrived at JFK International in New York.

Marcia was waiting for him. She had driven from West Point with John Buczacki. Buz was a classmate and close friend of Art's who taught math at the academy and had been appointed to serve as Marcia's "survival assistance officer." Sipping coffee from Styrofoam cups as dawn broke, they had spent the ninety-minute drive planning the funeral. "I want it to be a celebration of his life," she said. "I don't want people just thinking about how he died."

Although she was glad to have help in the preparations — and being involved seemed to make others feel better — Marcia reserved several important decisions for herself. One involved Joe Calek, another Nebraskan in the class of 1966 who had recently begun a tour in Korea with an engineering unit. Once the Bonifases and Calcks had been close friends — Joe was Art's best man — but in recent years Joe Calek had changed alarmingly. His overweening ambition, his drinking, and particularly his abusive treatment of his family had dismayed both Art and Marcia. So when Calek sent word that he wanted to escort Art's body back to West Point, Marcia replied sharply, "I'd rather have the North Koreans bring Art's body back than have Joe Calek do it."

On August 24, 1976, a day of dazzling sunshine, Art Bonifas was laid to rest at West Point. Nearly a thousand mourners attended the funeral mass at Most Holy Trinity Chapel, where nine priests in white vestments stood at the altar rail. In keeping with her desire to commemorate Art's life, Marcia wore a white suit with brown trim and white pumps. Hatless, tearless, her red hair flaming in the sunlight, she led the processional into the church and down the center aisle with an extraordinary radiance, singing, "Enter, Rejoice, and Come In." As Jim Ford had sought refuge in Psalm 31 during the hurricane, so Marcia selected a song of David — Psalm 143 — to read aloud in the church: "For the enemy hath persecuted my soul; he hath smitten my life down to the ground; he hath made me to dwell in darkness, as those that have been long dead."

The grave site in the academy cemetery was, in fact, just a few paces from "those that have been long dead" — the cluster of graves in Section XXXIV dominated by the '66ers killed in Vietnam. Art was buried at the foot of the pyramid housing the remains of Egbert Viele, the West Pointer who had been chief engineer of Prospect Park in Brooklyn, where Marcia had often played as a girl. Ray Bonifas, looking feeble and doomed in his best brown suit, sat on a folding chair. A doctor and nurse hovered nearby. Young Brian covered his ears and grimaced at the traditional three-round volley from the honor guard. After the flag was folded into its star-spangled wedge, Superintendent Berry handed it to Marcia, who tucked the flag beneath her arm in the familiar half-back's carry used by so many widows before her. Father Tom Curley read the homily:

> Deliberately, for this day at least, we place aside the political implications of so brutal and vicious an atrocity. Our Christian love forces us to remember Art Bonifas and what he meant to us.
>
> As in life, so even at death, Major Bonifas exemplified the ideals of his beloved West Point: duty, honor, country. Today, we his family and friends reverently prepare this hero's body for sacred burial. We commend his soul into the hands of the loving God who made him. Art, may the angels lead you into paradise. May the martyrs await your coming and escort you to the new Jerusalem, the holy city. May the choirs of angels welcome you, and with Lazarus — no longer poor — may you have eternal rest.

Escorted to an Army staff car by Buz Buczacki, Marcia climbed into the back seat and took one last glance through the rear window. An intricate weave of sunlight and shadow played across the casket, which still lay under a mimosa tree, awaiting interment. Marcia had kept her composure throughout the day, but she was undone by this sight. Sobs broke loose from deep within her as the car wheeled slowly from the cemetery, forever drawing her away from the only man she had ever loved.

Precisely two months later, on October 24, summer and sun had yielded to autumn and a miserable, pelting rain. Jack Wheeler stood near the same mimosa tree in Section XXXIV, surveying 150 of his classmates who had gathered for a Sunday memorial service to conclude the tenth reunion of the class of 1966. As Chaplain Ford offered a brief benediction, raindrops drummed on the crescent of black umbrellas, muffling the sounds of men and women weeping.

There had been very little discussion in the past forty-eight hours about the war, or Art Bonifas's death, or John Oi's murder, or any of the other tragedies that had befallen the class in the past ten years. For the most part, the classmates engaged in happy conversation — fueled with plenty of food and drink — about their cadet days, their families, their jobs. But the sight of so many graves, including the raw gash where Art lay buried, seemed to release a flood of pain and sad memories.

Some of those attending the reunion thought there was an unpleasant tension, a sense of competition between classmates. The men still in the Army were sorted into the fast burners and the also-rans, categories as evident as the rank insignia on their shoulders and the decorations on their uniform jackets. Those who had resigned were preoccupied with their new careers and efforts to find themselves in the civilian world. As one '66er observed, everyone seemed self-absorbed.

When Jim Ford finished his prayer, former first captain Norm Fretwell, now an attorney in Kansas City, stepped forward. In his clearest command voice, Fretwell offered an eloquent elegy to "our friends who no longer stand among us," confirming "to all who may hear that the unyielding standard of choosing the harder right rather than accepting the easier wrong, which was so deeply cherished by those who have gone before us, will be forever the hallmark of the class of 1966. As we depart today, may God grant each one of us the strength, the wisdom, and the courage to meet our destinies without fear and without hesitation, as those whom we honor have so nobly done before us."

With that plea, the reunion ended. Except for a few classmates who tarried to talk beneath their umbrellas or meditate on the graves, most hurried to their cars in the PX parking lot beyond the cemetery's northern hedgerow. But Jack turned and crossed the yard in the other direction, sidestepping puddles as he walked toward Section VI. There, in the lee of the boxy old cadet chapel, he found the tombstone he was looking for: Thomas Jay Hayes IV.

Although the lettering on the stone showed no signs of weathering, the manicured grass covering Tommy was well rooted. His grave looked no different from those of men buried near him who had died twenty, thirty, fifty years before. Jack found it hard to believe that his friend had so completely joined the dead.

In Jack's mind, however, Tommy still dwelt in a kind of purgatory. For the past several years, he had begun thinking of him automatically every April 17, the anniversary of his death. It was, Jack supposed, one way of paying tribute, of remembering. But who, besides those who had known and loved him, honored First Lieutenant Tommy Hayes? Who would remember him a generation from now? With the war over and all of Vietnam in the possession of the communists, Americans seemed determined to forget that 58,000 of their countrymen had died there. Tommy and Buck Thompson and Dick Hood and all of the other Vietnam KIAs buried here had tumbled into a void. Except for their individual grave markers, there was nothing to honor them, no acknowledgment of their service and sacrifice.

Regardless of the merits of the war, Jack believed that forgetting the dead was wrong, even shameful. He wanted to set it right, and he had come to the reunion with an ulterior motive: to enlist his classmates' help in building a memorial at West Point in honor of the academy's sons who had fallen in the war.

Like Norm Fretwell, Jack was trying to establish himself as a lawyer.

He had graduated with honors from Yale Law School in 1975, but not before enduring the same doubts and anxieties that had beset him during his years at West Point. In his first semester in New Haven, he had been so unhappy that he came close to quitting. Jack still felt like an alien in his own country — he was the only Vietnam veteran in his Yale class — and the strictures of torts and contracts seemed unbearably narrow for someone who preferred to think in grand terms about the future of the human race in general and his generation in particular.

Jack knew that a big part of his problem at Yale was loneliness. He missed Elisa Desportes desperately. Once or twice a month on Friday afternoon, he would race down I-95 in his Chevelle to see her, typically covering the 260 miles from New Haven to Washington in under four hours. He adored everything about her: the miniskirts she favored, her soft Southern accent, her boundless energy and commitment to social justice. As a girl in South Carolina, she had ignored her family's misgivings and worked in the civil rights movement. Now, as a researcher at the National Cathedral, she devoted herself to Project Test Pattern, the study of the life and death of Episcopal parishes. Jack found the results of her research fascinating, an intimate glimpse at the sociology of American spiritual life. And he loved the nickname that the bishop had given her: Miss Test Pattern.

Usually, they frittered away the weekend with long strolls along the C & O Canal towpath or through Georgetown's meandering lanes. When Art Mosley invited them to a Halloween costume party, they showed up as John and Martha Mitchell, the former attorney general and his loquacious wife. Jack would linger in Washington as long as he could on Sunday afternoons, then reluctantly climb back into the Chevelle and head north, usually stopping for a few hours of sleep at his parents' home in Aberdeen. At four A.M., Big Jack would roust his son with a mug of coffee and get him back on the road in time to make his nine o'clock class on Monday morning.

Not long after Christmas 1972, Elisa and Jack spent a weekend at the Woodstock Inn in upstate New York. In front of the fireplace in their room Jack asked Elisa to marry him. She promptly accepted and soon afterward announced the news to her family's old friend Kitsy Westmoreland.

"Kitsy," she exclaimed, "I'm engaged and he's a West Pointer."

"Elisa," the general's wife replied dryly, "you will never be bored."

Jack offered to buy Elisa a West Point miniature, but she preferred a conventional engagement ring. He knew she was interested in the academy and the deep ties that bound him to his alma mater, but he always sensed a certain ambivalence in her feelings. After all, West Point was a *Kriegschule* — a war school — and she most decidedly was a creature of peace; she even entertained hopes of returning to the seminary and someday being ordained as one of the few women priests in the Episcopal Church. The miniature didn't really matter, he decided. One gray hog in the family was enough.

On July 14, 1973, they were married in Trinity Cathedral in Elisa's home town, Columbia. After a honeymoon at Hilton Head, where they gorged on she-crab soup and romped in the Atlantic surf, they returned to New Haven for Jack's second year of law school. Fortified by his newfound domestic bliss, Jack threw himself into his studies and breezed through the final four semesters, graduating near the top of his class and landing the coveted position of note and comment editor on *The Yale Law Journal*.

With law degree in hand, he spent a year clerking in Washington for Judge George E. MacKinnon, who sat on the District of Columbia circuit of the U.S. Court of Appeals. Working for MacKinnon, Jack learned some invaluable lessons in practical jurisprudence, from how to read an indictment to how to read a jury. Among the cases that came before the court that year were the appeals filed by several Watergate defendants, including the former White House aides H. R. Haldeman and John D. Ehrlichman. When his clerkship ended, Jack accepted an offer from Shea and Gardner, a small firm with offices on 15th Street in downtown Washington.

Jack was happy enough with his life, but something still gnawed at him from within. In part, it had to do with the uncertainty he felt about his vocation. Did he really want to be one of the twenty or thirty thousand lawyers in Washington, adding his voice to the capital's litigious cacophony? One of his first big cases at Shea and Gardner involved a chemical-manufacturing company that was a codefendant in a class-action suit brought by a group of cancer victims. After reading all of the information that was available to the company in the 1940s and 1950s about the link between cancer and a particular chemical, Jack concluded that his client had knowingly disregarded the risks. Although he believed the company was entitled to a strong, competent defense, he found the whole affair distasteful. This was not the kind of commitment to public service that the academy demanded of her sons, and twelve generations of Wheelers in America had preserved some trace of the family's original Puritan impulse to right the world's ills. Jack wanted a cause in which he could passionately believe, something that would absorb his energy and talent, something that enhanced the common good.

"Go find your star, Jack," his mother had told him as he boarded the train for West Point at the age of seventeen. Now here he was, thirty-one years old, with what he called "a rococo assortment" of credentials from West Point, Harvard, and Yale. Was this the star he was meant to find, churning out obfuscatory legal briefs on behalf of a corporate client whose culpability he privately acknowledged? To ask the question was to answer it.

Then there was guilt, perhaps another Puritan inheritance. For ten years now it had festered: guilt at not seeking combat command; guilt over his failure to meet the highest standards of the long gray line; guilt at letting Tommy Hayes down. He knew that the sentiment was not rational; probably it wasn't even legitimate. Nonetheless, it was there, demanding expiation.

So, as he had pondered Tommy's death in April 1976, Jack began to consider how best to pay tribute to those who had given their lives. The proportion of his classmates killed in Vietnam — 7 percent — was almost identical with that of the academy's World War II classes, which had lost so many young officers against Germany and Japan. Yet they were hardly regarded with the same esteem. It was too late for ticker tape, he thought, but it was never too late for honor. Even if no one else in America was interested in remembering the Vietnam dead, Jack would honor them, perhaps with some kind of memorial at West Point. But he needed help.

He began by calling two classmates living in Washington, Wesley Clark and Matt Harrison, both of them now majors. One night in late spring, they met for dinner at Matt's house on Foxhall Road and talked late into the night. Superficially, at least, the alliance seemed unlikely. Although Jack's views had moderated considerably since his seminary declaration that most West Pointers were "morally reprehensible," he still believed that Vietnam had been a terrible and futile mistake. Wes Clark, on the other hand, still thought of the war as a noble cause. He had fervently defended American policy during several debates and speeches when he was a Rhodes scholar; in 1970, while recuperating from four gunshot wounds sustained during a firefight, he had bitterly regretted being evacuated from the war zone just before the invasion of Cambodia. The United States, Clark continued to believe, had "lost heart" and inexcusably "let the South Vietnamese down." Matt Harrison's views lay somewhere between those of Wes Clark and Jack; what most rankled was the scorn that had been heaped on the men who had done their duty by fighting the war. Matt's wide stubborn streak intertwined with an equally broad streak of loyalty. He often said that if so many people hadn't told him how fouled up the Army was in the early 1970s, he probably would have resigned; but with the brickbats flying, he was not about to bail out when the Army needed him most.

Despite their differences, the three men agreed that a memorial was a superb idea. It should be apolitical, they concurred, making no statement about the war other than to honor the West Pointers who had given their lives. To widen their base, they decided to include all of the classes from the 1960s. Matt pulled out his annual *Register of Graduates,* which listed every academy graduate since 1802. Combing through the '60s classes, they divided up the men they knew and roughed out a plan for soliciting money and support. When he left the house on Foxhall Road that night, Jack was jubilant.

Now, six months later, the drive for the memorial had gained momentum, although the project remained a long way from completion. Jack had enlisted another important ally, his old sailing partner Jeff Rogers, who was teaching in the academy's department of mechanics. "We don't want a statue of a guy on horseback with his sword drawn," Jeff insisted. What they did want, he suggested, was "a landscape solution," a memorial that somehow was so integrated into a tranquil setting as to encourage thoughtful reflection.

At the beginning of the reunion weekend, Jeff and Jack had walked around the academy examining potential sites. One possibility was the old "Plebe Flirty," a secluded glade of rhododendron and mountain laurel behind the superintendent's house. Another was the rocky outcropping on the western edge of Lusk Reservoir. *How many gallons in Lusk Reservoir?* For generations, every plebe had been required to know the answer to that query as well as he knew his own name. *Ninety point two million gallons, sir, when the water is flowing over the spillway.*

It's going to happen, Jack thought as he stood in the rain at Tommy's grave. We're going to make this happen. Just as West Pointers who survived the Civil War had sought to heal wounds from that conflict by founding the Association of Graduates — an alumni organization open to all graduates, Yankee or rebel — so this generation of survivors would try to bind its own wounds in its own way.

When Jack was a teenager, someone had given him a thick volume of Rudyard Kipling's poems and stories, which contained the poem "To Thomas Atkins." After Tommy's funeral, on a soggy day just like this one eight years before, Jack had thought of the lines:

> I have made for you a song,
> And it may be right or wrong,
> But only you can tell me if it's true.
> I have tried for to explain
> Both your pleasures and your pain,
> And, Thomas, here's my best respects to you.

Now the words occurred to him again, like a threnody. I have made for you a song, Tommy. And here's my best respects.

The tenth reunion made Marcia Bonifas uncomfortable. She had attended the parties and other festivities at the urging of her friends, but she felt like an outsider. Not knowing quite what to say to her, some of Art's classmates and their wives either kept their distance or, worse yet, were mawkish. She was astonished when perfect strangers rushed up and wrapped her in a bawling embrace. Small talk was difficult. When someone asked, "So, what have you been up to?" how was she supposed to respond? "Oh, not much. Burying my husband. Taking care of my fatherless children." The weekend strengthened her resolve to make a clean break, to leave West Point.

During the two months since Art's death, she had been preparing to do just that. But shortly after the funeral, one of the discs in her lower back finally gave out. Earlier in the summer, she had spent many hours hunched over a sewing machine, stitching drapes for the new house in Savannah. Aggravated by stress, the throbbing pain became so unrelenting that she could no longer lie down. Buz Buczacki gingerly loaded her into the back seat of a neighbor's Volkswagen camper and hauled her to the hospital, where the doctor prescribed two weeks of bed rest. When another sympathetic Army physician who happened to be an obstetrician-gynecologist stopped by the house at Stewart several times to check on her, his visits ignited a spate of rumors that she was pregnant. That provided Marcia with the first real laugh she'd had in weeks.

With her children ensconced at the McGuire house in Brooklyn, she used the recuperation period at Stewart as a time to think. "What am I supposed to do? How am I supposed to act?" she asked Buz. "Am I supposed to take off my wedding ring? What's my role now?"

She was no longer Art's wife, no longer Mrs. Major. She was simply Marcia. Having always submerged her own identity beneath that of her husband, she was frightened by the prospect of being on her own. The McGuires wanted her to move back to Brooklyn, but the thought of teaching again in the embattled New York public schools made her cringe. She appreciated the procession of neighbors who stopped by to wash the dishes and sweep the floors, yet their visits reminded her that these friends would all be moving on to other assignments in a year or two, leaving her behind. In Savannah, the builder kindly released her from the contract on the new house and returned the deposit. But if not Georgia, she wondered, then where?

The Army treated her with its usual blend of noblesse oblige and bureaucratic ham-handedness. Sidney Berry, outraged by the callous manner in which Marcia was informed of Art's death, waived the requirement that she vacate the house within ninety days. "We're not going to put you out in the street," the superintendent assured her. "We want you to stay right where you are for the next year. Leave the kids in school. No decisions have to be made now." Secretary of the Army Hoffmann even dropped by — with the retinue and fanfare befitting an emperor — to offer his condolences.

On the other hand, the Army began charging her rent, effective from the moment of Art's death. And the required payment was calculated on the basis of Art's promotion to major; but because he had not worn a major's oak leaves for twenty-four hours, as required by military regulations, Marcia received the widow's benefits of only a captain, a difference of $100 a month. Worse still was the Bronze Star that Art received posthumously. The decoration arrived from Washington in the academy's "message center," stuffed into a manila interoffice envelope.

"I'm not accepting this," she told Buczacki furiously. "Send it back. I refuse to take it under these conditions." He posted the medal back to Washington.

She fretted over finances. Art's life insurance policies had been in good order, leaving her a comfortable nest egg. But the money hardly sufficed to raise three children for fifteen or twenty years and put them through college. His salary had stopped on the day of his death except for a $3,000 severance check from the Army. That was supplemented by $31 a month in child support from the Veterans Administration and her widow's benefits of $500 a month. Social Security contributed a bit also. They were not penniless, but Marcia would unquestionably have to work, both for the sake of her sanity and as the family's new breadwinner.

One Saturday, the last of Art's personal effects arrived from Korea. She had already received a large photo that he mailed to her the day before he died. Taken right after he had finished a long run, the picture showed him sitting on a concrete step, face alight with his trademark grin. He had removed his big boots and positioned them neatly in front of the step. Sweat soaked his khaki T-shirt and fatigue pants, and a dark stain covered the concrete where his perspiration had puddled. She could see where the suntan ended on his biceps and in the V of his neck. It was a wonderful picture.

Now, unexpectedly, a shoebox arrived in the mail. Carefully packed inside were his wedding ring, West Point ring, wallet, and a cross he had been wearing when he died. As she fingered these talismans, her eyes flooded with tears. Later, when she was changing Megan's diaper before putting the children to bed in their bunks, the frustration overwhelmed her.

"Art, why did you do this to me?" she wailed, slamming both fists against the wall. Wide-eyed with confusion and alarm, the children watched silently until the storm passed.

In late October, she learned of a job opening in Colorado Springs as an assistant hostess at the Air Force Academy. From observing the hostesses at West Point over the years — she had first met Art on a blind date through the hostess Beatrice Holland in 1963 — Marcia knew that the position was a peculiar blend of chaperone, etiquette instructor, and surrogate mother. Patrolling the cadet hops, she would be a decorum enforcer who was supposed to watch for illicit drinking, PDA, drags with their shoes off, and so on. That didn't particularly appeal to her, but she liked the idea of a fresh start in a new environment. Colorado sounded like a good place for the children, certainly more wholesome than the scruffy, hard-scrabble avenues of Brooklyn.

She left Beth, Brian, and Megan with a baby sitter and flew west for an interview. Her parents were due back from a European vacation in two days, and Marcia left them a note in Brooklyn: "You have one day to do your laundry. Then won't you drive up to take care of the children? I've gone to Colorado to see about a job." (When Harriet McGuire dutifully arrived at Stewart, she rapped on the door and announced, "Your grandmother's here and it's time to behave. Get the toys picked up. I am not going to put up with the things your mother does.")

During her interview, Marcia immediately struck up a friendship with the cadet activities officer, an Air Force major named Dick Ryer, who had graduated from West Point in 1962. But the chief hostess was another matter. Having been at the academy almost since its founding in the 1950s, she affected an air of proprietorship — or so it seemed to Marcia. The cadets were tenants; she owned the place. When Marcia and Dick Ryer began chatting about West Point, the hostess interrupted. "I don't think Mrs. Bonifas will be able to understand the different terminology between the Army and the Air Force," she said. "Things are very different here. It would really be hard for her." Oh, come off it, Marcia thought, biting her tongue. When Ryer mentioned that they were also interviewing an Air Force widow, Marcia assumed the worst. I don't stand a chance, she told herself.

Even so, the next day she went househunting. Colorado Springs was a beautiful town, as breathtaking in its setting beneath Pikes Peak as West Point was in its Hudson gorge. Holding to the same $45,000 price she had used in Savannah, Marcia found a pleasant four-bedroom house in the northeast part of the city. With a large kitchen, full basement, and family room, the house seemed like a bargain. But the discovery depressed her. Why get your hopes up? she asked herself. This is just a wild goose chase. Driving back to the home of an old friend with whom she was staying, Marcia found herself praying for advice.

God, why am I doing this? she asked silently. I like this house, but I can't just come out here for no reason. I can't just pick up and move without having a purpose in being here. Give me a sign that this is where I'm supposed to be, that I'm doing the right thing.

Early that evening, Dick Ryer called. "Welcome aboard," he said. "We'd like you to start as soon as you can. When can you be here?"

Thrilled at getting the job, Marcia was even more pleased to receive the omen she had requested. This was it; this was where she was meant to be. She signed a contract for the house and flew back to New York, brimming with new confidence and vigor. We're going west, she told the children; Pikes Peak or bust. She scheduled the move for mid November.

One last loose end remained to be tied. Richard Stilwell, who had just retired after thirty-eight years in the Army, somehow learned of Marcia's abrupt rejection of Art's Bronze Star. Would you change your mind, the general asked, if I came to West Point to present the medal in a proper ceremony? She gratefully assented.

On November 11, several dozen classmates and other friends crowded into the superintendent's conference room in Building 600, the same chamber where Art had sworn his commissioning oath on the morning of June 8, 1966. Stilwell handed Marcia a packet of condolence letters from South Korea. "This volume," the general had written in a covering note, "tries to express the genuine sorrow and outrage — and at the same time, the profound appreciation — of the Korean people."

Then he offered her the five-pointed Bronze Star, with a tiny V for valor. "For heroism," the citation read. "Major Bonifas's outstanding performance of duty was in keeping with the finest tradition of the military service and reflected great credit upon him, his command, and the United States Army."

A week later, she rounded up the children and left West Point. They would stop in Omaha to see Ray Bonifas one last time — his cancer was in its final stages — and then fly on to Colorado. The Bronze Star was safely packed away with Art's class ring and other mementos. The medal meant a great deal to her, not just because of its obvious symbolism, but also because receiving the decoration had been her final act as Art's wife. Henceforth, she was Marcia, an independent woman, rising or falling on her own.

PART IV

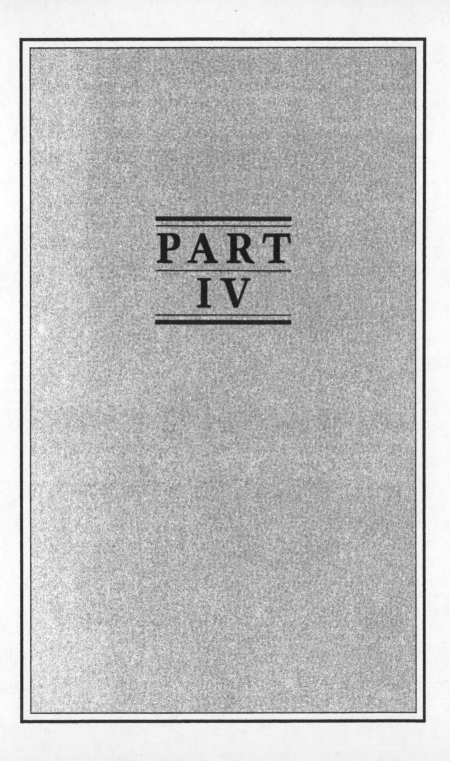

17

WALLS

JACK WHEELER rummaged through the pocket of his shorts and pulled out a palmful of change. "Here we go, John," he said to his two-year-old son, plucking a quarter from the silver pile. "I've got one." He handed it to the boy, who wrapped his small fist around the coin and grasped his father's finger with his free hand. Together they walked down the sandy driveway from the cottage. The early morning sun had barely breached the Atlantic horizon, but Jack felt its rays braising the back of his neck. With his fair skin and thinning hair, he would have to be cautious on the beach this afternoon; the day held promise of a first-rate sunburn for the foolhardy.

Father and son — John Parsons Wheeler III and IV — crossed the asphalt road and headed for the two newspaper vending boxes on the far side. Traffic was light at this hour, but Jack saw signs of people stirring in the neighboring cottages. Like many families among South Carolina's gentry, the Desportes had been coming to Pawley's Island for years, and Elisa had easily persuaded Jack to give the place a try for this year's vacation. North of Charleston in Georgetown County, the island had once been a retreat for the plantation gentry seeking relief from inland "summer fevers." Although somewhat more egalitarian now — and afflicted with the inevitable beach boutiques and T-shirt shops — the resort retained a whiff of antebellum charm, with its weathered cottages and cypress hummocks encased in marsh grass. A favorite local bumper sticker proclaimed, ARROGANTLY SHABBY — PAWLEY'S ISLAND, S.C.

After boosting up his son so that he could feed the quarter into the vending slot, Jack tugged open the rack and pulled a newspaper from the stack inside. The date on the front page was July 5, 1979. Returning to the cottage porch, he heard Elisa and young John's twin sister, Katie, puttering around inside. Jack spread the paper in his lap and skimmed the headlines.

NASA scientists continued to track the descent of Skylab, a seventy-seven-ton space station that was expected to plunge back into the atmosphere sometime next week; Nicaraguan strongman Anastasio Somoza — West Point class of '46 — was reportedly "very close" to abdicating in the face of a leftist revolt; Alexander M. Haig, Jr. — West Point '47 — had retired as NATO commander to become a political science lecturer at the University of Pennsylvania; tennis machine Björn Borg was breezing through Wimbledon; gasoline prices seemed to be stabilizing at a dollar a gallon — up 20 percent in three months — and the supply seemed adequate, though some service stations still reported long lines and occasional fistfights between motorists.

A brief Associated Press report inside the paper caught Jack's attention. Datelined Washington, the item noted:

> Jan C. Scruggs, a Vietnam veteran who once thought it would be easy to raise $1 million for a memorial to 57,000 Americans who died in Vietnam, says he was wrong. He's collected only $144.50 so far.
>
> But Scruggs, president of the tax-exempt Vietnam Veterans Memorial Fund, Inc., says he is still confident of ultimate success. "The whole idea behind this is a societal acknowledgment of the sacrifices and a national reconciliation after the war," Scruggs says.

Jack lingered over the article for a moment before tearing it from the paper and stuffing it into his pocket. He had never heard of Jan C. Scruggs, but the man sounded like a kindred spirit. Perhaps he could profit from Jack's experience in building the Southeast Asia memorial at West Point. Three years after he had first proposed that project, it was nearly completed; the academy classes from the 1960s had raised enough money for a large brass plaque honoring the war dead, and plans had been made for a formal dedication. In keeping with Jeff Rogers's proposal for a landscape solution, the plaque was set in a massive granite boulder sheltered by a pine copse on the shore of Lusk Reservoir. As modest and unobtrusive as the memorial was, Jack took immense pride in his achievement.

The past three years had been busy, turbulent, and often draining for the Wheelers. In late December of 1976, just five months after joining Shea and Gardner, Jack had been detached from his legal duties to help restore order to Jimmy Carter's inaugural preparations. After trudging through deep snow to the inauguration headquarters in Southeast Washington, he soon discovered that the planning was in chaos. The outgoing Republicans were being difficult; the incoming Democrats were confused; Carter's inner circle of Georgians was at loggerheads with the Washington establishment; and many details had been left to a spunky but inexperienced advance team from Carter's campaign.

Working for a savvy, thirty-two-year-old Atlanta banker named A. D. Frazier, Jack had labored sixteen hours a day for three weeks. Elisa was in her ninth month of pregnancy, and he and Frazier were afraid that the beeper Jack wore on his belt would suddenly summon him to the hospital before January 20. But they resolved each problem one by one — settling contract disputes, negotiating bus and subway schedules, and assuaging the fire marshal, who had threatened to shut down any inauguration event that violated safety codes. By the time Carter swore his oath to become the nation's thirty-ninth president, Jack was exhausted. Even the distasteful case involving the chemical company looked like a welcome return to the daily routine of a Washington lawyer.

Two weeks later, on February 4, Elisa was preparing to give birth to the Wheeler twins at Georgetown Hospital, when suddenly the fetal monitor showed that one of the babies was in serious distress. As a team of doctors and nurses wheeled Elisa away for a caesarean, Jack heard her scream careen down the corridor. For the next hour he was beside himself with anxiety. When the obstetrician reappeared, he gave Jack the grim news: both infants had serious birth defects. John suffered from a heart murmur and might require surgery. Katie had an improperly formed trachea. Every breath became a desperate gasp, drawn with a wheeze that made it sound as though she were drowning. She also was diagnosed as a probable SIDS baby, prone to sudden infant death syndrome.

A week later, while the babies and Elisa were still in the hospital, Katie suffered a seizure. At 4:30 A.M., the hospital called Jack at home and told him that his daughter may have suffered brain damage. Stepping into the shower, he leaned his head against the tile and wept as never before. Please God, he prayed, let her live long enough to know that she is loved.

Miraculously, both children had survived infancy. After a few weeks, the neonatal cardiac specialists decided that John's heart defect would probably heal itself. Katie's prognosis was less certain. She required a full-time nurse during the day and a special monitor in her crib that would sound an alarm whenever it detected any disruption in her breathing. On the many nights when the alarm beeped, Jack and Elisa took turns sitting beside her until dawn. Huddled beneath a blanket in the rocker next to the crib, struggling to stay awake, Jack felt like a sentry posted to keep death from entering the room. In the morning he would dress for work and head downtown, red-eyed and groggy, but triumphant for at least another day.

Only now, more than two years after the twins' birth, had Jack's life begun to resume some semblance of normality. In mid July 1979, after returning to Washington from Pawley's Island, he fished out the newspaper clipping he had saved and found Jan C. Scruggs's phone number through directory assistance in Columbia, a "planned community" midway between the capital and Baltimore. Still unsure how legitimate Scruggs was — the $144.50 announcement had provoked some condescension on the part of the media — Jack was intrigued enough to invite him to the Wheelers' house on Worthington Drive. After an hour of carefully sizing each other up in the living room, the two men agreed to collaborate on a national memorial. The next day, Scruggs wrote a thank-you note of sorts: "Dear Jack — We've got something good here. Write to anybody, ask for anything." Enclosed were ten lapel pins, inscribed with the initials VVMF: Vietnam Veterans Memorial Fund.

If Jack's alliance with Matt Harrison and Wes Clark had been unlikely, his new compact with Jan Scruggs was downright improbable. The son of a milkman and a waitress from Bowie, Maryland, Scruggs was a wiry, disheveled, chain-smoking, twenty-nine-year-old whose fondness for blue jeans and cowboy boots inevitably caused buttoned-down Washington to underestimate him. At eighteen, he had volunteered for Vietnam as an enlisted man, and returned home a year later with eleven fragments of a rocket-propelled grenade still in his body. After leaving the Army, he wandered for a while, as he put it, "smoking dope, raising hell, and hanging out on Indian reservations." Eventually, Scruggs put himself through college and took a part-time job with the Labor Department.

In March 1979, he went to see *The Deer Hunter*, a powerfully evocative movie about working-class grunts in Vietnam. The next day, after being up most of the night cradling a bottle of whiskey, he announced to his wife that he intended to build a war memorial containing the names of everyone who had died in Southeast Asia. With help from a lawyer named Robert Doubek, a former Air Force intelligence officer who had been stationed at Da Nang, Scruggs incorporated the VVMF. On May 29, 1979, ten years to the day after he lay wounded in the jungle, bleeding badly and reciting the Lord's Prayer, he had announced the project to the press. "The only thing we're worried about," he brashly predicted, "is raising too much money."

Scruggs had reason to be wary of Jack. For one thing, he distrusted officers, having seen more than a few in Vietnam who seemed perfectly willing to sacrifice their troops for the sake of reporting a high enemy body count or otherwise enhancing their own careers. And he was particularly leery of West Pointers; they were, after all, the self-proclaimed apotheoses of the officer corps. But if Scruggs found Jack's status as an academy graduate nettlesome, he also sensed a deep sincerity in his enthusiasm for the project. Besides, Scruggs concluded, at this point he could hardly be choosy about his allies.

He also appreciated two things that Wheeler sent him shortly after they met. The first was a poem, written by Jack: "We live in hope that in the final day / we will see our brothers again / face to face, where they shall know / us and we them, and we will not be / strangers." The second item was a memo:

> The need is not for a vindictive examination of the record. I see the need this way: very likely our own generation will be forced to consider committing American troops to combat. In making the policy judgment, we have to do our best to avoid the faulty reporting and thinking, both inside and outside of government, that went on in our country regarding Southeast Asia from 1946 to 1975 . . . Speaking personally, I think we have to try because, aside from my religious faith, that is the only way I can find meaning in the death of my friends.

With typical verve, Jack threw himself into the project. From the beginning, he was haunted by the experience of previous memorial builders. The Lincoln Memorial, undertaken in 1867, was not completed until 1922. Battle Monument at West Point was started in June 1864 but not dedicated until May 1897. Congress had approved the Franklin D. Roosevelt memorial in 1958, but it remained unbuilt because of a bitter dispute over the design — eight abstract marble slabs that critics dubbed Instant Stonehenge. Even when a memorial was completed with reasonable alacrity, the finished product often provoked ridicule; General Philip Sheridan, asked to comment on one scupture honoring Civil War veterans, replied, "I have only one fault to find: it's fireproof."

Jack also recognized that Scruggs was proceeding entirely on faith, which, however important, would not suffice to get the job done. "This guy Scruggs needs supervision," he told Doubek. "What we need are more horses." Among other recent changes in his life, Jack had left private practice in 1978 and taken a job as assistant general counsel to the Securities and Exchange Commission. Public service employment was more to his taste — he thought of himself as a cop, policing the nation's securities industry — and the new post expanded his network of friends and contacts. After four years in Washington, he now had an impressive list of potential "horses" — all listed alphabetically in his desktop Rolodex — and he was not reluctant to round them up. Some, like Joe Zengerle, West Point '64, had worked with Jack at Shea and

Gardner (and had also been in law school with Tom Carhart); others, like Sandy Mayo, a lawyer, and Bob Frank, an accountant, Jack had met through the Army-Navy Club; still others came from the academy's old boy network, including classmate Art Mosley and Dick Radez, class of '67, who had been at Long Binh with Jack.

One horse whose help VVMF desperately wanted was a former Marine captain turned lawyer and author. His name was James Henry Webb. On an August afternoon in 1979, Jack, Scruggs, and Doubek met Webb for lunch at Gusti's, a sidewalk bistro at 19th and M streets in downtown Washington. Over plates of antipasto and linguine, they laid out their scheme while Webb listened. "We think we can get a site on the Mall," Jack said, referring to the grassy rectangle where many of the antiwar protests had taken place. "At least it's something we can ask for. And one of the points we can make is that now it's *our* turn on the Mall."

Jim Webb was not sure what to make of this group, but he liked their animating passion. It resonated with his own feelings about the war. "The first duty," he had once said, "is to remember." Handsome and articulate, with curly hair and a powerful torso, he already was being lionized as one of his generation's premier men of letters, "the kick-ass troubadour for a generation of combat veterans," as an acquaintance later called him. Like Jack, he was the scion of military men. His ancestors had fought in the Regulator War — the taxpayer revolt in the Colonial Carolinas — as well as in the Revolution, the War of 1812, the Mexican War, and the Civil War. His grandfather, Robert E. Lee Webb, was a sharecropper, his father an Air Force colonel who had conducted Saturday morning inspections of his children's bedrooms. At the Naval Academy, Webb had been a fine boxer, losing a final, legendary bout to a classmate and rival named Oliver L. North.

After graduating in 1968, Webb was commissioned in the Marines. Finishing first among 256 others in the basic officers' course at Quantico, he shipped out for Vietnam, where he won the Navy Cross, the Silver Star, two Bronze Stars, and two Purple Hearts. According to one account, fifty-six men in his platoon had been killed or wounded during Webb's stint as a commander. Medically discharged in 1972 because of a frail knee that had been shattered by grenade fragments — he occasionally walked with a limp and, like Scruggs, still carried shards of shrapnel in his body — he enrolled at Georgetown Law School, from which he graduated in 1975. Emulating Ernest Hemingway, who once claimed he had learned to write by studying Paul Cézanne, Webb trekked to the National Gallery of Art every Thursday afternoon to study the Cézanne canvases. Then he began work on a novel. In what he described as "my personal catharsis," he labored over the book for months, fourteen hours a day, six days a week, rewriting the manuscript seven times from cover to cover in longhand with a ballpoint pen. The result, *Fields of Fire,* was published in 1978 to laudatory reviews.

At Gusti's, Webb offered some practical advice. A former Democrat who had converted to the Republican Party after Jimmy Carter offered amnesty to draft evaders in 1977, he had worked for a spell as the assistant minority counsel on the House Veterans Affairs Committee. Webb knew his way through the political labyrinth on Capitol Hill. Any memorial built on federal land required legislative approval, and that meant finding friends in high places in both the House and Senate. He ticked off several names of congressmen to avoid and several others whose favor should be curried. Webb lived in Annapolis, but he expected to be moving back to Washington soon. When Scruggs asked whether he would help, Webb nodded. "Yeah, okay," he replied. "Sure."

As they pushed away from the table, Scruggs felt elated. Here was precisely the kind of shrewd, well-connected veteran that VVMF needed. But a worry lodged in the back of his mind. Some of Webb's comments about antiwar protestors were tinged with animosity — he reputedly had once quipped that he "wouldn't cross the street to see Jane Fonda cut her wrists." In Scruggs's view, one thing they did not need was an ally who viewed the project as an opportunity to vent his spleen or make a political statement justifying the war.

Jack had no such reservations. Jim Webb struck him as most impressive, a little hard-boiled perhaps, but also imaginative, competent, and self-controlled. They had, he sensed, much in common: nearly the same age, they were both military brats and service academy graduates; both were lawyers; both had been young officers in Vietnam; both enjoyed writing. Always drawn to men who had been heroic in combat, Jack thought Jim would make a fine friend, not to mention a welcome addition to the other horses stabled in his Rolodex. Before they parted, he told Webb, "The ending of *Fields of Fire* is very similar to how my classmate Tommy Hayes died in Vietnam." Webb nodded appreciatively.

Others had noticed Jack's preoccupation with Tommy. One day, when Jack first asked Art Mosley for help on the memorial over lunch at the Metropolitan Club, he began his pitch in what Art called "that earnest tone."

"Art, what do you think of Tommy Hayes's death?"

For fifteen years, Art had considered it his duty to "periodically pull Jack off his high horse." Now duty called again.

"Jack," he answered, "I think that it's whatever you want to make of it. You think one thing about it. I think something else. Others may think something different from either of us." Vague as the response was, Art thought he had said precisely the right thing.

Scruggs, who had first heard of Tommy Hayes during his initial meeting with Jack on Worthington Drive, recognized the symptoms of "survivor's guilt," something he had once studied while working as a counselor. Anyone who lived through a catastrophe in which others had been killed — whether a car wreck or Hiroshima or the Vietnam War — was susceptible to guilt pangs. Survivor's guilt often afflicted soldiers, Scruggs knew, and Jack had the syndrome in spades. Although no rational connection linked Jack's survival to Tommy Hayes's death — Tommy had not flung himself on a grenade while they shared a foxhole — the link nevertheless persisted in Jack's mind.

Regardless of Jack's psychological complexities, Scruggs was grateful for his driving commitment to the project. Cool and composed before the public, in private VVMF brainstorming sessions Jack was, as Scruggs observed, "the world's worst poker player." Sometimes, on the verge of tears, he would yell or pound the table with his fists, demanding that they get on with the business at hand. In drafting legislation for a memorial site, Jack was shrewd enough to throw in a few extraneous clauses, which could later be bargained away during negotiations. "This," he told Scruggs with a grin, "is the type of law they teach at Yale." Building anything on the hallowed ground of the Mall, Jack warned, was "like adding an extra face to Mount Rushmore." In order to avoid offending anyone, VVMF had to veer away from all political statements. "We," he added soberly in a memo, "have become trustees of a portion of the national heart."

By midautumn, they were ready to ask Congress for two acres of that sacred ground. The spot they coveted had been suggested by Senator Charles Mathias of Maryland. During a meeting in an ornate anteroom just off the Senate floor, Mathias unfolded an Exxon map of Washington and pointed with his thumb to Constitution Gardens, a peaceful bower barely a hundred yards from the Lincoln Memorial. As the bill took final form, VVMF laid plans for a concerted publicity offensive to coincide with Mathias's introduction of the legislation on Veterans Day.

Meanwhile, Jim Webb had returned to Washington and was trying to help in the House. He had received a packet of information from VVMF, including a draft of the proposed bill, which he took to Representative John Paul Hammerschmidt of Arkansas, a former lumberman who was the ranking Republican on the Veterans Affairs Committee. Hammerschmidt promptly introduced the bill and read a floor speech that Webb had written for him. Then Webb called Doubek.

"Hey, Bob, guess what? Your bill was introduced in the House today."

The painful silence that followed was broken only when Doubek muttered a dour "Oh, shit."

When Scruggs learned that the legislation had been introduced prematurely, he was furious. He called Hammerschmidt's office, accusing the congressman of botching VVMF's plans and attacking Webb as a publicity hound. Jack also was irate. That night, he called Webb at his fiancée's house. "What the hell are you Arkansas Republicans up to?" Jack demanded.

Webb stood in a darkened bedroom, unable to reach the light switch because the phone cord was too short. He had spoken with Jack only once before, and he was taken aback by his acerbic tone. "What are you talking about?" he asked. In high dudgeon, Jack recounted the elaborate preparations that had been laid for Veterans Day.

"I didn't mean to stir your waters, Jack."

"The point I'm making is that we have to coordinate what we're doing. If you're going to do that kind of thing, we have to know about it. That's basic first-year tactics at either of our academies: tell your friends what you're doing."

That did it. Webb's temper had a short fuse and the last thing he needed was this Long Binh West Pointer lecturing him on tactics. "Go fuck yourself, man!" he snapped, slamming down the receiver.

Five minutes later Jack called back to apologize. They smoothed over the quarrel, but both men felt uneasy as they hung up the second time. As auguries went, this one was hardly auspicious.

While the federal legislation began working its way through Congress, money became the biggest obstacle. Scruggs had vowed that the memorial would be built without a dime of government funding, yet private donations were not exactly flooding in. VVMF was about to rent an office on Connecticut Avenue for $350 a month, but the cubicle had scarcely enough room for two desks and a telephone, much less a sophisticated fund-raising operation. Art Mosley, who pointed out that the Hammerschmidt incident had demonstrated that "we need to run this thing more like a business," drafted an organizational chart with six subcommittees and a master chronology detailing each step toward raising $10 million and dedicating the memorial in November 1982. The plan was brilliant, but as 1979 drew to a close, VVMF had a grand total of $9000 in the bank.

Senator John Warner of Virginia offered to help by inviting a dozen defense contractors to a fund-raising breakfast at his house. VVMF balked. Warner, who had been secretary of the Navy during the war, was good-hearted if somewhat melodramatic; during one meeting he had waggled his hand in the air and murmured, "This is the hand that signed the orders that sent thousands of men to Vietnam." But the memorial builders were wary of allying themselves with the defense industry. After considerable debate, they pushed aside those scruples.

"If their money is green," Doubek argued, "who the hell are we to make judgments?"

At 7:30 A.M. on December 20, Jack Wheeler, Jan Scruggs, Bob Doubek, Art Mosley, and several others gathered with the contractors at Warner's house in Georgetown. The Warner cook, outfitted in black livery, served scrambled eggs and sausage in the drawing room at the rear of the house. After forty-five minutes of awkward chitchat, Warner breezed in from the kitchen and announced, "Gentlemen, the chef." On his heels, dressed in a pink housecoat and slippers tufted with white pompoms, came the senator's new wife, Elizabeth Taylor.

The two dozen men leaped to their feet as though someone had barked, " 'TEN, HUT!' She circled the room, shaking hands and chatting gaily, while the men balanced their plates of congealing eggs and toed the rug like nervous schoolboys. They really are violet, Jack thought, maneuvering for a direct look at the actress's famous eyes.

"May I have one of those?" she asked Bob Doubek, pointing to his VVMF lapel pin. "Sure," he answered, plucking the insignia from his jacket. Then he hesitated. Rather than risking a trespass on the Taylor bosom, Doubek simply handed her the pin. On reaching Art Mosley, the actress cooed, "You, you'll be my doughboy." Art smiled, mute with adoration.

With his wife hugging her knees from a perch on the edge of a divan, Warner stood near the french doors leading to the garden and delivered his spiel to the contractors. "These are fine men and they have a fine cause," he said, gesturing to the VVMF group. "They deserve to be supported." After a few more minutes of arm twisting, the senator ushered everyone to the door. Scruggs and Doubek lingered with Miss Taylor for a few clumsy words of praise for her role in *National Velvet*.

Outside on the sidewalk the veterans regrouped. They had not exactly shown themselves to be the sharpest blades in Washington's beau monde, but at least the affair had achieved its purpose. They would net $40,000 in donation pledges from the breakfast. That was a start. Now, Jack calculated, all they had to do was find another $9,951,000.

Art Mosley was bothered that of the inner circle running VVMF, only Scruggs was a genuine combat vet. "You know," he told Doubek over a cup of coffee one day, "I wasn't all that gung ho about the war. In fact, I was a dissenter. Not only that, I got an Article 15. A West Pointer with an Article 15."

"Well, Art, I wasn't an Air Force intelligence officer because I wanted to lead men up the hill," Doubek replied.

"I guess I wonder," Art persisted, "who are we to do this?"

"Art, who *aren't* we to do this? When you're playing football and you see a ball bounce in front of you, do you leave it alone and say, 'I'm only a tackle,' or do you pick the ball up and run with it?"

Yet the more he considered the issue, the more convinced Art became that the memorial builders would benefit from the perspective — and the cachet — of someone who had been in the shit rather than a Dial soaper at Long Binh or Da Nang. Art thought he knew just the right fellow, a classmate who had once helped him steal the Navy goat, a man with combat experience and an artistic temperament to boot. "Jack, we really ought to get him involved," he told Wheeler, "because there are some things we're going to miss if we don't. And it would be right."

So it was that in mid April 1980 Art arrived at a VVMF meeting with Tom Carhart in tow. Tom, who had just moved to Washington from Amherst, listened quietly as the veterans discussed how to raise the additional $31,000 they needed to mail a million fund-raising letters. After a few minutes of debate, Tom stood up. "I think I can get the money," he offered.

Tom happened to know an officer at the First American Bank in Washington. Soon after the VVMF meeting, with Bob Doubek at his side, he walked into the bank on 15th Street and made his pitch.

"We want to borrow $30,000, unsecured."

The bank officer blinked. "I'm sorry, Tom, but we just can't loan you $30,000 unsecured."

Tom also knew that the president of First American was a retired Army colonel — West Point '44 — named Charles D. Daniel, a highly decorated combat veteran who had won Silver Stars in World War II and Vietnam. "Why don't you go in to Mr. Daniel's office," Tom told the bank officer, "and tell him that I'm here, that I'm a West Point graduate, and that I want to talk to him about something affecting our nation's military service."

A few minutes later, the banker returned. "That's interesting," he told Tom. "Mr. Daniel just threw the people he was talking to out of his office and says he'll see you."

After listening to Tom, Daniel paused for a moment before replying. "I'll tell you what," he said. "We'll lend you the $30,000 unsecured. And we'll lend you another $15,000 on top of that. All I can ask of you is what our Founding Fathers said: they pledged their lives, their fortunes, and their sacred honor. I won't ask you for your life or your fortune, but I will ask you for your sacred honor."

"Sir, you have it," Tom answered solemnly. "I pledge my sacred honor." An hour later he walked out of the bank with a check for $45,000 in his pocket.

Since returning from Brussels after the death of his sister, Tom had been experiencing the same kind of "personal catharsis" that Jim Webb had when he wrote *Fields of Fire*. Living at his parents' house in Amherst — Colonel and Mrs. Carhart had left on a long, therapeutic trip through the Far East and South Pacific — Tom attempted to restore some discipline to his life. He removed his wristwatch, ran six miles every day, read *The New York Times* religiously, shunned television, dined on a freezer full of stews and chilies that his mother had left, and labored on his memoirs of Vietnam. By June 1979, he had completed a 1450-page manuscript. While looking for a publisher, he passed the Massachusetts bar, hung out his shingle, and earned $300 or so a month handling cases for the public defender's office.

In August 1979, a friend arranged a blind date for him with a young stockbrocker named Jan Barbour. Nine years Tom's junior, she had auburn hair, dark eyes, and a sweet, easy smile. Her father, after graduating from Princeton in 1950, had entered the Army and received an OCS commission. Assigned to West Point as part of the cadre training cadets for the Korean War, he contracted polio and died at the academy hospital in August 1952, five months before Jan was born.

At first blush, Jan and Tom appeared to have little in common. A therapist friend, who was an aficionado of the Myers-Briggs personality-typing system, once described Tom as "a perfect ENFP" — extroverted, intuitive, feeling, perceptive. Jan, by contrast, was an INTJ — introverted, intuitive, thinking, judgmental. When Jan was three, her mother had married a New York banker, who raised his stepdaughter in the New Jersey suburbs. In high school, Jan worked ardently for the peace candidacy of Senator Eugene McCarthy, even sporting a black armband during the 1969 war moratorium. At Smith College, she majored in English and continued her antiwar activism. After teaching at a private school outside Washington, she had moved to Massachusetts for a new career as a stockbroker and was earning more than ten times Tom's income.

Jan Barbour could not quite get a fix on Tom Carhart. On that first date, at Judy's Restaurant in Amherst, she liked his openness, his gift with words, and his eagerness to talk about the war without apologizing for it. Still, he seemed to lend himself to stereotyping; for one thing, he talked a great deal about combat and Vietnam. And before they closed down the restaurant bar that night, she heard all about a man named Buck Thompson, and how he supposedly had once shot a swayback nag in a girls' dormitory at the University of Kansas. As a self-described save-the-whales type, Jan found that a little hard to stomach.

But when she tried to push Tom into the pigeonhole of the benignly loony veteran, he wouldn't quite fit. She discovered, among other things, that he was doing pro bono work for several juvenile delinquents and represented a retarded woman whom he visited every day in the state hospital. His complexity was beguiling. What's wrong with this picture? she asked herself.

Never one to camouflage his feelings, Tom pursued her through the fall. Smitten himself, he wanted her to be smitten, too. "Faint heart ne'er fair maiden won," he joked. "If you don't back off," she countered, eyebrows arched, "I'm going to bow out." Despite the painful lesson of his first marriage, he still struggled to master some rudimentary facts about modern women. One evening, as Jan was describing a particularly brutal day at the brokerage, he interrupted. Kissing her toes, he murmured, "Oh, sweetie, here. Relax. Sit down on the couch."

"Damn it!" she snapped. "Don't kiss my toes. *Listen to me.*"

In October, they moved in together. In January 1980, they married. Tom borrowed $3000 on a ninety-day note to take his bride on a stylish honeymoon in France; they made an excursion to Fontainebleau to visit the old Carhart estate with its regal chestnut trees. On their return — having won his fair maiden, finished his manuscript, and ensured his domestic tranquillity — Tom began chafing at the sedate pace of life in Amherst. He yearned for a city large enough to hold his ambitions, and that meant Washington. Jan agreed, and in the spring they packed up for the capital. Tom accepted a job in the Office of Personnel Management while hoping for something grander should Ronald Reagan snatch the presidency away from Jimmy Carter in the fall.

Beginning with his adroit feat of securing the $45,000 loan with only his word as collateral, Tom became a vigorous supporter of the memorial effort. When the legislation stalled in Congress, he hurried up to Capitol Hill for a brief — and fruitful — chat with the man who had appointed him to West Point, Representative Lucien N. Nedzi of Detroit, chairman of the House subcommittee on libraries and memorials. Frequently, he dropped into the VVMF office on Connecticut Avenue to stuff envelopes, answer the phone, and grouse about the federal government. ("Ah dee-spise the boor-acracy," he often sneered in his best Rhett Butler drawl.) He and Bob Doubek grew close. Sometimes, as they hiked through White Oak Canyon in the Shenandoah or drove to a concert together at Wolf Trap, Tom would talk about his adventures in Vietnam or his fantasy of searching for American POWs in Laos and Cambodia. "If I lost my life doing something like that," he told Doubek, "that would be a good death."

An even closer friend was Jim Webb. This is one guy I've got to meet, Tom had told himself after reading a review of Webb's novel in *News-*

week. Before long, they became regular fishing companions. Webb often swung by in his pickup truck for the drive south to Lake Quantico, where they would bob about with their lines over the gunwales, drinking Coke, chewing tobacco, and ventilating their feelings about the war. One weekend they went bar hopping together in Annapolis. "Jim," Tom confided after a few beers, "I like you so much I'd like to fight you."

Like Jack, Tom thought he had much in common with Webb: they were both oldest sons of men who had come up through the ranks of the Army Air Corps in World War II; they both had older sisters; both had lived in Europe as children, Tom in France, Jim in England; both were lawyers who had been divorced and written books; both had been infantry line doggies with an abiding affection for grunts; both were Aquarians, born in February. And, significantly, both resented the prevailing American attitude toward Vietnam veterans as losers. Tom had completely shed the rhetoric of his days with the student left in Ann Arbor. "Damn it, I don't remember losing in Vietnam," he once said heatedly. "I remember killing gooks."

Curiously, the admiration that separately drew Jack Wheeler and Tom Carhart to Jim Webb did not extend between the two West Pointers. Although they had known each other for nearly twenty years, including two years as company mates in Easy Deuce, Jack and Tom had never been much more than nodding acquaintances. Jack thought of Tom Carhart as he thought of Tom Sawyer: a clever free spirit who could persuade others to whitewash the fence and still remain in their good graces. Tom thought of Jack as a classic academy hive: brainy, bookish, and starchy. The word *prig* had come to mind on occasion.

On a blistering summer day in 1980, when the memorial legislation was at last ready for Jimmy Carter to sign into law, Carhart, Doubek, and Wheeler shared a taxi to the White House for the Rose Garden ceremony. Doubek joked in the cab about reorganizing the VVMF fund raising along ethnic divisions. "Tom, you can take the Irish Catholics," he said. "I'll take the Czechs and Slovaks. Wheeler can take the Episcopalians." When that failed to rile Jack, they needled him about his ancestor, the Confederate general Fightin' Joe Wheeler. Jack, who was intensely proud of his heritage, snapped back, "Damned fine cavalryman." Tom and Doubek rolled their eyes.

Yet at times the memorial drew the two classmates together as never before. One occasion was Memorial Day 1980. VVMF had planned a quiet ceremony in Constitution Gardens, where they hoped to stake a claim to the site and perhaps garner a little publicity. Doubek borrowed a load of folding chairs from the Old Guard at Fort Myer and drove to the Mall at eight A.M. in a twenty-foot Ryder rental truck. Tom was waiting for him. For a few minutes, they laboriously unloaded the truck, chair by chair.

"C'mon," Tom said impatiently, "get in the truck."

"Get in the truck? What are you doing? Can you drive this thing?"

Tom grinned. "Can *I* drive a truck?" Shifting into first, he popped the clutch and floored the accelerator. Around and around in a great spinning circle he drove. As the Ryder built up speed, centrifugal force began to fling the chairs from the back until they lay in a gray circle. "There," Tom said cheerfully, switching off the ignition. "All done."

Hundreds of people came to the ceremony, including several amputees and other veterans in their jungle fatigues, boonie hats, and campaign ribbons. Following the speeches, Jack, who had been sitting next to Ellsworth Bunker, former ambassador to Vietnam, spoke briefly to the crowd. "There's no more sacred part of a person than his name. We have to start remembering real, individual names." At his invitation, a line formed and people stepped forward to recite the names of loved ones they had lost in the war. A park ranger named her husband. A woman and two little girls, in unison, named the girls' father.

Then suddenly a beefy black man began ranting furiously into the microphone. "You no-good capitalist pigs!" he shrieked. "Killing the people — genocide — these poor Vietnamese!" A wave of alarm swept the crowd. Tom, who had been positioned as a bouncer, took four quick steps, grabbed the man by the shoulders, and ran him off into the fringe of the crowd. When the last person had spoken, Tom reappeared at the mike.

"Richard W. 'the Immortal Buck' Thompson!" he proclaimed.

As Tom moved aside, Jack stepped forward. "Thomas Jay Hayes the Fourth!"

After the crowd dispersed, the two classmates met as they prepared to leave the Mall. Without a word, they locked eyes, shook hands, and went their separate ways. "Who was Tommy Hayes?" Doubek later asked Tom. "He was a friend of ours and a good guy," Tom replied. "A real good guy."

With the two-acre tract of hallowed ground secure, VVMF turned to the issue of precisely what kind of memorial to build. After weeks of internal debate, the veterans decided to offer a $20,000 prize in an international design competition, the winning entry to be selected by a jury. To oversee the competition, they hired Paul Spreiregen, an experienced architect who had supervised such contests before. Jack insisted — again thumping the table with his fist — that any jury include a black, a woman, and representatives from the VVMF board of directors, of which he was now chairman.

"How does this guy Spreiregen feel about having board members on the jury?" he asked at one meeting.

"I don't know, Jack," Doubek answered.

"There are going to be two members of this board on that jury," Jack insisted. "Jan and me. My intuition tells me we should do that and my intuition is always right."

Doubek scoffed. "What do you mean, your intuition is always right?"

As the cut and thrust went back and forth, Jack exploded in anger. "You pissant!" he hollered at Doubek.

Doubek, who had recently read a book on assertiveness, fired back, "Don't yell at me, Jack. Don't yell at me, Jack. Don't yell at me, Jack. I'm *not* a pissant. I'm *not* a pissant."

One veteran had brought his young daughter to the meeting. When discussion turned to argument and argument dissolved into strident clamor, she began to cry and had to leave the room before order was restored.

Eventually Jack yielded, convinced in part by Art Mosley's low-key persuasiveness. In November 1980, VVMF announced the design competition. The eight jurors selected were all male, all white, all prestigious professionals — architects, sculptors, critics. Because none had served in Vietnam, Jack assembled a reading list to give the jury some notion of the sensibility VVMF sought.

But fund raising remained a problem. VVMF had appointed a "national sponsoring committee" of prominent Americans, including Rosalynn Carter, Gerald Ford, William Westmoreland, Bob Hope, and Jim Webb. But they were still a long way from $10 million. The mass mailing that Tom had helped underwrite netted $120,000, but the design competition alone was expected to cost $160,000.

Into the breech rode the same Texas billionaire who had helped the Reverend Jim Ford finance his trans-Atlantic voyage five years earlier. H. Ross Perot, who had lost one of his closest friends from the Naval Academy in a helicopter crash in Vietnam, had once proposed building a war memorial that could be seen from the White House and bore this inscription: FIRST COMMIT THE NATION, THEN COMMIT THE TROOPS. Having already donated $10,000 to VVMF, Perot now agreed to finance the competition. "Promise me one thing," he asked Scruggs, "that the men we're trying to honor like the memorial."

Despite some concern that Perot's largesse would give him excessive control over the project, VVMF accepted the gift with thanks. At least now they could survive until the spring of 1981, when the winning design was to be unveiled.

But the essential question remained: What should the memorial look like? The Iwo Jima statue? The unbuilt FDR tribute? One day, Jim Webb came across an article in *Texas Monthly* about a furor in Austin over a proposed Vietnam memorial. The city's arts council had picked a design that resembled a large egg carton with twenty holes. One hole was painted black. The other nineteen were white, emblematic of the nineteen Austin men killed in the war. Webb, who thought the design was ludicrous, sent the article to Jack with a note: "We aren't going to get an egg carton, are we?"

Jack didn't know. That was up to the creative genius of the design contestants and the sagacity of the jury. But Webb's point was well taken. "Whatever design we come up with will be one thousand degrees hot," Jack observed. "There will be a fight."

Tom had also been thinking about the design. He had urged VVMF to come up with its own idea. "Why don't we just do it ourselves?" he asked repeatedly. Tom was so certain that he could conjure up a suitable design that Scruggs began thinking of him as "some kind of goddamn Leonardo da Vinci." When the formal competition was announced, Tom decided to enter. He did not really expect to win — and becoming a contestant meant that he would have to sever his ties to VVMF — but the exercise would be cathartic, just as writing a book had allowed him to purge some of the war's emotion.

Tom often wandered into Arlington Cemetery to visit the grave of his sister, whose ashes lay buried less than fifty yards from the vast necropolis inhabited by the Vietnam dead. Walking among the tombstones of men from the 1st Cav and the 101st Airborne — his old unit — he thought of their sacrifice in terms of an offering, as Abraham had offered to sacrifice his son as an earnest of his devotion to God. One image in particular from his own experience lingered with Tom. Near the A Shau Valley on June 3, 1968, when Tom was wounded for the second time, his radioman, Lou Lopez, had been killed by NVA machine-gun bullets. Under fire, Tom had dragged Lopez's body eighty yards down a hill before hefting it in a fireman's carry to the helicopter landing zone. Soaked in the dead man's gore, Tom stood knee-deep in a rice paddy to hoist the corpse into a Huey.

After sketching that scene on a pad of paper, Tom went to the public library and checked out several books, including *Anyone Can Sculpt*. He made a model of the sculpture and then fashioned an armature from coat hangers. Working at night and on weekends, he kneaded the clay around the wire frame before placing the figure on the oven door, where the sculpture slowly hardened. Then he painted it gold. For a base, he fashioned a rice paddy in the shape of a heart, painted purple. Since the contest rules decreed that each design entry had to include the names of those killed in the war, Tom planned to enclose the figurine with a circular white wall upon which the names would be carved.

The finished sculpture, showing an officer struggling to lift the body of a slain soldier into an unseen helicopter, was amateurish. Tom joked that it resembled "the Pillsbury dough boy." But once again he had vented his feelings about the war. His intent was not to glorify battle, but rather to glorify those who had offered the last full measure of devotion. He thought of the war in the same paradoxical terms that he had once seen expressed by William Broyles, Jr., a Marine combat veteran who had later become an author and the editor of *Newsweek*. Vietnam, Broyles had written, evinced "the awesome beauty, the haunting romance of a timeless nightmare."

The damp chill in Hangar No. 3 at Andrews Air Force Base on Friday morning, May 1, 1981, reminded Jack of the Venturi effect at West Point. *Conveying a fluid through a constricted passage will increase the velocity of said fluid.* The principle had stuck with him, drummed into his head during mechanics class at the academy and made real by the north wind whipping through the Hudson gorge during many a reveille formation. This mammoth, drafty hangar southeast of Washington was simply an oversize Venturi tube. He hugged his chest for warmth.

Jack and the other VVMF vets sat on metal chairs at one end of the hangar. Facing them, in a parallel line of chairs, sat the eight jurors, who, for four days, had been studying the 1421 entries in the memorial competition. Arranged side by side in rows that snaked for more than a mile through the hangar, the designs ranged from the elegant to the crackpot. Among the proposals rejected by the jury were a steel helmet as tall as a house, an assortment of stone and metal abstractions, and a gold statue of a soldier lifting a dead comrade skyward.

After Paul Spreiregen, the competition impresario, had spent half an hour explaining the jury's deliberations, he unveiled the first and second runners-up. They were good, even excellent, Spreiregen said, but they weren't quite good enough. Instead, the jurors had unanimously decided on entry number 1026, a simple pastel drawing that had caught their collective imagination early on and never let go. Dramatically, he tugged away the cloth covering the sketch.

A tense, four-count pause followed. Jan Scruggs, who had been fidgeting in his chair, thought the design looked like a bat. Against a smudgy green background stood two black slashes, joined at an obtuse angle. Perhaps it's a boomerang, he thought. Art Mosley, sitting on Jack's left, had been studying architectural drawings for ten years and he instantly recognized that the black wings were meant to be gradually sloping walls set into a hillside. Jack wasn't sure what the sketch showed — he tried to make sense of Spreiregen's preparatory comments about how it tied in to the Lincoln Memorial and Washington Monument — but he recognized that if they faltered now the cause was lost.

"This," he said firmly, rising from his seat, "is a work of genius." He began to clap, and was quickly joined by the other veterans and jurors, who applauded vigorously.

Art leaned over and hugged him. "Boy, Jack, this is it. We got it. A gem bubbled to the surface."

"Aw, Art," Jack said, smiling, "you just like it because it looks like a baseball diamond."

Everyone laughed. It did resemble a baseball field, though second base was missing. The design also looked like a bat and a boomerang and the rank chevrons on a cadet's uniform. At any rate, this was it, whatever *it* was. The *pock-pock-pock* of applause reverberated through the cavernous hangar like tiny shots.

The artist, as VVMF quickly learned, was a young Chinese-American woman with hip-length black hair who was studying architecture at Yale. Born in 1959 — the year of the first American death in Vietnam — Maya Ying Lin came from Athens, Ohio, where her father was an accomplished ceramicist and her mother was a literature professor. Before the family immigrated to the United States, her grandfather had been a lawyer who served in the Chinese delegation to the League of Nations in 1921. Maya — the name, that of Buddha's mother, meant "illusion" — was strong-willed, self-contained, and wholly American. (She had even worked at McDonald's as a teenager.) Confessing to a "morbid" streak, she was fond of roaming among the big crypts in New Haven's Grove Street Cemetery, though no one she loved had ever died. Her winning memorial design, sketched for a class on funerary architecture, was awarded a B+ by her instructor at Yale.

VVMF quickly rendered Lin's pastel into a three-dimensional model. Now that there was something tangible to show the public, the memorial fund-raising drive caught fire. Thousands of letters poured in, most of them containing checks. The design easily gained the blessing of Washington's taste mavens by receiving unanimous approval from the city's Fine Arts Commission and the National Capital Planning Commission.

But the enthusiasm was hardly universal. Shortly after the winning entry was selected, Ross Perot called Scruggs. Their chat turned rancorous. "You've made a big, big mistake," the Texan warned. "It'll only be nice for the guys who died."

Jack was given the task of mollifying Jim Webb, who also had misgivings. The design was not an egg carton, but it wasn't the Iwo Jima sculpture either. Since their spat over the Hammerschmidt affair, the two men had forged a fragile peace. Webb had asked Jack to read and comment on the galleys of his second novel, *A Sense of Honor;* when Jack responded with four pages of incisive analysis, Webb repaid the debt by thanking him on the book's dedication page. During one conversation, both remarked how similar their fathers were to the character portrayed by Robert Duvall in *The Great Santini,* a movie about a tough Marine fighter pilot.

Now Jack was eager for Webb's support. Sitting down at his battered old typewriter, he pecked out a note. "Jim, it's the Eiffel Tower," he pleaded. "The design needs time to understand."

But Webb figured he could stare at the thing until doomsday without seeing the Eiffel Tower. The analogy he preferred was that of a "mass grave." He was inclined to agree with *The National Review,* which called the design "Orwellian glop." When it became clear that Jack and Scruggs were in no hurry to push for modifications, Webb and some of the other dissidents began to get angry. Sometimes they met at the Vietnam Inn in Arlington to smoke cigars, swig Ba Muoi Ba beer, and air their grievances. The memorial, they agreed, needed a flag, an appropriate inscription, and white walls. Furthermore, the structure should be aboveground.

Among those most upset in the indignant discussions at the restaurant was Tom Carhart. "Oh, boy, what did you guys do?" he asked Doubek after first seeing the design. "It should have been a statue." To Art Mosley, Tom added, "I just can't live with this."

Tom denounced Maya Lin's proposal as "an open urinal." But his anger went beyond simple esthetics. The congressional mandate called for a memorial "in honor and recognition of the men and women of the armed forces of the United States who served in the Vietnam War." What honor or recognition is there in this? Tom demanded. One arm of the wall pointed toward the Lincoln Memorial, the other toward the Washington Monument. Both of those were majestic white edifices that soared above the ground. This was just the opposite — black and subterranean. What did that say? To Tom, Lin's memorial offered no thanks to those who had served honorably; instead, it said, you are a disgrace.

He was also growing a little weary of John P. Wheeler III. Although some of Tom's friends thought he was preoccupied with Jack's bloodlines — the quintessential WASP, descendant of soldiers, son of a West Pointer — what really bothered Tom was his classmate's presuming to speak for the warriors who had actually fought the war. Tom had always had a special contempt for REMFs; he now began referring to Jack derisively as Mr. Vietnam Veteran and Sergeant Rock. Jack had spent the war in air-conditioned Long Binh, yet every time Tom turned on the television or radio he seemed to find Wheeler promoting himself as the voice of the fighting man. Tom considered him a fraud. He's wrapped himself in Tommy Hayes's bloody shirt, Tom thought bitterly, yet he's not half the man Tommy was.

Finally, he seethed at the selection of an artist who knew nothing of war or the brotherhood of combat. Although Tom later denied any racial animus toward Maya Lin, several men — including Bob Doubek and Art Mosley — noted his scorn at the selection of an Asian woman. Doubek reported that when he had asked for possible inscriptions for the wall, Tom replied, "How about 'Designed by a gook'?"

His anger simmered through the summer and into the fall. On October 9, Scruggs learned that Tom planned to go public with his dissent at a meeting of the Fine Arts Commission scheduled for the thirteenth, after the Columbus Day weekend. Scruggs called Jack; nothing good, they agreed, would come of this eleventh-hour protest, particularly from someone as articulate and impassioned as Carhart. Jack then called Art Mosley, who after a decade in Washington had recently packed up and moved to Key West. Art, he asked, will you mediate?

Art had watched Jack and Tom for nearly two decades, since the days when they were all naïve teenagers. He knew the great strengths of each. Jack had fervor and a matchless ability to get things done. You wanted to be sure you were on his side, Mosley believed, and Art remained steadfastly loyal to VVMF. But he did not underestimate Tom. Sure, Art thought, Carhart could be obstinate and obnoxious, but he was also smart, very smart. And he had an uncanny knack for rallying the troops, as he had done in the goat heist. On the night of October 12, Art called Tom from Key West.

"I know why you're calling me," Tom said. "I'm not going to change my mind. I have to do this."

"Hey, Tom, listen. You do it. I think you should do it. You feel strongly about this and you should speak your mind."

"That Wheeler," Tom continued. "Son of a bitch. He didn't do anything in Vietnam. What does he know?"

"Tom, there's a system and a way to do this thing that has been established. If you've got problems with it, come up with another design, sell that, and get it built."

At one A.M., Art called Jack to tell him that Tom was determined to speak his mind. "You'd better brace yourself, Jack," he added.

The Fine Arts Commission met the next day in one of the elegant town houses on Lafayette Square, across Pennsylvania Avenue from the White House. Tom arrived in a three-piece black suit with both Purple

Hearts pinned to his jacket breast. This was the only occasion he had ever worn the actual medals rather than the service ribbons. Knowing that his repudiation of the design would make good copy, he had alerted the television stations and the newspapers. But now he was scared. Here I am again, he thought, walking into enemy fire with my head exposed. By publicly traducing the wall, he knew that he was pitting himself against some powerful figures, including General Michael Davison, the former West Point commandant who was a VVMF ally and was about to become president of the academy's Association of Graduates. In August 1980, the general and Tom had jointly sent a memorial fund-raising appeal to all West Pointers. But now Tom was locking horns with Big Mike Davison. He wondered whether this dissent could cost him his new job as a civilian attorney in the Army chief of staff's office.

Yet, as in Vietnam, he thought of the issue in terms of pure principle. Strong belief required forceful action without regard to personal consequence. That was the West Point way, wasn't it? Anything less amounted to temporizing, a shirking of absolute commitment to principle. At the Vietnam Inn, he had urged the other dissenters to join him in speaking out. When they squirmed and demurred — complaining that "I'm a political appointee," or "The military won't let me," or "My wife will kill me" — Tom was disgusted. "All right," he muttered at last, "fuck it. I'm gonna say something."

Tom memorized a ten-minute statement and, in a hearing room crowded with journalists and TV cameras, he launched into his protest.

> Unless something unexpected happens, ground will soon be broken for the Vietnam Veterans Memorial on the Mall here in Washington. Although I have long awaited this moment, as it now approaches I feel only pain.
>
> I believe that the design selected for the memorial in an open competition is pointedly insulting to the sacrifices made for their country by all Vietnam veterans. By this will we be remembered: a black gash of shame and sorrow, hacked into the national visage that is the Mall.
>
> The winning design was chosen by a jury made up entirely of civilians . . . The jurors know nothing of the real war in Vietnam — the television portrayal was far from adequate. But the political war cut so deeply through society that everyone had to take sides . . . It may be that black walls sunk into a trench would be an appropriate statement of the political war in this country. But that is not the war whose veterans the fund has been authorized to memorialize.
>
> The proposed Vietnam memorial is anti-heroic . . . Black walls, the universal color of sorrow and dishonor. Hidden in a hole, as if in shame.
>
> President Reagan has called the nation's Vietnam experience a noble

cause. I hope that he and the rest of America do not want us to be remembered by posterity in this way.

The commission listened politely and then immediately reaffirmed its earlier decision to proceed with construction.

On the steps outside the town house, General Davison pulled Tom aside for a moment. "Okay, Tom, you've had your say and I respect your right to stand up and say it. I hope now you will close ranks with us so that we can get the job done."

Tom shook his head. That missed the point entirely. How could he speak his mind and then pretend that he did not believe his own words? Big Mike didn't understand.

Suddenly Jan Scruggs appeared on Tom's left. "Way to go, Carhart," he muttered. "You're a traitor. You stabbed us in the back. Where'd you learn to be a traitor? You learn that at West Point?"

As Scruggs turned away, Tom suppressed the urge to lash out. But the gibe left him in a smoldering rage. He resolved to speak out again and again, if necessary, until the entire country finally understood the reasons for his antipathy toward this dark wall.

Two weeks later, on Friday, October 23, Jan Carhart gave birth to a baby boy, whom the parents named Thomas. That weekend was the happiest of Tom's life. His Fine Arts Commission speech had set off a storm of controversy. Tom's arresting phrases — particularly "a black gash of shame and sorrow" — were eminently quotable, and the media had pounced on the schism over the memorial. But the dispute seemed trivial compared with the joy he felt at the birth of his first child.

His jubilation was short-lived. On Monday morning, after examining Tommy, the neonatologist told Jan, "Mrs. Carhart, I think you may have some problems with your child." The doctor suspected Down's syndrome, a severe congenital defect. Even if the baby survived, he would be mentally deficient and physically deformed. More tests were needed, but Tom had little doubt that something was drastically wrong.

As he drove home from the hospital that night, Tom cried so hard that the road dissolved into a black blur and he had to pull over. Later, he called his mother in Amherst. "Tommy," she said hopefully. "they still don't know. It's fifty-fifty until the tests come back."

"Mother, you don't understand. It's so difficult for me to accept the possibility that he might be so badly flawed."

When Tom hung up, he abruptly realized that he was not weeping for his little son. He was crying for himself, for his dashed expectations, the most cherished of which was that his son might someday follow him to West Point.

That epiphany dazzled Tom, altering his mood radically. He stopped crying. A powerful gust of adoration for his child swept aside his despair and self-pity. The tiny baby struggling in the hospital needed him as no one else in the world needed him. When the test results confirmed the doctor's suspicion of Down's, Tom shrugged. "Okay, it's okay," he told Jan, brimming with strength and confidence. He was lucky, really. He had a new son and a sweet wife. He had his life, his fortune — modest as it was — and he had his sacred honor. As he had overcome other tribulations, so he would overcome this one because, most important, he also had love.

The battle over the memorial settled into brutal, bitter trench warfare. Jack was reminded of an old legal saw which held that if you've got the facts on your side, argue the facts; if you've got the law, argue the law; if you've got neither the facts nor the law, call the other guy a scoundrel. Both camps engaged in a great deal of scoundrel calling.

No one was happy. Jim Webb wryly observed that it was as though the disputants were "throwing Purple Hearts at each other." Convinced that he was being flimflammed by Jack and Jan Scruggs, whom he called "pathetic creatures," Webb resigned from the sponsoring committee and threatened legal action if his name was not removed from the VVMF letterhead. Scruggs rounded up a group of Gold Star mothers, handed each a bottle of Wite-Out fluid, and put them to work for several days eradicating James H. Webb from the stationery.

In addition to the design opponents' other demands, Ross Perot insisted that the names on the memorial be alphabetized, rather than listed chronologically in the order of their deaths. "Do you know how many Smiths there are?" Mike Davison asked Perot over lunch in Washington one day. "There are six hundred and some. It would be like being buried in a telephone directory. How would you like it if you were the father of a Fred Smith who died in Vietnam? How would you like him to be there in the midst of six hundred and umpty-ump other Smiths?"

VVMF parried Tom Carhart's accusations as best it could. No, black was not the color of shame; both the Seabee and Iwo Jima memorials in Washington contained black granite. Besides, white stone would make the names difficult to read. No, the memorial was not a gash cut into the ground; the wall would actually be set into a hillside with a clear vista of the Mall. No, the memorial was not a V mimicking the antiwar peace sign; no human fingers could form a 125-degree V.

Ironically, the public flap was a boon to fund raising. After Tom's denunciation, contributions jumped to $50,000 a week, including handsome donations from Getty Oil, Boeing, Exxon, and Henry Kissinger. By early 1982, the fund had amassed $8 million.

Then serious trouble came from an unexpected quarter. The secretary of the interior, a pugnacious lawyer named James Watt, sympathized with the design opponents. On January 4, 1982, he decreed that there would be no work on the memorial until further notice. As the government's guardian of federal land, Watt could make the order stick. The project came to an abrupt halt.

Clearly, the time had come to compromise. But how? VVMF and the opponents seemed too far apart in their respective visions of the memorial to find common ground. At the invitation of Senator Warner, both sides met at three-thirty on January 25 in room 412 of the Russell Office Building on Capitol Hill. For more than four hours, in an ad hoc group therapy session, the parties decanted their spleen in the smoky room. When someone objected to the esthetics of placing a "stringy" American flag next to the wall, Tom Carhart, who sat next to Ross Perot, leaped to his feet and howled, "Take that back, you motherfucker!" Scruggs, equally enraged at the opponents' naysaying, jabbed his finger at Perot's crowd. "Where were you during the past three years?" he yelled. "Why didn't you help? Why are you trying to destroy this memorial now that it's ready to be built?"

At seven-thirty, Mike Davison stood up. In all the bickering, Davison thought he detected one thread: an abiding respect for the individual soldier who had answered his country's call during the war and done his duty. Was there some way to honor that without desecrating Lin's wall? Davison had a mental picture of the *Follow Me* statue in front of Infantry Hall at Fort Benning. In his left hand, the bronze soldier carried a rifle; his right hand was raised to summon the troops from behind.

"Look, this has gone on for too long," Davison said calmly. "Let's be reasonable. Why don't we just add a statue?"

Tom leaped to his feet again. "If you're going to give us a statue, you've got to let us have an American flag."

"We've got it," Warner said gleefully. "Let's pull together."

On March 26, after Secretary Watt lifted his stop order, VVMF broke ground with another ceremony in Constitution Gardens. The crowd sang "God Bless America." Then bulldozers slashed into the hillside, and pile drivers began hammering 140 concrete pillars into bedrock, thirty-five feet below the surface. Construction engineers issued orders to ship thirty truckloads of black granite from Bangalore, India, to Barre, Vermont, where the stone would be cut with a diamond-tipped saw into twelve dozen rectangles, each three inches thick and forty inches wide. After polishing with tin oxide, the slabs would be trucked to Memphis, where workmen waited to sandblast 58,000 names into the stone, in letters half an inch high.

As part of the compromise deal, Jack appointed Jim Webb, Art Mosley, and two other men to a committee that would select the memorial sculpture. Tom fervently wanted a seat on the panel, but Jack refused. Carhart, he concluded, was too volatile, too likely to upset the delicate chemistry that was needed. On July 1, the VVMF board accepted the committee's recommendation for a life-size statue of three soldiers by Frederick E. Hart, a thirty-eight-year-old sculptor who had finished third in the original design competition.

One afternoon in late summer, Jack wandered down to the memorial site. Although the two acres were unsightly, strewn with construction equipment and debris, the graceful angle of the wall was already apparent. Several dozen finished panels had arrived from Memphis and were now in place. Maya Lin had likened this gradual accretion of names on the memorial to the inexorable death toll during the war. Jack paused in front of panel 50 East, which was part of the wing that stretched toward the Washington Monument, eight hundred yards away. Small flecks of mica gave the black granite a reflective luster, and Jack could see himself clearly in the stone. Set within his own image, he found the name he sought: Thomas J. Hayes IV. Only a hand's breadth away were the names of the men Tommy had been trying to save when he was killed.

The sight gave Jack a gratifying sense of accomplishment at a time when he needed something to lift his spirits. A melancholy had settled over him in the past few months; the harder he worked at bringing the memorial to life, the more despondent he grew. Scruggs even worried that he was close to a nervous breakdown. As chairman of the VVMF board, Jack was a lightning rod for those disgruntled with the design. After Warner's compromise meeting, Jack's "coterie of devoted enemies," as Scruggs described them, had continued to pelt him with maledictions. Even the fact that he had been only a cadet sergeant at West Point was cited as evidence of his shortcomings. ("Like Eisenhower," Jack replied dryly.)

Ross Perot had concluded that Jack Wheeler was a shameless "opportunist." Listening to Jack, he complained, "you'd think he spent thirteen months in the field armed only with a dull knife and choking guys to death with his bare hands." In one phone conversation with Perot, Jack understood the Texan to say "I'll wap you out." He was not sure whom the "you" referred to, and he sure as hell didn't know what "wap" meant. Perot later denied making the comment, but not before Jack asked, "Mr. Perot, do you have counsel?"

"Sir," Perot thundered, "I am surrounded by counsel!"

Jim Webb, despite his new position on the sculpture panel, was convinced that Jack was both incompetent and manipulative, promising solutions for the sake of expediency. When Jack wrote that "the war sundered our generation," Webb also accused him of being "MacArthuresque." Jack could live with that. In fact, he liked to think of himself as a battle captain in the memorial fight. But the suggestion that he had been dishonorable in misleading Webb about modifications to Lin's design was harder to take. That, he believed, was hitting below the belt.

Jack again scanned the construction site. It was muddy and cluttered, but in just a few months the mud and debris would be gone, replaced by a thing of beauty that would honor the veterans of Vietnam for generations to come. Jack could see the finished work in his mind's eye as clearly as he could see the Lincoln Memorial through the grove of trees behind him. Why couldn't everyone else see the same thing?

By trying to appease all parties, he realized, he had managed to anger everyone. Even the VVMF inner circle watched him suspiciously, fearful that he would forge a separate peace with Webb and company. One particularly divisive issue involved the memorial dedication, now scheduled for Veterans Day in November 1982. Webb insisted that the formal dedication be delayed until the sculpture was finished, sometime in 1984. But the American Legion, which had donated $1.2 million, was threatening to revoke its contribution if the ceremony did not proceed as planned during the grand National Salute to Vietnam veterans.

"If Jim Webb wants to leave a fence around the memorial," Scruggs said, "let him get his jackboots and a Mauser and let him fire a round over the heads of the Gold Star mothers." When the issue was put to a vote, the VVMF board decided six-to-one to proceed with the dedication. Jack cast the sole dissenting vote. "Jack, haven't you figured it out yet?" Dick Radez asked with exasperation. "Who do you think has been working against you for two years? It's Webb!"

The stress wasn't doing Jack's home life any good, either. While devoting fifty to a hundred hours a week to the memorial and working full bore at the Securities and Exchange Commission, where he was now special counsel to Chairman John Shad, Jack worried about neglecting his wife and the twins. After two years of seminary work, Elisa had just been ordained an Episcopal priest at St. Columba's Church in Northwest Washington. He was enormously proud of her; the family had even danced a little jig outside the cathedral on learning that she had been admitted to the seminary to study for the divinity degree. But the special intimacy they once shared seemed to be fading.

Jack regretted that Elisa had never "bonded" with West Point the way he wanted her to, and now she seemed to keep her distance from the memorial. Although the priest in her appreciated the need for a touchstone to help heal the nation's war wounds, living with a husband who seemed to be back in Vietnam most of the time was burdensome. The threatening, anonymous phone calls Jack received at home also frightened her, particularly after young John burst into tears one day, wailing that "they want to hurt my daddy." Jack conceded that Elisa had ample grounds to criticize him; among other things, he tended to neglect paying the bills and doing other mundane household administrative chores. And the nights of vigil at Katie's bedside — not to mention the repeated trips to Boston for surgery and medical consultations — were enough to strain even the strongest marriage.

As he lingered by the unfinished wall, Jack wondered again whether he should resign from the board. If the brawl got ugly enough, his opponents might try to get him fired from the SEC. Losing his job would mean forfeiting his medical benefits, and that would be catastrophic. Perhaps, he thought, it would be best if he bowed out. Mike Davison, who admired Jack but privately thought he was "a worrywart almost to the point of paranoia," had urged him to stand fast. "For you to resign would be a grave mistake," Davison declared. "The memorial fund needs you."

Facie Tenus. Stand Fast. That was the Wheeler family motto. Jack had stood fast. But at what price? he wondered as he stared at panel 50E. Where was this all leading? To his left was the vertex of the two wings; here the memorial's inscription would be carved. VVMF had settled on a brief ode of gratitude, which in part read: "Our nation honors the courage, sacrifice, and devotion to duty and country of its Vietnam veterans." Duty. Honor. Country. Without telling anyone, Jack had arranged to have the lines contain the three words of West Point's credo. It was his secret.

He glanced around. The workmen had quit for the day and the site was empty. Jack was alone. He took several steps back from the panel, studying the reflections in the granite. Now, Saint Paul had written in First Corinthians, we see through a glass darkly. Was it the mirror of the wall, he wondered, that so bothered Tom and Jim Webb and the others?

Whatever happens, Jack thought, I will be able to look at myself in this black stone without shame. His eyes again locked on the half-inch letters that spelled Tommy's name. On another summer day in another place, they both had been taught the gesture of respect that every cadet learned in the first hours of Beast Barracks. Standing at attention now, with fingers rigid, Jack raised his right hand to his eyebrow in salute and then snapped it back to his side.

*

By the time the November dawn finally arrived in a seepage of grays and pinks, several dozen veterans had gathered along the wall. Individually or in small groups, they watched in silence as the chiaroscuro of morning light played across the 140 black panels. The names of the 57,939 dead stretched for five hundred feet in cyclical chronology. The first American casualty, Major Dale R. Buis, killed by Viet Cong machine-gun fire while watching a movie at Bien Hoa on July 8, 1959, was listed at the top of panel 1E, just to the right of the vertex. The last name, Richard Vandegeer, killed during the bloody rescue of the U.S.S. *Mayaguez* on May 25, 1975, appeared on the bottom of panel 1W, just left of the vertex. On the wall, as Maya Lin had envisioned, the dead met the dead, alpha and omega. Now, with the imminent dedication of the memorial, the wall would become, as writer Christopher Buckley noted, "a liminal place," a threshold where the dead also met the living.

William G. Haneke, West Point '66, sat in his wheelchair, taking it all in. Dressed in jungle fatigues, Bill had left his blue station wagon on Constitution Avenue and wheeled himself to the memorial. He was able to walk with his artificial right leg, but he planned to spend some time in meditation, and the chair would be more comfortable. There were, he thought as he parked himself, at least two miracles here. The first was that he was visiting the wall instead of being memorialized on it. By all rights, his name should have been grit-blasted over there on panel 39W with the rest of those killed on November 13, 1968.

The second miracle was that he could see the wall rather than simply feel the stones. Four years after Bill was wounded by the booby trap, a team of surgeons had operated on his left eye — the right one was completely gone — though they cautioned him that the odds were only one in a hundred that his sight could be restored. "You were warned," the distraught ophthalmologist told Mary Haneke after the surgery. "Everything that could go wrong did go wrong. He's fully blind, permanently."

But the next morning, when the bandages were removed, Bill could see a blurry Mary standing at the foot of the hospital bed. "Skirt's a bit short, isn't it?" he quipped. The surgeon was flabbergasted. "If I never believed in God," he said, "I do now."

Perhaps because he had been so close to death, Bill had taken more than a casual interest in the memorial. Tom Carhart had called him several times in Richmond, trying to enlist Bill in the ranks of the opposition. Bill listened attentively as Tom ticked off his objections to the "black gash" and the Asian woman who had designed it. But he was not convinced. He had always been impressed with Jack Wheeler, even when they were teenagers at Fort Monroe. After two or three calls, Bill tried to talk to Carhart like a Dutch uncle.

"Look, Tom," he said, "Jack's involved in this thing and he's going to have the interest of the Vietnam veterans at heart. He's not going to allow anything that reflects badly on us."

And here's the proof, Bill thought. He had been apprehensive about driving up alone for the dedication while Mary and their four children remained in Richmond, but now he was glad that he had. He needed this immersion to help complete his own recovery. The wall tapped some extraordinary force, a power latent in the mass of so many names. One of Jan Scruggs's favorite lines was from F. Scott Fitzgerald: "Show me a hero and I will write you a tragedy." Here were written the names of more than 58,000 heroes, which made for a tragedy of epic magnitude. Somehow, though, the memorial moved beyond death and grief to a celebration of the mysteries of life. It's supposed to heal, Bill thought, and it does.

After an hour of gazing at the memorial from a distance, he wheeled himself along the walkway running parallel to the panels and began to search for the names of classmates. On 42E, he found his old roommate Bob Luecke, the pride of Parma, Ohio. Billy Wayne Flynn, the first man in the class to be killed, was listed on 14E. Halfway up 19E was Frank Rybicki, shot with his own rifle in the Rung Sat Special Zone. Fred Bertolino, who had died in a delta rice paddy while George Crocker listened helplessly on the radio, was on 22E. A few lines below, Bill found another of his roommates, Dick Hood, and not far from Hood was Don Judd. They had died together, their bodies discovered by Matt Harrison after the ambush outside Dak To on June 22, 1967.

Where's Buck? Bill wondered. A friendly Coast Guard officer helped him to thumb through one of the alphabetical directories until he saw: Thompson, Richard William. 1Lt Army. 10 March '41. 19 November '67. Atchison, Kansas.

With Pete Lantz and most of the other dead men from Hill 875, Buck was immortalized on panel 30E. Just as the bodies on the hill had been stacked, so the names on the wall were stowed one atop another. Buck was the last soldier listed on line thirty-four. A narrow seam separated his name from the next panel. In the future, the crease would provide a perfect holder in which his widow, Fran, could slip the stem of a red rose. The wall, Bill thought, transformed the dead into something immutable, something eternal.

As the hour for the dedication ceremony approached and the crowd grew larger, Bill spotted Jack sitting on the dignitaries' platform. With difficulty, he inched the wheelchair through the throng. "Jack!" he called. "Hey, Jack!"

Peering down, Jack saw a vaguely familiar face behind thick eyeglasses. Who is that? he wondered. The face and body looked as though they had been fractured and reassembled, like a jigsaw puzzle that hadn't quite come together properly. When Bill identified himself, Jack crouched at the edge of the platform and shook his hand, trying not to show how shocked he was by the contrast between this battered figure and the Bill Haneke he remembered. Here, he thought, are all the wounds of the war in one body. After chatting for a moment, Bill said, "You've done a great job, Jack. Thanks." Then he pivoted the chair and was gone, swallowed by the crowd.

Jack felt strangely calm. The past few days had been hectic, with a thousand last-minute details to attend to. Wave on wave of veterans had swept into the nation's capital, which, belatedly, had embraced them in a warm homecoming. Strangers clapped the vets on the back, pumped their hands, and insisted on paying for drinks and dinner. A long parade had snaked down Constitution Avenue, with Jack, Jan Scruggs, and Bob Doubek riding in the lead jeep. Jack could almost imagine that it was 1945. His mother and father had watched from the bleachers until Janet sought a warmer haven in the Metropolitan Club. "It's cold and I'm from Texas," she complained with the same words that she had used to avoid meeting Big Jack at West Point in 1942; yes, she was cold, but the real reason for her retreat was the wrenching sight of so many broken, legless young men wheeling themselves down the broad avenue.

One particularly poignant ceremony in the Salute took place at the National Cathedral. Volunteers, working in half-hour shifts for fifty-six hours, read aloud all the names of the dead in alphabetical order, from Gerald L. Aadland of Sisseton, South Dakota, to David L. Zywicke of Manitowoc, Wisconsin. A Polish priest, a Spanish teacher, and a rabbi stood by to help with pronunciations. Before taking their turns, each volunteer practiced reciting without crying.

Now, as the dedication ceremony began at the memorial with prayers and speeches, Jack sat on a platform above the wall, gazing at the crowd. Considering how huge the throng was — 100,000 people stretching from the Reflecting Pool in the south to the low-slung buildings across Constitution Avenue — it seemed preternaturally quiet. When his turn came to speak, Jack was brief. "This memorial," he said, "should serve as a major step in the process of healing the wounds of the war. We ask for grace to face our past."

But as he sat down again, he knew that healing would take more than supplication or a parade or Maya Lin's wall. There was too much bitterness. Even Jan Scruggs had confided to Jack a secret fantasy of dragging former defense secretary Robert McNamara before the wall and shouting, "Read the names! Read the fucking names!"

Jack also saw no sign that Carhart and Webb and Perot were about to relent in their campaign against VVMF. A few weeks before, CBS had aired on *60 Minutes* a segment called "Lest We Forget."

"I don't see how a black ditch — underground, no flag, no inscription, a jumble of names — I don't see how that honors anyone. It's a black sarcophagus," Tom had told Morley Safer. "The license of Congress is to honor and recognize those who served in Vietnam, not Jane Fonda and her friends."

"You really think — you really feel that's what it leaves it open to?" Safer asked.

"I don't know," Tom replied. "I'm emotionally caught up in this, obviously, and so perhaps I can't see the great splendor and so on. Well, most of us aren't artists. We want something that will make us feel a part of America."

Ross Perot was demanding an independent audit of the memorial books, bluntly suggesting that Jack and the others had something to hide in their management of the fund's $10 million. That could drag out for years. Tom and Jim Webb were also furious at Jack for asking the Episcopal Church of America to issue a proclamation of "reconciliation," which included "those who actively sought a change in the policy regarding U.S. involvement in Indochina, and those who chose to resist military service." In their eyes, Jack had lumped together brave men who had done their duty and a bunch of craven draft dodgers. This is beyond the pale, they thought, even for Wheeler.

Jack sighed. At least for these few hours, the anxiety and emotional battering were quieted by the satisfaction of getting the job done. He thought of MacArthur's words: there is no substitute for victory. In the war, for reasons beyond the control of Jack's generation, victory had been unattainable. Now it seemed beside the point; human tragedy and the need to bind the nation's wounds had transcended the issue of winning or losing. There would have to be a substitute, MacArthur notwithstanding.

And here it was. Like Bill Haneke, Jack thought of miracles when he looked at the wall, though in somewhat different terms. His favorite author, C. S. Lewis, had warned that one should always be careful in praying for miracles because they were inevitably accompanied by a great shaking of the earth. The earth had indeed shaken. Now Jack could only hope that the trembling signified what he thought it did: the grace to face the past.

18

URGENT FURY

TWO SURPRISES awaited Lieutenant Colonel George Crocker as he walked down the ramp of the C-141 on the morning of October 26, 1983. The first was the balmy climate. Trade winds stirred the coconut fronds and provided a briny tonic to a man who had been cooped up for nearly four hours in the bay of the transport jet with a hundred other nervous soldiers. As expected, the island was warm and humid — particularly for an invader liveried in battle dress uniform and a heavy Kevlar helmet. But George had anticipated tropical heat akin to Vietnam, and this was nothing like the first wilting blast that he remembered on the tarmac at Bien Hoa.

The second surprise, considerably less pleasant, was that the fighting was both intense and very close. Operation Urgent Fury had been under way for more than twenty-four hours, yet the Rangers and first wave of paratroopers from the 82nd Airborne had barely advanced beyond the perimeter of the airport at Point Salines. George heard the familiar popping of small-arms fire; to the east, squads of American soldiers scuttled across the terrain, maneuvering for better firing positions. On a hillside next to the airport, large white letters spelled SIEMPRE ES 26 — It Is Always 26 — a reference to July 26, the date celebrated as the beginning of the Cuban revolution in 1953. Throughout the morning a medley of fire from helicopter gunships, artillery tubes, and Navy bombers had been raking targets farther inland.

Grenada was supposed to be a simple operation. U.S. intelligence analysts had predicted little or no resistance from the Cubans working on the island and only token opposition from the PRA, the People's Revolutionary Army. Plainly, the intelligence was wrong. As he moved away from the plane, George felt his pulse quicken. Nothing pumped the adrenaline like live ammunition. More than twelve years had passed since he last heard shots fired in anger; no matter how diligently he and his soldiers trained for battle, it was impossible to simulate the hot churn of fear and exhilaration that only enemy bullets could provoke.

A decade had also passed since George last commanded troops at the cassern in Erlangen. He had dutifully marked time as a major and a junior lieutenant colonel. The three years at West Point were followed by tours as a staff officer in the Pentagon and at Fort Bragg until, at last, his name had appeared on the command list. Leading this unit — the 1st Battalion of the 82nd Airborne's 505th Infantry Parachute Regiment — was the fulfillment of a dream, the culmination of a career that began when he left Arkansas for Beast Barracks in 1962. And, though rarely given to doubts about his abilities, he found it hard not to be jittery after waiting so long for this chance. He was now wholly responsible for eight hundred heavily armed men. They were good soldiers — in the three months since taking command George had been impressed by their motivation and discipline — yet very few of them had ever been in combat. Every commander could appreciate the old maxim, usually attributed to the Duke of Wellington, which held that there are no bad troops, only bad officers. George did not want to be unworthy.

While waiting for the rest of his battalion to arrive at Point Salines, he jumped into a jeep with the brigade commander and drove to the east end of the airport. In an area called Frequente, soldiers from the 2nd Brigade had just captured an arms cache, killing a dozen Cubans and capturing nearly a hundred others. Munitions sufficient to arm several battalions stood stacked from floor to ceiling in one warehouse. Among the nearly five hundred tons of weaponry that would be seized on the island were 16,000 AK-47s; 5 million rifle rounds; 86,000 rounds of antiaircraft ammo; and nearly 2,000 grenades. All in all, George concluded as he surveyed the warehouse, the arsenal, should it ever explode, contained enough latent power to demolish half the island in a spectacular fireball. At that moment, AK rounds began pinging off the tin roof. He hurried out to the jeep and drove back to the unloading area. If he was going to get shot or blown up, he didn't want it to happen before his entire unit had arrived.

Because the airport was so congested — only one or two planes could land and unload at the same time — mustering the battalion took all afternoon and much of the night. After the seventh and final C-141 had arrived, George bedded down the troops. In another captured warehouse not far from the Frequente arms cache, he stretched out on the floor for a few hours of sleep. The cartons on pallets around him were crammed with sundries apparently intended to provision the Marxist paradise:

toilet seats, Romanian beef, Soviet salmon and vodka, banana liqueur, Cuban cigars, even baseball bats and gloves. His sole mission thus far had been to deploy the battalion ready for combat. We're in it now, he thought as he drifted off to sleep amid the spoils of war. In the morning, they would join the fight.

Perhaps unconsciously, the American military had been waiting ten long years for Operation Urgent Fury. Symbols like Maya Lin's wall in Washington were important to help heal the rift between the Republic and its armed forces. But for professional soldiers, the demons of Vietnam could be fully exorcised only by the passage of time and an opportunity to demonstrate again valorous competence on the battlefield. If few wished for war — and few did who had experienced the carnage of Southeast Asia — nevertheless there persisted a yearning among military men to prove themselves. When that chance came on an obscure Caribbean island in October 1983, the Army and its sister services leaped to seize both the island and, they hoped, renewed self-confidence.

Grenada seemed an unlikely target for the fury, urgent or otherwise, of American military power. Barely twenty miles long and twelve miles wide, with the ragged oval shape of a crab's claw, the isle had been discovered by Columbus on his third voyage to the New World, in 1498. Not much had happened since. The somnolent capital of St. George's — population, 35,000 — was wrapped picturesquely around a small harbor on the west coast. Grenada's principal industries centered on nutmeg, bananas, and tourism.

The politics of this tiny, torpid remnant of the British Empire, however, were complicated. In 1979, a pro-Western prime minister had been toppled in a bloodless coup by Maurice Bishop, a lanky, articulate Marxist who sported a salt-and-pepper beard and headed a home-grown political organization called the New Jewel Movement. Finding the taste of autocratic power to his liking, Bishop quickly aligned himself with Moscow and Havana, and reneged on his promise to establish a modern democracy.

To Ronald Reagan, already obsessed with the new leftist state in Nicaragua, Bishop was one more intolerable neighbor, particularly when he began to build a nine-thousand-foot runway on the sandy promontory of Point Salines. Events came to a head in mid October 1983, when Bishop was placed under house arrest by one of his more radical New Jewel minions, Bernard Coard. Six days later, on Wednesday, October 19, Bishop was freed by several thousand chanting supporters. Three armored personnel carriers manned by Coard's PRA troops fired on the crowd, killing at least fifty people. The soldiers again seized Bishop and several others. At one P.M., as he knelt against a stucco wall beneath a basketball backboard, Bishop was executed by a four-man firing squad.

Preliminary U.S. military planning had begun on October 14, when the National Security Council asked the Joint Chiefs of Staff to begin considering the evacuation from Grenada of several hundred Americans, most of them students at St. George's University School of Medicine. Yet the Pentagon's zeal to prove itself — to exorcise those demons from Vietnam — quickly colored the planning and influenced the shape of Urgent Fury. Precisely because Grenada was the first sustained American military action in a decade, each of the four services was hungry for a piece of the action. "It doesn't matter which war you were in," according to a military truism, "as long as it was the last one." No one wanted to be left behind.

Moreover, the psychology of the American military had been deeply affected by the catastrophic rescue attempt in April 1980 of the embassy hostages in Tehran. Led by Charlie Beckwith, the mission had been aborted after a helicopter and a C-130 fuel tanker collided in the Iranian desert, burning eight servicemen to death. Many factors contributed to the flaming debacle at Desert One, but one of the catastrophe's lasting effects was an overkill mentality. "If a mission requires two divisions, send four. If it requires ten aircraft, send twenty," said one Army general in describing the military's state of mind before Grenada. "Don't go at the margin. Double it. We're not going to fail because of a lack of troops."

The original American plan, then, which involved a surgical attack on Grenada by special operations forces, became immensely complicated by the inclusion of conventional troops in a full-blown invasion scheme. Most amphibious operations, from Guadalcanal to Inchon, required months of detailed planning. In Grenada the military had only a few days to prepare, and Reagan did not sign the final invasion order until six P.M. on October 24, less than twelve hours before the operation was to commence.

Under Urgent Fury, a contingent of Marines — designated Task Force 124 — would seize the small airstrip at Pearls and the adjacent town of Grenville on the island's northeast coast; two Ranger battalions — Task Force 121 — and the 82nd Airborne — Task Force 123 — would secure Point Salines and the southern portion of Grenada.

As the invasion began, before dawn on October 25, the Marines — their morale stiffened by a showing of John Wayne in *The Sands of Iwo Jima* the night before — quickly seized their initial objectives on the northern half of Grenada, encountering very little resistance. Elsewhere on the island, however, the invasion began to foul almost immediately.

A team of Navy SEALs — special operation commandos — was lost when four men drowned, apparently after being knocked unconscious when they were dropped into the sea from the rear of a low-flying plane. Other special operations also went awry, including attempts to destroy the island's radio tower, to rescue the British governor-general, and to capture a prison near St. George's.

Along with these difficulties, the Army encountered unexpected resistance at Point Salines. Part of the invasion plan called for a platoon of Delta Force commandos to parachute onto the promontory before dawn, where they were to secure the airport for the Ranger battalions. But Grenadian forces and the Cuban construction workers spotted the Delta troops, pinning them down with an intense fusillade.

Rather than landing on a secure airstrip, as planned, the Rangers parachuted from five hundred feet, less than half the usual height and the lowest combat jump since World War II. They had expected to face six hundred pacific Cubans and twelve hundred poorly equipped, petrified PRA troops. Instead, they found themselves pitched into "absolute, total warfare," as the senior Army commander, Major General H. Norman Schwarzkopf, later described the scene.

The battle raged throughout the morning of the twenty-fifth. At two o'clock, despite harassing sniper fire, the runway was secure enough to allow the first paratroopers from the 82nd Airborne to land at Salines. But an hour later the defenders counterattacked from the north with three armored personnel carriers and mortar fire in an attempt to sweep the runway. The Americans shattered two of the APCs with 90mm recoilless rifle rounds; aircraft cannon fire destroyed the third. The airport was reopened, but the invasion commander, Vice Admiral Joseph Metcalf, surprised by the intensity of the fighting, asked the Joint Chiefs to send four more battalions from the 82nd. Nearly five thousand paratroopers would enter the fray, three times the number originally estimated by the invasion planners.

As the Marines continued to roll through the north, the chairman of the Joint Chiefs, General John Vessey, reportedly called the commander of the 82nd, Major General Edward L. Trobaugh. "We have two companies of Marines running all over the island and thousands of Army troops doing nothing," Vessey fumed. "What the hell is going on?" The rebuke was to linger for years with the paratroopers, who bitterly resented Vessey's censure as a classic example of know-nothing meddling from Washington.

Nowhere were the shortcomings of military intelligence more apparent than in the efforts to rescue the American medical students, on behalf of whom, nominally, the invasion had been launched. The American troops presumed, wrongly, that the students would all be found near the Salines airfield at the university's True Blue campus. But on securing True Blue on the morning of the twenty-sixth, the U.S. soldiers were "shocked and stunned," in the words of General Schwarzkopf, to learn that 224 additional students were nearly surrounded by enemy soldiers at Grand Anse beach, a campus annex midway between Salines and St. George's. By telephoning Grand Anse, the rescuers learned that Cuban and Grenadian troops had dug in only 250 yards from the students, facing south in the direction of the expected American attack.

After five hours of planning, gunships, naval batteries, and bombers from the U.S.S. *Independence* unleashed a barrage that reduced several buildings at Grand Anse, including two hotels, to rubble. Twenty seconds after the supporting fire lifted, in a scene likened by one student to the popular Vietnam movie *Apocalypse Now,* three waves of Marine helicopters carrying Army Rangers swooped in from the Caribbean. The Grand Anse beach was only a few yards wide, and palm trees grew nearly to the water's edge. Several Marine pilots thought of the fiery collision at Desert One. "Regardless of what happens to any of our aircraft or any of the Rangers on that beach," warned one lieutenant colonel, evidently thinking along the same lines, "it's going to go down."

As door gunners hammered the Cuban and PRA positions with .50-caliber fire, the Rangers sprinted through the campus buildings, rounding up students who had barricaded the windows with mattresses. Everyone was herded to the beach, where a flock of empty Sea Knight helicopters waited. The only mishap occurred when the blade from one chopper sliced into a palm tree; the trunk tumbled onto the rotors, destroying the helicopter. The Rangers inside escaped safely, and subsequently paddled to sea in a life raft; they were picked up by the Navy destroyer U.S.S. *Caron.*

In a campaign thus far devoid of glory, the Grand Anse operation had been an unblemished success. In less than half an hour, the Marines and Rangers had executed the plan perfectly without a single friendly casualty. The sole sour note was the certainty that had the PRA or Cubans been inclined to atrocity, they would have had thirty-six hours since the beginning of the invasion to execute the students, leisurely. Moreover, the rescue operation would take yet another day and a half to complete — because elsewhere on the island nearly two hundred additional students remained hidden, waiting, as it turned out, for a lieutenant colonel named Crocker.

George pulled the sheaf of papers from the deep thigh pocket in his fatigues. He now had four or five maps of Grenada, although none displayed the kind of topographical detail that a commander hoped for. On one, the photocopier had even washed out the southern shoreline, so he could no longer tell where land ended and sea began; George had drawn a dotted line with his pen to approximate the coast at Prickly Point.

Each map also had its own grid system, which made any coordination with the artillery firebases difficult. Grenville on St. Andrew's Bay, for example, was located on either vertical axis twenty or axis forty-two, depending on which map he looked at. Invasion planners on the U.S.S. *Guam*, according to one account, had even consulted a map last updated in 1895. It was hardly surprising that the usual fog of war was especially murky during the three days that George had now been on the island.

The best map in his collection was a four-foot tourist guide bearing the legend "Grenada: The Isle of Spice." He opened the map and spread it on the ground. There on the southern coast, only a couple of miles from the airport at Point Salines, was the battalion's new objective: a tiny peninsula called Lance aux Épines, which bore an uncanny resemblance in shape to the boot of Italy. The third and presumably final group of American students had been discovered hiding in the small hotels and posh houses dotting the promontory, and brigade headquarters had ordered George to seize the peninsula and evacuate the students.

The battalion fanned out from Calliste at the east end of the airport runway. George pushed two rifle companies down the high ground on either side of Lance aux Épines and a third company down the center. Armed resistance seemed unlikely, but the troops had already found one antiaircraft gun, and a die-hard Cuban or Grenadian defender might still be lurking with a rifle behind a palm tree. Of equal concern in George's mind was the reaction of the students. Although he had witnessed neither the True Blue nor Grand Anse evacuation, as far as he knew both had gone smoothly. But little was known about the group at Lance aux Épines. Did they want to be rescued? Or would they react to the American uniforms with contempt, as their older brothers and sisters had during Vietnam? He half expected the paratroopers to be greeted with profanity and spit.

The war — if the three-day firefight could be called a war — was nearly over now. Resistance had disintegrated. Hundreds of PRA soldiers were fleeing for the hills, leaving behind little piles of hats, belts, uniforms, and rifles. Once the shooting lessened, most Grenadians had happily welcomed the Americans, offering coconuts, bananas, and abandoned hand grenades. Children capered in the GIs' wake, scooping up instant coffee and ketchup packets that had been discarded from ration cartons. The liberation fervor had even spread to the Grenada zoo, where the resident alligator and anteater had been freed from their cages to lumber off into the jungle, leaving behind only a solitary vulture.

Although the invasion was hardly a model of military precision, George was pleased with the performance of his paratroopers. As he had hoped, they had shown themselves to be physically fit, well disciplined, and eager to fight, a far cry from the Magnificent Seven types that he had commanded at Erlangen. They had spent most of the past forty-eight hours patrolling near Point Salines, searching for pockets of defenders. The only casualty in the battalion thus far was a soldier who had broken his foot while kicking in a door.

Other units, he knew, had not fared as well. George had been lying about a thousand yards from the 2nd Brigade's tactical operations center (TOC) at Frequente when a Navy A7, misdirected by a Marine liaison team attached to the 82nd, raked the TOC with 20mm cannon fire. Seventeen men had been wounded; one later died. After the strafing run ended, George listened to the chaos on the radio before walking another two hundred yards down the road, where he happened on the Marine fire controller, staring at the ground.

"Do you know that air strike just hit the 2nd Brigade?" George asked. In a voice choked with remorse, the Marine had simply murmured, "Yes," and hung his head a little lower.

Two of George's classmates from '66 were also on Grenada. Both commanded battalions in the 82nd and both had been involved the day before in the final major action on the island, the storming of the Cuban barracks complex at Calivigny. Freddy McFarren, a droll, stocky Texan who had been one of George's old F-2 company mates, now led an artillery battalion. (During high-level planning sessions before the invasion, McFarren had delighted in surreptitiously making faces at George across the room, as though they were again twenty-year-old cadets in the academy barracks.)

The other classmate was the division's aviation battalion commander, Bob Seigle, an animated extrovert from Cincinnati who had been one of Bobby Knight's guards on the academy basketball team. As part of the secret planning for Urgent Fury, Seigle had been asked to calculate how long it would take fifteen Blackhawk helicopters to fly from Fort Bragg to Grenada. The answer, he reported, was 15.9 hours, including eleven refueling stops. That was clearly unacceptable, so the invasion planners decided instead to ferry the helicopters to Barbados aboard gigantic C-5 cargo planes, each of which could hold half a dozen Blackhawks.

By the evening of D-Day, October 25, Seigle was at Salines, where he discovered that the Army's special operations helicopters had not fared well in the early fighting. About ten aircraft from Task Force 160, a secret unit based at Fort Campbell, Kentucky, had been supporting Delta and the other commando forces. Nicknamed the Night Stalkers, their motto was "Death Waits in the Dark." TF 160 pilots were the Army's best — combat blooded, with at least two thousand hours of flying time each — and they had just been riddled with gunfire. Every TF helicopter was full of holes; at least one had been destroyed. The Night Stalkers' experience on Grenada, Seigle realized, did not bode well for the 82nd's pilots, who averaged only six hundred hours of flying time.

After assembling his Blackhawks on Barbados, Seigle received orders on Thursday, October 27, to send his helicopters into the Calivigny barracks complex on Grenada's southeast coast. The 82nd pilots considered the mission, apparently ordered specifically by the Joint Chiefs, to be suicidal, because PRA and Cuban defenders were believed to be firmly entrenched at Calivigny. "Guys, we don't know what's out there," Seigle told his crews. "Just remember that your primary job is to fly that aircraft until it won't fly anymore. Concentrate on that."

The Blackhawks would carry a company of Rangers in the assault. After Navy bombers, AC-130s, and Fred McFarren's artillery tubes had pounded the target, the first flight of four helicopters — Chalk One, Chalk Two, Chalk Three, and Chalk Four — swooped across Westerhall Bay at 4:15 P.M., just about the time that the 2nd Brigade TOC was being accidentally strafed. From satellite photos, the only suitable landing zone appeared to be in the middle of the compound. But when the pilots veered over a steep coastal embankment at eighty knots, they suddenly spotted the landing zone directly below them, half a mile short of where they expected it. As the Blackhawks decelerated, the Rangers — who had not trained with the 82nd pilots and were accustomed to leaping for the ground before the helicopters actually touched down — began jumping out. It was too soon. Several tumbled twenty feet; at least two suffered broken legs.

Chalk One landed, hard but safe, followed by Chalk Two. As Chalk Three was slowing, ground fire from the weeds near the barracks struck the tail rotor. The Blackhawk began to counterrotate out of control, smashing into Chalk Two. In a violent spray of metal fragments, the two helicopters flung chunks of rotor blade back and forth at each other, leaving four Rangers dead in a bloody mangle.

In a desperate effort to avoid the carnage below, Chalk Four veered 90 degrees to the right. The Blackhawk slammed into the ground so hard that the rotor blade flexed down, slicing out a section of the aluminum tail rotor drive shaft. When the pilot, unaware that his tail was gone, pulled up to leave a moment later, the Blackhawk spun wildly. After two gyrations, the Chalk Four pilot deliberately crash-landed his helicopter.

The second flight of four Blackhawks set down without mishap south of the barracks. The Rangers quickly swept through Calivigny, where they found the camp largely deserted. Like most of their comrades elsewhere on the island, the Cubans and PRA were dead, captured, or hiding in the hills. Bob Seigle spent most of the next twenty-four hours trying to mollify the furious Rangers and salvage what was left of the three shattered hulks lying at the edge of Westerhall Bay.

Now, on Friday, October 28, virtually all that remained before victory could be declared in Urgent Fury was the evacuation of the last group of students from Lance aux Épines. The operation went smoothly as George's paratroopers searched the beaches, jetties, and inland hills without finding any enemy soldiers. Two hours after he had dispersed his battalion down Lance aux Épines, the peninsula was secured without a shot being fired. The paratroopers then moved from house to house, rapping on doors, as wary of the American students as of the PRA. But the students, delighted to be rescued after four tense days of hiding, emerged without delay, profusely thanking the soldiers. Near the north end of the peninsula, the paratroopers established a landing zone as an assembly point for those who wanted to decamp. The Libyan ambassador, repeatedly drove past the site in his Honda, waving his passport; George suppressed the impulse to have his tires slashed. An eighty-year-old expatriate British woman with gin on her breath walked out of one house, elegantly dressed in an evening gown, white gloves, and diamonds. George personally escorted her to the LZ.

There, as the helicopters began to arrive in a boil of dust and noise, he beheld an amazing scene. One hundred and eighty-three students, many of them wearing cut-off blue jeans and sandals, mobbed the soldiers — hugging, kissing, weeping. "God bless America!" they shouted. "God bless you!" Partitioned into groups of twenty-five, their names recorded on a manifest, they were ushered into the Blackhawks for the short hop to the airstrip, where transport planes would ferry them north to the United States.

George watched the helicopters lift the students, cheering and waving, into the overcast sky. His soldiers waved back, some with tears in their eyes. Things have sure changed, he thought. The war was over. And this time he wasn't thinking about Grenada.

The invasion forces evacuated 740 American citizens from the Isle of Spice, 595 of whom were students. As the hostilities ended, casualty estimates varied widely. The Pentagon initially announced that 59 enemy soldiers had been killed in the invasion. Two weeks later, General Schwarzkopf put the tally at 160 PRA troops and 71 Cubans. Additionally, civilian casualties were estimated at 45 dead — some of whom died when a mental hospital was bombed accidentally — and 300 wounded. The U.S. government listed 19 U.S. troops killed and 115 wounded (although some analysts believed that the number would be considerably higher if all casualties among the secret, special operations forces were included).

Ronald Reagan called Urgent Fury a "brilliant campaign." Army Secretary John Marsh praised the invasion as "a great success." In truth, it was neither. The Pentagon's own afteraction analyses sharply criticized the operation, particularly the communications and intelligence snafus. "When you dismember it in retrospect as a Monday morning quarterback," one general commented, "I wasn't too happy." As one earthy Pentagon civilian put it, Grenada was "fucked up just like all wars are fucked up."

In the wake of Grenada, the United States Army added the 168th campaign streamer to its flag. Streaked with brown, yellow, green, and other earth tones, the ribbon was of precisely the same dimensions as the more venerable swatches won at Ticonderoga and Antietam and Anzio. The service also awarded nearly nine thousand medals for valor and achievement, far more than the number of soldiers actually on Grenada. An Army spokesman, somewhat self-consciously, defended the cascade of decorations as "a valuable and effective leadership tool to build unit morale and esprit."

Therein lay the crux of Urgent Fury. For all of its shortcomings, for all of the derisive commentary about the pathetic stature of the enemy against which American power was hurled, the invasion of Grenada was a victory. Armies fight with morale and esprit as much as they fight with tanks and bullets; after Grenada, soldiers walked a little taller, not because of their battlefield exploits but because of the huzzahs from the rescued students and an appreciative citizenry at home. The United States Army, its self-esteem battered in Southeast Asia, needed to win a war, any war. That slender campaign streamer from Grenada buried beneath it the seventeen preceding ribbons from Vietnam.

The invasion, by chance, coincided with what appeared to be a new era of stability in the Army. For twenty-five years, since before the class of 1966 reported to Beast Barracks, the Army had been in upheaval. As officers, George Crocker and his classmates had known nothing but war and the confused aftermath of defeat. Now, on the verge of inheriting command of the Army of the 1990s — the class could expect its first general's stars in another five years — they were part of a service that seemed more sure of itself than at any time since the end of World War II. The Army knew how it wanted to fight; it had confidence in the troops now filling the ranks; and it was benefiting from Ronald Reagan's $2 trillion defense build-up, a windfall that bought new weaponry and equipment at a pace unprecedented in American peacetime history.

This return to health had been a long time coming. Army doctrine, for example — the basic blueprint of how to fight — had been in constant turmoil since the atomic battlefield debates of the 1950s. Every few years, a virtual revolution had taken place within the councils of military thinkers. In Vietnam, the early dalliance with counterinsurgency doctrine succumbed in time to the traditional reliance on firepower. (Against the North Vietnamese and Viet Cong, that tactic was likened to "elephants chasing jack rabbits.")

But in 1973, the world had changed abruptly. The Yom Kippur War demonstrated for the first time how lethal the modern battlefield had become through the use of accurate, computer-guided "smart weapons." In two weeks of fighting, Egypt and Syria lost 2000 tanks of an initial 4500, and 500 planes of an initial 1100. Israel lost 800 of 2000 tanks, and 114 of 550 planes. Combined casualties exceeded 25,000.

A new certainty had come to the killing ground. In World War II, for instance, an American tank had to fire thirteen rounds to obtain a 50 percent probability of destroying a stationary enemy tank a mile away; by the mid 1970s, that PK — probability of kill — ratio had improved to one round. (Less comforting for the tankers was the knowledge that a TOW antiarmor missile had the same PK at a distance of more than two miles.) The Yom Kippur War held portents for twenty-first-century conventional warfare in much the same way that the Russo-Japanese War of 1905 had for the twentieth: by exhibiting an order-of-magnitude increase in technological killing power.

After studying the results of Yom Kippur and analyzing the Soviet military, which had steadily modernized while the United States was mired in Vietnam, the Army unveiled a new doctrine on July 1, 1976, in a revised version of Field Manual 100-5. It was apocalyptic, revolutionary, and immediately controversial. The doctrine warned that "the U.S. Army must prepare its units to fight outnumbered and to win." Furthermore, because of the "new lethality" of modern weapons, "the first battle of our next war could well be its last . . . The United States could find itself in a short, intense war — the outcome of which may be dictated by the results of this initial combat. This circumstance is unprecedented: we are an Army historically unprepared for its first battle."

The new doctrine stressed an "active defense," in which division commanders would quickly have to shift six or eight battalions to repel the spearhead of twenty to twenty-five Soviet battalions. As if to stress how pleased the Army was to leave Southeast Asia behind and concentrate once again on Central Europe, FM 100-5 contained reams of practical data about rainfall, mean temperatures, and the frequency of morning fog in Germany. Army strategists began to speak in terms of a "battle calculus," which would identify enemy targets to be "serviced" at a quantifiable "kill rate."

Active defense did not sit well with an Army proud of its traditional "offensive spirit." The new doctrine was likened to the French Maginot Line mentality of 1940. Officers familiar with the cluttered landscape of Europe scoffed at the notion of quickly shifting battalions laterally to outmaneuver a Soviet juggernaut. Many also criticized the doctrine for focusing excessively on war in Europe, which seemed less probable than conflicts elsewhere. Moreover, battle calculus struck some officers as sheer eyewash, a phony, mechanistic concept of war that ignored the confusion of real battle and devalued the timeless variables of leadership, courage, and endurance that determined victory and defeat.

After six years of vigorous debate — secret, at first, then very public — Army thinkers at Fort Leavenworth's Department of Tactics and Fort Monroe's Training and Doctrine Command finally proposed an alternative to active defense. Making a virtue of necessity, the doctrine called for battle commanders to "look deep," up to ninety miles behind the front lines. Enemy echelons were to be disrupted in the rear with air, artillery, and special operations strikes, and with electronic warfare tactics. American forces would emphasize maneuver in the spirit of Robert E. Lee and Stonewall Jackson, as well as mobility, which "protects the force and keeps the enemy off balance."

Because of its stress on coordination between ground and air forces, the new doctrine was called AirLand Battle. Once again, the Army emphasized campaigns and battles, rather than a single, decisive battle. Lateral, defensive movements fell from favor. AirLand was considered useful in a variety of potential war theaters, from Korea to Iran.

Using the war manual written by George C. Marshall in 1941 as a model of clarity, planners unveiled the AirLand battle doctrine in August 1982 in yet another revision of FM 100-5. Unlike active defense, Airland was greeted with widespread enthusiasm and a pervasive conviction that the doctrine would remain the Army's gospel on how to fight for at least a decade. The unveiling coincided with the beginning of the Reagan rearmament program, which outfited theory with hardware. By stressing leadership, initiative, and a commander's intuitive sense of timing and maneuver, AirLand was viewed as a final rejection of the systems analysis management philosophy personified by Robert McNamara.

Having a new doctrine and new weaponry was one thing; finding soldiers capable of using them adroitly was quite another. The Army had spent the 1970s trying to cure itself of the ills of Vietnam, including the racial strife, drug addiction, and inferior soldiers that George had seen at Erlangen. Even by December 1979, a confidential Army report rated six of ten divisions based in the United States as "not combat ready." In the arresting phrase of Chief of Staff Edward C. Meyer, America possessed a "hollow Army" that was desperately short of experienced NCOs and skilled technicians. In 1980, only two thirds of Army recruits were high school graduates; of nearly 101,000 new enlisted soldiers that year, only 25 had college degrees. Nearly half of the recruits in 1979 were rated CAT IV, the lowest mental category, which meant they were harder to train and more inclined to indiscipline than brighter soldiers.

In the early 1980s, things began to change. Two quick pay raises, totaling 25 percent, lured better soldiers into the service. A reinvigorated basic-training program stressed marksmanship, conditioning, and — after a ten-year hiatus — bayonet drills. The shortage of sergeants and skilled technicians shrank from seventeen thousand in 1979 to five hundred by early 1983.

The sociology of the ranks began to change dramatically as well. One soldier in ten was a woman; nearly a third of the Army's sergeants major were black; half of the enlisted troops were married. As the Army regained its self-confidence, it lost patience with drug users and racist troublemakers — black, white, and brown — who were summarily booted from the service.

In the officer corps, the Army tried to repair some of the damage done in the name of efficiency. Battalion command tours were extended from twelve to thirty months for the sake of stability and to ease the "ticket punching" mentality. The Army also tried to be more forgiving by allowing soldiers to learn from their mistakes; a young officer fearful of making a career-crushing error was hardly likely to be the audacious innovator that the new fighting doctrine demanded.

Nettlesome problems persisted, to be sure. At the time of Grenada, nearly half the Army was deployed overseas, from West Germany to South Korea. The service was as far-flung as the legions of Rome had been. Given the American commitment to defend dozens of allies, many generals fretted that the Army was stretched dangerously thin. And with the abolition of conscription in 1972, the Army once again became isolated from the Republic. The phrase "when *I* was in the Army" was heard less often, because an entire generation of young Americans — particularly those from the middle and upper classes — was essentially exempted from what has been called "the social chit" of military service that free men owe one another. In some respects, the nation had bought itself a mercenary Army.

All of these issues were of more than passing interest to George Crocker and his classmates. By 1984, fewer than half of the 579 men who had graduated from West Point in June 1966 remained in the service, and that number would drop sharply when the officers became eligible for retirement benefits in June 1986. Many of those still in uniform now commanded battalions. In three or four more years, a lucky few would command brigades; three or four years after that, fewer still would command divisions. By the mid 1990s, as they moved closer to thirty years of service, fewer than a dozen would command a corps or ascend to the pinnacle of Army leadership.

But who? The Darwinism that had begun on R-Day in Beast Barracks had continued for more than two decades. The rank of lieutenant colonel was a watershed; fewer men would be promoted to full colonel than would be passed over. Under the up-or-out philosophy adopted after World War II to promote younger officers into the senior ranks, a lieutenant colonel who had been passed over twice was forced to retire (although he now was permitted to remain in the service for a total of twenty-eight years). Competition for promotion was fierce, the selections often fickle. Like any organization, the Army suffered from the Peter Principle; officers were sometimes promoted until they had reached their level of incompetence. A capable company commander might make a wretched battalion commander; a fine battalion commander might be lost leading a division.

Promotion in peacetime was always different from promotion during war. Because the Army was smaller, advancement was slower and less likely. Furthermore, some of the qualities most admired in combat — audacity, for example — were less prized when the nation was at peace. In a confidential survey of officers conducted in 1984, half agreed with the proposition that the "bold, original, creative officer cannot survive in today's Army."

Other factors also figured in the fate of the class of '66. For one thing, they were part of what was widely known as a "bubble in the system." The near doubling of the size of the Army during Vietnam meant that an unusually large number of young officers had been commissioned in the 1960s; despite several "RIFs" — reductions in force — "year group" '66 remained abnormally large, which meant more officers competing for advancement. A West Point pedigree offered no guarantee of success:

7 percent of the second lieutenants commissioned in 1966 were academy graduates; by 1983, only 11 percent of the lieutenant colonels and 16 percent of the Army's full colonels were West Pointers. (The academy connection manifested itself at higher ranks, however; 40 percent of the Army's 395 generals were graduates in the early 1980s.)

Although most of the officers from '66 studied the tea leaves of promotion politics to one degree or another, by and large they were fatalistic. If they were destined to wear a colonel's eagles or a general's stars, so be it. Otherwise, the selection process was largely beyond influence other than by a lifelong effort to demonstrate competence, loyalty, and commitment. Given the realities of up-or-out, most spent at least some time mulling over what they would do if forced to begin a second career in their early forties.

Between the great wave of resignations in the early 1970s and the impending wave of retirements in the mid 1980s, relatively few men from the class of '66 had left the Army. But there were notable exceptions, particularly among men who felt disgruntled or in danger of compromising their principles. John McKnight, for example, resigned at the ten-year mark. An accomplished boxer who had been one of the Army's pre-eminent snipers in Vietnam, McKnight had later served in Buenos Aires and as an intelligence officer in Panama. When Juan Perón returned to power in Argentina, McKnight wrote an analysis of the political situation and asked that his report be sent to Washington. It was not. When Captain McKnight asked why, his boss, a major, put a thumb under his collar tab, pointed to the oak leaf insignia, and snapped, "That's why." McKnight resigned to become a lawyer, convinced that "my net worth was going to be based on rank rather than knowledge and ability."

Jerry Cecil was a short, engaging Kentuckian, the most highly decorated officer in the class because of the Distinguished Service Cross he had won with the 173rd Airborne in the Central Highlands in 1967. Cecil was an outspoken traditionalist who resented what he viewed as rampant, self-centered careerism in the officer corps. "You really need two armies," he complained publicly in 1981, "one for all the guys who don't want to get their hands dirty and another for the guys who are interested in being ready to fight . . . Everybody's interested in being fat, dumb, and happy. If you take 100,000 officers and count up how many are really interested in being soldiers, it'll scare you." After eighteen years in the Army — just two years short of retirement — he resigned to run the family tobacco-and-dairy farm in Kentucky.

Bill Rennagel was cut from the same cloth. Rennagel had lost his right hand in June 1967, when a hand grenade detonated prematurely as he was trying to flush the enemy from a streambed in Vietnam. After spending a year in the hospital, he attended graduate school and then taught at West Point. Because of his injury — classmates called him Captain Hook — the Army insisted that he leave the infantry to become a military intelligence officer. Rennagel responded by scoring 450 of a possible 500 points on a physical aptitude test and qualifying on all of the small arms in the Army inventory. The Army still insisted. In 1979, he was posted to NATO headquarters in Belgium, where he wrote speeches, first for Alexander Haig, then for Bernard Rogers. But he was continually troubled by an officer corps that he perceived as little different from the white collar executives in any other corporation. In 1980, Rennagel resigned with a blunderbuss resignation letter:

> The Army has changed and today my impression of "professional" officers is that of a corps corrupted by many self-serving individuals who are governed by expediency and careerism . . . In the modern volunteer Army, the profession of arms has become, in many instances, merely an organization managed by job holders and careerists — individuals whose conduct, and hence loyalty and integrity, tend to be governed by perceptions of personal gain rather than by the health of the Army as an institution.

Other classmates viewed the resignations with alarm and regret. Some agreed with the protests; others thought they were exaggerated. But all of those who remained in uniform concurred that the best way to correct whatever ills persisted in the service was to stay the course; someday, for a very few, their turn would come to run the Army.

It was very dark, almost as dark as night could get. In military terms, 100 percent illumination meant a full moon and clear sky. On this night, May 15, 1985, the illumination was 3 percent. The paratroopers on Green Ramp formed two lines, or "sticks," behind the yawning tailgate of the C-130. The hot, foul prop wash from the plane's four engines gusted through the ranks. In winter, the warm miasma felt good; now it was so scorching that the soldiers hunched over with their backs to the engines to avoid having their faces burned. Sometimes, when the dust swirled and blinded on a dirt airstrip, the men had to walk toward the plane with arms linked to avoid blundering into the slashing propeller blades.

The jumpmaster worked the sticks, methodically checking the soldiers' harness straps, main parachutes, and reserves. He ran a finger beneath the rims of their helmets, feeling for sharp edges. On command, the sticks surged forward into the plane. The paratroopers waddled like pregnant women; the cumbersome chute, rifle, rucksack, web belt, and other equipment brought the weight of each man to nearly three hundred pounds.

George Crocker was the last to board, which put him in the seat closest to one of the two jump doors. By tradition, the battalion commander would be the first to leap. Web seats lined both sides of the plane, and two more rows ran back to back down the middle of the bay. In the crowded plane hip rubbed hip, knee rubbed knee. To preserve the paratroopers' night vision, the only lights burning were a half-dozen soft red bulbs. As the plane taxied to the end of the runway for takeoff, the crew passed out air sickness bags. Under the best conditions the back of a C-130 was nauseatingly uncomfortable; in turbulent weather it was horrid. Occasionally, even the jumpmaster was too sick to stand.

After revving the engines into a shrill whine, the pilot released the brakes. The plane hurled down the tarmac, lifted into the night, and headed south. Tonight's mission involved jumping into Remagen Drop Zone and seizing a tiny dirt strip near Canoochee Creek on the Bryan-Evans county line in eastern Georgia. Two other battalions would join the attack from Fort Campbell.

This exercise, codenamed Solid Shield, would be one of George's last adventures with the battalion. He had already been picked to serve as the 82nd's G3 — the division's operations officer — beginning in July. After completing that plum assignment he was scheduled to attend the Army War College at Carlisle Barracks in Pennsylvania. That guaranteed promotion to full colonel, and chances were fair that he could expect to command a brigade following the year at Carlisle. Settling into his seat among the catnaping soldiers, he felt as content as a man could feel in such cramped quarters with a huge wad of nylon lashed to his chest.

After Grenada, life as a battalion commander had settled into an irregular routine of alerts, exercises, inspections, personnel issues, and — as always in the Army — plenty of paperwork. He enjoyed every minute of it. His headquarters occupied a white cinder block building on Ardennes Street — known simply as the Street — which ran through the main barracks cluster at Fort Bragg. Directly across the Street stood the division museum. George occasionally wandered among the exhibits just to savor the heritage of being a paratrooper in the 82nd. Was there a unit in the United States Army, he wondered, with a prouder tradition? In World War I, the division had fought with distinction at St. Mihiel, Meuse-Argonne, and Lorraine. On October 8, 1918, one of the 82nd's corporals — a former conscientious objector from Pall Mall, Tennessee, named Alvin York — had singlehandedly shattered a German attack on Hill 223 in the Meuse-Argonne, knocking out thirty-five Maxim machine guns, killing 20 enemy soldiers, and capturing another 132.

In World War II, employing the new and radical concept of attacking by parachute, the division had jumped at Sicily, Salerno, Normandy, and Holland, before fighting brilliantly on the ground at the Bulge. Matthew Ridgway, James Gavin, William Westmoreland — many of the finest soldiers in the history of the Army — had been commanders in the 82nd.

Not a great deal had changed in airborne combat since Operation Neptune at Normandy. The Air Force was a bit more adroit now in dropping paratroopers where they were supposed to be dropped, as well as in dropping heavy equipment like tanks and howitzers. Weapons had grown more powerful, of course, and fighting at night had become much more common. Otherwise, the principles of "forced entry" remained basically the same: jump, consolidate, seize the objective, establish perimeter responsibilities, exploit terrain features, maintain a small, mobile reserve.

As always, the basics appealed most to George. As a company commander, he had relished teaching the fundamentals of fighting that had been taught to young soldiers for centuries: marksmanship, discipline, fire-and-maneuver. Now, after nearly twenty years in the officer corps, he had boiled down his principles of leadership to one sentence: set the example and hold the soldiers to high standards. A good commander radiated concern for the welfare of his soldiers, endured what they endured, and provided them with a model to emulate (including, as he put it, temperance in "drinking, chewing, dipping, and spitting"). For the past two years, that was what he had tried to do with this battalion. On occasion he had insisted, gently but firmly, that several of his young lieutenants find a different line of work. They simply were not qualified to be infantry officers in this division, the essence of which was leading men through the woods in the dark of night.

Vonda had been a great help, a true partner. Her affection for Army life burned brighter than ever. She enjoyed even the disruptive excitement of frequent moves. The role of Mrs. Battalion Commander at Fort Bragg suited her perfectly; on occasion she unconsciously lapsed into military time, talking of seventeen hundred hours instead of five P.M. She had organized a family support group, which brought together officers' and enlisted men's wives. Occasionally they chartered buses for a trip to the linen and glassware outlets in Burlington, or held a lingerie show, with a guard posted at the door to keep out unwelcome husbands. Although she had a strong sense of propriety — live-in girlfriends were pointedly excluded from those activities reserved exclusively for wives — Vonda insisted that the women call each other by their first names, regardless of whether their husbands were privates or majors.

When tensions began to build in Grenada, George and his battalion had suddenly vanished. Unaware that their men were secretly staging for the invasion, the women felt panicked and confused. One wife even walked into the judge advocate's office to demand a divorce from her husband, who had not been heard from in three days. Vonda organized a telephone tree to call every wife — and girlfriend — in the battalion, and published a regular newsletter during the four weeks that the battalion remained on the island.

As the Army had changed, so had Fayetteville. No one called the city FayetteNam anymore. Young soldiers, often dressed in coats and ties, courted secretaries at the fern bar in Bennigan's or chatted up high school girls at the Cross Creek Mall. Vonda no longer kept two loaded pistols under her pillow when George was away (although she continued her karate training, steadily ascending through the black belt ranks). Whereas soldiers had once refused to wear their uniforms off post, now they seemed to insist on wearing their distinctive maroon paratrooper berets everywhere. Of course, troopers — being troopers — still liked to raise a ruckus in the few remaining topless bars on Bragg Boulevard. But the Army's tolerance for inebriation had ended; a single arrest for driving while intoxicated was likely to end the career of an officer or NCO.

Occasionally, George and Vonda chatted idly about what they would do after George retired from the Army. One pipe dream was to buy a big Harley-Davidson and tour the country by motorcycle. At a costume party one night, George wore a phony black beard, Harley T-shirt, biker's cap, and a tattoo inked on his right biceps; Vonda went sheathed in black leather. Another fantasy involved buying a little inn near a ski slope in Vermont. But the question seemed too remote to contemplate seriously. Sometimes they joked about a retirement scheme that involved recklessly spending every cent they owned and then winning the Pennsylvania lottery.

"Twen-ty minutes!"

The jumpmaster's cry sounded above the engine drone in the C-130 bay at midnight. Those paratroopers who had been dozing began to stir as a surge of excitement rippled through the sticks. Even after a hundred jumps, George felt the electricity. Parachuting was safer than it looked; the division injury rate was about one in a thousand jumps, mostly wrenched knees and twisted ankles. But George had never forgotten a magazine photograph he had once seen when he was in the ninth grade. William Westmoreland had just assumed command of the 101st Airborne Division at Fort Campbell. After personally checking the wind conditions and seeing the all-clear puff of green smoke below, Westmoreland had jumped with one of his brigades. Suddenly, a twenty-mile-an-hour gust whipped through the drop zone, jerking Westmoreland across the ground for several hundred yards before he finally collapsed his chute. The picture George had seen showed the bodies of seven soldiers strewn across the DZ, where they had been dragged to death.

"Ten minutes!"

The soldiers checked their harnesses for the last time. Parachute failure was a rare tragedy. Every day, the professional riggers at Bragg packed more than a thousand chutes. Each unfurled T-10, made of ripstop nylon and thirty suspension lines, was winched to the top of a tall tower to shake out the dirt and allow moisture to evaporate. Although it took an average of ten minutes to pack the nylon into a bundle the size of a laundry basket, the best riggers at Bragg could do it in four, nimbly tugging the lines through the harness with a metal stow hook at such speed that the eye could barely follow the blur. After a chute was packed, the rigger and an inspector signed a log book sewn into the harness. They then sealed the chutes inside a metal bin and shipped them by truck to Pope Air Force Base, where they were randomly distributed to the troopers.

"Get ready! In-board personnel — STAND UP!" The jumpmaster made an exaggerated upward gesture with his open palms, like a puppeteer jerking the soldiers to their feet. A black gale roared past the open doors. Every movement by the jumpmaster was carefully choreographed. He scrupulously avoided turning his back on the door to guard against a sudden lurch of the plane that could pitch him into the night. Bracing both hands against the bulkhead, he thrust his head out the doorway. The 125-mile-per-hour wind distorted his features, grotesquely flattening his lips and nose. All clear ahead. All clear to the rear. The trailing planes carrying the rest of the battalion were properly aligned. Somewhere, two or three miles ahead and a thousand feet below, Remagen DZ awaited.

"One minute!"

The jumpers stood in two tight files, facing the rear and rocking slightly with the motion of the C-130. They had latched their static cords to the anchor lines, which ran the length of the plane above each stick. The red lights flashed green.

"Go!"

George leaped. The slipstream whipped him away, a rag doll snatched by a tornado. He felt the familiar tug of his parachute unfurling as a hundred other chutes opened sequentially above him, like time-lapse photographs of a flower blooming. Whenever paratroopers came within fifty feet of one another, they were supposed to yell "Slip away!" More typically, however, the night was filled with curses: "Get away from me, you ugly sumbitch!"

As he drifted closer to earth, George spotted a broad black line on one side of Remagen DZ. Aw, shit, he thought. The trees. Although the Air Force had dropped them within the DZ, which measured a thousand by two thousand meters, he saw that the wind was blowing nearly the entire battalion into the pine forest bordering Remagen's western edge. George had landed in trees nine or ten times before. Sometimes the branches had let him down as gently as a feather; usually, though it was nothing but trouble.

The black trees rushed up to grab him as his boots sliced through the upper boughs. Then the nylon canopy snagged across the top of a tall pine, abruptly stopping his descent. He dangled for a moment, groping with his feet until he found a branch stout enough to stand on. As pine needles scratched at his face and hands, he lowered his rucksack with a long cord. In the inky darkness, George could hardly see his hand when he held it in front of his nose. Fishing a slender tube of "chemical light" from his pocket, he dropped it to gauge his height; the stick glowed green on the forest floor forty feet below. Grasping the pine trunk like a treed bear, he wriggled free of the parachute and gingerly began to climb down.

With a sharp *crack* the bough snapped beneath his boots, dropping him as swiftly as if he'd fallen through a trap door. George felt himself plummet for two eternal seconds before smashing into the ground on his back. An agonizing jolt of pain ripped through his arm and torso, followed by a black wave of unconsciousness.

The rude jangle of the telephone woke Vonda at three A.M. It was never good news when someone called in the middle of the night, not when your husband jumped out of airplanes for a living. She sat up, instantly alert. The battalion chaplain was on the line.

"Vonda," he said quietly, "George has been in an accident. The Air Force dumped them all into the trees and he fell climbing down."

"How bad is it?" she asked, attempting to remain calm.

"It's pretty bad. He broke a bunch of ribs and it looks as if one of his lungs is punctured. They don't know what else."

"Do you think I should come right now?"

"The doctors don't think you need to come at all," the chaplain said. "He seems to be doing okay."

"Well, I can't just sit here and wonder how he's doing long distance. Do they think it's going to be detrimental if I come? Is there a reason why I shouldn't?"

"No," the chaplain answered. "*I* think you should come."

She rose and dressed, sifting the chaplain's words for nuances. *It's pretty bad . . . He seems to be doing okay.* What did that mean? Was there something they weren't telling her? Vonda called Adele Crocker in Arkansas, trying to sound both nonchalant and reassuring.

She checked to see that the refrigerator was stocked with food for the children. Cheryl was a high school senior and could take care of Tara and Brackett. Neighbors would look in on them as needed. Then, early in the morning, she made the twenty-minute drive across town to Douglas Byrd Junior High School, where she taught. In the principal's office, while asking for a few days' leave, she broke into sobs. When the tears stopped, she got back in the car and drove to Georgia.

In the intensive care ward at the Army hospital outside Savannah, George was conscious but incoherent. Because of his thoracic injuries, doctors had propped him into a sitting position. An epidural catheter dripped morphine into his spinal column and a drain had been inserted into his chest because of internal bleeding. Twelve ribs and a shoulder blade were broken, and his right wrist was badly shattered. A bruise the size of a dinner plate covered one hip, where he had landed on his canteen. He had only fragmentary memories of the fall and its aftermath: the agony of being jostled onto a stretcher board; the whir of helicopter blades; a cheerful Asian doctor in the emergency room proclaiming, "Wunnerful news. Your back no broken." Oh, Lord, George had thought before losing consciousness again, I've been captured by the VC.

Shortly after Vonda arrived, he nearly died. One lung was already punctured, and, abruptly, the other lung showed signs of collapse. Vonda wasn't sure what was happening, but suddenly the hospital room seemed to erupt in panic. As she was shooed into the corridor, she caught a terrifying glimpse of doctors and nurses swarming around her husband.

The crisis passed within a few hours. George's condition was critical but stable. Ten days later he was moved from intensive care; four days after that he was flown to the hospital at Bragg.

The long recuperation began. Every few days, he marked another milestone in his recovery: reclining a few degrees in bed; lying flat on his back; getting out of bed unassisted; walking at an old man's gait for one block; walking the same block quickly. To repair his wrist, surgeons inserted bone pins through the back of his right hand and through the forearm near the elbow. He suffered a setback when a nasty infection set in and the upper pin literally fell from his arm one day. That crisis also passed, but the wrist never completely regained its flexibility and strength.

He returned to work, an hour at a time at first, usually clad only in a T-shirt and running shorts, since even the weight of a fatigue blouse on his upper body was painful. Vonda carried a pillow for him to sit on whenever they went out together. One Sunday the division commander stopped by the house after church on a social call; suspecting that he was being sized up to determine whether he was physically capable of handling the G3 job, George took two tablets of the painkiller Percocet, removed his wrist brace, slipped into a clean T-shirt, and tried to exude an air of well-being.

After the accident, a squad from the battalion had returned to the pine grove at Remagen DZ. In an echo of Operation Paul Bunyan in Korea, the men vengefully cut down the tree from which George had fallen. On June 14, the 82nd's chief of staff circulated this message:

> 1) Fort Stewart, Georgia, Remagen DZ is inadequate for mass tactical operations. 2) Until a major clearing effort and a resurvey of the DZ have been completed, Remagen DZ is not authorized for airborne operations by the 82nd Airborne Division.

On July 16, as scheduled, George relinquished the battalion that he had led for 106 weeks. Although he refused Vonda's pillow, the pain was still so intense that he again took two Percocets to make it through the morning ceremony. The troops turned out smartly with the traditional pomp of pennants and brass and crisp salutes. Command changes were always emotional events; this one was especially so, since George had the nagging sense of having let the men down in the final two months.

One day in early November, he drove out to a Bragg airstrip with his sergeant major. New troopers coming into the division after parachute training usually were first assigned to a replacement detachment; before joining one of the airborne regiments, they made their initial jump from a helicopter so that when they reached their unit they were no longer considered "cherry." As the division G3, George had responsibility for this replacement detachment, and he knew that a Blackhawk helicopter was waiting to take some new jumpers aloft. Also waiting, by chance, was the division chief of staff. "Are you cleared to jump?" the colonel asked. "Well, sir," George replied, "I'm not uncleared."

More precisely, he hadn't bothered to ask. Any paratrooper who went six months without a jump was required to take remedial training; such a hiatus also became an administrative vexation that could affect the $110 a month he collected in jump pay. But, of course, there was more to it than that.

The Blackhawk took off and circled toward the drop zone. The only equipment George wore was a parachute harness, one of the MC1-1 steerable chutes instead of the standard T-10. He felt slightly nervous as the jumpmaster hooked the ripcord to a cable ring behind the helicopter transmission. The day was clear and cool, with good visibility and little wind. Traveling at ninety knots, the Blackhawk leveled off at fifteen hundred feet, its deafening rotor din pulsing through the cabin. George saw the DZ below, broad and beckoning, with hardly a tree in sight. In paratrooper training years before, the instructors had urged each jumper to fix his gaze on the horizon rather than on his true destination. Crouching in the Blackhawk doorway, George scanned the flat, endless terrain of the Carolina countryside.

He knew what to do now. He jumped.

19

FIREBASE

THE EDUCATION of Matt Harrison in the ways of the civilian world began on a balmy Sunday evening in mid June 1986, twenty years and one week after his graduation from West Point.

Suitcase in hand, Matt emerged from the La Guardia Airport terminal in Queens, jostling through the curbside crush to queue up at the taxi stand. His new boss's secretary had suggested that until Matt moved his family to New York, he could temporarily take a room in Ardsley, a Hudson River village just south of the Tappan Zee Bridge in Westchester County. From there, he would have a simple commute through Yonkers to the company headquarters in the Bronx.

"Where to?" asked a bored cabbie.

"Ardsley, please," answered Matt, slinging his suitcase into the trunk.

"What?"

"I want to go to the Ardsley Manor in Ardsley."

The driver peered at him skeptically, as though he had suggested a jaunt to Wyoming or Paris. An hour later, having emptied his wallet to pay the $56 fare, Matt emerged from the cab and checked into the hotel, making a mental note to cash a check after a good night's sleep.

The next morning, he rose before dawn to shave, dress, and begin his new life. But first he needed money.

"I'm a little short of cash," he told the desk clerk. "Can I get you to cash a $25 check for me?"

"No way," the clerk replied. "And you need to pay for the room in advance. The whole week."

"Look, why don't you charge this to my company?"

The clerk scoffed. "You gotta be out of your mind, mister. We've just gone through nine months and a debt collection agency to collect our bills from those bastards. No way. Cash in advance."

Matt wasn't sure what to do in the face of such hostility. *Those bastards?* He briefly considered pawning his watch. "All right," he said, "you've got my suitcase. I'll give you that until I redeem my check with cash tonight. If the check bounces, you've got three suits, two pairs of shoes, and a shaving kit."

Reluctantly, the clerk agreed, and Matt left the hotel with $25 in hand. Okay, he thought, this is New York, right? The most civilian city in the civilian world. You had to expect these things. It wasn't Fort Devens, where an officer's word was worth at least $20 in a pinch. He spent $5.00 of his precious cash on cab fare to the Ardsley train station, where $3.00 more went to buy a ticket to 240th Street in the Bronx. With ninety blocks still to travel after disembarking, he flagged another taxi, acutely aware that he was about to arrive on the job penniless, in debt, and with his clothes held hostage by a cynical hotel clerk in a place called Ardsley.

No matter. For the past three or four years Matt had carefully contemplated the pros and cons of retiring from the service after his twenty years were up, and nothing was going to dampen his enthusiasm now that the deed was done. Like his classmate George Crocker, he loved the Army and had been an exemplary officer: highly decorated in Vietnam; early promotion to major; early selection to the Command and General Staff College; early selection to battalion command. He had enjoyed the rare good fortune of commanding two battalions successively, the first at Fort Ord, California, and the second at Fort Devens, outside Boston. He had been chosen to attend the War College at Carlisle and seemed a sure bet for promotion to O6 — "oh-six," or full colonel. Among his classmates, he was considered an exemplar of rectitude. "Matt Harrison," an admirer once declared, "is *more* honest than the day is long."

Yet the cost of success in the service had been dear. In the 1970s, Matt had married a slender, dark-haired woman from St. Louis. Judy Harrison was an editor and writer when they met; among other accomplishments, she had worked as Dean Acheson's researcher on his Pulitzer Prize–winning memoirs, *Present at the Creation*. After their marriage, Judy had quit her job to follow her husband from Army post to Army post, and Matt now thought she should have an opportunity to resume her career again. He also wanted more time with their two young daughters, Cecily and Page; Matt had missed five of Cecily's seven birthdays. Even when he was not deployed in the field with his unit, he typically worked from five-thirty in the morning until seven-thirty or eight at night. That was the Army way, but it didn't seem fair to the girls.

His future in the Army was clear enough to see. After the year at

Carlisle, he would owe the service two more years; promotion to colonel would mean an obligation of another three years. If he stayed in for twenty-six years, he would be powerfully tempted to remain in uniform for at least thirty, when his pension would increase from half to three quarters of his active duty pay.

Furthermore, he had long ago transferred from the infantry to military intelligence, and MI colonels in the Army tended to be a paper shufflers rather than troop commanders. Being a bureaucrat in the Pentagon or at Forces Command held little appeal. He could do that at General Foods or General Motors or General Whatever and earn two or three times what the Army paid him. Wouldn't it make more sense, he asked Judy, to begin a new career when I'm forty-one instead of waiting until I'm in my fifties?

Judy resisted. It wasn't that she loved the Army. But Matt's blood, she knew, was Army green. As the son of a West Pointer, he had never known any life except the military. His father, class of '41, had been on track to earn a general's stars when he abruptly retired, in 1964. Colonel Matt Harrison, Sr., regretted the decision; wouldn't Lieutenant Colonel Matt Harrison, Jr., also regret it? Let's think this through, she urged.

For many months Matt had pondered the proper course. He wanted greater control over his life, and in the Army that wasn't possible. "We're not going to just continue in the service because we have good assignments or because it's the path of least resistance," he said. "And we're not going to second-guess ourselves. We're going to be happy with the decision."

Retirement came with more whimper than bang. A pair of enlisted men processed the paperwork at Fort Devens, and, with a scratch of the pen, he was transformed from Lieutenant Colonel Harrison into Mr. Harrison. It surprised Matt that after twenty years the end was so quick and painless.

He had undertaken the search for a new career with his usual methodical deliberation. Many retired officers went to work for Beltway bandits, the vast network of defense contractors and consultants ringing Washington, D.C. But Matt concluded that if he was going to be out of the Army, he wanted to be all the way out. "I don't want to dabble on the edges," he declared. The notion of going through the so-called revolving door between the military and defense industry made him queasy. It smacked of incest.

His search soon produced three firm offers. But two came from defense contractors who wanted to exploit his expertise in electronic warfare, so he had settled on the third, from an obscure but booming manufacturer in the Bronx. The money was attractive — the company offered $9000 more a year than either of the defense contractors, plus a car and the promise of a bonus after six months on the job. His retirement pension would provide another $20,000 or so. And he would immediately become an executive, the company's vice president for administration.

He had been guided by advice from his classmate and closest friend, Bob Cresci, who had left the Army in 1970 and was prospering as an investment banker in New York. "You don't have the opportunity to start over as somebody's assistant and work your way up through a large corporation," Bob observed. "You should be with a smaller, younger, growing company, where you can earn a living wage and get a lot of stock or options."

Matt was pleased at the prospect of starting over with a new job, a new city, a new life. Only one issue really gnawed at him. Whatever its shortcomings, the Army had bedrock. Certain standards and values — sanctified by two hundred years of blood and sacrifice and tradition — were immutable. The usual shorthand for describing those precepts was duty, honor, and country. Occasionally the ideals seemed more honored in the breach than in the observance, but in times of moral quandary a conscientious officer could anchor himself with a few simple questions: Is it good for the troops? Is it good for the country? Is it honorable?

But where was the bedrock in the corporate world? Before leaving Fort Devens, Matt had had several long discussions with a woman who was a senior officer with Digital Equipment Corporation and a warden at the Harrisons' church. "I'm apprehensive about finding myself in an organization in which profits are a justification for doing things that I find uncomfortable, ethically and morally," Matt told her. "I think I can pretty much adapt to any kind of culture except one in which I'm expected to lie, cheat, or steal." The woman's advice was disarmingly simple. Trust your instincts, Matt, and you'll be all right. Her words had been reassuring.

The taxi pulled up to 595 Gerard Avenue at East 150th Street. If a United States Army post could be said to have an antithesis, the South Bronx was a likely candidate. Toward the Harlem River, the Hispanic American Import Corporation advertised *productos tropicales*. The Bronx jail squatted farther down the street, and beneath the green girders of the Major Deegan Expressway thrived a chop shop with a dozen stolen cars in various states of evisceration. Prostitutes in slit skirts and threadbare furs solicited motorists at the stoplight outside the Bronx Terminal Market.

Matt's company occupied most of one block. He saw a long, single-story brick building with frosted windows and five strands of barbed wire encircling the roof. The parking lot, roughly an acre in size, was a paved pit wrapped in chain-link fencing and concertina wire, not unlike a firebase in the Central Highlands. It abutted Yankee Stadium Lot No. 11; just to the north loomed the fabled House of Ruth itself.

The executive offices were housed in a three-story annex crowned with a flagpole. The new vice president for administration handed over the remainder of his $25 to the cab driver and walked briskly through the double glass doors into a small lobby with a dirty linoleum floor. On one wall, in block letters as shiny and bold as a summer morning, was the name of the outfit to which he had hitched his star: WEDTECH CORPORATION.

It took less than a day for Matt to realize that Wedtech was very different from the Army. The Army abhorred chaos; Wedtech embodied chaos. After waiting in the lobby for forty-five minutes, he was shown to his new office, which had the unmistakable air of having been quickly and recently evacuated. None of the other executives seemed to be in the building. In the parking lot, an attendant issued Matt a new Cadillac; he noticed, to his surprise, that the company owned forty or fifty other cars, including nine Mercedes and a half-dozen Lincoln Continentals. And life in the plant seemed equally odd. The vast majority of Wedtech's eleven hundred employees in the South Bronx were Puerto Rican, most of them evangelical Christians. They listened all day to religious radio broadcasts, read their Bibles during work breaks, and greeted one another in Spanish or English with cheerful benedictions, like "Jesus loves you" or "The Lord is with you." A Pentecostal chapel in the plant offered regular lunch-hour services.

Actually, Matt knew very little about Wedtech. The firm had been founded in 1965 as the Welbilt Electronic Die Corporation by John Mariotta, the son of Puerto Rican immigrants. Mariotta was joined in 1970 by Fred Neuberger, a Romanian Jew who claimed to have escaped the Nazis by walking to Palestine. After years of struggling as a small machine shop, the company had landed a $32 million contract in 1982 to build six-horsepower engines for the Army. More than $200 million in additional Pentagon contracts followed, including one for building ninety-ton pontoons for the Navy as part of the U.S. rapid deployment force. In 1983, the company had gone public by offering two million shares of stock at $16 each; two more stock offerings in the next two years raised another $70 million in capital. Almost overnight the company had become one of Wall Street's darlings, and analysts began referring to "the miracle of the South Bronx." During a 1984 campaign stop in New York, Ronald Reagan had praised John Mariotta as "a hero for the '80s." But a year later, Mariotta was ousted during an internal power struggle.

Matt rolled up his sleeves and got to work. His duties were never specifically defined, and three days passed before he ever saw his boss, Anthony Guariglia, the thirty-five-year-old company president. If ever a company needed a West Pointer to take charge — someone who could bring order and efficiency to the place — Matt figured it was Wedtech.

His initial impression of chaos was vigorously reinforced during his next two months on the job. The company had no system for hiring, firing, affirmative action, apportioning raises, or anything else. No one knew exactly how many workers Wedtech employed. The employees held 170 job titles, many of them apparently concocted on a whim. A clerk might be called a junior accountant, an accounting clerk, or an accounting assistant; he might earn $250 a month or $600, with no rational basis for the discrepancy. Because the company kept few records, bookkeeping was a shambles. A year before, Wedtech's salary system had been disallowed by the Defense Contract Audit Agency, but the company had never replied to the government audit. After spending a month writing an employee handbook that explained everything from health benefits to vacation schedules, Matt sent the draft to Guariglia and other company officials. No one ever responded.

Nevertheless, everything about Wedtech fit Matt's expectations of the "entrepreneurial culture" that he had studied in management courses at Harvard before leaving Fort Devens. In one class, the students had spent hours analyzing how a company successfully marketed a new strain of grass seed; now he could see the same process of American capitalism in action. Wedtech was precisely like some of those Harvard case histories: a classic "start-up" company founded by two or three hustling entrepreneurs who knew how to get a better mousetrap out the door but had outgrown their management acumen. In his mind, the very fact that Guariglia and the others recognized that they needed a Matt Harrison was a sign of how shrewd they were. "We've got problems," Guariglia had admitted. "We need somebody to come in here and get things under control, get them organized."

If Tony Guariglia seemed a little gaudy, with his European silk suits and heavy gold jewelry, that also was part of the pattern: someone who was rough around the edges but had energy and drive. In some respects, Matt thought, Guariglia was not very different from many Army officers who lacked a patina of sophistication but were nonetheless talented and capable. Guariglia had been an accountant at Main Hurdman before joining Wedtech in 1983; within the company he had the reputation of possessing a brilliant mind and photographic memory. Although Matt had never seen Guariglia's reputed genius at work, he figured that brilliance was heavily discounted in the South Bronx.

If the work was frustrating at times, Matt presumed that was because he had come from the overly bureaucratized culture of the Army and was not yet acclimated to a freewheeling world of savvy entrepreneurs. Even the incompetent old-timers who sat around doing nothing seemed to fit his preconceptions: they were the "keepers of the corporate folklore" he had read about. Everything was falling into place. Out of sheer luck, Matt told himself, I've stumbled into the perfect situation.

"I hate to sound as if I'm tooting my own whistle," he told Bob Cresci in one of their weekly phone conversations a few months after starting at Wedtech, "but I'm now the second or third most important guy in the company. They almost never make any decisions without consulting me. They're even thinking of forming a five-man office of the president, and I'd be one of the five."

Not everything at Wedtech, to be sure, quite fit the Harvard definition of entrepreneurial culture. He began to hear rumors, disquieting rumors, that were hard to rationalize. According to office scuttlebutt, Guariglia and three other senior executives often left the office lugging briefcases stuffed with cash for wild gambling sprees.

In late September, Matt mentioned the rumors to Cresci. "They supposedly have condos in Atlantic City," Matt told him on the phone, "and they'll go off for forty-eight-hour binges, sometimes blowing as much as $100,000 in a weekend."

There was a long pause. "That's bad," Cresci finally replied. "That means they're stealing."

Now Matt paused. "What do you mean?"

"They're ripping off the company. They're stealing. I don't know how, but I guarantee you they're stealing."

"Naw, that's crazy. They may be stealing legally. Big option programs, big bonuses, big salaries. But that's all approved. It's all disclosed. They're not stealing."

"Matt, I'm telling you they're stealing. I guarantee it. I've been in the business world for fifteen years and I've never seen the executives in a company gamble like that unless they were also stealing. They're stealing everything that's not locked down."

"How do you know?"

"I don't *know*. But no one gambles $100,000 in a weekend and goes back the next weekend to risk another $100,000 unless they're doing it with somebody else's money. Do you have any conception of how much money it takes to have $100,000 you can piss away? You have to be a

Saudi prince. Even people who make a million or a million and a half a year don't piss away a hundred grand."

Matt was unconvinced. Cresci worked with Fortune 500 companies, run by men with Ivy League educations and high-society manners. The Wedtech executives were a different breed; instead of attending the symphony or the opera, they drove to Atlantic City to play roulette and blackjack. To accuse them of stealing was outrageous, and Matt dismissed the allegation out of hand.

But Cresci's instincts proved shrewder than Matt's. A few weeks later, in October, the first intimation of scandal appeared in the newspapers. INVESTIGATORS PROBE BRONX FIRM, read one headline, and subsequent articles hinted at bribery, kickbacks, conspiracy, embezzlement. Matt still didn't believe any of it, not initially. Just two months earlier, a large investment bank had shown enough confidence in the company to underwrite $75 million in junk bonds; even *The New York Times* continued to list Wedtech among twenty companies offering "low-priced stocks with strong fundamentals." Two full audits by reputable accounting firms had given Wedtech a clean bill of health. The innuendoes, Matt was convinced, could not be true. Apparently impressed with his vice president's loyalty, Guariglia appointed him spokesman for the company, the front man who fielded reporters' phone calls and issued denials. Every morning Matt started his day by skimming the latest bad news in the packet of photocopied clippings prepared by the receptionist.

By early November, he could no longer delude himself. These men, he thought, really did do some of the things they're accused of doing. One newspaper article suggested that the company had bribed Representative Mario Biaggi, a scrappy former policeman who had served in Congress for nearly twenty years. Another stated flatly that Wedtech had fraudulently received $6 million in government progress payments. Customers began to cancel their contracts; on December 15, Wedtech abruptly declared bankruptcy.

Matt was appalled, sick at heart. Did I know and not admit it? he asked himself. Should I have known?

To his chagrin, he realized that he had outsmarted himself with his Harvard case histories and mumbo jumbo. Cresci had been absolutely right. Now what? He thought about quitting, just walking out the door and leaving the whole rancid affair behind. But he had a family to support and the mortgage to pay on a new house the Harrisons were buying in Westchester County. I know I haven't done anything wrong, he told Cresci, so why should I penalize myself and my family with what would amount to a damaging and futile gesture? He also felt a certain fascination with this catastrophe, like a motorist who can't help staring at a grisly car wreck.

The same stubborn streak that had kept him from resigning when the Army was in trouble in the early 1970s asserted itself again. He had made a commitment, and while the company may have been riddled with corruption at the top, Matt knew that more than a thousand workers still needed someone to look after their interests. Wedtech's new management, appointed by the company's creditors, desperately wanted him to remain on the job; Matt was one of the few certifiably honest executives who knew anything about the corporation's internal workings. After considerable soul searching, he agreed to stay.

In mid January, he got his first good look at the company's books and records, such as they were. Working with federal, state, and local investigators, he began to piece together an ugly picture of greed and perfidy. Though the full panorama took months to assemble, the outlines of venality quickly came into focus. Tony Guariglia and perhaps as many as fifty other Wedtech employees were, Matt concluded, "garden-variety crooks." Some pilfered petty cash or cheated on their expense vouchers; others stole millions.

Mariotta had looted the company of $12 million before his ouster. Guariglia, it turned out, had been hired from his accounting firm after discovering during a 1983 audit that Wedtech's executives had set up a private slush fund. Instead of reporting the corruption, Guariglia had joined in bleeding the firm.

The bribery and kickback schemes seemed unending. Biaggi, whom prosecutors later called "a thug in a congressman's suit," had been appeased with 225,000 shares of stock when he threatened to cut off support to Wedtech from the Small Business Administration. The former Bronx borough president had been bribed, as had a former SBA administrator, two Teamsters officials, two former Maryland state senators, and others.

The Army engine contract hadn't been earned in 1982 — it had been bought. The company had hired the former White House aide Lyn Nofziger as a lobbyist only three months after he left government service. The company also hired E. Robert Wallach, a close friend of White House counselor and future attorney general Edwin Meese III. Wallach, an elfin lawyer who affected a yellow rose in his lapel and liked to spell his name in lower-case letters, had peppered Meese with memos on Wedtech's behalf. In May 1982, Meese ordered a White House review of the Army engine contract; four months later it was awarded to Wedtech without competitive bidding, even though the company had never built an engine before and was insisting on payments that were twice what the Army thought was fair.

Every week, Matt felt a little more stupefied by the extent of the pillage. Wedtech's executives had been so greedy, he realized, that while stealing millions of dollars, they had refused to reimburse a dozen workers $40 each for the steel-toed safety shoes the men were required to buy.

That was the hardest part for Matt: the devastation wreaked among the workers who lost not only their jobs and health insurance benefits but also their self-esteem. As it became evident that Wedtech would be unable to reorganize and reopen, the new management team cut the labor force from a peak of fourteen hundred to fourteen. New jobs in the Bronx were hard to come by, especially for those who were unskilled, spoke little English, and owned no automobile. Matt tried to find them positions with other companies but with limited success. The employees' tearful pleas for assistance were echoed by similar cries from the company's subcontractors and bond holders.

Matt found himself in the role of avenging angel. The crooks, he believed, must be made to pay for the suffering they had caused. At every opportunity he urged prosecutors to "squeeze the culprits hard" to make certain they didn't have a hidden cache of ill-gotten money to fall back on after being released from jail. Wedtech lawyers also filed civil suits against those who had looted the company. But vengeance was an expensive undertaking; the company's legal bill quickly soared to $3 million.

Two weeks before four company executives pleaded guilty to bribery, Matt happened to walk into a small office at the plant, where he found Guariglia dejectedly staring at the wall.

"How are you doing, Tony?" Matt asked, unable to stifle forty-one years of good manners even in the presence of avarice personified.

"Not all that well, Matt," Guariglia replied. "You know, I still believe that I haven't done anything wrong."

Matt turned on his heel and walked out. What more was there to say? Slowly, some things about the vast world beyond the sanctuary of the United States Army were becoming clear, certainly much clearer than they had been in the classroom at Harvard. Guariglia and his kind truly believed that bribes were a necessary component of success in the corporate jungle. Otherwise, in their view, a Puerto Rican toolmaker in the South Bronx could not rise above his circumstances. In the absence of an old boy network or university connections or social contacts, corruption was the only way to level the playing field. "The Jews and Italians just got to America too late," Matt was told by one prominent lawyer, who reputedly had underworld ties. "The WASPs already stole the best stuff."

Matt knew that Wedtech was not typical of corporate America. He also knew it was unfair to suggest that Tony Guariglia, with his silk suits and gold chains and cash-stuffed briefcase, typified the nation's business executives. But Matt's fretful concern about bedrock seemed more legitimate than ever. As an Army officer, he had recognized that one of his duties was to serve as a civilizing influence, especially in the uncivil stress of combat; a good officer perpetuated the standards and principles of military honor that had been handed down from generation to generation. But such absolutes, he concluded, rarely obtained in the business world.

He wondered whether it was possible to survive *out here* without turning a blind eye to corruption. Was it just New York, or was it everywhere? Certainly in this city — at least in such businesses as construction, garbage collection, airports, trucking, shipping, parking — there seemed to be no limit to the kickbacks, payoffs, shakedowns, and sundry forms of turpitude. The salient questions that a dedicated military officer could use to chart his course — Is it good for the troops? the unit? the country? — were largely supplanted by the fundamental query of commerce: Will it earn a buck?

He was learning a great deal, although this was not the kind of education that he had sought. Cresci thought Matt had been "incredibly naïve," but that the naïveté was bred of admirable innocence. He also found that Matt had demonstrated his maturity in the Wedtech affair. "Ten years ago," Cresci later said, "Matt probably would have quit on the spot — leaving himself in the lurch with no income for his family — or he would have taken Tony Guariglia out back and beaten him half to death."

Ironically, the collapse of Wedtech was beneficial for Matt Harrison. The company's creditors needed someone competent to liquidate the assets, cooperate with investigators, and help coordinate the legal processes. His working hours became even more onerous than those of a battalion commander. He was rarely home now before nine P.M., and in the first five months after Wedtech's bankruptcy he worked every day except for one Saturday, when he broke free to take his daughters to the circus. But his salary had been doubled — he was earning more than he had expected to make after ten years in civilian life — and he and Judy bought a handsome Victorian house in Rye Brook, just a few blocks from the Connecticut line. Here, he realized, was yet another contrast with the Army, where officers were expected to share the hardships their men endured. At Wedtech, the grunts were jobless in the South Bronx while Matt drove home to comfortable Westchester County every night.

He never regretted his decision to retire, though the news of a classmate's promotion to full colonel occasionally stirred a wistful pang. Some old military habits were hard to break. He still rose every morning at 4:45 to jog five miles before heading off to work. As the liquidation of Wedtech settled into a routine, Judy and the girls were delighted to see him pull into the driveway at 7:30 one evening. Two days later he was actually home by 6:30.

One morning, a pair of FBI agents showed up at Wedtech in the company of Lawrence Shorten, the company's former chief financial officer. Shorten, who had pleaded guilty to bribery, was now being allowed to review certain records before testifying as a government witness. Matt despised the man's arrogance and mediocrity, but when Shorten entered the office and stuck out his hand with a cheerful "great to see you again," Matt reflexively shook it.

He immediately wished he hadn't. Why did I do that? he wondered. Few events in the past six months troubled him more than this gesture. It made him feel tainted somehow, soiled. A handshake was a sign of mutual respect, whether between Army officers or between civilian gentlemen. Shorten was neither. And for weeks Matt remained angry with himself for not being more discriminating.

As the Wedtech scandal festered, the class of 1966 held its twentieth reunion at West Point in mid October. More than three hundred classmates showed up for the event, lured from all over the world by that irresistible compulsion that drew them back to West Point periodically, like spawning salmon or migrating fowl. As cadets, they sometimes had ridiculed the aging veterans who returned to the academy again and again to bear-hug one another and reminisce about yesteryear. Yet here they were, yesteryear's children flocking home, now indistinguishable from the vets of Normandy and Okinawa who had strolled the Plain at their twentieth reunions in the early 1960s. In a hundred huddled conversations the men of '66 congratulated one another on preserving their youthful trim — while privately wondering how so many had grown so old so quickly. Some of those still in uniform were also struck by the fixation with Vietnam that seemed to grip many classmates who had resigned in the early 1970s. That preoccupation irritated the officers, who felt that it belittled the Army's accomplishments since the war.

By now, the reunions had assumed a certain routine. The classmates and their wives took a river cruise aboard the superintendent's steamer and danced to the low moan of big brass beneath the mess hall poop deck. They held a solemn memorial service and wreath-laying ceremony in Section XXXIV of the cemetery, and a boisterous dinner in the Hotel Thayer, where, this year, the men twirled their red napkins overhead and chanted "Beat Holy Cross!" just as they had chanted "Beat Penn State!" during the Great Mess Hall Riot in 1963.

On Friday morning, October 17, as sunlight flooded through the high bay windows of the Officers Club ballroom, more than a hundred classmates gathered for a prayer breakfast. Over eggs and hash browns, they sang the same hymn that had been sung during Art Bonifas's funeral:

> Enter, rejoice, and come in,
> Today will be a joyful day,
> Enter, rejoice, and come in.

Then Marcia Bonifas stepped to the podium, wearing a red paisley dress and gold earrings, her copper hair brilliantly backlit by the sun rising over the Hudson. Two months before, she had flown to Korea, where, on the tenth anniversary of Art's death, Camp Kitty Hawk on the DMZ had been renamed Camp Bonifas.

"The last time we sang that song together," she said, "everybody cried. Please put your tissues away. We're not crying today. I can't give another talk and have everybody crying.

"I was thinking how long ago it seems that Art and I were at our first assignment at Fort Benning. I can remember being frantic about having white gloves and the proper calling cards. Remember how you needed three cards if there was a daughter over the age of eighteen in the house you were visiting? We were so concerned about doing the right thing. And I was having a tough time just keeping Art's shorts laundered and starched.

"Our children were three, six, and eight when Art was killed. He treated those North Koreans with respect, as human beings. He trusted them. What greater love does a man have than to lay down his life for his friends? Now he's flying around heaven without a care in the world, leaving me with three kids." She paused, smiling mischievously. "I'll get even. There will be pain in heaven when I get there."

The smile faded. "It has never been rock 'n' roll. It has never been straight. And it has never been easy. But we're doing fine."

Art was ten years in his grave. At first, Marcia was frightened whenever she returned to visit him in the cemetery. The headstone was such a tangible reminder — as if she needed reminding — that he was gone forever. But over the years the fear was replaced by a gentle tranquillity, a communion that reminded her of their late afternoon chats at Stony Lonesome — their "private time" when he changed his clothes after riding the Daddy Bus up the hill from Thayer Hall.

She often spoke to him in the cemetery: "You know, I think I've done the right thing, Art. Do you think so, too?" And he would answer, as the dead speak to those they love, by wrapping her in a cloak of peaceful reassurance.

The job of assistant hostess at the Air Force Academy had occupied Marcia for a year after Art's death. Although she was supposed to be the enforcer of decorum at hops, she was usually too busy dancing with the cadets to prowl around for amorous couples or girls smoking in the bathrooms of Arnold Hall. Because the academy had so few female cadets, she occasionally drove to Denver to round up busloads of coeds from Regis College or Colorado Women's College. Recalling an old custom from West Point, she slyly instituted a pig pool to which each cadet contributed a dollar for the poor wretch judged to have the homeliest date.

The cadets adored her; sometimes they invited her out for pizza and beer, or dropped by the house to pour out their troubles. And when the shrewish senior hostess retired in the spring, the academy offered her job to Marcia. She pondered the offer for weeks. Is this how I want to grow old, she asked herself, playing chaperone to four thousand cadets who are perpetually twenty years old? After returning from a summer vacation in Europe with her three children, she resigned.

She returned to graduate school to earn a master's degree in public administration, and sold real estate for a while. Holding the family together was her first priority, and she worked at the task relentlessly. Nothing bothered her more than watching Brian grow up without a father. Her parents adored the children, but they lived two thousand miles away and could hardly provide Art's gentle nurturing. (When Peter McGuire came for a visit that first Christmas, he had insisted that his grandson forgo the usual kiss. "You're six years old and you must shake hands now, Brian. You're a man.") Marcia enrolled her son in the Colorado Springs Big Brother program, which paired Brian with a wonderfully crusty Air Force sergeant who often took him swimming or camping or go-carting.

Then, during a visit to Washington one spring, she paid a courtesy call on Richard Stilwell, who was now deputy undersecretary of defense. "What are you doing with the rest of your life?" Stilwell asked bluntly.

Taken aback, Marcia replied that she was "still trying to figure it out." Stilwell promised to help her find a suitable position. A year later — after proving that she was a loyal Republican and drafting a résumé with help from Wes Clark — she won a political appointment in Denver with CHAMPUS, the Civilian Health and Medical Program for the Uniformed Services. She liked the job, though the 120-mile round-trip commute from Colorado Springs had gradually worn her down. Now, again with Stilwell's help, she was trying to arrange a transfer to work in the Pentagon for the official who managed the military's health programs. Colorado had been a fine place to raise the children, but the day would come when they were gone and she was left behind. In Washington, where so many military acquaintances were stationed or had retired, she would be surrounded by old friends.

One day, long after the murders at Panmunjom had faded from most memories, an Army officer who had served with Art in Korea called Marcia in Colorado. "I'm sending you some pictures," he said mysteriously. "Don't look at them with anyone else." A few days later, a packet of slides arrived in the mail, carefully wrapped inside an eyeglass case. That night, she set up the projector in the basement recreation room. The pictures had been taken from one of the checkpoints above the poplar tree on August 18, 1976. She could see the cluster of arguing soldiers; the North Korean truck on the bridge; the fatal melee. According to the narrative description that the officer included with the slides, there was a brief period in which Art, injured but still alive, had been left alone by the fleeing South Korean and American soldiers. Then, the pictures seemed to show, the North Koreans had returned and bludgeoned him to death. A last slide showed his body sprawled in the dirt.

Marcia shut off the projector, horror giving way to hysteria. There had never been any hint in the investigations of the murder that Art had been abandoned. These pictures suggested that his death might have been prevented, though the evidence was ambiguous. Sobbing bitterly, Marcia scooped up the slides. The children must never see these, she told herself. What difference did it make now? August 18, 1976, had been Art's day to die. Nothing could change that. She threw the slides away without ever looking at them again.

After the prayer breakfast at the twentieth reunion, she once again visited the cemetery. Although she had long ago removed the wedding ring from her left hand as a gesture of independence, Marcia had never remarried, never found anyone with whom to share the same easy intimacy. Soon the children would be fully grown and on their own. Beth was studying to be a nurse on an ROTC scholarship at Georgetown University; Brian, who at six feet seven inches was a startling replica of his father, attended prep school in Vermont; Megan, an aspiring actress at fourteen, had inherited her dad's perfect smile.

Marcia was proud of how well they had turned out. Art, she thought, would also be proud. No, it had never been straight or easy. It had never been rock 'n' roll. But they were doing just fine.

I think I've done the right thing, Art. Do you think so, too? she wondered, standing beneath the graceful mimosa tree. In his warm presence, she had her answer.

The reunion allowed the men of 1966 to take the measure of West Point after twenty years much as they took the measure of one another. At first glance, they found the academy reassuringly familiar, tucked between the looming parapets of the chapel and the green ribbon of the timeless Hudson. Cadets marched across the Plain with the same smart precision in the same gray tunics, no doubt whispering the same ribald jokes *sotto voce* in the ranks. *The New York Times* was still delivered outside each barracks room at dawn, leadership class was still known as leadersleep, and Sylvanus Thayer's system of small classes and daily recitation still endured. On R-Day, just as on July 2, 1962, tearful parents surrendered their petrified children, who scrambled about collecting uniforms and equipment before marching raggedly to Trophy Point to vouch fidelity to "the sovereignty of the United States." Harried plebes could be seen pinging across Thayer Road at 120 steps per minute, or reciting the same nonsensical answers to the same nonsensical questions that had been asked of their fathers: "How's the cow?" "Sir, she walks, she talks, she's full of chalk, the lacteal fluid extracted from the female of the bovine species is highly prolific to the *n*th degree." Even much of the slang, from quill to slug, was preserved intact, although brown boy comforters had somehow become green girls, and a few terms, such as *spoony* and *drag*, had nearly vanished.

Vietnam had also receded as a presence. Fewer and fewer faculty members were men who had fought in the war, which, like the world wars and Korea, was largely relegated to history classes. Cadets entering with the class of 1991 were born as the American involvement in Southeast Asia had begun to ebb. For them, the war lingered in small fragments, as in a jody call used to count cadence while marching:

> Ranger on a hilltop
> Weapon by his side
> Sole intent and purpose
> Is just to stay alive.
> In Vietnam, Vietnammmmm,
> Late at night
> While you're sleepin'
> Charlie Commie comes a creepin'.

Cadets were conservative, staunchly patriotic, and as bewitched by Ronald Reagan's charisma as their fathers had been by John F. Kennedy's. Once again, the academy could — and did — boast that it attracted many of a generation's best and brightest. For approximately 1400 openings in each plebe class, West Point now received 15,000 applications. Moreover, graduates tended to remain in the Army even after their obligations had expired: after six years in the officer corps, a third of the class of 1966 had quit; for the class of 1981, the resignation rate would be only 18 percent. The cadets' patriotism was stiffened with viewings of *Patton, MacArthur,* and slick "Be All You Can Be" films.

More than a few cadets were known as Rambo or the kill-a-commie-for-mommy type. Watching tensions heat up in the Persian Gulf, they joked nervously about mustering for war, just as an older generation had during the Cuban missile crisis. As Morgan Roseborough, a '66 graduate who now worked in the superintendent's office, observed, "They remind me of us."

Yet, despite the similarities, West Point was not the same place, not at all. By the end of the reunion weekend, the men of '66 could see that as many profound changes had taken place at the academy in the past two decades as in the preceding 160 years. The transformation that George Crocker and his classmates had witnessed in the mid 1970s had accelerated in the 1980s, partly as the result of reforms adopted in the aftermath of the EE304 scandal and partly as a reflection of contemporary thinking in pedagogy and officer training.

In 1962, cadets had had just two elective classes in a four-year curriculum that was otherwise fixed and inviolable. Now, electives had become commonplace, cadets declared academic majors like other college students, classes had been shortened, and the general order of merit had been abolished (along with the custom of showering the class "goat" with dollar bills on graduation day).

Eleven percent of the corps was now female. In 1980, the first group of sixty-two women had graduated, slightly more than half of those who had entered the academy in July 1976. Despite a few untoward incidents — such as women once being forced to slaughter chickens with their teeth — much of the harassment had subsided after two or three years. Officially, West Point maintained that female cadets were completely integrated. An accomplished female might occasionally draw praise from her male classmates as "a real stud," the highest of accolades.

Unofficially, however, the women remained problematic. Outnumbered ten to one, they were an oddity in the masculine world of the military academy, particularly since the country continued to exclude them from service in the combat arms. "We bring them to an institution where officers are being prepared to fight the nation's wars," one colonel observed, "and then we tell the women that they won't really be equal to the men once they join the Army."

The overwhelmingly white male corps of the early 1960s had changed dramatically in other ways. West Point now had more than three hundred black cadets — only three blacks had graduated in 1966 — as well as nearly four hundred Hispanics and Asian Americans. The corps' first black first captain had been appointed in 1979, and in 1987 the academy would welcome its first black commandant, Brigadier General Fred A. Gorden, an artilleryman from Anniston, Alabama.

In the aftermath of EE304, the honor code remained intact, but the system for enforcing and perpetuating the code was radically different. No longer were honor boards drawn solely from the ranks of the upperclass-dominated honor committee. Of twelve board members hearing a case, four came from the committee and the other eight were picked randomly from the corps, two per class. To forestall "jury tampering," an accused cadet could be convicted by only ten guilty votes out of a possible twelve, rather than the previously required unanimity. And those convicted no longer faced automatic expulsion. The superintendent now had the "discretion" to suspend or reinstate the guilty. In 1986, in twenty-six honor cases the superintendent exercised that privilege eight times. One plebe, for example, who told an upperclassman that he'd been given a haircut, later confessed to cutting his hair himself; found for lying, he was suspended for a year. In an earlier era the young man would have faced certain dismissal.

Although West Point still implicitly believed in a moral gyroscope that allowed cadets to distinguish right from wrong, no longer did the academy presume that its neophytes arrived on R-Day with that ability securely in place. Honor instruction, once relatively informal, now entailed a four-year, highly structured indoctrination in ethics. Lectures and seminars in Beast Barracks culminated in a viewing of *Breaker Morant* — a film about two soldiers who were executed for killing prisoners in the Boer War — and a formal address by Buddy Bucha, the Medal of Honor winner from the class of '65.

After plebe year, the injunction against lying, cheating, and stealing was intended to "ramp up" toward a wider understanding of professionalism and integrity. Discussions ranged from the fatuous — Am I dishonorable if I've told two women at the same time that I love them? Why is a clipping penalty in football not an honor violation? — to profound questions about illegal orders and the Law of War, such as this example used in one ethics class:

> Captain Jones's company has been engaged in an effort to take a fortified enemy area for over three days. All attempts to breach the enemy defense have failed, and the company's losses are approaching sixty percent in equipment, and over forty-five percent killed or wounded. In an extremely emotional state, Captain Jones orders Lieutenant Pointer to take a patrol and poison the water in a stream which runs through the enemy-fortified area.

What was a young lieutenant to do? "Lieutenant Pointer," according to the ethics booklet, "is under both a moral and legal duty to confront his commander and advise him that the order is illegal and will not be carried out."

Perhaps the most controversial changes had taken place in what was benignly known as the Fourth Class System — the rigorous cosmology governing the life of every plebe. The term Beast Barracks had been replaced — in policy if not in practice — by the supposedly less degrading Cadet Basic Training, or CBT. "Demanding but not demeaning" was the new motto for the CBT cadre, who had strict orders to treat new cadets more humanely. Upperclassmen had to remain at least eighteen inches from plebes. Tag team harassment — the hazing of plebes by more than one upperclassman — was prohibited, as was the ancient practice of forcing plebes to eat any Ranger ropes — stray threads — found on their uniforms.

The mess hall, once a torture chamber for new cadets, had become a sanctuary. An upperclassman caught depriving cadets of food was punished, severely, and any plebe whose weight dropped by more than 3 percent was moved to a well-lardered training table with double rations. Some hazing was still permitted, certainly. A plebe who botched the carving of a "Martha Washington sheet cake" at supper might be marched outside to the equestrian statue of George Washington, told to beg the general's pardon — "General Washington, sir, I apologize for destroying your wife's sheet cake" — and ordered to "hold your salute until the general salutes back." But the sadism of an earlier age was largely gone. Plebes even kept boodle in their rooms legally, in contrast to the men of '66 who had nibbled on hidden candy bars after taps. And traditional reveille calls had been replaced with blaring recordings of Bruce Springsteen's "Born in the U.S.A." or the Blues Brothers' rendition of the theme from *Rawhide*.

Predictably, such reforms garnered mixed reviews. Upperclassmen sneeringly referred to Beast as "Beach." Reactionary grumbling that the corps had "gone to hell" since one's own cadetship had been the practice of graduates for nearly two hundred years, of course. For the men of '66, twenty years' remove from cadet gray was sufficient to qualify them as full-fledged DOGs — Disgruntled Old Grads — and some bitterly resented the changes. "They called it Beast for a reason — it was beastly," said Mike Hustead, a '66er who taught electrical engineering in the mid 1980s and whose son was a cadet. "You were supposed to be broken down into your basic components and then built back up. You were supposed to be tested . . . to learn how to stay cool, collect your thoughts, to have a sense of humor, to develop all of the things you need as an officer. If you couldn't take it, you left . . . I violently disagree with what's happening now."

Others, however, were dismayed by what they viewed as the glacial pace of change. Some officers found it ironic that one of the required memorizations for every plebe was the definition of discipline offered by Major General John M. Schofield in 1879, which stated in part:

> The discipline which makes the soldiers of a free country reliable in battle is not to be gained by harsh or tyrannical treatment. On the contrary, such treatment is far more likely to destroy than to make an army . . . He who feels the respect which is due to others cannot fail to inspire in them regard for himself, while he who feels, and hence manifests, disrespect toward others, especially his inferiors, cannot fail to inspire hatred against himself.

Yet in the century since Schofield uttered those words, West Point had moved only slightly toward putting his definition into practice, recent reforms notwithstanding. The academy continued to expect each cadet to offer blind obedience from the moment he or she was ordered to "drop the bag!" on R-Day. Autocracy remained the heart of West Point's leadership system. Some critics, like Larry Donnithorne, a soft-spoken '66 graduate who served as the superintendent's long-range planner, found that autocracy at odds with the modern Army's desire for for an independent and creative officer corps. In a fighting force that valued initiative, Donnithorne believed, officers had to learn how to think and experiment, how to understand a commander's intent while feeling free to act with creative innovation in executing that intent.

"But at West Point we drive a lot of creativity out," Donnithorne said. "We put the cadets into a mode in which they say, 'Just tell me what to do or say or think, and I'll do it.' In some respects, our environment is excessively controlling and insists on conformity in a blind way."

The issue, of course, was a variation on precisely the same enigma that had puzzled West Point since Thomas Jefferson founded the academy in 1802: How can the nation best produce the capable military officers it needed? Many of the men of '66 believed that the academy had done exceptionally well in the past and would, no doubt, continue to do so. Some regretted what they saw as an overly somber corps that no longer seemed to tolerate high-spirited iconoclasts; as the academy had loosened some of its strictures, the imps and mischief makers, paradoxically, seemed to grow fewer.

Leigh Wheeler, now an Army doctor stationed at the academy, phrased those concerns in a way that every man in the class of '66 would understand, though he might not agree with it: "Today's cadets are very serious. If there is a wild spark in them when they get here, it's extinguished very quickly. A Tom Carhart would not survive today."

A Tom Carhart would not survive today. Perhaps not, though the demise of Thomas M. Carhart III had been predicted before. By now, if nothing else was certain about Tom — and, in truth, nothing else was — he clearly was a survivor. He had arrived at the twentieth reunion in full-blown flamboyance: mustache, tweeds, and a handsome, broad-brimmed hat that gave him the jaunty look of a Hapsburg duke. Throughout the long weekend he seemed to be everywhere at once — laughing, reminiscing, spinning yarns — as full as ever of charm and panache. That Tom, his classmates said. And nothing more needed to be said.

As the reunion drew to a close, Tom bumped into an old company mate from Easy Deuce. Jack Wheeler stood in the lobby of the Hotel Thayer, waiting for the elevator. He and Tom shook hands. "I'd like to sit down and talk, but I'm under the gun right now," Jack said. "Sure," Tom replied, "I'd like to talk, too."

Not surprisingly, they never did. The bad blood had continued to flow long after the Vietnam memorial was dedicated in November 1982. Tom's anger, though now largely dissipated, had lingered for many months after the wall was a *fait accompli*. When the General Accounting Office audited the VVMF books because of allegations that Jack and others had misspent much of the memorial money, Tom had lashed out. "Mr. Carhart stated," according to one investigator's notes, "that he had been told that John Wheeler, Jan Scruggs, and Bob Doubek, and their girlfriends spent $20,000 in one weekend at the Hay-Adams Hotel in Washington, D.C., in order to promote a book that Wheeler wanted to write." No evidence was ever found to support the wild accusation.

Tom never thought of the memorial fight now without pain. He had foreseen that his opposition to the wall would cause him nothing but trouble, and he was right. He had agreed to "bell the cat," as he put it, to speak publicly for those too timid to protest. "The reasonable man adapts himself to the world," he sometimes explained, quoting George Bernard Shaw. "The unreasonable one persists in trying to adapt the world to himself. Therefore, all progress depends on the unreasonable man."

But soon this unreasonable man was being caricatured and vilified. Crank calls to the Carhart house became so numerous that Tom requested an unlisted phone number. An article in *The Washington Post* quoted him as saying of his combat experience, "I killed and I enjoyed it"; though not disputing the accuracy of the quote, he complained in a letter to the newspaper that the article unfairly portrayed him as a "blood-crazed killer."

When the memorial statue was nearly complete, someone suggested privately that he break into the foundry and steal the sculpture as a prank, as he had once stolen the Navy goat. Tom was offended by the proposal. What do they think I am, he wondered, somebody's tool? Some wacko? He took pains to curb his excesses. One night, after swapping war stories and drinking a case of beer with a vet from the 1st Cav, Tom was arrested for driving while intoxicated; humiliated and furious at himself, he never took another drink.

His old fishing companion Jim Webb, smoother and more politic than Tom, had continued to ascend; he was appointed assistant secretary of defense and, later, secretary of the Navy. For Tom, there was no ascent. He continued to labor in the federal bureaucracy that he despised, waiting for the high-level political appointment that never materialized. A friend in the government told him that a "Do Not Touch" warning had been placed on his file in the White House; he was considered too controversial and unpredictable for a senior management position. Worn out by the turmoil, chagrined by his failure to advance, he agreed to move to Connecticut to be the state director of the Vietnam Veterans Leadership Program, a federally funded effort to promote the image and circumstances of veterans. As he left Washington for Hartford with Jan and little Tommy in 1983, Tom felt as though he had been run out of town.

The New England sojourn provided a needed respite, allowing him to speak boldly for his brother veterans on television and radio shows and in the opinion pieces he wrote for *The Hartford Courant*. "This is scandalous," Tom declared in one interview. "Men and women offered their lives for their country in time of war, and now they need a federal program to allow them to be reaccepted by society with something approaching grace, or even neutrality." Smoking Connecticut Valley cigars in his Hartford office, he organized a job fair and pressured the state's insurance companies and defense contractors to hire unemployed veterans. The job was well suited to his convictions. He was, as he described it, "shaking the moral responsibility tree," calling on the country to recognize its debt to veterans. Tom had always had a knack for shaking trees, and this time the results were gratifying.

Unfortunately, Jan was miserable. In order to care for young Tommy, whose medical condition required full-time attention, she had not returned to work. With no job and few friends in the unfamiliar city, she spent many afternoons trapped in the Carharts' house on the Connecticut River in Windsor with little to occupy her except television soap operas. One bright moment in both their lives came on February 16, 1984 — Tom's fortieth birthday — when Jan bore another child, a robust, healthy boy whom they named Jason.

A year after leaving Washington, they were back. Tom had intended to remain in New England to practice law, but that summer he was asked to return to the capital to be the last national director of the Leadership Program, which would soon close down after five years of operation. (Jack Wheeler, ironically, had been the program's first director during a leave of absence from the Securities and Exchange Commission.) In the back of his mind, Tom hoped the appointment would be a steppingstone to bigger things. "I can't resist reaching for the brass ring," he explained. Yet when the program ended there was still no political appointment. In early 1985, he returned to work as an Army lawyer, a GS-13 in the civil service, or, in Tom's words, "a GS-Nothing." Once again, his ambitions had been thwarted. Once again, he described himself as a "faceless bureaucrat."

Some months after the twentieth reunion, Tom returned to West Point for a more private visit. As a child, he had adored the academy, the way little boys adore toy soldiers. Then, as a cadet, he had despised it, the way adolescents despise authority and restriction. Now, at the age of forty-three, he found that the rough edges of those cadet years had worn away. Once again he adored the academy, this time for the simple reason that West Point was the fountainhead of his youthful ideals.

In a chill drizzle, he strolled the grounds with his familiar athlete's strut, shoulders rolling, elbows slightly cocked, reviewing the landmarks of his coming-of-age: the piny copse beneath Thayer Road, where he had lost his virginity; the chandeliers in the wainscoted mess hall, where cadets had swung like apes during the pep rally riot; the old gymnasium, where he had hurtled about the obstacle course; the barracks Area, where he had walked so many tours as a much-slugged member of the Century Club and where he had spattered the upperclassman with shoe polish; the gray span of Bear Mountain Bridge, where so many dreams had died in the wreckage of Bob Albright's Corvette; the cluster of graves, where so many other dreams were buried with John Hoskins and Art Parker and the immortal Buck Thompson.

Never again, Tom thought, would the flame be quite as bright as it had been in those days twenty years before, when the world was still his oyster and life's possibilities seemed boundless. He thought of himself as "burned off," shunted aside. As a cadet he had been, in his own phrase, "a classic underachiever," and that pattern had persisted. "I keep dancing from ice floe to ice floe," he told a friend. He still dreamed of glory and thunder, of course; his latest ambition was to move to Massachusetts and run for the Senate seat held by Edward Kennedy. But those dreams were being crowded by a sense of limits. Even less grandiose aspirations, such as living in Paris for a few years, now receded beyond his grasp.

As he grew older, the real West Point became clearer to him. It was not the place of brass buttons and plumed shakos that the public saw. For Tom, the academy was a crucible in which young men of assorted weaknesses had been invested with the will power, self-discipline, and desire to overcome their shortcomings in pursuit of a greater good. If some had been stymied — "burned off" — at least the effort had been made in valiant good faith.

Tom's memoirs of Vietnam, a candid, compelling account entitled *The Offering,* had finally been published that spring. When the book received a tepid review in *The Assembly,* the academy alumni magazine, Tom wrote a response in which he tried to explain his own strivings:

> I do not believe that I always took the wisest or most effective path in my decisions. But I tried to tie my actions to pure principle, and always did what I thought was right . . . The basic question is, as it always has been, how much do you adhere to absolute principle, and how much do you sell out for what seems like personal advantage?
>
> That answer, at West Point, is a pure, almost holy commitment to absolute principle, with complete disregard for any personal price that must be paid in the process. That requires a belief in absolutes, of course, and the wise relativists will quickly assure us that such do not exist. As I approach middle age, I must admit that I have made some compromises now and again, either because I was weak or perhaps because I recognized that a subtle and tactful approach will often attain the desired end, or a close approximation thereof.

Compromise? Subtlety? Tact? Those were not the characteristics that first popped into the minds of his classmates whenever they thought of Tom Carhart, a man who had twice been relieved of command for following his own drummer. "I love to fight," he had told one interviewer in 1983. "I don't think you've won unless you've won everything. I want the whole thing." That was the Tom who sounded familiar to his old friends.

But in the same 1983 interview he had added, "Part of growing up is you gotta realize when you lose." If he now understood the need for occasional compromise, he was also shrewd enough to realize that concessions of any sort would never come naturally to him. Once, the West Point conception of honor had seemed to preclude giving ground. Now, he recognized that certain nuances of honor not only admitted compromise but required it.

His love for Jan was an absolute. He and she were partners, sharing hardship and prosperity. Jan was his best friend, his refuge, the counterbalance to whatever vicissitudes had befallen him. At times he was amazed at the serendipity that had brought him this loving wife and two beautiful sons. Their domestic life had assumed a routine that Tom came to cherish. Jan would drive him to work in the morning and pick him up in the afternoon. Those two half-hour interludes amid the grinding commuter traffic of suburban Washington were the best times of the day for them. After supper, he would bathe the boys, read them a story, and put them to bed. Stroking first Tommy's face and then Jason's, he would sing them a lullaby with his own nonsensical lyrics:

Good-night, moon,
See you soon.
That's the tune.
Daddy's croon.

Now, at West Point, in the gray drizzle, he stood on Trophy Point and contemplated how different that murmuring, affectionate Tom Carhart was from the obstreperous young man who had worn cadet gray or the combat soldier who had "killed and enjoyed it." It hardly seemed conceivable that they were the same person, and in many ways they were not. He much preferred this incarnation of himself. He exulted in the peace that this Tom had found, and the love that swelled inside him whenever he thought of his wife and sons. He had not won "the whole thing," but he had won a great deal.

Climbing into the car, Tom drove down Thayer Road toward West Point's main gate. If he hurried, if he left the academy right now, he could get back to Washington in time to bathe the boys and tuck them in and sing them his silly song. He could get home, where he belonged.

20

A Dark Wood

IF TOM CARHART had resembled a Hapsburg duke at the twentieth reunion, Jack Wheeler — impeccably dressed in a blue pinstripe suit, red silk tie, and polished black shoes — looked like a British banker. On the verge of his forty-second birthday, Jack was balder now, and the blond hair that remained had begun to gray. Yet friends could still glimpse the boyish towhead beneath those signs of middle age — particularly when Jack's sudden, shrill laugh erupted in the Hotel Thayer lobby or beneath the wainscoting of Washington Hall.

Characteristically, he had moved through the reunion festivities, as he moved everywhere, behind a relentless barrage of interrogatories. At the same Friday morning breakfast where Marcia Bonifas had reminisced about being a second lieutenant's wife, Jack walked up to the Officers Club podium to subject his classmates to the questions he had asked himself ever since he wore cadet gray.

In a voice Art Mosley had once called "that earnest tone," Jack asked, "What things are worth dying for? Is anything worth dying for? In the sixties, it became fashionable to wonder about these things, to wonder if anything was worth the price of your life." The audience shifted uneasily in their chairs, wary of this plunge into the metaphysical.

Then he offered his own thoughts on the matter. "I believe that, yes, there *are* things worth dying for. Of course there are. And it's because of love. Even being a soldier was an act of love."

As he left the podium, buoyed by his classmates' applause, Jack smiled wanly. But he returned to his seat and sat down without asking the other question that perplexed him even more now, perhaps because he was less certain of the answer: What things are worth living for?

Since 1979, Jack had lived in large measure to build and promote the Vietnam Veterans Memorial. That, too, had been an act of love, an undertaking that seemed worth living for. Yet now, having invested thousands of hours in seeing Maya Lin's wall completed, Jack thought of it as a nightmare. In constructing the memorial, he had come close to destroying himself.

As he had sensed in November 1982, the dedication of the wall had offered merely a respite from the controversy and recriminations. But while sitting on the dignitaries' platform on that glorious autumn day, contemplating miracles and grace, even Jack had not fully foreseen the pain that was yet to come.

He and Jim Webb had confronted each other in a final, ugly rupture. After the wall was dedicated, the two men had agreed to thrash out their differences over lunch. Jack arrived at the restaurant; Webb did not. Jack ate a bowl of soup and walked back to his office at the Securities and Exchange Commission, where he found a last-minute cancellation message. A few weeks later they both attended a reception for the Disabled American Veterans. "Why did you cancel the lunch?" Jack asked. "We've got to talk about these things."

But Jim Webb had been talking to Jack Wheeler for years. He'd had enough talk. As Jack later recounted the episode, Webb snapped, "You can either leave me alone or get a punch in the face." Jack retreated.

Ross Perot also continued to press his demands for an independent audit of VVMF's books. He hired the attorney Roy Cohn, who had gained infamy as Senator Joseph McCarthy's assistant during the red scare in the early 1950s. Cohn sent a letter to VVMF's lawyer, a 1966 Air Force Academy graduate named Terrence O'Donnell, who worked in the prominent firm of Williams and Connolly. Cohn notified O'Donnell that he had been retained to examine "what funds were raised and in what manner and on whose authority they were expended."

Several months later, the simmering questions about how the money had been spent caught the attention of a reporter for WDVM, the CBS affiliate in Washington. Carlton Sherwood, a former Marine who had seen action in the Dominican Republic and Vietnam, had won national acclaim as both a print and broadcast journalist with a nose for corruption. In probing VVMF's finances, Sherwood thought he had the makings of another explosive exposé; among other things, he discovered that Jack Wheeler's war record included disciplinary action — an Article 15 — for using a stolen jeep at Long Binh.

As Sherwood doggedly pursued the story, Jack thought he had better inform John Shad, chairman of the SEC, of the impending storm. "I used a hot jeep in Vietnam," he told Shad. The chairman smiled. "Don't ask me about the jeep I used in China," he replied. A short while later, Shad called back. "Jack, I've been thinking about what you're doing.

At a time like this, you feel that you don't have friends. Listen, you have friends. And this will pass."

Two days later, on Monday, November 7, 1983, the first of Sherwood's five planned segments aired on the evening news. VVMF, the reporter charged, "collected at least $9 million, yet spent less than a third of those contributions for construction of the memorial itself." Laden with innuendo, the report hinted at dark misdeeds.

Part two appeared the next night. Jack watched the segment in O'Donnell's tenth-floor office in the Barr Building on Farragut Square, two blocks from the White House. "At the helm of VVMF," Sherwood began as a picture of Jack flashed onto the screen, "is this man, John Wheeler. Since 1979, Wheeler has served as the organization's chairman . . . Army records show that after Wheeler graduated from West Point in 1966, he asked to be sent not to Vietnam, where 10 percent of his classmates gave their lives, but to Harvard, where he earned a master's degree in business. Records also show that he never served in combat, but was assigned to Army division headquarters at Long Binh as an administrative officer.

"Within several weeks of arriving in Vietnam in 1969, Captain John Wheeler became the subject of disciplinary action for misappropriation of government property. He was cited for 'conduct totally unbecoming an officer.' In 1971, with the Vietnam War at its height, he resigned his commission from the Army. As the chairman of the memorial fund, Wheeler can authorize expenditures of up to $5000."

When the report ended, Jack remained very quiet. O'Donnell thought he looked devastated, almost as though someone had struck him. At home that night, Jack wondered what to do next. He was shocked and then furious. Sherwood had all but accused him of being a thief. Elisa too was angry, not only at the aspersions cast at her husband, but also at the disruption the memorial had caused in the Wheeler household for the past four years.

Part three on Wednesday night showed Ross Perot complaining of VVMF that "nobody can get in, nobody can replace the directors, and nobody can look at the money." Tom Carhart, identified as a "highly decorated, twice-wounded Army officer," was even more intense: "If they've done nothing wrong, why not show the books? . . . If it comes out that they . . . misused money given by widows and orphans and people who were hard up, and they used it in ways other than they were legally allowed to use it, then I will feel that they have been slimy, treacherous, dishonorable, dirty people, and I won't rest until I see that things have been righted."

VVMF counterattacked forcefully. In a written rebuttal, Jan Scruggs accused the television station of libel, malice, and a "reckless travesty." Carlton Sherwood, the rebuttal charged, had ignored the satisfactory audits of VVMF's books that had been completed by Peat Marwick Mitchell and Company and the Internal Revenue Service. The station canceled the last portion of the series.

In May 1984, in an investigation triggered by the television reports, the General Accounting Office concluded that VVMF's financial dealings had been "proper" and that "management decisions were made in a prudent and cost-conscious manner."

"From the start," Jack said in a statement to the press, "the memorial fund operated with complete integrity and now we have proved it." To stave off a libel suit in the wake of the GAO vindication, the television station broadcast an extraordinary apology to Jack and the other VVMF officers, and donated $50,000 to the memorial's maintenance fund.

A few months later, in late 1984, Frederick Hart's statue was unveiled in Constitution Gardens. Hart's three bronze soldiers stood several hundred feet from the apex of Maya Lin's wall, heads cocked warily, as though emerging from a bamboo brake to discover this black apparition before them. The sculptor had taken great pains to achieve verisimilitude: insect repellent in a hat band; a dogtag tucked into the laces of a boot; the safety on an M-60 machine gun flipped to the on position. At last, the memorial was complete.

Jack's reputation had been restored by the GAO audit, and with the deeding of the memorial to the United States government, his role in VVMF became largely ceremonial. Yet he felt that his life was coming unraveled. He seemed destined to fling himself into worthy causes that paid nothing, dragged him away from his family, and exploded in controversy. In 1985, he volunteered to help Mothers Against Drunk Driving, an organization founded by Candy Lightner, a Sacramento real estate agent whose thirteen-year-old daughter had been killed by a hit-and-run drunk. In five years, MADD had expanded to nearly four hundred chapters with a $10 million budget. Jack found an enterprise that had grown too big too quickly, and was being legitimately criticized for spending too much money on fund raising and not enough on programs to combat drunk driving. MADD needed, Jack believed, "to become organizationally mature." In a bitter coup, MADD's board removed Candy Lightner as chairman and chief executive and replaced her with Jack. Lightner remained president and chief spokesman, but she angrily charged that the directors were out "to undermine me." Much of her ire was directed toward Jack.

The involvement with MADD placed further strains on Jack — and on Elisa. The years of turmoil had taken a heavy toll on their marriage.

The Wheelers had been through so much together — the anxiety of the twins' birth, the countless nights of keeping vigil at Katie's bedside, the unending furor over the memorial — all of which, Jack told a friend, "has been hell on Elisa." Sometimes he wondered why he couldn't concentrate on earning a living and tending to his family like an ordinary lawyer. Although Elisa was working as a priest at St. Columba's Church and he was earning $65,000 a year as secretary of the SEC, somehow they seemed to argue more frequently about money. Jack felt the distance between them inexorably widen, although he continued to deny the estrangement.

And then another woman entered his life. Her name was Linda Smith, a tall, slender blonde from San Diego, who was the sole heiress-apparent to the McDonald's fast-food empire, a fortune estimated at $600 million. Her mother, Joan, had divorced her first husband in the late 1960s and married a hustling entrepreneur named Ray A. Kroc; when Kroc died in January 1984, his widow inherited the McDonald's empire of seventy-five hundred restaurants in thirty-two countries. Among other possessions, the family also owned the San Diego Padres baseball team, of which Linda's husband, a former criminal defense lawyer named Ballard Smith, was now president.

Deeply moved by the Vietnam Veterans Memorial during a visit to Washington in April 1985 — she wept before Hart's sculpture, which she thought radiated the same ineffable sorrow as Michelangelo's *Pietà* in the Vatican — Linda had established an organization called Mothers Embracing Nuclear Disarmament. MEND, she hoped, could be patterned loosely after MADD. As she began gathering more information, Linda discovered that the chairman of the Vietnam memorial fund and the chairman-designate of MADD were the same person: Jack Wheeler.

Jack first talked to Linda on July 10, 1985, in a forty-five-minute phone call from his SEC office. She told him about MEND, the peace march she was organizing in San Diego's Balboa Park, and her emotional experience at the memorial that spring. He talked about VVMF, faith, grace, and C. S. Lewis. Jack, who often interpreted coincidence as the manifestation of the supernatural, was struck by the fact that Mrs. Smith had first visited the wall on April 16, the anniversary of Tommy Hayes's death if the International Date Line was taken into account. A few days later, while vacationing on Pawley's Island, he followed up their phone conversation with a fourteen-page letter.

In early September, they met face to face for the first time. Linda flew to Washington with a film crew to make a videotape for distribution to MEND chapters around the country. Part of the video would be shot at the wall. Jack secured permission from the Park Service for the taping, and agreed to appear on camera to discuss the memorial. The morning was already insufferably hot when, as arranged, Jack showed up in Constitution Gardens in his tan poplin suit, the unofficial summer uniform of the federal city. Linda arrived with her four young daughters in tow. In their pretty summer dresses, with their California tans, they reminded Jack of five flowers. After the taping was completed, he took them to the Hyatt Regency near his office for soft drinks and a salad. Then the Smiths flew home to San Diego and Jack returned to work at the SEC. Life resumed its usual routine except for one nettlesome development: Jack Wheeler was falling in love with Linda Smith, and she was falling in love with him.

For more than a year he tried to pretend that it wasn't so, that his marriage was solid, that his infatuation with Linda would pass. He tried to pretend until he could pretend no longer. His marriage, he confided to a friend in late 1986, was "dead." Although the breakup would be hard on his twins, he believed that it would be even worse to raise them in a home from which, as Jack described it, "love and mutual support had fled." He moved out, taking up temporary residence at the Watergate complex. As the Wheelers petitioned for divorce, so did Linda and Ballard Smith.

Jack began to spend more and more time in La Jolla, the beautiful coastal town north of San Diego where Linda lived. He believed that his work in the East was finished, that the moment to move on had arrived. The wall was now the most popular memorial in Washington. Thirty million visitors had come to pay homage already. Sometimes Jack imagined that the men whose names were inscribed in black granite had sent Linda Smith to him in tribute for his role in honoring the dead. "Wheeler's not exactly John Wayne," he imagined these spirits telling one another, "but he got the job done. Why don't we arrange to send this woman to him, to give him a little happiness?"

There was happiness, for a time. Jan Scruggs, who on several occasions had worried that Jack was close to a nervous breakdown, thought that his friend seemed content for the first time since they had met. After eight years at the SEC, Jack quit his job to work full time at the Center for the Study of the Vietnam Generation, a nonprofit organization he had founded the year before. In an office donated by the Smithsonian Institution, he devoted himself to raising money for the center and meditating on the cosmic questions that occupied him. Sixty million Americans formed what Jack defined as the "Vietnam generation, the richest and most powerful one percent of the planet." In describing the center's mission, he wrote, "We need an agenda for our stewardship of this country. We need to plan, not just four years into the future, but forty. What kind of world will we have made by the year 2030?"

Some friends thought this new venture was noble if quixotic; others thought it perplexing and even downright daffy. Typically, Jack had framed his personal search for answers within a grander quest on behalf of the entire generation. He had always been, as his father said, "a seeker of the stars." One journalist writing about the center noted that the Spanish philosopher José Ortega y Gasset had once described modern man as a being fabulously capable of creation but uncertain what to create; that apothegm could well have served to describe Jack.

In the spring of 1987, he moved to La Jolla. In his imagination, before fleeing west, Jack tossed a final salute to the 58,000 souls on the wall — as he had once privately saluted Tommy Hayes's name on panel 50E. In California, he settled into the empty house of an academic who was spending the term teaching at Harvard. Life in La Jolla was slower, sunnier, idyllic. Hummingbirds flitted through the orange and plum trees in the back yard, and morning thermals rising from Torrey Pines canyon scented the air with eucalyptus. Summer fog shrouded the Pacific headlands before burning off to reveal yet another perfect day. Jack studied for the California bar exam and contemplated writing several books. In the study, he carefully arranged his papers into seventy-six piles on the floor, each internally coherent and contributing to a larger chaos.

He spent most of his spare time with Linda, who lived nearby with her daughters. At a 1950s theme party to benefit the La Jolla County Day School, Jack bid $150 for the right to name a new street being built in the subdivision of Mira Mesa. He chose Thomas Hayes Lane. Later in the summer, he took Linda and the girls on a trip to West Point, where they strolled down Flirtation Walk and posed for pictures on the granite benches at Trophy Point that were inscribed with DIGNITY, DISCIPLINE, COURAGE, and the other soldierly virtues. He bought Linda a West Point miniature ring with the academy crest engraved on one side and the Wheeler family crest on the other. They set a date for their wedding, despite Joan Kroc's reluctance to accept this interloping suitor from Washington; for a processional hymn Jack selected "When Morning Gilds the Skies," which he could remember Tommy Hayes singing in his adjutant's bass as the academy choir marched into the chapel.

Then, abruptly, his happiness tottered and collapsed. A few weeks before the wedding, Jack balked. He loved Linda; unpretentious, committed, and good-humored, she was an extraordinary woman. But he had underestimated the tugs he felt from back east, tugs from his twins, his parents, his friends. The prospect of working as just another San Diego lawyer left him feeling flat and uninspired.

"Jack," Bruns Grayson told him, "you will never be satisfied doing *work* work. You need to do something you believe in. If you become rich, it will be purely incidental." Jack was also bothered by the number of young professionals in La Jolla who cared so much for affluence and private pleasures and so little for the commonweal. "In San Diego," another friend warned, "you'll be a battleship in a bathtub." Jack's impulse toward public service was no less forceful now than it had been when he stepped off the bus at the Hotel Thayer a quarter century before, although he was again confused over how best to commit himself. Capable of creation, he was uncertain what to create.

Remarriage, moreover, frightened him. He and Linda were about to wed only weeks after their divorces were final. The failure rate for second marriages, he knew, was very high. Had they thought this through sufficiently? Were they hurrying into something that they would regret? Perhaps, Jack told her, it would be prudent if he learned to live alone first, learned to be comfortable with himself, learned to *like* himself. After weeks of denial, bargaining, and anger — the fundamental stages of grief triggered by a loss — he and Linda agreed to break their engagement. Jack flew back to the East Coast, where he moved in with his parents in Aberdeen.

Suddenly, he was very tired, "ten years' tired," as he described it. The pain of his divorce, of forfeiting life with his children, of building the memorial — all of which had been temporarily held at bay by the joy of his California interlude — now came crashing down. Shortly after arriving home he slipped into a black depression, the deepest and most paralyzing despair of his life. He couldn't sleep, couldn't eat, couldn't think. While talking with friends, he would abruptly burst into tears, sometimes two or three times an hour. In his meditative writings, Jack had lauded the virtues of commitment and faithfulness. Now, he concluded, his life made a mockery of those precepts.

He had long doubted his ability to meet the iron standards of West Point's ideals. Now those perceived shortcomings seemed like damning deficiencies in his character. What was he doing? Where was he going? At the age of forty-three, he felt adrift and alone. Was pain, he wondered, the inevitable price for being too prideful, too full of himself? Lance Morrow, a friend and an essayist for *Time* magazine, reminded him of the opening passage in Canto I of Dante's *The Divine Comedy:* "In the middle of the journey of our life, I came to myself in a dark wood where the straight way was lost."

A few months after returning from California, Jack accepted a speaking invitation in Britain. In London on a crisp blue morning, he rented a car and drove north. Thirty miles beyond the city, he came to the double chimneys and hip roofs of the South Midlands village of Cranfield. It was here that his forefather, Thomas Wheeler, had lived a dozen generations ago before sailing to the Massachusetts Bay Colony in 1635.

As in his ancestor's day, Cranfield was still dominated by the parish church of St. Peter and St. Paul, with its lancet windows and red rooster weathervane crowning the square Norman tower. Colored light from a small stained glass window washed over the simple altar. A plaque near the arched doorway listed the forty-nine rectors of Cranfield in gilt lettering, beginning in 1133 with a priest listed simply as Geoffrey.

For an hour, Jack strolled among the canting headstones in the weedy churchyard. One corner of the yard had been reserved for victims of the Black Death. In another corner, he found a few Wheelers — a Lillie and an Isabel and a Leonard. One strain of Wheelers who remained in England rather than striking off for America, he learned, had become Cranfield's most prominent Quaker family. Jack wondered whether he wouldn't have been better suited to life here among the peaceful Society of Friends, rather than as the descendant of men who had emigrated to become soldiers in the New World.

Among the more recent gravestones stood several belonging to young men who had died in the Battle of Britain. One commemorated F. G. Harrington, whose marker read simply: "Pilot. Royal Air Force. 16th December 1940. Age 19." Another was inscribed: "Sergeant R. S. C. Lawson. Royal Air Force. 10th June 1940. Tread Softly, for You Tread on Our Dreams." Jack trod softly, and he wept.

Not long after returning home, he drove with his parents to a funeral at Arlington National Cemetery. Big Jack's roommate from the West Point class of January 1943, Jack Fontaine Dulaney of Greenville, Tennessee — nicknamed Dopey — had died at the age of sixty-seven. A champion boxer at West Point, Dulaney was known for his custom of solicitously hugging his battered opponents after each bout. The winner of a Silver Star and two Purple Hearts in Europe during World War II, Dopey Dulaney had been Jack's godfather.

Thirty classmates from '43 gathered at the grave site. Jack heard the familiar *thacka-thacka-thacka* of a military helicopter skimming over the Potomac. The honor guard stood at rigid attention with ceremonial M-14 rifles at the ready, the same weapon Jack had used during marksmanship training in Beast Barracks. I know that rifle, he thought, I know it the way I know my own hands.

Big Jack, his thick silver hair glinting in the sunlight, spoke at the grave. Although he had just turned seventy years old, his command voice carried across the headstones with the crisp authority of a young man.

"Dopey and I," he recalled, "met nearly fifty years ago in old E Company. It's no secret that he and the academic departments had their ups and downs. But there's one thing we all know about Dopey: he was one of the best soldiers in our class.

"He jumped into Normandy on D-Day. He was wounded and then, some days later, wounded again. His leg wound stayed with him all his life. He married the nurse who tended his wounds. All these years, he has been an important part of our class fellowship."

Big Jack's voice dropped to a raspy whisper. "He was a soldier's soldier. God will keep him."

The rifle squad fired three volleys. Jack scooped up two of the ejected brass cartridges and slipped them into his pocket as keepsakes, one for himself and the other for Big Jack. Yes, in the middle of his journey he was in a dark wood where the straight way was lost. But he would find his way again because, simply, that was what West Pointers did. They embraced their opponents after thrashing them senseless in the boxing ring. They spoke, even as septuagenarians, with impassioned conviction about duty and honor and country. And when they were lost, they pushed on until they were found.

Someday, Jack would speak at his father's funeral. He had occasionally wondered what he would say when that day came. Now he knew precisely: "He was a soldier's soldier. God will keep him." Dry-eyed, fingering the brass cartridges in his pocket, Jack walked briskly from the cemetery, leaving the dead behind.

In the fall of 1987, George Crocker also traveled through a dark wood, but, as usual, he knew exactly where he was.

The brigade command post — *his* brigade command post — lay in a pine thicket about fifty yards from the runway that had been seized the night before by the 82nd Airborne. Next to a communications truck, on a table jerrybuilt from plywood and 105mm ammunition crates, George studied a map labeled "Lake Istokpoga Region." The map showed the brigade's deployment through a swatch of swamp in south-central Florida, near the village of Avon Park. A few miles farther south was the town of Sebring, famous for its Grand Prix racecourse. But it was Sebring's airport, not the raceway, that held the commander's attention, for tonight his troops had orders to attack the control tower and kill or capture everyone inside. He studied the runway configuration, the taxi apron, and the arrangement of the airplane hangars. He contemplated the angle at which the moon would rise and the distance at which helicopter rotors would first be audible. He pondered fields of fire.

George's face was smeared with green "cammie" stick. His wrists were cross-hatched with red and blue Magic Marker ink, from leaning on the map. The silver eagle insignia of a full colonel — now blackened in camouflage — adorned his helmet. This exercise, codenamed Sand

Eagle, had gone reasonably well thus far, though nearly two dozen paratroopers had suffered assorted sprains and bruises in the jump at Avon Park. George had landed on the soft runway apron barely three feet from the concrete, a near miss for which his forty-four-year-old knees and back were grateful. The terrain was utterly flat, pocked with limestone sinkholes and meandering sloughs. To the southeast lay the ruins of Fort Kissimmee, an outpost from the Seminole Wars of the 1830s. The sloughs and sand creeks reminded George of Charlie Beckwith's Ranger camp at Auxiliary Field Seven in the Florida panhandle; the humidity and sparrow-size mosquitoes reminded him of Vietnam.

Under the Sand Eagle scenario, Florida had been transformed into two nations. Pinea, a struggling democracy friendly to the United States, occupied the northern half of the peninsula; Marcala, its Marxist southern neighbor, had abruptly mounted a hostile invasion across the Pinean border. Heeding Pinea's plea for help, the Americans decided to parachute behind the Marcalan lines and seize the airfield at Avon Park. B-52s from Texas and Louisiana, along with F-111s from Idaho, had feinted toward Cuba — Marcala's fellow traveler — before simulating bombing runs on central Florida. The bombers had flown more than a hundred sorties against Avon Park before George's troopers jumped, shortly after sundown. The Marcalan defenders — played by soldiers from the 10th Mountain Division, who wore black stocking caps and wrote 82ND SUCKS with red spray paint wherever they had the opportunity — had been routed. The world, or at least this imaginary world, was a little safer for democracy. Now all that remained before packing up and returning to Fort Bragg was the raid on Sebring. According to G2 intelligence reports, several senior Marcalan commanders would meet in the airport control tower at 2230 hours — 10:30 P.M. — for a strategy session.

Although the absence of live ammunition in Sand Eagle took some of the edge off, George was delighted just to be back in the field — "doing men things in a manly manner with other men," as his executive officer, Lieutenant Colonel Tim McMahon, put it. After a year at the Army War College in Pennsylvania, the Crockers had returned to Fort Bragg in the summer of 1987 — the seventeenth move George and Vonda had made in twenty-one years of marriage. They now lived in a spacious stucco house with a red tile roof near the Bragg parade ground. Their neighbors were the division's other colonels and generals, who lived in *their* spacious stucco houses with red tile roofs. A tidy sign on the corner lauded the YARDS OF THE MONTH.

Before addressing his soldiers at the change-of-command ceremony in October, George wrote himself a note: "Stay brief." He was. The

82nd Airborne Division's 1st Brigade — or, in the Army's regimental system, the 504th Parachute Infantry Regiment — comprised twenty-three hundred men divided into three infantry battalions and an artillery battalion. Roughly half the size of a Roman legion, the regiment had a distinguished heritage, which George studied assiduously. In World War I, the 504th fought at St. Mihiel, Lorraine, and the Meuse-Argonne. In World War II, it jumped on Sicily in July 1943 and, in September 1944, on Holland, fifty-seven miles behind the German lines. The regiment liked to call itself "Those Devils in Baggy Pants," an epithet found in the diary of a German officer who had opposed the 504th at Anzio.

William Westmoreland had once been the regimental commander, but George's favorite predecessor was Reuben H. Tucker III, West Point '35. According to one bit of lore, the paratroopers had been rowdy while storming through Italy, and Tucker had filled a footlocker with court-martial papers. After Anzio, or so the story went, General Mark Clark had told Tucker to be sure to dispose of his disciplinary problems. Tucker saluted and, while the 504th was sailing back to England in 1944, pitched the footlocker into the Mediterranean. His portrait hung in a place of honor just inside the door of the brigade headquarters.

George knew that this tour with the 82nd, his fourth, was likely to be his final command assignment with the division. Although many of his admiring classmates assumed that he would be promoted to brigadier general in another four or five years, the odds against that were about fifty-to-one. Even promotion to 06 — full colonel — was an achievement denied most of the class. Of the 179 men from '66 who remained in the Army, 46 were now colonels, 127 were lieutenant colonels, and 6 were majors. The class of '66 had come "into the zone" for O6 promotions that summer; those passed over were unlikely to rise any higher. The proportion of active-duty '66ers who would be promoted to full colonel — about four in ten — was exactly that of "promotable" lieutenant colonels in the Army as a whole; in other words, there was still no statistical advantage to being a West Pointer.

The politics of promotion had never held much interest for George and he rarely thought about it now. Having the good fortune to command a battalion and then a brigade in the 82nd was about as much luck as an infantry officer could hope for. George Marshall had once suggested in World War II that no regimental commander should be older than forty-five. If that was so, then George Crocker had made the cut by less than six months. His overriding ambition was to lead the 504th honorably and capably for two years; the future would take care of itself. Someday, perhaps he and Vonda would buy that ski lodge in Vermont or tour the country on a Harley or win the Pennsylvania lottery and retire in style.

In the two weeks between the time he took command of the brigade and the start of Exercise Sand Eagle, George had concentrated on getting to know his regiment. A battalion was considered the largest unit a commander could address with his unamplified voice; commanding a brigade was like steering a much larger and less responsive ship. The mass and momentum were awesome, but trying to change direction took time. He still had not met all of the company commanders, and so many lieutenants served in the regiment — seventy-five — that he would never get to know all of them. Two of his three infantry battalion commanders had been blooded in Vietnam, but their younger successors would probably lack that experience. The Army's combat expertise — once so vast that it wasn't uncommon to find soldiers who had fought in World War II, Korea, and Vietnam — was rapidly dissipating. Some lessons, such as the art of remaining cool amid the dead and wounded, would have to be learned all over again by the officer corps if and when the next war erupted.

Now, in the pine thickets of Avon Park, the next "war" was the nocturnal raid on Sebring. Planning began just before noon. The orders from division headquarters read: "The intent of this operation is to make a bold surgical strike to remove key C3 [command, control, and communications] assets, including high-level personnel." Ten Blackhawk helicopters had been assigned to the mission, sufficient to carry one paratrooper company.

At 12:40 P.M., division intelligence reported that the target was more complex than originally thought. In addition to occupying the control tower, the enemy had established a headquarters and a communications facility; the Marcalans also manned two 57mm antiaircraft guns near the runway. Among the enemy leaders expected to gather at the planning session were a brigade commander and possibly the Marcalan commander-in-chief. Intelligence also passed on a warning that the XVIII Airborne Corps commander, a three-star general, might be present as an observer.

With a dozen of his officers gathered around the map table, George scribbled some notes in a small loose-leaf book that he kept in his breast pocket. "Let's concentrate on the tower," he said after listening to the G2 report. "Easy in, easy out. I'd like us to be on the ground for no more than ten minutes. If they want to surrender, strip them down to their shorts, handcuff them, and sit on them.

"Unless," he added with a chuckle, "it's the corps commander. And there's a case of beer bounty for any soldier who can capture the enemy commander."

The discussions continued for three hours. Chewing on a pine needle, George walked around barefooted while his boots dried on a log nearby.

As his captains and majors put the finishing touches on the battle plan, he hovered at their elbows, silent except to ask an occasional question. An arriving officer interrupted the serious business at hand to report that the paratroopers had invented a sport called "cattle tipping": a soldier would sneak up behind a sleeping — albeit standing — cow, place two hands on its rump, and shove. The cow would topple nose first into the grass with a puzzled *mooo*. George roared with laughter at the image.

At four P.M., what the Army referred to as "real-world restrictions" suddenly complicated the brigade's planning. The city fathers of Sebring, alarmed at the prospect of dozens of heavily armed paratroopers storming across their airport, had placed the control tower off limits. "Burning pyrotechnics" were also proscribed, which meant that M-16 and machine-gun blanks would be permitted but no heavy ordnance. The meeting of Marcalan commanders, G2 reported, had been moved to a tent next to the airport runway.

At sunset, the raiding party gathered for a dress rehearsal. Under the plan, the Blackhawks would drop the soldiers six hundred yards from the target, retreat a mile or so to the north, and loiter until hearing the code word "red," the signal to pick up the raiders. One battalion commander pointed out that if the enemy tent was protected with triple-strand concertina wire, the raid would probably take longer than ten minutes. "Well," George advised, "it may be that your men will just have to kneel and hose down the tent, or else toss hand grenades inside."

The ten Blackhawks stood silently in single file near the old World War II hardstands at the Avon Park airstrip. Thirty yards from each helicopter, a dozen paratroopers waited on the dewy grass, slapping at mosquitoes. At precisely ten o'clock, the Blackhawk turbines erupted in a shrieking whirl of diesel exhaust. Then the heavy rotors began to crank. On signal, the paratroopers scrambled aboard in that awkward, running crouch so familiar in the age of the helicopter. George, whose call sign was Devil Six, climbed into the third Blackhawk as an observer. At ten-thirty, the Blackhawks lifted into the night and turned south in a procession of dark shapes and blinking red lights.

A huge three-quarter moon silvered the orange groves and karst lakes several hundred feet below. Chill night air blasted through the bays at ninety knots. Each paratrooper wore PVS-5 night-vision goggles under his Kevlar helmet. The heavy headsets positioned a four-inch cylinder over each eye, amplifying the ambient light so that the landscape glowed with a monochromatic, daytime brilliance. The Army considered the goggles so valuable that they were kept under lock and key when not in use, just like the troopers' M-16s.

At eleven, the raiders swooped onto the outer runway at Sebring. In the distance, they saw the black silhouettes of the forbidden control tower and hangars. As the Blackhawks touched down, paratroopers spilled from the helicopters and sprinted across the grass. Crimson muzzle flashes peppered the night. One platoon veered to the right, hunting — futilely, as it turned out — for the Marcalan communications center. Another platoon raced toward the darkened command tent.

Devil Six lingered in the rear. He sprawled in the wet grass, watching the action through his PVS-5. Ten yards in front of him, the company commander issued a steady patter of orders into his radio handset. The din of shouted commands, curses, and automatic weapons fire built to a frenzied crescendo and then began to ebb. An enemy machine-gun nest to the left fell silent. After ten minutes, the paratroopers began drifting back across the airport, and the flock of Blackhawks again swooped in after being summoned with the code word. Twenty minutes after the first shots were fired, the raid was over.

At best, the operation had been a mixed success. The paratroopers reported "killing" six Marcalan soldiers, including two women, in the command tent, where they also scooped up an armload of maps and documents. But the highest ranking officer shot was only a major. The intelligence reports had been wildly inaccurate. There had been no meeting of senior commanders, no communications center, no Marcalan general to strip, handcuff, and sit on. Had the intense antiaircraft fire been real, George calculated that his raiders would have lost at least two Blackhawks.

Nevertheless, the adventure had been good training for his troops. War, even make-believe war, was an inexact science. Nothing ever went precisely as planned. "Nine-tenths of tactics are certain, and taught in books," T. E. Lawrence had written. "But the irrational tenth is like the kingfisher flashing across the pool, and that is the test for generals." It could also be the test for colonels commanding a paratrooper regiment in the Florida sloughs.

Back at Avon Park, George met briefly with his battalion and company commanders. "Your first platoon gaggled around a bit when they couldn't find the commo site," he noted, "but I thought you did a good job on the plan-up. Have your men get some sleep."

At one A.M., he returned to the brigade command post. Twenty-five yards from the communications truck, George scooped together a bed of pine needles, careful to avoid the gray mound of a fire ant nest. Hollowing out a depression for his hips and shoulders, he spread a tarpaulin on the damp needles and wrapped himself in a blanket. Night sounds — crickets, an owl — were punctuated by men sounds — the distant hum of a diesel generator, a garbled shout from the deep woods.

A few feet away lay the dark fetal forms of a half-dozen sleeping paratroopers. Several of them were born the year George Crocker first went to Vietnam; he had been leading men in the dark of night when these soldiers were still in swaddling clothes. For a quarter of a century, since the class of 1966 marched out to Camp Buckner for its first sustained taste of Army life, he had been bedding down in woods like these. It was not the way most men, on approaching their forty-fifth birthday, would choose to make a living. But then that singularity, that sense of being called, had always been one of the attractions of military life. Maxwell Taylor was right: the Army, like the Church, was not for everyone.

Through the upper boughs of the pine trees, George could see the Big Dipper, washed pale by the brilliant moon. He had been blessed. Fate had steered him into a profession that perfectly suited his character and his talent. Fate also had spared him when, by all rights, he should have died a dozen deaths in shootings, booby traps, helicopter crashes, parachuting accidents, and God only knew how many other assaults on his mortality.

But why? To what end? The answer was easy. To snatch a few hours of sleep in a dark wood; to ponder the "irrational tenth" flashing like the kingfisher across a pool; to rise with the sun for yet another day of soldiering; "to maintain and defend the sovereignty of the United States"; to do men things in a manly manner with other men.

At 10:30 A.M. on October 4, 1987, the Reverend James D. Ford slipped from Quarters 60 into the West Point chapel through the sacristy passageway, just as he had on a thousand previous Sabbath mornings. Despite a freak autumn storm that had blanketed the Hudson Valley with snow and sleet, the chapel was packed. Ford walked briskly down the east aisle, hymnal in hand. Beneath the two-handed Crusader's sword crowning the main door, he took his place behind the cadet choir. The forest of eighteen thousand organ pipes burst forth with the processional, a hymn that was Ford's favorite:

The church's one foundation
Is Jesus Christ Her Lord.
She is His new creation,
By water and the word.

The choir moved slowly down the center aisle, four abreast in dress gray, legs swinging in slow cadence to the swelling voices of the congregation. The gloom outside — a reminder that winter was West Point's natural state — dulled the stained glass and the old flags unfurled in the triforium. As the hymn ended and the cadets shuffled into the choir pews, Ford settled back in his carved oak clergy stall. The chair felt comfortable, as though molded to his form by countless Sunday sittings.

Yet he was here not as the chaplain but as an invited guest. After eighteen years, Ford had left West Point in December 1978 to become chaplain of the U.S. House of Representatives. Politics had always intrigued him — "send your good men into the ministry but your best men into politics," he often quoted — and now he was immersed in "the art of the possible." His office, a crypt in the Capitol basement below the Rotunda, had once served as Henry Clay's hideaway. The room was walnut dark with a domed ceiling, a marble fireplace, and a sweet fragrance as of pipe smoke. On one wall, Ford kept a framed fragment of a prayer written in Swedish that had been handed down from his grandfather, and on his stout desk sat a coffee mug inscribed WEST POINT CLASS OF '66.

Ford's affection for the academy and the cadets had never slackened. But he had grown weary of the perpetual friction between his theology and West Point's precepts. A man who believed that life's cornerstone was the grace of unmerited favor — "when you're loved by God and don't deserve it" — would always be an odd duck in a place where everything that befell a cadet for good or ill was deemed deserved. Ford believed that, like many institutions, West Point had a propensity for confusing morality and religion. Year after year, he had battled all attempts to make the chapel a conservatory of moral instruction rather than a simple temple of worship.

His favorite parable was Luke's tale of the prodigal son. He likened morality to the parable's elder son, who dutifully obeyed the rules yet never understood the essence of his father's love. Religion was personified by the prodigal, who discovered the transcendent mystery of that love. "My dish isn't morality," Ford sometimes said; "it's religion."

Likewise, he privately thought that the much-venerated Cadet Prayer had become something of a period piece. Written in the 1920s, the prayer was, he believed, overly duty-bound, with too little stress on forgiveness and humility. Some of the language had become anachronistic, such as the plea for "clean thinking," or elitist, such as "encourage us in our endeavor to live above the common level of life." Finally, he wondered whether any group — cadets, clergymen, congressmen — should feel self-important enough to have its own prayer.

But Ford was gone and the Cadet Prayer was still recited at West Point, chiseled into a stone monument next to the chapel. In fact, the prayer was being murmured by the congregation on this snowy Sunday morning. Fifteen hundred voices intoned together, "Make us to choose the harder right instead of the easier wrong, and never to be content with a half truth when the whole can be won."

When the prayer ended, Ford was introduced by his successor, a rangy Baptist named Richard Camp. Rising from the clergy stall to stand at the pulpit, Ford rocked slightly on the balls of his feet, perfectly balanced as always. At the age of fifty-six, he had grown even more owlish behind his horn-rim glasses, and the surplice draped his thick frame like the robe in Rodin's masterly sculpture of Balzac. "The weather's a little nasty this morning," he began, eyes twinkling, "but it doesn't really bother me. I'm from Minnesota, where we have nine months of winter and three months of poor sledding."

For twenty minutes, he offered not so much a sermon as a reminiscence. The current cadet choir leader, he noted, was the son of the first cadet Ford could recall meeting at West Point in 1961. The scripture lesson from Matthew had been read by a cadet who was the daughter of the second couple Ford had married in the chapel, also in 1961. At a recent Founders Day banquet in Heidelberg, he added, "there were 830 people in the room, and when I asked how many I had married, 75 stood up."

He recounted sailing the Atlantic in the *Yankee Doodle* and being invited to Annapolis as a guest chaplain a few months after his voyage. "And when I was introduced," he recalled, "someone mentioned that I had just crossed the ocean. 'Yes,' I told the middies, 'I've just crossed the Atlantic, six thousand miles. To do it, I read six books, bought a small boat, and took two West Pointers with me. What do you midshipmen *do* here for four years?' "

As the cadets guffawed appreciatively, Ford laughed with them, that throaty *heh-heh-heh* that he saved for the times when he had gotten someone's goat.

After the service, after he had shaken the last of the many hands eager to greet him, Ford tarried in the empty chapel for half an hour. "There are so many memories," he had told the congregation, "that flood the mind at a time like this, in this place of blended beauty and strength."

So many memories indeed. There, near the main door, was where Ross Perot had placed his Stetson on a folding chair before playing "Anchors Aweigh" on the chapel bells. In the narthex was the spiral staircase where the outraged cadets had dragged Perot down from the loft and off to jail. Across the apse stood the baptismal font, where he had anointed so many squawling babies, including Buck Thompson's son, the Deuce. And set high above the nave on the west clerestory, in the window dedicated to the class of 1966, he spotted the stained glass visage of Saint Valeria. Ford still remembered the baccalaureate sermon he had preached when that window was consecrated. During the service, Paul's Epistle to the Ephesians had been read by Bob Luecke, who was killed in an ambush near Saigon less than two years later:

> Put on the whole armor of God, that ye may be able to stand against the wiles of the devil. For we wrestle not against flesh and blood, but against principalities, against powers, against the rulers of the darkness of this world.

Ford peered outside at the portico, now dusted with snow. Nearly twenty-four years before, he had stood there with Ted Speers on that terrible November afternoon, watching as scores of cadets trudged up the steps to pray for the soul of John Kennedy. Jim Ford had been a young man then. Wasn't everyone young in those days? he wondered.

Shrouded in a white bed sheet, he had played ghost in the chapel with his children, perhaps without realizing what a tabernacle of ghosts the place would become. *For we wrestle not against flesh and blood, but against principalities, against powers, against the rulers of the darkness of this world.*

As always when he visited West Point, Ford made a private pilgrimage to the cemetery before returning to Washington. He knew the nooks and crevices of this churchyard at least as well as he knew the Gothic crannies of the chapel. So much of his youth had been left in this hallowed ground. *The funerals aged us pretty quickly,* Choirmaster John Davis once said. Were Ford to call for an accounting of the dead, as he had called on Founders Day for an accounting of those he had married, how many shades would rise? He had lost track. Sixty or seventy funerals from Vietnam alone. Perhaps several hundred altogether.

For two and a half hours Ford strolled about, lost in meditation. White-tail deer often browsed boldly among the tombstones, oblivious of both the quick and the dead. The dogwoods and cherry trees were already flushed with autumn; soon enough, the yard would be entombed in deep snow. At Ted Speers's headstone he paused, prayed, and walked on, passing first Tommy Hayes's grave in Section VI and then the graves of Winfield Scott, Sylvanus Thayer, and George Custer. As always, the illustrious and the infamous slept side by side.

On the northern border, beyond the ornate pyramid housing Egbert Viele's sarcophagus, he paused again, by the simpler graves in Section XXXIV. No spot on earth was more sacred to him, no memories more precious. The names on the stones ran together like a lullaby, a benediction, an American haiku:

Booth. Bonifas. Brown.
Luecke. Hoskins. Rybicki.
Wilson. Lantz. Thompson.

I loved these men, Jim Ford thought. *I loved Peter Lantz. I loved Buck Thompson. I loved these men with all my heart.*

Afterword
to the Tenth Anniversary Edition

In serried ranks they find themselves deep in the back country of middle age. Nearly four decades have passed since they first reported to the man in the red sash on R-Day, that sun-splashed morning when God was in His heaven and all was right with the world—or at least the American world. More than thirty years have gone since they heaved their hats at the sky and bolted off to war. Today, clearly, they are on the gray side of the Long Gray Line: West Point has turned out more young officers since the class of 1966 graduated—about thirty thousand—than in the entire preceding 164-year history of the academy. Among the boys of '66, only the dead remain boys.

The reunions have continued apace—the twenty-fifth in 1991, the thirtieth in 1996—and it is at these ritual conclaves that they take their own measure and reaffirm the brotherhood. "To those of you with sagging chests, thick bifocals, balding pates, and pronounced limps: take ten, smoke 'em if you got 'em," an anonymous classmate wrote in a reunion publication in the early 1990s. "We've made fortunes and war; created companies, loving families, and the world's finest soldiers. We've lost classmates and wives, children and body parts. We've got millionaires and paupers, pompous asses and clowns. We've got killers and lovers, movers and shakers, thinkers and doers, the brave and the timid, the youthful and the aging."

The accidents of history have continued to mesmerize them—how they unwittingly straddled a fault line in the American saga. "We did not know," another classmate wrote, "that America would erupt in debate over every basic value in society, including the bond between country and soldier." Remedial swimmers assigned to the Rock Squad during plebe year could still recall instructor Robert Sorge ordering them away from the pool walls, as they thrashed about in fatigues, boots, and brick-laden backpacks. "There are no walls out there," Sorge had declared, and the admonition seemed enduringly apt.

Yet age and perspective brought a certain clarity. Some saw the class of 1966 as an avatar of other callow war classes graduated into combat—1848, 1861, 1898, 1917, 1941, 1950—and drew comfort from the lineage. Most would agree with classmate Jerry Cecil that "our experience as cadets, officers, and blood brothers is strengthened with each passing year as people discard the superficial and meaningless parts of their lives." And it seemed fair to assert that the values they hold dear, and the struggles they have joined individually and collectively, offer a prism through which one can consider what the nation holds dear. Certain themes run through the best of their history and the best history of the country like veins of ore: Duty, honor, country. Service, sacrifice, valor.

With the century drawing to a close, fewer than a dozen remain in uniform. The generation of officers who swore on June 8, 1966, to "maintain true faith and allegiance" has all but gone. Wesley K. Clark, the valedictorian and Rhodes scholar, fulfilled his great promise by becoming the four-star supreme commander of NATO. Freddy E. McFarren wore two stars as the commander at Fort Riley, after tours as an artillery brigade commander in the Persian Gulf War and as West Point's commandant. Robert H. Scales, Jr., was also a major general and commandant of the Army War College. John A. Dubia was a three-star lieutenant general as director of the Army staff; David J. Kelley, another three-star, ran the Defense Information Systems Agency, and Lieutenant General Edward G. Anderson III was the chief strategist for the Joint Chiefs of Staff. Roger G. Thompson, Jr., Robert R. Hicks, Jr., James B. Peake, Edward L. Andrews, Emmitt E. Gibson—each had become senior generals.

And George Crocker. Widely recognized as one the finest combat soldiers in the Army, George's ascension through the ranks continued apace. After leaving brigade command at Fort Bragg, he had commanded the U.S. Army in Panama and U.S. Special Operations in the Pacific before returning for a fifth tour with the 82nd Airborne—this time as commanding general. For a man as devoted to the division as George, the assignment fulfilled a dream he had never dared consider possible. In 1997, he received the third star of a lieutenant general and was given command of I Corps, the Army on the West Coast. With the three children grown, he and Vonda—now a black belt in karate—moved into the sprawling commanding general's mansion at Fort Lewis, Washington. They also bought a house in Choctaw, Arkansas, which awaited them whenever retirement came. For now, George focused on the task at hand, which after more than thirty years he had whittled down to a five-word phrase: "warfighting and care of soldiers."

Tom Carhart, as full of vigor and ambitions as ever, received his Ph.D.

in American history from Princeton University in June 1998. He titled his dissertation, "A Narrative History of African-American West Pointers in the 19th Century." The achievement, Tom suggested in a note to his classmates, meant "academic splendor still awaits you, even the stupidest of you from the lower third of the class." Tom had written two more books—*Iron Soldiers* and *Battlefront Vietnam*—before retiring as an Army civilian in 1997; he and Jan and their two sons moved to an affluent, leafy neighborhood in the Virginia suburbs of Washington, D.C. "I've got another twenty years or so of productive life," he declared. "I want to teach and write and do the Vietnam thing." The "thing" involved a project with classmates Sam Champi and Vince Casillo to build forty thousand low-cost apartments outside Ho Chi Minh City, one of the largest American business investments ever in Vietnam. A *New York Times* article on the enterprise in September 1998, quoted Tom: "You could say this is an accident, but it ain't no accident."

At the thirtieth reunion, Tom threw an arm around Jack Wheeler's shoulder. "I hope everything you do flourishes," Tom said. It was a reconciliation, of sorts. Jack, in fact, *had* flourished, in his own searching fashion. A hasty marriage in late 1988 was soon annulled by mutual consent. Jack would come to consider the late 1980s and early 1990s as his "burned-up period." He sought rejuvenation among Trappist monks in the Abbey of Gethsemani, in Kentucky, where he began to retreat annually for periods of solitude and prayer; he also helped confect thirty thousand fruitcakes, which the monks sold to help keep the monastery solvent.

With Jack, of course, there were causes and campaigns. For President George Bush, he ran the Earth Conservation Corps, a federal environmental initiative. He also was president of the Vietnam Children's Fund, a charity devoted to building new elementary schools in Vietnam, and he organized Beyond the Wall, which assembled a permanent exhibit at the Smithsonian Institution of artifacts left by mourners at the Vietnam Veterans Memorial. He was special counsel to the chairman of Macy's, during the department store's successful turnaround in the mid-1990s, and he helped build a memorial at Arlington National Cemetery to the victims of the terrorist bomb that destroyed Pan Am Flight 103. In June 1997, Jack became president of the Deafness Research Foundation and launched a national effort to conquer deafness, which, perhaps inevitably, offended many of those he sought to help by implying that they were impaired. He married Katherine P. Klyce, who had two grown daughters and lived in New Haven; Jack's own twins both chose colleges in the South, where they are scheduled to graduate in the year 2000.

Like many classmates he welcomed the resurgent national interest in World War II, in part because it implied eventual homage for Vietnam

War veterans; moreover, in Jack's estimation, "it affirmed that there are things worth dying for." On September 29, 1995, the feast day of St. Michael, patron saint of soldiers, Jack's father died. Big Jack was buried with honors at Arlington; the band played *Garry Owen*, anthem of the cavalry. Janet Wheeler survives him in Maryland. After the funeral, Jack removed his own class ring and took to wearing his father's, from the class of 1936.

Others flourished. Marcia Bonifas moved to Washington, D.C., and became director of customer service for TRICARE, the health care program for the uniformed Armed Services. Daughter Beth became a nurse practioner after a decade as a nurse, including four years in the Army; she also gave Marcia a grandson, Andrew Arthur. Brian married and became a firefighter in Fairfax County, Virginia. Megan graduated from Georgetown University and became news media director for the Houston Comets. Marcia's father, Peter McGuire, who had reluctantly surrendered his daughter's hand to Art, died in November 1998, at the age of eighty-eight, and was buried in Arlington.

Matt Harrison's harrowing experience with Wedtech left him with an enduring interest in moribund companies. He subsequently served as "chief restructuring officer" of a corporation that operated ski resorts and amusement parks. Other ventures included helping to manage a mail-order jewelry company, a nonprofit operator of schools and churches in the South Bronx, and a regional parking-lot company. With both daughters in college and Judy running an interior-design business, Matt in February 1998, became chief executive officer of the bankrupt bookstore chain Lauriat's, Inc., which he labored to make solvent. "It wouldn't be fun if it wasn't challenging, would it?" he told a friend.

Ron Cox, who had been Matt's roommate, became an appeals court judge in Washington State.

Norm Fretwell, the class first captain, returned home to his native Missouri and built a law practice in Kansas City.

Bill Haneke continued working in the Richmond health care industry for various hospitals, clinics, and managed care plans.

Jeff Smith, who had been Tom Carhart's classmate at both West Point and in law school, served for many years on the staff of the Senate Armed Services Committee and then as general counsel of the CIA, before joining a private law firm in Washington. He was instrumental, with support from Tom and others, in securing the nation's first posthumous presidential pardon, granted in February 1999 by Bill Clinton to Henry O. Flipper. Born a slave, Flipper became the military academy's first black graduate; but in 1882, he was convicted of racially tainted charges of conduct unbecoming an officer. Now, more than a century later, his name was cleared.

Art Mosley spent five years in Atlanta as the director of venue acquisition for the 1996 Summer Olympics; after returning to Key West for a final real estate development project, he moved to Washington in early 1999 to join his old Easy Deuce company mate, Jack Wheeler, as vice president of the Deafness Research Foundation.

Ron Bartek, who had testified about alleged war crimes on Capitol Hill, left the State Deparment for a six-year stint on the House Armed Services Committee staff before joining a private firm cultivating business opportunities in central and eastern Europe.

Tom Beasley, who served as best man at the Crockers' wedding, founded the hugely successful Corrections Corporation of America, of which classmate Doctor R. Crants, Jr. eventually became chairman.

Michael B. Fuller, who had ridden the train with Jack to New York from southern Virginia in July 1962, became president of local communications for Sprint, the telecommunications giant.

Tommy Hayes's obituary was published in *Assembly*, the academy alumni magazine, in time for the thirtieth reunion in 1996. General Hayes, who also was at the academy that spring attending the sixtieth reunion of his own class, had needed much time to draft the last word on his son. Tommy's name endured on the street in San Diego, on a Boy Scout camp in Nebraska, on a hall at the Army Engineer Center in Missouri, and on Hayes Gymnasium at West Point.

Jim Ford passed his twenty-first year as chaplain of the House of Representatives, another institution that sometimes confused religion and morality. At the age of sixty-seven he had taken up ultralight piloting, flying his own forty-horsepower aircraft over the Virginia countryside with other enthusiasts, dropping water balloons on targets far below. He continued to visit West Point routinely, always lingering at the cemetery. He still loves these men with all his heart.

No longer could West Point fairly be said to represent two centuries of tradition unhampered by progress. Change—gradual but relentless as the glaciers that carved the Hudson Valley—continued through the 1990s, as the academy adjusted to the end of the Cold War and to contemporary thinking about how best to build an Army officer. West Point contracted in the mid-1990s, from 4,400 cadets to 4,000, a reduction much more modest than the Army as a whole, which had shrunk by more than one-third. By 1999, the academy provided nearly one-quarter of all new lieutenants entering the Army, a far bigger share than at the peak of the Vietnam War when roughly one new butterball lieutenant in twenty was a West Pointer. That meant the academy had a proportionately greater impact on the officer corps; it was the acknowledged "wellspring of professional values" for the Army, as it had been during other quiescent periods in the nation's history. In a time of national emergency, West Pointers were to provide a cadre of martial competence and a requisite warrior ethic.

The academy's rigid math-and-engineering curriculum continued to evolve. Of the forty courses needed over four years to graduate, thirty-one are required for all cadets—evenly divided between mathematics, science, and engineering classes on one hand and humanities and social science classes on the other—reflecting the conviction that a modern officer should have a broad, liberal education. Cadets took another nine courses for a "field of study," or thirteen for an academic major. Hazing, now defined as "abusive and inappropriate leadership," was not tolerated. The corps had been restructured to more clearly reflect the Army hierarchy, with plebes officially known as cadet privates; yearlings were corporals, cows were sergeants, and all firsties became cadet officers. (And, for reasons unknown, the term "yearling" vanished from the barracks, replaced by "yuk.") Privileges expanded—drawing more howls of outrage from the Old Grads—with cadets allowed to own cars in their third year and to have telephones in their rooms. Those twenty-one or older could even drink alcohol in Eisenhower Hall.

"More important than what has changed is what has *not* changed. And what has not changed is a set of core values that a George Crocker or a Wes Clark would recognize," said the current superintendent, Lieutenant General Daniel W. Christman, who graduated first in the class of 1965. "Those things will endure here."

Racial and gender diversity in the corps increasingly reflected diversity in the Army and in the country. More than 9 percent of the academy's bicentennial class of 2002 was African-American, the highest proportion of any West Point class ever, and more than one cadet in five was a minority of some kind. (The Army in 1999 was 27 percent black and 60 percent white.) Women accounted for 15 percent of the corps. No longer were they considered curiosities—or monstrosities—as in the 1970s; Kristin M. Baker, the daughter of a '66 graduate, was selected as the academy's first female first captain for the class of 1990.

The academy continued to draw roughly ten applicants for every position; about 80 percent of those who survived cadet basic training—née Beast Barracks—held on to graduate four years later. The honor system remained paramount, but clearly with shades of gray. The academy no longer assumed that neophytes arrived with a sense of honor in full flower; integrity was taught, robustly, and honor violators were subject to a broad range of punishments, including penance as an enlisted soldier in the Army for a year. Honor jurisprudence continued to kindle inflamed debate, including, most recently, the question of whether cadets who borrowed things without asking were thieves or just boors.

Keen to divine formulas for success, the Army scrutinized its young officers relentlessly. Such studies in the 1990s showed that West Pointers did uncommonly well within the officer corps, scoring significantly higher than average in securing exemplary efficiency reports, early promotions, and command positions. More troubling was the retention rate. The traditional tendency of West Point graduates to remain in the Army longer than non–West Pointers had eroded to the point that they were now *less* likely to stay once their five-year obligation expired. About 40–45 percent of graduates from the academy classes of the mid-1960s had stayed in the Army for at least twenty years; for the classes of the mid-1970s, that slipped to 30–35 percent. For the classes of the 1980s the Army now could project that only 25 percent or so were likely to remain in the service for twenty years. Factors included a booming economy, which offered lucrative civilian jobs to those with West Point credentials, as well as the increasing number of working spouses and the concomitant difficulty of juggling the life of an Army nomad with a spouse's career. Pay and living standards for young officers had eroded, too. One study found that a captain in the early 1980s could expect military housing that provided him roughly the same living space enjoyed by his typical civilian contemporary; by the late 1990s, however, a captain's living space averaged less than half that of a civilian peer.

Perhaps most perplexing to the academy's stewards was how to preserve the bond between the military and the broader republic at a time when the two cultures had again drifted apart. "We always have a problem, historically, when an institution like the Army becomes so isolated that it begins to look inward rather than outward. It can tend to think too highly of itself," said Colonel Kerry K. Pierce, director of West Point's policy, planning, and analysis office. "The worst thing an army can do in a democratic society is think that it's better than the society it is sworn to protect."

Few American institutions had changed as much in a decade as the United States Army. If the Army's core values were of a piece with an earlier time—and the basic writ was still to fight and win the nation's wars—little else remained unaltered. The force had shrunk from 770,000 when the Berlin Wall fell to 474,000 as the century drew to a close. That contraction brought the most radical restructuring in a generation.

Within five years after German reunification in 1990, for example, the Army in Europe bore little resemblance to the force that had occupied the continent for half a century. The ranks in Europe dwindled from 213,000 to 62,000, including a three-quarters reduction in combat battalions. An Army that for decades considered itself "forward deployed"—troops weren't going any further—was stunned to find

European bases serving as launch pads for missions in Africa, Asia, the Balkans, the Middle East, and eastern Europe. In 1998, Army contingents operated in eighty-three countries. And within this welter of post–Cold War change, the military fought one major war—in the Persian Gulf—and several brushfires, in places as improbable and diverse as Panama and Somalia and Bosnia and Kosovo.

Officers junior and senior worried about "mission creep," the transformation of the Army into a go-anywhere, do-anything expeditionary legion. Soldiers were expected to be proficient in warfighting, peacekeeping, peace enforcement, counterinsurgency, drug interdiction, humanitarian assistance, counterterrorism, and WMD (weapons of mass destruction) antiproliferation. As one senior general put it, "We don't have the luxury of hanging a sign in front of the Pentagon that says, 'We only do the big ones.'" The demands on officers and enlisted troops, with frequent deployments and reductions in combat training, contributed to what the Pentagon called "personnel turbulence." By 1999, with the nation's economy booming, the Army faced severe recruitment shortfalls; fewer junior officers, moreover, believed they could count on the service for a guaranteed twenty-year career with a decent pension. Peace had often been curiously hard on the Army, and this peace—at the end of the millennium—had its own unique difficulties.

For nearly all the men in the class of 1966, such challenges of officership no longer fall to them. They are simply citizens, not soldiers. Their fight has been fought. They are left, as Jerry Cecil recently wrote to his classmates, with "an unparalleled camraderie forged in good times and bad, friendships made and interrupted by death, bonds of marriage that became stronger after each test, and a family of dear friends that will sustain us through the next phase of our lives. We stand by what we did, and we did it well."

Of the 579 cadets who graduated in June 1966, 48 have passed, including the 30 killed in Southeast Asia. Far fewer died in the nearly three decades since America pulled out of Vietnam than perished during their relatively brief stint in harm's way. For those who survived, the odds of living to middle age and beyond were excellent. Wars are like that.

Rick Atkinson
Washington, D.C. June 1999

Author's Note

This book is largely the result of interviews, beginning in June 1981 and ending in February 1989, with approximately two hundred people, some of whom consented to as many as fifteen or twenty separate sessions. My debt to them is matched only by my gratitude. The West Point class of 1966 as a whole was unstinting in its cooperation and enthusiasm for this project. Members of the class fed, housed, transported, humored, and otherwise indulged me with extraordinary generosity. In this regard, I am particularly indebted to Marcia Bonifas, Tom and Jan Carhart, George and Vonda Crocker, Jim Ford, Norm Fretwell, Mike Fuller, Matt and Judy Harrison, Mac and Cathy Hayes, and Jack Wheeler. From the bottom of my heart, I thank them.

Writing a narrative that spans twenty-five years of recent American social history is a tricky business. Perhaps the most lucid summary of the perplexities involved was written by Arthur M. Schlesinger, Jr., in his Foreword to *A Thousand Days:* "The reconstruction of past events is exceedingly difficult, if not impossible; and, when I have been confronted by diverging judgments and memories, I have had no choice but to consider the evidence as best I could and draw conclusions on my own responsibility."

Memories slip and shade, recollections differ drastically even among eyewitnesses. I have attempted to re-create the past as faithfully as possible. All characters in this book are real; the names of only a few minor figures have been changed, none of them West Pointers. Whatever dialogue is used is based on the account of at least one direct participant. For the sake of narrative continuity, I have recounted several events in a sequence that is slightly altered from their actual chronology. Although a great many people helped me by donating their time, memories, and expertise, any shortcomings are entirely my own responsibility.

The United States Military Academy provided invaluable assistance and cooperation. Among those I wish particularly to acknowledge are Lieutenant General Dave Richard Palmer, the superintendent; Kenneth W. Hedman, chief librarian; Marie Capps, Suzanne Christoff, and Dorothy Rapp of the library's Special Collections Department; Richard P. Butler and Robert F. Priest of the Office of Institutional Research; Andrea Hamburger, Colonel Jack Yeagley, and Lieutenant Colonel Bruce K. Bell of the Office of Public Affairs; and the staffs of *Assembly* magazine and the *Register of Graduates*.

The Kansas City Times, my former employer, encouraged my pursuit of this project when it was only an inchoate idea for a newspaper series. Particular thanks to the publisher, James Hale; the former editor-in-chief, Michael J. Davies; and the former managing editor, Chris Waddle.

The Washington Post, my current employer, generously granted me the time and freedom to write this book. Thanks to Benjamin C. Bradlee, Leonard Downie, Jr., Robert G. Kaiser, Dan Balz, Bob Woodward, Charles R. Babcock, and head librarian Jennifer Belton.

Among the Army's officers and civilian employees who have been particularly helpful: Lieutenant Colonel Rick Kiernan and Major Mike Nason, of the XVIII Airborne Corps and 82nd Airborne Division Public Affairs Offices respectively; Colonel Anthony F. Caggiano and Jim Kelly of the Public Affairs Office at the U.S. Army Training and Doctrine Command, Fort Monroe, Virginia; Colonel Bill Smullen and Lieutenant Colonel Greg Rixon of the Army's Public Affairs Office at the Pentagon; Colonel James N. Hawthorne, Jr., of the U.S. Army War College in Carlisle, Pennsylvania (and later, of West Point); Steve Moore of the Public Affairs Office at Fort Benning, Georgia; Lieutenant Colonel Andrew Dulina and Captain Charles Aycock of the 1st Special Operations Command Public Affairs Office at Fort Bragg; Betty C. Van Sickle, reference librarian at the Infantry School, Fort Benning; Janet Wray of the Fort Leavenworth Public Affairs Office; and Geraldine Judkins of the U.S. Army Center for Military in Washington. I have a special affection for the officers and men of the 504th Parachute Infantry Regiment at Fort Bragg, "Those Devils in Baggy Pants."

Thanks also to Henry Mayer, assistant branch chief of the Military Field Branch at the National Archives; David Wigdor and Ronald Wilkinson of the Manuscript Division of the Library of Congress; Paul G. Dickhaut, superintendent of the Massachusetts Correctional Institute at Lancaster; Shirley Job, librarian of *The Boston Globe;* Evan Thomas, Washington bureau chief of *Newsweek* magazine; and attorney Richard Heller.

My researcher, Michelle Hall, showed exceptional patience and ingenuity in pursuing a thousand arcane details. Janet Thompson spent hundreds of hours transcribing interview tapes.

Michael B. Fuller, West Point '66, first alerted me to the powerful epic that was the story of his classmates. Colonel Rance Farrell, also West Point '66, was kind enough to read the manuscript and offer valuable suggestions.

Particular thanks to my friend and agent, Rafe Sagalyn, an unflagging supporter of this project from the beginning.

The term "born editor" is regrettably overused; that accolade would best be reserved for a man like John Sterling, the editor-in-chief of Houghton Mifflin, whose extraordinary intelligence, talent, and enthusiasm are reflected on every page.

My manuscript editor at Houghton Mifflin, Frances Apt, improved my work in a thousand ways, large and small, for which I am deeply grateful. I also appreciate the care lavished by Marie B. Morris, assistant editor, and Rebecca Saikia-Wilson, manuscript editing supervisor.

Finally, I would like to thank my father, who demonstrated through twenty-eight years of service in the Army officer corps that West Pointers have no monopoly on the virtues of duty, honor, and country.

INTERVIEWS

Robert H. Albright; Edward G. Anderson III; Virginia Stuart Anderson; Eugene D. Atkinson; Kristin Baker; Blaine Ball; Ronald J. Bartek; Samuel W. Bartholomew, Jr.; Thomas W. Beasley; Lester E. Bennett; Sidney B. Berry; Marcia Bonifas; Thelma Bonifas; Charles C. Boyce; G. C. Brunnhoeffer III; John C. Buczacki; Francis Richard Callahan; Richard Camp; Jan Carhart; Thomas M. Carhart III; Kenneth G. Carlson; Gerald T. Cecil; Mark A. Centra; Wesley K. Clark; Stephen D. Clement; Frank C. Cosentino; Michael K. Collmeyer; Sean Corrigan; Ronald E. Cox; Danny L. Crawford; Robert J. Cresci; Adele Crocker; George A. Crocker; Vonda Crocker; Thomas J. Curley; James M. Daly, Jr.; Charles D. Daniel; John Davis; Michael S. Davison; Chris Detoro; Larry R. Donnithorne; Robert W. Doubek; J. Gary Droubay; Andrew Dulina; Carroll Hilton Dunn, Jr.; John S. DuVall; Michael Easterling.

Henry R. Farrell; Susan Farrell; Celia FlorCruz; James D. Ford; Joseph P. Franklin; A. D. Frazier; Billy W. Frazier; Norman E. Fretwell; Michael B. Fuller; William B. Fulton; John T. Gatesy; Brad Gericke; Holly Getz; David Goldie; Alan Goldstein; Richard V. Gorski; Philip W. Gray; Bruns Grayson; Janice Grice; Kenneth R. Grice; Norman E. Gunderson, Jr.; Robert Hammond; Mary Haneke; William G. Haneke; Glen M. Harnden; Anne Harris; Judith Harrison; Matthew C. Harrison, Jr.; Franklin Y. Hartline; Cathy Hayes; James M. Hayes; Thomas J. Hayes III; Bruce B. Hedrick, Jr.; Morris J. Herbert; Robert R. Hicks, Jr.; Theodore P. Hill; John G. Hoffman; Kelso Horst; William F. Hughes; Michael W. Hustead; Russell W. Jenna, Jr.; Edward P. Kane; Chester E. Keith, Jr.; Susan P. Kellett-Forsyth; Tom Kelly; John S. Kelsey; Robert H. Kesmodel; Howard C. Kirk III; Richard D. Kline.

Cheryl Lau; Lanse M. Leach; Sharon Leach; Ronald Leonard; Peyton F. Ligon III; Arthur F. Lincoln, Jr.; Alfred A. Lindseth; Jon W. Loftheim;

David F. Martin; Myres McDougal; Richard J. McDowell; Freddy E. McFarren; Craig McGinnis; Kenneth McGraw; William R. McKinney; John T. McKnight, Jr.; Randall P. Medlock; Michael C. Mewhinney; Arthur C. Mosley, Jr.; Arthur G. Mulligan; Daniel Mulligan; Richard N. Murray, Jr.; Alan B. Nason; Garner M. Nason; George E. Norton III; Patrick V. O'Donnell; Terrence O'Donnell; Lee D. Olvey; William S. Otto; Dave R. Palmer; Robert D. Paulson; James B. Peake; H. Ross Perot; Brad Pippin; Walter S. Piskun, Jr.; Richard Potter; Richard E. Radez; Robert B. Ramsay; Harry G. Rennagel, Jr.; William C. Rennagel; Donald A. Renner; Glenn F. Rogers, Jr.; Susie Rogers; Martha Roseborough; Morgan G. Roseborough, Jr.; Pierce A. Rushton, Jr.

Malcolm Schaefer; Jan Scruggs; Fran Seaman; Robert E. Seger; Robert N. Seigle; Tracy Seymour; Sidney Shachnow; Ed Shirron; Thomas C. Shull; Michael B. Silliman; Stephen L. Singer; Alfred J. Sirutis, Jr.; Claudia Smith; Jeffrey H. Smith; Linda Smith; F. William Smullen; Donald J. Soland; Robert W. Spanogle; Richard G. Stilwell; Carl W. Stiner; Harry G. Summers, Jr.; Gregory A. Stone; Joseph S. Stringham III; Armand Therrien; Douglas S. Thornblom; John C. F. Tillson IV; Walter F. Ulmer, Jr.; George B. Utter III; James Wallace; Lee Walters; John M. Wattendorf; John W. Weatherford; James Webb; William L. Weihl; A. Clark Welch; William C. Westmoreland; Janet Conly Wheeler; John P. Wheeler, Jr.; John P. Wheeler III; Leigh F. Wheeler, Jr.; Robert Wheeler; Lee Ann Wilson; Piers M. Wood; Edgar Wright III; John P. Yeagley; Robert G. Yerks; Joseph C. Zengerle III.

Notes

Prologue and Chapter 1. Beast

Through the generosity of the Military Academy and the class of 1966, I was able to attend the class's twentieth reunion in 1986, as I had attended the fifteenth reunion in 1981.

The original Penn Station is described in an article by Carter Wiseman, "You Must Remember This: Penn Station," in *New York.*

Profile material of the class of '66 is drawn from studies compiled by West Point's Office of Institutional Research, particularly E. B. Piccolino's "Comparative Report on Selected Characteristics of Entrants to the USMA and Entrants to Four-Year Colleges Nationally."

The thumbnail sketch of the 1950s is drawn from William Manchester's *The Glory and the Dream: A Narrative History of America, 1932–1972.*

Throughout this book, for details regarding the academy's history I have drawn on Stephen E. Ambrose's *Duty, Honor, Country;* Thomas Fleming's *West Point: The Men and Times of the Military Academy;* Sidney Forman's *West Point: A History of the United States Military Academy;* and Russell F. Weigley's *History of the United States Army.*

An exceptional account of Benedict Arnold's treason can be found in Dave R. Palmer's *The River and the Rock.* Douglas MacArthur's arrival at the academy in 1899 is described by William Manchester in *American Caesar.*

Details about the history of drill are found in FM 22-5, "Drill and Ceremonies," published by the Department of the Army. I am also endebted to Sergeant Major Patrick V. O'Donnell of West Point for further assistance on this subject.

Evelyn Nesbit as the possible model for *Fame* is mentioned in *West Point Today* by A. C. M. Azoy and Kendall Banning. The description of Richard Stilwell's "trust in authority" comes from Neil Sheehan's *A Bright Shining Lie: John Paul Vann and America in Vietnam.* Stilwell's gaze and work habits are described by General Bruce Palmer, Jr., in *The 25-Year War.* Faulkner's visit to West Point is described by *The New York Times* of April 21, 1962. John

Kennedy's graduation address is printed in "Administration of National Security, Selected Papers," published by the U.S. Government Printing Office in 1962.

Eisenhower's comment about the "bewildered" Army is noted in A. J. Bacevich's *The Pentomic Era.*

The Roman *sacramentum,* or soldier's oath, is mentioned by John Keegan in *The Mask of Command.*

The description of Leslie Groves as a "sonovabitch" is contained in Richard Rhodes's *The Making of the Atomic Bomb.*

MacArthur's valedictory speech is described by Manchester in *American Caesar.* The full text of the speech is printed in *Bugle Notes,* the so-called plebe bible issued to each new cadet.

The disproportionate influence of rural Southerners on the Army is outlined by Morris Janowitz in *The Professional Soldier.*

Eisenhower's quip about taking "the next train out" is cited in *School for Soldiers: West Point and the Profession of Arms* by Joseph Ellis and Robert Moore.

Patton's remark about a three-minute accumulation of yeas and nays is noted in *The Challenge of Command* by Roger H. Nye (who was one of Jack Wheeler's instructors at West Point).

Chapter 2. Year of the Tiger

The various clothing flags are described in *West Point Today* by Azoy and Banning. Fleming describes the runt-flanker tradition in his *West Point.* Project Equality is mentioned in John P. Lovell's *Neither Athens Nor Sparta?*

The account of the horse auction in 1947 is drawn from Lovell. The account of George Patton weeping as his men stacked their sabers is drawn from Janowitz's *The Professional Soldier.*

Details about the Wheeler clan's history are drawn from a genealogy compiled by the family. Other details come from Allen French's *Old Concord;* Dickson J. Preston's *Talbot County: A History;* and Townsend Scudder's *Concord: American Town.* Nye, in *The Challenge of Command,* describes the yellow scarves and tanker boots of armor officers.

Some details about the curriculum are drawn from West Point catalogues published in the early and mid 1960s. For historical data about the academy's academic regimen I have used Ambrose's *Duty, Honor, Country,* and Fleming's *West Point.* The former is the source for the anecdote about the arrest of the would-be math wit; the latter is the source of the Horace Mann quote and the description of instructors in their swallowtail coats. Other useful sources are *School for Soldiers* by Ellis and Moore, and Forman's *West Point.* Charles W. Eliot's attack is noted in Manchester's *American Caesar.* "The complete freedom of choice" exercised by cadets in selecting their lot — a statement made by Colonel James W. Green, Jr., chairman of the electricity department — is quoted in Lovell, as is Gar Davidson's "blood was drawn" witticism. "The best school" quote from Andrew Jackson is cited in *The Best School in the World* by James L. Morrison, Jr.

The overhaul of the curriculum under Davidson was reported in *The New York Times* on August 23, 1959.

Historical information about the cadet uniforms comes from exhibits in the academy museum and Weigley's *History of the United States Army*.

The sliding scale of demerits for exhaustion is noted in *West Point Today* by Azoy and Banning. Fleming mentions the Black Hole of Calcutta in *West Point*.

Statistics on minority cadets are from a June 1974 article in *Assembly*, the academy's alumni magazine. James Smith's ordeal in cleaning up tobacco spittle is noted by Fleming. Flipper documented his own ordeal in *The Colored Cadet at West Point*. General Davis's comment about "silent friends" was quoted in a United Press article on June 5, 1987.

The Army's description of blacks having "less developed mental capacities" is quoted in George H. Walton's *The Tarnished Shield*. Two studies by the Office of Institutional Research were particularly useful: "An Overview of the Success of Negro Cadets at West Point," in October 1969; and "Survey of Negro Graduates: One Hundred Years of Blacks Among the Gray," in July 1971.

General Westmoreland in an interview described his cemetery encounter with MacArthur; he also mentions it in his autobiography, *A Soldier Reports*, which is the source for some of the details about his background. His speech to the class of '64 is noted in Lovell's *Neither Athens Nor Sparta?* and Ivan Prashker's *Duty, Honor, Vietnam*. Westmoreland's hiring of Paul Dietzel is described in *School for Soldiers* by Ellis and Moore; the general also discussed the episode with me.

Chapter 3. Year of the Rabbit

The account of the corps marching to Boston to hear John Quincy Adams, as well as many other useful bits of history, is in a 41-page booklet, published by West Point, entitled, "Fourth Class Knowledge: History, Legends, and Traditions of the Corps." Summer encampments in Gilbert and Sullivan uniforms are described by Fleming in *West Point*, as is the overhaul of training that took place in World War II. The background on Sergeant F. D. R. Smith comes from the Middletown (New York) *Times-Herald Record* of August 23, 1965.

For details on the Army during and after World War II, I have relied on two comprehensive books by Russell F. Weigley, *The American Way of War* and *History of the United States Army*. A useful, succinct account of ROAD and other aspects of the postwar Army is Robert A. Doughty's essay "The Evolution of U.S. Army Tactical Doctrine, 1946–1976," published by the U.S. Command and General Staff College. Bacevich describes the atomic cannon in *The Pentomic Era*.

The suggestion to convert the Army to a home guard civil defense force is described by Harry G. Summers, Jr., in *On Strategy: A Critical Analysis of the Vietnam War*.

Janowitz in *The Professional Soldier* describes the extraordinary expansion of the officers corps in World War II.

Washington's comment about an "army of asses" is quoted in Kenneth W. Rapp's *West Point: Whistler in Gray and Other Stories*.

Neil Sheehan's assessment of "the senior leadership of the American armed forces" is on page 285 of *A Bright Shining Lie.*

Athletics at West Point are described by Fleming in *West Point.* The behavior of Taylor Locke and Bobby Knight was described to me most vividly by Bob Seigle and Richard Murray, both of whom played on West Point's basketball team.

The account of the World's Largest Blind Date is drawn from various newspaper clippings in the 1963 scrapbook maintained by the USMA Library.

Chapter 4. Year of the Dragon

Details about the history and architecture of the West Point chapel come from *The Cadet Chapel* by George S. Pappas. I am also endebted to the Reverend Richard Camp for a tour of Quarters 60 and to John Davis for arranging my visit to the chapel belfry and parapet.

The War Department order notifying cadets of Lincoln's death is described by Forman in *West Point.* Details of the academy's ceremony mourning John Kennedy are described in the *Newburgh Evening News* of November 23, 1963.

The friction between Army and civilian chaplains over West Point is noted in Roy J. Honeywell's *Chaplains of the United States Army.* For other details about the history of religion at the academy I have referred to Ambrose's *Duty, Honor, Country;* Lovell's *Neither Athens Nor Sparta?;* Fleming's *West Point;* and Forman's *West Point.* The Episcopal leanings of the Army are noted by Janowitz in *The Professional Soldier.*

MacArthur's funeral is elegantly described by Manchester in *American Caesar.*

The concept of the Good Bad Boy in American mythology is that of Leslie Fiedler; see, for example, "Good Good Girls and Good Bad Boys" in *Love and Death in the American Novel.*

The escapades of Jefferson Davis, E. A. Poe, and J. M. Whistler are from Fleming's *West Point.* More details on Poe are in an article in the Middletown *Times-Herald Record* of January 1, 1966.

The belief that cadets' milk was spiked with saltpeter is mentioned by Dale O. Smith in *Cradle of Valor.*

Lucian K. Truscott, in his novel *Dress Gray,* amusingly describes the cadet fondness for "rack."

Thayer's efforts to keep the cadets on the academy grounds is mentioned in Ambrose's *Duty, Honor, Country.* The practice of wagering on whether a cadet could get to New York and back between roll calls is described in Fleming's *West Point.* Manchester notes MacArthur's foray to Rector's in *American Caesar.*

A concise history of "West Point's First Captains," written by Robert J. Nicholson, appeared in the winter 1970 issue of *Assembly.*

Jim Ford was convinced that the chief chaplain's job would go to Arie D. Bestebreurtje, a prominent Louisville clergyman who later drowned after falling through the ice while skating on a reservoir near Charlottesville, Virginia.

The account of the posthumous medal awarded to Spruill is drawn from the New York *Herald Tribune* of October 15, 1964.

Chapter 5. Year of the Horse

Janowitz in *The Professional Soldier* notes the general lack of correlation between class standing at the academy and achievement in the Army.

Sources of commissioning for new lieutenants who entered the Army in 1965 and 1966 are listed in an August 1984 memorandum compiled by the Office of Institutional Research, "Battalion/Brigade Commanders by Source of Commission."

The up-or-out policy adopted after World War II is described by James Fallows in *National Defense.* The promotion pyramid is described in the 1966–67 edition of *The Officer's Guide.*

Ambrose, in *Duty, Honor, Country,* describes the origins of the four-year obligation in 1838.

Nuances regarding the Year of Fire and the Horse can be found in *The New York Times* of January 15, 1987. Saint Valeria is described by Agnes B. C. Dunbar in *Dictionary of Saintly Women,* volume two.

Hubert Humphrey's graduation address is excerpted in the summer 1966 issue of *Assembly.*

Grant's comment on graduating from West Point is quoted in *School for Soldiers* by Ellis and Moore.

Chapter 6. Ranger

I am grateful to Richard J. McDowell, Colonel A. Clark Welch, Colonel Ronald Leonard, Colonel Joseph S. Stringham III, John McKnight, Lieutenant Colonel Peyton Ligon, and Al Lindseth, all of whom were Ranger instructors in the 1960s, for details on the cadre and course of instruction. The Infantry School library at Fort Benning provided documents on Ranger course 7-D-F4 and the history of American Rangers. Captain John W. Weatherford, senior tactical officer at Harmony Church in 1987, was kind enough to locate records from Ranger 2 and 3 in 1966; he also provided information on attrition rates and the grading system. An article in the October 16, 1965, issue of *Journal of the Armed Forces* discusses efforts to incorporate lessons from Vietnam in the Ranger curriculum.

Details of the Doolittle raid are drawn from Quentin Reynolds's *The Amazing Mr. Doolittle.* Al Lindseth of '66, who later returned to the Florida camp as an instructor, told me that he had confirmed with Doolittle that Aux Field Seven was used by the raiders in their training.

Charlie Beckwith provides some background on himself, as well as a brief description of his tenure in the Ranger camp, in his autobiographical *Delta Force.*

For insights into the American experience with guerrilla warfare, I have relied on Weigley's *The American Way of War* and *History of the United States Army,* Dave R. Palmer's *Summons of the Trumpet,* and *The 25-Year War* by Bruce Palmer, Jr. Omar Bradley's comment about guerrilla warfare in Korea is quoted in Summers's *On Strategy,* which is also the source for the disagreement between General Decker and John Kennedy. Another useful source is Douglas S. Blaufarb's *The Counterinsurgency Era,* which notes the spreading of c.i. gospel into the Finance School and Cooks and Bakers School.

Chapter 7. Benning

Janowitz, in *The Professional Soldier,* draws an exceptional portrait of Old Army protocol. He is the source for details about the wives of George Patton and George Marshall. Details on etiquette are drawn from *Mrs. Lieutenant* by Mary Preston Gross; *Service Etiquette* by Oretha D. Schwartz; and the 1966–67 edition of *The Officer's Guide.* Thomas Fleming's novel *The Officers' Wives* also provides rich detail on military protocol. I have drawn, too, on my own experience as an Army brat.

The letter sent to artillerymen who washed out of Ranger is quoted in Robert Leider's study "Why They Leave: Resignations from the USMA Class of 1966."

I am grateful to Major Mike Nason for giving me a primer on the art of artillery. Other details about the branch are drawn from Weigley's *History of the United States Army* and Doughty's essay on "The Evolution of U.S. Army Tactical Doctrine, 1946–1976."

The study on alcoholism in the Army was reported in *The New York Times* on April 9, 1976.

The lines from Stephen Crane are taken from *The Collected Poems of Stephen Crane,* edited by Wilson Follett. *The Officer's Guide* quote about the adaptability of Army wives is contained in Fleming's *The Officers' Wives.*

Tom Carhart's recollections of getting lost in the Florida Ranger camp were supplemented by Colonel Ronald Leonard, who was a student in the same Ranger cycle.

Jack Wheeler mentions his experience in airborne training and the West Point hospital in his insightful meditation, *Touched With Fire.*

Details on the opening of the summer festival at Saratoga are drawn from "Festivals: A Place, A Show, A Win" in the July 22, 1966, issue of *Time,* and "Dancing in the Rain" in the August 1, 1966, issue of *Newsweek.*

Bacevich discusses the Nike Hercules system in *The Pentomic Era.* Jack's recollections of duty at a Nike base were supplemented by Fred McFarren, one of his classmates who served at a similar base in Milwaukee.

Chapter 8. United Hearts and Minds

The welcoming speech at Bien Hoa is quoted by James Sterba in "Scraps of Paper from Vietnam," *The New York Times Magazine,* October 18, 1970.

A particularly thorough account of the 9th Division's combat experience is contained in William B. Fulton's *Riverine Operations, 1966–1969,* which also summarizes the history of riverine operations by the American Army. General Fulton discussed his experiences as a brigade commander with me in an interview. Another useful source is *Riverine Force* by John Forbes and Robert Williams. Westmoreland's comment about "a protracted war of attrition" is cited in Palmer's *Summons of the Trumpet.*

Cu Chi is described in *The Tunnels of Cu Chi* by Tom Mangold and John Penycate. Historical details on the Wolfhounds are contained in *The Forgotten*

War: America in Korea, 1950–1953 by Clay Blair. Colonel Morris Herbert described his experiences on the Pusan perimeter to me in an interview.

The obituary for Frank Rybicki appears in *Newsweek*, June 5, 1967. Patton's diary entry about ruthlessness is in Nye's *The Challenge of Command*.

The battle of Ap Bac is described in detail in Sheehan's *A Bright Shining Lie*. The description of a claymore mine, as well as details about life as a combat lieutenant, are contained in James McDonough's *Platoon Leader*. S. L. A. Marshall's studies are discussed in Nye's *The Challenge of Command* and Keegan's *The Face of Battle;* recently, Marshall's work was assailed by two historians and a military writer, who contended that his conclusions were based on faked evidence. See *The New York Times*, February 19, 1989, page 1.

Chapter 9. Eight Seven Five

The *Newsweek* article "West Point Goes to War" is in the July 10, 1967, issue.

Details about *Sgt. Pepper's Lonely Hearts Club* are in a retrospective piece by Walt Harrington published by *The Washington Post* on May 31, 1987. Details about the Summer of Love are in an Associated Press article of June 6, 1987.

The Civil War expression for experiencing combat — "seeing the elephant" — is noted by James M. McPherson in *Battle Cry of Freedom*.

For details regarding the fighting in the Central Highlands in the latter half of 1967, I have relied largely on combat-action reports compiled by the 173rd Airborne Brigade and now in the possession of the Office of the Chief of Military History at the National Archives. Particularly useful was "Operational Report: Lessons Learned, 1 Nov. 1967–31 Jan. 1968." A number of participants in the fighting were generous in recounting their experiences, including Matt Harrison, Ron Leonard, Al Lindseth, Peyton Ligon, Jerry Cecil, and Bob Cresci.

Henry V's participation in Mass at Agincourt and the role of clergymen in Wellington's army are both chronicled in John Keegan's *The Face of Battle*. Other historical information about men of the cloth in battle is drawn from Honeywell's *Chaplains of the United States Army*.

The NVA offensive in the Central Highlands as part of a diversion before Tet is mentioned in Dave Palmer's *Summons of the Trumpet*. Other useful sources are Shelby L. Stanton's *The Rise and Fall of an American Army* and F. Clifton Berry's *Sky Soldiers*. Michael Herr's brilliant *Dispatches* describes the evacuation of Hill 875 and the subsequent memorial service at Dak To. The *Time* issue of December 1, 1967, and the *Newsweek* issue of December 4, 1967, also provide some details. Churchill's comment about victory being almost indistinguishable from defeat is quoted in *Soldiers: A History of Men in Battle* by John Keegan and Richard Holmes. Westmoreland's comment about "the beginning of a great defeat" for the enemy is cited by *The New York Times* of November 23, 1967.

The telegrams sent to Buck Thompson's family and his Silver Star citation were provided to me by the Army under a Freedom of Information Act request. His widow, Fran Seaman, and his sister, Lee Ann Wilson, were very kind in recounting details about the burial, as well as Buck's background. Jim Ford and the former chapel music director John Davis took pains to reconstruct the funeral.

Chapter 10. Screaming Eagle

Tom Carhart's excellent memoir of his year in Vietnam, *The Offering*, was an invaluable resource, helping me not only to reconstruct his experiences but also to understand the duties and conflicts of a platoon leader in combat.

Historical background on Officer Efficiency Reports is drawn from Janowitz's *The Professional Soldier*.

The number of '66ers earning Silver Stars and Purple Hearts is drawn from biographical notations in the *Register of Graduates*, published by academy's Association of Graduates. While laudably accurate, the entries occasionally are incomplete, and the actual numbers may in fact be higher.

Details of Tommy Hayes's death, as well as a copy of his last letter home, were provided to me in San Francisco by his father, Major General Tom Hayes. Several of Tommy's classmates offered recollections of his funeral, including Jack Wheeler, Art Mosley, George Crocker, Jim Peake, Jack Gatesy, and Bob Kesmodel.

John Hoskins's poetry is printed in his obituary, carried in the spring 1970 issue of *Assembly*.

General Wheeler's simile, in which he likened U.S. advisers to "the steel reinforcing rods in concrete," is quoted in Dave Palmer's *Summons of the Trumpet*, which is also the source for the number of enemy killed under the Phoenix program.

Tom Carhart's account, in *The Offering*, of being relieved of duty the second time differs slightly from the account cited here. After Tom's memoirs were published, one of his former NCOs helped to refresh his recollection, particularly about the commander's anger over Tom's participation in Phoenix.

Chapter 11. Long Binh

In *Touched With Fire*, Jack Wheeler poignantly describes meeting his father in California before leaving for Vietnam.

The survey of attitudes toward the war at Harvard Business School is cited in the school's 1969 yearbook.

For the physical layout of Long Binh, I am indebted to the descriptive powers of Bruns Grayson. Michael Herr's account of "Dial soapers" is in *Dispatches*. Saigon's nightlife is described in *Time* magazine, December 1, 1967. Sheehan also describes Long Binh in *A Bright Shining Lie*.

Ted Hill in Atlanta, Art Mosley in Key West, and Jack Wheeler in Washington each recounted for me the story of the jeep. For the political discussion at the Loon Foon, I have relied on the memories of Wheeler, Mosley, Bruns Grayson, Dick Radez, and Al Goldstein.

Isaiah Berlin's insight into Churchill's imagination is contained in *Mr. Churchill in 1940*.

Details on the tactical successes of 1969 are found in Palmer's *Summons of the Trumpet*.

Statistics on officer casualties, fraggings, and medal inflation are drawn from *Crisis in Command* by Richard A. Gabriel and Paul L. Savage. Statistics on Civil War casualties are cited by McPherson in *Battle Cry of Freedom.* The proportion of '66ers killed and wounded is compiled from biographical information in the *Register of Graduates.*

Patton's quote regarding "the warrior's soul" is cited in Fallows's *National Defense.*

The song of the Synanon garbage men can be found in David U. Gerstel's *Paradise Incorporated: Synanon.*

Da Lat is described by Palmer in *Summons of the Trumpet.*

Chapter 12. Wounds

Janowitz in *The Professional Soldier* notes the contrast between public support for World War II and support for Vietnam.

Jim Ford's quip about "two boats which are sinking" is cited in Ward Just's *Military Men.*

Details about the impact of wars on West Point are drawn from Forman's *West Point;* Fleming's *West Point;* Ambrose's *Duty, Honor, Country;* and Lovell's *Neither Athens Nor Sparta?*

Superintendent Dave Palmer told me about cadets wearing wigs when they went on leave in the 1960s.

The resignation of General Koster is described by Just in *Military Men,* and in the spring 1970 issue of *Assembly* magazine.

The Reverend George Bean's sermon on Saint Paul is noted in Lovell's *Neither Athens Nor Sparta?*

Details on the French heritage at West Point are drawn from *Ambrose's Duty, Honor, Country;* Fleming's *West Point;* Lovell's *Neither Athens Nor Sparta?;* and Forman's *West Point.*

Tom Carhart describes his *marraine de guerre* in *The Offering.*

Some details about the hospital are drawn from the Walter Reed Army Medical Center annual report for 1968. John Keegan, in *The Face of Battle* and *The Mask of Command,* offers insight and statistical data regarding "combat fatigue" and the comparative care of casualties given in various wars.

Chapter 13. Farewell to Arms

Details on the Single Integrated Operational Plan are drawn from *S.I.O.P.: The Secret U.S. Plan for Nuclear War* by Peter Pringle and William Arkin.

Public opinion surveys showing the esteem in which military officers were held are cited in Janowitz's *The Professional Soldier.*

"Why They Leave: Resignations from the USMA Class of 1966" was written by Robert Leider. I am grateful to the U.S. Army War College library at Carlisle Barracks for providing me with a copy of the study in 1981. The Office of Institutional Research also conducted interviews with several resigning members of the class in the spring of 1970. Details on the different characteristics of those who resigned versus those who remained in the Army are in Richard P. Butler's

"Survey of Careerists and Non-Careerists from the USMA Classes of 1963–1967," published by the Office of Institutional Research.

Historical data on resignations by West Pointers are drawn from Fleming's *West Point* and Janowitz's *The Professional Soldier*. An article written by Seymour Hersh regarding the high number of resigning West Point instructors appears in *The New York Times* of June 25, 1972.

The decline in first classmen who said they would again attend the academy if given the opportunity is cited by Lovell in *Neither Athens Nor Sparta?*

General Fred Weyand's comment about the "tradition of irreverence" is quoted in Summers's *On Strategy*.

Ron Bartek's testimony about "war crimes," which was extensively covered in the newspapers, is also discussed in *West Point: America's Power Fraternity* by K. Bruce Galloway and Robert Bowie Johnson, Jr.

Chapter 14. A Hard Peace

James McPherson, in *Battle Cry of Freedom*, notes Lincoln's "soft peace" policy.

The article "The Forgotten Seventh Army" appears in *Time* magazine, October 4, 1971. Patton's "born at sea" quotation is contained in "The Neglected and Troubled Seventh Army," *Newsweek*, May 31, 1971.

Two well-documented books on the Seventh Army in Germany were particularly useful to me: *Army in Anguish* by Haynes Johnson and George C. Wilson, and *A History of U.S. Forces in Germany* by Daniel J. Nelson. The former offers a vivid portrait of life inside the barracks; the latter was especially helpful because of the author's laborious review of German newspapers and periodicals.

Nineteenth-century drug addiction in the Army is cited in Walton's *The Tarnished Shield*. Keegan in *The Mask of Command* notes the issuance of triple rations of brandy to Napoleon's troops before Austerlitz.

Drug overdose deaths in Vietnam are cited by William L. Hauser in *America's Army in Crisis*. Gabriel and Savage also document indiscipline and other problems plaguing the Army in *Crisis in Command*.

Statistics on blacks in the officer corps are cited by Bernard C. Nalty in *Strength for the Fight: A History of Black Americans in the Military*. Nelson in *A History of U.S. Forces in Germany* notes the disproportionate number of blacks charged with serious crimes in Europe.

The reference to "raggedy-ass little bastards" is in Sheehan's *A Bright Shining Lie*.

The Army War College study in 1970, as well as the follow-up study in 1971, which referred to "an Army which bordered on self-destruction," are discussed in depth in *Crisis in Command* by Gabriel and Savage. The remark about the Army's being "overstaffed, overmanned, [and] overofficered" is drawn from Hauser's *America's Army in Crisis*.

Westmoreland's breast pocket quotation is mentioned by Johnson and Wilson in *Army in Anguish*.

Fallows's assessment of the damage done to the professional soldier by Vietnam is in his *National Defense*. Alfred de Vigny, the nineteenth-century French poet, wrote of an army searching high and low for its soul.

The advice about paying, commanding, and hanging well is in *Soldiers: A History of Men in Battle* by Keegan and Holmes.

Washington's comment about discipline being "the soul of an army" is noted in Weigley's *History of the United States Army.*

The description of Hitler in his Landsberg prison cell is taken from John Toland's *Adolf Hitler.*

Desertion rates in 1966 and 1971 are taken from *The New York Times,* September 5, 1971. The rate for 1944 is in *Crisis in Command* by Gabriel and Savage. Desertion in the nineteenth century is discussed by Weigley in *History of the United States Army,* as is Washington's lamentation about his rioting Army. The inspector general's complaint about the Army of Northern Virginia is noted by McPherson in *Battle Cry of Freedom.*

Ambrose, in *Duty, Honor, Country,* recounts the national contempt for the military before the Civil War, as well as Grant's chagrin at being ridiculed. Congressional reluctance to pay the Army is noted by Fleming in *West Point.*

General Knowlton's observations about "living in a kind of aberrated period" is in "West Point Cadets Now Say, 'Why, Sir?' by Thomas Fleming in *The New York Times Magazine,* July 5, 1970.

Details about the battle of Waterloo are drawn from Keegan's *The Face of Battle* and *The Mask of Command.*

For the account of the killing of John Oi, I interviewed the man convicted of his murder, Armand Therrien, in prison in Massachusetts. Therrien gave me a copy of the trial transcript. Oi's widow, Cheryl Lau, who now lives in California, was very helpful. *The Boston Globe* and *The Boston Herald* covered the murder extensively. Calvin Trillin also wrote a gripping piece about the crime in *The New Yorker;* it later appeared as a chapter in his anthology *Killings.* Oi's obituary, published in the December 1983 issue of *Assembly,* provided useful information about his background. Classmate Larry Donnithorne offered some details about the funeral.

Chapter 15. Dishonor

The means by which Jim Ford financed his expedition across the Atlantic first came to my attention in an article by Leslie Marshall, "Acts of Faith," in *The Washington Post Magazine* of January 9, 1983.

Sidney Berry's comment about never being "in more of a combat situation than I am now" is quoted in *Time,* June 7, 1976. Berry described to me in an interview the session he had with Creighton Abrams.

The best synthesis of the EE304 scandal is contained in the *Report to the Secretary of the Army by the Special Commission on the United States Military Academy,* headed by Frank Borman and Harold K. Johnson. I am grateful to Tom Kelly, a staff member on the commission, for insights into the inner workings of the investigation. Fleming in his *West Point* describes the nineteenth-century attitude toward cheating at the academy. The Reverend Thomas Curley told me about the accused cadets referring to themselves as "the Liars, Cheaters, and Thieves."

Abridgement of the Blue Book is reported by *The New York Times* of August 29, 1973. Other modifications are noted in Lovell's *Neither Athens Nor Sparta?*

The discovery of the tragus is reported in *School for Soldiers* by Ellis and Moore.

Lieutenant General Walter Ulmer told me about the fireworks fiasco.

News of the affidavits accusing nearly seven hundred additional cadets of honor violations was first reported in *The New York Times* on September 9, 1976.

Westmoreland's dismissal of women at West Point as "silly" was reported by the Associated Press on May 31, 1976. Sid Berry's contemplation of resignation was reported in *Newsweek* on December 1, 1975. Some details regarding the academy's preparations to receive the first class of women are drawn from "Women at West Point," in the June 1976 issue of *Soldiers* magazine.

The Office of Institutional Research studies on cadet attitudes toward women, most of which were directed by Robert F. Priest, are cited in the Bibliography under his name.

The New York Times of August 24, 1976, reported Martin Hoffmann's decision to readmit the cadets expelled for cheating.

A good feature article on the filming of *MacArthur* at West Point appears in *The New York Times* of November 19, 1976.

Chapter 16. The Poplar Tree

Much of the description of the Korean DMZ is drawn from my visit to Panmunjom while traveling in Korea with Defense Secretary Caspar Weinberger; details appeared in *The Washington Post* on May 16, 1984. Another helpful article from *The Post* on the poplar tree appeared on August 27, 1976.

Three publications were particularly useful in reconstructing the murders and subsequent military actions: "Murder at Panmunjom: The Role of the Theater Commander in Crisis Resolution," an article by Conrad De Lateur; *Timber: The Story of Operation Paul Bunyan* by Wayne A. Kirkbride; and *Crisis Resolution: Presidential Decision Making in the Mayaguez and Korean Confrontations* by Richard G. Head, Frisco W. Short, and Robert C. McFarlane.

I have also drawn on "Sudden Death at Checkpoint Three" in *Time*, and "The War of the Poplar Tree" in *Newsweek*, both in the August 30, 1976, issues. The Army's public affairs office in the Pentagon provided me with the official chronology of the incident, as well as a broader account entitled "The U.S. Military Experience in Korea, 1871–1982," by James P. Finley, command historian at the headquarters of U.S. Forces, Korea.

The Reverend Tom Curley generously provided me with a copy of the homily he read at the funeral.

Chapter 17. Walls

Two sources were invaluable in my research on the Vietnam Veterans Memorial: *To Heal a Nation* by Jan C. Scruggs and Joel L. Swerdlow, and Christopher Buckley's article "The Wall," which appeared in *Esquire* in September 1985. Scruggs also gave me access to the vast files of the Vietnam Veterans Memorial Fund, now on deposit at the Library of Congress. I have also drawn on the numerous newspaper articles that tracked the progress of the memorial, particularly in *The Washington Post*. Among the principals interviewed at length for this chapter, Robert W. Doubek was especially helpful in describing the chronological sequence and the behind-the-scenes maneuvering; I have also used some details from his article on the memorial in the November 1983 issue of *The Retired Officer*.

Some information on James Webb's background is drawn from "The Private War of Ollie and Jim" by Robert Timberg in *Esquire*, March 1988, and "Never Give an Inch: James Webb's Struggles With Pen and Sword," in *The Washington Post Magazine*, December 8, 1985.

Details on the difficulty in building Battle Monument are noted in Forman's *West Point*.

Biographical information about Maya Lin is drawn from "Maya Lin and the Great Wall of China," an article by Phil McCombs in *The Washington Post*, January 3, 1982.

A long excerpt of Tom Carhart's testimony before the Fine Arts Commission appeared on the Op-Ed page of *The New York Times* of October 24, 1981. The VVMF files at the Library of Congress contain a memo, written by Wheeler and dated May 5, 1982, regarding his phone conversation with Ross Perot.

The *60 Minutes* segment "Lest We Forget" aired on October 24, 1981. A transcript is in the VVMF files.

Chapter 18. Urgent Fury

Because of the volume of contradictory information about Operation Urgent Fury and the Defense Department's reluctance to release afteraction reports, reconstructing the American invasion of Grenada was more difficult than expected. Some of the participants, including George Crocker, Fred McFarren, Bob Seigle, and others, were enormously helpful in recounting their involvement. I have also drawn on two of my experiences as a reporter for *The Washington Post*. One was attending the briefing conducted at Hunter Army Air Field, Georgia, in early November 1983 by then Major General Schwarzkopf and then Lieutenant Colonel Wesley Taylor, who commanded the Rangers on Grenada. That briefing was the fullest official account of the invasion by the Army. The other experience occurred two days later at Andrews Air Force Base outside Washington, where the U.S. government unveiled the spoils of war seized on the island.

Other useful sources are the chapter on Grenada in *Secret Armies* by James Adams, and Ronald H. Spector's official account, "U.S. Marines in Grenada — 1983." Richard A. Gabriel's *Military Incompetence: Why the American Military Doesn't Win* is the most ambitious effort to understand the special operations missions in Urgent Fury.

I have also drawn on *American Intervention in Grenada* by Peter W. Dunn and Bruce W. Watson; *Grenada 1983* by Lee E. Russell and M. Albert Mendez; and *Revolution and Intervention in Grenada* by Kai P. Schoenhals and Richard A. Melanson.

The source of the "elephants chasing jackrabbits" analogy is Doughty's "The Evolution of U.S. Army Tactical Doctrine, 1946–1976." The impact of the Yom Kippur War on the Army's thinking is explained very well by John J. Romjue in *From Active Defense to Airland Battle: The Development of Army Doctrine, 1973–1982*. Weigley in his *History of the United States Army* also writes about the new lethality of "smart weapons." I consulted "Tactics and the Operational Level of War," an essay by Colonel William J. Bolt and Colonel David Jablonsky in the February 1987 issue of *Military Review*.

Weigley describes the ill-advised selling of Army wagons in 1895 in his *History of the United States Army*.

The New York Times on September 9, 1980, documented concerns about six of ten divisions being "not combat ready"; the resumption of bayonet training was reported by the newspaper on November 7, 1981; concerns about the Army being stretched thin were reported on August 10, 1983; results of the confidential survey of Army officers appeared in an April 21, 1985 article; details regarding the Reagan administration's military pay raises appeared on May 16, 1985.

The number of CAT IVs is noted in Weigley's *History*, which also documents the poor pay of enlisted men in the late 1970s; Fallows in *National Defense* cites the number of recruits with college degrees.

I appreciate the efforts of Colonels Rance Farrell, Bob Seigle, Bob Hicks, and Harry Summers in helping me to understand the mysteries of the Army's promotion system.

To further my education and allow me to see the inside of a C-130 during a night parachute operation, George Crocker arranged for me to accompany his men on a jump at Fort Bragg in the winter of 1987.

Chapter 19. Firebase

For the saga of Wedtech's undoing, I have relied principally on Matt Harrison's vivid recollections and the fine reporting of George Lardner in *The Washington Post*.

A portrait of the Corps of Cadets in the 1980s was compiled by the Office of Institutional Research in "Development of Values and Moral Judgments of West Point Cadets," written by Claude Bridges and Robert Priest, August 1983.

The incident in which women were forced to slaughter chickens was reported in *The Washington Post* on November 10, 1979.

For insights into how the honor system was modified in the wake of EE304, I am grateful to Major Gregory A. Stone, the commandant's special representative for honor issues.

The Vietnam Veterans Memorial Fund, using the Freedom of Information Act, obtained the notes of the General Accounting Office investigator who interviewed Tom Carhart. The document is contained in the VVMF files at the Library of Congress.

The article in which Tom Carhart was quoted as saying "I killed and enjoyed it" appeared in the Style section of *The Washington Post* on November 9, 1984; Tom's explanatory letter ran in the newspaper on November 12. Tom's observations on the "scandalous" treatment of Vietnam vets is drawn from *The Baltimore Sun* of November 14, 1983, which is also the source of his "I love to fight" quote.

Chapter 20. A Dark Wood

Roy Cohn's letter demanding access to the VVMF books is in the fund's files in the Library of Congress. The files also contain a letter dated March 14, 1983, to Jan Scruggs from Elliot L. Richardson, in which the former attorney general says that Ross Perot has "hired a mean lawyer [in Cohn]. I have known Roy Cohn since 1947, and if you want me to make him feel embarrassed for taking Ross Perot's cause, I would be glad to oblige." A transcript of the WDVM broadcast is also in the files; Christopher Buckley describes the controversy over Carlton Sherwood's investigation in "The Wall," his *Esquire* article.

Some biographical details about Linda Smith are drawn from "Linda Smith: Mother Power," by Virginia Butterfield in *San Diego* magazine, April 1986. In La Jolla, Linda told me of her emotional 1985 visit to the memorial.

George Crocker was kind enough to arrange for me to spend several days with the 82nd Airborne in Florida on Exercise Sand Eagle.

George Marshall's reflections on an age ceiling for regimental commanders is noted by Clay Blair in *The Forgotten War.*

T. E. Lawrence's "the irrational tenth" is cited in Roger Nye's *The Challenge of Command.*

I attended the October 4, 1987, chapel service at West Point, where Jim Ford delivered his guest sermon.

BIBLIOGRAPHY

Adams, James. *Secret Armies*. New York: Atlantic Monthly Press, 1987.
Ambrose, Stephen E. *Duty, Honor, Country: A History of West Point*. Baltimore: Johns Hopkins University Press, 1966.
Azoy, A. C. M., and Kendall Banning. *West Point Today*. New York: Coward-McCann, 1963.
Bacevich, A. J. *The Pentomic Era*. Washington, D.C.: National Defense University Press, 1986.
Beckwith, Charlie A., and Donald Knox. *Delta Force*. New York: Harcourt Brace Jovanovich, 1983.
Berlin, Isaiah. *Mr. Churchill in 1940*. Boston: Houghton Mifflin, 1949.
Berry, F. Clifton, Jr. *Sky Soldiers*. New York: Bantam, 1987.
Binkin, Martin, and Shirley J. Bach. *Women and the Military*. Washington, D.C.: Brookings Institution, 1977.
Blair, Clay. *The Forgotten War: America in Korea, 1950–1953*. New York: Times Books, 1987.
Blaufarb, Douglas S. *The Counterinsurgency Era*. New York: Free Press, 1977.
Blumenson, Martin. *Patton: The Man Behind the Legend*. New York: William Morrow, 1985.
Bolt, William J., and David Jablonsky. "Tactics and the Operational Level of War." *Military Review*, February 1987.
Bowman, William, Roger Little, and G. Thomas Sicilia, ed. *The All-Volunteer Force After a Decade*. Washington, D.C.: Pergamon-Brassey's, 1986.
Bridges, Claude, and Robert F. Priest. "Development of Values and Moral Judgment of West Point Cadets." West Point: USMA Office of Institutional Research (OIR), August 1983.
Buckley, Christopher. "The Wall." *Esquire*, September 1985.
Butler, Richard P. "Survey of Careerists and Non-Careerists From the USMA Classes of 1963–1967." West Point: USMA OIR, April 1971.
Butterfield, Virginia. "Linda Smith: Mother Power." *San Diego Magazine*, April 1986.
Carhart, Tom. *Battles and Campaigns in Vietnam, 1954–1984*. New York: The Military Press, 1984.

———. *The Offering*. New York: William Morrow, 1987.

Carter, Ross. *Those Devils in Baggy Pants*. Kingsport, Tennessee: Kingsport Press, 1951.

Chaplin, Gordon. "Battalion Commander." *The Washington Post Magazine*, May 10, 1981.

Coffman, Edward M. *The Old Army: A Portrait of the American Army in Peacetime, 1784–1898*. New York: Oxford University Press, 1986.

Cortwright, David. *Soldiers in Revolt*. New York: Anchor Press/Doubleday, 1975.

Crane, Stephen. *The Collected Poems of Stephen Crane*. Wilson Follett, ed. New York: Alfred A. Knopf, 1930.

Croizat, Victor. *The Brown Water Navy: The River and Coastal War in Indo-China and Vietnam, 1948–1972*. Poole (U.K.): Blandford Press, 1984.

"Dancing in the Rain." *Newsweek*, August 1, 1966.

De Lateur, Conrad. "Murder at Panmunjom: The Role of the Theater Commander in Crisis Resolution." Rosslyn, Virginia: U.S. Department of State Foreign Service Institute, March 1987.

Desportes, Elisa L. *Congregations in Change*. New York: Seabury Press, 1973.

Dickinson, Hillman, Jack V. Mackmull, and Jack N. Merritt. "Final Report of the West Point Study Group." Washington, D.C.: Department of the Army, July 1977.

Doughty, Robert A. "The Evolution of U.S. Army Tactical Doctrine, 1946–1976." Fort Leavenworth, Kansas: U.S. Command and General Staff College, Combat Studies Institute, August 1976.

"Drill and Ceremonies," (Field Manual 22–5). Washington, D.C.: Department of the Army, December 1986.

Dunbar, Agnes B. C. *Dictionary of Saintly Women* (vol. two). London: George Bell & Sons, 1904.

Dunn, Peter W., and Bruce W. Watson, eds. *American Intervention in Grenada*. Boulder: Westview Press, 1985.

Dupuy, R. Ernest. *The Compact History of the United States Army*. New York: Hawthorn Books, 1973.

———. *Men of West Point*. New York: William Sloane Associates, 1951.

Dusenbury, Mary E. (Carhart). *A Genealogical Record of the Descendants of Thomas Carhart of Cornwall, England*. New York: A. S. Barnes & Company, 1880.

Ellis, Joseph, and Robert Moore. *School for Soldiers: West Point and the Profession of Arms*. New York: Oxford University Press, 1974.

Fallows, James. *National Defense*. New York: Random House, 1981.

"Festivals: A Place, A Show, A Win." *Time*, July 22, 1966.

Fiedler, Leslie. *The Collected Essays of Leslie Fiedler* (vol. one). New York: Stein & Day, 1971.

FitzGerald, Frances. *Fire in the Lake*. New York: Vintage Books, 1972.

Fleming, Thomas. *The Officers' Wives*. New York: Doubleday, 1981.

———. *West Point: The Men and Times of the United States Military Academy*. New York: William Morrow, 1969.

———. "West Point Cadets Now Say, 'Why, Sir?' " *The New York Times Magazine*, July 5, 1970.

Flipper, Henry O. *The Colored Cadet at West Point*. New York: Homer Lee, 1878.
Forbes, John, and Robert Williams. *Riverine Force*. New York: Bantam Books, 1987.
Forman, Sidney. *West Point: A History of the United States Military Academy*. New York: Columbia University Press, 1950.
"Fourth Class Knowledge: History, Legends, and Traditions of the Corps." West Point: USMA booklet, 1962.
French, Allen. *Old Concord*. Boston: Little, Brown, 1915.
Fulton, William B. *Riverine Operations, 1966–1969*. Washington, D.C.: Department of the Army, 1973.
Gabriel, Richard A. *Military Incompetence: Why the American Military Doesn't Win*. New York: Hill & Wang, 1985.
———, and Paul L. Savage. *Crisis in Command*. New York: Hill and Wang, 1978.
Gailey, Phil. "West Point Goes to War." *Newsweek*, July 10, 1967.
Galloway, K. Bruce, and Robert Bowie Johnson, Jr. *West Point: America's Power Fraternity*. New York: Simon & Schuster, 1973.
Gerstel, David U. *Paradise Incorporated: Synanon*. Novato, California: Presidio Press, 1982.
Gross, Mary Preston. *Mrs. Lieutenant*. Chuluota, Florida: Beau Lac Publisher, no date.
Hagan, Kenneth J., and William R. Roberts, eds. *Against All Enemies*. Westport, Connecticut: Greenwood Press, 1986.
Hamill, Pete. "The New York We've Lost." *New York*, December 21, 1987.
Harding, Stephen. *Air War Grenada*. Missoula: Pictorial Histories Publishing, 1984.
Harris, Boyd M. "West Point Journal." Unpublished manuscript.
Hauser, William L. *America's Army in Crisis*. Baltimore: Johns Hopkins University Press, 1973.
Head, Richard G., Frisco W. Short, Robert C. McFarlane. *Crisis Resolution: Presidential Decision Making in the Mayaguez and Korean Confrontations*. Boulder: Westview Press, 1978.
Herr, Michael. *Dispatches*. New York: Avon Books, 1978.
Hersh, Seymour M. "The Decline and Near Fall of the U.S. Army," *Saturday Review*, November 18, 1972.
Holm, Jeanne. *Women in the Military*. Novato, California: Presidio Press, 1982.
Honeywell, Roy J. *Chaplains of the United States Army*. Washington: Department of the Army, 1958.
Houston, John W. "Characteristics of the Class of 1977." West Point: USMA OIR, November 1973.
Huntington, Samuel. *The Soldier and the State*. Cambridge, Massachusetts: Belknap Press, 1957.
Janowitz, Morris. *The Professional Soldier*. New York: Free Press, 1971.
Johnson, Haynes, and George C. Wilson. *Army in Anguish*. New York: Pocket Books, 1972.
Just, Ward. *Military Men*. New York: Alfred A. Knopf, 1970.
———. "West Point Rendezvous." *Atlantic*. January 1975.

Karnow, Stanley. *Vietnam: A History.* New York: Viking, 1983.
Keegan, John. *The Face of Battle.* New York: Viking, 1976.
———. *The Mask of Command.* New York: Viking, 1987.
———, and Richard Holmes. *Soldiers: A History of Men in Battle.* New York: Viking, 1985.
Kemple, C. Robert. *The Image of the Army Officer in America.* Westport, Connecticut: Greenwood Press, 1973.
Kipling, Rudyard. *Kipling: A Selection of His Stories and Poems.* Edited by John Beecroft. New York: Doubleday, 1956.
Kirkbride, Wayne A. *Timber: The Story of Operation Paul Bunyan.* New York: Vantage Press, 1980.
Langguth, A. J. *Patriots: The Men Who Started the American Revolution.* New York: Simon & Schuster, 1988.
Lapham, Lewis H. "Case Study of an Army Star." *Life,* September 1970.
Leider, Robert. "Why They Leave: Resignations from the USMA Class of 1966." Washington, D.C.: Department of the Army, July 1970.
Lemley, Brad. "Never Give an Inch." *The Washington Post Magazine,* December 8, 1985.
Lovell, John P. *Neither Athens Nor Sparta?* Bloomington: Indiana University Press, 1979.
Manchester, William. *American Caesar.* New York: Little, Brown, 1978.
———. *The Glory and the Dream.* New York: Bantam, 1975.
Mangold, Tom, and John Penycate. *The Tunnels of Cu Chi.* New York: Random House, 1985.
Mardis, Jaime. *Memos of a West Point Cadet.* New York: David McKay, 1976.
Marshall, Leslie. "Acts of Faith." *The Washington Post Magazine,* January 9, 1983.
Mason, Robert. *Chickenhawk.* New York: Viking, 1983.
McDonough, James. *Platoon Leader.* Novato, California: Presidio Press, 1985.
McFeely, William S. *Grant.* New York: W. W. Norton, 1981.
McPherson, James M. *Battle Cry of Freedom.* New York: Oxford University Press, 1988.
Morrison, James L., Jr. *The Best School in the World.* Kent, Ohio: Kent State University Press, 1986.
Nalty, Bernard C. *Strength for the Fight: A History of Black Americans in the Military.* New York: Free Press, 1986.
Nelson, Daniel J. *A History of U.S. Forces in Germany.* Boulder: Westview Press, 1987.
Nicholson, Robert J. "West Point's First Captains." *Assembly,* Winter 1970.
Nye, Roger H. *The Challenge of Command.* Wayne, New Jersey: Avery Publishing Group, 1986.
Official and Social Courtesy. West Point: USMA Department of Tactics, 1947.
Palmer, Bruce, Jr. *The 25-Year War: America's Military Role in Vietnam.* Lexington: University Press of Kentucky, 1984.
Palmer, Dave R. *The River and the Rock.* New York: Greenwood Publishing Group, 1969.
———. *Summons of the Trumpet.* New York: Ballantine, 1978.
Pappas, George S. *The Cadet Chapel — United States Military Academy.* Providence: Andrew Mowbray, Inc., 1987.

Piccolino, E. B. "Comparative Report on Selected Characteristics of Entrants to the USMA and Entrants to Four-Year Colleges Nationally." West Point: USMA OIR, January 1967.

Prashker, Ivan. *Duty, Honor, Vietnam: Twelve Men of West Point*. New York: Arbor House, 1988.

Preston, Dickson J. *Talbot County: A History*. Centreville, Maryland: Tidewater Publishers.

Priest, Robert F. "Cadet Attitudes Toward Women — 1975." West Point: USMA OIR, May 1976.

———. "A Comparison of Faculty and Cadet Attitudes Toward Women." West Point: USMA OIR, May 1976.

———. "Content of Cadet Comments on the Integration of Women." West Point: USMA OIR, August 1977.

———, Stephen B. Grove, and Jerome Adams. "Institutional and Historical Perspective on Women in Military Academy Roles." West Point: USMA OIR, April 1981.

———, and John W. Houston. "Analysis of Spontaneous Cadet Comments on the Admission of Women." West Point: USMA OIR, May 1976.

———, Howard T. Prince, and Alan G. Vitters. "Women Cadets at the United States Military Academy." West Point: USMA OIR, October 1977.

Pringle, Peter, and William Arkin. *S.I.O.P.: The Secret U.S. Plan for Nuclear War*. New York: W. W. Norton, 1983.

Race, Jeffrey. *War Comes to Long An*. Berkeley: University of California Press, 1972.

Rapp, Kenneth W. *West Point: Whistler in Gray and Other Stories*. North River Press, 1978.

Reeder, Russell P., and Nardi Campion Reeder. *The West Point Story*. New York: Random House, 1985.

Report to the Secretary of the Army by the Special Commission on the United States Military Academy (Borman Commission). Washington, D.C.: Department of the Army, December 1976.

Reynolds, Quentin. *The Amazing Mr. Doolittle*. New York: Appleton-Century-Crofts, 1953.

Rhodes, Richard. *The Making of the Atomic Bomb*. New York: Simon & Schuster, 1986.

Rogan, Helen. *Mixed Company: Women in the Modern Army*. Boston: Beacon Press, 1981.

Romjue, John J. *From Active Defense to Airland Battle: The Development of Army Doctrine, 1973–1982*. Fort Monroe, Virginia: U.S. Army Training and Doctrine Command, 1984.

Russell, Lee E., and M. Albert Mendez. *Grenada 1983*. London: Osprey Publishing, 1985.

Samuel, Gertrude. "Where Junkies Learn to Hang Tough." *The New York Times Magazine*, May 9, 1965.

Saunders, Mary H. "Characteristics of the Class of 1988." West Point: USMA OIR, September 1984.

Schoenhals, Kai P., and Richard A. Melanson. *Revolution and Intervention in Grenada*. Boulder: Westview Press, 1985.

Schwartz, Oretha D. *Service Etiquette*. Annapolis: U.S. Naval Institute Press, 1985.
Scruggs, Jan C., and Joel L. Swerdlow. *To Heal a Nation*. New York: Harper & Row, 1985.
Scudder, Townsend. *Concord: American Town*. Boston: Little, Brown, 1947.
"Senior Level Leadership: Selected Readings." Fort Leavenworth: U.S. Command and General Staff College, April 1987.
Sheehan, Neil. *A Bright Shining Lie*. New York: Random House, 1988.
Smith, Dale O. *Cradle of Valor: The Intimate Letters of a Plebe at West Point Between the Wars*. Chapel Hill: Algonquin Books, 1988.
Spector, Ronald H. "U.S. Marines in Grenada — 1983." Washington: History and Museums Division, U.S. Marine Corps, 1987.
Stanton, Shelby L. *The Rise and Fall of an American Army*. Novato, California: Presidio Press, 1985.
Sterba, James P. "Scraps of Paper From Vietnam." *The New York Times Magazine,* October 18, 1970.
"Study on Military Professionalism." Carlisle, Pennsylvania: U.S. Army War College, June 1970.
"Sudden Death at Checkpoint Three." *Time,* August 8, 1976.
Summers, Harry G., Jr. *On Strategy: A Critical Analysis of the Vietnam War*. New York: Dell, 1984.
Terry, Wallace. *Bloods: An Oral History of the Vietnam War by Black Veterans*. New York: Random House, 1984.
Timberg, Robert. "The Private War of Ollie and Jim." *Esquire,* March 1988.
Todd, Frederick P. *Cadet Gray*. New York: Sterling Publishing Co., 1955.
Toland, John. *Adolf Hitler*. New York: Ballantine, 1977.
———. *The Rising Sun*. New York: Random House, 1970.
Truscott, Lucian K. *Dress Gray*. New York: Doubleday, 1979.
Ulmer, Walter F., Jr. "The Army's New Leadership." *Parameters,* December 1987.
Wallace, J. Richard. "Status of EE304 Honor Incident Cadets." West Point: USMA OIR (memorandum for superintendent), December 5, 1986.
Walton, George H. *The Tarnished Shield*. New York: Dodd, Mead, 1973.
"The War of the Poplar Tree." *Newsweek,* August 30, 1976.
Webb, James. *Fields of Fire*. New York: Bantam, 1978.
Weigley, Russell F. *The American Way of War*. Bloomington: Indiana University Press, 1973.
———. *History of the United States Army*. Bloomington: Indiana University Press, 1984.
Westmoreland, William C. *A Soldier Reports*. New York: Doubleday, 1976.
Wheeler, John. *Touched With Fire*. New York: Franklin Watts, 1984.
Wiseman, Carter. "You Must Remember This: Penn Station." *New York,* December 21, 1987, p. 84.
Woodward, Bob. *Veil: The Secret Wars of the CIA, 1981–1987*. New York: Simon & Schuster, 1987.

INDEX